Dartington Hall

ANTHONY EMERY

DARTINGTON HALL

The Clarendon Press · Oxford 1970

Designed by David Pelham

Printed and bound in Great Britain by Jarrold and Sons Ltd, Norwich

Oxford University Press, Ely House, London W.1
GLASGOW NEW YORK TORONTO MELBOURNE WELLINGTON
CAPE TOWN SALISBURY IBADAN NAIROBI LUSAKA ADDIS ABABA
BOMBAY CALCUTTA MADRAS KARACHI LAHORE DACCA
KUALA LUMPUR SINGAPORE HONG KONG TOKYO

© Oxford University Press 1970

To Dorothy and Leonard Elmhirst

Foreword

This book is a survey of the owners, history, and architecture of what is essentially a late fourteenth-century residence. The text is divided into two parts; Part One is an account of the owners and history of Dartington Hall and Part Two describes the existing remains. Each part is preceded by an introductory chapter; the first is a short survey of the restoration of the Hall and the second describes the architectural history and significance of the building.

A few words are perhaps necessary about certain aspects of the text. First of all, I have essentially concerned myself with the history of the Hall and its owners and not with the manor of Dartington. The two subjects are quite different, and although the descent of the manor and other aspects of its early history are considered in the first chapter, little reference is made to the subject thereafter. Small consideration will, therefore, be given to such matters as the economic and social changes of the manor in the fifteenth or nineteenth centuries, or to the financial transactions involved in its passage through several hands in the mid sixteenth century.

Secondly, the material concerning the owners of the Hall is extremely patchy. It might be expected that there would be more documentary evidence for the last three hundred years than for the previous three centuries. Yet the records of the Champernowne family who owned the Hall between 1559 and 1925 are not very extensive, and those that have been deposited in Exeter City Library are essentially legal and estate documents. The rewards to be garnered from sorting through them are strictly limited for there are few personal papers, no diaries, and only a handful of letters. Only occasionally do they afford a glimpse of the personalities writing them or of their family home near Totnes. Almost the opposite is true of their medieval predecessors, the Holand family, for although few of their personal records are known, a wealth of documentary material refers to them. John Holand, the half-brother of Richard II, was responsible for much of the Hall as it stands today and in the absence of any previous biography about him, it was decided that his career should be followed in some detail.

Thirdly, the history does not include that of the Elmhirst family or of their work at Dartington, for the study of the many social, cultural, educational, industrial, and agricultural activities that have centred on the Hall since 1925 need quite a different author. Victor Bonham-Carter has already written about their many achievements since the 1920s, and I have confined myself to recording their careful rehabilitation of the building.

Fourthly, the architectural descriptions of the Hall are prefaced by a chapter summarizing the development of secular architecture in the late fourteenth century. Too many buildings are still studied in isolation and I have, therefore, tried to draw together some of the strands that make the late fourteenth century an important period in the development of English architecture. The study of secular work has lagged behind that of ecclesiastical architecture and I fear that my summary is all too brief.

Finally, all documentary, excavated, and other material gathered in the preparation of this book has been deposited in the Records Office of the Dartington Hall Trustees at Totnes for the benefit and use of future students.

Acknowledgements

Although this book was planned to be written in three years, it has grown in scope and content and taken almost nine years to complete. Throughout this period, I have received unstinted support and facilities from the Trustees of Dartington Hall. In particular, I would like to express my very deep gratitude to Dorothy and Leonard Elmhirst whose encouragement, generosity, and enthusiasm made my task one of continual pleasure.

I am also deeply indebted to several other people who gave up a considerable amount of their time to help me with the text and illustrations. Dr. C. H. Talbot transcribed and translated nearly two hundred Latin documents relating to the Holand family. Professor Dorothy Whitelock translated the Charter of 833, and J. McN. Dodgson commented on the origin of the place-name *Dartington*. R. Welldon Finn read and commented on that part of Chapter 1 dealing with the Domesday Survey, James Sherborne improved Chapters 2 and 3, and Dr. Joyce Youings commented on Chapters 4 and 5. I am also grateful for the advice received on historical matters from Sir Anthony Wagner, Professor Maurice Beresford, Cecil Gould, Claud Blair, and Madeleine Ginsburg.

My architectural work was made considerably easier by a most valuable report prepared for me by Stanley Jones on the roofs at Dartington Hall. Mr. Jones also prepared the associated cross-sections which form the basis of those included in Chapters 7, 9, and 13. Professor Scott Simpson contributed a report on the building stones used in the construction of the Hall (Appendix 7), and Anthony Clark undertook two resistivity surveys and prepared the report given in Appendix 5. Dr. Colin Platt led the excavations on the site of the south court in 1962, assisted by students of Leeds University and the London Institute of Archaeology, whilst John Hurst advised me on the finds recovered from this site and from the east range during its reconstruction in 1963. Chapter 6 has benefited from the comments of Dr. C. A. Ralegh Radford, and Chapters 7 to 16 from those of Dr. W. A. Pantin, Dr. Eric Gee, J. T. Smith, and A. W. Everett.

Nearly all the photographs of the Hall have been specially taken for this book by Humphrey Sutton, and they have been supplemented from the collection of the Dartington Hall Trustees. Miss C. E. Champernowne, D. G. Champernowne, W. R. U. Litton, Robin Johnson, the University of Exeter, and the staff of the British Museum helped me to obtain illustrations for the historical chapters. The plans of the Hall were originally prepared by four students of the Architectural Association's School of Architecture, Miss D. L. Smith, C. Carter, H. E. Evans, and R. Tuck, and they were redrawn by Colin Spooner to take account of subsequent alterations and my suggested dating of the structure. Mr. Spooner has also taken considerable trouble over redrawing all the other plans and diagrams from my measurements and sketches.

I would also like to thank Victor Bonham-Carter, John Harvey, N. E. Pugsley, and the owners of many private residences who generously allowed me to invade their homes with notebook and measuring tape. Finally, my thanks are due to a number of my friends who read and commented on the manuscript and made me rewrite several parts of it again.

London, July 1968

Contents

Part One   The Owners and History of Dartington Hall

Introduction	The Restoration of Dartington Hall	3
Chapter 1	The Descent of the Manor of Dartington prior to the Late Fourteenth Century	13
Chapter 2	John Holand, Earl of Huntingdon: Mid Fourteenth Century to 1390	23
Chapter 3	John Holand, Earl of Huntingdon: 1390 to 1400	38
Chapter 4	The Later Holands and Their Successors: 1400 to 1559	55
Chapter 5	The Champernowne Family: 1559 to 1925	73

Part Two   The Architectural History and Description of Dartington Hall

Introduction	The Architectural History and Significance of Dartington Hall	95
Chapter 6	Major Residential Architecture during the Late Fourteenth Century	103
Chapter 7	The Entrance Block and North Courtyard	139
Chapter 8	The Porch Tower and Great Hall	150
Chapter 9	The Lower Residential Block	165
Chapter 10	The Kitchen and Offices	171
Chapter 11	The Upper Residential Block	177
Chapter 12	The Site of the South Court	185
Chapter 13	The West Range of Lodgings	203
Chapter 14	The East Range of Lodgings	215
Chapter 15	The Barn	222
Chapter 16	Dartington Hall and Aspects of Residential Design in the Late Fourteenth Century	226

Appendix 1	The Charter of 833	260
Appendix 2	The Estates and Income of John Holand, Earl of Huntingdon, in the Late Fourteenth Century	260
Appendix 3	The Authorship of the *Chronique de la Traison et Mort de Richard II*	263
Appendix 4	An Early Medieval Building on the Site of Dartington Hall	264
Appendix 5	Report of a Resistivity Survey at Dartington Hall	266
Appendix 6	Furnishings at Dartington Hall: 1400–1401	267
Appendix 7	The Building Stones of Dartington Hall	268
Appendix 8	Masons Marks at Dartington Hall	272

List of Plates	274
List of Figures and Maps	279
Index	281
Plans of Dartington Hall	

List of Abbreviations

Antiq. Jour.	The Antiquaries Journal
Arch. Aeliana	Archaeologia Aeliana
Arch. Cambrensis	Archaeologia Cambrensis
Arch. Cantiana	Archaeologia Cantiana
Arch. Jour.	Archaeological Journal
Assoc. Arch. Soc. Reports	Associated Architectural Societies, Reports
B.M.	British Museum, London
Bull. Inst. Hist. Research	Bulletin of the Institute of Historical Research
Cal. Inq. Misc.	Calendar of Inquisitions, Miscellaneous
Cal. Inq. Post Mortem	Calendar of Inquisitions, Post Mortem
Cal. Pat. Rolls	Calendar of Patent Rolls
Eng. Hist. Rev.	English Historical Review
Jour. Arch. Archaeol. and Hist. Soc. of Chester and N. Wales	Journal of the Architectural, Archaeological and Historical Society of Chester and North Wales
Jour. Brit. Arch. Assoc.	Journal of the British Archaeological Association
Jour. R.I.B.A.	Journal of the Royal Institute of British Architects
Med. Archaeol.	Medieval Archaeology
Ord. Privy Council	Ordinances of the Privy Council
P.R.O.	Public Record Office, London
Proc. Brit. Acad.	Proceedings of the British Academy
Proc. Devon Arch. Exploration Soc.	Proceedings of the Devon Archaeological Exploration Society
Proc. Somerset Arch. & Nat. Hist. Soc.	Proceedings of the Somerset Archaeological and Natural History Society
R.C.H.M.	Royal Commission on Historical Monuments
Rot. Franc.	Rotuli Francorum
Rot. Lit. Claus.	Rotuli Litterarum Clausarum
Surrey Arch. Coll.	Surrey Archaeological Society, Collections
Sussex Arch. Coll.	Sussex Archaeological Society, Collections
Trans. Birmingham Arch. Soc.	Transactions of the Birmingham Archaeological Society
Trans. Bristol and Glos. Arch. Soc.	Transactions of the Bristol and Gloucestershire Archaeological Society
Trans. Cumb. & West. Antiq. and Arch. Soc.	Transactions of the Cumberland and Westmorland Antiquarian and Archaeological Society
Trans. Devon Assoc.	Transactions of the Devonshire Association
Trans. Exeter Diocesan Arch. Soc.	Transactions of the Exeter Diocesan Archaeological Society
Trans. Hampshire Field & Arch. Soc.	Transactions of the Hampshire Field Club and Archaeological Society
Trans. Leic. Arch. Soc.	Transactions of the Leicestershire Archaeological Society
V.C.H.	Victoria County History
Wilts. Arch. & Nat. Hist. Mag.	Wiltshire Archaeological and Natural History Magazine
Yorks. Arch. Jour.	Yorkshire Archaeological Journal

Part One

The Owners and History of Dartington Hall

Introduction

The Restoration of Dartington Hall

Leonard Elmhirst first saw the grey stone walls of Dartington Hall in February 1925 when he was searching for an estate that could form the nucleus of the enterprise which he and his wife had agreed to launch together. Two London property agents had proffered him nearly forty addresses in the west of England that met Elmhirst's minimum requirements—a house with historical associations and a large number of rooms, situated in the middle of an impoverished but fertile estate. The first place visited by Leonard, Syon Abbey near South Brent, was unsatisfactory and so he turned to a second address in Devon nearly eight miles away.

The Dartington Hall estate covered a low hill overlooking a wide bend of the river Dart, two miles north-west of Totnes. It consisted of 600 acres of farmland, 190 acres of woodland, and 33 acres of private grounds. This was all that remained of the several thousand acres formerly in the hands of the Champernowne family who had owned Dartington since the mid sixteenth century. But although the estate was in low water, land was cheap in the 1920s and there was the likelihood that the property could be extended by purchasing several adjacent holdings. On the other hand, much of the Hall was derelict and those parts that were roofed were in a bad state of repair.

After walking past several outbuildings, Leonard Elmhirst entered the main courtyard of a large medieval house. The ranges on either side, once occupied by the retainers of a large household, still remained in a mutilated state. Part of the right-hand range was in use as a farmhouse while the rooms in one corner sheltered a cider-press and an apple store. The range on the left-hand side had been used until a few years earlier as a coach-house, cowhouse, and hayloft, but it had begun to fall into disrepair. The two ranges were linked by a barn, still in fair condition and fulfilling its original purpose. A seven-foot wall ran across the middle of the courtyard, separating the farmstead with its clutter of equipment, machinery, and wire fencing from a lawn in front of the great hall. The ruins of this apartment and the adjacent service rooms completed the fourth side of the courtyard. The wind and rain swept through the roofless hall, grass covered the floor, and ivy entwined the empty window tracery. The rooms above the entrance tower were not in good shape and those at the lower end of the hall were in a state of collapse. A passageway, half of it open to the sky, gave access to the gaunt shell of the original medieval kitchen. Only the living-rooms in the south-west angle of the courtyard were still weather-proof and even these had not been inhabited for the previous four years. The prospect of restoring such dilapidated property did not seem very attractive on a cold winter's day. Yet the Hall, like the estate, almost fully satisfied Leonard Elmhirst's needs. It was extensive enough to accommodate a large staff and to form the centre for several of the enterprises envisaged. It had historical associations as well as architectural distinction, for it had been built by the half-brother of Richard II and occupied for the past 350 years by the Champernowne family. Finally, it possessed, even in its ruined state, an atmosphere of beauty, quietness, and mellow dignity. Leonard searched no further. Dorothy Elmhirst, arriving from America

North court from the entrance passage: 1925

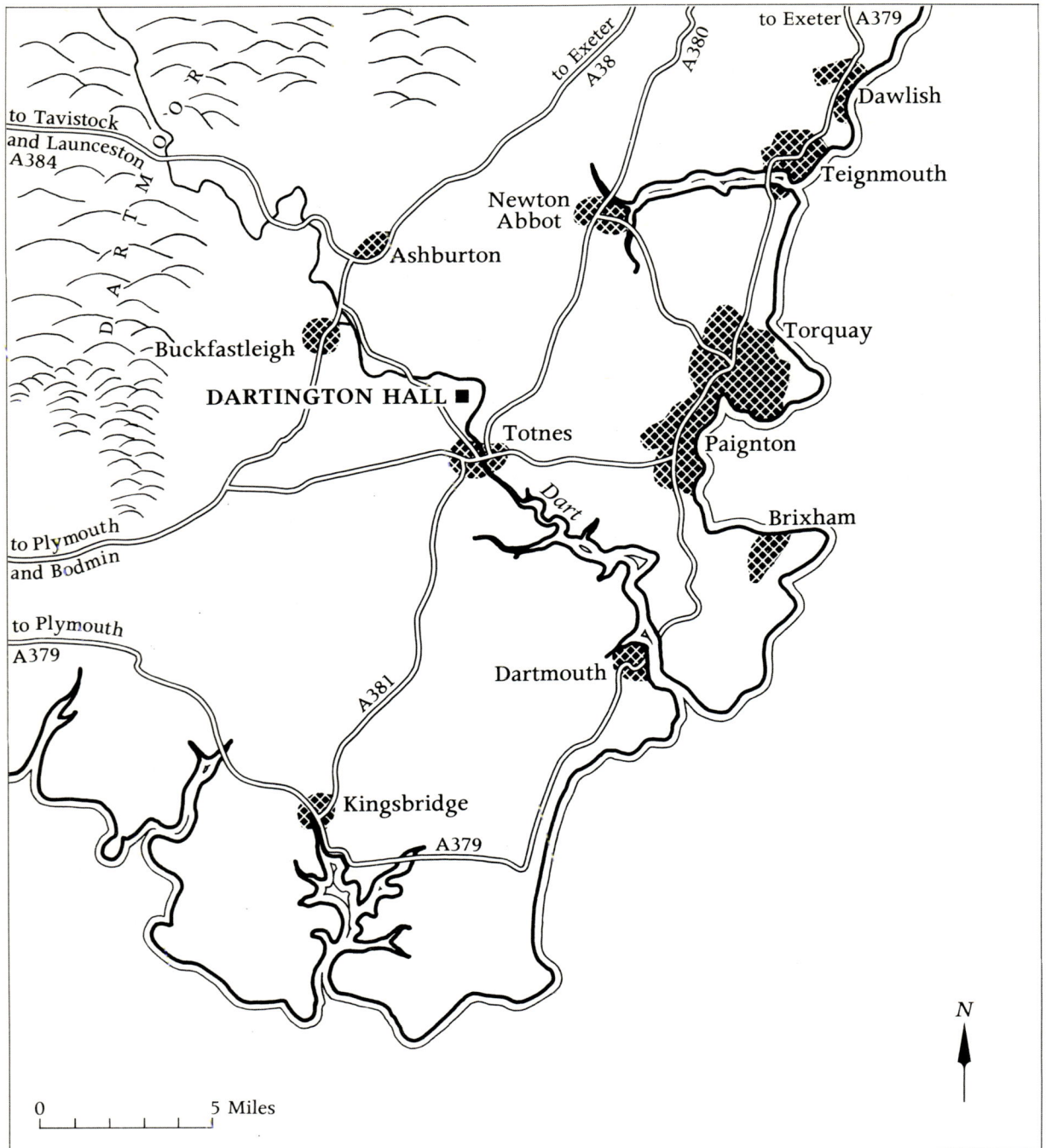

Fig. 1 South Devon showing the position of Dartington Hall

in June 1925, agreed with his choice and their purchase of the Hall and the estate was completed in the following September.

The story of the development of the estate and the work that has been carried out there since 1925 has been described by Victor Bonham-Carter and it is not intended to repeat it again.[1] But the extensive restoration of the Hall and the adjacent gardens was undertaken at the same time as the Elmhirsts were launching their educational and economic programme and was closely associated with it. To that extent, it is necessary to indicate briefly the nature and purpose of their work.

Leonard and Dorothy were fired with the enthusiasm, endowed with the ability, and commanded the fortune to carry out three major projects. The first was the revival of farming and forestry and the general rehabilitation of the estate, together with the development of associated industries, on a sound economic basis. The second was to start a progressive co-educational boarding-school, and the third was to create a centre for the study and performance of the arts, particularly music, drama, and the dance. Research

[1] Victor Bonham-Carter and W. B. Curry, *Dartington Hall—The History of an Experiment* (1958). Other publications on the work of the Elmhirsts at Dartington are L. K. Elmhirst, 'Some Aspects of the History of Dartington Hall', *Trans. Devon Assoc.* vol. 91 (1959), and the guide-book, *The Story of Dartington* (1967).

Porch tower: 1925

departments dealing with the economics of agriculture and forestry were associated with the first of these projects, and it was complemented by the introduction of adult education classes and all kinds of facilities for recreation so that everyone concerned with the enterprise might have the opportunity of leading as full a life as they wished. A visionary programme of this breadth and scale was bound to run into difficulties and Dartington has certainly not been short of them. Yet experience has brilliantly justified these early ideals, and Dartington has thriven economically, culturally, and socially.

Most of these undertakings were launched before 1930. It had always been intended that the cultural enterprises should be centred upon the medieval buildings at Dartington, but the school and several of the industrial projects were temporarily accommodated round the courtyard until new buildings could be erected for them elsewhere. Therefore, the first task was to put as many of the existing buildings to work as possible and then, more gradually, to restore and reconstruct each part of the Hall in turn.

The Elmhirsts were fortunate in their choice of architect. William Weir was responsible

Interior of great hall: 1925

for almost all the work carried out at the Hall between 1926 and 1938, apart from some minor alterations to the private house undertaken shortly after the Elmhirsts arrived there. Weir had established a considerable reputation for his sympathetic restoration of ancient buildings during the first quarter of the twentieth century. His work was scholarly and unobtrusive and it was probably his self-effacing manner, common to both himself and his work, which explains why it is not more well known today. He had particularly demonstrated his ability by restoring Tattershall and Bodiam castles for Lord Curzon immediately before and after the First World War, but his work at Dartington involved far more than consolidation and restoration—it was an extended task of sympathetic reconstruction and re-creation.

Weir was an architect with an extensive knowledge of the practical aspects of construction, both past and present. Until the outbreak of the First World War, he employed a small team of craftsmen whom he had personally trained. Later conditions made it impossible to continue methods so reminiscent of medieval times, but he was fortunate in having a

West range from the north court: 1925

group of skilled workmen assembled for him at Dartington whom he similarly imbued with enthusiasm and pride. 'If only present-day visitors could have seen that diminutive Scotsman in action, his cat-like figure moving up ladders and over scaffolding as he applied his broad grasp of medieval design and gave intimate attention to the smallest detail. How Weir's keen eye could twinkle appreciation of honest and solid craftsmanship, a man of few words.'[2]

[2] L. K. Elmhirst, *Dartington Hall: News of the Day* (13 August 1952).

Weir was as adept at plastering the walls of the great hall by hand as in designing its roof or the hinges for its doors. He made it axiomatic of his work that different but subtly chosen materials should be used for all repairs. There was to be no faking; all his work would be visible to those who looked but it was not to be immediately apparent. Furthermore, the original buildings were to be adapted boldly to new purposes wherever necessary although with the minimum of disturbance to the original fabric. Weir's work was exceptionally successful and very little modification has been necessary to the Hall since its restoration was completed. It is in a large measure due to the skill of William Weir that the Hall

East range from the rear: 1925

Reconstruction of the roof of the great hall: 1932

Restoration of the private house and great hall: 1933

Private house, great hall, and kitchen from the stone terrace

The Hall and tournament ground from the upper terrace

radiates that atmosphere of quiet beauty and dignity which has captivated generations of residents and visitors alike.

Weir's first task was to save the rooms at the lower end of the great hall and above the entrance tower which were in imminent danger of collapse. He designed a new ceiling for the large first-floor room which could then be used as a school hall. This was followed between 1926 and 1927 by the reconstruction of the east range as a series of single bedrooms for the school and the restoration of the entrance block as a group of classrooms. The private house, where the Elmhirsts have always lived, had already been made habitable by the end of 1925 but more substantial work was carried out between 1928 and 1930. Saving the roof of the entrance block took place in 1930–31 and was followed by the major task of re-roofing and restoring the great hall. Weir's plans for this project had been prepared four years earlier, but it had been necessary to allow plenty of time for the oak chosen for the beams to undergo preliminary seasoning in the open. All the wood used in the restoration came from trees felled on the estate except for one tie-beam in the great hall and four in the kitchen which came from Lord Churston's estate. The restoration of the hall was one of the triumphs of Weir's career and it was probably the most successful single task he undertook. The work was not so much a restoration as a re-creation and it was so sympathetically undertaken that the hall gives the impression of being in no way inferior to its medieval predecessor, either in spirit or in detail. It was followed by the restoration of the great kitchen. This similarly lacked a roof, but whereas Weir had at least been able to base his design of the hall roof on existing evidence left in the plaster on one of the end walls, his reconstruction of that in the kitchen had to be entirely conjectural. The rehabilitation of the west range so that it could be used for office, classroom, and residential accommodation, begun in association with Robert Hening in 1934, was completed in the following year, while the conversion of the barn into a theatre took place between 1933 and 1938 under the direction of Walter Gropius and Robert Hening. By 1938, Dartington Hall had assumed the appearance it wears today. Later work has been of a minor nature, apart from Robert Hening's internal reconstruction of the east range of the courtyard in 1963 as the Devon Centre of Further Education.

The planning of the gardens was conditioned by the desire to relate them to the medieval buildings, and therefore they can hardly be divorced from the Hall.[3] Preliminary work began in 1927 with the planning of the lawns immediately south of the great hall. The modification of the ground between the terraces to form an open-air theatre was carried out between 1927 and 1931 and the proportions of the north court were restored and

[3] They are described by Dorothy Elmhirst, *The Gardens at Dartington Hall* (1961); and E. Hyams and E. Smith, *The English Garden* (1964), 242–8.

The gardens from the roof of the great hall

enhanced by Beatrix Farrand's design of a central lawn and encircling drive in 1935. An imaginative planting scheme was put in hand, combined with an architectural treatment of the natural features of the gardens. After the Second World War, new vistas were opened out by Percy Cane and the long flight of steps created down the heath bank. In 1955, the open-air theatre was levelled to give the tournament ground its present appearance, and the south lawn was re-laid in 1962 following the excavation of that area as part of the study work for this book.

It is due to the ideas, resources, and enthusiasm of the Elmhirsts that Dartington Hall did not suffer the fate that has befallen so many large houses and estates in the twentieth century. The land was not divided up and sold in a series of small lots, but enlarged from a holding of 823 acres to one of nearly 4,000 acres. The remains of the Hall were not pulled down and replaced by a smaller residence in the pseudo-Georgian style so fashionable at that time, but infused with new life by an extensive and sympathetic restoration. As a result, the Hall fulfills its purpose today as the centre of an integrated community more closely than at any time since the fifteenth century. Yet the story of the Hall and its owners can by no means be read from the stones that stand today. Nor do they immediately reveal the complexity of the original design and the series of alterations to which it has been subject. It is therefore the purpose of the following chapters to describe each part of the building in some detail, and to tell the story of the families who have been associated with Dartington Hall during the past eleven centuries.

Dorothy and Leonard Elmhirst

Chapter 1

The Descent of the Manor of Dartington prior to the Late Fourteenth Century

Anglo-Saxon Dartington

It was not until the mid seventh century that the Saxons began to establish themselves in Devon. The course of their occupation is still not clear but it seems likely that it was essentially completed by the end of that century, except perhaps for the lowland south of Dartmoor between the estuaries of the Teign and Tamar, and even this region had been overrun by 712.[1] The existing evidence is meagre, but it suggests that the Saxon settlement of Devon was a comparatively peaceful one. By the beginning of the eighth century, all the inhabitants of Devon were subject to the laws of Wessex, paid dues to the kings of Wessex, and looked to them for protection. Despite periodic raids from the West Welsh of Cornwall, the slow task of settlement and the clearing of land in the thickly wooded Dart valley proceeded gradually, and there is clear evidence of habitation at Dartington by the second quarter of the ninth century.

Early in that century, three sisters, Beornwynn, Aelfflaed, and Wealhburgh had inherited ten hides of land at Wennland[2] and divided the property equally between themselves. Unfortunately they lost the original title-deed to their inheritance, and sought confirmation of their rights from King Egbert.[3] His charter, given at Dorchester on 26 December 833, recounts this story and adds that when the sisters received a further portion of their inheritance, Beornwynn renounced her heritage at Wennland and retired to *Derentunehomm* in Devon leaving Aelfflaed and Wealhburgh to share the land at Wennland between themselves. A translation of this charter of confirmation is given in Appendix 1.

The place-name *Derentune* is composed of two Old English elements, *Derent* meaning the river Dart and *tun* meaning a farm. Dartington is *the farm on the river Dart*. The charter of 833 refers to the Dartington *homm* or more precisely the *hamm* of Dartington. It used to be thought that this element generally meant a bend in a river, and in this example referred to the prominent bend in the river Dart, nearly three miles upstream from Totnes. It is not possible, however, to read the meaning of the seventeenth and eighteenth centuries into an Old English word and this interpretation can no longer be supported on philological grounds. A second interpretation was put forward by the English Place Name Society in 1931 which considered that the element *hamm* referred to a large area centred round *Derentune*.[4] As far as present knowledge allows, it is now considered that *hamm* probably means an area of enclosed pasture or more precisely meadow land.[5]

In considering this place-name, J. McN. Dodgson has pointed out to me that field work frequently shows that a *hamm* is situated at the bottom of a valley or stream. Furthermore, the more notable estates and settlements in Anglo-Saxon Devon were located in valleys and combes wherever there was good *hamm* land.[6] A charter of 847 shows that the whole region between Plymouth and the Dart estuary was called the Hams,[7] and this could mean not simply an area of enclosed pasture or meadow land but rather a district where settlements

---

[1] W. G. Hoskins, *Devon* (1954), 41–5.

[2] Not yet identified. Professor Whitelock suggests that it may be Woolland in Dorset, Old English *Wynnland*. H. P. R. Finberg, *The Early Charters of Wessex* (1964), 157, concurs.

[3] F. M. Stenton notes that this is one of the earliest records of the loss of a charter by a private person. *Latin Charters of the Anglo-Saxon Period* (1955), 14.

[4] J. E. B. Gover, A. Mawer, and F. M. Stenton, *Place Names of Devon*, 2 vols. (1931–2), 265, 297, 678. Also W. G. Hoskins and H. P. R. Finberg, *Devonshire Studies* (1952), 303 n. Mrs. Rose Troup, *Trans. Devon Assoc.* vol. 61 (1929), 249–80 went further and conjectured that this estate originally extended from the river Dart on the east to Dartmoor on the north, Ugborough Moor, Glaze Brook and the river Avon as far as Gara Bridge and then to the sea on the west.

[5] A. H. Smith, *English Place-Name Elements*, pt. 1 (1956), 229–31.

[6] See the map facing page 307 in W. G. Hoskins and H. P. R. Finberg, *Devonshire Studies* (1952).

[7] W. de Gray Birch, *Cartularium Saxonicum*, vol. 2 (1887), 33–5. The English Place Name Society considered that this simply meant a large district of uncertain area. Gover, Mawer, and Stenton, *Place Names of Devon*, vol. 1 (1931), 264–5.

The deer-park wall looking towards Staverton

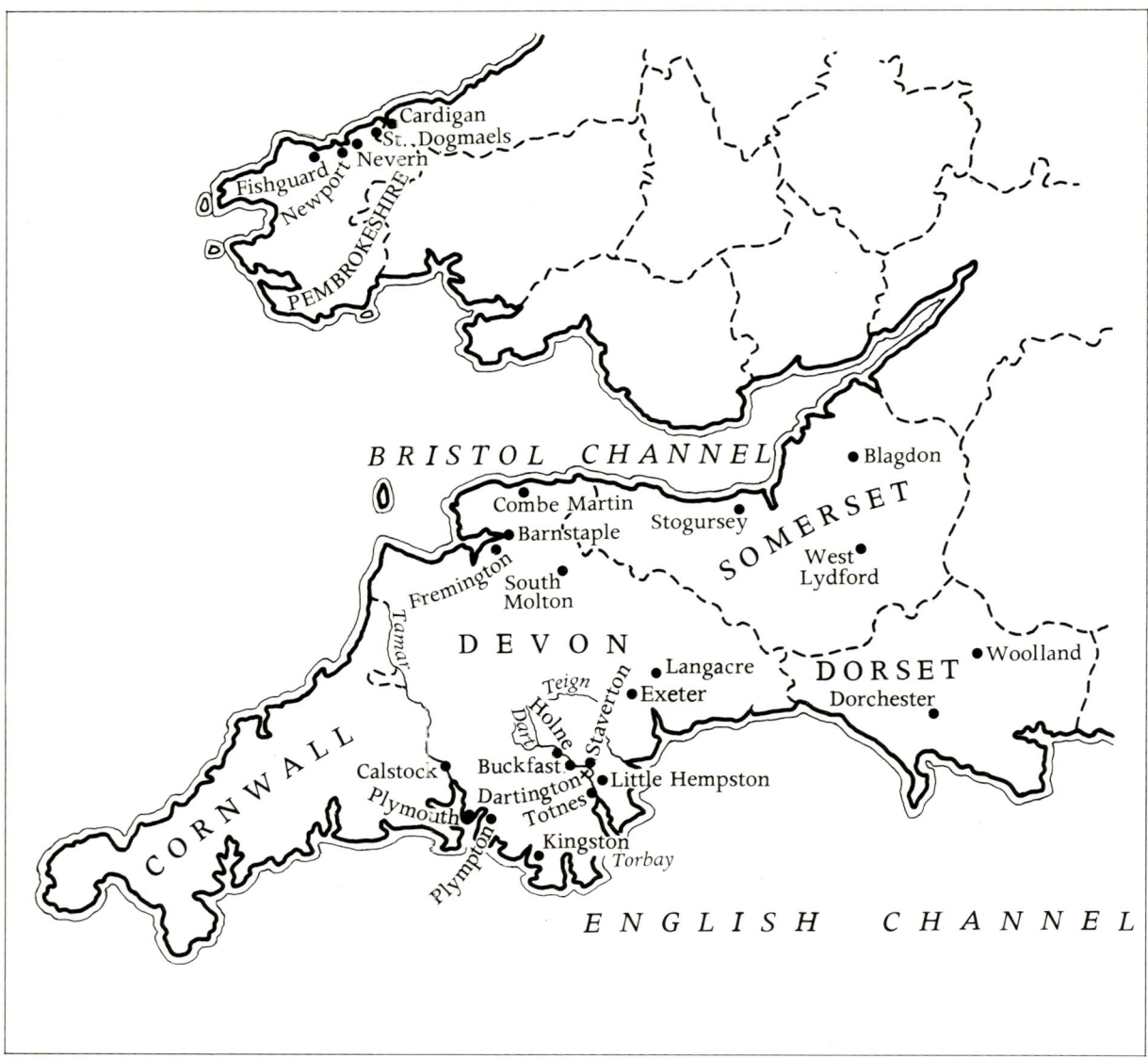

Fig. 2 Map showing places mentioned in Chapter 1

were characteristically in *hamms*. Hence *hamm* can almost have come to signify *a homestead in a valley bottom*. It is possible that *Derentune-homm*, or more precisely the *hamm Derentune*, should therefore be interpreted as *the valley bottom farm on the river Dart*. Confirmation of Mr. Dodgson's suggestion must await further research. All that may be said with certainty is that written evidence indicates that there was a settlement with enclosures of meadow land at Dartington in 833, suitable for a lady of substance, situated close to the river Dart and possibly in the river valley itself. Although there has been a residence on the site of Dartington Hall since at least the thirteenth century, any association between this and Beornwynn's homestead more than four hundred years earlier cannot be entertained on the evidence available.

Any possibility of further raids in south Devon by the West Welsh of Cornwall was eliminated by King Egbert in 838 when he defeated a combined force of West Welsh and marauding Danes, gathered on Hingston Down above Calstock in preparation for a united attack into Wessex. However, the security achieved by this victory was short-lived. The Danes, who had first plundered the English coast in 835, reached Devon in force sixteen years later. Their devastation of coastal settlements and their predatory forays up river valleys and trackways in search of plunder were maintained at irregular intervals throughout the second half of the century. Dartington may have suffered during this period, but the settlement does not seem to have been eradicated by these or by the renewed Danish raids

[8] Chapter Library, Exeter: Exon Domesday, fol. 368b. Translated in *V.C.H. Devon*, vol. 1 (1906), 491. P.R.O. Exchequer Domesday, f. 111a.2.

[9] Half of them were grouped in the lower Dart valley and the remainder were situated in the southern and eastern parts of the shire. Sir Henry Maxwell Lyte suggested that the manor of Stogursey in Somerset was probably William's principal residence. 'Burci, Falaise and Martin', *Proc. Somerset Arch. and Nat. Hist. Soc.* vol. 65 (1919), 2.

[10] This view is implied, but not stated by Lyte in his article in *Proc. Somerset Arch. and Nat. Hist. Soc.* vol. 65 (1919), 2–3. It is more clearly enunciated by J. F. A. Mason, 'The Date of the Geld Rolls', *Eng. Hist. Rev.* vol. 69 (1954), 284. Mason points out that as William's estates in Devon descended to the son of Geva by her first husband, Martin, rather than to her daughters by her second husband, William of Falaise, the latter must have held them in right of his wife. As Geva's father, Serlo de Burci, was alive when the Domesday Commissioners visited Somerset, he must have died during the course of the inquest, for property in Devon held by his son-in-law had presumably descended to him through his wife only a very short time before. Serlo's other daughter was ineligible to hold property as she had taken the veil at Shaftesbury Abbey.

[11] H. C. Darby and R. Welldon Finn, *The Domesday Geography of South-West England* (1967).

[12] This includes the 2½ plough teams on Anschetil's holding. Chapter Library, Exeter: Exon Domesday, fol. 368b. P.R.O. Exchequer Domesday, f. 111a.2. R. Lennard, 'Domesday Plough-teams: the South-western Evidence', *Eng. Hist. Rev.* vol. 60 (1945), 233, states that the number of oxen in a plough team varied from 4 to 6, 8 or even more. H. P. R. Finberg, 'The Domesday Plough-team', *Eng. Hist. Rev.* vol. 66 (1951), 67–71, prefers the more traditional reckoning of 8 oxen to a team. R. Welldon Finn has pointed out to me that 1086 seems to have been a bad weather year and mortality in beasts may have been considerable at the time.

[13] Unfortunately, the interpretation of the information about plough teams is still so doubtful that it is not yet possible to make full use of the statistics given in Domesday Book. There were 10¼ teams for 3 ferlings at Dartington and 2½ teams for 1 ferling at Luscombe. William of Falaise used 2 teams for 1 ferling, while his villagers had four times that number for 2 ferlings.

which again afflicted the south-west coast nearly a century later until Devon passed into the hands of the Danish conqueror, Cnut, in 1016.

Fifty years later, the manor of Dartington was held by Alwine, one of the many thegns who held property in late Anglo-Saxon Devon.[8] Domesday Book records that at least forty-six estates in the county were held by a person of that name in 1086, but it is unlikely that they were all held by the same individual. Alwine was a very common name at the time and had one person held over forty-six holdings, his *honour* would have been granted *en bloc*, or almost so, to a newcomer in the great redistribution of land which followed the Norman Conquest in 1066. Like nearly all the other thegns in the shire, the Alwine who held Dartington in 1066 was a victim of a gigantic revolution. His property was rudely taken from him and granted to a Norman holder, and he was left to fend for himself as best he could. For Alwine, the Norman Conquest with its consequent loss of estate, privilege, and social consideration, was an unqualified disaster.

Anglo-Norman Dartington

The greatest single change in the history of landownership in Devon occurred in the years following the Norman invasion. By 1086, approximately 55 per cent of the shire was held by the king and Church, and the remainder was divided between seventy-seven tenants-in-chief. The ownership of Dartington during the years immediately following the Norman Conquest is not entirely clear. It was held in 1086 by William of Falaise, a follower of the Conqueror who probably came from the town of Falaise in Normandy. At the time of the Domesday survey, William held nineteen manors in Devon including Dartington, and it is most likely that they formed the initial group of holdings granted to him by the Conqueror.[9] It has been suggested that Dartington may have been among the estates which he acquired in right of his wife, Geva, through her father but the evidence is far from conclusive and rests on hypothesis rather than on unimpeachable supporting evidence.[10]

The lower Dart valley was not an area of close settlement in the late eleventh century, but one of large manors and considerable prosperity compared with the greater part of Devon.[11] The manor of Dartington was bounded on the north and east by the river Dart and to the west and south by the manors of Dean, Rattery, and Follaton and the borough of Totnes. It included a small holding at Luscombe in Rattery which had been held as a separate manor until the Conquest and which William of Falaise let out to an under-tenant, Anschetil.

Nearly every entry in Domesday Book includes two statistics which, although still subject to considerable discussion concerning their precise interpretation, give some indication of the wealth and size of a holding. The first is the recorded population within different grades of society and the second is the number of plough teams necessary to till the potential arable land. According to Domesday Book, there was sufficient land available at Dartington for 15 plough teams.[12] At that time, 824 or two-thirds of the settlements in Devon were incapable of supporting more than 5 plough teams and of the remainder, only 133 had land for 10 or more teams. Dartington's ability to support 15 teams marks it as among the more prosperous settlements in the county and one of the most valuable held by William of Falaise.[13] The recorded population of 33 villeins, cottagers, and slaves indicates that the

15

manor was a sizeable settlement by Devonshire standards. There were 13 villein families, possibly living in a small hamlet rather than in detached farms, and the manor also supported 7 bordars or cottagers, 9 slaves, 2 swineherds, and 2 fishermen. Anschetil had a further 4 villein families and a slave at Luscombe. As it is usually considered that the figures given in Domesday refer to heads of households and not to individuals, they should be subject to a multiplication factor of something like 4 or 5 to obtain a closer assessment of the population of the manor.[14]

The Torbay region was the principal sheep-rearing area in the county at the time of the survey, but although it records that William and Geva kept 72 sheep, no information is given here or elsewhere about the number maintained by the villeins. The payment of a rent of 19 swine indicates that pig farming was undertaken at Dartington, as in other parts of the shire, on quite a large scale and the reference to a single *porcus* might be to a boar, rented out by William for breeding purposes. Fish was an important item in the medieval economy and the presence of two fishermen who paid an annual rent of 80 salmon to their lord is an early recorded example of the fishing value of the river Dart. The large area of woodland, ½ league by 2½ furlongs,[15] and 30 acres of coppice reflect the importance of woodland in this area. 100 acres of pasture land (presumably common-pasture) were available throughout the year for feeding cattle and sheep, but the absence of any record of meadow land, other than ½ acre held by Anschetil, is surprising in view of the proximity of the manor to the river Dart. This is probably a clerical error for hay must have been obtained from somewhere. The manor apparently increased slightly in value from £4. 15s. in 1066 to £5 in 1086.[16] This may indicate that Dartington was participating in the general prosperity of the Torbay hinterland where values were rising, rather than in the declining values of the area between the Dart and Tamar estuaries.[17] It is possible, however, that the increase was the result of stiffer rents. Only Anschetil's holding had risen in value and this was rather well-teamed and populated for a small hamlet.

It should be observed that the present estate still shows traces of a form which may be traced as far back as the eleventh century. There has never been a village of Dartington. It is quite clear that the estate has consisted for several centuries of the lord's demesne and a number of scattered hamlets and farmsteads, and Domesday Book suggests that this pattern was in existence in 1086. Coppice and woodland formed a substantial part of the estate then as they do now, while the existing cultivation pattern of large irregular fields possibly reflects a long-established system. The present landscape has hardly changed since the tithe map of 1839 was prepared and this valuable source for early cultivation patterns gives no evidence that the open-field system was practised in medieval Dartington as in some parts of Devon.[18]

William of Falaise's wife, Geva, was the daughter of Serlo de Burci who had been granted a group of fifteen estates in Somerset and Dorset within two years of the Conquest.[19] Her first husband was Martin, the founder of the family of that name, but on his death she had married William of Falaise. A charter drawn up between 1100 and 1107[20] shows that both William and Geva were still alive at the beginning of the twelfth century, but on William's death all his Devon holdings reverted to Robert, Geva's son by her first husband, and the long tenancy of Dartington by the Martin family began.

[14] It is still not known whether slaves were recorded as heads of households or as individuals. H. C. Darby and E. M. J. Campbell, *The Domesday Geography of South-East England* (1962), 588–90.

[15] As there was no standard league or furlong at the time, it is not possible to discover the area covered by woodland in 1086. H. C. Darby, *The Domesday Geography of Eastern England* (1952), 335–6.

[16] The entry for Dartington in the Exchequer text differs from, or omits, some of the information given in the Exeter book. The former values Luscombe at 5s. while the latter values it at 15s. This makes all the difference between a decline or an appreciation in the total value of the manor. Other differences between the texts include the omission by the Exchequer scribe of the 2 fishermen and their rent, a record in the Exchequer volume of 8 rather than 8½ villeins, and 21 swineherd against the 19 ($x^i x$) noted in the Exeter text.

[17] F. W. Morgan, 'The Domesday Geography of Devon', *Trans. Devon Assoc.* vol. 72 (1940), 318–20.

[18] P.R.O. Tithe Map of Devon, 1839. See also W. G. Hoskins and H. P. R. Finberg, *Devonshire Studies* (1952), 265–88.

[19] H. W. C. Davis, *Regesta Regum Anglo-Normannorum*, vol. 1, 1066–1100 (1913), 7. Blagdon in Somerset was possibly the most important of his holdings. Sir Henry Maxwell Lyte, 'Burci, Falaise and Martin', *Proc. Somerset Arch. and Nat. Hist. Soc.* vol. 65 (1919), 2.

[20] William and Geva gave the church of St. Andrew of Stogursey, Somerset, with a hide of land and all tithes of Cockington, Williton, and Lilstock to the abbey of Lonlay. The charter also gives details of an endowment to the abbey at Teignton, Devon, and Treguz, Glamorgan, by Robert Fitz Martin. The charter was witnessed by Miles Crispin who died in 1107. T. D. Tremlett and N. Blakiston, *Stogursey Charters*, Somerset Record Society, vol. 61 (1946), 1–2.

The Martin Family: c. 1107–1359

Eight generations of the Martin family held the manor of Dartington between the early twelfth and the mid fourteenth century, but few records have survived concerning their tenure of the property.[21] There is documentary evidence which suggests that the family were resident at Dartington in the mid twelfth century, and excavations have revealed evidence of an apparently late thirteenth-century building on the site of the later Hall. No part of the present structure, however, can be clearly assigned to this family although they may have been responsible for the deer-park wall.

[21] For accounts of this family, see: Tristram Risdon, *Chorographic Description or Survey of the County of Devon* (1605–30; published 1811); Thomas Westcote, *View of Devonshire* (1630; published 1845); Sir William Pole, *Collections towards a Description of the County of Devon* (early 17th century; published 1791); W. Dugdale, *The Baronage of England*, vol. 1 (1675), 729; John Prince, *Worthies of Devon* (1701); J. L. Vivian, *The Visitations of the County of Devon* (1895); J. Collinson, *The History and Antiquities of the County of Somerset* (1791, ed. 1898); J. Hutchins, *The History and Antiquities of the County of Dorset* (3rd ed., 1861–70); George Owen, *The Description of Pembrokeshire* (1603 ed., 4 vols., 1892–1936); R. Fenton, *Historical Tour through Pembrokeshire* (1811). More recent books are of little value: E. M. Pritchard, *History of St. Dogmael's Abbey* (1907); W. G. W. Watson, *House of Martin—chapters in the history of the West of England branch of that family* (1906); Lady Lloyd, *The Lords Marcher of Kemes* (1930). There are several relevant articles. In order of value they are Sir Henry Maxwell Lyte, 'Burci, Falaise and Martin' in *Proc. Somerset Arch. and Nat. Hist. Soc.* vol. 65 (1919), 1–27; V. Gibbs and H. A. Doubleday, 'The Martin family', *The Complete Peerage*, vol. 8 (1932), 530–9; J. H. Round, 'The Lord of Kemes' in *Family Origins and other Studies*, ed. W. Page (1930), 73–102, and H. R. Watkin, *History of Totnes Priory and Medieval Town*, vol. 2 (1917), 745–56.

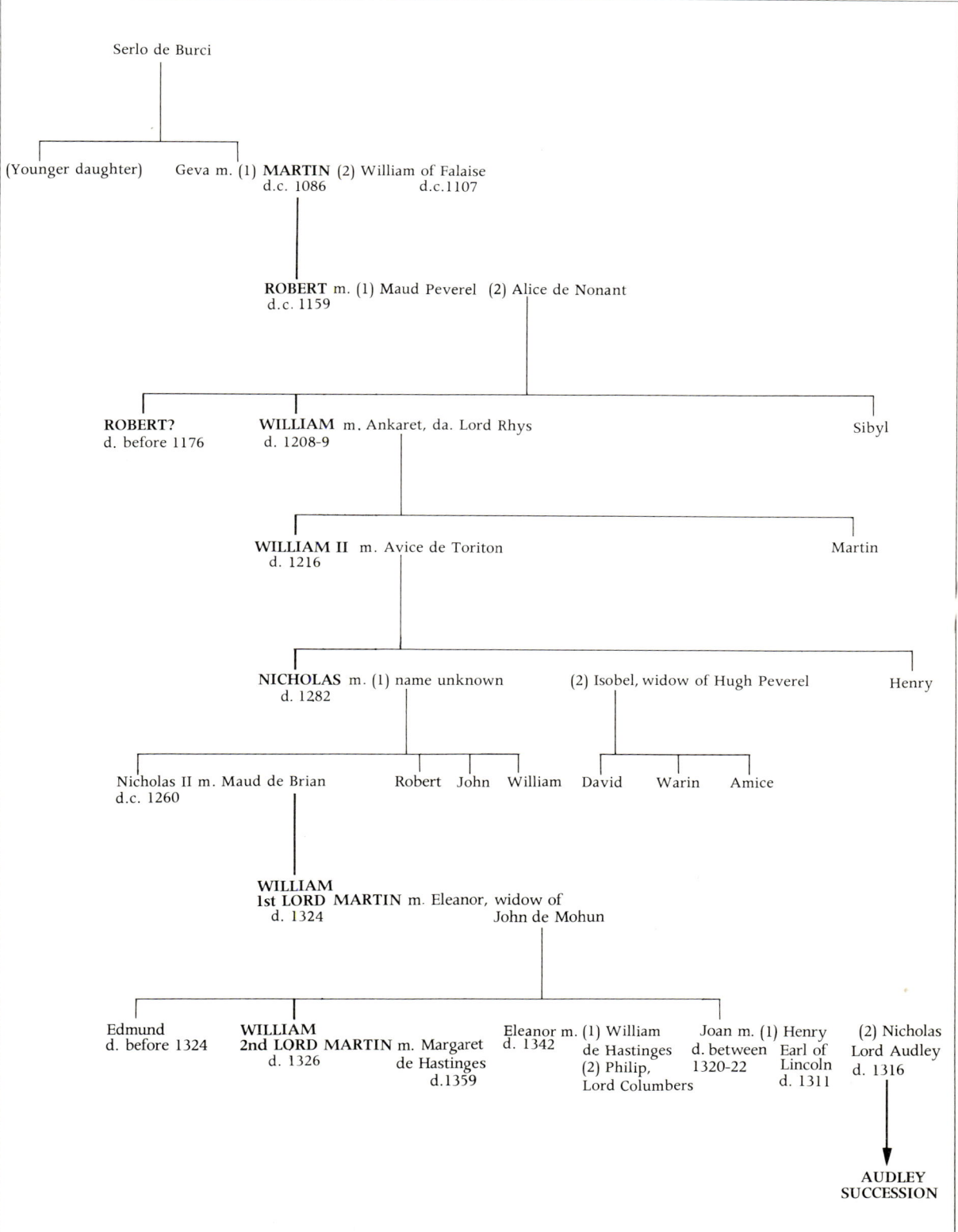

Fig. 3 The Martin succession from the 11th to the 14th centuries

The Martins were among the first generation of Normans in England but nothing is known about the founder of the family apart from his name, that of his wife, and the fact that he died before the completion of the Domesday survey for Devon in 1086.[22] His son, Robert, entered into the manor of Dartington during the early years of the twelfth century and spent much of his life extending the family holdings by conquest in South Wales. He was one of the Norman lords who gradually subjected South Wales to foreign rule during the late eleventh and early twelfth centuries and who carved out regions for themselves and their families. Robert seems to have been the first Norman lord of the cantref of Cemaes, that district which stretched along the north coast of Pembrokeshire from Fishguard to the neighbourhood of Cardigan, and he held this region from about 1115 onwards.[23]

Most of the surviving records of Robert and his first wife, Maud Peverel, refer to their religious benefactions and particularly to the priory founded by them at St. Dogmael's in Cemaes in about 1115.[24] Among such benefactions, given at unspecified dates, may be noted the conveyance of a fourth part of the lands of Fenna in the manor of Dartington to the canons of Plympton,[25] and the gift of land in *Derteland*—an area possibly reclaimed from the river Dart—to the monks of Totnes Priory.[26]

The succession of the Martin estates immediately after Robert's death in about 1159 is uncertain, for there were apparently two sons, Robert and William, by his second wife, the young Alice de Nonant. The references to Robert are meagre and it is not even clear whether he was the elder brother or not.[27] Robert's tenure of the Martin estates therefore, even if it occurred at all, must have been very short-lived, for they were certainly held by William when he attained his majority in 1176.[28] Dartington, however, was one of the family estates granted to Alice de Nonant as part of her dower after her husband's death. A deed dating from the third quarter of the twelfth century records that Robert was buried in the chapter house of Totnes Priory and that Alice gave some land to the monks of the priory. As the deed was drawn up at Dartington, it implies that she was resident there at the time.[29] It is possible that she had associations with Dartington before her second marriage, for her first husband, Roger de Nonant, apparently held property there at the beginning of the century.[30] Alice's grant to Totnes Priory, however, is the earliest known documentary evidence suggestive of a Martin residence at Dartington.

Although she had already survived two husbands, Alice was still young enough for the king to claim his right to find her another husband. But she took the matter into her own hands in about 1175 by remarrying without royal permission. Her temerity resulted in the forfeiture of her estates at Dartington, Langacre, and Holne from 1176 until at least 1189 when the sheriff of Devon collected all their profits on behalf of the Exchequer.[31] A gap in the sheriff's accounts after 1189 makes it impossible to establish when Alice died or when the sheriff ceased to collect these profits, but these events had occurred before 1194 when Richard I confirmed all the lands and liberties of Serlo de Burci to Alice's son, William Martin.[32]

William was head of the family for at least thirty-five years and possibly for far longer. His estates consisted of a compact holding in South Wales and a number of manors in the three western counties of Dorset, Devon, and Somerset.[33] He hoped that his marriage to a daughter of Lord Rhys, the most powerful Welsh prince of his day, would strengthen

[22] It is possible that he was the Martinus de Walis who witnessed the foundation charter of Totnes Priory. H. R. Watkin, *History of Totnes Priory and Medieval Town*, vol. 1 (1914), 9–10.

[23] J. E. Lloyd, *History of Wales*, vol. 2 (1911), 425, considers it unlikely that the conquest took place before this date.

[24] J. H. Round, *Cal. Docs. France: 918–1206*, xxxv–vi, 352–4. The house was raised to the dignity of an abbey in 1120.

[25] Probably land at Venton. The grant is recorded in a confirmation of the priory's possessions by Henry II. G. Oliver, *Monasticon Dioecesis Exoniensis* (1889 ed.), 135.

[26] The grant was made after September 1120 as it was witnessed by Fulchard, abbot of St. Dogmael's, who was installed there in September of that year. H. R. Watkin, *History of Totnes Priory and Medieval Town*, vol. 1 (1914), 26.

[27] Robert is not mentioned in the article by Sir Henry Maxwell Lyte or by the editors of *The Complete Peerage*. The evidence for his existence is:
(i) A grant to Totnes Priory by Alice de Nonant which specifically refers to her two sons, Robert and William, and to her daughter. See p. 19, n. 29.
(ii) Robert, son of Robert, son of Martin, witnessed a deed of Roger de Nonant which also refers to the boundaries of property held by Robert, son of Martin. The date of this document is not known. It survives in an early 14th-century cartulary of Buckfast Abbey (no. 44), ed. F. C. Hingeston-Randolph, *Register of John of Grandisson, Bishop of Exeter, 1327–69*, pt. 3 (1899), 1594–5.
(iii) There are at least two returns from Robert, son of Martin, and although they were made some years after Robert Martin's death in about 1159, it is usually assumed that they refer to him. The scutage returns from the sheriff of Devon in 1162 record the payment of 22s. 6d. from Robert, son of Martin, and the outstanding debt of 44s. 2d., Pipe Roll, 8 Henry II, 6. In 1166, the bishop of Bath confirmed that Robert, son of Martin, held ¾ knight's fee from him. H. Hall, *Red Book of the Exchequer* (1896), 221. In view of the date of these entries, it is just possible that they refer to the son rather than the father as considered hitherto. The fact that the abbot of Glastonbury reported that an unnamed son of Robert, son of Martin, held 5 knight's fees from him at the same time as the bishop of Bath made his return, lends some colour to this view. Ibid., 223.

[28] *Pipe Roll, 22 Henry II*, 156, which records his fine of £10 for defaulting before the justices in Somerset.

[29] H. R. Watkin, *History of Totnes Priory and Medieval Town*, vol. 1 (1914), 57. The grant was made after the death of Alice's husband in about 1159 and before her remarriage in 1175. Watkin ascribed it to the period 1162–5 (p. 59) but subsequently amended this to 1166–71 (p. 1121b).

[30] H. R. Watkin, *History of Totnes Priory and Medieval Town*, vol. 2 (1917), 698. C. Johnson and H. A. Cronne, *Regesta Regum Anglo-Normannorum, vol. 2, 1100–1135* (1956), 50.

[31] See entries in Pipe Rolls, 22 Henry II–35 Henry II.

[32] P.R.O. Ancient Petitions, no. 2978.

[33] The estates in south-west England formed the barony of Blagdon. Dartington is sometimes referred to as the head of this barony, e.g. *Cal. Inq. Post Mortem*, vol. 2, 263, but Blagdon has the greater claim. I. J. Sanders, *English Baronies* (1960), 15.

[34] *Pipe Roll, 11 John*, 102, under Dorset and Somerset which records the large sum of £200 paid by his son as relief on entering into his patrimony.

[35] *Rot. Lit. Claus*, vol. 1 (1833), 248, 293, 457; ibid., vol. 2 (1844), 23; *Cal. Close Rolls, 1227–31*, 553. William Martin II had married Avice de Toriton, apparently a sister of Fawkes de Breauté. Custody of the Martin estates was granted in the first instance to de Breauté, but after the exile of this ruthless soldier of fortune in 1225, their wardship was held by Henry de Trubleville, later seneschal of Gascony and Lord of the Channel Islands.

[36] *Cal. Inq. Post Mortem*, vol. 1, 71. For a summary of Nicholas Martin's career, see C. Moor, *Knights of Edward I*, vol. 3 (1930), 124–5.

[37] *Cal. Charter Rolls*, vol. 1 (1226–57), 307; ibid., vol. 2 (1257–1300), 53.

[38] In 1326 William Martin was receiving £11. 7s. 2d. in rents from the 68 burgesses in this settlement. P.R.O. C 134/99, no. 14.

[39] *Cal. Pat. Rolls 1225–32*, 105. In 1288, the church was valued at £6. 12s.

[40] When the church was restored in 1852, the foundations are said to have been discovered of an earlier transeptal church with a west tower and no aisles. W. Grey, *Trans. Exeter Diocesan Arch. Soc.* vol. 2 (1870), 113.

his territorial position and help to preserve peace between the Normans and the Welsh. However, the latter swept across Cemaes in 1191, forced William to abandon the family stronghold at Nevern and to establish Newport as the principal seat of his family. He died in 1208 or 1209,[34] followed by his son eight years later.

The estates passed through a period of wardship until Nicholas Martin was of age to take possession of them in about 1231.[35] A constant supporter of Henry III, Nicholas played an active part in Welsh affairs throughout his life and had been knighted for his services by 1253.[36] Sir Nicholas added to the family inheritance by acquiring the hundred and manor of South Molton and obtaining a life interest in West Lydford. He also contributed to the prosperity of some of his Devon estates, as well as to his own pocket, by obtaining the right for fairs and markets to be held at South Molton and Combe Martin in 1246 and 1265 respectively.[37] Sir Nicholas was also possibly responsible for founding the extension of the borough of Totnes known as North Ford outside the north gate of the town. It was adjacent to the manor of Dartington and covered the most direct approach to the Exeter road.[38] The church at Dartington may have been built during his lifetime for the earliest record of a rector dates from 1226[39] and the foundations of a building, earlier than the structure pulled down in 1878, are said to have been discovered during a restoration twenty years before.[40] Dartington also knew a less generous side of Sir Nicholas's character, for he was summoned in 1280 for holding free warren and view of frankpledge, and for exacting fines

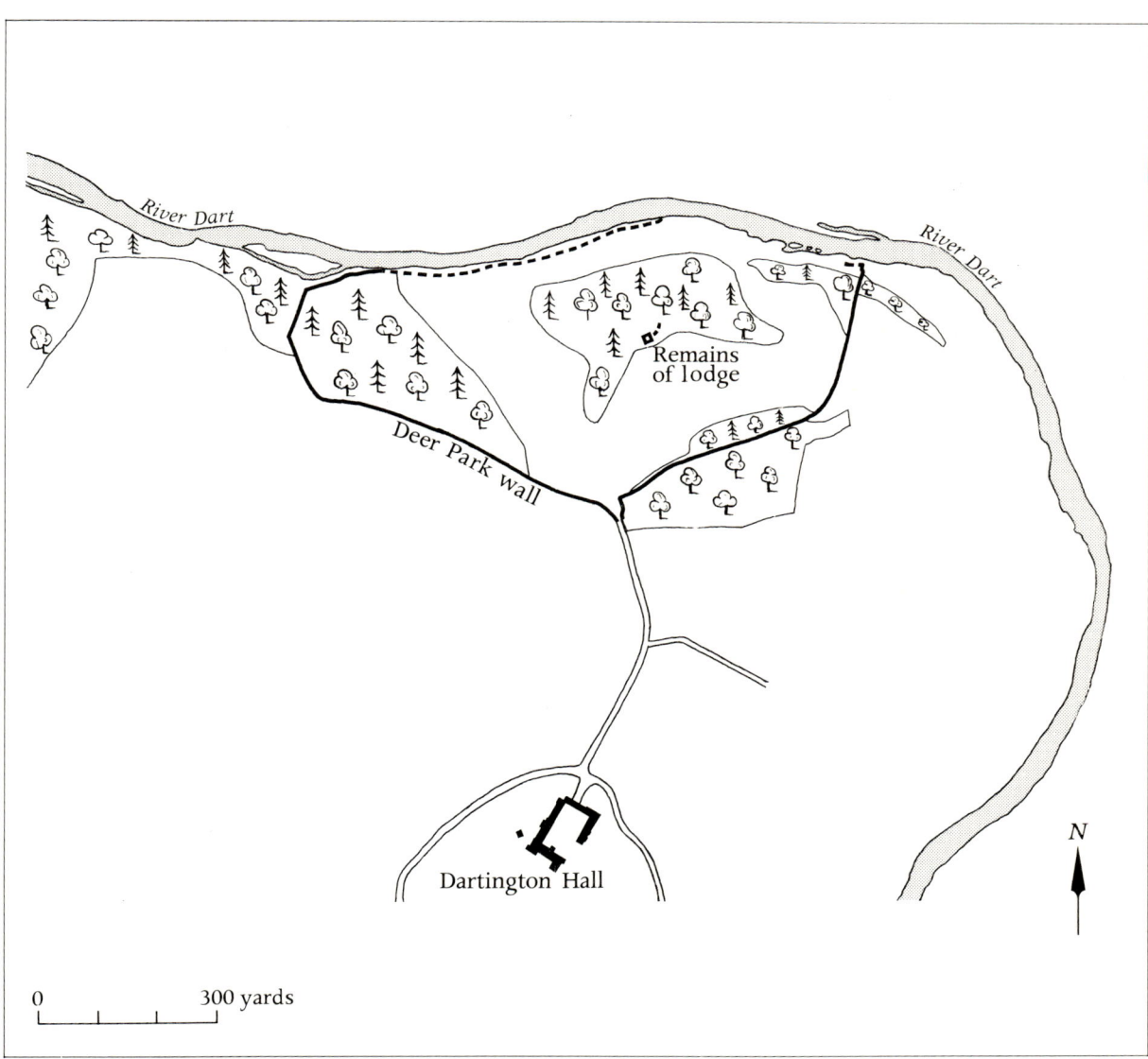

Fig. 4 The deer-park wall at Dartington

for breaking the assizes of bread and beer at Dartington without royal licence.[41]
His grandson, William Martin, spent much of his life in the service of the Crown, first in military service with Edward I against the Welsh and then as a supporter of Edward II in the party struggles of his reign.[42] He received a personal writ of summons to Parliament in 1295 whereby he is held to have become Lord Martin, and although his principal estates were in Wales, he spent more time in Devon than many of his forbears. In 1301 and in several subsequent years, Lord Martin was a commissioner of oyer and terminer in Devon,[43] and in 1305 Edward I gave him the custody of the lands and marriage rights of the heir of Henry de la Pomerai.[44] Two years later and on subsequent occasions, he was one of the keepers of the peace in Devon[45] and in 1308 his estates were extended by the addition of his mother's inheritance which included the barony of Barnstaple.[46] Lord Martin had received a grant of free warren in some of his estates in Devon and Somerset in 1293 including Dartington,[47] and he had obtained a licence in 1305 enjoining the manor of Totnes to maintain the two causeways and bridges leading from the north gate of Totnes to Dartington.[48] It is also likely that he was responsible for the earliest known residence on the site of the present Hall, for the foundations of a building, discovered in 1962 south of the great hall, probably date from the late thirteenth century.[49]

Lord Martin was survived by his second son, William, and his elder daughter, Eleanor. William, thirty years old at the time of his succession in 1324,[50] died less than two years later.[51] He had married Margaret, daughter of John Lord Hastinges, but in the absence of any children, the estates were divided between William's co-heirs, his forty-year-old sister and James, the fourteen-year-old son of his younger sister Joan by her second husband, Nicholas Lord Audley.[52] The manor of Dartington was among the estates apportioned to James Lord Audley, but it was granted on his behalf to Margaret, Lord Martin's widow, as part of her dower. She held it from June 1326 until her death in 1359 when it reverted to Lord Audley.[53] In 1326 it was stated that the manor covered 968 acres and was worth £55. 17s. 7½d., only approximately half the value of three of the Martin estates in north Devon.[54] Yet Dartington and Kingston were their richest holdings in south Devon and were worth more than the castle and town of Newport in Cemaes or the manors of Barnstaple or Combe Martin.[55] James became sole heir to the Martin estates on Eleanor's death in 1342[56] although he did not obtain possession of Dartington until seventeen years later.

The Martin family had held Dartington for well over two hundred years. They had lived there intermittently and in an unspectacular fashion, cultivating the land, serving the king in his wars, sometimes helping to maintain the king's peace in Devon as well as in Wales. On the whole, the repercussions of the family on Dartington and its neighbourhood were less than on many of their properties, and little trace of their tenancy is visible today. The earliest known buildings on the site of the present Hall can be attributed to them and part of the existing stone wall enclosing a deer-park north of the Hall may well have been their responsibility.[57] But although the estate was still bringing in a substantial return in 1326, the capital messuage or homestead was beginning to succumb to a period of neglect and apart from the easement of the houses, it was worth nothing at that time.[58] The passing of the estate to the Audley family in the mid fourteenth century failed to bring about any improvement in its condition, and the Martin residence was in ruins by 1388.

[41] Assize Roll, 1280.

[42] See C. Moor, *Knights of Edward I*, vol. 3 (1930), 125-7 for details of Lord Martin's career.

[43] *Cal. Pat. Rolls 1301–07*, 79, 354.

[44] Ibid., 376. E. B. Powley, *The House of De La Pomerai* (1944), 44, 51.

[45] *Cal. Pat. Rolls 1307–13*, 30; *Cal. Pat. Rolls 1313–17*, 108.

[46] *Cal. Fine Rolls 1307–19*, 30; I. J. Sanders, *English Baronies* (1960), 104–5.

[47] *Cal. Charter Rolls 1257–1300*, 433.

[48] *Cal. Pat. Rolls 1301–07*, 385.

[49] See Appendix 4. The late 13th-century remains at Newport Castle, Pembrokeshire, are also attributed to William Martin. *Arch. Jour.* vol. 119 (1962), 340.

[50] *Cal. Inq. Post Mortem*, vol. 6, 358.

[51] Ibid., 446–53. It records his lands in Cemaes, his estates in London, and his manors in Somerset, Dorset, Devon, and Cornwall.

[52] *Cal. Inq. Post Mortem*, vol. 6, 446–53. Joan had died between 1320 and 1322.

[53] *Cal. Close Rolls 1323–27*, 483; *Cal. Inq. Post Mortem*, vol. 10, 390; *Devon Feet of Fines*, ed. O. J. Reichel, F. B. Prideaux, and H. Tapley-Soper, Devon and Cornwall Record Society, vol. 2 (1939), 386–7.

[54] P.R.O. C 134/99, no. 14. The acreage excludes the land taken up by the capital messuage or homestead.

[55] *Cal. Close Rolls 1323–27*, 483.

[56] *Cal. Fine Rolls 1337–47*, 319.

[57] The wall is devoid of datable features. The park was enclosed and stocked with deer by 1325. *Cal. Inq. Post Mortem*, vol. 6, 448. In May 1326, it was estimated that the park covered 100 acres. P.R.O. C 134/99, no. 14. The present stone wall encloses an area of 66 acres.

[58] P.R.O. C 134/99, no. 14.

The Audley Family and their Immediate Successors: 1359–1388

The Audley family did not rise to prominence until the first half of the thirteenth century when they acquired a substantial amount of property in north Shropshire and north-west Staffordshire.[59] A rapid succession of deaths, seven between 1272 and 1317, made it difficult to develop or enlarge their inheritance and it was not until the young James Lord Audley inherited the patrimony in 1316 that it experienced a period of settled ownership.

Lord Audley's life is devoid of major interest, but his disagreeable nature brought him into conflict with the law on several occasions[60] and he was indirectly responsible for Dartington and other family property passing into the king's hands. Lord Audley became sole heir to the estates of his maternal uncle in 1342 and took possession of them in 1359. Six years earlier, Audley had made an agreement with Edward III whereby some of the estates of the Martin family were to be enfeoffed to the Crown at once, some were to be re-enfeoffed to Lord Audley for his lifetime with remainder to the king, and some were to be re-enfeoffed to Lord Audley and his second wife Isobel with remainder to their son, James, and then to the king in the absence of any heirs by either father or son. This third group of estates included the manors of Barnstaple, Combe Martin, and Fremington, and the reversion of the manor of Dartington which Audley claimed were worth £266. 13s. 4d. a year, although he agreed to furnish additional estates if it was found that his reckoning was inaccurate.[61] The reasons for this agreement with the king are not clear but reference to

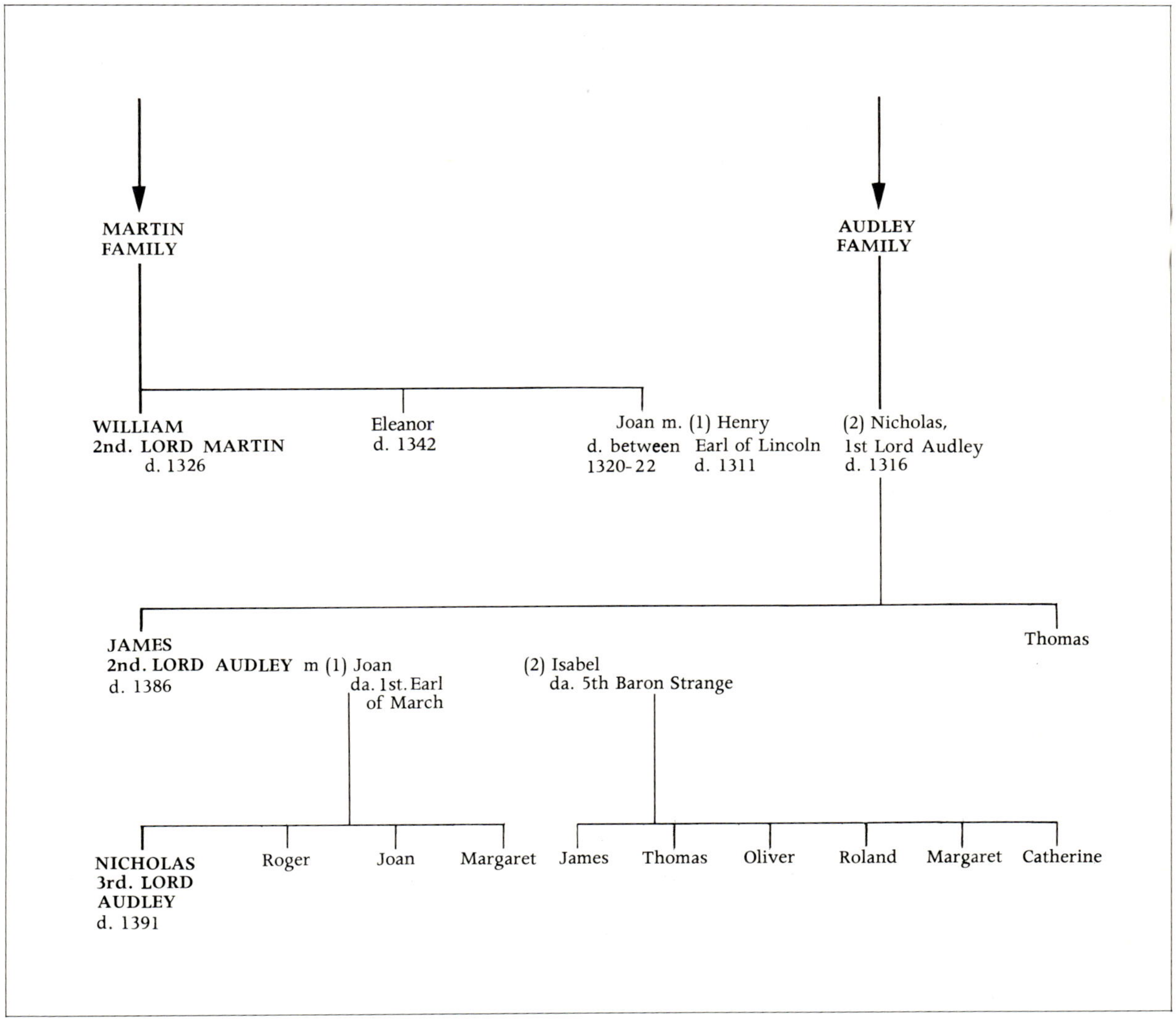

---

[59] No detailed study has yet been made of this family. Early accounts include W. Dugdale, *The Baronage of England*, vol. 1 (1675), 746–51, and S. Erdeswick, *Survey of Staffordshire* (1844 edition; ed. T. Harwood), 92–106. A brief but useful summary is given in V. Gibbs and H. A. Doubleday, *The Complete Peerage*, vol. 1 (1910), 336–46. The early history is discussed by J. H. Round, *Peerage and Pedigree*, vol. 2 (1910), 22–36, and J. Wedgwood, 'The Parentage of Sir James de Audley', *Collections for a History of Staffordshire*, vol. 9 (1906), 259–66. A. L. Reade, *Audley Pedigrees*, 3 pts. (1929–36) does not include the Barons Audley of Audley, Staffordshire in his text.

[60] *Cal. Pat. Rolls 1343–45*, 192–3; F. C. Hingeston-Randolph, *Register of John of Grandisson, Bishop of Exeter, 1327–69*, pt. 3 (1899), 1294–5, 1310, 1379, 1472; V. Gibbs and H. A. Doubleday, *The Complete Peerage*, vol. 1 (1910), 339, 340.

[61] *Cal. Close Rolls 1349–54*, 594; *Cal. Pat. Rolls 1350–54*, 427, 445.

Fig. 5 The Audley succession in the 14th century

an Inquisition Post Mortem held on the death of Lord Martin's widow six years later indicates that it was in settlement of a fine levied against Lord Audley in the king's court for an unnamed offence.[62] As Audley's eldest son by his second wife died without heirs in 1370 and all their other sons died without heirs before their father, it was only a matter of time before these estates passed into the king's hands.

There is no evidence to suggest that Audley spent any time at Dartington after he had obtained possession of the manor in 1359.[63] It was simply one of the more prosperous of his estates, offering a regular income towards the end of his life of just over £50 per year without taking into account the sale of any woodland.[64] Audley tried to increase his income in 1380 by building six weirs at Dartington, Staverton, and Little Hempston so that he could take advantage of the rich fisheries which bordered his estate. The abbot of Buckfast Abbey, five miles upstream, protested vehemently, claiming that he and his fellow monks were being deprived of the salmon which they had been catching in their weir near the abbey for many generations. Protracted negotiations over a three-year period finally led to a settlement in December 1383 when Lord Audley undertook to destroy the offending weirs, whilst the abbot and monks agreed to say masses for Lord Audley and his family and to insert their coat of arms in the west gable of the abbey church and the gable of the lady chapel.[65]

Lord Audley died in April 1386.[66] Richard II had taken advantage of Audley's advancing years to grant the reversion of Dartington and other Audley estates to two of his friends in turn. The first recipient was his half-brother, John Holand, who held them for a period of less than four months from mid December 1384 to April 1385.[67] Six months later, Richard re-granted them to his chamberlain and favourite, the handsome but incompetent Robert de Vere, earl of Oxford, shortly before he embarked on his expedition to Ireland.[68] After the earl's defeat at Radcot Bridge in December 1387 and his subsequent flight from England, the manor of Dartington again passed to the Crown, now lacking the woodland which de Vere had stripped and sold for £95. 5s. 8d. in an effort to meet his commitments in Ireland.[69] In the following July, the manor was re-granted to its former holder John Holand, and it is with this particular event and person that the story of Dartington Hall as it stands today truly begins.

[62] *Cal. Inq. Post Mortem*, vol. 10, 390.

[63] *Cal. Close Rolls 1354–60*, 589.

[64] *Cal. Inq. Misc. 1387–93*, 4. The value of the manor in 1388 was made up of £28. 8s. 2d. from the rent of assize, £14 from the farm of the demesne lands, £4 from the farm of the mill, £1. 10s. 0d. from the perquisites of the court, £1. 6s. 8d. from the aid of the villeins, and £2. ?s. 10d. from the sale of boon works.

[65] *Cal. Close Rolls 1377–81*, 303; *Cal. Pat. Rolls 1381–85*, 344.

[66] Nicholas, Lord Audley's eldest and sole surviving son by his first wife, died without heirs in 1391. The barony passed into the Tuchet family through the marriage of Nicholas's sister, Joan, to Sir John Tuchet.

[67] *Cal. Pat. Rolls 1381–85*, 515–16.

[68] *Cal. Pat. Rolls 1385–89*, 115, 112–13.

[69] *Cal. Inq. Misc. 1387–93*, 4. Sir Philip Courtenay was granted custody of the park at Dartington in March 1388, but he held it for less than 3 months. *Cal. Pat. Rolls 1385–89*, 413.

Chapter 2

John Holand, Earl of Huntingdon: Mid Fourteenth Century to 1390

Youth and Upbringing

The life of John Holand, earl of Huntingdon and later duke of Exeter, spans the second half of the fourteenth century. He was born at a time when fear of recurrence of the plague which had wreaked such damage between 1349 and 1351, was almost overshadowed by the seemingly glorious victories of the early part of the Hundred Years War against France. The defeat of a large French army by the Black Prince near Poitiers in 1356 and the capture of King John had endorsed the earlier victories of Edward III, and there was almost complete harmony for a time between the king and his magnates. But as Holand grew up, this co-operation gradually diminished and many of the problems which Edward's successor had to face and in which Holand was involved, stemmed from the fierce antagonism which arose between the Throne and a group of powerful and impolitic magnates.

John Holand's father, Sir Thomas Holand, was a cadet of a minor Lancashire family originating from the village of Upholland near Wigan.[1] The earliest record of the family occurs early in the thirteenth century, but the family did not rise in importance until Sir Robert Holand became an official of the household of Thomas, earl of Lancaster, in the first quarter of the fourteenth century.[2] Sir Robert's second son, Thomas, was born in about 1317, and shortly after he had been appointed steward to the youthful earl of Salisbury, he fell in love with Joan, the 'Fair Maid of Kent'.[3] Joan, whose beauty and personality aroused comment when she was still very young, was the daughter of Edmund, earl of Kent, Edward I's youngest son. She married Sir Thomas by contract in or before 1339 when she was not more than eleven years old and he, already a proven soldier, was about twenty-two, and before his death late in 1360, Joan had borne him two daughters and two sons, Thomas and John.[4]

Very little is known about John Holand's infancy and youth. The date of his birth is unknown and no documents or chronicles give any indication of his age at any point in his life. All that can be said with certainty is that he was born after his elder brother in about 1350 and before November 1360 when his parents apparently granted him two manors for life.[5] There is no evidence to confirm the statement that John was born in about 1352;[6] in fact, it is possible that he was born in the mid or late 1350s for he was not knighted until 1380 and none of his contemporaries is known to have received a knighthood later than his twenty-fourth birthday.[7]

Ten months after Sir Thomas's death in December 1360, Joan married the thirty-year-old prince of Wales, Edward, the Black Prince. The Holand brothers therefore spent the remainder of their early years with their step-father. During the first few months of their married life, Joan and her family lived with the Black Prince at Berkhamsted where John Holand was under the direct supervision of the prince's yeoman, John de la Haye.[8] But

---

[1] For the history of this family, see W. Dugdale, *The Baronage of England*, vol. 2 (1676), 73–82; Bernard Holland, *The Lancashire Hollands* (1917); the relevant entries in *The Dictionary of National Biography*; and the more carefully compiled ones in V. Gibbs and H. A. Doubleday, *The Complete Peerage*, particularly under Exeter, vol. 5 (1926), Holand, vol. 6 (1926), and Kent, vol. 7 (1929).

[2] *V.C.H. Lancashire*, vol. 4 (1911), 92–3; V. Gibbs and H. A. Doubleday, *The Complete Peerage*, vol. 6 (1926), 528–33.

[3] W. Dugdale, *The Baronage of England*, vol. 2 (1676), 74a. Joan's soubriquet does not seem to be a contemporary one.

[4] Another son, Edmund, is mentioned by W. Dugdale, *The Baronage of England*, vol. 2 (1676), 74b. No reference is given and he cannot be traced in any known documents. It is possible that Dugdale confused him with Edmund, the second son of Thomas Holand, earl of Kent and grandson of Sir Thomas Holand.

[5] *Cal. Pat. Rolls 1358–61*, 480.

[6] T. F. Tout, *Chapters in the Administrative History of Medieval England*, vol. 4 (1928), 23, states that he was 45 in 1397 but there is no evidence to show that he was born in 1352. W. J. Hardy suggested in *The Dictionary of National Biography*, vol. 9 (1921), that he may have been born between 1350 and 1352, but he gave no supporting evidence. It is unfortunate that Huntingdon is the only major figure in Richard's reign whose age is in doubt.

[7] It is not always certain when contemporary members of the greater baronage were knighted, but their ages can be accurately established in the case of 18 members born during the third quarter of the 14th century. Except for the earl of Rutland who was 4 years old at the time, the average age was 17 years. However, the earl of Devon and Thomas Despenser, later earl of Gloucester, did not receive their knighthoods until they were 23.

[8] *Black Prince's Register 1351–67*, 467.

23

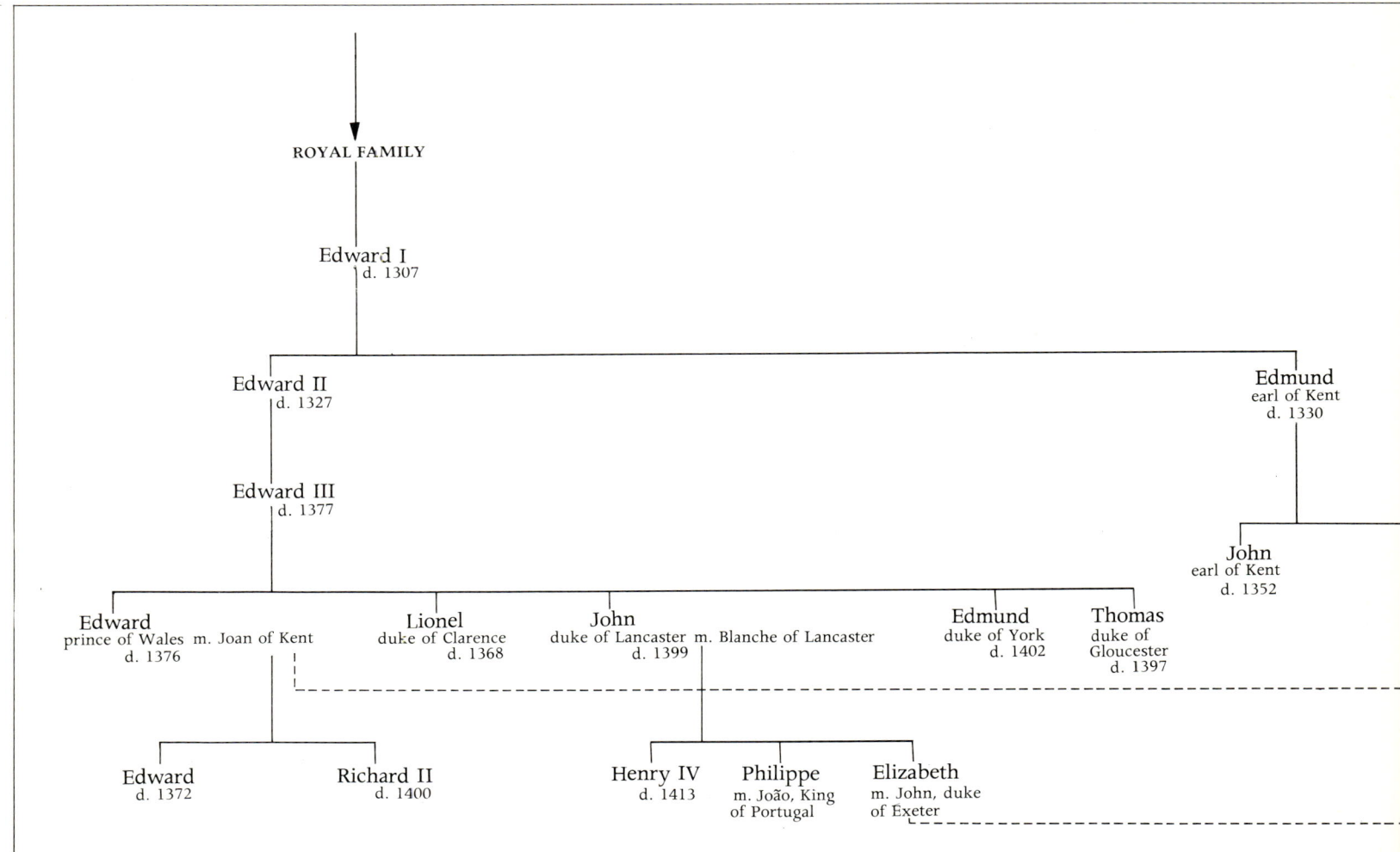

Fig. 6 The Royal and Holand families in the 14th century

the battlefield appealed far more to the Black Prince than the green fields of Hertfordshire and Edward III's gift of Aquitaine and Gascony to his eldest son in 1362 gave a new lease of life to the prince's energy. Within seven months, he and his household had left for Gascony and there is no reason to doubt that John and Thomas spent their next few years abroad.[9] While in Aquitaine, Joan gave birth to two sons by her second husband, the short-lived Edward of Angoulême and Richard of Bordeaux. However, the climate ill favoured the Black Prince's health and he returned home four years later to drag out his last few years of life. Until his death in 1376 at the age of forty-six, he and his family lived mainly at Berkhamsted Castle,[10] remembering a past age of glory and learning of successive English defeats at the hands of a rejuvenated French command.

The early upbringing of the Holand brothers must be set against the background of the Hundred Years War. Both John and Thomas were no doubt brought up and tutored in the conventional way of the time, playing games, dancing, shooting, wrestling, and skating with bones under their feet in winter on the frozen moats surrounding Berkhamsted Castle. Successful battles, valuable prisoners, ransoms, and rich booty would have been their everyday conversation, and success in arms the ambition of most young men. Their father had spent the majority of his life in France fighting for his king, and he had built up the family fortunes with the help of a ransom of £12,000 obtained through capturing the count of Eu in 1346. The reputation of their step-father was even more widespread. To a greater extent perhaps than Richard, the Holand brothers were brought up in the shadow of England's most chivalrous knight—a prince great in war and tournaments, courteous,

[9] Thomas certainly took part in some of his step-father's campaigns and was knighted by him in 1367 while fighting in Castile. Froissart, *Chronicles*, ed. Kervyn de Lettenhove, vol. 7 (1870), 169.

[10] *V.C.H. Hertfordshire*, vol. 2 (1908), 166.

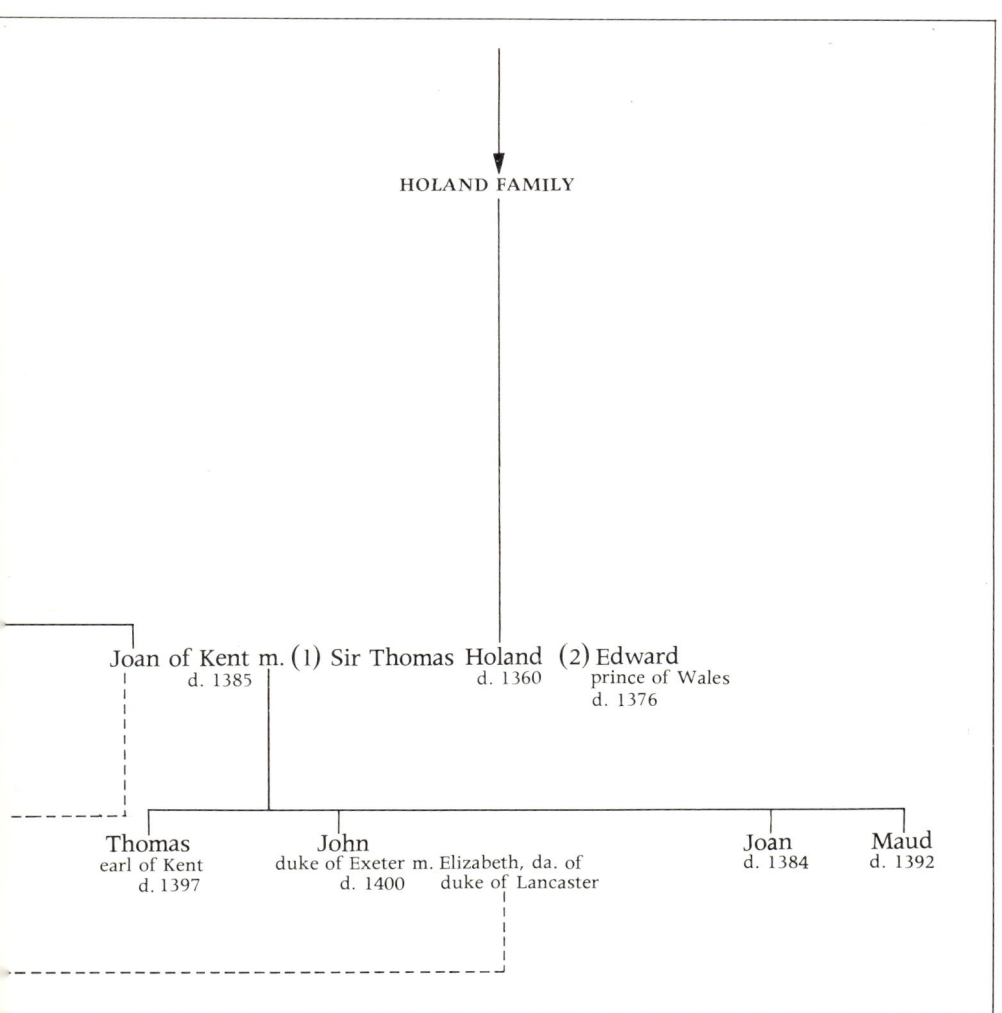

Edward, the Black Prince: 1377–80

Joan, the 'Fair Maid of Kent': c. 1380

John, duke of Lancaster. (Early 15th century)

extravagant, and almost entirely indifferent to any class other than his own.

Richard was considerably younger than his half-brothers. At the time of his accession as king in 1377 he was only ten years old, whereas Thomas was twenty-seven and John between seventeen and twenty-six. This difference in their ages makes it likely that John, and certain that Thomas, were not brought up with him. In any case, it is unlikely that either of the Holand brothers were very sympathetic to Richard's sensitive nature. John possessed far more of the militant spirit of his father than the tenderness of his mother, and therefore his allegiance lay more with his soldier uncle, the thirty-seven-year-old duke of Lancaster, than with the princess of Wales or her youngest son.

The death of the Black Prince in June 1376, and the dotage of Edward III meant that the king's third son, the duke of Lancaster, virtually became the representative of the monarchy. Until now, he had been principally concerned with military campaigns in France and with his vast English estates, but the torpor into which both his father and elder brother sank before their deaths made it easy for him to dominate English politics and encouraged him to do so. He never aimed at taking over the English Throne as his contemporaries often suggested, but he was a competent politician (even if a second-rate soldier), thrust into the forefront of government and politics through his position and prodigious wealth and the absence of anyone more capable. Towards the close of 1376, Lancaster tried to curry favour with a number of grants to the heir apparent and his mother and several magnates, and it was possibly at this time that he first sought the active support of his nephew, John Holand.

Berkhamsted Castle. Remains of motte, encircling bailey wall, earthworks, and moats

Early Years of Manhood

The association between Holand and his uncle, a close one throughout their lives, began with a military fiasco. Richard II's accession in June 1377 had been marked by a series of French attacks upon many of the towns and villages of the south coast. Lancaster retaliated in the following year with an attack on St. Malo in which both Thomas and John Holand participated.[11] The walls of the port were bombarded with cannon, and extensive mining operations were put in hand, but the careless watch of the earl of Arundel enabled the garrison to make a successful sortie and completely wreck the work of the attacking force. The siege had to be abandoned and Lancaster was forced to sail home, discredited and unpopular.

Holand was probably knighted two years later in the spring of 1380[12] and was appointed justice of Chester for life nearly twelve months later.[13] But in between this appointment and its confirmation in August 1381,[14] he had been embroiled in one of the great social revolutions of the medieval world. An awareness by the depressed classes of the growing prosperity of labourers not tied by bond services had not been stifled by a series of repressive and selfish acts, imposed by the government over a period of nearly thirty years in an attempt to deal with an unprecedented labour shortage. Twelve years of military, political, and financial incompetence had aggravated an intolerable situation, and the decision in 1380 to impose a poll tax throughout the country which would hit the poorest classes hardest led directly to the so-called Peasants' Revolt.

[11] Froissart, *Chronicles*, ed. Kervyn de Lettenhove, vol. 9 (1870), 68.

[12] The first reference to his knighthood is dated 8 June 1380. *Cal. Fine Rolls 1377–83*, 200–1. The creation is confirmed by a document of 10 July 1380. *Cal. Pat. Rolls 1377–81*, 526. It is likely that he was created a knight of the Garter in the following year. As a knight of the royal household, Holand was numbered among the élite of such men.

[13] *Cal. Pat. Rolls 1377–81*, 624. Richard II had been created earl of Chester in November 1376, and the honour had been merged with the Crown on his accession 7 months later.

[14] *Cal. Pat. Rolls 1381–85*, 36; P.R.O. Chester Rolls 2/53.

The Peasants' Revolt. John Ball and Wat Tyler leading the insurgents, 1381. (*c.* 1460–80)

It must have seemed to the ruling classes as if the very foundations of society were crumbling as rumours of unruly hordes of peasants, advancing on London, gave way to grim reality. Richard took refuge in the Tower with a number of friends and immediate counsellors, while the insurgents from Kent poured over London Bridge to meet their fellow supporters from Essex and Hertfordshire. While Richard's ministers were paralysed with fright, helplessly listening to the cries of the looters, the fourteen-year-old king averted disaster by riding from the Tower to Mile End and promising the rebels pardons and charters abolishing villeinage. At the same time, the Holand brothers took the opportunity to leave Richard and flee from the terrors of London to the comparative safety of the country.[15] It is with this incident that John Holand makes his bow on the stage of English politics. There is nothing inherently impossible in the story and Holand's subsequent actions as a bully are not incompatible with those of a coward. But the only authority for this story is a chronicler who was not present in England at the time of the rising. Froissart's account of the Revolt of 1381, like so much of his immensely readable work, is full of colour and vivid action. Yet it is often based on hearsay, garnered from many sources, and frequently idealized in the cause of chivalry. There are several more reliable chroniclers for the events of this Revolt than this Flemish writer, and until the Holand incident can be confirmed by an independent source, doubt must be cast on its authenticity. Yet even if this incident did, in fact occur, John did not suffer sufficient loss of face with his half-brother to prevent him from leading the embassy sent by Richard to Calais at the end of the year to meet the future queen of England and escort her back to England.[16]

A brief reference in August 1382 indicates that Holand was Richard's lieutenant in Ireland at that time,[17] but the mounting problems of English rule in Ireland were considered unimportant compared with the renewal of the war against France. When the attempt by the bishop of Norwich to lead an army through Flanders ended in fiasco, Lancaster's counter-proposal to attack France through Spain received more sympathetic support. His aim was to isolate France by a series of truces with her allies, defeat Scotland and Castile in turn, and then vigorously pursue the war against France. Apart from the fact that the proposals were tactically sound, they had the additional merit in Lancaster's eyes of furthering his own claim to the throne of Castile—an ambition never far from his thoughts.[18] That the scheme came anywhere near to success was due in no part to Holand, whose temper and ineptitude conspired to frustrate it.

Lancaster successfully negotiated a short truce with France in January 1384,[19] and he followed it up with a raid against Scotland in the following spring. But ever since Richard had encouraged the bishop of Norwich's 'crusade', Lancaster's relations with his nephew had grown increasingly strained. The Crown had been subject to a series of bitter attacks from many of Lancaster's supporters, including Holand, so that the Parliament which assembled at Salisbury in April 1384, met in an atmosphere of hostility and recrimination between the magnates and the courtiers—a war and a peace party—heightened by many personal feuds. An attempt was made to impeach the royalist chancellor on the grounds of corruption, John Holand complained about the cancellation of grants made to him by the king,[20] and the stormy session was abruptly terminated after some of its members had become involved in a particularly squalid scandal.

[15] Froissart, *Chronicles*, ed. Kervyn de Lettenhove, vol. 9 (1870), 68.

[16] T. Rymer, *Foedera*, Rec. Edition, vol. 4, 136; *Cal. Close Rolls 1381-85*, 97; E. Perroy, *L'Angleterre et Le Grand Schisme D'Occident* (1933), 155.

[17] *Cal. Pat. Rolls 1381-85*, 160.

[18] M. V. Clarke, *Fourteenth Century Studies* (1937), 44; A. Steel, *Richard II* (1941), 103. That a burning ambition should outweigh political expediency was typical of the period.

[19] Holand was among those who had accompanied Lancaster on his visit to Calais in November 1383. French Roll, 7 Richard II. The embassy left on 8 November and returned on 2 February 1384. Holand was paid a wage of £2 a day and, with costs of £16. 11s. 4d., his total expenses came to £188. 11s. 4d. He was also at Calais with Lancaster from 30 June to 26 September 1384, when his costs were £13. 18s. 4d. and his total expenses were £187. 18s. 4d. P.R.O. Exch. L.T.R. Foreign Accts., no. 17 m.D.d.

[20] *Rolls of Parliament*, vol. 3, 177.

Richard II: c. 1390–95. Artist unknown

A Carmelite friar, celebrating mass before the king at the residence of his great friend, the earl of Oxford, suddenly accused Lancaster of plotting to murder Richard and asked Richard to agree to Lancaster's immediate death without a trial.[21] The king was restrained from taking any hasty action and the friar was held in custody until the charges could be examined in detail.[22] On being taken to Salisbury Castle, however, he was seized by a group of soldiers, led by Holand, and hustled away. Once in their clutches, the friar was interrogated and tortured but completely failed to add anything more to what he had already said before Richard. Lord Zouche was implicated but he denied all knowledge of the accusations and Lancaster likewise protested his innocence. The friar died a few days later from the injuries inflicted upon him, without any further explanation or elaboration of his story. An attempt was made to hush up the incident,[23] and no action was taken against the accused or the miscreants, but it led to the break-up of the Salisbury Parliament in a vitriolic atmosphere of accusation and recrimination.

Lack of further information makes it difficult to discern the motives behind the friar's story, and it is impossible to tell whether it was a personal outburst of enmity against Lancaster or, more likely, an artless attempt by the earl of Oxford and his friends to discredit the duke. Walsingham, violently anti-Lancastrian, clearly believed that Holand was responsible for the outrage, but the more balanced opinion of the Westminster Chronicle is not so assertive. Holand seems to have been the leader of the interrogators, but he was probably merely working on a directive from Lancaster. In fact, he was helped by some of the king's followers who were equally eager to get to the bottom of the accusations.[24] Lancaster certainly cannot be exonerated from connivance at Holand's butchery and he apparently tried to shift the blame for the friar's death on to the custodian of Salisbury Castle.[25] But even if responsibility for this outrage cannot be attributed entirely to Holand, the unsavoury part played by him in this affair is hardly in doubt.

Holand made his first acquaintance with Dartington only a few months after this incident. Holand was not a wealthy landowner. Considering his age and position, he held remarkably little property, but the situation was substantially improved by the grant made to him in December 1384 when the agreement between Edward III and Lord Audley was recalled. Now that Lord Audley was seventy-one, much of his property would inevitably be reverting to the Crown within the next few years and in anticipation of an event which occurred only sixteen months later, Richard granted his half-brother the reversion of Dartington and several other Audley manors in the west of England. Holand held them from mid-December 1384 until April 1385 when his three and a half months ownership was abruptly terminated by the surrender of the relevant letters patent to the king who ordered the chancellor to cancel and destroy them.[26] Unfortunately, the motives behind these actions have not been recorded, but it is likely that Richard intended to elevate his half-brother to the peerage, for this group of manors was almost identical with that granted to him after he had been created earl of Huntingdon in 1388. A personal quarrel with the king or antagonistic counsellors may have been responsible for the abrupt change in plan, possibly furthered by Holand's friendship with Lancaster who was becoming increasingly unpopular with the Crown.

Tension between Richard and Lancaster and their respective supporters had not diminished

[21] There are two contemporary accounts of this incident, one by the St. Albans chronicler, Thomas Walsingham, and a much longer version by an anonymous monk of Westminster. Both versions agree in substance although not in detail, but the fact that the author of the Westminster version benefited from close proximity to the court and included details given by one of Richard's courtiers, Sir John Clanvowe, makes his the more circumstantial version. For Walsingham's account, see *Historia Anglicana: 1272–1422*, ed. H. T. Riley (1863–4), 112–15, and an analysis of this author's work by V. H. Galbraith, *The St. Albans' Chronicle: 1406–1420* (1937). For the Westminster version, see Ralph Higden, *Polychronicon*, ed. J. R. Lumby, vol. 9 (1886), 33–40, and for the authorship of the continuation from 1381 to 1394, J. A. Robinson, 'An Unrecognised Westminster Chronicle, 1381–94', *Proc. Brit. Acad.* (1907–8), 61–77. The Salisbury incident is also described in the chronicle attributed to an anonymous monk of Evesham, but as this work closely follows Walsingham's chronicle until 1390, it cannot be considered an independent authority. The author, however, adds the friar's name, John Latimer, *Historia Vitae et Regni Ricardi Secundi*, ed. T. Hearne (1729), 50–2.

[22] Richard's demonic fury on this occasion when he is alleged to have thrown his cloak and shoes out of the window has been shown to be due to a textual misunderstanding of the Westminster chronicler. It refers not to the royal temper but to a ruse by the monk to extricate himself from the situation which he had precipitated. See L. C. Hector, 'An Alleged Hysterical Outburst of Richard II', *Eng. Hist. Rev.* vol. 68 (1953), 62–5.

[23] It is not mentioned for instance in the Rolls of Parliament.

[24] Among those who took part in the outrage, the Westminster Chronicle mentions Sir William Elmham and one of the sons of the earl of Devon, either Sir Philip or Sir Peter Courtenay, both of whom were antagonistic to Lancaster. He also states that Sir Simon Burley and Sir John Montague, Richard's steward and vice-chamberlain respectively, stood by during the torture. Walsingham transposes Courtenay's actions to Sir Henry Green, father of Richard II's later favourite.

[25] Ralph Higden, *Polychronicon*, ed. J. R. Lumby, vol. 9 (1886), 39.

[26] *Cal. Pat. Rolls 1381–85*, 515–6.

as a result of the threat of invasion from France and Scotland, or by Parliament's decision to support Lancaster's plan to invade and defeat Scotland. Preparations were made throughout the spring of 1385 for a highly impressive and splendidly arrayed force to march against the northern insurgents, and nearly every magnate of note was a member of this, the first military enterprise of the reign to be led by the king. Writs demanding fulfilment of feudal levy were issued[27] and Holand attended with a force of 100 men-at-arms and 160 archers, the largest force of any knight present.[28] Troops were assembled at Berwick and the court moved northwards early in July. During Richard's brief stay at York, the court was disturbed by a quarrel between two of Holand's armour bearers and two grooms of the earl of Stafford which led to the death of Holand's followers. Although the king promised his wrathful half-brother royal justice and particularly forbade him to take personal revenge,[29] Holand preferred to take the law into his own hands and a chance meeting between Stafford's son and himself not far from York led to insults, blows, and his adversary's death. The demise of Sir Ralph Stafford, a member of the queen's household and one of Richard's close companions, unleashed a paroxysm of royal rage and grief. Holand fled to Lancashire[30] and all his possessions and positions were confiscated.[31] Richard swore that he should be judged as a murderer by common law, while his mother entreated her son to have mercy on his half-brother. Her pleas received a very chilly reception and she died a few days later 'burdened by her excessive grief'.[32] The death of the princess Joan and the delay of the invasion caused by Holand's brawl exacerbated an already tense relationship between Richard and his half-brother. For a few months, Holand was an outcast and an outlaw. He failed to answer the summons to appear before the King's Bench as a common murderer,[33] but just as suddenly as his prospects had been jeopardized, so did they dramatically change once more following the partial success of the Scottish campaign and the radical improvement in Lancaster's claim to the throne of Castile.

The Castilian Campaign

England's entanglement in Spanish and Portuguese affairs during the second half of the fourteenth century is one of the more tangled skeins in our national history. Since 1335, both England and France had been eager to gain control of Castile and its royal fleet which swept the coasts from the Mediterranean to the English Channel. In 1366 France succeeded in deposing England's Castilian ally, Pedro the Cruel, but by marrying Pedro's elder daughter, Constanza, Lancaster was able to lay claim shortly afterwards to the throne of Castile on behalf of his wife. It was impossible for him to press his claim to any great advantage for several years, but a spectacular Portuguese victory over the Castilians in 1385, followed by an appeal to Lancaster for help, radically altered the situation. His preparations for the conquest of Castile were encouraged as much by his critics as by his supporters, and although the invasion was a semi-private venture, manned and financed by Lancastrian supporters, Parliament no longer wished to cavil at the *chemin d'Espaigne* and eagerly helped it with a grant of £47,500.[34]

Relations between Richard and Lancaster improved at once, partly because the duke rapidly lost interest in English politics, and partly because Richard anticipated that his

[27] This force was the last one raised by feudal levy in the Middle Ages, a system practised in England since the Norman Conquest. N. B. Lewis, 'The Last Medieval Summons of the English Feudal Levy, 13 June, 1385', *Eng. Hist. Rev.* vol. 73 (1958), 1–26.

[28] Holand's contract is summarized by Dugdale in *The Baronage of England*, vol. 2 (1676), 76b, but no details are given. The most satisfactory text of the army summons is given in S. Armitage Smith, *John of Gaunt* (1904), 437–9; but see the comments made by N. B. Lewis, *Eng. Hist. Rev.* vol. 73 (1958). Only the contingents of the duke of Lancaster, the earls of Northumberland, Cambridge, Warwick, Buckingham, Stafford, and probably of Oxford were larger than those of Holand. Lancaster arrived with 1,000 men-at-arms and 2,000 archers, and Stafford with 119 men-at-arms and 180 archers. The forces brought by the earl of Devon and Lord Neville were approximately similar in size to those of Holand.

[29] Ralph Higden, *Polychronicon*, ed. J. R. Lumby, vol. 9 (1886), 61–2.

[30] Ibid., 62. Apart from the reliability of the Westminster chronicler, Holand's escape to Lancashire is more convincing than sanctuary at Beverley mentioned by Walsingham, *Historia Anglicana*, ed. H. T. Riley (1863–4), 130, and followed by the Evesham chronicler, *Historia Vitae et Regni Ricardi Secundi*, ed. T. Hearne (1729), 63.

[31] *Cal. Fine Rolls 1383–91*, 123–4. It is noteworthy that Richard ordered the revenues and profits from Holand's forfeited lands to be paid into the chamber, an exceptional practice at this time, but possibly carried out so that the property could be held in friendly hands. T. F. Tout, *Chapters in the Administrative History of Medieval England*, vol. 4 (1928), 313 n. 2.

[32] Walsingham, *Historia Anglicana*, ed. H. T. Riley (1863–4), 130. She died during the second week of August at Wallingford Castle.

[33] Ralph Higden, *Polychronicon*, ed. J. R. Lumby, vol. 9 (1886), 72.

[34] P. E. Russell, *English Intervention in Spain and Portugal in the Time of Edward III and Richard II* (1955), 403 n. 1.

English ships arriving at Lisbon in 1385 to support the Portuguese against Castile. (Late 15th century)

uncle's absence from England would be a protracted one. As Lancaster was anxious to appoint Holand constable of his army, it was essential that a reconciliation between Richard and his half-brother should be effected as quickly as possible. Taking advantage of his recent rise in stock, the duke persuaded Richard to listen to his half-brother's apology[35] and on 2 February 1386, Holand was led by the archbishop of Canterbury and the bishop of London into the royal presence, dressed in mourning and making abject prostrations.[36] In pleading for mercy before the king, Holand promised to found a chantry for three chaplains and he was finally, if unwillingly, received back into royal grace.[37] All his goods and chattels were returned to him and his estates were restored a few weeks later. As it was agreed that the difference between their estimated value of £333. 6s. 8d. and their true value of £200 should be paid by the Exchequer,[38] this episode of mayhem and murder ultimately proved financially beneficial to Holand although at the cost of several months anxiety for his life.

Lancaster immediately showed his confidence in Holand by appointing him constable of his new army and choosing one of his confederates in the Salisbury outrage, Sir Thomas Morieux, as marshal under him.[39] The army began to assemble at Plymouth, and Lancaster and his family left London towards the end of March and, in stately array, progressed towards the west of England. They arrived in Devonshire during the last days of April,[40] but difficulties in obtaining sufficient shipping delayed their departure until July. Troops were constantly arriving in Devon, and Holand had as much difficulty in housing them as he did in coping with their urgent claims for pay. He found time, however, to court

[35] *The Chronicle of Henry Knighton*, ed. J. R. Lumby (1889–95), 206.

[36] Ralph Higden, *Polychronicon*, ed. J. R. Lumby, vol. 9 (1886), 79.

[37] *Cal. Pat. Rolls 1385–89*, 114, 368, 99. The royal pardon was granted on 8 February.

[38] Ibid., 122, 130.

[39] Morieux was also Lancaster's son-in-law by his mysterious daughter, Blanche.

[40] E. Perroy, *L'Angleterre et le Grand Schisme D'Occident* (1933), 236 n. 6.

João I entertaining the duke of Lancaster, 1386. (Late 15th century)

Lancaster's second daughter, Elizabeth, with the result that the preparations for sailing were suddenly interrupted by her announcement of pregnancy by the constable of the army.[41] A shot-gun wedding was hastily arranged at or near Plymouth on 24 June[42] and Lancaster, accompanied by an army of about 8,000 men and his new son-in-law, sailed from Plymouth Sound two weeks later.

Richard was as glad to see the back of Holand as he was of Lancaster. Holand had never disguised the fact that his allegiance lay with his uncle rather than with the king and court, and since his embroilment in the deaths of the Carmelite friar and Sir Ralph Stafford, his character and temper had become anathema to Richard. For his part, Lancaster had shown his regard for Holand by helping to secure his pardon and by appointing him constable of an army that was going to win European glory for the House of Lancaster. To Richard, the whole Castilian project was an all-embracing opportunity for the prolonged riddance of some of his outstanding opponents.

After a brief delay at Brest to help the beleaguered garrison in its fight against the duke of Brittany, the army landed unopposed at La Coruña close to the north-west tip of Spain and marched directly to Santiago de Compostela.[43] At Lancaster's instigation, Holand ordered that the local population should be treated with respect and that food should be purchased at local prices, for the expedition was dependent for its supplies on local goodwill. Once he had secured a foothold, Lancaster negotiated a marriage alliance between his eldest daughter and his ally, the Portuguese king, Dom João I,[44] while his constable and marshals led a series of detachments through north-west Spain to quell any areas of

[41] Ralph Higden, *Polychronicon*, ed. J. R. Lumby, vol. 9 (1886), 96–7. As Elizabeth was probably born in 1364, she was about 22 at the time. She had married the 8-year-old earl of Pembroke in 1380 but the marriage had been dissolved just over 3 years later. G. H. Cowling has suggested that Chaucer's 'Complaint of Mars' and 'Complaint of Venus' refer to the events of this marriage. *Review of Eng. Studies*, vol. 2 (1926), 405–10.

[42] *Cal. Close Rolls 1402–05*, 425.

[43] Nine years later, Thomas Bony, the master of Holand's barge 'la Marie', obtained permission to take 80 pilgrims to Santiago. *Cal. Pat. Rolls 1391–96*, 566. This was only 1 of at least 12 boats taking pilgrims there at the time.

[44] Fernão Lopes, *Chrónica de Dom João I*, 2a parte, ed. M. Lopes de Almeda and A. de Magnalhaes Basto (Pôrto, 1949), 203. Lopes was a Portuguese chronicler writing about 1440 who consulted many relevant contemporary documents in the royal archives under his care.

opposition. According to Froissart, only the town of Ribadavia put up a stout defence and that crumbled after an assaulting force, led by Holand and the marshals, had breached the walls.[45] But much time was wasted on diplomatic negotiations and minor affrays so that when João and his forces finally met the English army not far from Braganza in the middle of March 1387, the joint invasion of Castile began in an atmosphere of mutual distrust. The unsuccessful siege of Benavente at the beginning of April was followed by a steady deterioration in the relationship between the two forces, heightened by the lack of any striking success against the Castilian forces who were following a policy of attrition. During the next five weeks, a number of medium-size towns were taken, but the enemy refused to be drawn into battle and the Castilian policy of waiting for disease, fatigue, lack of supplies, and internal disagreements to disseminate the Lancastrian-Portuguese army gradually paid dividends. Lancaster had no alternative but to retire as gracefully as possible to the friendly soil of his ally and to consolidate the secret overtures for peace which he had already been making with the Castilian king.

The force which retreated from Castile, less than a year after it had sailed in such splendid array from Plymouth Sound was exhausted, undisciplined, and hungry. The remnant of Lancaster's army struggled southwards through Ciudad Rodrigo and as soon as it was in sight of the Portuguese frontier early in June, Holand and some of his companions announced their intention of leaving immediately for England. Their interest in the campaign had completely seeped away. Their sole aim now was to get away from this

[45] Froissart, *Chronicles*, ed. T. Johnes, vol. 2 (1839), 219–20. Froissart gives an extremely colourful and detailed account of Lancaster's expedition to Castile, but it is almost entirely dependent on hearsay which the chronicler had no way of checking. He had no access to diplomatic records and no knowledge of the geography of Spain and Portugal, with the result that his attractive account is also inadequate and ill-informed and must be treated with caution.

Joust between John Holand and Regnault de Roye, 1387. (Late 15th century)

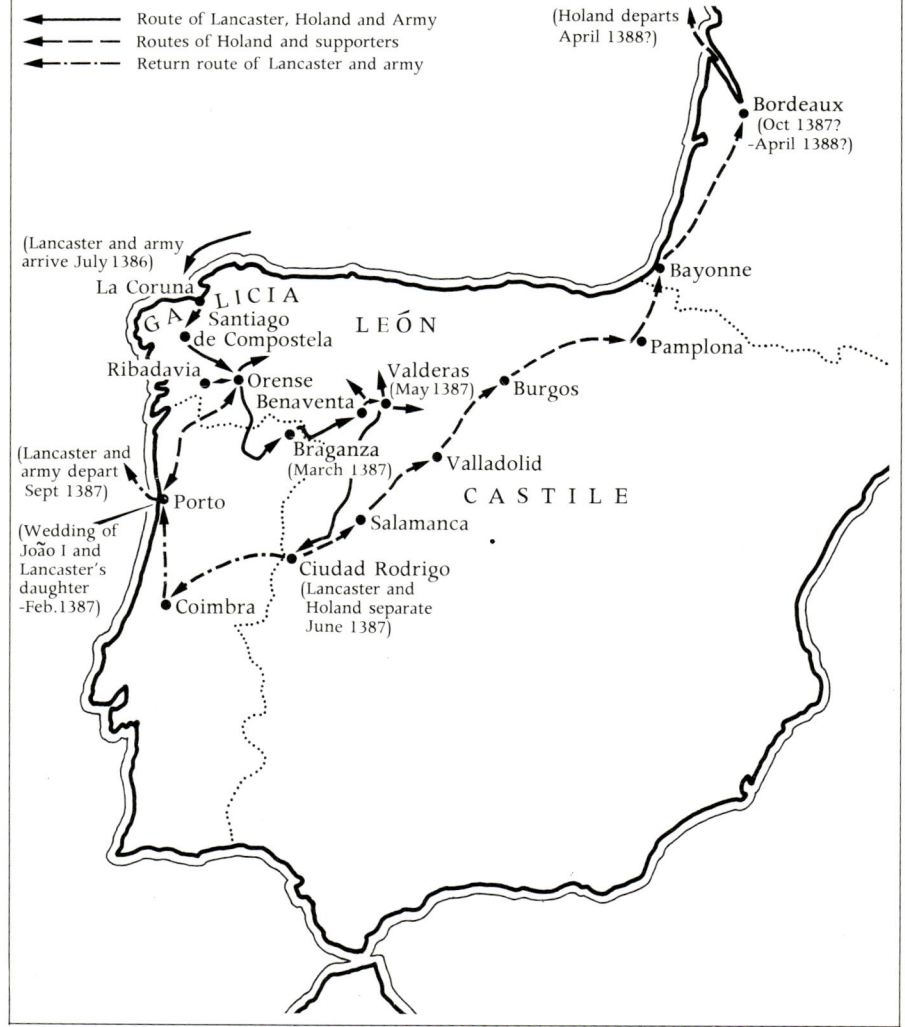

Fig. 7 Map of the Castilian campaign: 1386–7

disease-ridden country as quickly as possible and to return to the softer climes of England. Within a few days, Holand and his wife, some ladies, and a group of knights, left the Lancastrian force for home and, with the aid of safe conducts, passed through the territory of the enemy they had just been trying to defeat.

The failure of the expedition was partly due to the adoption of tactics by the Castilian king which Lancaster had no way of countering, but the principal reason lay in the military incapacity of Lancaster and his constable. Holand undoubtedly worked under difficult conditions. He had to lead his men through an uncongenial country, handicapped by bad weather and hampered by ladies, clerks, chaplains, servants, and all the paraphernalia of the Lancastrian court. Disease ravaged the expedition so seriously that it was only possible to muster about one-quarter of the total force which had landed in Spain for the invasion of Castile. The fact that the Portuguese joined the English with a larger army than they promised merely emphasized the inadequacy of Lancaster's force and its reliance for any success on its ally. But the constables of the English and Portuguese armies never worked together harmoniously. Holand, supported by Lancaster, insisted that English banners should fly over all towns occupied during the course of the invasion, even though they may have been captured by the Portuguese, and when it came to sacking a town such as Valderas in May 1387, the Lancastrian leaders demanded that their troops should have priority for several hours before the Portuguese be allowed to enter the town. Holand was imperious and sensitive about his position, and quite unable to work with someone whose

The siege of Ribadavia, 1386. (Late 15th century)

military ability and knowledge of the enemy's terrain was far greater than his own. Despite the fact that some measure of agreement between the two constables was essential to the success of the invasion, Holand made no attempt to minimize the friction between himself and the Portuguese commander, or to curb the constant bickering between the two armies and the steady deterioration in their relationship. Nor was Holand a disciplinarian. He preferred to share rather than to check the contempt his subordinates showed towards their allies. Morale was low under his command and made worse by the fact that he failed lamentably to organize the supplies necessary for carrying on a war in a difficult country. Holand never held such a responsible military position again, but the complete lack of military or administrative competence he displayed during the Castilian campaign made his limitations all too clear.

Political Support and Reward

The effect of Lancaster's absence on English politics was profound. Although some of the unruly elements at court were absent in Spain, the removal of the duke's strong but often ameliorative influence meant that some of the more extreme magnates were given free rein. The baronial opposition was directed at first against the royal ministers and favourites, but later it turned against Richard himself. The opposition was headed by five magnates —that persistent nuisance and royal enemy, the thirty-year-old duke of Gloucester; his kinsman, the earl of Arundel; the militant earl of Warwick; Lancaster's aloof but calculating son, the earl of Derby; and Richard's former friend, the earl of Nottingham, who had married Arundel's sister. The rout of the royal forces gathered by Richard's bosom friend, the twenty-six-year-old earl of Oxford, at the battle of Radcot Bridge in December 1387, was followed by the famous 'Merciless' Parliament. Richard's chief supporters were either executed, removed, imprisoned, or exiled while the 'appellants' (i.e. those who appealed or accused) took over control of the government and rewarded themselves with honours, appointments, and money.

It was possibly at this point that Holand returned from Spain, bringing news of Lancaster's expedition. Although Holand had left Lancaster and the remnant of his army at the beginning of June 1387, it is unlikely that he arrived in England before April 1388.[46] No doubt he painted a biased picture of the difficulties attending the expedition so as to conceal the measure of its failure, whilst the leaders of the 'Merciless' Parliament also glossed their recent acts. But Holand had probably witnessed a number of their activities and therefore it was deemed expedient to bribe both Lancaster and his constable to prevent them from joining forces with the king. The appointment of the duke as lieutenant of Aquitaine, a post of honour and some responsibility, was intended to gratify his pride, and on 2 June 1388, Holand was led into the king's presence in Parliament by the earls of Warwick and Salisbury[47] and created earl of Huntingdon with a grant of lands valued at £1,333. 6s. 8d. per annum.[48] It has been thought that the award was a very liberal one in view of the fact that Richard's younger uncles had been allowed no more than £1,000 at the time of their creation as dukes, three years earlier.[49] But the award specifically included Holand's existing lands valued at £200 per annum, and whereas the holdings of the royal dukes were already appreciable, those of the new earl were noticeably small. It is more

[46] Ralph Higden, *Polychronicon*, ed. J. R. Lumby, vol. 9 (1886), 172. According to Froissart, Holand passed through Castile to Bayonne where he and his wife remained for some time. The same chronicler mentions that they had left for Bordeaux not long before Lancaster reached Bayonne in October 1387. It is probable that Holand stayed at Bordeaux throughout the winter, although P. E. Russell, *English Intervention in Spain in the Time of Edward III and Richard II* (1955), considers that he returned to England either in the early summer of 1387 (p. 493) or the early autumn (p. 504). His absence from any of the records of the time until the following June, when his support would have been valued by either side, in itself makes such an early return unlikely. Walsingham and the Evesham chronicler both indicate that Huntingdon returned from overseas shortly before he received his earldom in June 1388. *Historia Anglicana: 1272–1422*, ed. H. T. Riley (1863–4), 177, and *Historia Vitae et Regni Ricardi Secundi*, ed. T. Hearne (1729), 106. Dugdale states that his return was made at the request of Parliament. *The Baronage of England*, vol. 2 (1676), 78b.

[47] Ralph Higden, *Polychronicon*, ed. J. R. Lumby, vol. 9 (1886), 157.

[48] *Cal. Pat. Rolls 1385–89*, 494–5; *Rolls of Parliament*, vol. 3, 250b–251b. He was also granted £20 per annum from the profits of Huntingdonshire. *Cal. Close Rolls 1385–89*, 515, and *Cal. Close Rolls 1422–29*, 436.

[49] H. Wallon, *Richard II*, vol. 1 (1864), 373. A. Steel, *Richard II* (1941), 163.

significant that the creation was made two days before the conclusion of the 'Merciless' Parliament, and that Holand's appointment was made at the same time that some of the appellants were being rewarded with honours.[50] One of the results of this award was that Dartington passed once more into Holand's hands, and the plans he may have dreamt about in Spain for building a new residence in Devon could now be put into action.

The appointment and grant to the new earl of Huntingdon did not have the effect that had probably been intended. Although Richard had been isolated and deprived of his friends, he displayed an unusual ability to rebuild a group of supporters round him. He was helped by the selfish and incompetent record of the appellants who burdened an already precarious economy with crippling expenditure, and in May 1389 Richard quietly but dramatically announced his intention of personally assuming control of the government. Gloucester and Warwick were dismissed from the council, and the earl of Arundel was relieved of his appointment as admiral of the Fleet and captain of Brest. Huntingdon was appointed admiral of the Fleet from the river Thames westwards during Richard's pleasure,[51] and at the beginning of June he was also granted custody of the castle, town, and bastide of Brest for a period of three years.[52] Richard made no attempt to revoke the work of the 'Merciless' Parliament or to emulate the slippery path of Edward II by recalling his boon companions from abroad. But he was clearly moving towards a more personal rule, supported by a group of friends and relations who would counter-balance any anti-royalist moves.

It is impossible to avoid the conclusion that the Castilian campaign had wrought a marked change in Huntingdon. That there was no repetition of his earlier violent outbursts might simply be attributed to his growing maturity, but it is also possible that the disease which had ravaged the Lancastrian army had physically weakened Huntingdon too. Furthermore, Lancaster and his constable were almost certainly informed of all the altered political circumstances in England after their departure in 1386,[53] and their decision to support Richard may have arisen from their discussions in Spain concerning the relationship and attitude of their Houses to the Throne. Lancaster could be hot-tempered and explosive, but he was always mindful of the dignity of the Crown and had little sympathy for the appellants. Where Lancaster led, Huntingdon usually followed. He had returned from Spain in time to witness much of the appellant triumph and to see the extent to which Richard had been reduced to a cipher. Yet he must also have noticed that some of Richard's acts were bearing the stamp of maturity and even ability in the face of formidable opposition. A word to Richard that he could rely on the support of his elder uncle, as well as himself, considerably strengthened the royal hand at this critical time. A peremptory command brought Lancaster home in October 1389 and the period of co-operation between the king and his uncle which mark the last ten years of Lancaster's life amply confirmed Huntingdon's whispered promises. A great hunting party given by Lancaster at Leicester in August 1390 for Richard and his queen, his brothers of York and Gloucester, his son-in-law Huntingdon, and many lords, bishops, and ladies,[54] was symptomatic of the change in outlook and (except for Gloucester) the restoration of family unity. Both Huntingdon and Richard were apparently prepared to bury the past, and the future augured far better for both of them than at any time, so far, throughout their lives.

[50] Of the 13 witnesses of Holand's charter of appointment, 11 were members of the commission of 14, appointed in 1386 to guide Richard. *Rolls of Parliament*, vol. 3, 251b; T. F. Tout, *Chapters in the Administrative History of Medieval England*, vol. 3 (1928), 438 n. 3.

[51] French Roll, 12 Richard II, mems. 4, 26.

[52] Huntingdon's command was later extended to a period of nearly 8 years. T. Rymer, *Foedera*, Hague ed. vol. 3, pt. iv, 39.

[53] Probably by Lancaster's agent, Sir Thomas Percy.

[54] *The Chronicle of Henry Knighton*, ed. J. R. Lumby, vol. 2 (1895), 313.

Chapter 3

John Holand, Earl of Huntingdon: 1390 to 1400

Richard II's Personal Rule

Although the feudal organization of society changed during the fourteenth and fifteenth centuries, the political and social dominance of a small group of magnates which had characterized lay society for more than three hundred years remained unimpaired. Their number rarely exceeded more than twenty families at any time throughout the fourteenth century and was rather less towards the end of Richard's reign. In 1389, for example, there were three dukes—all uncles of the king—and thirteen earls, and they nearly all represented large aggregations of family and territorial authority. Although not a politically homogeneous group, they were the natural leaders of the baronage and may be considered apart from the fifty lay barons who formed the remainder of the nobility.[1]

No earl could maintain his position during this period on an annual income of less than about £700,[2] but most of them could be certain of a revenue considerably in excess of this figure. Huntingdon, as the younger member of the Holand family, was unlikely to inherit the family holdings and therefore he was almost entirely dependent for his income on the lands granted to him in 1388. It is possible that the annual revenue from his estates was between £2,000 and £2,500 (see Appendix 2), whereas Lancaster, admittedly the most powerful and wealthy magnate of the day, received an annual income from his English lands alone of over £12,000 a year.[3] Huntingdon's wealth and position were entirely due to his close family ties with the king. Wealth and position, however, did not necessarily mean indulgence in political intrigues. State affairs during Richard's personal rule were almost entirely avoided by the duke of York and the majority of the earls, so that the political fortunes of the country between 1389 and 1397 lay in the hands of a very small group of magnates—the dukes of Lancaster and Gloucester, and the earls of Arundel, Derby, Nottingham, and Rutland. They wielded an influence out of all proportion to their numbers, although not to the size of their estates. Huntingdon was neither politically nor territorially influential, but his close relationship with the king and the support he accorded the Crown prevented him from becoming a nonentity during this period.

Richard's personal rule between 1389 and 1397 was a comparatively quiet one. His policy of peace at home and abroad was more advantageous to him and to England than the desultory war with France which had been followed for so long, and it enabled him to build up a new court party, independent of appellant influence. As a founder-member of the new party, Huntingdon was rewarded with a shower of royal grants and appointments. In less than four years, he was granted the castles at Berkhamsted,[4] Tintagel,[5] Horston,[6] and Trematon,[7] the custody of Rockingham[8] and Haverford,[9] and the constableship of Conway Castle.[10] To the military and naval commands bestowed on him in 1389, the important position of chamberlain of Richard's household was added early in 1390, an appointment soon confirmed for life.[11] In the same year, he was appointed a justice of the

[1] At least 6 barons were minors in 1389, and of the remainder, only the lords Cobham, Despenser, Lovell, and Neville were of more than local importance.

[2] G. A. Holmes, *The Estates of the Higher Nobility in Fourteenth Century England* (1957), 4.

[3] This was for the years ending Michaelmas 1394 and 1395. R. Somerville, *History of the Duchy of Lancaster*, vol. 1 (1953), 91–3.

[4] The grant in October 1388 was first of all during pleasure and later extended for life. *Cal. Pat. Rolls 1385–89*, 518; *Cal. Pat. Rolls 1388–92*, 372.

[5] January 1389. *Cal. Pat. Rolls 1385–89*, 537.

[6] September 1391. Horston in Horsley, Derbyshire. *Cal. Pat. Rolls 1388–92*, 488.

[7] Probably granted during this period. Huntingdon's servants there were assaulted in September 1393. *Cal. Pat. Rolls 1391–96*, 357.

[8] April 1391. *Cat. Pat. Rolls 1388–92*, 394. The grant included the stewardship of Rockingham Forest.

[9] January 1392. *Cal. Pat. Rolls 1391–96*, 15, 70.

[10] May 1389. The grant was made by Queen Anne. Ibid., 208, 501. Huntingdon held the post for 9 years.

[11] He was holding the position by March. *Rolls of Parliament*, vol. 3, 264. The appointment for life was made on the last day of May. *Cal. Pat. Rolls 1388–92*, 252. Huntingdon received summer robes for the office in 1390. P.R.O. EA 402/5.

[12] *Cal. Pat. Rolls 1388–92*, 344, 130, 196, 242–3; *Cal. Pat. Rolls*

peace for Devon, and was commissioned to hear a plea in the Court of Chivalry.[12] Huntingdon's star was in the ascendant and his help was sought at the time in furthering petitions to the king.[13] But there is little indication that he deserved or possessed the administrative ability necessary to cope with the responsibility vested in him.

Huntingdon was admiral of the king's fleet from the Thames westward from May 1389 onwards,[14] and although the lack of any naval engagements during this period prevented him from openly demonstrating the inadequacy of the ramshackle collection of ships in his charge or the quality of his leadership, the records of the Court of Admiralty give no evidence of any sustained administrative capacity on his part. Details of two cases which came before Huntingdon's jurisdiction reveal a lack of firm direction,[15] while three out of the six other cases known to have been held during his brief tenure of office support the unsatisfactory state indicated by the more detailed records.[16] Complaints made against the Court, and its unpopularity with the mayor and sheriff of London,[17] suggest that it may have been the irregularities committed during Huntingdon's term of office which led to the passing of the important statutes in 1389 and 1391, clarifying and restricting the jurisdiction of the Court's officials. Nor is confidence in Huntingdon's judgments encouraged by the knowledge that he had tried some years earlier to use his official position as justice of Cheshire and Flint to add estates to his own property in North Wales which rightly belonged to the earl of Arundel.[18]

Huntingdon was appointed chamberlain of the royal household in order that Richard could be certain of the wholehearted support of that office. The chamber was essentially a royal 'privy purse', accountable solely to the king, and its staff were frequently used by Richard for his confidential business. It was vital to Richard's independence that he should have complete control over the chamber's activities and throughout his personal rule, Richard made certain that the offices of chamberlain and sub-chamberlain were held by strong supporters of the court party.[19] As far as can be judged on the scanty evidence available, Huntingdon looked upon his office as essentially a formal but financially rewarding one, and left the bulk of the work to the under-chamberlain.[20] Nor did Huntingdon exert any appreciable political influence, either in Parliament or the council chamber, except to rubber stamp a number of royal actions during the last two years of the reign. Huntingdon was summoned to all but one of the ten Parliaments held between June 1388 and September 1399,[21] but none of the chroniclers, the parliament rolls, or the statute book give any indication that he took part in their proceedings in any material way. This does not in itself indicate a lack of political strength, for the average life of these Parliaments was only about three weeks and most political matters at this time were thrashed out in meetings of the great and small councils. Huntingdon was present at five out of the six council meetings held between August 1389 and the following April where the names of attending members are known. But his initial enthusiasm quickly waned. He attended only three out of the forty meetings recorded between January 1392 and February 1393,[22] and there is no reason to believe that the situation materially altered in later years. Huntingdon certainly proved useful to Richard during the months immediately following the dismissal of the appellants and he continued to use his half-brother on diplomatic missions such as those to France in 1389 and 1392,[23] but Huntingdon's infrequent

---

1396–99, 28. Huntingdon was commissioned to hear various pleas in 1393 and 1394. *Cal. Pat. Rolls 1391–96*, 237, 306, 390. In 1397, he was appointed justice of the peace for the 10 counties in which he held property at that time. *Cal. Pat. Rolls 1396–99*, 230.

[13] *Cal. Pat. Rolls 1388–92*, 116, 366. B.M. MS. Cott. Vespasian F. XIII, f. 12.

[14] French Roll, 12 Richard II, mem. 4.

[15] R. G. Marsden, *Select Pleas in the Court of Admiralty*, vol. 1 (1894), Li, 1–26, 149–72. No other detailed records of this Court earlier than the 16th century have survived.

[16] *Cal. Close Rolls 1389–92*, 31, 94, and *Cal. Pat. Rolls 1388–92*, 159, 412, 425, 458, 473, 487, 491.

[17] In January 1391, a committee was set up headed by Lancaster and the bishops of London and Salisbury to hear Huntingdon's complaints against the mayor and sheriffs for conduct prejudicial to his office and Court of Admiralty. *Cal. Pat. Rolls 1388–92*, 436.

[18] *Cal. Pat. Rolls 1385–89*, 25–6.

[19] In 1393, Aubrey de Vere, earl of Oxford, claimed the position as a hereditary right. His plea failed and a fresh grant of the office was made to Huntingdon. *Cal. Pat. Rolls 1391–96*, 312. When the attainder of Robert de Vere, duke of Ireland, was reversed in 1397, his uncle, Aubrey de Vere, became entitled to the chamberlainship, but Richard wanted to be certain of an unquestionably loyal holder and forced de Vere to give up all claim to the position. Richard confirmed his earlier grant to Huntingdon in February 1398, extending the honour to include his male heirs. *Cal. Pat. Rolls 1396–99*, 290.

[20] T. F. Tout, *Chapters in the Administrative History of Medieval England*, vol. 4 (1928), 337, 341, and S. B. Chrimes, *An Introduction to the Administrative History of Medieval England* (1952), 199, tend to over-emphasize Huntingdon's activity as chamberlain.

[21] He was probably abroad at the time of the January Parliament of 1395.

[22] Proceedings given in J. F. Baldwin, *The King's Council in England during the Middle Ages* (1913), 489–504.

[23] *Proceedings and Ordinances of the Privy Council*, ed. Sir Harris Nicolas, vol. 1 (1834), 7; and P.R.O. Council and Privy Seal, file 3. The delegation in 1392 consisted entirely of friends or relations of Lancaster.

attendance at council meetings is telling evidence that he was not to be numbered among Richard's active political supporters during the majority of his personal rule.

Had he been questioned, Huntingdon would have probably replied that he was a soldier and not an administrator, but he found little outlet for his military enthusiasm in the course of this period. Responsibility for the defence of the Scottish border for a short time had taken him to Berwick-on-Tweed in August 1392,[24] and he was abroad during the greater part of 1394 on a quasi military and diplomatic mission and did not return until about February 1395.[25] According to Froissart, Huntingdon went on a pilgrimage to Jerusalem and Mount Sinai and returned to England through Hungary,[26] but what may have been originally planned as a pilgrimage became an instrument by which Richard explored the first of several hare-brained schemes. His brother-in-law Sigismund, king of Hungary, had appealed for help against the Turks who were threatening his borders, and Richard took the opportunity to appoint his half-brother an ambassador to discuss with Sigismund 'certain negotiations touching the king and his realm'.[27] The Pope granted Huntingdon an indulgence on learning of his departure to fight the infidel,[28] and the mission bade fair to be the spearhead of a grandiose plan. But nothing came of the discussions. It was left to the French to heed Sigismund's appeals and to be routed by the Turks in battle. By that time, Richard was wisely contenting himself with the more practical aims of consolidating the peace that he had finally achieved with France.

Yet just as Richard was displaying signs of statesmanship, the stability of his personal rule began to crumble. When his attempt to support a French expedition against Italy was firmly squashed by Parliament early in 1397, he interested himself in the proposals put forward by Huntingdon for an Italian 'crusade'. His plan was to lead a force to Italy which would exterminate all schismatics and rebels, and although Pope Boniface IX could hardly have felt that Huntingdon was pre-eminently suited to the role of crusader, any support against his many enemies was most welcome. In March 1397, the Pope appointed Huntingdon gonfalonier of the Holy Roman Church and vicar in temporals in the papal lands, with privileges throughout England and Italy which were quite extraordinarily extensive. He received crusading indulgences for himself and his friends, a part of all benefices in England and Ireland, and exorbitant privileges from the English clergy.[29] These suggest that Huntingdon's scheme was nothing less than a plan to end all schism in the Church by a personal crusade, with far wider powers than those granted a few years earlier to the bishop of Norwich or the duke of Lancaster. The grant may have been made in response to a genuine desire on Huntingdon's part to undertake a crusade, but he lacked the ability to fulfil any such grandiose scheme and inevitably nothing came of his proposals.

The support given by Richard to these and other wild schemes during the first six months of 1397 proved very disquieting to some of the appellants who began to unite in their alarm, but it was not until late June or early July that the flames of discontent were fanned into open discord. The causes are by no means clear, but according to the French chronicle known as the *Traison et Mort*,[30] Gloucester took the opportunity at a royal feast to criticize most forcefully Richard's recent withdrawal of English forces from Brest.[31] Heated words were exchanged with the king and despite an apparently amicable parting, the incident seems to have marked the close of Richard's peaceful rule and led to those events which

[24] T. Rymer, *Foedera*, Hague ed., vol. 3, pt. iv, 82. It is possible that Huntingdon was deliberately appointed warden of Carlisle and the western marches to act as a check on the Percies.

[25] There is no evidence recording Huntingdon's movements in England between February 1394 and February 1395. He was absent from Richard's autumn campaign in Ireland and from the parliamentary summons of November 1394. Huntingdon joined Richard in Ireland in March 1395 when his name begins to appear as a witness to the submissions made by the Irish chiefs. E. Curtis fails to give his evidence for including Huntingdon among the nobles who accompanied Richard to Ireland in September 1394. See his *Richard II in Ireland, 1394–5* (1927), 26, and 'Unpublished Letters from Richard II in Ireland', *Proc. Royal Irish Acad.* vol. 37, Sec. C (1924–7), 289.

[26] Froissart, *Chronicles*, ed. T. Johnes, vol. 2 (1839), 568. Huntingdon may have been anxious to emulate both the earl of Derby and the earl of Arundel who had been to Jerusalem a year or two earlier. Huntingdon had also agreed in about 1395 to be a patron of a crusading order, the Order of the Passion, founded and exhaustively canvassed by Phillippe de Mézières, Charles VI's adviser. An abbreviated text of de Mézières's plea for this crusade was given to Huntingdon in about 1395 and may well be that preserved as Ashmole 813, Bodleian Library, Oxford. See M. V. Clarke, 'The Wilton Diptych', *The Burlington Magazine*, vol. 58 (June 1931), 290–4.

[27] T. Rymer, *Foedera*. Hague ed., vol. 3, pt. iv, 93. A letter from Richard II to a German prince c. January 1394, also mentions Huntingdon's journey to Hungary. *Diplomatic Correspondence of Richard II*, ed. E. Perroy (1933), 144–5, and 244, which shows that the plans for the journey had been made by December 1393.

[28] *Cal. Papal Registers: Papal Letters. Vol. 4. 1362–1404*, 489.

[29] Walsingham, *Annales Ricardi II*, ed. H. T. Riley (1866), 200–1. *Cal. Papal Registers: Papal Letters. Vol. 4. 1362–1404*, 294–5, 300. A. Theiner, *Codex Diplomaticus*, vol. 3, 91.

[30] *Chronique de la Traison et Mort de Richard II*, ed. B. Williams (1846), 1, 117. The possibility that this chronicle was written by a member of Elizabeth Holand's household is discussed in Appendix 3.

[31] In 1370, the duke of Brittany had pledged the town of Brest to England for the duration of the

war with France. With the cessation of hostilities, the pledges for Brest were reclaimed by the duke. Huntingdon had been governor of the town since 1389 and had been granted £2,000 each year for paying his forces and maintaining the fortifications there. P.R.O. E 101, Box 68/11, no. 270 and E 101, Box 69/1, no. 278. He had made some attempt to maintain the defences in 1390 and 1394 by ordering bows and other equipment. *Cal. Close Rolls 1389–93*, 134, and *Cal. Close Rolls 1392–96*, 309, but a record of his movements do not suggest that he resided at Brest for any length of time between 1389 and 1392 as stated by W. Dugdale, *The Baronage of England*, vol. 2 (1676), 78b. To compensate him for the loss of this command, Huntingdon was appointed governor of Calais, and keeper of the New Tower there in February 1398 for a period of 15 years.

[32] *Traison et Mort*, ed. B. Williams (1846), 5, 125.

[33] Neither the *Traison et Mort* nor John Gower in his *Cronica Tripertita* refer to this feast. *Complete Works of John Gower*, ed. G. C. Macauley, vol. 4 (1902), 316. On the other hand, Walsingham, *Annales Ricardi II*, ed. H. T. Riley (1866), 201, states that the feast was held at Huntingdon's mansion near St. Paul's, whereas the *Rolls of Parliament*, vol. 3, 436, state that it was at the home of the chancellor, Edmund Stafford, bishop of Exeter. It is surprising that Richard did not include the charge of conspiracy against the Crown in his formal accusations if he had known of the plot against him. For that reason, the account given by the anonymous French chronicler has been rejected by several historians. The absence of any other contemporary account makes it difficult to check the accuracy of the *Traison et Mort* and Gower. The incident is not mentioned by Walsingham but the fact that a member of his religious house was probably involved in the plot may well account for his silence. Froissart is quite unreliable, but the Lancastrian supporter, Adam of Usk, does confirm the incident to some extent as he states that Warwick claimed to have been lured on by Gloucester, the abbot of St. Albans, and a monk recluse of Westminster.

[34] See the Evesham Chronicle, an original source from 1391 onwards.

[35] *Cal. Fine Rolls 1391–99*, 219.

culminated in his downfall. Full of anger and contempt, Gloucester, who had never disguised his animosity for Richard or Lancaster, sounded out a small number of like-minded associates, including the archbishop of Canterbury and the earls of Warwick, Arundel, and Nottingham.[32] Any plot they contemplated against Richard, however, was quickly frustrated by its betrayal. As soon as Richard learnt of their scheme from Nottingham's lips, he apparently rushed to Huntingdon and prepared a counter-plan to invite the three principal conspirators to a feast and then arrest them. Gloucester pleaded ill-health and took refuge at Pleshey Castle, Arundel sent his excuses and locked himself in Reigate Castle, while Warwick, accepting the invitation, was cordially received by Richard and conducted to the Tower of London.[33] Aware of the dangers attendant upon a plan which had proved only partially successful, Richard and Huntingdon acted with speed. On 10 July, they rode with a large force to Gloucester's country residence at Pleshey, awoke the duke in his bed[34] and took him to London where he was entrusted to Nottingham for custody in prison at Calais. Huntingdon arrested the earl of Arundel two days later and seized Arundel Castle before the end of the week.[35] These arrests created a sensation: so much so that Richard had to proclaim that he had been advised by eight specified counsellors who would appeal Gloucester and his supporters at the September Parliament.

Owing to the reconstruction of Westminster Hall, all those attending the September meeting assembled in a temporary wooden building, surrounded by Richard's personal

The arrest of the duke of Gloucester, 1397. (*c.* 1460–80)

archers from Cheshire and the retinues of only a few selected magnates.[36] As a punishment for their actions against the Crown between 1386 and 1388, the archbishop of Canterbury was sent into exile, Gloucester was murdered in prison, Arundel was executed, and Warwick, recently in Huntingdon's custody at Tintagel Castle,[37] was banished to the Isle of Man. The flamboyant but not entirely unprecedented distribution of honours which followed this display of Machiavellian justice included the elevation of Huntingdon to the dukedom of Exeter.[38] Other supporters were rewarded with lesser titles, and lands forfeited by Gloucester and Warwick were divided among those whom Walsingham contemptuously referred to as 'dukelings'.[39] Richard and the new duke of Exeter shared Arundel's lands between them[40] and Arundel's only son was handed over to Exeter for safe keeping.[41] Parliament was adjourned on the last day of September and the meeting concluded with a great feast at which the duchess of Exeter received a prize as the best dancer present.[42]

Huntingdon's Household

The rebuilding of Dartington Hall began immediately after Huntingdon had been raised to the earldom in 1388 and probably continued until the close of the century (see Introduction, Part 2). It was intended that the Hall should reflect the position and wealth of its owner and the porch tower, great hall, and kitchen still testify to this. Part of Huntingdon's private apartments are incorporated in the rooms immediately behind the dais of the great hall, and it is possible that he and his family used some of the rooms south of the great hall which have been revealed by excavation. The buttery and pantry survive at the lower end of the great hall and the rooms above were possibly used by the steward and other members closely associated with the organization of the household. The need to accommodate a large staff and retinue also had to be taken into account in planning a residence of this nature, and part of the lodgings built by Huntingdon for his household still remain on the east and probably on the west side of the great court. Although they are a rare survival, what is particularly interesting is that several contemporary records enable us to people these rooms.

The household of any magnate principally consisted of two groups; those engaged in the administration of his residences and estates, and the soldiers who were fed and paid to

Royal retinues watching Edward III paying homage to Philip VI of France, 1331. (Late 14th century)

[36] Lancaster, Derby, York, and Huntingdon were among the chosen few. T. Rymer, *Foedera*, London ed., vol. 8, 147. The new appellants were singularly undistinguished as a group. Nottingham, the most able of them, was a few months older than Richard. Neither Huntingdon, Salisbury, nor Sir William Scrope were particularly competent politicians, while the earls of Kent, Rutland, and Somerset and Lord Despenser were still in their mid twenties and inexperienced. They obviously set out to enjoy the occasion to the utmost. They were dressed uniformly in robes of red silk edged with white, and decorated with gold letters. *Chronicon Adae de Usk*, ed. E. Maunde Thompson (1904), 13.

[37] *Cal. Close Rolls 1396–99*, 167.

[38] *Rolls of Parliament*, vol. 3, 355a. Edward III had established a precedent in 1337 by creating 5 earls in 1 day.

[39] Walsingham, *Annales Ricardi II*, ed. H. T. Riley (1866), 223.

[40] According to the admission of 1433, Exeter may be considered to have become the earl of Arundel. V. Gibbs and H. A. Doubleday, *The Complete Peerage*, vol. 1 (1910), 245.

[41] *Cal. Pat. Rolls 1396–99*, 214. This son was later confined in his father's old castle of Reigate under the custody of Exeter's steward. Walsingham comments that he was subject to many humiliations, *Annales Ricardi II*, ed. H. T. Riley (1866), 241, while the *Traison et Mort* notes that he worked for Exeter like a slave and continually blacked his boots. *Traison et Mort*, ed. B. Williams (1846), 97, 253–4.

[42] *Traison et Mort*, ed. B. Williams (1846), 11, 140.

[43] *Cal. Close Rolls 1399–1402*, 58–9.

[44] *Traison et Mort*, ed. B. Williams (1846), 96, 251.

[45] Described in 1405 as late steward of the late duke of Exeter. *Cal. Pat. Rolls 1401–05*, 450. Huntingdon's treasurer is mentioned, but not named. Ibid., 26.

[46] P.R.O. Misc. Inq. C 145/275, no. 8.

[47] P.R.O. Misc. Inq. C 275/30 and C 276/12.

serve their lord. The household was the outward display of a noble's wealth and importance, often maintained at a heavy and sometimes disastrous cost to his finances. All magnates had a household through which they controlled their possessions, and this was the basis of their central authority. Three of the most important members of Huntingdon's household were his steward, treasurer, and wardrober. The last-named was in charge of all his furniture, plate, clothes, and jewels, and at the end of the century this position was held by one Alexander.[43] The treasurer looked after all financial matters connected with the earl's household, while the steward, usually a person of rank and influence, held all courts on behalf of his lord, installed local officers, and seized the goods of outlaws. Huntingdon had more than one steward. Sir Thomas Shelley,[44] Richard Shelley,[45] and his chaplain John Holand[46] were all so described and were responsible for property in Devon, while William Curleston and John Lankey were his stewards in Dartmouth and Cornwall respectively.[47] Sir William Coggeshall was Huntingdon's chamberlain,[48] while other members of his household included Warin Waldegrave, one of his attorneys,[49] three clerks, Walter Lambard, Robert Bays, and John Belle,[50] his butler, Hugh Cade,[51] his panter, Thomas Blakesley,[52] and William Warde, keeper of the park at Dartington at a wage of 2d. a day.[53]

All magnates were surrounded by a body of retainers which varied considerably in number, depending on the wealth and standing of their lord. Since at least the close of the previous century, the system had been practised whereby liveried retainers, bound by written indenture and usually paid an annual wage, agreed to serve their lord in times of peace and war. This system of contract was one of the principal characteristics of what has been called 'bastard feudalism' and although its origins lay in military necessity, it came to be applied to officials and even servants. Chaucer's gentle knight shows that not all military retainers were brigands, but the difficulties of controlling an unruly retinue had already become apparent during the second quarter of the fourteenth century, although the worst evils of the system were not fully revealed until the following century.

Numerous contracts survive to show that the Black Prince and the duke of Lancaster supported hundreds of retainers, but very few indentures, for instance, have survived for the earls of March and Salisbury[54] and even less have been found for Huntingdon. Two contracts exist, dating significantly after the success of Henry IV's venture in the summer of 1399. In September 1399, Thomas Proudfoot was retained by Huntingdon for life on the payment of an annual wage of £10 which ensured his personal attendance on the earl and his family.[55] In the same month, Huntingdon also retained an esquire, John Trenarke, for life in return for an annual payment of the same amount 'and in time of war, such wages as others of his estate'.[56] Such people would wear the earl's livery and declare themselves to be of his company, a body described in January 1400 as 'associated with very many evil deeds'.[57] It is likely that Sir Benedict Cely[58] was a member of his company as well as William Allington,[59] Alexander Bouer,[60] Robert Cary,[61] William Cresshill,[62] and others,[63] all described as esquires of the earl and some of whom bore Devonshire names. It is impossible to obtain any idea of the size of Huntingdon's retinue. It would be increased in times of war, as was the case when Huntingdon went to Ireland in 1399,[64] but the fact that the contingent accompanying him to Scotland in 1385 was the largest of any knight

---

[48] P.R.O. Misc. Inq. C 145/275, no. 30. Sir John Yard is noted as his receiver of moneys in 1399. P.R.O. Misc. Inq. C 145/275, no. 4.

[49] *Cal. Pat. Rolls 1385–89*, 213.

[50] *Cal. Pat. Rolls 1396–99*, 279; *Cal. Close Rolls 1396–99*, 374–5; *Cal. Pat. Rolls 1388–92*, 194, 365.

[51] *Traison et Mort*, ed. B. Williams (1846), 97, 252.

[52] *Cal. Pat. Rolls 1391–96*, 639.

[53] *Cal. Pat. Rolls 1399–1401*, 405–6. He had been keeper of the park since August 1387.

[54] G. A. Holmes, *The Estates of the Higher Nobility in Fourteenth Century England* (1957), 62–6.

[55] *Cal. Pat. Rolls 1399–1401*, 244. This record, made in March 1400, confirms a grant given in the previous September.

[56] Ibid., 255. The existence or otherwise of such documents is entirely haphazard and is, of course, no indication of the size of Huntingdon's retinue.

[57] T. Rymer, *Foedera*, London ed., vol. 8, 120.

[58] *Cal. Pat. Rolls 1391–96*, 535.

[59] J. S. Roskell, 'William Allington of Horseheath, Speaker in the Parliament of 1429–30', *Proc. Camb. Antiquarian Soc.* vol. 52 (1958), 32–3.

[60] *Cal. Pat. Rolls 1399–1401*, 378. He was granted 2d. a day from the issues of the manor of Dartington.

[61] *Cal. Pat. Rolls 1391–96*, 46. Cary was the son and heir of Sir John Cary who had been banished to Ireland by the 'Merciless' Parliament in 1388.

[62] *Cal. Pat. Rolls 1396–99*, 276. Huntingdon appointed him constable of Berkhamsted Castle in 1398.

[63] Richard Cryse, *Cal. Pat. Rolls 1399–1401*, 186. Ranlin Covely, P.R.O. Misc. Inq. C 145/275, no. 29. Robert Feriby, *Cal. Pat. Rolls 1391–96*, 46. John Hobildoe, *Cal. Pat. Rolls 1401–05*, 26. John Pasford, *Cal. Close Rolls 1396–99*, 374–5. John Savage, Froissart, *Chronicles*, ed. T. Johnes, vol. 2 (1839), 410. John Verdon, *Cal. Pat. Rolls 1391–96*, 208. *Cal. Pat. Rolls 1396–99*, 349. William Yerde, *Cal. Close Rolls 1413–19*, 486. Walsingham also states that one of the earl's soldiers, John Schevele, was with him in Essex at the beginning of 1400. *Annales Ricardi II*, ed. H. T. Riley (1866), 327.

[64] *Cal. Pat. Rolls 1396–99*, 540, 573.

present, that the great hall built by him a few years later at Dartington was almost the largest raised during the last quarter of the fourteenth century, and that the lodgings built for his household at Dartington were particularly extensive suggest that Huntingdon always supported a retinue of considerable size.

Huntingdon would be accompanied by a disordered array of jostling retainers wherever he travelled. It is not surprising that such bands of supporters frequently distressed the innocent and particularly those who had offended their lord. Consequently, the practice of livery was closely associated with that of maintenance, whereby a person granted his lands to a powerful lord on payment of an annual fee and received them back with a guarantee of the lord's protection. The earliest record of this nature associated with Huntingdon dates shortly after he received his earldom. In December 1388, William Howell granted all his lands and tenements in the town of Stratton and the manor of Hilton in Cornwall to Huntingdon and received them back in February 1389 in return for an annual payment of 6s. 8d.[65] In April 1396, several of Huntingdon's friends witnessed a deed made at Dartington whereby Nicholas Tremayn, John Isaac, and John Prouse granted Huntingdon the reversion of the Devonshire manor of Flute Daumarle and a third of the manor of Holbeton in return for his protection.[66] In 1400, the jurors reported at an inquisition at Exeter that Richard Spicer of Plymouth had enfeoffed the earl some time beforehand of all his lands, tenants, goods, and chattels.[67] As a magnate, therefore, Huntingdon's responsibilities were wider than merely those to his family: he was the head of an extensive household, lord of a large body of retainers and supporters, and patron of a considerable number of small landholders.

The Fall of Richard II and His Supporters

Parliament reassembled at Shrewsbury at the end of January 1398, in fear of the newly created 'dradde dukis'.[68] Within four days, it had repealed the acts of the 'Merciless' Parliament of 1388 and provided Richard with sufficient money to stabilize his financial position. None of the quarrels which broke out between the victorious lords hindered its work, not even the famous abortive one at Coventry between Lancaster's son and the duke of Norfolk which led to their banishment for ten years and life respectively.

Richard's recent successes went to his head. The rigged appointment of royalist sheriffs, the exaction of forced loans, arbitrary fines, and demands for oaths of loyalty became a common feature of his rule. These and other capricious actions of a sick mind, merely strengthened the very opposition that Richard was bent on crushing. Liberal rewards were granted to the little coterie of friends and advisers who clustered round him, but Huntingdon was not among them. He had been thrust into prominence during the arrest and trial of the appellants, possibly more so than any other of Richard's supporters, and had been well rewarded with lands and title. But Richard, jealous of the over-mighty subject, preferred to rule through less exalted men. Exeter was valuable as an older member of the court party and useful as a passive supporter, willing to lend his name to the air of verisimilitude which covered some of Richard's actions,[69] but his value to the king as an active supporter of his policies was very limited.[70]

Despite the growing lack of confidence in his rule, Richard chose this moment to threaten

[65] P.R.O. E 40/11030, 10932.

[66] P.R.O. E 40/6964. See also Cal. Close Rolls 1405–09, 301.

[67] P.R.O. Misc. Inq. C 145/275, no. 4.

[68] 'Richard the Redeless', ed. W. W. Skeat in Piers Plowman, Pt. 3 (1883), 475, 476.

[69] He was a member of the committee set up at the end of the January Parliament of 1398 to deal with outstanding petitions left unanswered by Parliament. Rolls of Parliament, vol. 3, 368b.

[70] The comment by the author of 'Richard the Redeless', written in the summer of 1399, that the king relied on young and frivolous courtiers who had never worn armour, supports the view that Exeter was not numbered among them. W. W. Skeat, Piers Plowman, Pt. 3 (1883), 474, 476, 495.

[71] Huntingdon was retained by indenture to serve Richard with 140 men-at-arms and 500 archers. There was to be 1 mason and 1 carpenter for every 20 archers. P.R.O. E 101, Box 69, no. 300. W. Dugdale, *The Baronage of England*, vol. 2 (1676), 79b. Rutland attended with 140 men-at-arms and 200 archers. Ibid., 156b.

the right of inheritance by confiscating Lancaster's estates immediately after the latter's death in February 1399, and followed it up by using them to finance a second expedition to Ireland. Exeter, Rutland, the young earl of Gloucester, and a number of other friends accompanied the thirty-two-year-old king, but most of the magnates were discouraged from attending.[71] Consequently, the nobility with their private armies, remained in England at the very time that the Crown and its forces were leaving the country.

The inadequate preparations, dilatoriness, and indecision which marked this brief, but futile Irish campaign are so redolent of the Castilian campaign of 1386–7 that it is possible to see the hand of Exeter asserting itself again. By avoiding a pitched battle, the Irish encouraged Richard to waste his energies on futile marching, and declining food supplies forced him to withdraw his army to Dublin to await reinforcements.

With Richard II's departure in May 1399, mounting unrest and confusion in England was reinforced by rumours that he intended to rule from Ireland and Cheshire through his minions. The earl of Arundel, recently escaped from Exeter's custody, joined Archbishop Arundel and Henry Bolingbroke, Lancaster's son, in Paris. Towards the end of June, this small group and their supporters made their way to Boulogne and sailed to England with the sole declared intention of claiming Bolingbroke's inheritance. Nevertheless, they carried the forces which inexorably led to Richard's deposition and the death of Exeter.

As soon as Bolingbroke and his companions landed in Yorkshire at the end of June or the beginning of July, nobles, knights, and peasants, as well as the riff-raff so often found in the van of any band of adventurers, flocked to his cause. With the assured support of the great northern magnates, Bolingbroke marched southwards towards Bristol. Richard

Richard II prepares to leave for Ireland, 1399. (*c.* 1460–80)

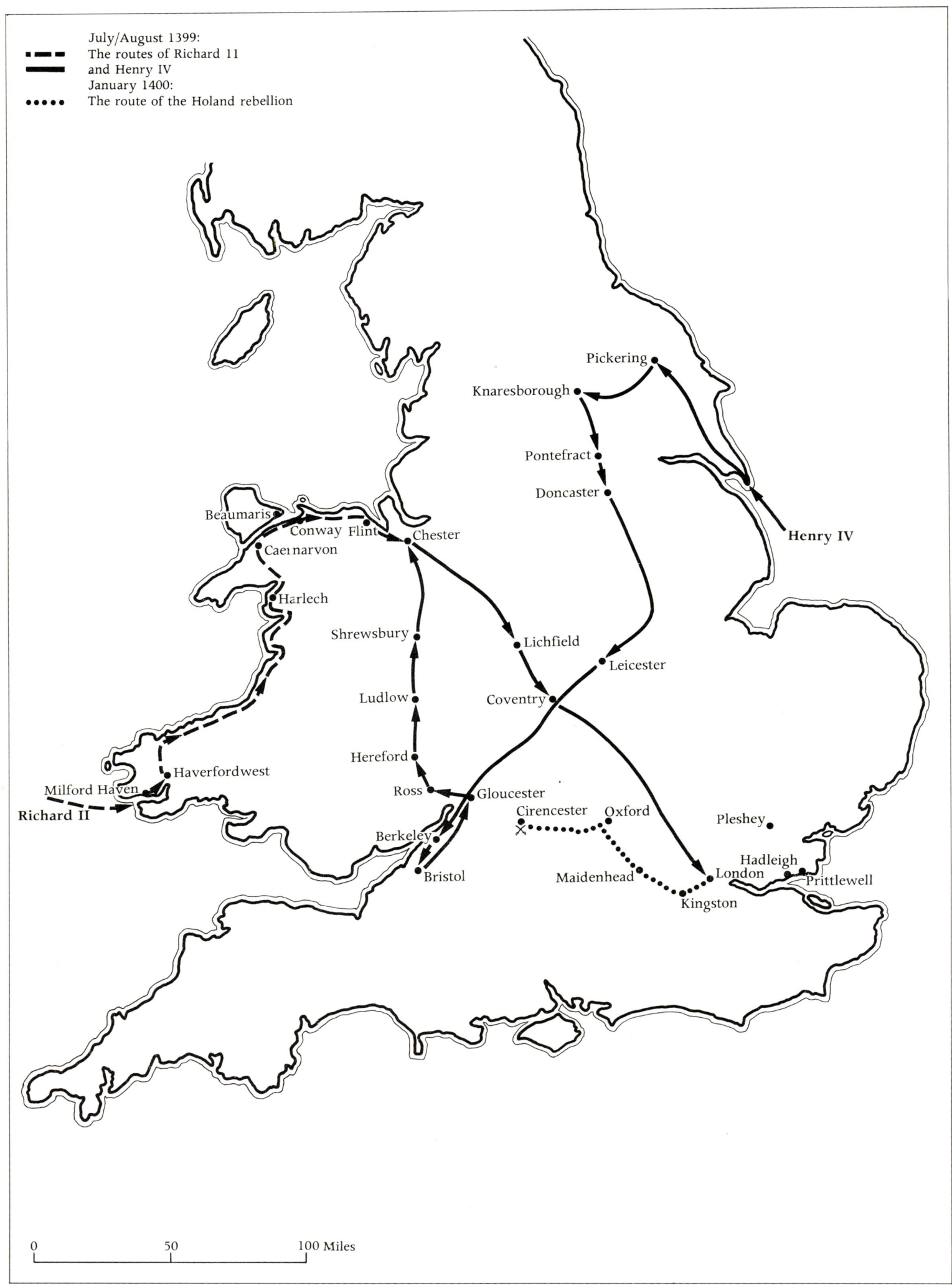

Fig. 8 Map showing the routes of Richard II and Bolingbroke in 1399, and the Holand rebellion in 1400

[72] P.R.O. TRE. Enrolled Accounts, 364/34.

[73] *Traison et Mort*, ed. B Williams (1846), 43–5, 191–2. Exeter may have known the castle as he had been its constable for 9 years.

[74] The chronicler known as 'Creton' gives both names but the *Traison et Mort* mentions Exeter only. *The Deposition of Richard II*, ed. J. Webb, *Archaeologia*, vol. 20 (1824), and reprinted separately in 1823, 109. *Traison et Mort*, ed. B. Williams (1846), 45, 192.

[75] Neither 'Creton' nor the *Traison et Mort* mention Arundel, but his name may have been added by the Lancastrian chroniclers to give an air of verisimilitude to Northumberland's actions.

[76] *Traison et Mort*, ed. B. Williams (1846), 193.

[77] According to 'Creton', Richard saw Exeter at Chester, but neither was allowed to speak to each other, and while Richard languished in prison, Exeter sat at his brother-in-law's table. *The Deposition of Richard II*, ed. J. Webb (1823), 174.

unaccountably delayed returning to England until about 24 July[72] and as soon as he landed in Pembrokeshire, his army melted away leaving him with only a small group of friends and foreign soldiers. Most of the king's friends urged him to withdraw to Bordeaux where he could gather sufficient strength to renew the attack against the invader, but Exeter favoured their flight to Conway where Richard could make a stand and yet escape to France if necessary.[73] Disguised as a priest and accompanied by about fifteen companions, the king hurried northwards as quickly as possible.

At the same time that Richard was riding hard up the west coast of Wales, Bolingbroke, aware of his opponent's plan, was following the parallel road along the border country from Bristol to Chester. By 9 August, the two opposing forces were less than forty miles apart. Both sides sent envoys to discuss terms with each other. Exeter and possibly the duke of Surrey went as Richard's representatives to Chester,[74] while the earl of Northumberland and possibly Arundel set out for Conway.[75] Exeter's attempt to persuade Bolingbroke to sue for pardon was doomed to failure for Richard not only seriously underestimated the purpose and strength of his opponent, but he failed to realize the precariousness of his position in a remote part of the country with only the haziest notion of the position and strength of the enemy. Exeter's meeting with Bolingbroke was none too cordial and terminated in the duke's arrest.[76] Meanwhile, Northumberland arrived at Conway Castle bearing counter-proposals. Vainly trusting in the strength of his position as the anointed ruler of England, Richard agreed to meet his opponents and on about 15 August, he left the security of Conway Castle, his last stronghold and source of escape. Once on the road which threaded its way over the hills edging the coast, Northumberland had little difficulty in ambushing his adversary. That night, Richard and his small band of companions were brought as prisoners to Flint Castle, lodged in Chester Castle on the following day, and began their journey to London a few days later.[77]

At an assembly held at the end of September, Richard's abdication was read out, the

The seal of John Holand, 1st duke of Exeter: 1399

throne declared vacant, and Bolingbroke chosen as king. Richard was condemned to perpetual imprisonment and his supporters were brought before the new king and his council to account for their complicity in the murder of the duke of Gloucester two years earlier. Exeter declared that he knew nothing about Gloucester's death until the duke of Norfolk had informed him of it, and as for the other judgments made in the Parliament

Richard II at Conway Castle, 1399. (Early 15th century)

The dukes of Exeter and Surrey leave for Chester, 1399. (Early 15th century)

48

[78] *Rolls of Parliament*, vol. 3, 450.

[79] The appointment of Rutland as Justiciary and Keeper of the New Forest and all forests of the Trent at the beginning of November, and the presence of both Rutland and Huntingdon as members of the council are indicative of Henry's lack of resentment to his former adversaries at this time. *Ord. Privy Council*, i, 100.

[80] *Rolls of Parliament*, vol. 3, 451–2.

of 1397, he was not a party to them and lamented them in his heart, but dared say nothing for fear of death.[78] Henry IV was not disposed towards exacting vengeance.[79] Exeter and his friends were ordered to forfeit all holdings awarded to them since September 1397, and to revert to their former titles. They were stripped of all offices, ordered to reduce their retinues, and warned in the clearest terms of the dangers of treason.[80]

Henry Bolingbroke receives the dukes of Exeter and Surrey at Chester Castle, 1399. (Early 15th century)

Henry Bolingbroke delivers Richard II to the citizens of London, 1399. (Early 15th century)

The Holand Rebellion

The attempt made by a small group of Richard's supporters to kill Henry IV and to restore Richard to the throne centred on the Holand family. It is not clear who was responsible for organizing this rebellion but its leaders numbered John Holand, once more earl of Huntingdon; his twenty-nine-year-old nephew, Thomas Holand, earl of Kent; his twenty-seven-year-old half-cousin, the earl of Rutland; the latter's twenty-six-year-old brother-in-law, Lord Despenser; and the earl of Salisbury who was about the same age as Huntingdon and whose father had been married for a time to Huntingdon's mother. They were supported by several of Richard's friends including the Oxfordshire knight, Sir Thomas Blount; the deposed archbishop of Canterbury; the bishop of Carlisle; a royal clerk and Richard's physician. The foundations of the rebellion were laid in the middle of

The Holand rebellion, 1400. (c. 1460–80)

[81] The rebels may also have been swayed by the unrest already present in Kent and the fact that Sir Stephen Scrope was accused of plotting against the king at Binbury. T. Rymer, *Foedera*, London ed., vol. 8, 170. The part played by Huntingdon in this rebellion is by no means clear. The version given by the author of *Traison et Mort* is so markedly different from the accounts given by the English chroniclers that they are irreconcilable. The *Traison et Mort* has been dismissed by Sir James Ramsay as 'a mere jumble unworthy of criticism', *Lancaster and York*, vol. 1 (1892), 20, and the belief that it is unsupported to any marked extent by any other chronicle has led to its frequent dismissal. The fact that much of the chronicle can be shown to be extremely reliable has been ignored and the reason why so many statements have been fabricated if they are not true, has never been explained. The support given to Walsingham's version by the other Lancastrian writers, Adam of Usk and the author of the *Continuation of the Eulogium Historiarum* is considered sufficient evidence of the reliability of the English version, although Usk's account is very brief and the *Continuation of the Eulogium Historiarum* does not clearly indicate Huntingdon's part in the rebellion. Walsingham's story is that the earls of Kent and Salisbury were the leading rebels and that Huntingdon played the coward's part by remaining in London until he had seen whether the conspiracy was successful or not. Doubts about this view are suggested by the fact that Henry's warrant for the arrest of the leading rebels expressly names only Kent and Huntingdon and that we have no evidence that Huntingdon was a coward in the field of battle. The Lancastrian

December 1399 when the conspirators apparently agreed at a meeting held in the rooms of the abbot of Westminster that Henry and his sons should be captured under cover of a tournament to be held at Windsor early in the New Year. From the first, it was intended that the royal clerk should impersonate Richard so as to attract supporters to the rebel side until it proved possible to reach the deposed king and gain his active co-operation.

The restoration of their recently lost titles and possessions may have motivated the rebels as Walsingham and Adam of Usk assert, but there was also the hope that whilst Richard was still alive, the people would prefer to support the king *de jure* rather than the king *de facto*. The fact that Henry's popularity was still in the ascendant did not deter Huntingdon and his confederates for one moment.[81]

After spending Christmas and New Year's Day at Windsor, Huntingdon, Kent, and Rutland left the court, ostensibly to prepare for the forthcoming tournament, but in fact to arm themselves and to meet again at Kingston on 4 January with their supporters.[82] Rutland, however, failed to join them at the appointed time and the letters sent by the rebels urging him to support them were discovered by Rutland's father, the duke of York, who promptly set out for Windsor to alert the king to the conspiracy. Forewarned of the danger, Henry IV left immediately for London, meeting the mayor on his way bringing him news of the rebellion. Henry immediately issued a warrant for the arrest of Huntingdon and Kent 'and whomsoever else there is in their company, as betrayers of ourselves and our realm',[83] dispatched copies of it to every sheriff in England, and took the field against the insurgents. Meanwhile Kent, Despenser, and Salisbury, arriving at Windsor and learning that their opponent had escaped,[84] rejoined Huntingdon and made towards Gloucestershire, possibly with the intention of trying to reach Cheshire but more probably Wales or the west of England. Huntingdon led the rebels westwards while Kent held the bridge at Maidenhead and delayed the vanguard of Henry's forces.[85] The first night was probably spent not far from Oxford, and by the following evening, the rebels had reached the Cotswolds. They spent the night in the fields near Cirencester while the leaders stayed at a hostelry in the town. Unfortunately, one of Henry's archers, staying at the same inn, was recognised by Kent who promptly ordered the constable of Cirencester to hang him. The constable attempted to arrest Kent instead, and in the scuffle which ensued, both Kent and Salisbury were killed.[86] Realizing their difficulty, Huntingdon and Gloucester jumped through a window and tried to create a diversion by firing some houses. Huntingdon found his steward with his horses during the ensuing confusion and fled towards Essex, while Despenser turned towards Wales and was captured at Bristol. Many of those who failed to escape from Cirencester were taken prisoner and the heads of Kent and Salisbury accompanied Henry IV on his triumphant return to London.

The rebellion collapsed in ignominy because it failed to receive substantial support. Men in towns close to the rebels' route, such as Wantage and Faringdon in Berkshire and Bampton in Oxfordshire, rose in favour of Henry and harassed the fleeing insurgents.[87] Sympathetic disturbances in Cheshire were quickly put down,[88] while the rebellion received little support from Huntingdon's estates in the west of England. Two canons of Exeter Cathedral had been won over with jewels and silver and gold plate worth £200, while John Kem of Yeovil had received a fur-lined coat and a jewel-embroidered tunic worth

---

writers seem to have felt that Huntingdon's dramatic arrest and death in Essex precluded him from having been with Kent and Salisbury, particularly as they met their deaths over 100 miles away at Cirencester. But it does nothing of the sort. Kent and Salisbury died 2 or 3 days before Huntingdon was arrested and that gave him plenty of time to make his escape from Gloucestershire. Furthermore, although the author of the *Traison et Mort* is as biased in favour of the rebels as Walsingham is against them, he offers far more precise detail about the rebellion than any other writer of the time and, despite several minor inaccuracies, betrays a knowledge of events which is only likely to have been gained by close proximity to the principal personalities. On the whole, 'Creton' supports the story given in the *Traison et Mort* but entirely omits the part played by Huntingdon. 'Creton', however, was now relying for his information on a French priest who had accompanied Bolingbroke on his invasion in 1399.

[82] *Traison et Mort*, ed. B. Williams (1846), 80, 233. It is probable that the description of the leave-taking between Huntingdon and his wife described at this point by the author of the *Traison et Mort*, is the record of an eye-witness.

[83] T. Rymer, *Foedera*, Hague ed., vol. 3, pt. iv, 175.

[84] Neither the *Traison et Mort* nor the *Continuation of the Eulogium Historiarum* mention this visit to Windsor, but it is reported by 'Creton', Walsingham, and Archbishop Arundel in a letter written on 10 January 1400. *Literae Cantuarienses*, ed. J. B. Sheppard, vol. 3 (1889), 73.

[85] Walsingham mentions that the rebels visited the queen at Sonning near Reading to rally supporters to their cause, but although one of the leaders may have done so, it is extremely unlikely that they all rushed to a child and her attendants at such a critical time, merely to gather a small number of additional supporters. *Annales Ricardi II*, ed. H. T. Riley (1866), 323–4.

[86] This account is supported by an entry in the Issue Roll 1 Henry IV where John Cosin of Cirencester was paid £66. 13s. 4d. a year for resisting Kent. Froissart and the *Chronique du Religieux de St. Denys*, ed. M. L. Bellaguet, vol. 2 (1840), 736, both add that Huntingdon was present at Cirencester.

[87] T. Rymer, *Foedera*, Hague ed., vol. 3, pt. iv, 192.

[88] Sir H. Nicolas, *Proceedings and Ordinances of the Privy Council*, vol. 1 (1834), 109.

Pleshey Castle: *c.* 1803

£20. Weapons had been widely distributed in anticipation of the rebellion and caches of them were later found in north Devon, Bovey Tracey, and Dartmouth.[89] As soon as news of the rising reached Devon, Simon Gall had ridden from Barnstaple to Combe Martin and summoned all the villagers there to rise against King Henry and go to the help of their lord, John Holand. At Dartmouth, servants of William Curleston had gone round the town urging the inhabitants to join them in meeting Richard II and the earl of Huntingdon now that they were in the field with a great host of people, while Ranlin Covely had strutted round the town wearing Huntingdon's livery and refusing to take it off. At Exeter, one of the bribed canons had gathered forty archers and was holding out there in Huntingdon's name.[90] But there was no great rush to join the insurgents as had been the case with Bolingbroke's progress six months beforehand, for most people preferred to wait and see if the rebellion was likely to succeed before publicly nailing their colours to Huntingdon's mast.

Meanwhile, Huntingdon and his steward, Sir Thomas Shelley, had ridden across England and reached Prittlewell in Essex.[91] It is difficult to understand why Huntingdon failed to escape to his estates in Devon and thence abroad, for his chances of discovery would have been far less and those of escape far greater. Walsingham's story that he tried to seek refuge at Hadleigh Castle, the home of the earl of Oxford, is reasonable enough for the earl's son, Richard, had almost certainly married one of Huntingdon's daughters and he had been a visitor to Dartington Hall not long beforehand.[92] However, before Huntingdon and his steward could arrange for a boat to take them to the Continent, they had been captured and taken to the residence of the countess of Hereford at Pleshey about thirty miles away.[93] Word of Huntingdon's capture was reported immediately to the king who gave orders for the constable of the Tower to receive Huntingdon 'from one who will

[89] P.R.O. Misc. Inq. C 145/275, nos. 34, 7, 9, and 30.

[90] Ibid., and also no. 29.

[91] The journey could probably not be accomplished by hard riding in less than 20 hours.

[92] V. Gibbs and H. A. Doubleday, *The Complete Peerage*, vol. 10 (1945), 235, note h. It was stated by the Commons to Henry IV in October 1399, that Richard, earl of Oxford, 'had espoused the daughter of your sister'. *Rolls of Parliament*, vol. 3, 441. De Vere had recently left some armour belonging to him at Dartington Hall, *Cal. Close Rolls 1399–1402*, 58–9, and his knights had distributed armour at Combe Martin at the time of the Holand rebellion. P.R.O. Misc. Inq. C 145/275, no. 30.

[93] It is possible that the men of Essex had not yet forgotten the forced contribution of £1,333. 6s. 8d. which Richard had exacted between May 1398 and January 1399 and which they had paid, apparently with great difficulty. A. Steel, *Receipt of the Exchequer: 1377–1485* (1954), 118. The opportunity to exact revenge on one of Richard's supporters would not have been lost on the men of Essex.

[94] T. Rymer, *Foedera*, Hague ed., vol. 3, pt. iv, 175, and *Cal. Close Rolls 1399–1402*, 34.

[95] Jean Le Beau, *Chronique de Richard II, 1377–99*, ed. J. A. Buchan (1826) and *Chronique du Religieux de St. Denys*, ed. M. L. Bellaguet, vol. 2 (1840), 742, support the *Traison et Mort*, ed. B. Williams (1846), 97, 253. This action is far more likely than Walsingham's story that the countess tried to save Huntingdon from the mob in order that the king might interview him. Huntingdon's steward, Sir Thomas Shelley, however, was handed over to the king and imprisoned in the Tower. *Cal. Letter Books of City of London. Letter Book I. c. 1400–1422*, ed. R. R. Sharpe (1909), 2.

[96] *Cal. Close Rolls 1402–05*, 425.

[97] According to the *Traison et Mort* and the *Chronique du Religieux de St. Denys*, ed. M. L. Bellaguet, vol. 2 (1840), 742, Arundel paraded Huntingdon's head through the streets of London on a pole and took it to the king. Henry expressly ordered that it should be set upon London Bridge 'and remain there so long as it might last'. However, his wife's petition for it to be taken down and delivered to her for burial was granted on 19 February. *Cal. Close Rolls 1399–1402*, 56.

[98] Nothing remains of the tomb today. The remains of an inscription upon part of a

give you his custody on our behalf'.[94] But the matter was taken out of his hands. Huntingdon had been taken to the sister of the murdered earl of Arundel and mother-in-law of the murdered duke of Gloucester. According to the French chronicles, the countess was quickly joined by the nineteen-year-old earl of Arundel who had so recently been a prisoner in Huntingdon's custody, and it was at their orders that the earl was executed.[95] In a moving scene described in great detail by the author of the *Traison et Mort*, Huntingdon was beheaded on 10 January 1400,[96] and his head sent to London for display on London Bridge.[97] He was buried in the collegiate church at Pleshey, founded six years beforehand by his enemy, the duke of Gloucester, and the severed head was united with the body towards the end of February 1400.[98] Shortly afterwards, Richard II died, probably murdered within the walls of Pontefract Castle.

Huntingdon's Character and Ability

As is so often the case with medieval personalities, we can only judge Huntingdon by his actions. Of his opinions, his affections, and his health, we know nothing. No contemporary portrait of him exists, and the representations of him in two of the drawings illustrating 'Creton's' chronicle are lacking in detail (see pages 48 and 49).[99] Some of his friends are known[100] and the presence of Thomas Litlington, the king's painter, in his company during the expedition to Ireland in 1399, is suggestive of artistic appreciation.[101] He was probably given a sound education and the presence of several books among his personal possessions at Dartington Hall in 1400 suggests that he may have been literate.[102]

He was a well-known jouster, for it was said that he liked nothing better than fighting:[103] it was a challenge to his skill, an appeal to his spirit of adventure, and a path to European fame. Unfortunately, his record on the tournament ground is little happier than that on the field of battle. In Spain, for instance, he gained a preliminary success at the festivities organized in February 1387 to celebrate the marriage of Lancaster's daughter to the king of Portugal, but he fared less happily a little later in meeting an opponent of the calibre of Sir Reginald de Roye.[104] He met de Roye again at St. Inglevert in March and April 1390, when the earl of Nottingham, Sir Peter Courtenay, and he accepted de Roye's challenge to hold the field against all comers.[105] However, the French considered that Nottingham was the finest English knight present and there is no record that Huntingdon participated in any further tournaments during the last ten years of his life.

Huntingdon's character rests almost entirely on his actions as recorded in official documents and contemporary chronicles. It cannot be said that historians, any more than his contemporaries, have given him a good press. They have unanimously endorsed Bishop Stubbs' opinion that he was a royal companion 'of the worst sort, violent, dissipated, and cruel'.[106] Supporting evidence for Walsingham's assertion that Huntingdon was greatly hated by the people during the closing years of Richard's reign is lacking, although it is extremely probable that he was associated with the opprobrium of Richard's rule, and it was widely believed that he was responsible for Gloucester's death.[107] The chroniclers' opinion, however, that he was one of Richard's principal advisers is not borne out by the evidence except at times of crisis.

Huntingdon was unimaginative but impetuous—a follower rather than a leader—whose

---

dismembered monument is recorded in J. Weever, Ancient Funerall Monuments (1631), 637. 'Here lyeth John Holand, Erle of Exeter, Erle of Huntingdon and Chamberlyne of England. Who dyed. . . .' (In the official record of Henry IV's coronation, Bolingbroke is similarly described as the earl and not as the duke of Hereford. T. Rymer, Foedera, London ed., vol. 8, 90.)

[99] Sir E. Maunde Thompson, 'A Contemporary Account of the Fall of Richard II', 2 parts, *The Burlington Magazine*, vol. 5 (May and June 1904). Maunde Thompson considered that they were probably drawn in the first quarter of the 15th century, but that the artist was copying from authentic contemporary drawings.

[100] He was particularly friendly with the earl of Devon, and other members of the Courtenay family, one of whom had married Huntingdon's sister, Maud. The earl of Salisbury, his companion in the 1400 conspiracy, was also a friend of both John and his wife. Elizabeth Holand had interceded on Salisbury's behalf after his imprisonment in the Tower in October 1399 for complicity in Gloucester's death.

[101] *Cal. Pat. Rolls 1396–99*, 573.

[102] An antiphoner and a great breviary containing two books, confiscated as Huntingdon's property by the escheator of Devon in 1400, almost certainly came from Dartington. They were found in the hands of the priest of the near-by manor of Woodland. P.R.O. Misc. Inq. C 145/278, no. 1.

[103] Froissart, *Chronicles*, ed. Kervyn de Lettenhove, vol. 8 (1870), ch. 31.

[104] It is likely that this famous meeting occurred towards the end of the Spanish campaign when a safe conduct was given by Lancaster to de Roye and 50 other knights and squires to pass through the English lines. *John of Gaunt's Register: 1379–83*, ed. E. C. Lodge and R. Somerville (1937), no. 1233. The Portuguese chronicler Fernâo Lopes describes the *pointes d'armes* and notes that Huntingdon came off second best. *Chrónica de Dom Joao I*, 2a parte, ed. M. Lopes de Almeda and A. de Magnalhaes Basto (1949), 233–4.

[105] T. Rymer, *Foedera*, Hague ed., vol. 3, pt. iv, 55.

[106] W. Stubbs, *The Constitutional History of England* (1880), 505.

[107] Walsingham, *Annales Ricardi II*, ed. H. T. Riley (1866), 224. The people of Exeter had no doubt in March 1400 that he was responsible. P.R.O. Misc. Inq. C 145/275, no. 3.

other characteristics have been overshadowed by the dramatic outrages of his youth. His performance in the Castilian campaign was quite devoid of the military ability shown by his father and step-father, and this is emphasized by his inability to extricate Richard from the difficult position in which the king found himself in the summer of 1399. Lassitude and indifference afflicted his administrative work as well as his military record, possibly heightened by physical weakness after the Spanish campaign. The *Traison et Mort* suggests that Huntingdon was not devoid of charm or warmth towards his wife and children, but birth and background thrust mediocrity into a position where it could do the greatest disservice to himself and to his family. Like other magnates of the period such as Bolingbroke, Gloucester, and Northumberland, Huntingdon was to some extent a typical product of late fourteenth-century chivalry—aggressive in temper and militant in taste. Where he differed from most of his fellow magnates was not so much in outlook as in the degree of his competence. Possibly highly strung like his mother, Huntingdon's birth and position were no substitute for ability, and of the last-named, he had but small measure.

The jousts of St. Inglevert, 1390. (*c.* 1460–80)

Chapter 4

The Later Holands and Their Successors: 1400 to 1559

The Aftermath of the Holand Rebellion

With the collapse of the Holand rising early in 1400, all the estates, goods, and chattels belonging to the earl of Huntingdon and his accomplices were automatically forfeited and delivered to the treasurer.[1] By 23 January, the escheator of Essex had collected everything belonging to the earl in that county,[2] the mayor had seized all his London possessions by 18 February,[3] and an inventory of Huntingdon's goods at Dartington Hall had been completed within a further seven days (see Appendix 6). The work needed to be accomplished swiftly for many of his chattels disappeared overnight as soon as it became known that Huntingdon's property was to be seized by the Crown. Bulls belonging to the earl at Bovey Tracey and horses at Harbertonford and Dartmouth were stolen and sold. Goods of his in Cornwall were swiftly put on board ship and taken away. Silver which bore his crest was taken to Exeter and melted down to avoid identification.[4] Proceedings were being taken against the escheator of Essex in 1403 to determine whether he had declared all the earl's sequestered possessions,[5] while Henry IV was still trying to establish four years later whether one of the commissioners in the west of England had returned a true record of everything due to the Crown.[6]

In this work, the innocent suffered as well as the guilty. At the beginning of February, Richard Cryse had to claim back all the goods and chattels 'which the escheator of Kent [had] seized because he was lately with the earl of Huntingdon, deceased, supposing him to be of his company, which he was not'.[7] Two weeks later, four of Huntingdon's servants, innocent of the rebellion, had to seek protection from the king because their enemies had denounced them as accomplices of the benighted earl.[8] Military equipment which the earl of Oxford's son had recently left at Dartington Hall on his way to Ireland, was hastily claimed before it was swept away in the general inventory.[9] Thomas Proudfoot, to whom Huntingdon had granted the Devon manor of Winkleigh in September 1399, was summarily ousted from all his property on the pretext that he had been beheaded as a rebel.[10] Warin Waldegrave, one of Huntingdon's attorneys, was having similar trouble with property belonging to him in Yorkshire, while a former retainer, William Yerde, whose Somerset manor of West Lydford had been hastily seized and granted to the monks of St. Mary Graces by the Tower, had to be reimbursed with an annual grant of £20.[11]

With certain exceptions, it was intended that the revenues from the rebels' estates should be applied to the expenses of the royal household.[12] Henry IV's half-brother, the earl of Somerset, and the king's son, John, received some of the furniture that Huntingdon had held in Devon, while another son, Humphrey, received some of the goods and chattels from Dartington Hall.[13] The monks of St. Mary Graces by the Tower finally received the lands formerly owned by Lord Audley which Edward III had promised them over thirty years earlier but which Richard II had diverted into Huntingdon's hands.[14] Any wholesale redistribution of Huntingdon's property, however, which Henry IV might have envisaged

---

[1] *Cal. Pat. Rolls 1399–1401*, 180; *Cal. Fine Rolls 1399–1405*, 35; *Rolls of Parliament*, vol. 3, 459a.

[2] *Cal. Close Rolls 1399–1402*, 42. A list of jewels and clothes belonging to Huntingdon and Sir Thomas Shelley, confiscated in Essex, is given in P.R.O. E 101/335, no. 7. It is unfortunate that the respective owners of the goods listed are not identified.

[3] *Cal. Pat. Rolls 1399–1401*, 206.

[4] P.R.O. Misc. Inq. C 145/278, nos. 6, 8, 17, 20, 31.

[5] *Cal. Close Rolls 1402–05*, 165–6; also *Cal. Pat. Rolls 1405–08*, 151.

[6] *Cal. Close Rolls 1405–09*, 270; also *Cal. Pat. Rolls 1401–05*, 274.

[7] *Cal. Pat. Rolls 1399–1401*, 186.

[8] Ibid., 204.

[9] *Cal. Close Rolls 1399–1402*, 58–9.

[10] Proudfoot had to appear in person before the king and council before the mistake was admitted. *Cal. Close Rolls 1399–1402*, 72, 137–8.

[11] *Cal. Pat. Rolls 1399–1401*, 256, 348.

[12] Ibid., 475.

[13] Ibid., 387, 394 (Somerset), 435 (John), 439 (Humphrey).

[14] March 1400. *Cal. Pat. Rolls 1399–1401*, 274–5, 457.

Elizabeth Holand, 1st duchess of Exeter: c. 1425

was forestalled by the king's formidable sister, Elizabeth Holand. Elizabeth's effigy in Burford Church indicates that she was a tall, slender featured woman.[15] She was some years younger than her husband, and the *Traison et Mort* suggests that her relationship with Huntingdon towards the end of their marriage was not without strain.[16] Yet her marked determination after her husband's execution to ensure the restoration of as many of his estates and possessions for their children as possible, betokens a woman of strength who coped extremely well in the face of difficult circumstances.

The immediate problem facing Elizabeth was to see that she had sufficient income to support herself and her children. She held a certain amount of property in Cornwall in her own name valued at £40 a year,[17] and she was allowed to retain this as well as the Cornish properties granted to her and her husband in July 1395.[18] But these were not sufficient to enable her to maintain an estate befitting the king's sister. Within six weeks of her husband's death, Henry IV had granted her £666. 13s. 4d. per annum from the petty customs of the Port of London until he could provide her with lands to the value of this sum.[19] Gradually she began to regain possession of many of the estates which her husband had formerly held in the west of England. In August 1400, two small manors in Bedfordshire and Berkshire were liberated to her,[20] and in the following May, she was granted some of the property which her husband had held in Devon including the manor of Dartington where their children had been living during the past year.[21] Despite the declared forfeiture of all her husband's property, this record suggests that Elizabeth and her children were never evicted from Dartington Hall. Three years later, Parliament agreed that she should recover all the lands which Huntingdon had formerly held in Devon, Somerset, and Huntingdon,[22] and she was still engaged in litigation in 1411 to recover property in Pembrokeshire which had been seized eleven years earlier.[23]

[15] The effigy is completely devoid of any artistic quality. It is local workmanship that has the sole merit of including certain physical characteristics.

[16] *Traison et Mort*, ed. B. Williams (1846), 232–3.

[17] *Cal. Pat. Rolls 1396–99*, 22.

[18] *Cal. Close Rolls 1399–1402*, 271–2.

[19] *Cal. Pat. Rolls 1399–1401*, 201.

[20] *Cal. Close Rolls 1399–1402*, 168.

[21] The manors and borough of Combe Martin, Barnstaple, and South Molton, the manors of Blackborough, Dartington, Winkleigh, and Fremington, valued at £218. 15s. 8d., were to be held by Elizabeth in trust during the minority of John Holand II. *Cal. Pat. Rolls 1399–1401*, 241, 445, 483, 550. The Issue Rolls for 22 November 1401 record the payment by Henry IV of £14. 13s. 4d. to the sheriff of Devon on behalf of the three sons and daughters of Huntingdon at Dartington.

[22] June 1404. *Cal. Close Rolls 1402–05*, 342–3; *Rolls of Parliament*, vol. 3, 483, 533. The manors granted to the abbey of St. Mary Graces were excluded.

[23] *Cal. Pat. Rolls 1399–1401*, 187, 233; *Cal. Close Rolls 1402–05*, 21; *Cal. Close Rolls 1409–13*, 163–4.

Elizabeth Holand and Sir John Cornwaille: mid 15th century

[24] *Cal. Pat. Rolls 1399–1401*, 206, 244.

[25] Ibid., 398. For a further extensive list of goods granted to Elizabeth, see ibid., 513–4. Elizabeth had 3 sons and at least 2 daughters by John, earl of Huntingdon. Only one of the sons lived to manhood. The eldest daughter, Constance, born in 1387, was espoused to Thomas, son of the earl of Nottingham in October 1391. *Cal. Papal Registers. Papal Letters: Vol. 4. 1362–1404*, 396. She had married him before 18 October 1402. *Cal. Close Rolls 1402–05*, 91. Thomas was beheaded in 1405. It was probably the second daughter who was espoused to Richard, eldest son of the earl of Oxford in 1399. See Chapter 3, n. 92.

[26] *Cal. Pat. Rolls 1399–1401*, 409. According to Walsingham, Elizabeth met Cornwaille at a tournament at York in July 1400. *Annales Ricardi II*, ed. H. T. Riley (1866), 333. Elizabeth died on 24 November 1425 and was buried in Burford Church, Shropshire, adjacent to the home of her second husband.

[27] P.R.O. Inq. Post Mortem, Henry V, file 35, no. 58, translated in *Trans. Devon Assoc.* vol. 73 (1941), 174–6. The statement that he was 9 years and more on 5 May 1406, slightly favours the later date. *Cal. Pat. Rolls 1405–08*, 174.

[28] P.R.O. Inq. Post Mortem, Henry V, file 35, no. 58.

[29] P.R.O. Inq. Post Mortem, Henry V, file 21, no. 50; *Cal. Close Rolls 1413–19*, 483–6; V. Gibbs and H. A. Doubleday, *The Complete Peerage*, vol. 5 (1926), 205. His younger brother, Edmund, was still alive in 1415 when he and John Holand were granted liveries. P.R.O. Exch. Accts. 406, 26.

[30] *Cal. Pat. Rolls 1399–1401*, 241.

Elizabeth also assiduously recovered many of the furnishings which had formerly been in their homes in London and Devon. During the early months of her widowhood, she was concerned with her possessions in London,[24] but later in the year, she was intent on replenishing the furnishings at Dartington Hall so that at least her children could live there in comfort.[25] Finally, having regained possession of many of her late husband's estates and goods, Elizabeth married Sir John Cornwaille before the close of 1400 and began the gentle process of adjusting herself to a less turbulent life than she had formerly known.[26]

John Holand II, Earl of Huntingdon and Third Duke of Exeter: 1400–1447

The careers of Elizabeth's son and grandson, John and Henry Holand, third and fourth duke of Exeter respectively, differ markedly from each other. The former achieved distinction abroad in the wars against France whereas the latter became ensnared in the political rancour and domestic misfortunes of the Wars of the Roses. Hardly any records refer to their presence or activities at Dartington. This is not to say that they never knew their Devon estate, but the fact that most of their lives were spent in serving the king meant that their visits to Dartington Hall were probably infrequent.

John Holand II was born and baptized at Dartington on 29 March 1395 or 1396.[27] He was carried to his christening by the wife of Sir John de la Pomerai, preceded by twenty-four men carrying torches which were lit as soon as he had been baptized. After the service was over, one of his godfathers, the abbot of Tavistock, gave him a gold cup filled with 10 pounds of gold whilst his other godfather, the prior of Plympton, gave him 20 pounds of gold.[28] His father's execution and the death of his elder brother, Richard, only eight months later[29] probably made little immediate difference to Holand's upbringing, but nothing is known of his childhood except that part of it was spent at Dartington Hall.[30]

His subsequent career suggests that he was well grounded in the art of warfare, possibly under the tuition of his step-father, Sir John Cornwaille, whom he later joined in active service. In 1407, Henry IV awarded his nephew a grant of £66. 13s. 4d. a year for his maintenance during his minority and this was renewed by Henry V shortly after his accession in 1413.[31] Many of the new king's actions during the first few months of his reign were to further his policy of peace and conciliation with those whom his father had upset, and it was no accident that the order of knighthood was conferred on Holand on the eve of Henry's coronation only thirteen years after the rebellion of 1400.

Holand reached maturity at the same time that the second part of the Hundred Years War with France broke out. Hostilities were renewed in 1415 and Holand first witnessed active service during that year at the siege of Harfleur and the battle of Agincourt. In the following year, he commanded the supply force sent to help the beleaguered Englishmen at Harfleur and was created a Knight of the Garter less than three weeks later.[32] During his absence, Parliament heard his petition seeking livery of his father's lands and earldom on the occasion of his majority in March 1417.[33] His royal friendship and proven ability contributed to its favourable reception, and he signalled his coming of age in June 1417 by attacking and defeating a French fleet of twenty-six ships and nine Genoese carracks stationed off Harfleur.[34] After a three-hour fight, Holand captured four of the carracks and their commander, scattered the remainder of the fleet, and thereby cleared the coast for Henry V's second invasion of Normandy. John, now earl of Huntingdon, was promised a royal reward of £1,000.[35]

During the next four years, John took part in a series of campaigns in northern France and achieved considerable success leading forces sent to capture strategic towns or to destroy pockets of resistance. It was not until 1421 that the English army suffered its first

[31] *Cal. Pat. Rolls 1405–08*, 385 and *Cal. Pat. Rolls 1413–16*, 136; *Cal. Fine Rolls 1405–13*, 117.

[32] T. Rymer, *Foedera*, Hague ed., vol. 4, pt. ii, 158; *Cal. Pat. Rolls 1416–22*, 112.

[33] *Rolls of Parliament*, vol. 4, 100–1. The enrolment was not made until October 1418. *Cal. Close Rolls 1413–19*, 483–6, 467. Holand had been styled earl of Huntingdon since he had been involved in preparations for the expedition to France in April 1415. P.R.O. E 101, Box 45/7, nos. 1 and 2.

[34] 'The Brut', ed. by C. L. Kingsford in *English Historical Literature in the Fifteenth Century* (1913), 307. J. M. Wylie and W. T. Waugh, *The Reign of Henry the Fifth*, vol. 3 (1929), 48–9.

[35] *Rolls of Parliament*, vol. 4, 247.

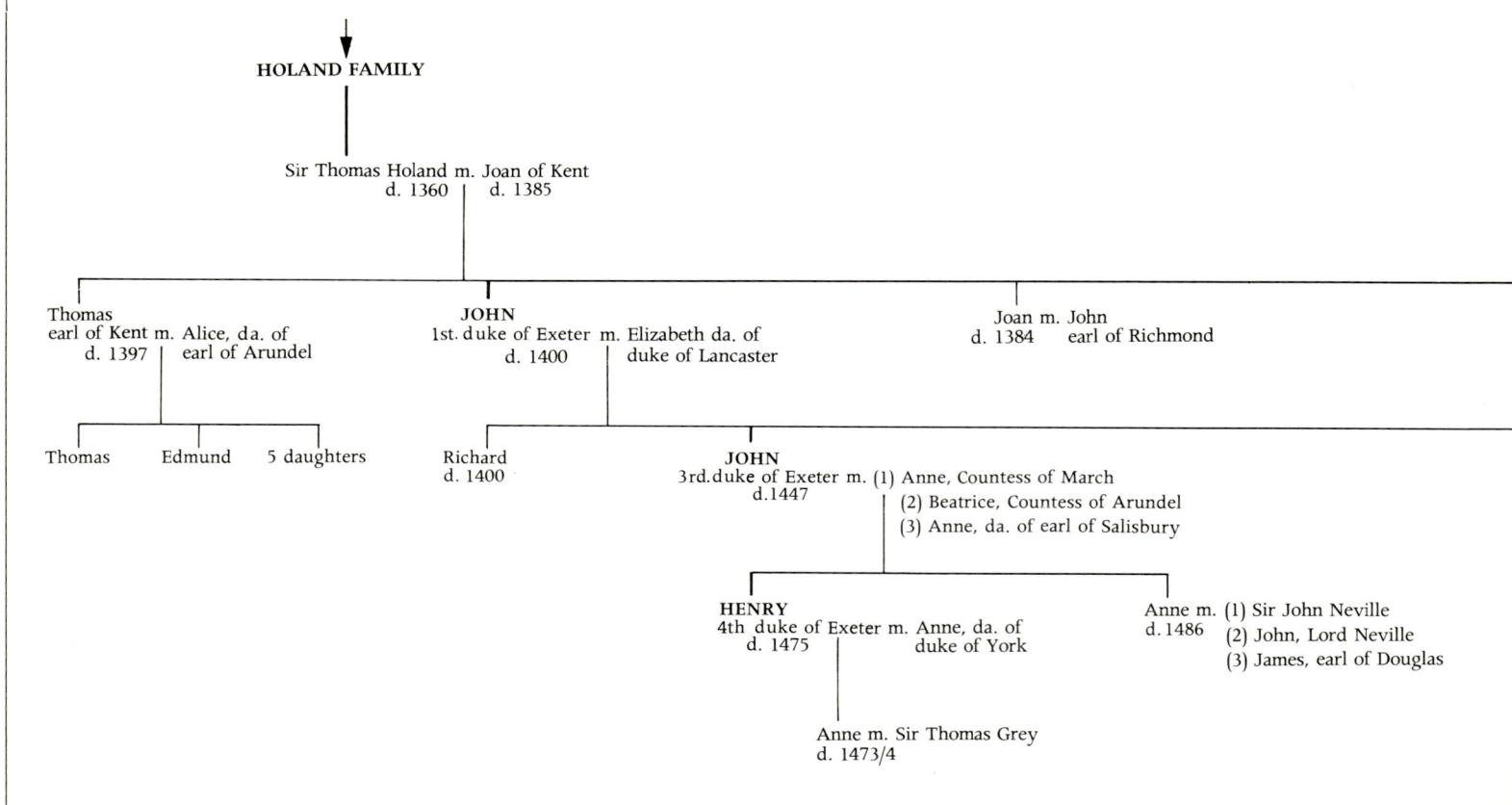

Fig. 9 The Exeter branch of the Holand family in the late fourteenth and fifteenth centuries

reversal when it was defeated at Baugé in the Loire valley through engaging the enemy before assembling all its forces. The English commander and heir presumptive was killed and Huntingdon was captured by the count of Vendôme.[36] The earl was a most valuable prize. He was young, a formidable soldier, and an able commander. The English were by no means short of competent leaders but they could ill afford to lose such a young and capable lieutenant. His ransom was appropriately high, even in an age of high ransoms, and it was more than four years before sufficient money could be gathered to pay a measure of the £13,333. 6s. 8d. demanded.[37] In 1423, Huntingdon was granted the rights to the ransoms of two French lords in part settlement of his own ransom[38] while Sir John Cornwaille, administering Huntingdon's estates during his absence, was allowed to appropriate part of their profits for the same purpose.[39] Cornwaille had paid £1,166. 13s. 4d. to the count of Vendôme by April 1425[40] and the earl was released a few months later and returned at once to England.[41]

Huntingdon had gained considerable experience of the two faces of war before he was thirty. His successes had brought him several honours including his life appointment in August 1420 of the constableship of the Tower of London.[42] He had accompanied Henry V on his entry into Paris, been appointed a custodian of Charles VI, the intermittently mad king of France, and granted a retinue of 500 men. On the other hand, he had suffered the heaviest financial loss that could befall a soldier—to be taken alive and ransomed. He had had to try and find more than £13,000 and yet was himself owed £8,157. 14s. 9d. for wages in France by Henry V who had bequeathed him only £1,333. 6s. 8d. in his will.[43] Unfortunately, Huntingdon was only one of the many victims of the short-sighted policy of the Lancastrian dynasty which constantly ignored the need to maintain a satisfactory balance of royal credit.

[36] C. L. Kingsford, *Chronicles of London* (1905), 74, 127; G. Chastellain, 'Chronique de Normandie', ed. B. Williams in *Henrici Quinti Gesta* (1850), 258. It was ironic that Huntingdon's captor had himself been taken prisoner by the earl's step-father at Agincourt only six years beforehand.

[37] *Rolls of Parliament*, vol. 4, 385.

[38] Ibid., 247, 284. These ransoms were in lieu of £2,333. 6s. 8d. due to Huntingdon from Henry V.

[39] Ibid., 283.

[40] *Cal. Pat. Rolls 1422–29*, 291.

[41] Cal. French Rolls, Henry VI, in *Forty-eighth report of the Deputy Keeper of the Public Records* (1887), 238.

[42] *Cal. Pat. Rolls 1422–29*, 41.

[43] *Rolls of Parliament*, vol. 4, 247. For Henry V's will see J. M. Wylie, *The Reign of Henry the Fifth*, vol. 1 (1914), 539–43. In March 1428, Henry VI granted Huntingdon an annuity of £133. 6s. 8d. in consideration of the heavy expenditure he had incurred during the recent wars and the fact that three properties formerly held by his father were now in the king's hands. *Cal. Pat. Rolls 1422–28*, 465.

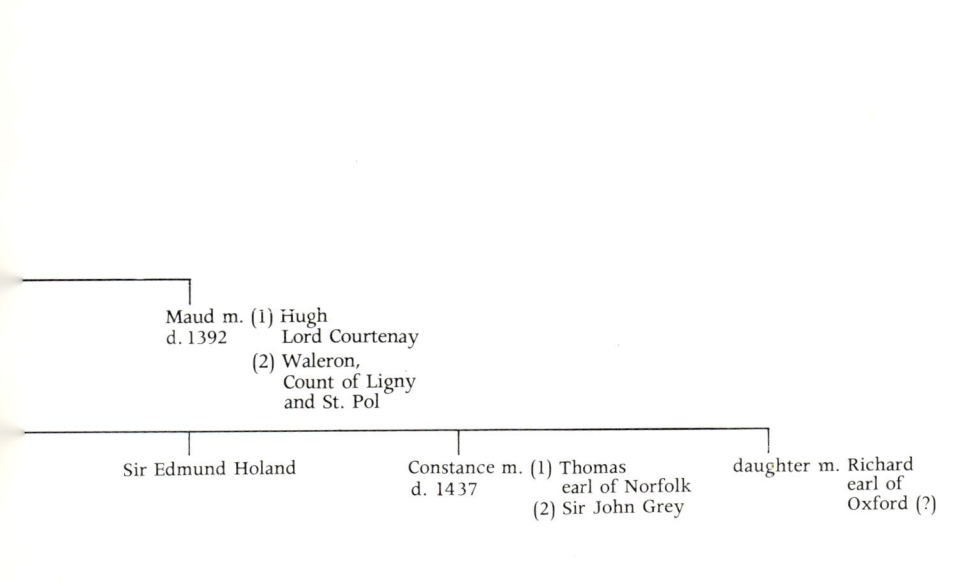

The siege of St. James de Beuvron, Normandy, 1418. (1487)

The Tower of London: c. 1500

As soon as he returned from imprisonment, Huntingdon began to recoup his finances by claiming payment for wages not yet received.[44] Although the results of this appeal are not known, his precarious financial position was much improved by the receipt in March 1426 of the lands which his recently deceased mother had held in her demesne and in dower, for life, of his inheritance.[45] About four months later, Huntingdon married Anne, widow of Edmund, earl of March, whose petitions to Parliament for help in securing the release of her future husband had been as prolific as Sir John Cornwaille's activities in other directions.[46] Nor were the financial benefits arising from this marriage in any way disturbed by the fine of £400 levied on Huntingdon two years later for failing to obtain royal permission to marry a widow.[47] By 1436 the annual revenue of the earl of Huntingdon and his wife was rated for income tax purposes at £1,002 per year, plus annuities worth £183 per year. This sum was apparently well above the average baronial income estimated

[44] P.R.O. E 101, 45/7, no. 5.

[45] *Cal. Fine Rolls 1422–30*, 127.

[46] *Cal. Close Rolls 1422–29*, 274. In November 1430, Huntingdon conveyed the greater part of his lands, including Dartington, to himself and his wife. *Cal. Pat. Rolls 1429–36*, 114–5; *Rolls of Parliament*, vol. 4, 384. Anne died at Bordeaux in September 1432.

[47] *Cal. Close Rolls 1422–29*, 408.

[48] H. L. Gray, 'Incomes from Land in England in 1436', *Eng. Hist. Rev.* vol. 49 (1934), 615. The average baronial income with annuities was £865.

[49] T. B. Pugh and C. D. Ross,

at £768 and fourteenth in a graduated table covering the incomes of fifty-one lay barons.[48] However, these figures are very suspect and are almost certainly lower than they should have been owing to the lack of strict control in carrying out the assessment, the failure to take into account any lands outside England, and the omission of royal grants and profits of wardship which were apparently outside the scope of the assessment.[49] Even if the tax returns of 1436 were not a fair indication of the gross income of Huntingdon and his wife, nevertheless they suggest that they were to be numbered among the wealthier baronial families of the time.[50]

Huntingdon returned to the battlefield in 1429. Henry V had died seven years earlier and desultory siege operations had continued during the early years of Henry VI's minority until the appearance, enthusiasm, and morale of Joan of Arc galvanized the French into a spectacular offensive. Huntingdon was appointed one of the commanders of a relieving army sent from England and was present at the siege of Compiègne in spring 1430. Despite Joan's capture outside the city, the siege was unsuccessful, partly because, as the duke of Burgundy later wrote to Henry VI, 'good cousin of Huntingdon could not, as he said, for want of payment, any longer keep his men together'.[51] An increasing number of military setbacks overtook the English cause. The earl returned to England to gather fresh forces for a renewed attack, but he was unable to reverse the English fortunes.[52] He was appointed one of the plenipotentiaries to attend the peace negotiations at Arras in 1435[53] but they proved abortive and he was busy during the next nine years defending English possessions, first in the Calais area and then in Aquitaine. Huntingdon succeeded in containing the French offensive launched against Aquitaine in 1438 and his counter attacks forced the invaders back and held them at the border of the duchy. But his work proved of little avail, for the brief peace that followed his return to England in 1444 was succeeded by a swift and successful offensive which sealed the collapse of English rule in France.

Huntingdon was the recipient of a series of honours during the last twenty years of his life. He had been a member of the Privy Council since November 1426, and continued to be so until at least October 1446 and probably until his death a few months later.[54] In November 1432, he was granted the post of deputy marshal of England for nearly four years during the minority of John, heir of the duke of Norfolk.[55] Huntingdon was appointed admiral of England, Ireland, and Aquitaine in October 1436,[56] but the crowning point of his career came on 6 January 1444, when he was granted the title of duke of Exeter[57] with precedence in Parliament and council next to the duke of York and his heirs.[58] The flow of honours continued unabated until his death. In successive years from 1444 to 1447 he was appointed captain of Calais, granted the lordship of Lesparre in Aquitaine and with his only son, awarded the offices of admiral and constable of the Tower of London in survivorship.[59]

No documentary evidence has yet come to light that Exeter spent any of his years of manhood at Dartington, although the discovery of a gold noble of 1420 during the restoration of the Hall in 1927 is indicative of its occupation later than the first quarter of the century. Exeter's bequest in his will of a set of vestments to the church at Dartington suggests that he was not indifferent to his boyhood home,[60] but he preferred to stay in London during his occasional visits to England in the later years of his life. It was in the

---

[48] 'The English Baronage and the Income Tax of 1436', *Bull. Inst. Hist. Research*, vol. 26 (1953), 1–28.

[50] Huntingdon was granted an annuity of £333. 6s. 8d. in July 1441 which was amended and renewed in November 1443. *Cal. Pat. Rolls 1436–41*, 565 and *Cal. Pat. Rolls 1441–46*, 242. W. J. Hardy suggests that this grant was made because many of the earl's offices were more honourable than remunerative, *The Dictionary of National Biography*, vol. 27 (1891), 49, but Huntingdon was not in a pecuniary position. During the last few years of his life he was one of the small group of magnates able to lend substantial sums to the Crown. He lent £1,000 in January 1441, a similar amount again in May 1442, and £1,816 between 1442 and 1447. A. Steel, *Receipt of the Exchequer: 1377–1485* (1954), 216, 219, 257. He also endowed a chest of £100 to the University of Oxford in 1442 to enable loans to be made to halls of residence. *V.C.H. Oxfordshire*, vol. 3 (1954), 16.

[51] *Letters and Papers of Henry VI*, ed. J. Stevenson, vol. 2, pt. 1 (1864), 159–60.

[52] *Cal. Pat. Rolls 1429–36*, 277; *Cal. Close Rolls 1429–35*, 243.

[53] T. Rymer, *Foedera*, Hague ed., vol. 5, pt. i, 18. Huntingdon obtained permission to take nearly £6,000 worth of plate and goods with him to this conference. Ibid., 21. This was very little less than the leading ambassador, Cardinal Beaufort, took and he was accustomed to surrounding himself with splendour. Huntingdon's role at the Congress is not known but his position in the embassy was an exalted one. J. G. Dickinson, *The Congress of Arras* (1955), 41–2.

[54] *Rolls of Parliament*, vol. 5, 407, and P.R.O. Council and Privy Seal, file 77.

[55] *Cal. Pat. Rolls 1429–36*, 242.

[56] Ibid., 488.

[57] *Cal. Charter Rolls 1427–1516*, 39. The title of duke of Exeter had been held between 1416 and 1426 by Thomas Beaufort, the youngest of the three illegitimate sons of the duke of Lancaster. John Holand II was therefore the 3rd duke of Exeter.

[58] *Cal. Pat. Rolls 1441–46*, 230. The duke of York's title dated from 1385.

[59] P.R.O. E 101/714, no. 915; *Cal. Pat. Rolls 1441–46*, 405, and *Cal. Pat. Rolls 1446–52*, 32.

[60] Lambeth Palace, Register of Archbishop Stafford, fols. 160–1.

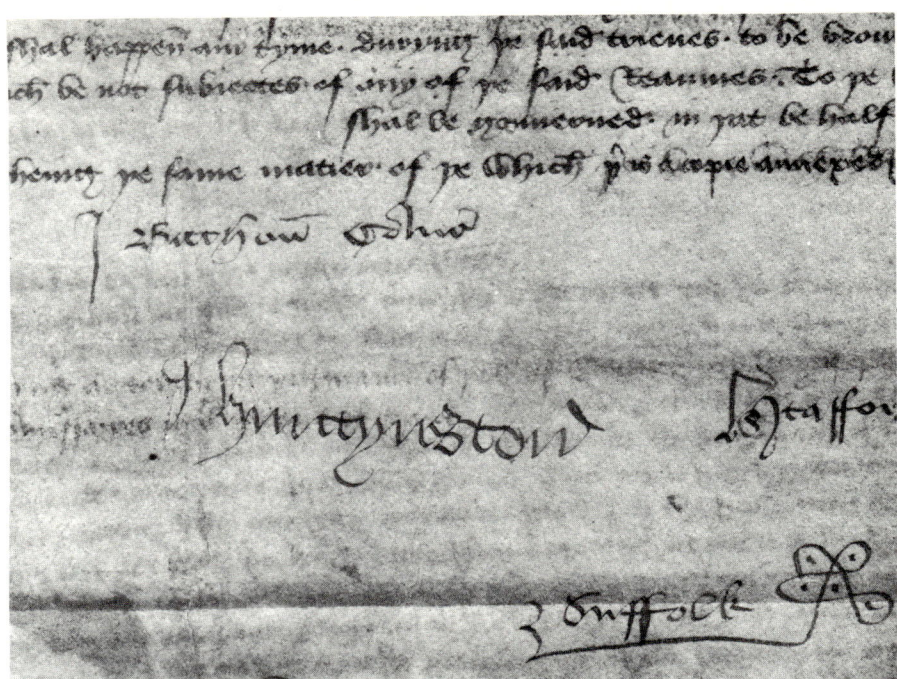

The seal of John Holand, earl of Huntingdon: 1436–44   The signature of John Holand, earl of Huntingdon: c. 1432

Tower of London that his son was born and that one of Exeter's companions was accidently killed by a bolt ricocheting off a tree as the duke and he were practising with their crossbows.[61] Exeter died on 5 August 1447,[62] and he was buried with his first and third wives in the chapel of St. Katherine, close to the fortress of which he had been constable for nearly thirty years.[63]

Exeter's effigy, now in the Tower of London, is a stylized work which in no way reflects the splendour of his physique mentioned by a contemporary chronicler.[64] He married three times,[65] but had only one son and a daughter although he left an annuity of £40 in his will to his two illegitimate sons, William and Thomas. His lengthy absences abroad meant that he had little time to take part in local politics but the fact that the duke of Gloucester had to intervene in 1428 in disturbances over shire elections in Bedfordshire between Exeter and his brother-in-law, the duke of Norfolk, indicates that he was not entirely devoid of interest in local political affairs.[66] It was probably this occasion that prompted the St. Albans chronicler to refer to a feud between Holand and the duke of Norfolk. The fact that he also mentions a quarrel in the following year between Holand and his brother-in-law, the earl of Stafford, which led to a decree that baronial servants were not to wear arms within royal palaces,[67] suggests that Exeter may have occasionally given vent to sharp, forthright words as military commanders are prone to do. For Exeter was essentially a soldier and one whose capabilities have not always been recognized. The chronicler known as the pseudo Thomas of Elmham, writing almost immediately after the duke's death, described him as 'a fine soldier of circumspection, integrity and wide military attainment, outstanding by reason of his extensive military achievements and particularly notable for his magnificent physique and kindness',[68] while another contemporary writer reflected that as 'The firy Cressett [Exeter] hath lost his lyght/Therfore Ingland may make great mone'.[69] Exeter is a shadowy figure today—a series of military achievements rather than a substantial personality on the field of battle. But in his time, he built up a powerful reputation as a soldier, statesman, and counsellor which has unfortunately been clouded by the more virulent personalities and politics of a flamboyant and turbulent age.

[61] November 1446. *Cal. Pat. Rolls 1446–52*, 18–9.

[62] P.R.O. Inq. Post Mortem, Henry VI, file 127, no. 25. There is an inventory of Exeter's jewels and debts drawn up in 1447 at Westminster Abbey, Muniment 6643.

[63] The church and hospital of St. Katherine were pulled down in 1825 and Exeter's tomb was moved to the new chapel and buildings erected near Regent's Park. The tomb was moved again to St. Peter ad Vincula within the Tower of London in 1951. R. Gough, *Sepulchral Monuments in Great Britain*, vol. 2, pt. 2 (1796), 155–6; *Survey of London*, ed. G. Gater and W. H. Godfrey, vol. 19 (1938), 110–12.

[64] Pseudo Thomas of Elmham, *Vita et Gesta Henrici Quinti*, ed. T. Hearne (1727), 181.

[65] Four months after the death of his first wife in September 1432, Huntingdon married Beatrice, widow of the earl of Arundel and Surrey who had taken a leading part in the death of Exeter's father in 1400. She died at Bordeaux in October 1439. Huntingdon's third wife, Anne, eldest daughter of the earl of Salisbury, whom he married after October 1442, died in 1457.

[66] Details in J. S. Roskell, *The Commons in the Parliament of 1422* (1954), 17 n.

[67] *Annales Monasterii Sancti Albani*, ed. H. T. Riley (1870), 25, 42.

[68] Pseudo Thomas of Elmham, *Vita et Gesta Henrici Quinti*, ed. T. Hearne (1727), 181.

[69] *Political Poems and Songs*, ed. T. Wright (1861), 221. The cresset was the badge of the Admiralty.

Henry Holand, Fourth Duke of Exeter: 1447–1475

Henry Holand, only son and heir of the third duke of Exeter by his first wife, was born in the Tower of London on 27 June 1430. On the same day, he was carried by his aunt to the family home at Cold Harbour and then taken by barge to St. Stephen's Chapel, Westminster, where he was baptized.[70] He was knighted just before his ninth birthday and at the age of seventeen, married Anne, the seven-year-old daughter of Richard, duke of York. Henry's father died only six days after the wedding and therefore his son, still a minor, was entrusted to the duke of York and granted a royal annuity of £221. 13s. 4d. for the remainder of his minority.[71] By virtue of the hereditary grants made to his father, the seventeen-year-old duke of Exeter was automatically admiral of England, Ireland, and Aquitaine, and constable of the Tower of London, but in view of his age, these offices were administered by deputies during the remainder of his minority.

Exeter was brought up during a period of growing disorder. The war with France had gone very badly and loss had followed loss until the English dream of continental expansion had crumbled beneath a series of French successes. At home, Henry VI's long minority had been followed by the chaotic government of squabbling and selfish lords. Unemployment, pestilence, a series of bad harvests, and an empty exchequer in a country dominated by great landed magnates had contributed to the growing anarchy of mid fifteenth-century England. Restlessness and lawlessness, furthered by disappointed creditors and unpaid soldiers accentuated trends which made civil war increasingly inevitable. The breakdown of order in 1450 was followed by the gradual emergence of the two baronial factions of Lancaster and York, led by the duke of Somerset—Lancaster's grandson—

[70] P.R.O. Inq. Post Mortem, Henry VI, file 170, no. 43.

[71] *Cal. Pat. Rolls 1446–52*, 86.

Henry VI and Queen Margaret of Anjou receiving a book from the earl of Shrewsbury: 1445

and Richard, duke of York—Edward III's great-grandson. The late duke of Exeter had arranged that both his children should marry members of the powerful Neville family,[72] but Henry Holand never supported the duke of York, possibly through resentment against his father-in-law and former guardian. Like the majority of lords, Henry preferred to support the Lancastrian party which stood for government by the baronage, rather than the Yorkists who strove for a strong monarchy and an efficient government. Unfortunately, Exeter's unswerving support of the Lancastrian cause combined with his markedly mediocre ability ultimately cost him his life and helped to bring about the ruin of his house.

Even as his minority came to an end in 1450, Henry was already participating in English politics, basking in the reflected glory of his father's name[73] as a supporter of Henry VI.[74] He participated in faction and seizure at an early age by claiming the manor of Ampthill in about 1452 from that formidable opponent, Lord Cromwell. Both parties were so heavily armed when they attended the assize at Westminster in the following year that they were both committed to prison.[75] In 1454, the twenty-three-year-old Exeter entered the political lists by joining the younger Percy in his long-standing feud with the Neville family, even though Exeter had no immediate association with the Percies. Henry VI's temporary insanity, the queen's ascendancy, and the appointment of York as protector of the realm contributed to the crisis which culminated in a warlike gathering of forces in Yorkshire, apparently led by Exeter. The protector took up arms against him[76] but Exeter fled and sought sanctuary in Westminster Abbey. York promptly arrested him and dispatched him to Pontefract Castle and then set about defeating the Percies.[77] A year later Exeter was still in prison[78] but Henry VI's recovery and reassertion of his will, meant the loss of York's power and Exeter's release.

During the next few years, both parties actively prepared for war. In October 1456, Exeter tried unsuccessfully to ambush York and his nephew, Richard Neville, earl of Warwick, after they had been arraigned by the Court at Coventry[79] and in the following year, Warwick worsted Exeter by obtaining the command of the fleet which the duke had held until then. Exeter's chagrin was in no way appeased by a grant of £1,000[80] and personal enmity between the two magnates deepened. Local conflict, growing disorder, and French raids on the south coast brought increasing tension and violence. Among such disturbances was Exeter's personal attack during 1458 on a judge within the Palace of Westminster, followed by his forcible shipment to the Tower and incarceration there. There was a public outcry even in this lawless age and Exeter was confined to Berkhamsted Castle until he was freed by royal compassion.[81] Meanwhile, preparations for open conflict became increasingly apparent with the result that hostilities broke out in the summer of 1459. Exeter joined the royalist army and experienced the defeat and sudden reversal of fortune which characterize this and later phases of the so-called Wars of the Roses. Before the close of the year, York had been forced to escape to Ireland and Warwick had fled to Calais after hiding in north Devon. Exeter joined the Lancastrian supporters in taking the oath of allegiance to Henry VI at Coventry in December,[82] and he was rewarded eight days later by his appointment as constable of his wife's birthplace, Fotheringhay Castle, and a grant of £100 a year for life for his services against the rebels.[83]

Disorder continued unabated as the government sought to restore its tottering authority

---

[72] His daughter, Anne, married before February 1441 Sir John Neville, son of the earl of Westmorland, and before September 1452 John, Lord Neville, her first husband's uncle. On Lord Neville's death at Towton, she married James, earl of Douglas. She died in December 1486.

[73] Jack Cade's manifesto of June 1450 includes the comment that Henry should take about his person those mighty princes, the dukes of Exeter, Buckingham, and Norfolk, together with the true earls and barons of the land. Then he would be the richest king in Christendom. *Three Fifteenth Century Chronicles*, ed. J Gairdner (1880), 94–9.

[74] 'John Piggot's Memoranda', ed. C. L. Kingsford in *English Historical Literature in the Fifteenth Century* (1913), 371, 372.

[75] G. L. Harriss, 'A Fifteenth Century Chronicle at Trinity College, Dublin', *Bull. Inst. Hist. Research*, vol. 38 (1965), 216.

[76] *The Paston Letters*, ed. J. Gairdner, vol. 1 (1910), nos. 195, 206.

[77] *Proceedings and Ordinances of the Privy Council*, ed. Sir N. H. Nicolas, vol. 6 (1837), 218; T. Rymer, *Foedera*, Hague ed., vol. 5, pt. ii, 62; *Incerti Scriptoris Chronicon Angliae de ... Henrici IV, Henrici V et Henrici VI*, ed. J. A. Giles (1848), pt. 3, 45–7; C. L. Kingsford, *Chronicles of London* (1905), 164. The most detailed account of this rebellion is by R. L. Storey, *The End of the House of Lancaster* (1966), 142–9.

[78] He had been transferred to Wallingford Castle. *Proceedings and Ordinances of the Privy Council*, ed. Sir N. H. Nicolas, vol. 6 (1837), 234, 246; *V.C.H. Berkshire*, vol. 3 (1923), 528.

[79] *Six Town Chronicles*, ed. R. Flenley (1911), 144.

[80] *The Paston Letters*, ed. J. Gairdner, vol. 1 (1910), nos. 313, 315.

[81] *Letters and Papers of Henry VI*, ed. J. Stevenson, vol. 1 (1861), 367–8; *Cal. Close Rolls 1454–61*, 318.

[82] *Rolls of Parliament*, vol. 5, 351.

[83] *Cal. Pat. Rolls 1452–61*, 547.

by such measures as forced loans, purveyances, and commissions of array. Exeter, fresh from seizing the late Sir John Fastolf's house and goods in Southwark on the flimsiest pretext,[84] joined the earls of Wiltshire and Shrewsbury in sacking the Yorkist town of Newbury and hanging some of its citizens. Fear of invasion and popular support for the rebels, drew the government's attention to the weak state of the royal fleet. Yet the expenditure of £2,666. 13s. 4d. incurred on building up the fleet was virtually wasted when it was associated with Exeter's appointment in March 1460 as admiral for a period of three years,[85] and demonstrated by Exeter's inability to intercept Warwick off the coast of Devon as he sailed towards Calais after visiting York in Ireland.[86] In the following month, a Yorkist army from Calais landed in Kent. Both sides secured their successes but the House of York proved triumphant in March 1461 at the hard-fought battle of Towton. The Lancastrian army was routed, Henry and his queen, Margaret of Anjou, lost control of southern England and fled to Scotland accompanied by Exeter, while York's son, Edward, assumed the throne as Edward IV.

There was peace for eight years, broken only by sporadic engagements in the far north of England arising from Margaret's attempts to win a foothold there. Exeter participated in the siege of Carlisle in May,[87] and unsuccessfully tried to stop the Welsh castles still holding out for Henry from surrendering to the new king. John Paston was assured in October that Exeter and the earl of Pembroke had been forced to take refuge in the Welsh mountains, hounded by many lords,[88] but Exeter managed to rejoin Margaret and shortly afterwards fled with her to the court of Louis XI of France to seek more material assistance. An attempt by Margaret and Exeter to capture and hold the major castles of Northumberland during the early months of 1463 with a small force of French supporters failed and they were forced to flee once more to France.[89]

No one had any illusions about Exeter's lack of ability. He possessed none of his father's qualities of leadership. It was impossible to entrust him with military command and his incompetence in the sphere of naval warfare had been emphasized by the success that had attended Warwick's naval exploits. He was intolerant and according to the Milanese ambassador in France, 'fierce and cruel'.[90] The absence of his name from the list of witnesses to royal charters and the lack of almost any judicial appointment suggest that the court distrusted him until at least the close of 1459 almost as much as his enemies disliked him. Yet his well-known name and valuable estates in Devon and elsewhere made him a useful supporter of the Lancastrian cause. Exeter latched himself to the fortunes of Henry VI despite his own marriage to Edward IV's sister, and he continued to support Henry and Margaret long after others had transferred their allegiance to the new king. Rumours spread in 1461 that Exeter wished to return and seek Edward IV's pardon but these were no more than idle hopes.[91] Exeter was temperamental, unstable, and possibly dominated by the queen's strong personality and favours. To his credit, he was one of the very few magnates who never forsook the cause he had adopted, but his inflexibility and hot-headedness showed that he failed to take the measure of the forces around him.

There is no record that Henry ever visited Dartington Hall, but Leland noted during his visit to Devon about eighty years later that everyone in the duke of Exeter's household there drank wine brought from France at the time when Sir Baldwin Fulford was under-admiral

[84] *The Paston Letters*, ed. J. Gairdner, vol. 1 (1910), no. 338.

[85] *Letters and Papers of Henry VI*, ed. J. Stevenson, vol. 2, pt. 2 (1864), 515–6.

[86] *Registrum Abbatiae Johanis Whethamstede*, ed. H. T. Riley, vol. 1 (1872), 369; G. Baskerville, 'A London Chronicle of 1460', *Eng. Hist. Rev.* vol. 28 (1913), 125–6; C. L. Kingsford, *Chronicles of London* (1905), 171; C. A. Scofield, *The Life and Reign of Edward the Fourth*, vol. 1 (1923), 60–4.

[87] *Cal. Pat. Rolls 1461–67*, 82.

[88] *The Paston Letters*, ed. J. Gairdner, vol. 2 (1910), no. 416.

[89] Pseudo William of Worcester in *Letters and Papers of Henry VI*, ed. J. Stevenson, vol. 2, pt. 2 (1864), 779.

[90] *Cal. State Papers, Milan: 1385–1618*, 76.

[91] Ibid., 100.

[92] John Leland, *Itinerary*, ed. L. T. Smith, vol. 5 (1907), 2. Sir Baldwin Fulford, beheaded in 1461, lived at Great Fulford about 20 miles north of Dartington.

[93] *Cal. Close Rolls 1447–54*, 9, 86, 145.

[94] *Cal. Pat. Rolls 1461–67*, 32, 35.

[95] *Rolls of Parliament*, vol. 5, 476–8. Among those proscribed was one of Exeter's supporters, Thomas Philip, late of Dartington, Devon.

[96] *Cal. Pat. Rolls 1461–67*, 104–5. In 1466, Exeter's daughter Anne, became a pawn in the politics of the time. She had been the intended bride of Warwick's nephew, the earl of Northumberland, but a bribe of £2,666. 13s. 4d. from Elizabeth Woodville, Edward IV's wife, persuaded the duchess of Exeter to change her affiliations, break off the negotiations, and agree to her daughter's marriage to Sir Thomas Grey, the queen's elder son by her first marriage. Pseudo William of Worcester in *Letters and Papers of Henry VI*, ed. J. Stevenson, vol. 2, pt. 2 (1864), 786. The ceremony took place in October 1466, and Anne died less than 8 years later between January 1473 and June 1474. *Rolls of Parliament*, vol. 6, 107.

[97] T. Rymer, *Foedera*, Hague ed., vol. 5, pt. ii, 110.

[98] *Mémoires de Philippe de Commynes*, ed. J. Calmette, vol. 1 (Paris, 1924), 195.

[99] Ibid., 211–2.

[100] *The Great Chronicle of London*, ed. A. H. Thomas and I. D. Thornley (1938), 214.

to the duke.[92] This reference to Fulford indicates that Leland was referring to the fourth duke of Exeter and his comment is supported by references in the Close Rolls to Henry Holand's importation of 144 tuns of wine from Gascony between May 1448 and February 1450.[93]

Some of Exeter's properties had been seized before his flight to Scotland in March 1461[94] but the remainder were forfeited, together with all his honours, after his attainder in Parliament in November 1461.[95] It was only his marriage to the king's sister that prevented him from losing his title. Meanwhile, the duchess of Exeter had been granted all the lands which she had held jointly with her husband, as well as some of his forfeited estates including the manor of Dartington. In the following December, these forfeited estates, with some additions, were granted to Anne and her heirs by the duke of Exeter for life,[96] and in July 1462 she was also given for her own use all the goods which had formerly belonged to her husband.[97]

Exeter, like the sovereign whom he had so unfailingly supported, was reduced to poverty and drifted to the court of Burgundy. According to the French chronicler, Philippe de Commynes, most of the fugitives from England were destitute. 'One of them was the duke of Exeter, but he concealed his name, following the duke of Burgundy's train, bare footed and bare legged, begging his bread from door to door . . . and being afterwards known, had a small pension allowed him for his subsistence.'[98]

Yet, even in these dire straits, fortune seemed to favour the Lancastrian cause again. Edward IV's capricious treatment of the earl of Warwick forced the latter to flee to France in 1470 where he brought himself to join forces with Queen Margaret in an unholy alliance to restore Henry VI. This association was as unpalatable to Exeter as it was to Margaret and in seeking release from Burgundy to return to England, Exeter promised the duke that he would be working against Warwick rather than for him.[99] Yet, however different their motives, the common cause of kingmaker brought Exeter to England in February 1471. He stayed a fortnight at his residence at Cold Harbour[100] before joining the forces gathering under Warwick's banner to face Edward IV's army marching southwards from Yorkshire. The opposing forces met at Barnet on Easter Sunday, 1471. For the first time

The seal of Henry Holand, 4th duke of Exeter: 1447–57 or 1460–1

in his life, Exeter was given command. He held the forces on the left wing of Warwick's line and fought bravely in the ensuing fog-bound battle, but he was 'gretely despolede and woundede, and lefte nakede for dede in the felde, and so lay ther from vii of clokke till iiii after none; whiche was take up and brought to a house by a manne of his owne; and a leche brought to hym, and so afterwarde brought in to sancuarii at Westmynster'.[101] The abbey served Exeter no better on this occasion than it had done seventeen years earlier. He was moved to the Tower, declared a traitor, and kept in solitary confinement.[102] No doubt Edward suspected that his brother-in-law would take the first opportunity to lead a faction against the Crown, or even possibly try to claim the throne for himself, unless his activities were permanently stifled.

Exactly four years later, Exeter sought, or was ordered by Edward IV, to join the royal army gathering for a new invasion of France. The army landed at Calais with much panoply, but the invasion was swiftly followed by a series of peace talks which led to the withdrawal of the English army in September 1475. Apart from some hostages lost in a foraging raid, only one man failed to return. Exeter was drowned between Calais and Dover as the army was sailing home. There is no evidence that foul play was suspected at the time in England,[103] although the Milanese ambassador to the Burgundian court wrote to his master less than three months later saying that the duke of Exeter was thrown into the sea by order of the king of England.[104] The facts are not clear but Edward certainly

[101] *Chronicle of the reign of Edward IV by John Warkworth*, ed. J. O. Halliwell (1839), 16. A. H. Burne, *The Battlefields of England* (1950), 108–16, makes no mention of Exeter's participation in this battle.

[102] T. Rymer, *Foedera*, Hague ed., vol. 5, pt. iii, 3, 5.

[103] R. Fabyan, *The New Chronicles of England and France*, ed. H. Ellis (1811), 663; C. L. Kingsford, *Chronicles of London* (1905), 186.

[104] *Cal. State Papers, Milan: 1385–1618*, 220.

The battle of Barnet, 1471. (Late 15th century)

The duchess of Exeter and Sir Thomas St. Leger: c. 1483

had no cause to regret the death of a leading supporter of the Lancastrian cause, while for more personal motives, his sister, the duchess of Exeter and her second husband had even greater cause to rejoice at his demise. The duchess had obtained a divorce from Exeter in November 1472[105] and promptly married Sir Thomas St. Leger, the second son of John St. Leger and Margery Donnet of Ulcombe in Kent.[106] Exeter's sole daughter had died before June 1474 and Exeter's fortuitous death enabled St. Leger to further his schemes to obtain his wife's property for himself with reversion to his own daughter by the duchess.

The death of the duke of Exeter at the age of forty-five meant that the House of Holand was no more. The suggestion that the fall of this House was consequent upon the Wars of the Roses is no more true than the belief that these wars were responsible for the decimation of the English aristocracy. They were essentially a struggle for power between irresponsible aristocratic factions and their supporters, and therefore they affected the baronage and gentry far more than other classes. Yet the baronage was by no means destroyed by the political upheavals of the period, although their ranks were certainly thinned. The failure of the Exeter line of the Holand family was not due to their support of the Lancastrian cause but to Henry Holand's failure to beget a male heir. The line had continued to flourish despite John Holand's execution and forfeiture in 1400, and it could have done so again had the fourth duke of Exeter been succeeded by a son. But he had no male heir and his only daughter died childless.[107] Few mourned Exeter's death in 1475. His wife had divorced him and married again. His daughter had died a year or so beforehand. He had suffered imprisonment, forfeiture, and destitution for a cause which had completely foundered. Exeter's bitterness was only assuaged by the wind-tossed waters of the English Channel, and in claiming him, they claimed the last member of the once noble House of Holand.

The Late Medieval Succession: 1475–1559

On the death of the duchess of Exeter in January 1476, Dartington, together with her other property, passed to her second husband. Sir Thomas St. Leger's marriage 'by seditious means as it is notoriously known' had aroused considerable gossip at the time and this had been furthered by his attempts to obtain the reversion of his wife's property to his own daughter by the duchess.[108] His scheme collapsed, however, when he lost both his property and his life in November 1483, for taking part in the duke of Buckingham's abortive rising against Richard III.[109] After St. Leger's execution at Exeter, all his estates and property passed to the Crown. For over seventy years, Dartington was held by a series of owners and tenants who took little personal interest in the property other than as a source of income. The fact that Leland noted during his perambulation of England in the early 1540s that St. Leger had formerly kept house at Dartington suggests that his was the last name associated at that time with personal occupation of the Hall.[110] It was certainly occupied by him in the year before his death, for he entertained one of his wife's relatives, Anne Stonor, the third wife of Sir William Stonor, at Dartington during the summer of 1482.[111]

The property was held between March 1487 and 1509 by Margaret Beaufort, countess of

---

[105] W. Dugdale, *The Baronage of England*, vol. 2 (1676), 82.

[106] E. Hasted, *History and Topographical Survey of Kent*, vol. 2 (1782), 422.

[107] K. B. McFarlane has pointed out that an examination of *The Complete Peerage* shows that the failure in the direct male line happened on an average to a quarter of the families listed every 25 years throughout the 14th and 15th centuries; and that the second half of the 15th century did not exceed the average. 'The Wars of the Roses', *Proc. British Acad.* vol. 50 (1964), 115–6.

[108] *Rolls of Parliament*, vol. 6, 242–4. The daughter of the duchess of Exeter and Sir Thomas St. Leger married Lord Roos and was buried with her husband in St. George's Chapel, Windsor Castle, in 1526.

[109] C. L. Kingsford, *Chronicles of London* (1905), 192. In 1481, St. Leger founded a chantry in the newly built chapel of St. George in Windsor Castle. Both he and his wife are buried in the north transept chapel where there is a memorial plate to them in the north-east wall (see opposite page).

[110] John Leland, *Itinerary*, ed. L. T. Smith, vol. 1 (1907), 219.

[111] *The Stonor Letters: 1290–1483*, ed. C. L. Kingsford, vol. 2 (1919), 147. Anne Stonor was a member of the Neville family.

Panoramic view of lower Dart valley showing Dartington Hall in upper left-hand corner: *c.* 1540

Richmond and mother of Henry VII.[112] On Margaret's death, Dartington reverted to the Crown which held it for the next sixteen years. In 1509, Henry VIII appointed Henry Assheton bailiff of the lordship and keeper of the park,[113] and presented to the living two years later. In 1514, Sir John Shilston was appointed bailiff of the manor and keeper of the chief mansion.[114] Eleven years later, Henry VIII gave the manor of Dartington to his cousin Henry Courtenay, earl of Devon, as part of the estates supporting his creation as Marquis of Exeter.[115] There is no evidence that Courtenay, any more than Margaret Beaufort, resided at Dartington and the property again reverted to the Crown on Courtenay's execution in January 1539 as part of Henry's policy of exterminating all possible Yorkist claimants to the Tudor throne.

Although Leland saw the Hall during his journeys through England between about 1534 and 1545, he gives no indication of its condition, merely contenting himself with noting that there was a great manor place within Dartington Park.[116] Repairs were carried out to the Hall in 1541 but as they came to no more than 19s. 9d., they cannot have been substantial and were probably incurred in maintaining rooms used for the court meetings held there each year.[117] The series of bailiffs' accounts for the closing years of Henry VIII's reign and Edward VI's reign make no mention of rents from the Hall itself.[118] Apparently it was unoccupied, no doubt because of its enormous size and remoteness, but its representation in a panoramic view of the coast from Exeter to Land's End, made in about 1540, does not suggest that the body of the Hall was in ruins at that time.[119] In 1550 it was reported that 'there are no weedes growinge upon the premises',[120] and it is clear from the accounts for the estate that the latter was providing a valuable and regular income.

After Courtenay's death, the property was held from the Crown by a series of tenants. In September 1539, it had been granted to John, Baron Russell,[121] who held it for only a few months before it was given to Queen Catherine Howard who held it from January 1541 until her fall from royal grace in February 1542.[122] The property passed shortly afterwards to Queen Catherine Parr[123] who leased the park to Jasper Horsey, its keeper during Courtenay's ownership.[124] The estate reverted to the Crown on Catherine's death in 1548 and in June 1550, it was granted to Nicholas Adam, a Dartmouth man, and to Henry Peckham, the second son of Sir Edmund Peckham, a Buckinghamshire squire, in exchange for the manor of Lavenden in Buckinghamshire.[125] Peckham sold the estate in April 1552 to John Aylworth, a member of a lesser west of England family and member of Parliament for Penryn in Cornwall.[126] Aylworth's acquisition of the property was the cause of extensive litigation with Nicholas Adams concerning the latter's right to the park and chase.[127] The passage of Dartington through several hands in a very short time during the mid sixteenth century was symptomatic of the development of a land market at this time. Both Peckham and Aylworth were motivated by speculation and profit. Neither of them was intent on building up an estate far from their principal landed interests and they only held the manor for two and seven years respectively. In 1559, Aylworth arranged with Sir Arthur Champernowne that the estate should be exchanged with that of Polsloe Priory,[128] and with his acquisition of the property, Dartington Hall entered upon a new phase of its history as the home of a local land-owning family.

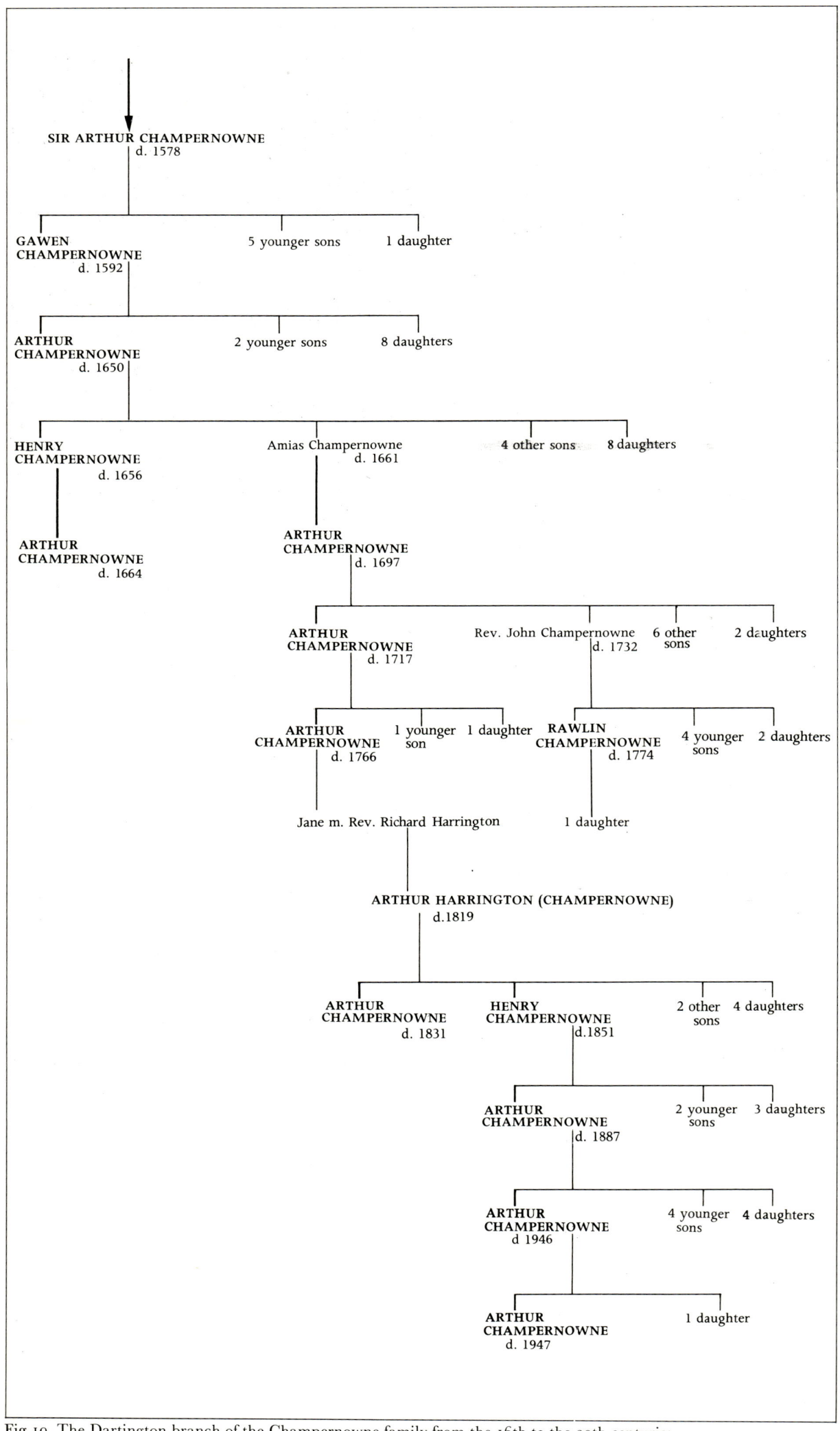

Fig.10 The Dartington branch of the Champernowne family from the 16th to the 20th centuries

Chapter 5

The Champernowne Family: 1559 to 1925

Champernowne has been a well-known surname in Devon for at least six hundred years. The family originated from Cambernon near Coutances in Normandy and apparently settled in England during the twelfth century. The main branch of the family lived at Modbury from the early fourteenth century until it died out in 1700 but a younger line, resident at Dartington Hall from 1559 onwards, maintained the family's association with the county until it was severed by their sale of the Hall in 1925.

Champernownes have been numbered among the lesser gentry of Devon for several centuries but they have rarely played a major part in the history of the county. The family have contributed little to the fields of politics, art, or science, and only two or three members have revealed more than an ordinary talent for government. Eleven generations of the family occupied Dartington Hall. Although a younger son would sometimes leave Devon to seek his fortune elsewhere,[1] the eldest born always lived at the Hall, performing local and private duties, supervising his estates and content to be surrounded by the large families his line usually favoured. The interest of this branch of the family lies less in the ability of individual members than in that quiet service they maintained to their tenants, to their home, and occasionally to the county.[2]

Sir Arthur Champernowne: 1559–1578

Arthur Champernowne was still a minor,[3] probably in his late teens, when his three-year-old nephew inherited the family estates at Modbury in 1545. Champernowne seems to have been imbued with a more adventuresome spirit than was usual in his family and the death of his brother and then his father perhaps encouraged his independence. In 1546, he enlisted as a member of the earl of Hertford's expedition to France. This was the tail-end of Henry VIII's last and disastrous attempt to display his power in Europe, and Champernowne witnessed only the final few weeks of fighting. He was amongst those whom Hertford noted 'brake their staves and did very honestly' in the fighting around Boulogne,[4] but the conclusion of peace shortly afterwards made his military career a very brief one. In the following July, the king granted Champernowne £40 towards the cost of fitting himself out as a member of an embassy to France,[5] and he was knighted by Edward VI two years later.[6]

Sir Arthur was a staunch adherent of the Protestant cause and his faith was a guiding principle behind many of his actions. The introduction of a new prayer book in English in 1549 was marked by the outbreak of the so-called Prayer Book Rebellion in Devon and Cornwall. Champernowne was quick to join the forces sent to quell it, and although the precise nature of the support given by Sir Arthur is not known, he was rewarded in 1550 by a grant of the clappers from many church bells in Devon and Cornwall. This punishment was imposed to prevent the insurgents from being readily called together again and Champernowne sold the iron, frequently to the parishioners, to make a handsome profit

---

[1] George, the second son of Sir Arthur Champernowne was killed in 1589 fighting in Ireland. *Historical Manuscripts Commission: Marquis of Salisbury*, vol. 3 (1889), 453. Charles, Sir Arthur's third son was a member of the expedition led by Sir Humphrey Gilbert in 1578. Francis Champernowne settled in the New World in the 1630s.

[2] Accounts of the family and descriptions of Dartington Hall are given in several histories of Devonshire, but most of these entries are very brief and contribute little to current knowledge. T. Risdon, *Survey of the County of Devon* (1630, pub. 1811), 161–2 gives a short history of Dartington. Sir William Pole, *Collections towards a description of the County of Devon* (early 17th century, pub. 1791), 296–7 briefly surveys the holders of the manor. J. Prince, *The Worthies of Devon* (1701, 2nd ed. 1810), 192–4, 500–4, gives a detailed account of the family and the Hall, and R. Polwhele, *History of Devonshire* (1797), 481–2, gives a useful description of the estate at the close of the 18th century. The entry in D. and S. Lysons, *Magna Britannia*, vol. 6, Devon (1822), cccxlviii, 152–3, is disappointing, but there is a contemporary description of the Hall by J. Britton and E. W. Brayley, *Devonshire and Cornwall Illustrated* (1832), 71–2. The history of the family given by Rev. T. Moore, *The History of Devonshire* (1829–31), vol. 2, 529–35 adds nothing to that given in earlier topographical volumes, while the pedigree in J. L. Vivian, *The Visitation of the County of Devon* (1895), 160–5, is inaccurate. A detailed history of the family by C. E. Champernowne was prepared and privately printed in 1954. There are copies at Dartington Hall, Exeter City Library, and the library of the Society of Genealogists.

[3] P.R.O. Inq. Post Mortem, series 2, vol. 73. f. 187, 11. A biography of Sir Arthur Champernowne is given by J. Roberts, 'The Parliamentary Representation of Devon and Dorset, 1559–1601', unpublished thesis (1958), University of London Library.

[4] *Letters and Papers, Foreign and Domestic: 1546*, pt. 1, 442.

[5] Ibid., 612.

[6] W. Metcalfe, *Book of Knights* (1885), 100.

on the whole transaction.[7] He added to this by selling the silver from Modbury Church 'for his necessities in the comocion tyme to serve the king's majestie'.[8]

Queen Mary's accession three years' later and the vigorous prosecution of her proposal to marry the king of Spain led to the outbreak of several associated rebellions in 1554, led by the hot-headed Sir Thomas Wyatt. Champernowne was implicated in the conspiracy in the west of England but washed his hands of the affair before it came to a head.[9] Nevertheless, he was arrested, despite his loud protestations of loyalty to the queen,[10] and taken to Exeter and then to the Tower of London for questioning. He was pardoned after examination[11] and allowed to return to Devon, but not before difficulties had been put in his way to prevent him from returning home immediately.[12] Two years later, another conspiracy to depose Mary, hatched by Sir Henry Dudley, revived all the old suspicions. Champernowne was not amongst those involved, but he was put under recognizance of £1,000 for his appearance in London and ordered to appear every day before a clerk of the Council from 14 May to 7 July.[13] He was only allowed to return home on condition that he would appear before the Council, whenever summoned, at twenty days' notice.[14]

An increasing number of public duties, such as his attendance on the earl of Lincoln during his visit to France in 1557,[15] the needs of a growing family, and a desire to increase his standing, encouraged Champernowne to seek a residence independent of the family home at Modbury. His father had left him a number of properties and he had added to them by purchasing Polsloe Priory in 1549.[16] A property so close to the thriving town of Exeter could only increase in value and Champernowne held it for only a few years before capitalizing on his investment. In 1554, he sold the manor of Polsloe to Sir John Peter, a merchant of Exeter, and five years later, exchanged the site of the priory with John Aylworth for the far more attractively situated manor of Dartington.[17] The younger branch of the Champernowne family now possessed a large estate of their own and it remained their home for nearly 370 years.

Dartington Hall had been held by a series of absentee landlords since its forfeiture by Sir Thomas St. Leger seventy-six years beforehand. There is little doubt that it had fallen on lean times, yet it was still a large residence, capable of adaptation to the standards of the time, and Sir Arthur apparently began to modify the Hall shortly after he had taken possession of it. An entry in the churchwardens' accounts of Ashburton for 1560–1 notes, 'xiiis. viiid. to divers persons labouring at Dertyngton with Arthur Champernown, knight'.[18] In the absence of any contrary evidence, the alterations made to the Hall in the second half of the sixteenth century may be fairly convincingly attributed to him and probably to this period when Sir Arthur would be anxious to make the property both habitable and comfortable. As he was capable of designing a banqueting house on an island for Richard Carew at Antony in Cornwall,[19] it is likely that he also deployed his talents on his own house at Dartington. The courtyard south of the great hall was finally abandoned, the upper and lower residential blocks were adapted to the needs of his family, and minor alterations were made to the ranges on either side of the main courtyard. The address given at the foot of most of the surviving letters written by Sir Arthur confirm that he spent the remainder of his life at his new family home.

The sea, as with so many Elizabethan men of Devon, played a major part in Sir Arthur's

[7] F. Rose-Troup, *The Western Rebellion of 1549* (1913), 375–7.

[8] Ibid., 508.

[9] *State Papers, Domestic: 1547–80*, 57.

[10] Ibid., 59.

[11] *Historical Manuscripts Commission: Records of the City of Exeter* (1916), 366–7.

[12] It was claimed that his pardon was invalidated because the seal had not been affixed. *Acts of the Privy Council, 1554–56*, 18.

[13] Ibid., 373, where the recognizance is struck out.

[14] Ibid., 304.

[15] *Historical Manuscripts Commission: Marquis of Salisbury*, vol. 1 (1883), 146.

[16] The priory had been granted by Henry VIII to Sir George Carew, Lady Champernowne's first husband, who had died in 1545 not long after their marriage. She retained it for some years after his death and it was not completely alienated by the Crown until 1549 when it was granted to the earl of Warwick. He immediately resold it to Sir Richard Sackville who, in turn, sold it a few months later to Sir Arthur Champernowne. *Cal. Pat. Rolls: Ed. VI*, vol. 3, 61; ibid., vol. 4, 43. See also Dr. J. Youings, *Devon Monastic Lands: 1536–1558* (1955).

[17] Exeter City Library: DD 41950. This transaction was not finally settled by the two families until 1618.

[18] J. H. Butcher, *The Parish of Ashburton in the 15th and 16th Centuries* (1870), 38. The churchwardens' accounts of Dartington for the late 15th and the 16th centuries are devoid of any references to the Hall or to the families who occupied it.

[19] Richard Carew, *Survey of Cornwall* (1602, ed. F. E. Halliday, 1953), 175–6. This house was similar in design to that built for Henry VIII at Nonsuch Palace between 1538 and 1546. John Dent, *The Quest for Nonsuch* (1962), 125.

life. His estates were located at the head of the tidal waters of the river Dart and he was related by marriage to some of the well-known seafaring families of the sixteenth century —Gilbert, Raleigh, Grenville, Seymour, and Carew.[20] He was granted a private licence in 1558 by the Court of Admiralty for the 'Galleon of Dartmouth' and although little is known of Sir Arthur's sea-going experiences, they were sufficient to warrant his appointment by 1562 at the latest as vice-admiral of the West. All matters touching the western seas came within Sir Arthur's purview, including, like an earlier owner of Dartington Hall, the Court of Admiralty. He was particularly concerned with the activities of pirate and enemy shipping off the western coast. On several occasions he was enjoined by the Privy Council to take piratical shipping, as in the case of the thirteen ships from Flushing which were blockading Torbay in July 1576.[21] French shipping received particularly short shrift at Sir Arthur's hands and he frequently forced the sale of their cargoes on the grounds that they would otherwise perish before reaching their destination. In 1575, for instance, bad weather drove a French vessel into Dartmouth and Sir Arthur promptly took the opportunity to relieve a local shortage of salt by enforcing the sale of the ship's cargo and distributing it round the countryside.[22] Complaints about similar actions were received by the Privy Council from the merchants of Rouen and Dieppe in 1577 and 1578,[23] but it is not clear whether these and comparable complaints stemmed from any piratical leanings or from a zealous regard for his duties.

Ever since the beginning of the sixteenth century, friendship between England and Spain had been one of the guiding principles of English foreign policy. The death of Mary and the accession of a Protestant queen in 1558 had not entirely endangered this relationship, but there were many acts of provocation on either side during the following quarter century before war finally broke out between the two countries. Among such acts was the seizure of the Spanish treasure fleet by the English in December 1568. King Philip of Spain had raised a loan of 800,000 ducats from the Genoese banking houses for the payment of the duke of Alva's troops in the Netherlands. The English Channel was swarming with both English and French freebooters but Philip hoped that his friendship with England would ensure that there was no interference with the treasure cavalcade as it slowly made its way through the Channel on its journey from Spain to Antwerp. Philip's confidence was misplaced. Autumn storms and Channel pirates drove the ships into Fowey, Saltash, and Southampton. The opportunity to avenge a recent treacherous attack on Hawkins and Drake off the Mexican coast was too good to miss and Cecil immediately suggested to Champernowne that he should remove the treasure from the ships under colour of friendship to the greater safety of Fowey and Saltash. On 19 December, Champernowne reported its successful movement to Cecil in a letter from Dartington, claiming that the Spanish 'seemed to take my said persuasions in good part. . . . The whole treasure in both places is such that it is supposed to be worth £40,000 sterling and therefore most fit for her majesty'.[24] Champernowne had read Cecil's mind correctly and reported the fact with a smack of self-satisfaction.[25] In the following month, John Killigrew and he conducted the ninety-four bags from the west of England to the Tower of London attended by fifty horse, and supported by fifty foot and artillery for its protection.[26] According to their contract with Philip, the loan was still the property of the Genoese bankers until it had

---

[20] Sir Arthur was an uncle of Sir John and Humphrey Gilbert and later of Sir Walter Raleigh through the marriage of his sister, Katherine, into the Gilbert and then the Raleigh family. A second sister Elizabeth, married into the Grenville family and his daughter married Sir Edward Seymour of near-by Berry Pomeroy Castle. His wife, Mary, had previously been married to Sir George Carew.

[21] *Acts of the Privy Council, 1575–77*, 172.

[22] Ibid., 88.

[23] *State Papers, Domestic: Addenda, 1566–79*, 524–5; *State Papers, Foreign: 1577–78*, 473.

[24] *State Papers, Domestic: 1547–80*, 324, 326; A. L. Rowse, *Sir Richard Grenville of the Revenge* (1937), 73.

[25] A. L. Rowse, *Tudor Cornwall* (1941), 380.

[26] *State Papers, Domestic: Addenda, 1566–79*, 72.

Sir Arthur Champernowne, d. 1578. Artist unknown

been delivered to Alva. Elizabeth I promptly borrowed it from the Genoese for herself, forwarded half of it to William of Orange to be used in his fight against the Spanish and spent the remainder on her navy. Philip fumed and his troops in the Netherlands mutinied, but Spain was not prepared to declare war over the incident.

Champernowne was one of Cecil's principal informants of affairs in Devon. His ardent

Gawen Champernowne, d. 1592. Artist unknown

support of the Protestant cause had already impelled him to write to Cecil in September 1568, offering him hearsay evidence about Mary, Queen of Scots, but Champernowne's news of the progress of the Protestant cause in France was far more valuable to the Secretary of State because it was first-hand information obtained initially from Champernowne's nephew until his death in France in 1570, and then from Champernowne's son after his marriage in 1572 to the daughter of a Huguenot leader.[27] For Sir Arthur was a staunch Protestant and patriot, feared by the French,[28] but quite unable to consider European politics from anything other than the insular viewpoint common to so many of his countrymen.

Like many members of Tudor society, Champernowne consciously strove to improve his status. Judicious investment in the 1540s substantially added to the tin-mines and estates which his father had left him, and his income was no doubt supplemented by the by-products of his post as vice-admiral of the West. He had sold part of Polsloe Priory at a profit and exchanged the remainder for a residence of a size and dignity befitting his aspirations. He was rated for £30 in lands in the subsidy of 1576, although he claimed that he had no land to spare when he wished to marry off his daughter.[29] He was returned as member of Parliament for Barnstaple in 1547, Plympton in 1555, Totnes in 1563, appointed sheriff of Devon in 1561, and a commissioner of peace on five occasions. He was the only member of his branch of the family to hold an important government position and he had added to his standing among the neighbouring gentry by arranging his son's marriage to the count de Montgommery's daughter, and his daughter's marriage to the heir of the Seymour family. Seymour had disapproved of the match but Champernowne took advantage of his friendship with Cecil to obtain letters of approval from both him and the queen, and the marriage took place unopposed.

Described by Richard Carew of Antony as 'that perfectly accomplished gentleman',[30] Sir Arthur was in tune with the vigorous, confident spirit of the Elizabethan Age, but his determination to improve the standing of himself and his line came to naught because neither his son nor his grandson had the same aspirations or ability. Only a handful of the 360 or 400 indisputable gentry in Devon rose within or out of their class in the early seventeenth century.[31] Despite Sir Arthur's efforts, the Champernowne family was not among them.

Dartington Hall was the home of Sir Arthur for nearly twenty years and he died not far from it at his sister's house at Slade on 1 April 1578. He was buried in Dartington Church a week later, and the tomb erected to him and his wife, who had died eight years earlier, now stands in the church tower overlooking their former home. He left five sons and two daughters and an eighth child who apparently died young.

The Late Tudor and Early Stuart Generations: 1578–1664

Gawen Champernowne, probably born in 1554, was eighteen-years-old when his father arranged his marriage to Robarda, the daughter of the count de Montgommery. An alliance between the families of a keen English Protestant and one of the principal leaders of the Huguenot faction against the House of Guise, inevitably led to Gawen's participation in the religious wars in France. Not surprisingly, the massacre of the Huguenots on St. Bartholomew's Day (1572) was responsible for the count de Montgommery seeking refuge with his daughter and son-in-law at Dartington Hall only a few months after their marriage. The possibility that the count might be assassinated by French royalists made it necessary for Sir Arthur Champernowne to order that no Frenchmen should be admitted to the count whilst he was at Dartington, unless he already knew them.[32] A loan

[27] *State Papers, Domestic: 1547–80*, 316, 384, 437, 439.

[28] After making diligent inquiries in 1574 about the arms and men that Sir Richard Grenville was gathering for his 7 ships, the French ambassador reported that their purpose 'be very suspect: the more so because I was told that the said Grenville had associated Sir Arthur Champernowne with him'. It was only after further inquiries that the ambassador established that Grenville's intention was not to attack France but to discover the South Sea passage. La Monthe-Fénelon, *Correspondance Diplomatique*, vol. 6, 127–8. Grenville's scheme never came to fruition.

[29] *Historical Manuscripts Commission: Marquis of Salisbury*, vol. 2 (1888), 112–3.

[30] Richard Carew, *Survey of Cornwall* (1602, ed. F. E. Halliday, 1953), 175.

[31] W. G. Hoskins and H. P. R. Finberg, *Devonshire Studies* (1952), 334.

[32] *State Papers, Foreign: 1572–74*, 430. For a biography of the count de Montgommery, see Michaud, *Biographie Universelle* (1854–7), vol. 29.

which Montgommery succeeded in raising during his stay in England was sufficiently large to enable him to equip a squadron for the relief of La Rochelle under his own and Gawen's command. The expedition was a failure and while Montgommery and Gawen were preparing a second expedition, peace was restored with the grant of freedom of worship for all Protestants. Montgommery's second expedition in 1574 terminated in his capture and death, although Gawen continued to fight for the Protestant cause in France for a further year.

Gawen's marriage was hardly more successful than his military ventures. His father-in-law refused to pay the agreed marriage allowance and it was necessary to try and recover it by law. Despite promises and procrastinations, it was still an item on the English ambassador's agenda of matters to be discussed in France in 1576.[33] Proceedings for Gawen's divorce were instigated in July 1582 on the grounds of his wife's misconduct with two domestic servants.[34] Both Robarda's mother and her brother sought Walsingham's intervention against he whom, it was claimed, 'has received too much favour from our said house'.[35] The countess wrote to Walsingham that 'what her daughter is accused of is pure calumny, far from truth and invented by her husband in his transport of unbridled passion'.[36] Reconciliation must have been effected, however, for Robarda proved her husband's will and she had three further children by Gawen, including one born after his death.[37]

The war with Spain which both Elizabeth and Philip had been trying to avoid for so many years broke out in 1588. Gawen, a friend of Sir Francis Drake,[38] contributed one of the eight ships which sailed from Dartmouth to repulse the Spanish Armada. The *Phoenix* was a vessel of 70 tons and 50 men,[39] but Gawen's appointment the previous December as Captain of Horse for the South Division of Devon prevented him from sailing with her.[40] In the following year, the churchwardens of Dartington paid 3s. 9d. for a shirt, a pair of stockings, and a pair of shoes for a straggler from the defeated Spanish fleet.[41]

Gawen died four years after the defeat of the Armada. The principal change made by him at Dartington affected the estates rather than the Hall itself, for it was he who was responsible for the construction of the weir on the river Dart just north-east of Totnes. This enabled him to recover the tidal area stretching from Pudhaven to the river, a marked feature of the landscape today near the lodge and the lower drive.

Arthur Champernowne, Gawen's eldest son, was nearly twelve-years-old at the time of his father's death. Whereas his grandfather had been responsible for the safe-keeping of the western shores and his father had participated in the religious wars in France, Arthur Champernowne set the pattern for succeeding generations by tending to confine himself entirely to local affairs. He was returned as member of Parliament for Totnes in 1624 and 1626 and was appointed a justice of the peace in 1639, but he had no intention of actively participating in the Civil War and answered Sir Edward Seymour's call in 1645 for horses and arms with 'a little pretty, fat old horse [and] nothing else'.[42]

Under the late Tudors and early Stuarts, the military traditions of the later Middle Ages were replaced by maritime ascendance, fostered by naval victories, exploration, and colonization. Arthur participated in them to the extent that he was the owner or part-owner of several vessels at Dartmouth[43] and he helped one of his sons, Francis, to colonize

[33] *State Papers, Foreign: 1575–77*, 302.

[34] *State Papers, Domestic: 1581–90*, 63.

[35] *State Papers, Foreign: 1583–84*, 469, 470.

[36] Ibid.

[37] A ghost story associated with Robarda's life at Dartington Hall is related, with others, in *Trans. Devon Assoc.* vol. 92 (1960), 368–9, and ibid., vol. 93 (1961), 114.

[38] Gawen left Drake a ring inscribed 'the remembrance of a Friend'. Lady Elliott Drake, *The Family and Heirs of Sir Francis Drake* (1911), 116–7.

[39] *Devon Notes and Gleanings*, vols. 1 and 2 (1888), 75.

[40] *Historical Manuscripts Commission: Manuscripts of the Dukes of Somerset and Others* (1898), 4.

[41] Dartington: Churchwarden Accounts, 1554–1639. Returns for 1589, f. 153.

[42] *Historical Manuscripts Commission: Manuscripts of the Duke of Somerset and Others* (1898), 85.

[43] In 1620, he is listed as the owner of *Chudleigh* (140 tons) and *Gidleigh* (140 tons); in 1627, part-owner of *Benediction* (160 tons), in 1629 *The Martin* (35 tons), *Mary* (25 tons), *Greyhound* (60 tons), *The Bridgett* (100 tons), and *The Francis* (40 tons).

lands in New England by raising a substantial mortgage of £1,118 in 1635 on local properties at Godmerock and Kingswear.[44] However, the finances of the family suffered heavily during Arthur's lifetime, partly because he became responsible for paying some of the debts of his cousin, Sir Richard Champernowne of Modbury, and partly because he had to support a large family of six sons and eight daughters.[45] Furthermore, he suffered financially during the war with Spain, although it is not known in what way, and successfully petitioned Charles I in 1634 for help by receiving the reversion of Plympton Priory which he already held in tail male.[46]

Arthur died in 1650 but his wife, Bridgett, lived at Dartington with her son and grandson for a further seventeen years. The daughter of Sir Thomas Fulford, Bridgett is responsible for the earliest surviving description of the Hall. Drawn up in 1663 when she was more than eighty years old, her notes show that some of the buildings round the main courtyard were part of the barton or home farmstead which remained there until 1925. Among the buildings on the west side of the courtyard apparently used for this purpose were 'the chamber in which the old woman now lodges and the chamber which next adjoins right, and the three old lofts there which belonging, the dairy, the larder, the meal house and the three lower piggs houses, the store house and the celler all adjoining to the hall'.[47] On the south side of the great court was a wood-house and hen-house and there was another wood-house lying on the south side of the old kitchen. Other buildings round the main courtyard included 'the four chambers which Mr. G. Champernowne usually maketh use of, two chambers lying on the east side of the court called Mr. Amias chambers, the gatehouse chamber and the gatehouse'.

'The old barn on the north-west half of the shippen and the hay loft over the same' may possibly refer to the barn which still exists a few yards from the north-west angle of the courtyard. The rooms in the private house used by the head of the family are not mentioned by Bridgett, but she had the partial use of the great dining chamber, the little dining chamber, and the count's chamber, which were apparently part of this residence. She also had the use of a brewhouse, wash-house, bakehouse, and the higher stable.

The Late Stuart and Early Georgian Generations: 1664–1774

The generations who span the second half of the Stuart period have left little mark on the history of the Hall. They took little part in politics and most of the records of this period deal with the management of their estates—the customs of the manor, the letting of farms, repairs to estate property, and the collection of annual rentals. Arthur Champernowne (d. 1697) was among the gentry who welcomed William of Orange when he landed at Brixham in 1688 and subscribed £30 of the £82. 10s. 0d. collected in Dartington as a loan to William.[48] Members of the family occasionally represented Totnes in Parliament, but in general they lived a private rather than a public life in a leisured and dignified manner.

In 1717 the estate passed to a nine-year-old child who, by the age of twenty-one, was cutting a very well-dressed figure. The bill presented to Arthur Champernowne by his tailor for purchases in 1729 came to £119. 5s. 10d. and that for 1730 began with comparable lavish expenditure.

[44] Francis Champernowne, b. 1614, d. 1687. He went to Kittery, southern Maine in 1637. See C. Penrose, *Old Kittery, Land of Adventure* (New York, 1947); C. W. Tuttle, *Capt. Francis Champernowne, the Dutch Conquest of Acadie* (Boston, 1889); P. Russell and G. Yorke, 'Kingswear and Neighbourhood', *Trans. Devon Assoc.* vol. 85 (1953), 68–9; and R. D. Brown, 'Devonians and New England Settlement before 1650', *Trans. Devon Assoc.* vol. 95 (1963), 219–43.

[45] It was possibly one of Arthur's children who was responsible in 1639 for incising the date on the left-hand side of the outer arch of the tower porch.

[46] *Historical Manuscripts Commission: Fourth report, Records of the Marquis of Bath*, pt. 1 (1874), 233

[47] Exeter City Library: 58/3/1/1. In 1701, this barton was described as 'one of the best, both for numbers of acres and goodness of land, in this county'. John Prince, *The Worthies of Devon*, 500.

[48] Exeter City Library: DD 40682.

31 Jan. 1730	Making a scarlet banion with lining	£3.	5. 4.
	Making a scarlet double breasted waistcoat	1.	7. 6.
	Making a superfine black cloth suit	7.	13. 7.
7 Feb.	Making a blue jocky coat and breeches with lining, silver garters	2.	13. 5.
14 Feb.	Making drab jocky coat and breeches	1.	17. 5.
28 Feb.	Making superfine cloth coat and breeches richly laced with gold. Gold wire on coat	13.	17. 10.
	6 yards of green baize for a case for your clothes and to lay over them in the box		16. 0.
14 Mar.	Cleaning a jocky coat and a horseman's		2. 0.
21 Mar.	Full trimming a black cloth coat etc.		12. 0.
	Making a fine black cloth mourning suit with lining	5.	2. 0.
	Making a grey cloth jocky coat	1.	12. 3.
	Making a drab cloth horseman's coat	1.	13. 1.
	Paid for carriage of 4 boxes to Exeter and porterage		16. 6.
25 Apr.	New making a grey silk banion	1.	3. 10.

During the remainder of the year, Champernowne also ordered two more cloth coats, three pairs of cloth breeches, a silk coat, a waistcoat and pair of breeches, a velvet waistcoat and a pair of silk garters.[49] In addition to the total charge of £58. 10s. 8d., there was a further bill for £5. 19s. 1d. for 'work done for your servants on 14th and 21st March, 1730'.[50] This extravagance was not intended to serve his needs in London, but simply those at Dartington. He rarely visited the metropolis and his lack of enthusiasm for the social season there contributed to his estrangement from his wife less than two years after their marriage. Arthur's bride was Jane, the daughter of Dr. Hollings, George II's physician, but rural life in Devon was not really conducive to her high spirits and she spent most of her time at the house in Soho Square which her father had bought her.[51]

Apart from its distance from London, it is possible that Jane also disliked Dartington because she found the Hall too uncomfortable and old fashioned for her tastes. A comparison between the engraving of Dartington made by the Buck brothers in 1734 with those of other major Devonian residences such as Powderham Castle, Buckland Abbey, and Forde Abbey shows how old fashioned the Hall looked at that time, an impression emphasized by the lack of a formal garden within the main courtyard. Arthur set about rectifying this by altering several of the rooms in the private house at the upper end of the great hall, and by creating a series of new rooms on the first floor of the west range overlooking the main courtyard. Broad pine panelling, larger windows, plastered ceilings, and a new staircase replaced medieval and Elizabethan features. The dates 1737 and 1741 on the bell and weather-vane above the porch tower are probably indicative of the years when this work was carried out, and apart from improving the comfort of the Hall, Arthur's efforts were finally rewarded by his wife's return to Dartington in about 1761.[52]

Illness seems to have dogged the last few years of Arthur's life. In 1762, his cousin, Sir William Courtenay, wrote to him, 'I am told that your leg is very bad and that you are advised to have it scraped again. If this is the case for God's sake submit, if you don't

---

[49] Exeter City Library: DD 41095.

[50] Exeter City Library: DD 41098.

[51] In 1762, a Charles Willes wrote to Jane Champernowne to say that his father's will, dated November 1737, had included a bequest 'to his good friend Mrs. Champernowne' who was bequeathed £100, and £40 was to be paid to her each quarter during the life of her husband 'and as long as she continues to live separate and apart from him ... and I do give the same legacy and annuity as a Testimony of my Respect for so good a woman that has been so very ill-used'. From documents held in 1962 by Miss C. E. Champernowne.

[52] In a codicil to the above-mentioned will dated August 1761, the legacy given earlier was revoked because Jane and her daughter 'are gone to live with her husband in Devonshire, who has promised, as he is very well able, to provide very handsomely for them'. From documents held in 1962 by Miss C. E. Champernowne who considered that Arthur had, in fact, heavily mortgaged the estate.

The north court from the east: 1734. By S. and N. Buck

approve of the surgeons in the country, come to Town where you are sure of the best advice, believe me....'[53]

Bills as well as illness continued to worry him during the last few years of his life. His daughter, Jane, was as fond of fine materials and clothes as her father had been in his youth, and among his surviving accounts is one for his daughter of £106. 4s. 2d. This

[53] Exeter City Library: DD 41129.

...MPLE, IN THE COUNTY OF DEVON.

THIS Place in all probability was an House of the Knights Templers, but the whole order was dissolv'd about the 5.th Ed. II. that but few particulars are to be found in History of them, Their great Possessions were given principally to the Knights Hospitallers, tho' some at that time came into Gentlemens Hands as all did at length in the common Dissolution.

S. & N. Buck, delin et Sculp. 1734

was for purchasing various fabrics such as poplin, brocade, satin, and lustring over a two and a half years' period prior to 1760, and although £90 had been paid off by 1762, the remainder was still outstanding at the time of Champernowne's death in 1766.[54] Among other outstanding bills at that time was one from his gunsmith for £7. 12s. 6d., still not paid five years later,[55] and one from his coachman for £8. 13s. 0d. for making a new set

[54] Exeter City Library: DD 41105; also DD 41119.

[55] Exeter City Library: DD 41128.

Arthur Champernowne, d. 1766. By Thomas Hudson

His wife, Jane Champernowne. By Thomas Hudson

Dartington Hall and church from the south: c. 1800. By R. H. Froude

The entrance block and north end of west range: 1805. By G. Saunders

of wheels, varnishing them with vermilion, and fitting them on a coach in return for keeping the old ones, and other sundry items.[56]

In the absence of a male heir, the estate passed on Arthur's death in 1766 to his cousin Rawlin, the son of the Rev. John Champernowne and Margaret Mallock. He was already forty-one-years-old when he entered upon Dartington and he lived there until his death eight years later. No family papers of his remain, and apart from the fact that he was fond of fishing,[57] very little is known about him.

Arthur Champernowne: 1774–1819

Rawlin was the last in the male line of the Champernowne family, and in 1774 the estate passed to another Arthur, the seven-year-old son of Jane and the Rev. Harrington, rector of Powderham. In accordance with the terms of his grandfather's will, Arthur immediately adopted the name and arms of Champernowne by deed-poll.

Arthur showed a marked talent for travelling at an early age and spent one of his youthful tours in the company of Richard Polwhele, the Devonshire historian. At the conclusion of their journey through Devon and Cornwall, Arthur presented Polwhele with his manuscript notes, considering that they might be of use for his projected history of Devon. However, the historian considered them 'rather puerile' and they found no place in his topographical volume.[58]

Arthur made the Grand Tour of Europe when he was seventeen years old. He began with a series of famous residences and gardens in Wiltshire—Stourhead, Fonthill, Wardour, Wilton, and Longford Castle—and after visiting Cambridge, travelled to Calais, Rheims, Strasbourg, Heidelberg, and Frankfurt. He returned imbued with the desire to fill his home with Old Masters comparable with those he had seen abroad. He bought a number of pictures at the famous Orleans sale of 1798 and sold property in London, Devon, and Cornwall to give him the £1,000 he paid annually 'for the pleasure of looking at the wonderful works of Rubens, Titian, Andrea del Sarto, Correggio, Van Dyke and Domenichino'.[59] Many of his purchases were made in Italy which he and his wife frequently visited, combining their activities with their talent for sketching and drawing. Champernowne was a discerning amateur collector, a friend of Buchanan, Carr, and Irvine, and in the forefront of that great trade in England in works of art during the late eighteenth and early nineteenth centuries.[60] Among Champernowne's purchases were Titian's *Noli me Tangere* and Rubens's *Horror of War* and *Triumph of Caesar*.[61] For a time, these and several other masterpieces adorned the walls of Dartington Hall, but heavy debts made it necessary to sell most of the collection shortly after Champernowne's death in 1819.

Arthur frequently thought of altering and enlarging the Hall but none of his ideas came to fruition. In 1805, he commissioned George Saunders to prepare a series of drawings showing the existing condition of the Hall and suggestions for restoring and enlarging it.[62] These drawings are a most valuable and accurate survey of the structure at the beginning of the nineteenth century and reference will frequently be made to them in subsequent chapters. Saunders' suggestions included proposals for restoring the great hall and constructing a new residential court to the south-east of it, but Champernowne's pencil comment on the title-page of the plan book notes that the work could not be carried out

---

[56] Exeter City Library: DD 41104.

[57] C. E. Champernowne, *The Champernowne Family* (1954), 274.

[58] Ibid., 276.

[59] Ibid., 276–7.

[60] W. Buchanan, *Memoirs of Painting* (1824), 2 vols.

[61] These 3 pictures were acquired by the National Gallery in 1856. Cecil Gould informs me that there may be other pictures in the Gallery which formerly belonged to Champernowne, but it will not be possible to determine this until the cumulative index of provenance has been completed.

[62] Saunders was born in 1762 and died in 1839. He was surveyor for the county of Middlesex and chairman of the commission of sewers for 28 years. He designed an extension of Montague House for the trustees of the British Museum and contributed several papers to *Archaeologia*. See P. Frankl, *The Gothic* (1960), 499–502.

Arthur Champernowne, d. 1819. By W. Brockedon   His wife, Louisa Champernowne, d. 1870. By W. Brockedon

'by any one who has not twenty thousand pounds and four thousand per annum <u>certain income</u> which does not happen to be the case with the present proprietor of Dartington Hall'.[63] In any case, any intention of implementing these proposals was curtailed by the development of more personal plans for in September 1807, Captain Hare of Curtisknowle wrote to his wife, 'You will be surprised when I tell you that Champernowne instead of building a house is on the matrimonial scheme and in a very few days we expect him and his wife. He is on the point of marrying Miss Buller I believe of Morval in Cornwall, a lady, I apprehend, in every way suited to him.'[64]

The Champernownes did not maintain a large household. At the end of that same September, Captain Hare wrote, 'Captain Champernowne and his wife seem to live very comfortable. They have only a curricle and pair and his old horse, and Drew the soldier servant, who is coachman and groom, and his old servant Charles. I do not know what female servants, I believe a soldier's wife to cook and her maid. I am not sure if there is any other or not.'[65]

Champernowne had helped to resist the Napoleonic invasion anticipated in 1803, by raising a corps of cavalry composed of persons of property in the neighbourhood. For a short time, he represented Saltash in Parliament and was sheriff of Devon in 1811, but most of his time and money were spent in collecting pictures and geological specimens. He was elected a member of the Society of Antiquaries in 1797 and a member of the Geological Society in 1807.[66]

An entry in the diary of Joseph Farington, the landscape painter, after his visit to Dartington in October 1809, gives an idea of the condition of the Hall and of Champernowne's estate at that time.

Dartington Hall is a very ancient building. The principal door opens into a hall which for length, breadth and height is remarkable for its size, appearing in dimensions like a large chapel. The roof is supported by timbers and the walls are whitewashed. It is in a state bare of ornament or furniture. We were shown into a sitting room and afterwards into a dining-room, a cold and comfortless looking room.—Several large pictures

[63] Exeter City Library: f. 009.4/113547. Volume of plans and drawings of Dartington Hall.

[64] C. E. Champernowne, *The Champernowne Family* (1954), 280.

[65] Ibid., 281.

[66] Ibid., 280, 281, 277.

The north court from the entrance block: 1797. By T. Bonner

by Artois with figures by Teniers covered part of the walls. The pictures not of good quality. Smaller pictures were hung without order, mixed with drawings. An imitation of Wilson—among them. A study by Sir Joshua Reynolds, for which Lady Maynard sat; a drawing by Canaletto etc.—In the sitting room there are two landscapes, by Salvator Rosa, and a Holy Family by Ludovico Carrach. . . .

We now returned to Totnes. Mr. Champernowne had talked of doing much at Dartington but has done nothing. His property is such as to afford him means for improving the place. He is reckoned to have £4,000 a year to expend. An eagle kept at Dartington engaged Sir William's [Elford] attention. . . . He made a sketch of it to add to a collection he has long been forming of English birds. . . .[67]

[67] *The Farington Diary*, ed. J. Greig, vol. 5 (1925), 281. A few days earlier, Farington had recorded in his diary that 'Mr. Champernowne's estate at Dartington is about £2,500 a year. He resides there but little, preferring to move about with his wife, and they amuse themselves with sketching.' Ibid., 275.

[68] Exeter City Library: 58/3/5/8.

Although the kitchen block had been ruined for many years, the condition of the roof of the great hall began to give Champernowne cause for concern. This apartment had stood empty for many years. An inventory of all the furniture and furnishings at the Hall made by the Rev. Harrington on his son's accession in 1774 shows that the only furnishings in the great hall were a sedan-chair, two old trunks of linen, and a chimney-stove grate.[68] It was sometimes used for storage purposes and only recaptured its former glory once a year when Champernowne gave a dinner for all the tenants on his estate. As he wrote to George Cumberland, the antiquarian, in 1791, 'You might then have a faint idea of the figure they must have cut when this place was inhabited by Holland, Duke of Exeter, when there was a christening here which cost more than a thousand pounds four hundred years since, and when the surrounding parishes, which now only pay me a chief-rent of a shilling or sixpense, all belonged to one person.'[69]

[69] C. E. Champernowne, *The Champernowne Family* (1954), 278.

In May 1813, Champernowne ordered his steward, Christopher Savery, to take all the slating off the roof of the great hall so that he could examine the condition of the timbers underneath.[70] Neither Savery nor his associates were in favour of leaving the woodwork open to the elements, but Champernowne overruled them. An estimate of more than £2,000 for rebuilding the roof was considered too high, particularly as Champernowne was considering spending only twice that amount on building an entirely new house near Aller Park. William Wilkins, the architect, examined the timbers and recommended that the Hall 'could not be made comfortable, and that the hall roof should be destroyed and

[70] All correspondence referring to the condition of the hall roof is in Exeter City Library: 58/3/1/11.

that the materials of your part of the house should be taken for the new house'.[71] Although these proposals did not come to fruition, Champernowne left the hall unroofed, considering that 'when the walls of the hall are overgrown with ivy, they will be as much admired as they are now. I shall have a coping put on the tops of them to preserve them.'[72] Champernowne lived well above his means throughout his life. The return from his estates and the mining interests in Cornwall which his great-grandfather had acquired on his marriage into the Courtenay family, were quite inadequate for Arthur's needs. His frequent travels abroad, his artistic purchases, and a family of eight children proved very expensive, while a property venture at Honiton was financially disastrous. Yet he was full of ideas for purchasing property, building houses, and rebuilding Dartington Hall until the end of his life, despite the debt of nearly £25,000[73] which he bequeathed to his heirs in 1819.

The Later Champernownes: 1819–1925

The estate passed to Arthur's eldest son, also christened Arthur, who died in 1831 before his eighteenth birthday. Throughout his short life, the estate was administered by a group of trustees, and for all practical purposes by the Rev. R. H. Froude, rector of Dartington from 1799 until his death fifty years later.[74] Many of the Champernowne papers now preserved at Exeter City Library date from Froude's stewardship and it is clear that he vigorously prosecuted the outstanding task of clearing his patron's debts. The sale in 1820 of many of the pictures and marbles so recently collected realized £6,187. 18s. 3d. and the debt was extinguished by selling the Champernowne estates in Cornwall and their family house in Montague Square, London.[75]

Froude's accounts for the period 1820 to 1828 show that Dartington and a small estate at Cowley, a hamlet of Upton Pyne not far from Exeter, provided about three-quarters of the total family income. The remainder was principally made up from revenues derived from the mansion house and gardens, dividend on stock, and the sale of wood, timber, and bark. Out of a total income in 1828 of £6,155—£1,131 was spent on maintaining the estate, £800 on the annual jointure settled on Mrs. Champernowne, £582 on investment stock, and £500 on repaying a loan of £10,000.[76] The balance of over £3,000 was higher in 1828 than at any time during the minority, for Froude's strict accounting and control ensured that the estate was solvent when he passed it to Henry Champernowne, Arthur's brother, in 1831.

Henry Champernowne was responsible for the only major alterations to the Hall during the nineteenth century, changes aimed at increasing its internal comfort rather than its overall appearance. This was not for lack of plans. Those put forward by Pugin in 1845 included proposals for restoring the great hall, altering the private house, and constructing a new residential court on the site of the kitchen block with the principal rooms on the first floor. Overwhelmingly confident, Pugin's designs included an abundance of oriel windows, chimneys, and steeply pitched roofs which made his proposals less severe than those put forward by Saunders, but quite out of harmony with the remainder of the Hall. Fortunately, Champernowne considered the estimated cost of between £4,000 and £5,000 prohibitive[77] and the alterations finally carried out between about 1846 and 1851 were on a far more modest scale. The rooms above the lower residential block and the hall porch

[71] C. E. Champernowne, *The Champernowne Family* (1954), 285.

[72] Ibid.

[73] Exeter City Library: 58/3/4/5.

[74] He was the father of three famous sons—all born at Dartington rectory—J. A. Froude, the historian, R. H. Froude, the divine, and W. Froude, the engineer. A description of the Rev. Froude and life at Dartington rectory at this time is given in J. A. Froude's autobiographical fragment included in *James Anthony Froude* by W. H. Dunn (1961), 12–25.

[75] Exeter City Library: 58/3/4/5.

[76] Ibid.

[77] Exeter City Library: DD 41575.

The south front of the Hall, incorporating suggestions for improving the private house: 1839. Artist unknown

were re-roofed, the kitchen ruins strengthened, and the battlements above the great hall restored. Alterations in the private house included redesigning the inner staircase, altering the south-facing windows, and constructing a new entrance leading to the upper drive. The opportunity was also taken about this time to remove the plaster ceiling in the dining-room which had given notice of its impending disintegration when a cherub's wing fell into a soup-tureen.[78] Correspondence shows that Pugin was responsible for some of this work, but it was not sufficient to allow him scope for his volatile talents and he did so little on one of his visits to Dartington that he testily wrote to Champernowne that he could have arranged to carry out six times the work if he had been allowed to do so.[79] It is probable that he also objected to the suggestions made by the Rev. Froude who was finally responsible for most of the alterations completed.

The only other Victorian addition was the extension of the ground-floor passage at the rear of the west range and the insertion of a staircase there, made by Arthur Champernowne in the third quarter of the century so that his wife did not have to meet the housemaids whenever she used the main stairs.[80]

The Champernownes of Victorian and Edwardian England took little part in the life of the county. Their sphere of influence extended no further than local affairs, and hardly beyond Totnes less than two miles away. They were simply lesser gentry, holding an estate of 2,385 acres,[81] and content to be quietly considerate landlords within their means. Henry built a group of cottages for his tenants in 1847 'so that they might acquire the habits favourable to health, decency and good morals', and employees who preferred 'a Tory landlord and not a great radical' sought his favour.[82] He built the church at Brooking, three miles from the Hall for the benefit of his distant tenants while his son, a noted geologist, built a new church at Dartington closer to Shinners Bridge. Designed by J. L. Pearson in 1878 at a cost of £8,000,[83] it was closely modelled on the original structure and incorporated several features from it. Apart from the tower which still remains, the medieval church which had so closely served the Hall and the estate for several centuries

[78] C. E. Champernowne, *The Champernowne Family* (1954), 289.

[79] Exeter City Library: DD 41575.

[80] C. E. Champernowne, *The Champernowne Family* (1954), 290.

[81] *Parliamentary Accounts and Papers, 1874*, vol. 72, pt. 1, Return of Owners of Land: 1872–3.

[82] Exeter City Library: 58/3/6/21. Henry was 'Greatly beloved by all around: dispensing benefits with a liberal hand: attending particularly to the wants of the poor and labourers on the estate in the comfort of suitable residences; and great attention by the ladies of the family in sickness: and provision for the aged in cottages in the style of almshouses, designed and carried out by the Ven. Archdeacon Froude, Rector of Dartington.' G. A. Cawse, *History of Modbury* (1860).

[83] Chiefly defrayed by the Champernownes. Kelly's *Directory of Devonshire* (1939), 192.

was pulled down in 1880, a typical misguided act of the age which had little time for the aesthetic values of past centuries.

Whilst their husbands were visiting different parts of the estate and supervising the work of the steward and tenantry, the ladies of the manor stayed at home, usefully employed in organizing the large household, dispensing hospitality, or busy at their needlework. There was considerable homely entertainment during this period and the Hall was continuously filled with the noise of children.[84] Yet the large families which were characteristic of the Champernownes were a heavy financial burden. Arthur (d. 1819) had four sons and four daughters, Henry (d. 1851) had three sons and three daughters, while Arthur (d. 1887) had six sons and four daughters. All had to be clothed and tutored. Sons had to be maintained at university[85] and daughters given a marriage dowry or a permanent allowance in the case of spinsterhood. Furthermore, wives had to be supported and a jointure made in their widowhood which maintained them in the style to which they had been accustomed. There were also payments to brothers and sisters and support given to aunts and uncles and their children, as in the case of the Buller family who stayed at Dartington Hall for several years in the 1820s. Only a portion of the total income from the estate proved to be available for the use of the head of the family who was ill able to afford such a heavy financial burden.

Although the outward appearance of a landed estate belied inner reality, the life of the gentry continued uninterrupted. The ordinary events of birth, marriage, and death were suitably marked as befitted the position and responsibility of the family. The tenantry of the estates expressed their joy or sorrow as was appropriate and participated in the annual events of a long-established tradition associated with those of superior estate.

In 1957 Miss Elizabeth Champernowne recalled that during the ownership of the property by her father in the late nineteenth century:

The Rent Day dinner was held in the 'solar' (the first floor room to the east of the great hall). We children used to look out of the dining room windows to watch the turkey and the sirloin and all the good things being carried out. And three months after my eldest brother was born, my mother carried him up to the tower to be shown to the tenants and Mr. Luscombe, the Steward, proposed his health, beginning, 'Since it hath pleased the Halmighty Hauthor of the Universe to grant us an heir . . . .'.[86]

The Champernownes were never a wealthy family. Their estates were not extensive and the sale of their interests other than those at Dartington during the nineteenth century meant that this single property with an estimated gross rental in 1872 of £3,388 per year[87] was almost their only source of income. The consequences of this were not felt until the great agricultural depression which extended from the late 1870s until the close of the century, and then, less severely, until the early 1940s. This unhappy period of economic history was essentially due to the rising flood of cheap food from overseas, and its consequences for the estates of the Champernownes, as for so many landed families, were fatal. They had neither the reserves nor the alternative income to offset the diminishing returns from their property and they were unable to break the vortex. The prints and drawings, including work by Rembrandt, collected by Arthur Champernowne in the early nineteenth century, were sold in 1911 and the sale of much of the estate in 1919 and again in 1921 reduced it from a holding of 2,385 acres to one of 876 acres. The contraction of

[84] C. E. Champernowne, *The Champernowne Family* (1954), 288.

[85] Usually Oxford and frequently Exeter College.

[86] Dartington Hall Records Office: Champernowne Papers. Mr. Luscombe was the steward from 1855 to 1904.

[87] *Parliamentary Accounts and Papers, 1874*, vol. 72, pt. 1, Return of Owners of Land: 1872–3.

Great hall and porch tower from the north court: *c.* 1870

West range from the north court: *c.* 1870

Private house and great hall from the south: *c.* 1870

Private house. Interior of the morning-room: *c.* 1870

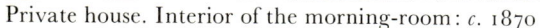

West range, great hall, and kitchen from the east: *c.* 1900

the family estate by the sale of outlying parts and using the capital for more profitable ends was part of a movement common throughout England in the years immediately following the First World War, but in the case of Dartington Hall, it merely postponed an inevitable decision for a few more years. It became necessary to sell the remainder of the estate in 1925 and in September of that year Dorothy and Leonard Elmhirst purchased the Hall and its immediate grounds, two farms of about 600 acres and the associated woodlands of about 190 acres. The Champernowne family passed quietly from the county with which they had so long been associated, the victims of changing values and economic forces which they could no longer withstand.

Part Two

The Architectural History and Description of Dartington Hall

Introduction

The Architectural History and Significance of Dartington Hall

The first impression of Dartington Hall is of an austere, almost cheerless building. It is only on closer examination that the pattern of dark grey stone walls is softened by trimmed lawns and the mellow warmth of flowering trees and climbers. Similarly, the use of undressed blocks of local limestone and Cornish slates throughout the Hall suggests a unity of design and planning which a more careful study shows is not entirely true. Abruptly terminating ranges, different window forms, and varying roof levels are all indicative that building has taken place at several different periods. But although the Hall as it stands today is the work of several generations, their alterations have added to the character of a residence which is still essentially the house of a fourteenth-century magnate, adapted to the comfort and needs of later generations.

Periods of Construction

Much of the present structure was built by the earl of Huntingdon during the last twelve years of the fourteenth century, but neither a study of the documentary evidence nor an examination of the building has yet clarified the date or responsibility for every part of the Hall.[1] The evidence for the different building periods based on records and other sources is given below, but dating determined solely on architectural grounds is reserved for detailed discussion in later chapters.

Although records show that members of the Martin family were resident at Dartington in the twelfth and thirteenth centuries, no evidence has been traced so far which indicates that the site of the present Hall was occupied before the thirteenth century. The recovery in 1962 of several sherds of pottery and other finds of that period close to the footings of a rectangular structure south of the great hall, suggest that a stone building may have been constructed on the site of the later Hall during the second half of the thirteenth century (see Appendix 4).

An inquisition taken at Dartington on 5 April 1388 states that '. . . the buildings and site of the manor and park are somewhat in ruin and decay through lack of repair'.[2] This confirms the existence of a residence at Dartington prior to the late fourteenth century. It also suggests that the buildings had probably been raised by the Martin family who held the property until 1359 and that they had been so little used by Lord Audley during his short-lived tenure of the estate that they had fallen into ruin.

The earl of Huntingdon first held Dartington between December 1384 and April 1385, but it is extremely unlikely that he launched any building programme during these few winter months. The attribution of any of the existing structure to this period may therefore be discounted. Huntingdon acquired the estate again on 16 July 1388 and the rebuilding of Dartington Hall apparently began at once. On 12 September, the dean and chapter of Exeter granted him '. . . slate from the quarry of their manor at Staverton for the roofing of the buildings of the said manor at Dartington'.[3] It would have been impossible

---

[1] The earliest description of the Hall is that by Jeremiah Milles, dean of Exeter, which he wrote in about 1755 as part of his history of Devonshire. It exists only in manuscript form, Bodleian Library, Oxford, MS. Top. Devon, c. 9. The descriptions by J. Prince in *Worthies of Devon* (2nd ed. 1810), 500, 504, and by J. Britton and E. W. Brayley in *Devonshire and Cornwall Illustrated* (1832), 71–2, are very brief, and this also applies to the account by J. H. Parker in *Domestic Architecture of the Middle Ages*, vol. 3, pt. 2 (1859), 353–4. Nine years later, Arthur Champernowne contributed a short note on the Hall to the *Proceedings of the Teign Naturalists' Field Club* (1868), 14–15. The first architectural description of serious intent was published in vol. 30 of the *Arch. Jour.* (1873), 440–2. A more detailed account was contributed by A. Hamilton Thompson to vol. 70 of the same journal (1913), 553–7. Nearly all the information included in the anonymous article in the *Jour. Brit. Arch. Assoc.* vol. 33 (1927), 123–35, is inaccurate or misleading, and this also applies to the anonymous work (but by J. Benson), *A Short History of Dartington Hall with Architectural Notes*, Dartington Hall (4th ed. 1937). A short report on the work of reconstruction was noted by *Country Life* in 1933, and two illustrated articles by Christopher Hussey were published in the same journal in 1938 (27 August and 3 September). 'Dartington Hall, Devonshire' by Anthony Emery in vol. 115 of the *Arch. Jour.* (1958), 184–202, was a brief survey, preparatory to the present book. Colin Platt's report on the excavations of the second court was published in vol. 119 of the same journal (1962), 208–24. Both reports were summarized in two illustrated articles by Christopher Hussey in *Country Life* in 1969 (23 and 30 January).

[2] *Cal. Inq. Misc.* 1387–93, 4.

[3] 'Petras tegulium de lapidicium manerii eorum de Stauerton pro domobus dicti manerii de Dertyngton. . . .' Exeter Cathedral Library: Dean and Chapter, Exeter, MS. 3550, f. 45 r. (Chapter Act Book).

North court from the entrance passage

for Huntingdon to have completed any permanent buildings less than two months after obtaining the property, and the slates must have been intended to cover a temporary structure or some of the existing ruined buildings so that they could be used as temporary lodgings, either by Huntingdon or more probably by the masons and other workmen on the site.

No other documentary evidence has been discovered referring to the building of the Hall before Huntingdon's execution in January 1400. Yet at least part of the hall range was constructed between 1390 and 1399. The wheat-ears which surround the central boss and the base of some of the ribs of the vault in the hall porch was the insignia of the earl and clearly indicates his responsibility for the work. But even more important is the crowned and chained hart of Richard II on the central boss of the porch vault.[4] The king did not adopt this badge before October 1390[5] and it would certainly not have been displayed after Richard's deposition in September 1399.[6] As the porch is an integral part of the hall range, it is possible therefore to confine the construction of the porch tower and probably the great hall to between these two dates. Additional but less reliable evidence for the responsibility for this work is recorded in William White's *History, Gazetteer and Directory of Devonshire* published in 1850, where it is stated that the ceiling of the hall was embellished with the arms of Richard II and the duke of Exeter.[7] This statement probably refers to the porch vault, but it is possible that White was recording evidence observed when the hall roof was pulled down less than forty years beforehand.

It is unlikely that Huntingdon made use of any earlier buildings on the site. Apart from their ruined condition, the accommodation suitable for the Martin family in the later thirteenth and early fourteenth centuries would probably not have satisfied the needs or standing of a great magnate in the late fourteenth century. In addition to the substantial increase in the living standards between the two periods, it would have been well-nigh impossible to accommodate a household the size of that maintained by Huntingdon in the earlier buildings without drastically altering and adding to them. All earlier buildings were probably pulled down in the summer of 1388 and work begun immediately afterwards on laying the foundations for an entirely new residence. It is possible that the private apartments were built before the great hall, as at Portchester Castle,[8] and this receives qualified support by a date for the porch tower not earlier than October 1390.

It was possibly to avoid the life and perambulations of the court that Huntingdon chose Dartington as his principal residence. Like Lord Scrope who refused to take office under Richard II after 1382 and retired to the isolated castle that he was building at Bolton in Wensleydale, Huntingdon also chose to build a residence far from the seat of government or important lines of communication. In deciding to build his mansion in Devon, Huntingdon chose a county with which neither he nor his family had any previous association. It was remote, thinly populated, and under-developed compared with many other counties. It cannot be stressed too strongly that Huntingdon, who had been brought up in the centre of court life and activity, chose to live in an area which many people, like Bishop Grandisson of Exeter, regarded at the time as almost on the edge of the known world. Whatever the reasons for his choice, work proceeded apace. At least part of the Hall must have been in use when Huntingdon stayed there in October 1393,[9] and his entertainment of

---

[4] Queen Philippa, the wife of Edward III, had adopted the white hind as one of her badges. It is believed that she gave it to her ward Joan, the 'Fair Maid of Kent', who added a gold crown about its neck and a pendant chain. This passed to her eldest son, Thomas Holand, earl of Kent. H. Stanford London, *Royal Beasts* (1956), 65; J. H. Harvey, 'The Wilton Diptych—A Re-examination', *Archaeologia*, vol. 98 (1961), 16. W. H. St. John Hope suggested that Richard II may have chosen the white hart rather than the white hind of his mother as a pun on his own name, Rich-hart. *Heraldry for Craftsmen and Designers* (1913). Heraldically, the hart differs from the hind by the addition of antlers. This makes it quite clear that it was Richard's badge and not that of Joan or Thomas Holand which was carved on the boss at Dartington. The rose on which the hart lies was associated with the royal family long before the 15th century and has no particular reference to the House of Lancaster. H. Stanford London, *Royal Beasts* (1956), 32.

[5] Richard had adopted the white hart as early as 1379 when he pawned some brooches bearing this device to the city of London. H. T. Riley, *Memorials of London* (1868), 429, 443, 550, but the Monk of Evesham clearly states that the white hart with a crown and gold chain was first worn by Richard II at the Smithfield Tournament in October 1390. *Historia Vitae et Regni Ricardi Secundi*, ed. T. Hearne (1729), 122.

[6] Nor would it have been possible to reproduce it again before Henry V's reign.

[7] Pages 518–9.

[8] *V.C.H. Hampshire*, vol. 3 (1908), 156. The hall, offices, kitchen, and state apartments at Portchester were built within 3 years. Work began early in 1397 and continued until August 1399, but apart from the fact that these buildings were smaller than those at Dartington, use was also made of existing outer walls.

[9] *Cal. Pat. Rolls 1391–96*, 639.

several members of the Courtenay family at Dartington in April 1396 indicates that much of the building was occupied by that date.[10] Huntingdon's wife and children were in residence in March 1400[11] and the inventories of goods and chattels drawn up only a few weeks earlier testifies to the richness and extent of some of the furnishings in the Hall at that time.

It is not yet possible to determine the precise limits of Huntingdon's work. It certainly included the porch tower, the great hall, the lower residential block, and the kitchen, and it is likely that it included the upper residential block and the south court. It is also reasonable to attribute the east range of the main court to the earl on architectural grounds while the west range may have been the last work undertaken by him before his death in 1400.

The presence of Richard II's badge on the boss of the hall porch raises the possibility that the king may have been personally associated with Huntingdon in the construction of his new residence. The insertion of a lord's shield on a building was quite common in the fourteenth century and occurs, for example, on John of Sutton's house at Lincoln where the arms of the duke of Lancaster are displayed on a gable.[12] But Richard's insignia was a more personal device than a coat of arms. Among the few surviving examples in stone are those on the string-course beneath the windows of Westminster Hall and the West Gate at Winchester, and that on the contemporary boss of the vaulted ceiling in the muniment tower of Winchester College.[13] Richard's badge was painted on the piers flanking Edward II's tomb in Gloucester Cathedral,[14] the wall of a chamber above the south transept of Westminster Abbey, and on the well-known Wilton Diptych probably painted between 1394 and 1399.[15] It also occurs on the garments of Richard's effigy in Westminster Abbey, ordered in 1395 and completed in 1399,[16] and on the canopy above his tomb. The white hart was similarly used as a decorative motif on the royal barge, banners, standards, and the walls and windows of several royal buildings which no longer exist.[17] The distribution of this device as a livery was Richard's own prerogative and he can be personally associated with all known examples. It occurs on the brass of Sir John Golafré, one of Richard's favourites, who died in 1396 and was buried in Westminster Abbey, and the presence of the royal badge at Dartington may be similarly indicative of Huntingdon's allegiance to the king. It is possible, however, that it signifies a more personal royal association with the Hall, and although no record of financial support or evidence of a royal visit to Dartington has yet come to light, Richard's pardon of Huntingdon's debts on at least two occasions during the building of the Hall deserved symbolic recognition.

What had been built for a member of the royal family in the late fourteenth century passed in the mid sixteenth century to a local landowning family. Sir Arthur Champernowne had no need for state rooms, galleries, or extensive lodgings and therefore his decision to make Dartington his home suggests that he was responsible for the alterations to the Hall in the second half of the sixteenth century. His known ability as an amateur architect strengthens this supposition. Part of the second court was pulled down and the remainder was left to stand as a ruin. He adapted several of the rooms in the south range to the greater comforts of the age, partly by altering and adding to the rooms of the upper residential block and partly by inserting new windows there and in the porch tower, the great hall,

[10] P.R.O. E 40/6964.

[11] *Cal. Pat. Rolls 1399–1401*, 241.

[12] J. W. F. Hill, *Medieval Lincoln* (1948), 168. Sutton held lands from Lancaster who was probably his patron.

[13] Richard took an active interest in Wykeham's foundations and endowed them with privileges in return for masses to be said for himself and Queen Anne. J. H. Harvey, 'The Wilton Diptych—A Re-examination', *Archaeologia*, vol. 98 (1961), 18 n. 1.

[14] Possibly added shortly after Richard's agreement with the abbot and convent in April 1391 to maintain lights and ornaments at the king's shrine. Ibid., 17 and n. 6.

[15] Ibid. which refers to all previous studies. See also M. V. Clarke, *Fourteenth Century Studies* (1937), 272–92.

[16] G. Scharf, *Description of the Wilton House Diptych* (1882), 43–5. J. H. Harvey, 'The Wilton Diptych—A Re-examination', *Archaeologia*, vol. 98 (1961), 8 n. 6.

[17] Ibid., 6–8.

and the lower residential block. An entry in the churchwardens' accounts of Ashburton in 1560–1, recording the payment of 13s. 8d. to several people labouring at Dartington with Sir Arthur, probably indicates the date of this work.[18] He also modified part of the west range of the north court to create a separate dwelling for farming purposes.

Changing tastes and the need for still greater comfort caused a later Arthur Champernowne to redesign some of the rooms during the second quarter of the eighteenth century. A new staircase was inserted in the upper residential block and part of the west range was altered to create a new suite of rooms on the first floor. No accounts have survived for this work, but Buck's engraving of the Hall in 1734 indicates that it had not taken place by that date, while Jeremiah Milles, dean of Exeter, noted in his description of Devon written in about 1755, that by laying two groups of chambers in the west range together, Mr. Champernowne had made them his best apartments.[19] It is probable that Arthur Champernowne's name and the date 1737 on the bell above the porch tower and his initials and the year 1741 on the weather-vane indicate when this work was carried out.

The alterations made by the Champernowne family in the nineteenth century were minimal. No doubt the lack of adequate funds to carry out the grandiose plans drawn up in 1805 and again in 1845 was not considered the blessing that it is now felt to have been. It was equally fortunate that the restoration of the Hall[20] between 1925 and 1938 was in the hands of an architect and patron who combined thoroughness with a rare spirit of sympathy for the original structure.

The Architectural Significance of the Hall

Dartington's claim to architectural significance is high. The reasons for this will become apparent as each part of the Hall is examined in turn, but it may be useful to summarize the more important considerations. Apart from the Bishop's Palace at Wells, Dartington Hall is the most important major example of medieval domestic architecture in the west of England. Cornwall has hardly any residences earlier than the Tudor period. Somerset and Dorset still retain considerable remains of several smaller medieval houses such as Clevedon Court, the Manor House at Meare, and Woodsford Castle, but their plan and design usually follows orthodox patterns which can be paralleled elsewhere. Several small fourteenth- and fifteenth-century houses of considerable charm and completeness survive in Devon, but only Dartington Hall can claim a plan and structure of more than regional interest.

Much of the present building, including the porch tower, great hall, lower residential block, and kitchen, are the distinguished remains of a late fourteenth-century mansion. Sufficient evidence survives for the plan and form of the contemporary upper residential block to be determined, while excavations have established the existence of a suite of apartments, grouped round a second court, which may be contemporary with this work. The form of an unusual series of lodgings flanking either side of the main courtyard may still be traced, and one group of lodgings in the west range survives in almost mint condition. The medieval entrance block and the eighteenth-century staircase hall include features of considerable local interest, while the restoration of the Hall in the twentieth century deserves appreciation in its own right as a major work of craftsmanship.

[18] J. H. Butcher, *The Parish of Ashburton in the Fifteenth and Sixteenth Centuries* (1870), 38.

[19] Bodleian Library, Oxford, MS. Top. Devon, c. 9, f. 72.

[20] The epithet 'Hall' is not very old. Reference was made in 1400 to the manor of Dartington, *Cal. Close Rolls 1399–1402*, 58, and in Henry VIII's reign, Leland refers to the building as a manor place. It was also described as a mansion and a castle in Henry's reign. *Letters and Papers: Foreign and Domestic, 1509–14*, 733 and *1538*, pt. 2, 292. The brothers Buck recorded in 1734 that the Hall was known as Dartington Temple but this was due to an erroneous association with the Order of Templars. The residence was more usually called Dartington House in the 18th century and it was still so called until at least 1860.

Dartington Hall is one of the very few non-defensive residences built during the reign of Richard II. The majority of castles and larger residences built between 1377 and 1399 were fortified structures, and although comfort played a far greater part in their planning than hitherto, defensive considerations were still an important factor in their design. The residences with which Dartington can most readily be compared are the contemporary educational foundations of Winchester College and New College, Oxford, and the royal apartments reconstructed during this period at Kenilworth and Portchester castles and the Palace of Westminster. Nevertheless, Dartington Hall is the only surviving example to show the plan and form adopted in a major non-defensive residence in the late

Aerial view of Dartington Hall

fourteenth century. Its construction by a half-brother of the king and its differences and affinities with contemporary castles and fortified houses adds to its value and interest, while the surviving remains also reflect the wealth and importance of its builder and the size of his household.

Finally, the Hall still survives in excellent condition—the centre of an extensive estate and a family home of warmth and charm. The administration of the estate is now carried out from a group of modern offices over a mile away, and part of the Hall is used for educational and artistic activities. Nevertheless, it is a living structure, neither a ruin nor a show-house, and preserves a continuity which has hardly been broken during the past six hundred years.

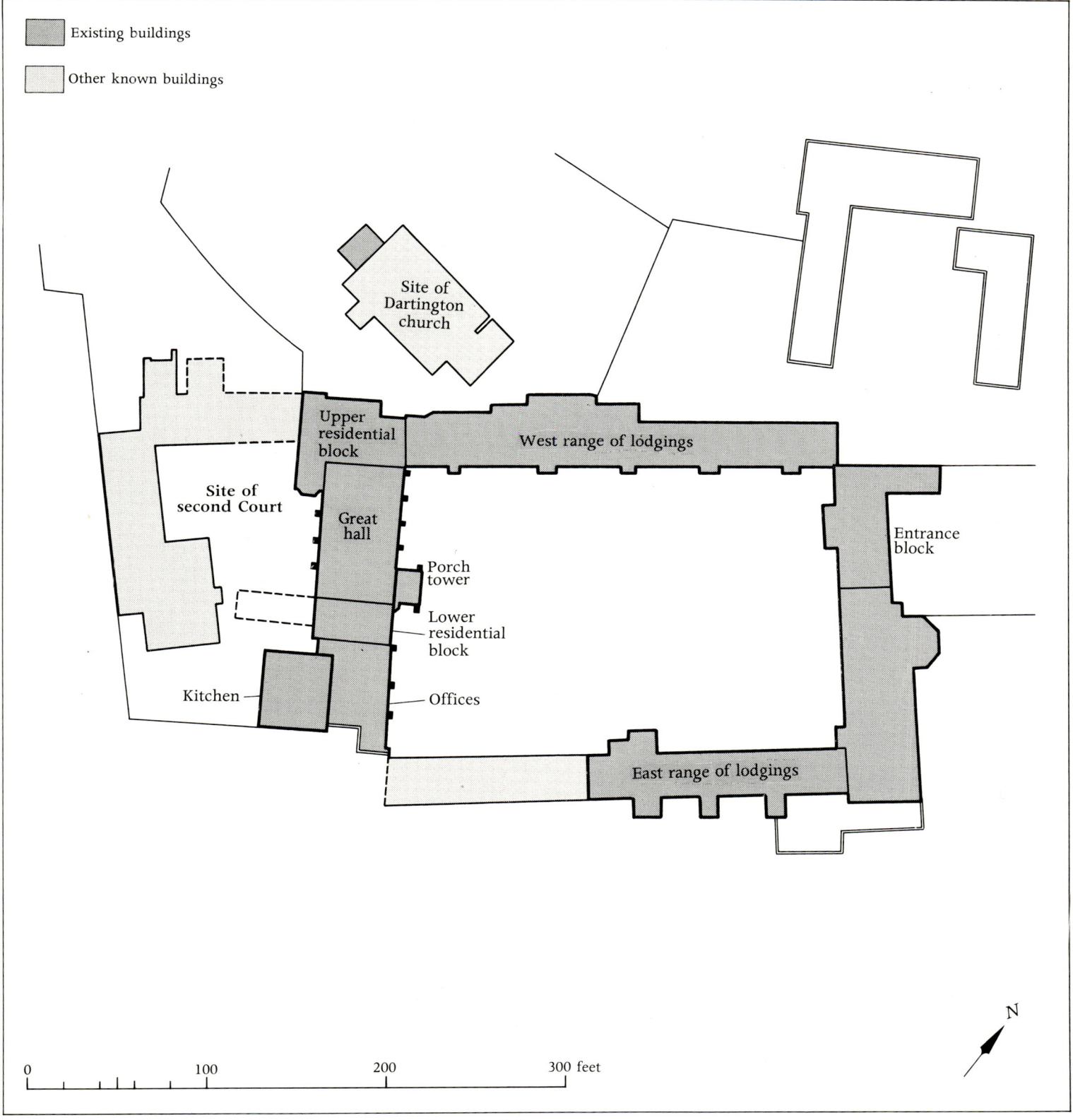

Fig. 11 Dartington Hall. General plan of existing and other known buildings

Fig.12 Major Residential Building Activity: 1377–99

Chapter 6

Major Residential Architecture during the Late Fourteenth Century

The architectural features and social implications of the original plan and design of Dartington Hall cannot be measured in isolation but need to be considered within the context of other comparable structures built at approximately the same time. This is not quite so easy as it sounds, for although it is not necessary to consider vernacular buildings, town dwellings, or the houses of minor landholders, the lack of precision in dating the majority of these buildings also applies to several larger and relatively more important residences. They are usually private rather than royal houses, partly because they have often been subject to several changes of ownership and lack a continuity of original documentation, and partly because private residences were usually built or altered by people lacking an enduring administrative organization like that within the royal household. The gap may be filled to some extent from four different sources—licences to crenellate, other documentary evidence, literary references, and heraldic devices—and it may be supplemented by dating based on the stylistic evidence of the existing remains.

Indiscriminate military building was checked from the thirteenth century onwards by the need to obtain the king's permission before a residence could be crenellated or embattled. Licences had to be sought for a minor fortified house as well as for a palace-fortress, and they were equally necessary for any defensive additions to an existing structure. The enrollment of these licences from about 1250 to 1530 provides an invaluable guide to the dating of many fortified residences and, incidentally, to the political climate of the time.[1] Licences to crenellate, however, must be treated with caution and particularly during the period under review. They were not, of course, needed for royal works, but members of the royal family were apparently exempted from any such restraint on their building activities by the late fourteenth century. Although the right to grant a licence within the county palatine of Durham lay with the bishop and not with the king, there is no record of one for the castle at Brancepeth, although it can be shown on other documentary evidence to have been constructed during the closing years of the century. Even more important are such obvious gaps as the absence of any licences for the new castles at Scotney and Wressell, and for the additions at Cockermouth, Warwick, and Saltwood which on other grounds can be firmly attributed to the last quarter of the century. The reasons for this capriciousness are not yet known. Verbal permission may have been sufficient in cases such as the work carried out by the archbishop of Canterbury at Saltwood Castle, and there is no doubt that the weakness of the monarchy to enforce its will and the strength of the baronage to dispense with royal permission explain why licences to crenellate became increasingly rare in the fifteenth century. Attempts were already being made in Richard II's reign to fortify sites without bothering to seek royal permission as at Farliegh Hungerford and *Ragley* castles.[2] Care must also be exercised in considering the date of these licences, for work would not only continue for several years after a licence

[1] All the licences in Richard II's reign were recorded in the Patent Rolls except for one included in the Charter Rolls in 1387. Most of them are conveniently listed in J. H. Parker, *Domestic Architecture of the Middle Ages*, vol. 3, pt. 2 (1859), 401–22. The inclusion of a residence on the map opposite to which no other reference is made in this chapter is based on the evidence of a licence to crenellate.

[2] *Cal. Pat. Rolls 1381–85*, 340, 64. It is clear that John Rous, the builder of *Ragley Castle*, feared little punishment for he repeated the practice 10 years later at *Stanley Pontlarge* in Gloucestershire. *Cal. Pat. Rolls 1391–96*, 46.

had been granted,[3] but the date of the grant is not necessarily indicative of the year when building began. A building contract for part of Bolton Castle was drawn up ten months before the licence to crenellate was granted. Moreover, the terms of the contract imply that it was a continuation of work already begun.[4]

Apart from the building activities mentioned in chronicles and other literary forms,[5] there are several other types of documentary evidence. The most precise are building contracts of which a number have survived giving details which can often be checked with existing remains.[6] Building accounts such as those from 1397 for New College, Oxford and founder's statutes as in the case of Winchester College are equally valuable. Only a little less precise are the records of official assistance for non-royal work, such as the licence granted to Lancaster's master mason at Kenilworth Castle in 1391 for the impressment of twenty men, or that granted to Gloucester in 1388 to cut down oaks for the repair of Caldicot Castle. Finally, there is the evidence of wills which sometimes refer to work under construction as at Amberley Castle in 1382 or include bequests for work to be carried out after death as occurred at Maidstone College after the death of Archbishop Courtenay in 1396.

Heraldic evidence must be treated with caution, but the insertion of coats of arms such as those at Saltwood and Howden helps to determine individual responsibility, and this may be delineated still further by the differencing or impaling of arms as at Raby and Cockermouth. Heraldic badges such as those at Warkworth and Dartington are also valuable evidence for limiting the years of building activity.

Finally, there is the evidence of architectural and stylistic forms. This is usually an imprecise and sometimes entirely conjectural basis for dating. It can be no more than an indication of a period of construction within fairly broad limits, ranging from a whole century to one or two decades. At best, dating based on such considerations must be treated with reservation until far more individual buildings have been analysed in detail and the results also measured against a series of regional studies.

This chapter is an attempt to summarize all known major residential building activity during the late fourteenth century in the absence of any comparable study. Consideration is given to some of the factors determining the planning and design of these residences and to their importance as a reflection of the social environment and standing of their owners. Only those buildings which can be accurately dated on documentary or other reliable grounds are included, with buildings no longer in existence printed in italics. The brevity of the text must necessarily make part of it read like a catalogue, but it is hoped that the illustrations will give an indication of the extent and richness of the surviving remains.

Building Activity

The absence of many magnates at war in France between about 1340 and 1360 and the high mortality caused by outbreaks of the plague in England from 1348 onwards, retarded but did not lead to the cessation of all building activity during the middle years of the century. The majority of military and domestic structures raised during this period, however, were built by the king rather than by his magnates and the onset of severe financial difficulties in about 1365, followed by the dotage of Edward III meant that no new royal

[3] It took more than 20 years, for example, to build the castles at Bolton and Sheriff Hutton.

[4] L. F. Salzman, *Building in England down to 1540* (1952), 454–6. Evidence that Cooling Castle was begun before the licence to crenellate was granted is discussed in *Arch. Cantiana*, vol. 2 (1859), 95–101, and ibid., vol. 11 (1877), 128–44. See also ibid., vol. 46 (1934), 52–6. The terms of the licence for Workington Hall also suggest that the house had already been built by the time that the licence was granted. *Cal. Pat. Rolls 1377–81*, 447.

[5] Thus the building works of Prior Chillenden of Canterbury (1391–1411) are listed in the monastery's chronicles. *Literae Cantuarienses*, ed. J. B. Sheppard, vol. 3 (1889), 119.

[6] Most contracts prior to the mid sixteenth century are printed by L. F. Salzman, *Building in England down to 1540* (1952), Appendix B.

projects were undertaken during the last twelve years of his reign. The recurrence of the plague in 1369, the renewal of war with France, a series of military disasters, and a crisis in government contributed to a severe slump in all building activity which was not reversed until about 1377 when political events in that and successive years, together with a period of economic recovery and prosperity, led to a revival and architectural flowering which continued until the close of the century. This age, coinciding with the reign of Richard II, was one of the great periods of building activity in medieval England. It covered nearly twenty-five years of intense patronage and industry, undertaken in the first full bloom of the Perpendicular style and particularly rich in comparison with the small amount of work undertaken in the years immediately preceding and those which followed the last quarter of the century.

1377–1388

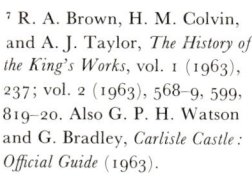
[7] R. A. Brown, H. M. Colvin, and A. J. Taylor, *The History of the King's Works*, vol. 1 (1963), 237; vol. 2 (1963), 568–9, 599, 819–20. Also G. P. H. Watson and G. Bradley, *Carlisle Castle: Official Guide* (1963).

The serious threat of invasion from both France and Scotland throughout Richard's minority, furthered by a succession of coastal raids and border attacks, was responsible for the castles and major additions to existing fortresses which make these years the last great era of military building in England. Although the king's advisers strengthened the northern castles at *Berwick* (1377–86), Carlisle (1378–83), and Roxburgh (1378–88),[7] the the defence of the border country was left almost entirely in the hands of the great northern

Sheriff Hutton Castle, Yorkshire. 1382–after 1402

Carlisle Castle, Cumberland. Outer gatehouse: 1378–83

Cockermouth Castle, Cumberland. Inner entrance range: 1383–5. Kitchen tower: *c.* 1388. Outer court: before 1408

Dunstanburgh Castle, Northumberland. Gatehouse of 1313–6 converted into keep: 1380–3

magnates whose rule there virtually replaced the king's writ. Lord Scrope built an entirely new palace-fortress at Bolton (c. 1378–99),[8] Lord Neville built a similar one at Sheriff Hutton (1382–after 1402),[9] and the earl of Northumberland built a compact tower-house at Warkworth (probably between c. 1377 and 1384).[10] Neville and Northumberland also made a series of major defensive and residential additions at Raby (1378–c. 90?)[11] and at Cockermouth (1383–before 1408)[12] respectively, while the duke of Lancaster strengthened the defences of his castle at Dunstanburgh (1380–3).[13] If the political uncertainty of the time made it necessary for the archbishop of York to obtain a licence to crenellate his essentially domestic residence at *Rest* (1383)[14] and to add several towers to his archiepiscopal residence at *Cawood* (between 1374 and 1388),[15] it is not surprising that smaller border landowners like John Fenwick at Fenwick in Northumberland (1378)[16] and Sir Gilbert Culwen at Workington were anxious to defend their property with at least a modest pele-tower (1380).[17]

The defences of the southern coast were reinforced from foreign attack by a combination of royal, municipal, and private effort. The king's advisers improved the defences at *Southampton* (1378–88) and Carisbrooke castles (1380–4),[18] the civic authorities strengthened the walls at Chichester and Rochester,[19] Archbishop Sudbury built a new town gate at his own expense at Canterbury (1380),[20] and Lord Cobham and Sir Edward Dalyngrigge

[8] L. F. Salzman, *Building in England down to 1540* (1952), 454–6, for the text of the building contract of September 1378. *Cal. Pat. Rolls 1377–81*, 369, for the licence to crenellate in 1379, and *Cal. Pat. Rolls 1396–99*, 489, for the licence to consecrate the chapel in 1399.

[9] *Cal. Pat. Rolls 1381–85*, 108. The four shields and garter above the entrance arch to the principal court indicate that the castle was not completed until after 1402.

[10] The construction of this tower-house used to be attributed to the first half of the 15th century, but an examination of the Percy accounts shows that no major building expenditure was incurred at Warkworth during that period. J. M. W. Bean, *The Estates of the Percy Family: 1416–1537* (1958), 105. As the Percy lion on the north front of the tower-house is not quartered with the Lucy arms, the structure may well have been built between about 1377 when Northumberland began to spend much of his time at Warkworth and 1384 when Northumberland agreed to quarter his family arms

Workington Hall, Cumberland.
Lower ground floor of pele-tower: 1380

Carisbrooke Castle, Isle of Wight.
Gatehouse of 1335–7 heightened in 1380–4

with the Lucy arms of his wife. Ibid., 8. It is likely that the rebuilding of the courtyard wall of the great hall with its terminal towers, the kitchen, and the collegiate church took place during the uneasy border peace at the close of the century and before Northumberland's participation in the rebellion of 1405.

[11] *Reports of the Deputy Keeper of the Public Records*, vol. 32 (1871), 292, for the licence to crenellate. The arms of Neville's wife indicate that the gatehouse named after him was built between 1382 and 1388. Neville died in 1388 and any work left unfinished at that time was presumably completed by his son.

[12] Northumberland acquired the property through marriage late in 1381. A contract was made in 1383 for completing the inner gateway and part of the flanking range by the end of 1385. J. H. Harvey, *English Mediaeval Architects* (1954), 26. The massive kitchen tower was built shortly afterwards to cope with the additional residential needs. The shields above the outer gatehouse indicate that the outer court and the lower part of the gatehouse were also built by Northumberland before his death in 1408.

[13] *John of Gaunt's Register: 1379–1383*, ed. E. C. Lodge and R. Somerville (1937), no. 922. Also L. F. Salzman, *Building in England down to 1540* (1952), 460–1, 463.

[14] *Cal. Pat. Rolls 1381–85*, 333.

[15] *Historians of the Church of York and its Archbishops*, ed. J. Raine, vol. 2 (1886), 425. Archbishop Neville held the see for 14 years before he was ousted from it.

[16] *Cal. Pat. Rolls 1377–81*, 290.

[17] Ibid., 447. The licence specifically refers to Workington's proximity to the Scottish border.

[18] R. A. Brown, H. M. Colvin, and A. J. Taylor, *The History of the King's Works*, vol. 2 (1963), 842–4, 593–5. The north-west angle of Cilgerran Castle, in the king's hands at the time, was also possibly subject to repairs in the late 1370s in anticipation of a French landing in Pembrokeshire. O. E. Craster, *Cilgerran Castle: Official Guide* (1957).

[19] *Cal. Pat. Rolls 1377–81*, 72, and *Cal. Pat. Rolls 1385–89*, 215. The royal castle at Rochester was also put into a state of repair at the same time. R. A. Brown, H. M. Colvin, and A. J. Taylor, *The History of the King's Works*, vol. 2 (1963), 813.

[20] *Cal. Pat. Rolls 1377–81*, 450, and *Cal. Pat. Rolls 1381–85*, 8.

Cooling Castle, Kent: 1381–c. 85

Amberley Castle, Sussex: 1377–c. 83

Halnaker House, Sussex. Entrance front: c. 1380

[21] *Cal. Pat. Rolls 1377–81*, 596. A plaque on the gatehouse specifically states that it was 'mad in help of the cuntre' and not for Cobham's personal aggrandizement. For the genuineness of this feature, see *Arch. Cantiana*, vol. 39 (1927), 176–80. Work proceeded rapidly during the national emergency. The east front and inner gatehouse were finished by July 1382, and the south gate of the outer ward by November 1382. Most of the castle had been completed by 1385. *Arch. Cantiana*, vol. 2 (1859), 98–9.

[22] *Cal. Pat. Rolls 1385–89*, 42. The licence for Bodiam Castle empowered Dalyngrigge to 'make a castle in defence of the adjacent countryside and for resistance against our enemies'. Work must have been completed with the utmost rapidity if the castle was to have any defensive value at all. This is supported by the uniformity of the plan and the architectural details.

Scotney Castle, Kent: c. 1378–80

Hever Castle, Kent. Gatehouse: 1383

[23] *Cal. Pat. Rolls 1377–81*, 76. Building was still in progress in August 1382 when Bishop Rede made his will. F. M. Powicke, *The Medieval Books of Merton College* (1931). 87.

[24] Architectural features such as the character of several four-centred arches, the moulding of the inner archway of the hall porch, and the design of the now destroyed hall windows indicate a late 14th-century date for both the defensive frontage and the great hall. Building probably occurred shortly after 1376 when Lord St. John inherited the property and French raids were making it necessary to defend Amberley and the city of Chichester only a few miles away. The defensive frontage firmly faces the sea for Halnaker was, if anything, even more vulnerable to attack than Amberley.

[25] This dating is partly based on the plan and existing architectural features such as the form of the machicolations, and partly on the political situation at the time and the ownership of the castle by a conservator of the peace for Kent and Sussex from about 1376 to 1380.

[26] *Cal. Pat. Rolls 1381–85*, 326.

[27] Courtenay sold the materials of Brochall, a house near Saltwood and other manor-houses in 1382, to defray the expense of his additions to the castle. Christopher Hussey, *Country Life* (4 December 1942). Courtenay's arms and those of the see of Canterbury which he held between 1381 and 1396 were inserted on either side of the entrance arch.

[28] *Cal. Pat. Rolls 1377–81*, 9, 10. There is no documentary or architectural evidence to prove that the bishop implemented any of these licences. He also obtained a licence for his house in *Fleet Street*, London.

[29] *Cal. Pat. Rolls 1377–81*, 377.

[30] Ibid., 491.

[31] *Cal. Close Rolls 1385–89*, 537–8.

[32] The house must have been substantially completed by 1392 when William Bonville was born there. Some of the rooms are listed in Sir William's will in 1408. F. C. Hingeston-Randolph, *Episcopal Registers of the Diocese of Exeter: Bishop Stafford* (1906), 390.

Shute Barton, Devon. Residential ranges: *c.* 1385–90

built entirely new castles at Cooling (1381–*c.* 85)[21] and Bodiam (1385–*c.* 90)[22] as part of the national scheme of defence. The series of French and Castilian raids during these early years of Richard's rule were also responsible for the defensive character of several residences in Sussex and Kent including those of the bishop of Chichester at Amberley (1377–*c.* 83),[23] Lord St. John at Halnaker House (probably *c.* 1380),[24] Roger Ashburnham at Scotney (*c.* 1378–80),[25] and the gatehouses built by Sir John Cobham at Hever (1383)[26] and Archbishop Courtenay at Saltwood Castle (probably *c.* 1382).[27] Further westward, the bishop of Salisbury took the precaution of renewing the licences for *nine* of his manors (1377) which his predecessor had obtained nearly forty years beforehand,[28] while the bishop of Exeter sought protection for his country house at *Chudleigh* (1379)[29] and Sir John Chideok renewed the ten year old licence for his Dorset manor at *Chideok* (1380).[30] Nothing gives a better idea of the fear of invasion which gripped the country during the early years of Richard II's reign, rising at times almost to panic, than this crop of licences to crenellate. Nor did the fear abate quickly. In 1388 the townspeople at Dartmouth were building a small fortress to protect their property from seaborne attack,[31] and Sir William Bonville was providing some measure of protection for his essentially domestic house at Shute Barton at about the same time (probably *c.* 1385–90).[32]

Not all castles built during Richard's minority were intended to defend the country from

Lumley Castle, Co. Durham. 1389–c. 92

invasion or to protect their inhabitants from coastal raids. Several residences were designed principally to minister to the pride of a rising family with the outward trappings of defence added only for appearances' sake. Two such examples are Shirburn Castle built by Lord Lisle in 1377[33] and that at Farleigh Hungerford built by Sir Thomas Hungerford between about 1370 and 1383.[34] Nor were such motives far from the thoughts of the earl of Suffolk who began Wingfield Castle in the same year that he received his earldom (1385),[35] or those of Sir Thomas Percy whose castle at Wressell (probably c. 1380–90)[36] emulated the richness of his brother's residence at Warkworth. Similarly, Sir William Asthorp and his wife, isolated in the hills of east Devon, built a new residence at Hemyock (1380),[37] while Sir Richard Abberbury added a commanding gatehouse to his modest and slightly earlier castle at Donnington (1386).[38]

Domestic building was not entirely unknown during these turbulent years. The earl of Arundel seems to have rebuilt the great hall at *Arundel Castle* shortly after entering into his wealthy inheritance in 1376,[39] while the duke of Lancaster raised a chapel and a group of domestic buildings within *Hertford Castle* (1380)[40] and added some rooms to his Yorkshire manor at *Cowick* (1381).[41] A local Cheshire landowner, John Leicester, built a timber-framed hall at Tabley (c. 1380),[42] John, Lord Neville added a hall with flanking domestic ranges at Bamburgh Castle between 1384 and 1387,[43] and the militant bishop of Norwich

[33] *Cal. Pat. Rolls 1374–77*, 434. It was begun 3 months before Richard's accession.

[34] Hungerford purchased the manor in 1369–70. The castle was completed by 1383 when he was pardoned for fortifying the site without royal permission. *Cal. Pat. Rolls 1381–85*, 340. See also *Wilts. Arch. and Nat. Hist. Mag.* vol. 106 (1956), 272–303, for an undated request for a licence to enclose with a wall of stone and lime, embattle and enfoss without fines or fees. The application was presumably made after the pardon of 1383.

[35] *Cal. Pat. Rolls 1381–85*, 555. Work must have proceeded apace, for although Suffolk was imprisoned for much of 1386 and had to flee the country at the end of 1387, the gatehouse bears the arms of the earl and his wife and not those of his son. Suffolk also fortified two other manors in the same county, built a house in London, and four brick houses in Hull, three of them with brick towers. W. Dugdale, *Monasticon Anglicanum*, vol. 6, pt. 1 (ed. 1846), 20–1.

[36] The dating is based principally on architectural grounds, although it is supported by Leland's statement that the castle was built in Richard II's reign. *Itinerary*, ed. L. T. Smith, vol. 1 (1907), 53. The castle was certainly in existence by 1403 when Percy forfeited it after the battle of Shrewsbury. *Cal. Pat. Rolls 1401–05*, 247.

[37] *Cal. Pat. Rolls 1377–81*, 552.

[38] *Cal. Pat. Rolls 1385–89*, 156.

[39] J. Dallaway, *A History of the Western Division . . . of Sussex*, vol. 2 (1819), 100; M. A. Tierney, *The History and Antiquities . . . of Arundel*, vol. 1 (1834), 51–2.

[40] L. F. Salzman, *Building in England down to 1540* (1952), 459–60. It is possible that some of Lancaster's work may be traced in a 16th-century plan reproduced in A. W. Clapham and W. H. Godfrey, *Some Famous Buildings and Their Story* (1913), 141–5.

[41] *John of Gaunt's Register: 1379–1383*, ed. E. C. Lodge and R. Somerville (1937), nos. 598, 599.

[42] Although the antiquarian Sir Peter Leicester states in his *Historic Antiquities of Cheshire* (1673), that the hall was built in about 1380 and also refers to the licence for an oratory granted by the bishop of Lichfield in 1387, ed. G. Ormerod, vol. 1 (1819), 456–60, I have been unable to trace Leicester's reference of *c.* 1380 to 'illud messuagium vocatum le New Hall de Tabley' quoted by Christopher Hussey, *Country Life* (July 1923).

Tabley Old Hall, Cheshire. Main truss of great hall: *c.* 1380. Taken in 1923

Tabley Old Hall, Cheshire. Taken in 1968

[43] R. A. Brown, H. M. Colvin, and A. J. Taylor, *The History of the King's Works*, vol. 2 (1963), 557; L. F. Salzman, *Building in England down to 1540* (1952), 465–6.

[44] *Cal. Pat. Rolls 1385–89*, 381.

[45] The house is dated entirely on architectural grounds, but it is quite likely that building began shortly after Gawen had purchased the manor. I owe this evidence of ownership to Norman Drinkwater.

[46] But uncertainty about the outcome of the negotiations with France is possibly reflected in the repair and strengthening of the walls and gates at Winchester shortly after 1390. *Cal. Pat. Rolls 1388–92*, 237 and *Trans. Hampshire Field Club and Archaeol. Soc.* vol. 16 (1944), 56–8.

[47] *Reports of the Deputy Keeper of the Public Records*, vol. 33 (1872), 71, for the licence granted by Bishop Skirlaw of Durham. It was confirmed by Richard II 3 years later, possibly when work was reaching embattlement stage. *Cal. Pat. Rolls 1391–96*, 188.

[48] The northern master mason, John Lewyn, was working for Neville near Brancepeth in 1391. *Reports of the Deputy Keeper of the Public Records*, vol. 33 (1872), 74. Part of the castle had certainly been completed by September 1398 when the walls of the Constable Tower were to be the model for the dormitory of Durham Priory. L. F. Salzman, *Building in England down to 1540* (1952), 473–5.

[49] *Cal. Pat. Rolls 1396–99*, 66, 524. The severely defensive gatehouse at Tynemouth Priory, built by the prior with the help of Richard II and Lancaster during the last years of the century, is another secular work designed as a border defence against Scottish raids. R. N. Hadcock, *Tynemouth Priory and Castle: Official Guide* (1952).

Shirburn Castle, Oxfordshire: 1377

North Elmham Saxon Cathedral, Norfolk. Residential conversion: 1387

built a new residence at North Elmham within the foundations of a late Saxon cathedral (1387).[44] Yet the only surviving domestic work of any significance attributable to this period is the modest but attractive remains of the manor-house at Norrington in Wiltshire, almost certainly built by John Gawen, a member of a local landowning family, after he had purchased this property in 1377.[45]

1388–1399

The desultory war between England and France which had been prosecuted vigorously and sluggishly in turn since about 1340, gradually petered out for want of enthusiasm or coherent direction on either side. With the signing of a three years' truce in 1389 and its prolongation for twenty-seven years in 1396, fear of French attack abated and was gradually replaced by a note of friendliness between the two nations. No castle was begun in the south of England during the last eleven years of the century[46] and work was started on only two palace-fortresses in the north of England, Lumley Castle, reconstructed by Lord Lumley between 1389 and about 1392[47] and Brancepeth Castle, built by Lord Neville's son, the earl of Westmorland from about 1391 to 1398.[48] The fortlet built at Penrith in 1397 by William Strickland, later bishop of Carlisle, was conceived entirely as a local defence against Scottish border raids.[49] The only other major defensive structure raised during the last years of Richard's reign was Guy's Tower at Warwick Castle (1394), completing an

111

entrance frontage begun more than thirty years beforehand, and undertaken not through fear of foreign attack but because of the earl of Warwick's absence from court after 1389 and his temporary retirement from the political fray.[50]

One of the consequences arising from the dotage of Edward III and the minority of his grandson was that the royal lead in building projects passed from the Crown to the duke of Lancaster whose sumptuous programme of defensive and residential works had been in progress since the early 1370s. Other members of the royal family also undertook important works. Nothing now remains at *Fotheringhay Castle* rebuilt by Lancaster's younger brother, the duke of York,[51] but the residential gatehouse and postern tower built by his other brother, the duke of Gloucester, at Caldicot Castle still survive (*c*. 1388)[52] as does much of the large and entirely non-defensive mansion begun by his nephew at Dartington in 1388. Lancaster's own work reached its apogee immediately after his return from Spain with the reconstruction of the great hall and domestic suite at Kenilworth Castle between 1389 and 1393.[53] By then, Richard had taken over the royal lead in building activity. His earliest work was modest enough—the construction of a timber-framed retiring house for himself and his wife at *Sheen* (1384–8).[54] Minor residential alterations and additions were carried out during his reign at *Eltham Palace* and *King's Langley*,[55] and later at the royal manor-house in *Windsor Park* (1394–7).[56] Nothing remains of these works or of the new house he began at *Sutton* near Chiswick (1396–9),[57] but his modifications to the great hall at Winchester Castle may still be traced (1394–5)[58] and his reconstruction of the great hall at the Palace of Westminster between 1394 and 1401[59] is one of the outstanding achievements of the Gothic world. At the same time, Richard reconstructed the great hall, offices, and state apartments at Portchester Castle (1396–9),[60] and although candles were used at night so that the work could be completed as quickly as possible, it is unlikely that Richard's eagerness to use his new apartments was ever satisfied.

It was only to be expected that others would emulate this large-scale display of royal activity. The archbishop of Canterbury added an audience hall and chapel at Saltwood Castle and he may have rebuilt the great hall of his palace at Croydon.[61] The bishop of Winchester improved the amenities at Wolvesey Palace, Winchester, and largely rebuilt his favourite manor at *Highclere* (*c*. 1387–94).[62] The bishop of Durham built a large manor-house at Howden in Yorkshire during the closing years of the century,[63] while a new hall and residential block were raised by the constable at the royal castle of Scarborough (1396–1400).[64] But despite the state of greater prosperity during the last decade of the century, few magnates or knights were anxious to follow the royal example or were willing to put their trust in the more peaceful conditions of Richard's personal rule. Sir John Devereux strengthened the defences of his manor at Penshurst in 1392,[65] and Lord Lovel built a fortified house of highly unusual design at Wardour in the following year.[66] Sir Hugh Cheyne crenellated his Shropshire border residence at Cheyney Longville in 1394,[67] Sir Thomas Brook built a defensive house at Holditch in 1397,[68] and Sir William Bagot probably raised his fortlet at Baginton, near Coventry at about this time.[69] The insecurity of the last two years of Richard's rule was also reflected in the request from the abbot of Chester in 1399 for permission to embattle *three* of his Cheshire manors,[70] for fear of political tyranny was heightened in this county by memories of a local rising a few years earlier and the

[50] W. Dugdale, *Antiquities of Warwickshire* (1656), 322a, 342b. See also p. 136, n. 155.

[51] Leland, *Itinerary*, ed. L. T. Smith, vol. 4 (1907), 91–2; *V.C.H. Northamptonshire*, vol. 2 (1906), 573–4. The precise years when this work was carried out are not known.

[52] The gatehouse and postern tower are associated on architectural grounds. Their ascription to Gloucester and his wife is based on two rare foundation-stones inscribed 'Thomas' and 'Alianore' found at the foot of the entrance to the postern tower and in the foundations of an adjacent free-standing structure respectively. Thomas, duke of Gloucester, married Eleanor de Bohun in 1376. Work was in progress in 1388 when he was granted permission to cut down 100 oak trees to help repair the castle. The timber would have been necessary for scaffolding, floors, and roofs. *Cal. Pat. Rolls 1385–89*, 511.

[53] Masons were being impressed for this work in 1391. *Cal. Pat. Rolls 1388–92*, 449. See also J. H. Harvey, 'Side Lights on Kenilworth Castle', *Arch. Jour.* vol. 101 (1944), 91–107.

[54] R. A. Brown, H. M. Colvin, and A. J. Taylor, *The History of the King's Works*, vol. 1 (1963), 245; vol. 2 (1963), 997–8.

[55] Ibid., vol. 2 (1963), 934–5, 975–6.

[56] Ibid., 1008.

[57] Ibid., 1003–4. Maintenance work was also carried out at several royal castles during Richard's reign. A new tower was added at Corfe (1377–9), the keep at *Gloucester* was repaired and several turrets added (1377–89), a wall was built at *Tintagel* (1385–6), and minor repairs and additions were carried out at *Wallingford* (1389–90 and 1398–9) and the *Tower of London* (*c*. 1384 and 1396–9). Ibid., 623, 656, 846, 851, 728.

[58] Ibid., 863–4. M. Portal, *The Great Hall of Winchester Castle* (1899), 57–9.

[59] R. A. Brown, H. M. Colvin, and A. J. Taylor, *The History of the King's Works*, vol. 1 (1963), 527–33. The outer gateway to the Palace, built by Richard between 1397 and 1399, has not survived. Ibid., 548.

[60] Ibid., vol. 2 (1963), 790–4.

[61] The residential work at Saltwood cannot be dated precisely but it was probably initiated by Courtenay (1381–96) who made the castle his principal residence. See also p. 109, note 27. As the chapel was consecrated by

his successor in 1401, the work was possibly begun late in Courtenay's life or by Archbishop Arundel. Only the porch remains at Croydon, and although it is usually attributed to Courtenay on stylistic grounds, the Lambeth Court and Account Rolls record extensive building work at Croydon by his successor during the last year of the century.

[62] *Med. Archaeol.*, vol. 11 (1967), 282. The bishop's accounts show that Wykeham built a new hall, great chamber, and chapel at Highclere. J. H. Harvey, *English Mediaeval Architects* (1954), 129, 248, 309; M. Girouard, *Country Life* (June 1959).

[63] Bishop Skirlaw who held the see of Durham between 1388 and 1405 is identified as the builder 'of the whole hall' by William de Chambre, *Historiae Dunelmensis Scriptores Tres*, ed. J. Raine (1839), 144. His arms also survive on the central boss of the hall porch and above its embattled parapet.

[64] *Cal. Pat. Rolls 1391–96*, 710.

[65] Ibid., 164.

[66] Ibid., 261.

[67] Ibid., 500.

[68] *Cal. Pat. Rolls 1396–99*, 85.

[69] The castle was excavated in the 1930s and firmly dated on architectural grounds to the late 14th century when it was owned by Sir William Bagot. William of Worcester's statement in about 1480 that Bagot built the fortalice does not seem to have been known to the excavators. *Itinerarium*, ed. J. Nasmith (1778), 352. The structure was probably built in the early 1390s after Bagot's royal friendship and financial standing had blossomed. The castle was certainly in existence in 1398 when Bolingbroke stayed there prior to his famous tournament with Norfolk at Coventry.

[70] *Cal. Pat. Rolls 1396–99*, 552. There is no work of this period at *Saighton* nor at *Sutton* and the evidence at *Ince* is in doubt. G. M. R. Davies who has examined the remains at Ince for me states that they are an architectural hotch-potch. Two ranges survive of a moated enclosure. One, converted into cottages after the Dissolution, contains Early English elements. The other, possibly the hall and now used as a barn, is Perpendicular work. Photographs taken by Mr. Davies suggest that it dates from the 15th rather than the late 14th century. The licence was renewed in 1410. I owe this communication to D. F. Petch of the Grosvenor Museum, Chester. See also *Jour. Arch., Archaeol. and Hist. Soc. of Chester and N. Wales*, vol. 16 (1909), 36–7.

Caldicot Castle, Monmouthshire. Gatehouse: *c.* 1388

Warwick Castle. Guy's Tower: 1394

Palace of Westminster. Great Hall: 1394–1401

Kenilworth Castle, Warwickshire. Great hall: 1389–93

Scarborough Castle, Yorkshire.
Hall and residential block: 1396–1400

Penshurst Place, Kent. Mid fourteenth-century manor with one of the additional towers: 1392

Carisbrooke Castle, Isle of Wight.
Upper residential block: 1385–97

New College, Oxford. Great quadrangle: 1380–6

implications of the extensive recruitment of local yeomen and archers in the king's service. Only the earl of Salisbury concerned himself with purely domestic building activities, and even the residential block and improvements he made to the great hall at Carisbrooke Castle between 1385 and 1397 were within the confines of a strongly defended fortress.[71]

Finally, two major residential buildings were under construction throughout the last twenty years of the century, regardless of the political troubles and conditions of the time. William of Wykeham's colleges at Oxford and Winchester, founded in 1379[72] and 1382[73]

[71] Richard II appointed Salisbury constable of the castle in 1382 and granted him the residence for life 3 years later. He died in 1397. Salisbury's work is marked by his arms on the south-west buttress of the residential apartments at the upper end of the hall and by those of his wife, formerly upon the fireplace in the great hall. Hardly any abbot or prior altered or improved his residential accommodation during the last quarter of the 14th century except the abbot of Wigmore, Herefordshire, whose lodgings date from this period.

[72] Quadrangle, hall, kitchen, and chapel 1380–6; cloisters 1390–1400; bell tower 1396–8; warden's barn c. 1402. V.C.H. Oxfordshire, vol. 3 (1954), 144–62. A. H. Smith, New College Oxford and its

Buildings (1952). No other contemporary collegiate work survives at Oxford. The most important project, apart from the building of New College, was the construction of the hall, kitchen, chapel, and library at *The Queen's College* between 1372 and 1402. These buildings were demolished in the early eighteenth century. Other destroyed work includes the library of *Exeter College* (1383), the chapel at *University College* (1399), and the new halls and chapels at *Balliol College* (1386–7) and *Canterbury College* (1394–6). Contemporary collegiate work at Cambridge was on a smaller scale. The quadrangle of Pembroke College, probably begun in about 1351 and completed by about 1398, survives in part. Half of the west range of King's Hostel, begun in 1375 and containing the master's *camera* still exists, but the hall and kitchen (1386–90) were pulled down in the 16th century when the hostel was incorporated in Trinity College. *R.C.H.M. City of Oxford* (1939); E. A. Gee, 'Oxford Masons: 1370–1530', *Arch. Jour.* vol. 109 (1952), 54–131; *V.C.H. Oxfordshire*, vol. 3 (1954); R. Willis and J. W. Clarke, *The Architectural History of the University of Cambridge* (1886); *R.C.H.M. City of Cambridge* (1959).

[73] Chamber court, hall, and chapel 1387–94; cloisters 1395; outer court and exchequer tower 1394–1401; stables 1400–1. J. H. Harvey, 'Winchester College', *Jour. Brit. Archaeol. Assoc.* vol. 28 (1965), 107–28.

[74] *Cal. Pat. Rolls 1391–96*, 658.

[75] The college was founded by the duke of Lancaster, his wife, and Bishop Houghton in 1365 according to letters patent of 1382 confirmed in 1400. *Cal. Pat. Rolls 1399–1401*, 310. It seems that it was some years before the foundation was established, for the statutes governing the college were not drawn up until 1372, W. Dugdale, *Monasticon Anglicanum*, vol. 6, pt. 3 (ed. 1846), 1390, and the first master was not appointed until about 1387, Edward Yardley, *Menevia Sacra*, ed. F. Green (1927). W. B. Jones and E. A. Freeman stated without reference that the college was founded in 1377, *The History and Antiquities of St. David's* (1856), 179, and all subsequent writers have attributed the present remains to that year. It is more likely that building was taking place in 1384 when extensive building operations were in progress which cannot be matched with any work in the cathedral, and that the college was ready for occupation by 1387. Chapter accounts in ibid., Appendix 4.

[76] *Cal. Pat. Rolls 1377–81*, 494.

[77] *Cal. Pat. Rolls 1391–96*, 363.

Winchester College, Hampshire. Middle gate from Chamber Court: 1387–94

by the leading political prelate of the age, are important for their planning and influence on collegiate design as well as for the breadth of their founder's conception of school and university education. Archbishop Courtenay established a college for priests at Maidstone in 1395,[74] and although Lancaster, Arundel, and Gloucester founded similar but smaller foundations at St. David's (1365),[75] Arundel (1380),[76] and *Pleshey* (1394),[77] it was the bishop of Winchester's twin educational foundations which particularly added lustre to the last quarter of the century.

Sources of Income and Expenditure

An analysis of the Receipt and Issue Rolls of Richard II has enabled a reasonably accurate estimation to be made of his annual income and expenditure.[78] The cost of several royal building projects has also been estimated with some fidelity.[79] But how did the magnates finance the building of their castles and palace-fortresses, and what measure of expenditure did they incur? Little research has been carried out so far into either of these aspects of economic history, with the exception of one or two studies of lay inheritances[80] and the private accounts of two or three later castles.[81] These questions can therefore only be answered in the broadest terms until far more research has been undertaken.

Of surviving military works, it is known that the outer gatehouse at Carlisle Castle was budgeted to cost the king £333. 6s. 8d.,[82] and that the earl of Warwick spent £395. 5s. 2d. on building Guy's Tower at Warwick Castle.[83] In 1378, John Lewyn received a fee from Lord Scrope of £33. 6s. 8d. for his work at Bolton Castle and he was paid at the rate of £5 for every length of masonry 20 feet long and 3 or 4 feet thick.[84] According to Leland, Scrope spent £666. 13s. 4d. each year for eighteen years on Bolton Castle, a total of £12,006.[85] If this figure has any validity, a further amount should be added for the work which is known to have been carried out during a further three years or more. Even then, if Edward III's expenditure of about £20,000 on *Queenborough Castle* is any guide,[86] the amount is still an underestimation of the total cost of the project. As for some domestic work, it has been estimated that Richard II spent just over £1,700 on rebuilding the residential apartments at Portchester Castle, while his reconstruction of Westminster Hall cost between £8,000 and £9,000.[87] Although it is difficult to translate these figures into modern money terms,[88] they give some indication that buildings for which no accounts are known such as Raby, Sheriff Hutton, Wardour, Lumley, and Dartington almost certainly stretched the financial resources of their owners, particularly since they were deliberate displays of magnificence, wealth, and position.

Comparatively few residences in the late fourteenth century were financed solely from what, in the previous century, had been the most important source of wealth—the profits of land-ownership. Such a source certainly paid for the additions at Warwick Castle made by an earl whose inheritance was spread over eighteen counties. It was also responsible for the alterations carried out at *Arundel Castle* by an owner whose father is reputed to have held a stock of about £67,000 in cash at the time of his death in 1375.[89] Yet the profits from land were far less likely to finance a long-cherished building project than the rewards from service to the Crown. The gatehouse at Donnington Castle, for instance, was built by Abberbury after nine year's service in the royal household, first as a guardian of the young king and then as chamberlain to his queen. Bolton Castle was built on the rewards of law and the offices of steward of the royal household, treasurer and chancellor of England, while the additions at Penshurst were financed from the profits of diplomacy and that same office of stewardship. Nor were such rewards limited to the Crown, for the merchant of Salisbury who became steward of Lancaster's southern estates purchased several manors including Farleigh Hungerford to herald his arrival as a man of property.[90]

The rewards from local administration were smaller but frequently more secure than those

[78] A. B. Steel, *The Receipt of the Exchequer: 1377–1485* (1954).

[79] R. A. Brown, H. M. Colvin, and A. J. Taylor, *The History of the King's Works*, vols. 1 and 2 (1963).

[80] R. Somerville, *The History of the Duchy of Lancaster* (1953). G. A. Holmes, *The Estates of the Higher Nobility in Fourteenth-Century England* (1957).

[81] H. D. Barnes and W. D. Simpson, 'The Building Accounts of Caister Castle, 1432–35', *Norfolk Archaeol.* vol. 30 (1951), 178–88. A. Hamilton Thompson and Sir Charles Peers, 'The Building Accounts of Kirby Muxloe Castle', *Trans. Leic. Arch. Soc.* vol. 11 (1915–16), 193–345. *The Building Accounts of Tattershall Castle: 1434–1472*, ed. W. Douglas Simpson (1960).

[82] L. F. Salzman, *Building in England down to 1540* (1952), 456.

[83] W. Dugdale, *Antiquities of Warwickshire* (1656), 342b.

[84] L. F. Salzman, *Building in England down to 1540* (1952), 454–5. Two years later, Lancaster paid Lewyn £6. 13s. 4d. for every perch of walling at Dunstanburgh 20 feet high and 4 feet thick. Ibid., 460.

[85] Leland, *Itinerary*, ed. L. T. Smith, vol. 5 (1907), 139.

[86] The building of *Queenborough Castle* and town between 1361 and 1377 cost Edward III about £25,000 of which about £20,000 is likely to have been spent on the castle. The inner court, the major part of the castle with its residential apartments and some defences, cost £14,621. R. A. Brown, H. M. Colvin, and A. J. Taylor, *The History of the King's Works*, vol. 2 (1963), 793–803.

[87] Ibid., vol. 2 (1968), 790; vol. 1 (1963), 533.

[88] Apart from the fact that modern money values are continually changing, the same multiplication factor does not apply to every commodity price.

[89] G. A. Holmes, *The Estates of the Higher Nobility in Fourteenth-Century England* (1957), 5. Both the Arundel and Warwick estates had been enlarged substantially during the previous 50 years. The acquisition of the Warenne inheritance in 1347 had nearly doubled the size of the Arundel holding, and the Warwick inheritance had been increased by the arbitrary acquisition of the Gower lordship in 1353.

for royal service. Cheyney Longville and Holditch, as well as at least six other residences were erected by justices of the peace, an office which had grown considerably in power since the mid fourteenth century. Hemyock and Fenwick were raised by sheriffs, Halnaker and *Chideok* by commissioners of array, and Scotney by a conservator of the peace.

The profits of war were inevitably less substantial during Richard's reign than that of his grandfather, but the castles at Cooling and Bodiam were built by successful veterans of Edward III's campaigns. Dalyngrigge honoured his chief, Sir Robert Knollys, at Bodiam by raising his shield and crest high above the postern gate, and Lord Lovel, probably Richard's most able commander, built Wardour Castle on a plan not unlike the duc de Berry's contemporary castle at Concressault in central France.

Dartington Hall could not have been built without royal support, while Sheriff Hutton, Brancepeth, and the additions at Raby and Bamburgh blazoned the rise of the Neville family through royal favour. It has been suggested that the work at Sheriff Hutton and Raby might have been financed by Lord Neville with the proceeds obtained through taking up the claims of Crown creditors at discount and obtaining payment for himself in full.[91] Yet this group of palace-fortresses stemmed from Richard's deliberate elevation of the Neville family as a counterbalance to the growing strength of the neighbouring Percy family. Since the middle of the century, the Percies had been extending their activities beyond border raids and petty feuds, and they had taken advantage of the lack of royal strength in the north to build up their power in becoming a bulwark against the Scots. The earl of Northumberland's financial and military skill, matched by his diplomatic and administrative abilities, was fittingly symbolized by the carefully planned and imposing tower-house at Warkworth Castle.[92]

The additions at Kenilworth and Caldicot were the fruits of successful marriages with the Lancaster and Bohun heiresses. Wingfield was based on a mercantile fortune, furthered by de la Pole's marriage with a Suffolk heiress and the acquisition of the estates of the extinct Ufford family in 1382. Ecclesiastical moneys might also richly supplement slender family resources. The Courtenay barony was probably the least powerful or well endowed in the late fourteenth century, but once the eldest son had been appointed an archbishop, he could afford to enlarge properties at Saltwood and possibly at Croydon. William of Wykeham similarly used the wealthiest bishopric in England, as well as the profits of office acquired during his meteoric rise to power, to fulfil his extensive architectural ambitions.

Planning Factors

The planning of residential accommodation in a series of ranges round a quadrangle was the basis of military, major domestic, and collegiate design during the later Middle Ages.[93] This form stemmed from the discipline imposed on defensive buildings in the late thirteenth century and accorded with the need for more private rooms, following the rise in the standards of living and the development of ranks and position during the fourteenth century. Growing prosperity and the increased availability of money undoubtedly encouraged the development and design of many new building projects during Richard II's reign, and an age which revelled in colour, fine fabrics, and the new fashion of tapestries also demanded well-lit rooms in which they could be displayed.

---

[90] The rise of this family continued unimpaired under the guidance of Sir William Hungerford's son and grandson. Administrative skill and successful marriages brought the total holding of this family to over 100 manors by the mid 15th century.

[91] Sir James Ramsey, *Genesis of Lancaster*, vol. 2 (1913), 53.

[92] Northumberland's political and financial position was furthered by his second marriage to an heiress with considerable estates in Cumberland including the castle and honour of Cockermouth. Furthermore, his brother's castle at Wressell acted as a keystone to the Percy encirclement of the Neville estates.

[93] Descriptive literature is extensive but extremely varied in quality. The most recent general survey is Joan Evans, *English Art: 1307–1461* (1949). For houses, see J. Hudson Turner and J. H. Parker, *Domestic Architecture of the Middle Ages*, vol. 2 (1853) and vol. 3 (1859), and Margaret Wood, *The English Mediaeval House* (1965), which includes a comprehensive bibliography. For castles and defensive works, A. Hamilton Thompson, *Military Architecture in England during the Middle Ages* (1912); S. Toy, *The Castles of Great Britain* (1953); R. A. Brown, *English Medieval Castles* (1954), and B. H. St. J. O'Neil, *Castles and Cannon* (1960). Apart from the individual works listed hereafter, see also the series of county guides by Nikolaus Pevsner (1951 onwards) for individual descriptions.

Shorn of the presence of the owner, there was little to distinguish a royal from a baronial residence, either by its size or its standards. The prestige of a magnate depended to a considerable extent on the size of his household and the numbers of his retinue as well as on the lavishness of his hospitality and the magnificence of his table. A magnate, like the king, had to provide accommodation for his family, personal retinue, household officials, chaplains, ladies-in-waiting, pages, and the administrators of his properties and estates.[94] In many cases, his household was a minor version of the royal court, although there was nothing provincial or small, for instance, about the courts of Lancaster or his son. And just as the king had more than two or three residences, so did the magnates who similarly frequented, altered, and favoured them in turn. The additions made by Northumberland and Neville transformed four minor castles into princely residences, while Neville created a further one on an entirely new site. Lancaster was responsible for major additions at twice that number of seats.[95] Suffolk sought permission to crenellate not one but three houses only a few miles from each other in 1385, while the bishop of Salisbury sought to embattle nine manors on his estates at the same time just a few years earlier. Not surprisingly, a social pattern which dictated and permeated the classes below, similarly affected the planning of their houses. Farleigh Hungerford and Bodiam gave no quarter in scale or comfort to Wingfield or Brancepeth. The social distinction between the residence of a knight and those of an earl tended to be in their number rather than in their standards or size. Even a local landowner like John Gawen could build a hall with flanking residential blocks just as Huntingdon did on a larger scale at Dartington. Finally, major residences were often designed by masons with extensive practices,[96] and built by a labour force drawn from many parts of the country. They tended therefore to follow common patterns of planning and design which might be affected by regional factors but which were rarely subject to local influences.

The great hall continued to be the social and domestic focus of both fortified and non-fortified residences. It was frequently warmed by large wall fireplaces, and the development of roof design—the one major constructional development of the later Middle Ages—enabled them to be spanned by far larger timber roofs than had been possible hitherto. This apartment was usually built at ground-floor level, but first-floor halls still persisted

[94] The complex hierarchy serving the Black Prince and Lancaster have been analysed in detail and those of the earls of March (d. 1398) and Salisbury (d. 1397) have been partially revealed. T. F. Tout, *Chapters in the Administrative History of Medieval England*, vol. 5 (1930), 289–400; R. Somerville, *History of the Duchy of Lancaster* (1953), 111–53; G. A. Holmes, *The Estates of the Higher Nobility in Fourteenth-Century England* (1957), 60–6. To take only two slightly later illustrations where the evidence is more plentiful. The household staff of the countess of Warwick at Berkeley Castle numbered 55 in 1421 and the household book for that year records the provision of between 60 and 100 meals a day. Later in the century, Lord Berkeley who might feed up to 300 persons in his hall, usually travelled with 150 servants. C. D. Ross, *Trans. Bristol and Glos. Arch. Soc.* vol. 70 (1951), 91–6; J. Smyth, *The Lives of the Berkeleys ... from 1066 to 1618*, ed. J. Maclean (1883–5).

[95] His early work includes improvements at *Kenilworth Castle* (1372), remodelling the upper part of the keep at *Pontefract Castle* (1374), and additions to *Savoy Palace* (1376).

[96] For the work of individual architects, see J. H. Harvey, *English Mediaeval Architects* (1954) and his *Henry Yevele* (1946).

Bolton Castle, Yorkshire: c. 1378–99

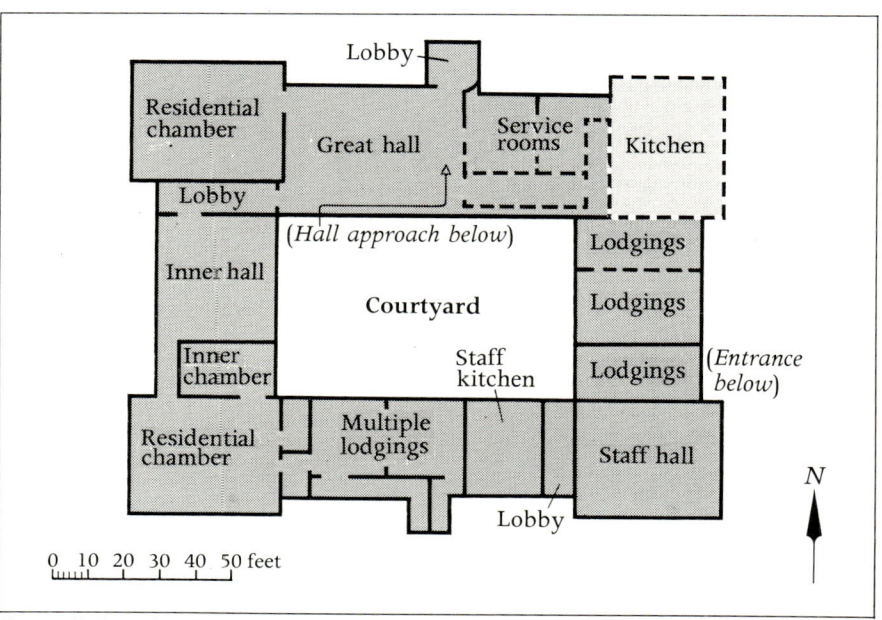

Fig. 13 Bolton Castle. First-floor plan

[97] At Raby, Neville built a hall directly above an earlier ground-floor hall. Wardour is an example of a southern castle with a first-floor hall.

for defensive reasons, particularly in the north as at Bolton and Wressell.[97] A restricted site or the presence of earlier buildings may have contributed to the decision to build the halls at North Elmham, Portchester, and Kenilworth at first-floor level, but considerations of estate were clearly most important at the last two named and they may have determined the design at Farleigh Hungerford where site restrictions did not exist. Suites of private apartments, frequently on two floors, and numerous small chambers were planned to meet the higher social standards of the period and the demand for greater privacy. Rooms in some of the larger residences such as Bolton were planned with ingeniously devised means of access, and they were frequently adorned with wall paintings and rich hangings as well as with more furniture than is generally credited.

Castles

[98] *V.C.H. Yorkshire: North Riding*, vol. 1 (1914), 272–3; P. A. Faulkner, *Arch. Jour.* vol. 120 (1963), 225–30.

[99] *V.C.H. Yorkshire: North Riding*, vol. 2 (1923), 174–6; *Arch. Jour.* vol. 91 (1934), 390.

[100] H. Avray Tipping, *English Homes. Period 1*, vol. 1: *1066–1485* (1921), 247–57; *Arch. Jour.* vol. 111 (1954), 212–13; *Lumley Castle: Official Guide* (c. 1955).

[101] J. F. Hodgson, *Trans. of Arch. and Archaeol. Soc. of Durham and Northumberland*, vol. 3 (1880–92), vol. 4 (1890–5); J. P. Pritchett, *Arch. Aeliana*, vol. 24 (1903), 65–8; O. S. Scott, *Raby, its Castles and its Lords* (5th ed. 1960); H. Avray Tipping, *English Homes. Period 1*, vol. 1: *1066–1485* (1921), 258–74. Alistair Rowan, *Country Life* (July 1969).

[102] W. Hutchinson, *The History and Antiquities of the County Palatine of Durham*, vol. 3 (1823), 377; E. W. Short, *The Story of Brancepeth Castle* (1942).

[103] W. Cotton, *Graphic and Historical Sketch of Bodyam Castle* (1831); G. T. Clark, *Medieval Military Architecture*, vol. 1 (1884); H. Sands, *Sussex Arch. Coll.* vol. 46 (1903); The Marquis Curzon of Kedleston, *Bodiam Castle* (1926); W. D. Simpson, *Sussex Arch. Coll.* vol. 72 (1931); 69–99; *V.C.H. Sussex*, vol. 9 (1937), 259–62. For interpretations of its plan, P. A. Faulkner, *Arch. Jour.* vol. 120 (1963), 230–4, and W. D. Simpson, *The Antiq. Jour.* vol. 26 (1946), 145–71.

[104] W. A. Scott Robertson, *Arch. Cantiana*, vol. 11 (1877), 128–44; also vol. 39 (1927), 176–80.

[105] S. E. Rigold, *Med. Archaeol.* vols. 6–7 (1962–3), 67–108, and *North Elmham Saxon Cathedral: Official Guide* (1960). *V.C.H. Worcestershire*, vol. 4 (1924), 202, 431, 433. No survey has yet been made of the two-storeyed ranges at Cheyney Longville.

Late fourteenth-century castles combined the twin roles of defence and residence more satisfactorily than at any other time during the Middle Ages. Their planning was dominated by two features: boldly projecting towers and the distribution of accommodation round each side of a regular quadrangle. Yet there are marked differences in the planning of fortresses in the north compared with those in the south of England, based on different interpretations of these two important features. The primary line of defence in a northern castle such as Bolton,[98] Sheriff Hutton,[99] and Lumley[100] lay in its massive angle towers rather than a dominant gatehouse. The ranges round the courtyard were integrated with the outer wall, and whereas the ground-floor rooms were vaulted and generally used for storage, the residential and service accommodation was located on two upper floors. Despite more irregular planning, Raby[101] and Brancepeth[102] also show the same primary characteristics. On the other hand, castles in the south such as Bodiam[103] and Cooling[104] were marked by powerful entrance towers, flanking and dominating the main approach. Round corner towers, considerably less bold than the more conservative square ones in the north, gave additional protection. The hall and offices were usually at ground level and the two-storeyed ranges round the quadrangle were not integrated with the outer wall but simply built against it. The site was protected wherever possible by water defences, including double moats as at North Elmham, Cheyney Longville, and *Strensham*.[105]

Brancepeth Castle, Co. Durham. South front: c. 1391–8. East front altered and extended: c. 1817

Raby Castle, Co. Durham. Neville gateway and west front: 1378–c. 90

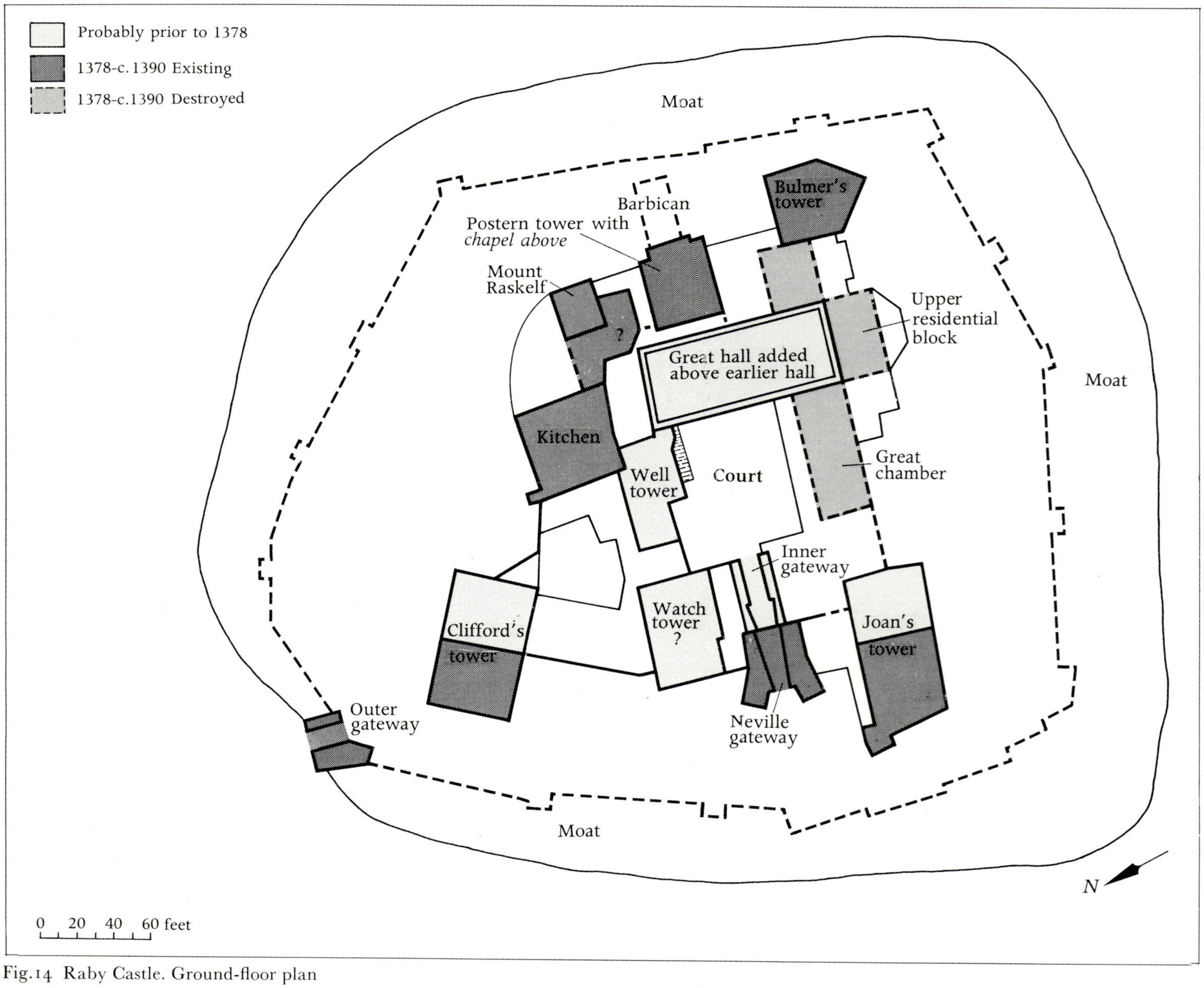

Fig. 14 Raby Castle. Ground-floor plan

Bodiam Castle, Sussex. Entrance and east frontages: 1385–c. 90

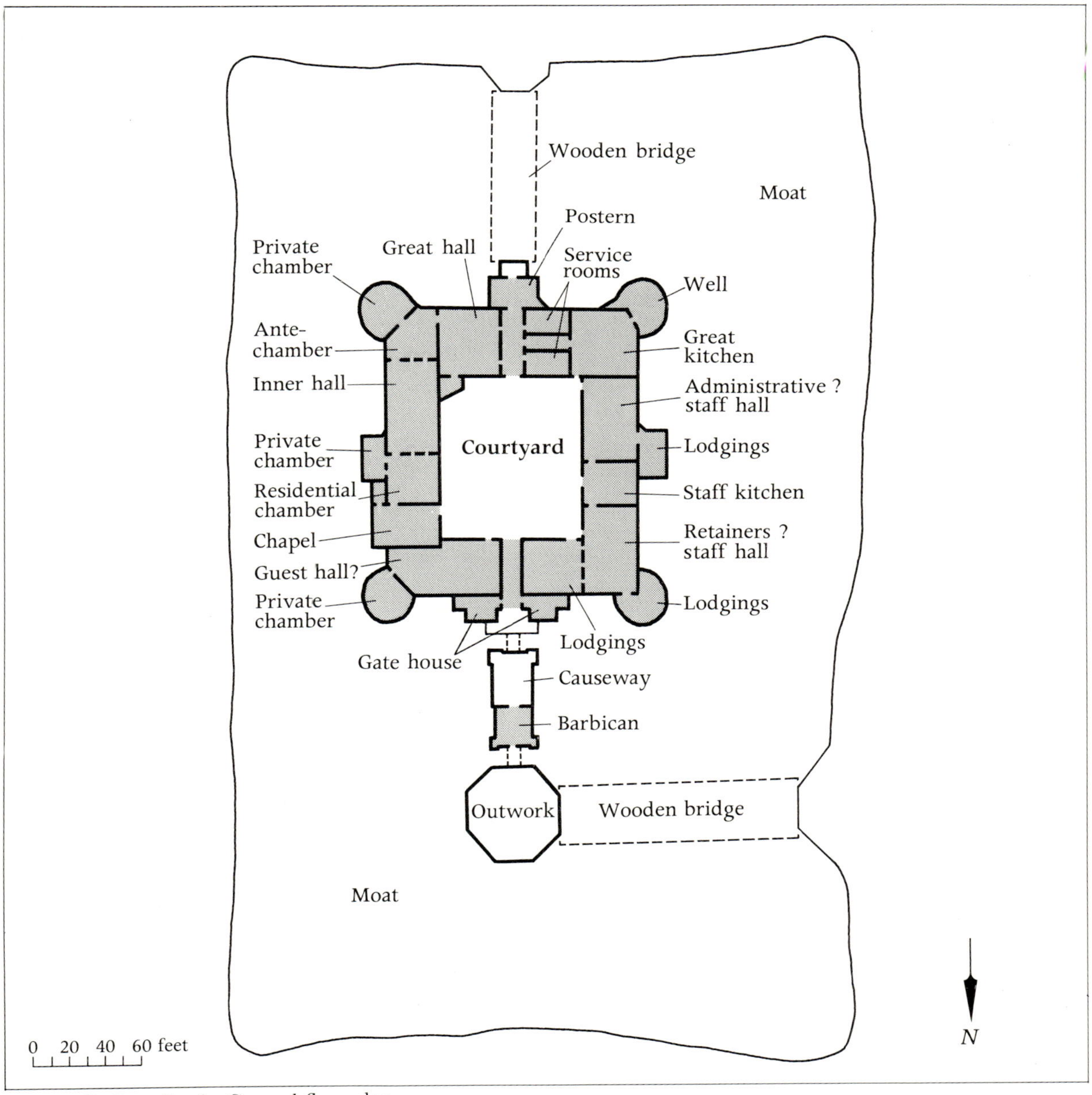

Fig. 15 Bodiam Castle. Ground-floor plan

Penrith Castle, Cumberland: 1397

Wressell Castle, Yorkshire. South front: c. 1380–90

Fortified houses

The prime considerations in determining the design of a fortified house were that it should afford its occupants a measure of protection against turbulent neighbours or local violence and yet give considerable scope to the increasing amenities of civilized life. The defences of a fortified house were therefore usually more impressive than effective, and in some cases, they were clearly designed as status symbols rather than as practical fortifications.

There were two important types of fortified houses at this time—the quadrangular house and the tower-house. The approach of a quadrangular house such as Shirburn,[106] Wressell,[107] Wingfield,[108] Hever,[109] and Hemyock castles, was defended by a gatehouse, angle towers, battlements, and a moat, although these features might be limited to just battlements and moats as at Cheyney Longville.[110] On closer examination, however, the thin outer walls and

[106] *V.C.H. Oxfordshire*, vol. 8 (1964), 179–81; Mary, countess of Macclesfield, *Scattered Notices of Shirburn Castle* (1887).

[107] J. Savage, *The History of the Castle and Parish of Wressle* (1805); *Yorks. Arch. Jour.* vol. 22 (1913), 182–93; *Arch. Jour.* vol. 91 (1934), 397.

[108] *Country Life* (June 1913); S. W. H. Aldwell, *Wingfield: its Church, Castle and College* (1925), 31–4; *Connoisseur Year Book* (1960).

[109] T. Garner and A. Stratton, *Domestic Architecture of England during the Tudor Period* (1911), 55–6; A. Oswald, *Country Houses of Kent* (1933), 9–10; Gavin Astor, *Hever Castle and Gardens: Official Guide* (1966).

[110] Gillow Manor, a border house with similar features, has been attributed on architectural evidence to this period. *R.C.H.M. Herefordshire*, vol. 1 (1931), 86–7.

Wingfield Castle, Suffolk. Entrance front: 1385

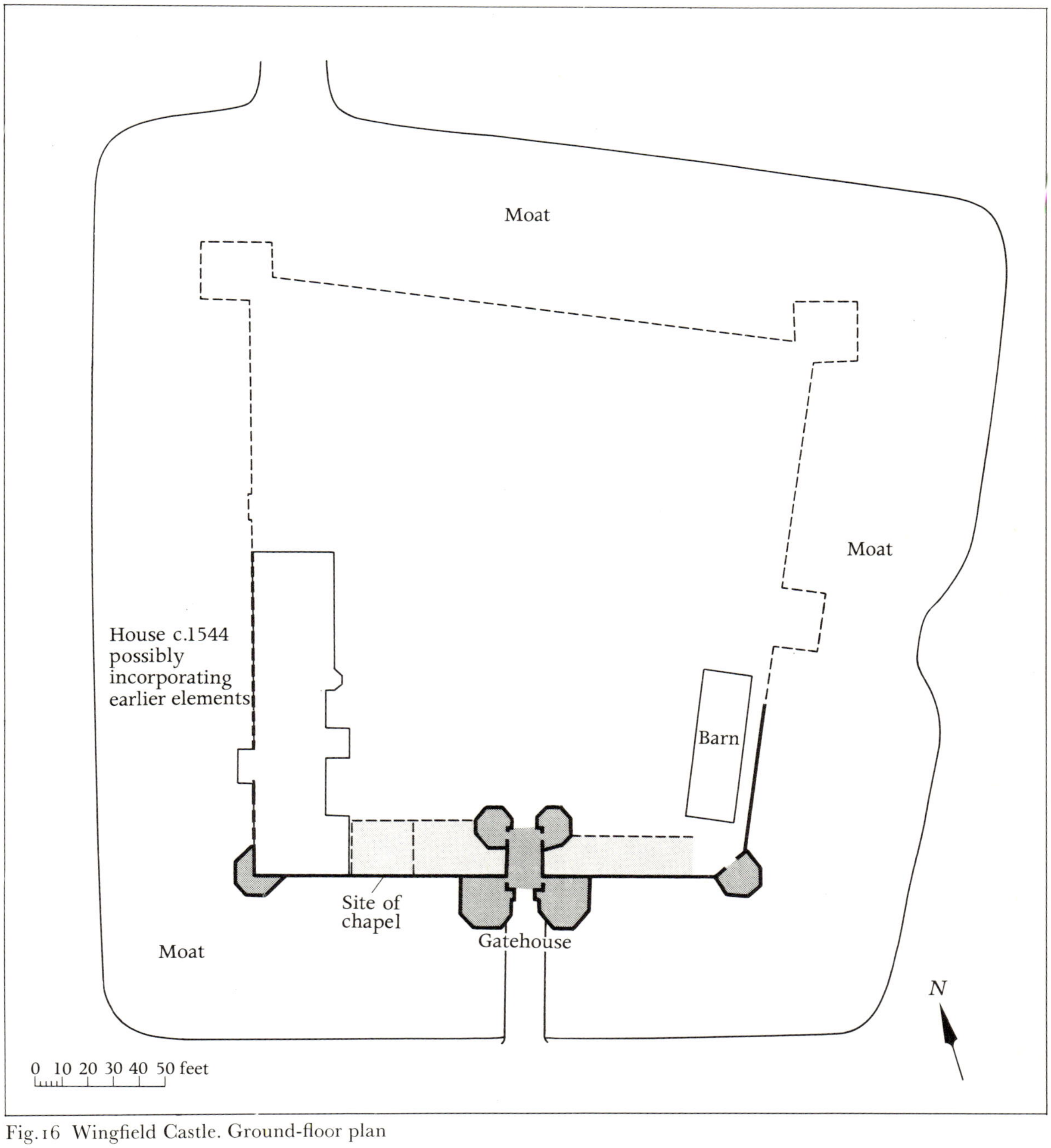

Fig.16 Wingfield Castle. Ground-floor plan

Farleigh Hungerford Castle, Somerset. Site of gatehouse and inner court: c. 1370–83

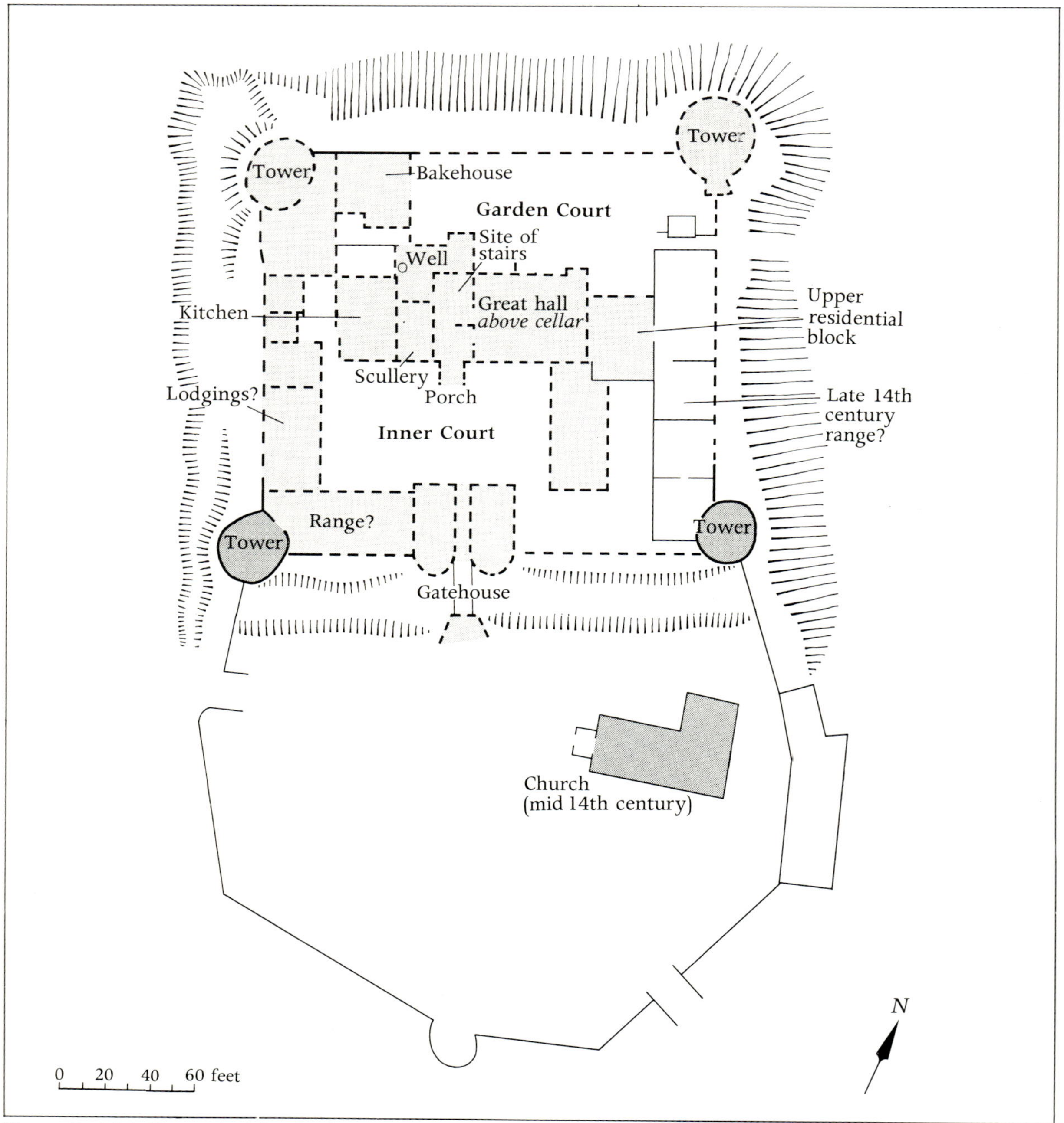

Fig. 17 Farleigh Hungerford Castle. Ground-floor plan

[111] Christopher Hussey, *Country Life* (February 1951).

[112] M. W. Taylor, *The Old Manorial Halls of Westmorland and Cumberland* (1892), 244–52. Also plan and notes on the site.

[113] *Med. Archaeol.* vol. 8 (1964), 276–7. The site was excavated in 1963.

[114] *Farleigh Hungerford Castle: Official Guide* (1962).

[115] Christopher Hussey, *A History of Scotney Castle* (1963); E. Hussey, *Arch. Cantiana*, vol. 17 (1887), 38–48.

[116] W. D. Peckham, *Sussex Arch. Coll.* vol. 62 (1921), 21–63.

[117] J. F. Curwen, *Trans. Cumb. and West. Antiq. and Arch. Soc.* vol. 16 (1900), 1–15.

[118] Only the lower part of the tower survives incorporated in some farm buildings. C. J. Bates, *Castles and Pele Towers of Northumberland* (1891) and E. Long, *Castles of Northumberland* (1967) for this and other castles in the county.

[119] *R.C.H.M. Dorset*, vol. 1 (1952), 247. The tower is virtually featureless.

[120] P. B. Chatwin, *Trans. Birmingham Arch. Soc.* vol. 67 (1947–8), 13–16; J. H. Edwards, *Trans. Birmingham Arch. Soc.* vol. 69 (1951), 44–9.

[121] John Bilson attributed its construction to Thomas de Etton, a family of local significance c. 1380–c. 1402. *Yorks. Arch. Jour.* vol. 19 (1907), 105–92; also *V.C.H. Yorkshire: North Riding*, vol. 1 (1914), 478–80.

[122] F. C. Rimington and J. G. Rutter, *Ayton Castle* (1967). The castle is attributed to Sir Ralph Eure, a northern administrator, who obtained the property through marriage in 1389. No examples of the much larger tower-house with defensive and residential towers projecting from a central block can yet be attributed to Richard's reign, but several examples were still under construction during his early years. Harewood (1366), Haughton (form adopted after 1373), and Langley (attributed to the late as well as to the mid 14th century) are of this type. The plan was not confined to the north, for Nunney (1373) is a well-known example in Somerset.

[123] *Northumberland County History, History of Northumberland*, vol. 5 (1889), 18–112; W. D. Simpson, *Arch. Aeliana*, vol. 15 (1938), 115–36; ibid., vol. 19 (1941), 93–103; C. H. Hunter Blair and H. L. Honeyman, *Warkworth Castle: Official Guide* (1963). At least two keeps were in the

process of construction at the same time, a cylindrical keep at *Southampton* and one in the shape of a fetterlock at *Fotheringhay*. Nothing remains of either structure but it is clear that they were both massive buildings. Even if the latter was a residential tower-house, the former was primarily a military structure, rare but not necessarily archaic in form, and a link with the 15th-century tower-houses and keeps which are still regarded as an isolated architectural phenomenon. For Southampton, see P. G. Stone, *Trans. Hamps. Field Club & Archaeol. Soc.* vol. 12 (1934), 241–70.

[124] R. B. Pugh and A. D. Saunders, *Old Wardour Castle: Official Guide* (1968); L. Keen, *Wilts. Arch. & Nat. Hist. Mag.* vol. 62 (1967), 67–78.

[125] C. H. Hunter Blair and H. L. Honeyman, *Dunstanburgh Castle: Official Guide* (1955); W. D. Simpson, *Arch. Aeliana*, vol. 27 (1949), 15–19, 21–5.

[126] J. F. Curwen, *Trans. Cumb. and West. Antiq. and Arch. Soc.* vol. 11 (1911), 129–58. Both the inner and the outer gatehouses combine defensive with residential needs.

[127] J. L. André, *Sussex Arch. Coll.* vol. 43 (1900), 210–13; W. H. Godfrey, *Sussex Arch. Coll.*, vol. 82 (1942), 59–64; F. W. Steer, *A Short History and Description of Halnaker House* (privately printed 1958).

[128] Margaret Wood, *Donnington Castle: Official Guide* (1964); *V.C.H. Berkshire*, vol. 4 (1924), 93–4.

[129] Christopher Hussey, *Country Life* (November–December 1942); H. Enterprise, *Historical Traces of Saltwood Castle* (1841); *Jour. Brit. Arch. Assoc.* vol. 20 (1914), 195–201; *Arch. Jour.* vol. 86 (1929), 309–10.

[130] H. Avray Tipping, *English Homes. Period 1*, vol. 1, *1066–1485* (1921), 67–82. The extension and enlargement of the gatehouse at the ecclesiastical castle at Llawhaden in Pembrokeshire has also been attributed on architectural grounds to this period. C. A. Ralegh Radford, *Llawhaden Castle: Official Guide* (1947). Gatehouses as a vehicle of display were not confined to secular owners for there are a number of comparable monastic structures culminating in that *folie de grandeur* at Thornton Abbey (1382). Other monastic gatehouses used for residential or administrative purposes include the more sober structures at Wigmore Abbey (c. 1379), Bridlington Priory (1388), St. Augustine's Abbey, Canterbury (Cemetery Gate c. 1390), and Ely Priory (1396–c. 1400).

Warkworth Castle, Northumberland. Tower-house: c. 1377–84

the large windows piercing them indicate that the residential accommodation was nearly always given priority over the defensive measures. Modified examples of this plan include Shute Barton[111] where there were only two residential ranges round the quadrangle, and Penrith[112] and *Rest*[113] where the principal apartments were confined to a single block and the remaining sides of the site were flanked by half-timbered ranges backed by a stone wall. Furthermore, with accommodation no longer needing to be planned so tightly as hitherto, it could be ranged round two courtyards instead of one, separated by the all-important hall with a residential block at either end. The castles at Farleigh Hungerford,[114] Scotney,[115] and Amberley[116] are three of the earliest examples of this double quadrangular design which, like its parent, gradually shed its defensive characteristics during the following century.

The second type of fortified house was the tower-house, a type of house usually confined to the border regions by the late fourteenth century. The simplest design, as at Workington Hall,[117] Fenwick,[118] and possibly Holditch,[119] was merely a small residential tower attached to one end of the hall range. A more elaborate form was the self-contained residential tower standing within an enclosure as at Baginton,[120] Gilling,[121] and Ayton[122] castles with the living-rooms on the first floor and the sleeping quarters on the second floor.

The most complex tower-houses of this period were the two spectacular and intricately planned examples at Warkworth[123] and Wardour.[124] Nearly all the accommodation enjoyed by a magnate in the more spacious palace-fortresses was united in each of these structures into a single comprehensive unit which was vigorous in conception and at Warkworth, aesthetically satisfying in execution.

If the tower-house was a complete residence in itself, many gatehouses of the period tended to be nearly so. Some were still primarily intended for defence, such as those at Dunstanburgh,[125] Cockermouth,[126] and Halnaker House,[127] but others were built primarily for purposes of accommodation in a form which gave an impression of dignity and strength as at Donnington,[128] Saltwood,[129] and Caldicot[130] castles.

Baginton Castle, Warwickshire. Foundations of west front: *c*. 1390–5

Wardour Castle, Wiltshire. Tower-house: 1393

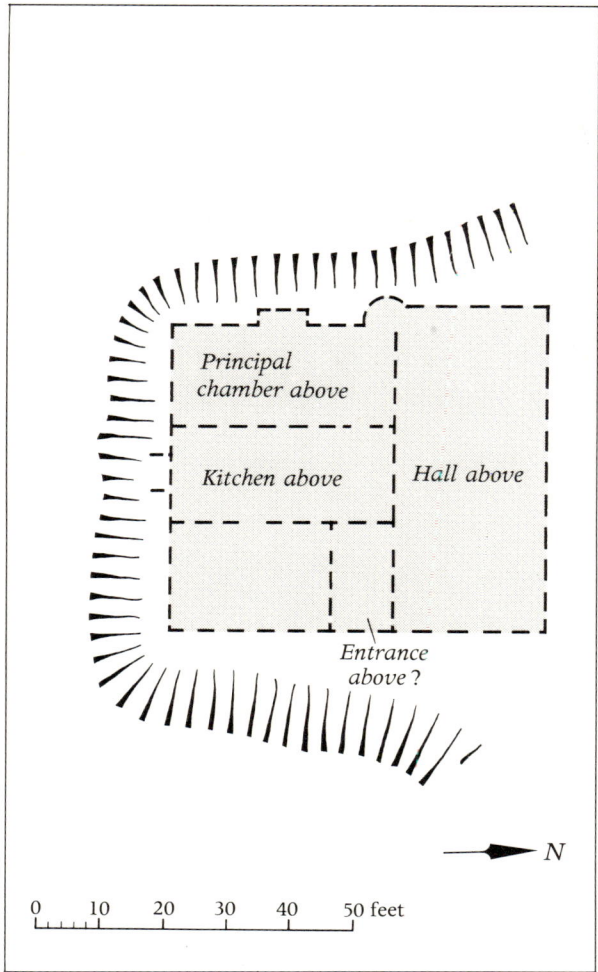

Fig.18 Baginton Castle. Lower ground-floor plan

Donnington Castle, Berkshire. Gatehouse: 1386

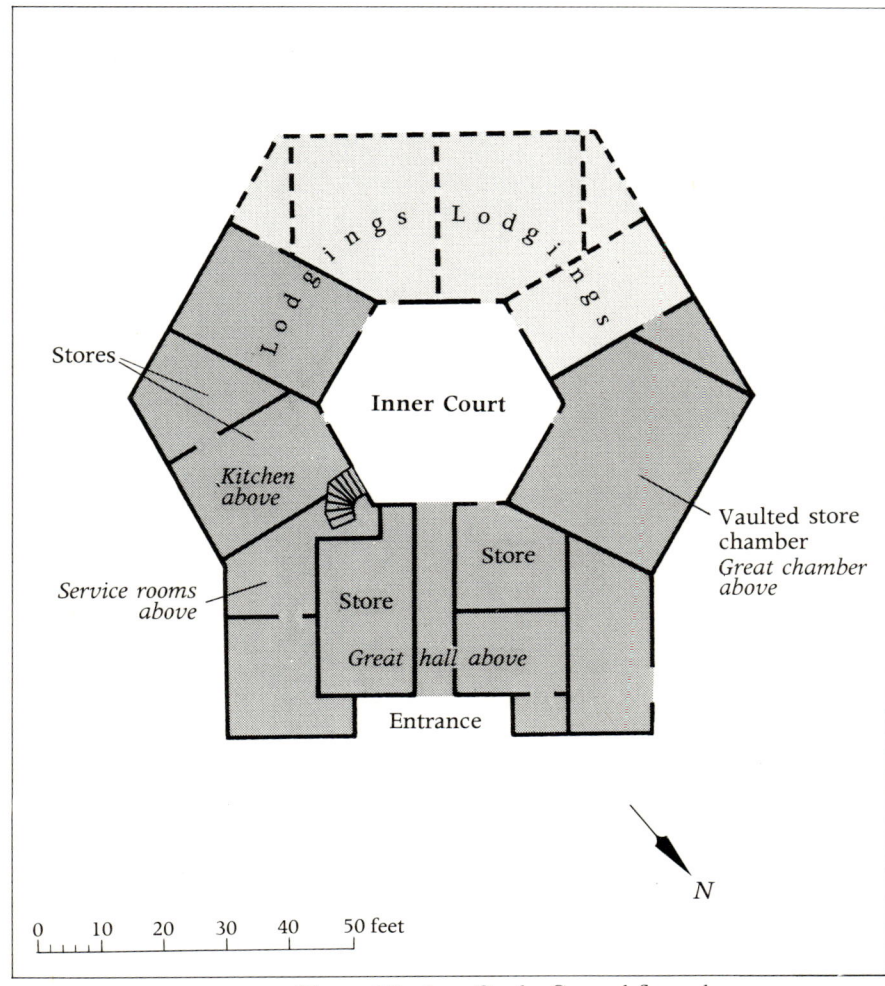

Fig.19 Wardour Castle. Ground-floor plan

Saltwood Castle, Kent. Gatehouse: c. 1382

Unfortified houses

Only the absence of any defensive features distinguish some of the larger fortified houses from their non-defensive brethren, for the quadrangular plan was common to them both. Very few unfortified residences of appreciable size were raised during the late fourteenth century and no complete examples are extant. Fortunately, the porch and remains of the hall at Howden Manor are supplemented by a description made in 1561 enabling the quadrangular plan of the house to be reconstructed in detail,[131] while the remains at Dartington Hall can be shown to be part of an even larger double quadrangular plan. In both cases, their form was determined by the need to provide extensive accommodation for the owners and their personal staff and in the case of Dartington, for a series of lodgings housing a large number of retainers and household officials.

The principal apartments at several major residences were reconstructed during this period, centred on the great hall and sometimes including the associated residential accommodation. The three regal halls at Westminster,[132] Portchester,[133] and Kenilworth[134] are still redolent of the grandeur and elegance of the king and prince who built them. The undercroft of the hall and flanking chambers remain at Bamburgh[135] and Scarborough[136] castles, the porch at Croydon,[137] and the undercroft and outer walls of an audience hall at Saltwood.[138] The two-storeyed range of princely apartments at Portchester and Kenilworth may be traced and a much smaller residential block at Carisbrooke,[139] but all these works were built within existing enceintes whereas the planning of Dartington and Howden was

[131] Canon Raine, *Assoc. Arch. Soc. Reports and Papers*, vol. 8 (1865–6), 295–302; W. Hutchinson, *Yorks. Arch. Jour.* vol. 9 (1886), 384–93; John Bilson, *Yorks. Arch. Jour.* vol. 22 (1913), 256–69.

[132] J. T. Smith, *Antiquities of Westminster* (1807); E. W. Brayley and J. Britton, *The History of the Ancient Palace and Late Houses of Parliament at Westminster* (1836); House of Commons, *Report from the Select Committee on Westminster Hall Restoration* (1885); Frederick Baines, *Report on the Condition of the Roof Timber of Westminster Hall* (1914); W. Harvey, *The Builder* (19 August 1921); *R.C.H.M. London*, vol. 2 (1925), 121–3; H. Cescinsky and E. R. Gribble, *The Burlington Magazine*, vol. 40 (1922), 76–84, and R. A. Brown, H. M. Colvin, and A. J. Taylor, *The History of the King's Works*, vol. 1 (1963), 527–33.

[133] S. E. Rigold, *Portchester Castle: Official Guide* (1965); *V.C.H. Hampshire*, vol. 3 (1908), 151–8; R. A. Brown, H. M. Colvin, and A. J. Taylor, *The History of the King's Works*, vol. 2 (1963), 790–1.

Dartington Hall, Devonshire. Great hall, entrance porch, and lower residential block: 1388–c. 1400. West range: c. 1393–1400, altered c. 1740

[134] P. K. Baillie Reynolds, *Kenilworth Castle: Official Guide* (1956); *V.C.H. Warwickshire*, vol. 6 (1951), 134–8.

[135] Several vaulted cellars and the mangled remains of the kitchen and offices survive, encased in a series of state rooms built by Lord Armstrong between 1894 and 1905 that are notably lacking in merit. *Northumberland County History*, vol. 1 (1893); H. Avray Tipping, *English Homes. Period 1, vol. 1: 1066–1485* (1921); *Arch. Jour.* vol. 82 (1925), 245–8.

[136] *The History of Scarborough*, ed. A. Rowntree (1931), 141–53; *Scarborough Castle: Official Guide* (1957).

[137] *Surrey Arch. Coll.* vol. 24 (1911), 81–91; *V.C.H. Surrey*, vol. 4 (1912), 206–13; A. Oswald, *Country Life* (April 1965).

[138] The remains were incorporated in an entirely conjectural restoration in 1936. Philip Tilden, *True Remembrances* (1954), 165. The adjacent contemporary chapel was left in ruins.

[139] *V.C.H. Hampshire*, vol. 5 (1912), 226.

Howden Manor, Yorkshire. Great hall and entrance porch: 1388–1405

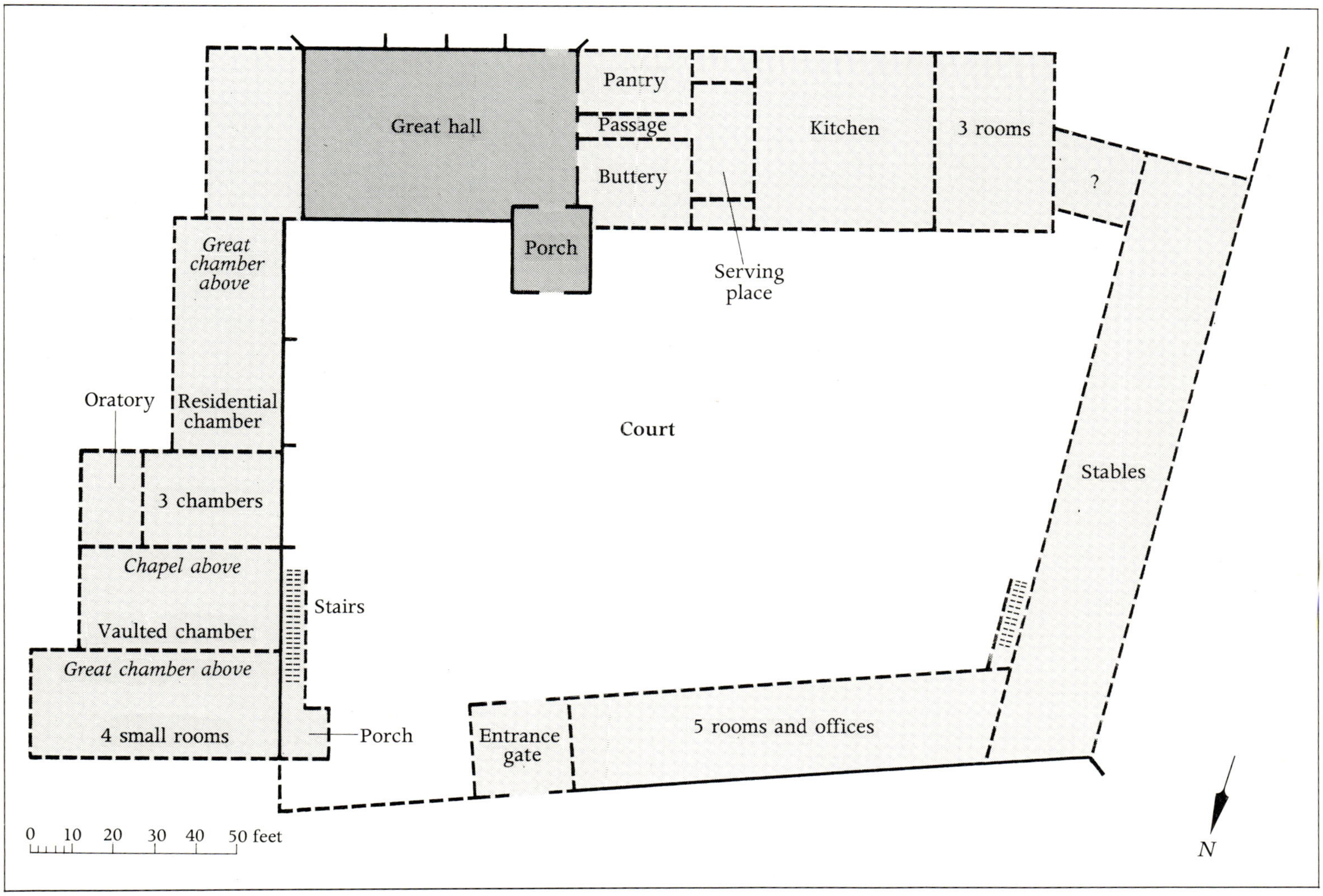

Fig. 20 Howden Manor. Ground-floor plan

Norrington Manor, Wiltshire. Great hall: c. 1380

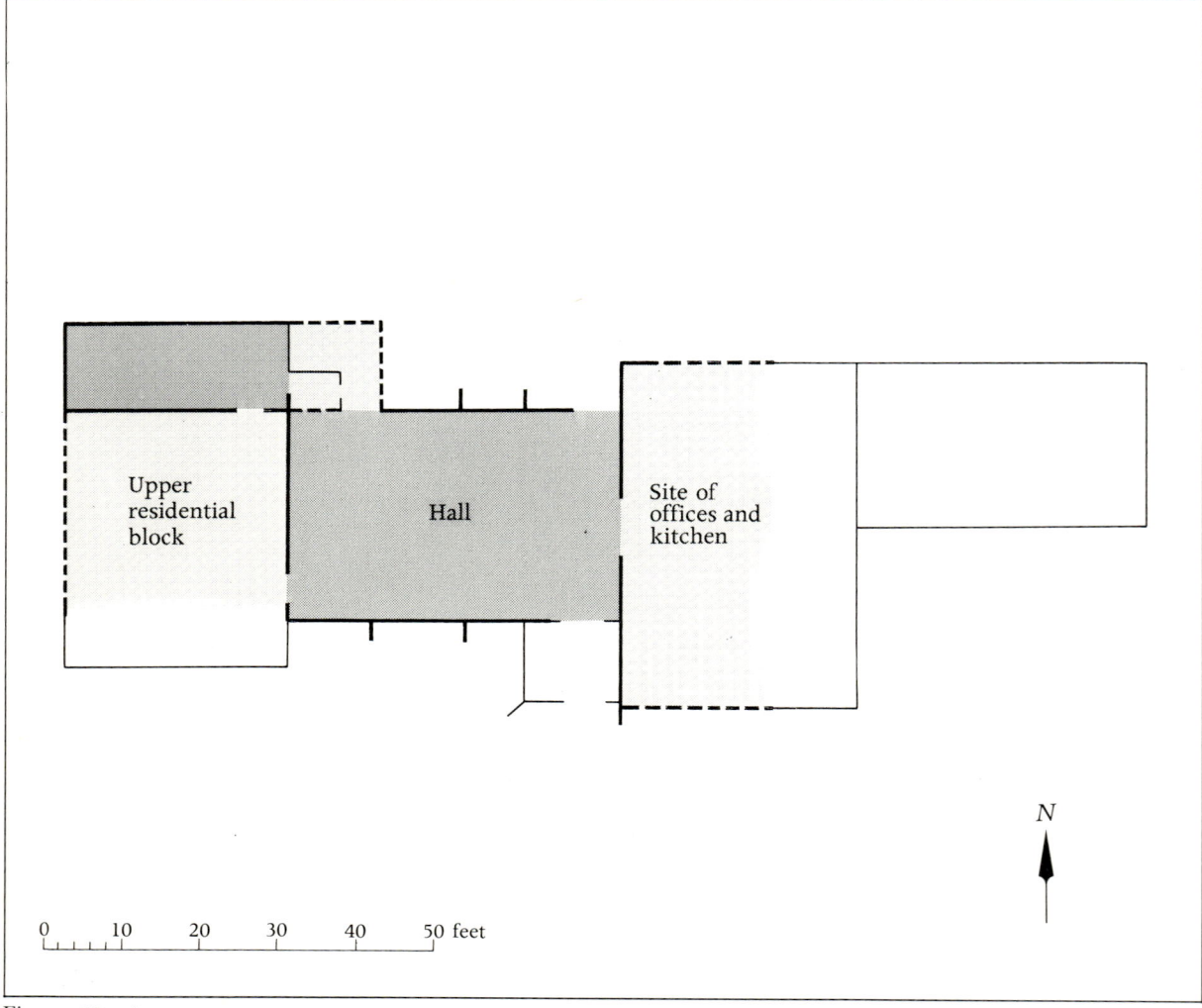

Fig. 21 Norrington Manor. Ground-floor plan

[140] Christopher Hussey, *Country Life* (July 1923); R.C.H.M. *Monuments Threatened or Destroyed: 1956–1962* (1963), 27–8. It is particularly regrettable that salt-mining subsidence and government indifference allowed the timber-framed hall and lower cross wing of this building to fall down in 1959.

[141] Preston Patrick Hall, Westmorland; Court House, Poyntington, Dorset; Manor Farm, Upton Scudmore, Wiltshire, and Knighstone, Devon are other examples of this design which have been attributed on architectural grounds to the late 14th century. *R.C.H.M. Westmorland* (1936), 195–6; *R.C.H.M. Dorset*, vol. 1 (1952), 189; *R.C.H.M. Monuments Threatened or Destroyed: 1956–1962* (1963), 65; Christopher Hussey, *Country Life* (September 1950).

[142] The development of this type of house has been attributed to the second half of the 14th century. J. T. Smith, *Arch. Jour.* vol. 122 (1965), 152. Wardes at Otham and Larkfield are early examples that have been attributed to the last quarter of the century.

[143] Aymer Vallance, *The Old Colleges of Oxford* (1912); *R.C.H.M. City of Oxford* (1939); *V.C.H. Oxfordshire*, vol. 3 (1954), 144–62; A. H. Smith, *New College Oxford and Its Buildings* (1952). A. F. Leach, *A History of Winchester College* (1899); Winchester College Arch. Soc., *Winchester College: its History, Buildings and Customs* (1926), and *Winchester: its History, Buildings and People* (1933); J. H. Harvey, *Jour. Brit. Arch. Assoc.* vol. 28 (1965), 107–28.

for a total residence, unhampered by any earlier buildings of consequence.

The smaller house of any architectural or social pretensions was usually based on the hall and end-block plan, derived from the planning of domestic quarters in larger residences. It consisted of a central hall with a two-storeyed residential block at the upper end and an office and domestic block at the lower end as at Tabley Old Hall[140] and Norrington Manor. This form usually fulfilled a different function from the larger quadrangular house and reflected the lesser standing of the owner. It was not the administrative centre of a network of estates but the single home of a small landowner. Nor was there any need to house a large retinue but merely the owner and his family and their servants. The hall and end-block plan is therefore the basic form of much lesser residential architecture during the late medieval period. Probably several examples date from Richard's reign but few can be ascribed with accuracy.[141] Furthermore, although this plan was widespread throughout the country, it was subject to several regional variations of which the most important was in south-east England where its execution in timber framing gave rise to a quite distinctive form of design known as the Wealden house.[142] The study of this and other forms, however, is outside the scope of this short survey.

Colleges and comparable ecclesiastical foundations

Surviving evidence indicates that the planning of collegiate residences round a quadrangle had been adopted at both Oxford and Cambridge by the second half of the fourteenth century. The importance of Wykeham's twin educational foundations at Oxford and Winchester lies in his insistence on a unified plan which complemented his innovation that the warden, fellows, and scholars should reside within one building.[143] Discipline was the keynote of Wykeham's statutes and therefore the warden, like many a magnate, was accommodated in the rooms over a prominent gateway so that he could maintain a keen vigilance over his students. Scholars and fellows were ranged round three sides of the quadrangle and the fourth side was closed by a chapel built back to back with the hall, an apartment used for communal work as well as for eating and modelled on the pattern familiar in larger private houses. Attention has been drawn to the similarity between this design and that of the royal apartments at Windsor Castle built in the mid fourteenth

Kenilworth Castle, Warwickshire. Great hall and residential range: 1389–93

Portchester Castle, Hampshire. Great hall, entrance porch, and lower residential block: 1396–9

century,[144] but it also bears a superficial resemblance to the colleges built for priests at Cobham (after 1362) and Arundel (1380).

The planning of colleges for priests, like vicars choral and hospitals, was determined by the same elements of hall, lodgings, and offices ranged round the sides of a court that characterize so much late medieval secular planning. The halls of the college at St. David's (c. 1384)[145] and the hospital of St. Cross, Winchester (possibly between 1383 and 1410)[146] are simply smaller and more sober versions of that at Kenilworth Castle. The college chambers at Arundel[147] are not unlike those at near-by Amberley Castle, while the principal gatehouse at Maidstone College (1395)[148] would not disgrace a major fortified house. A cursory glance at the vicars choral at Chichester (1397)[149] and the remnants at Exeter

[144] L. G. Wickham Legg, *Jour. Brit. Arch. Assoc.* vol. 3 (1938), 83–95.

[145] The hall, re-roofed in 1966, its bell tower, and the entrance to the college survive. W. B. Jones and E. A. Freeman, *The History and Antiquities of St. David's* (1856), 179–89. The cloisters were excavated in 1933. W. D. Caroe, *Arch. Cambriensis*, vol. 89 (1934), 279–90. The lodgings at

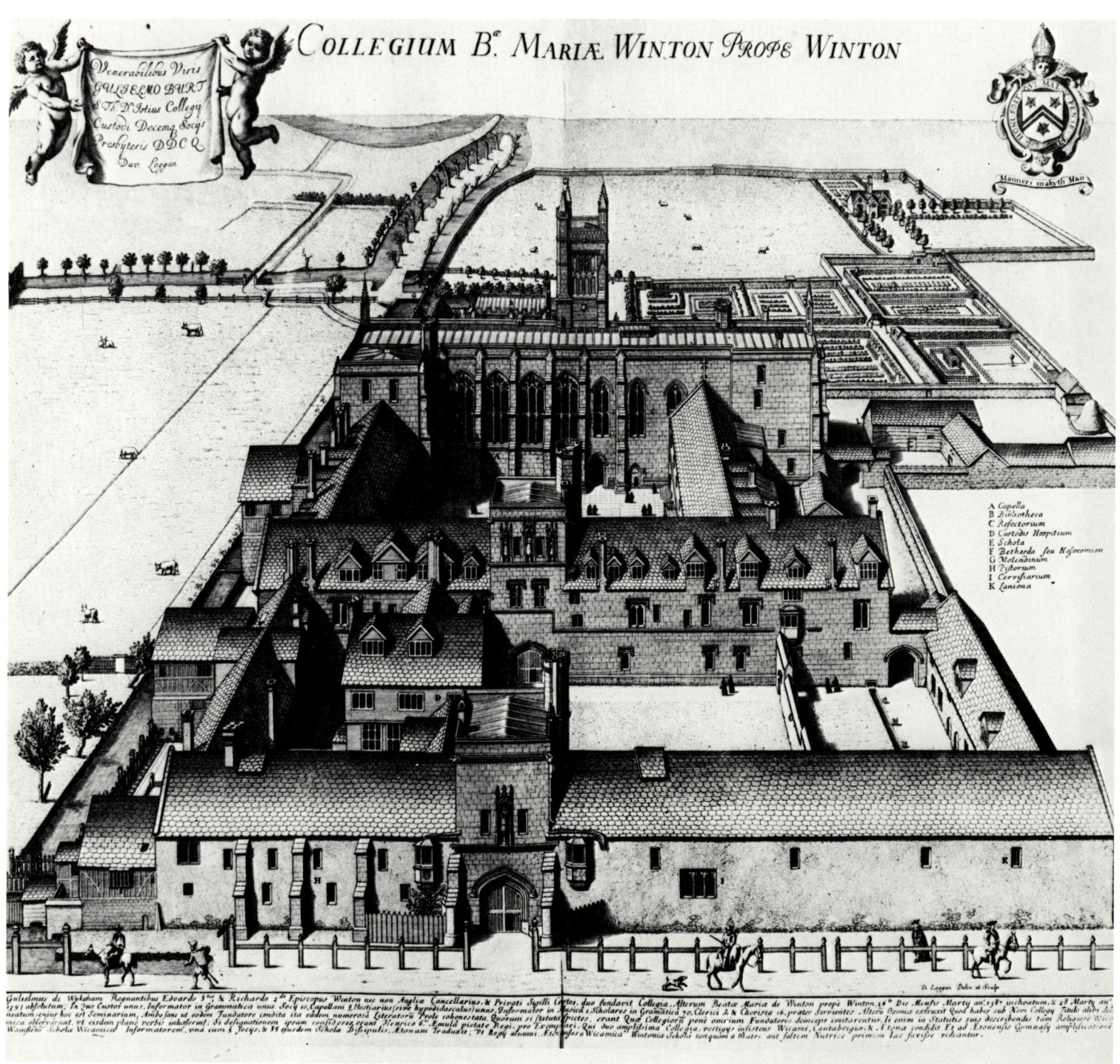

Winchester College, Hampshire: 1387–1401. Engraving by David Loggan, 1675

this college were not built round a quadrangle but grouped irregularly.

[146] The hall is traditionally attributed to about 1445, *V.C.H. Hampshire*, vol. 5 (1912), 66–9. Margaret Wood prefers the period from about 1383 onwards, *The English Mediaeval House* (1965), 29, 355, while John Harvey concedes that either date seems possible, *Arch. Jour.* vol. 123 (1966), 216. The hall may have been built by the Master John Campden, who spent considerable sums on building work between 1383 and 1410.

[147] M. A. Tierney, *The History and Antiquities . . . of Arundel* (1834); G. H. Cook, *English Collegiate Churches of the Middle Ages* (1959), 119–25. The buildings were incorporated in a lifeless reconstruction in the 19th century.

[148] B. Post, *History of the College of All Saints, Maidstone* (1856); G. H. Cook, *English Collegiate Churches of the Middle Ages* (1959), 128–35. The inner gatehouse, hall, and treasury tower survive and a ruined subsidiary gateway. The master's house is an earlier building of *c*. 1375.

[149] I. C. Hannah, *Sussex Arch. Coll.* vol. 56 (1913), 92–109; W. D. Peckham, *Sussex Arch. Coll.* vol. 78 (1937), 126–59; F. W. Steer, *The Vicars Hall, Chichester* (1958). The first-floor hall is complete. The western range of lodgings were refaced in the 18th century, the eastern range were turned back-to-front in 1825 and the quadrangle divided down the middle to create a series of back gardens, and the entrance gate was demolished in 1831.

[150] J. F. Chanter, *The Custos and College of the Vicars Choral at the Cathedral, Exeter* (1933). The last of the individual houses was pulled down in the early 20th century and the hall was reduced to a shell by bombing in 1940. Other contemporary work for vicars choral includes the entrance range at Lincoln with the arms of Bishop Buckingham (1363–93) and their original hall at Hereford, founded in 1396.

(1388)[150] hardly suggest that they had much in common with contemporary baronial accommodation, but a closer examination of the elongated court with its flanking residences and communal hall opposite the entrance approach is the same basic plan that Huntingdon adopted for the north court at Dartington Hall. However, the similarity between these elements and those in contemporary secular buildings must not be pushed too far. These foundations were all ecclesiastical-based and their lodgings were generally of equal importance, linked by a common hall. There is no dominant block of chambers equivalent to the lord's apartments or series of suites designed according to the rank of the occupants. Even the master of a college, dominant though he was within his community, lived on a far less lavish scale than a magnate and lacked an extensive personal household.

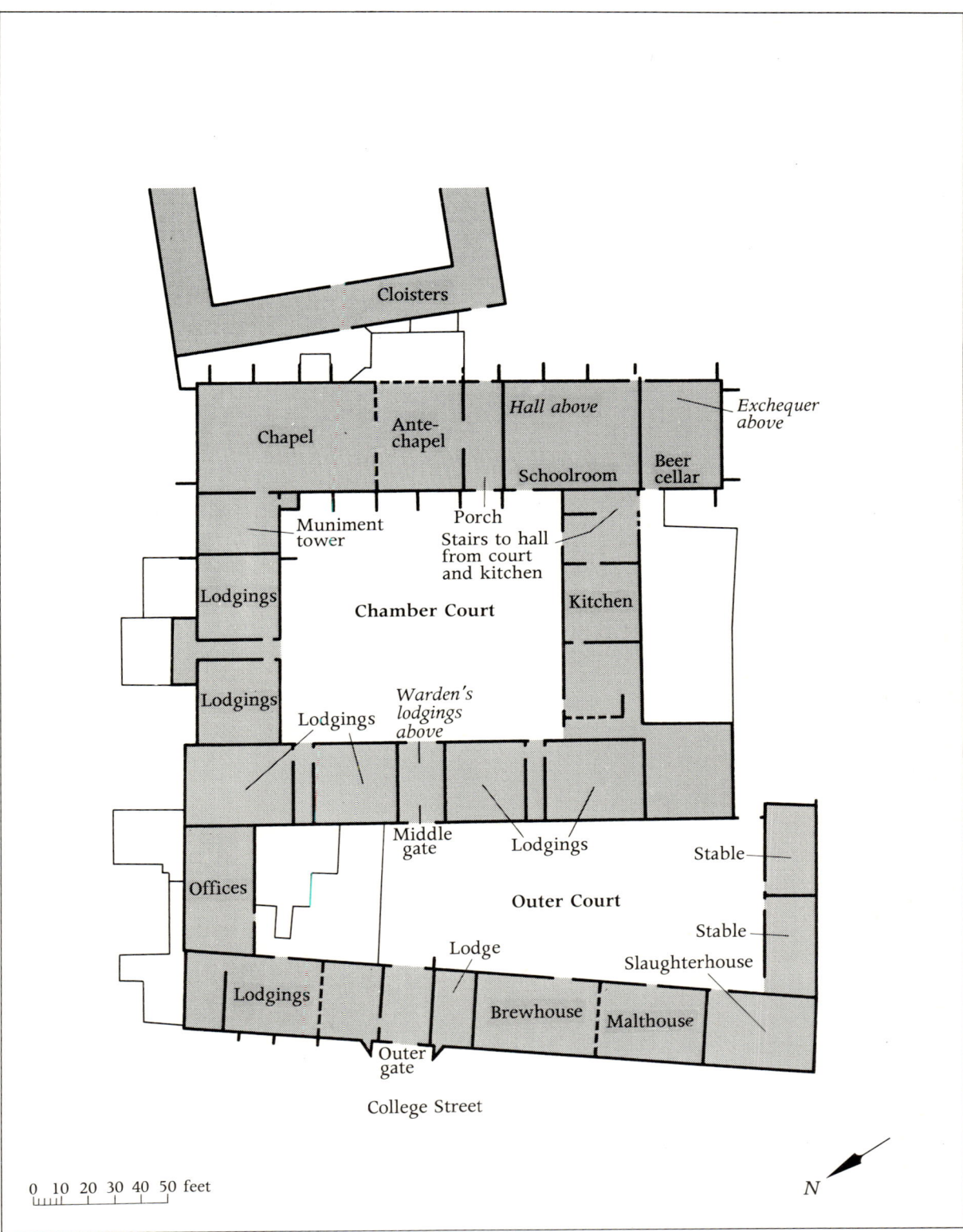

Fig. 22 Winchester College. Ground-floor plan

Architectural Character and Design

The emphasis on the vertical which is the keynote of late Gothic architecture in England led to particularly happy results in military and domestic architecture, for it gave considerable scope to the development of perpendicular members of many different heights without the repetitive decoration which makes so much ecclesiastical bay design seem monotonous. The readily identifiable characteristics of Perpendicular architecture such as vertical members of tracery cutting the heads of arches, panelled surfaces, four-centred arches, and slender pinnacles and turrets, are far more apparent in religious than in secular buildings. But the fundamental virtues of this national style such as the development of the balanced design, the enlargement of windows at the expense of wall, and increasing emphasis on space characterized military and residential design as much as ecclesiastical work, and raised secular architecture to an aesthetic standard which rivalled its ecclesiastical counterpart for the first time.

Design in England was helped by the availability of a wide range of building materials, a factor which contributed to the different appearance of two such closely situated and similarly planned castles as Bolton and Lumley. Flint was used at Donnington and in association with pebbles at Wingfield. Limestone was chosen for Wykeham's foundations at Oxford and Winchester, and massive blocks of Wadhurst stone at Bodiam. Shirburn is an early example of the use of brick, now wretchedly hidden beneath a thick coat of plaster. Oak is nearly always used for roof structures as at Westminster Hall but the widespread use of timber is not always appreciated, particularly since the destruction of the hall at Tabley Old Hall. The licence granted to the earl of Suffolk in 1385 stated that he could fortify Wingfield with a paling of timber as an alternative to the wall of stone and lime that

Warwick Castle. Caesar's Tower: c. 1370–85. Gatehouse and barbican: c. 1360–9. Guy's Tower: c. 1390–4

[151] *Cal. Pat. Rolls 1381–85*, 555.

[152] *Med. Archaeol.* vol. 8 (1964), 276–7.

[153] Leland, *Itinerary*, ed. L. T. Smith, vol. 1 (1907), 53. Leland suggests that this court was later than the main building

he actually built.[151] Excavations at *Rest* have shown that three of the ranges there were built of timber backed by an outer stone wall,[152] while Leland records that the outer court at Wressell was built entirely of timber.[153]

The adoption of the quadrangular plan and the principles of coherent design encouraged the development of symmetrical façades. There is little doubt that the keep at Warkworth and the north front of Bodiam, for example, were consciously planned for a balanced effect, and that many of the fortified houses in the last quarter of the century were designed with an eye to their aesthetic appearance. The fact that many of them were raised on new sites gave considerable scope to the application of these principles. The existence of previous buildings at Kenilworth, however, did not hamper the planning of the great hall and flanking towers where the outer façade is an early example of a symmetrical design applied to a domestic structure.

Residences of the early Perpendicular period tended to be inward rather than outward looking. This is inevitably so in defensive structures and palace-fortresses such as Bolton and Sheriff Hutton,[154] but it also applies to colleges such as Cobham and New College, Oxford, where the occupants were shut in by high walls and the gate was the principal and sometimes the only means of access. As far as can be ascertained, this characteristic also seems to have applied to several non-fortified buildings such as Dartington Hall where most of the rooms round the main courtyard were designed to face inwards rather than towards the outside world. Once inside a courtyard, however, external severity gave way to internal lightness. Large windows flooded the hall and the private apartments with light, and bay-windows such as that at Kenilworth developed from the smaller oriel chamber at the dais end of the great hall.

[154] See engraving by S. Buck, *Antiquities*, vol. 1 (1721), Yorkshire, No. 23.

Ornamentation was eschewed in secular structures throughout the early Perpendicular

Kenilworth Castle, Warwickshire. Windows of great hall: 1389–93

Tower of London. Byward Tower; painted wall decoration: *c.* 1380, with superimposed figures: *c.* 1400

period. Good proportions, boldly designed components, and the sure use of large areas of blank walling were the principal elements of design at this time. External decoration was confined to simple features such as the knapped flint and sandstone frontage of the gatehouse at Halnaker, the shields held by angels at Warkworth, the fleuron frieze at Wardour, or the window brackets and crockets at Caldicot. Internal ornamentation rarely extended beyond window and door mouldings and decorated shields. Only the great hall at Kenilworth shows an extensive and mechanical use of tracery panelling, and even this would originally have been offset by painted cloths or tapestries and a magnificent hammer-beam roof.

It is in the largest residences that the growing interest in the exploration of spatial effect in domestic architecture is most apparent during this period. Its development is immediately obvious by comparing the heavy timber roof built above the kitchen of the Bishop's Palace, Chichester, in the second half of the thirteenth century with the spacious vault and lantern of the kitchen of Durham Priory raised a hundred years later. The possibilities of spatial suggestion were extended throughout the fourteenth century by the development of the hammer-beam roof which led to the abandonment of intermediate columns in the larger halls and enabled attention to be focused on the upper spaces of the apartment. The thrilling effect of inventive and decorative genius exploring spatial enclosure would be far more apparent if the roof of the great hall at the Palace of Westminster and that reconstructed at Dartington were not the only such structures to have survived from the late fourteenth century.

It is qualities such as those displayed at Westminster which raised secular architecture to a new level of aesthetic achievement during the last quarter of the fourteenth century. The gatehouse at Saltwood and its prototype, the west gate at Canterbury, may or may not have been the work of the royal architect Henry Yevele, but their proportions, clean lines, and the quality of their workmanship are undeniable. Bodiam and Bolton demonstrate their designers' ability to create an integrated plan resolving the domestic and military demands of a major household within a single architectural concept. The entrance approach of Warwick Castle is the most imposing military frontage built in late medieval England,[155] and the tower-house at Warkworth Castle is a highly ingeniously planned residence which was both comfortable and aesthetically attractive. The halls at the Palace of Westminster and Kenilworth Castle were admirably designed as a stage to offset the estate and magnificence of their owners, while Wykeham's two colleges, both of noble design but with an even higher standard of workmanship at Winchester than at Oxford, still fulfil the function for which they were designed nearly six hundred years ago. It is buildings such as these and ecclesiastical works such as the cathedral naves at Canterbury (1378–81 and 1391–1411) and Winchester (1394–c. 1406) which make up and still identify the first peak of the Perpendicular style of architecture in England.

Interiors and Furnishings

Few of the buildings discussed in this chapter retain an unscathed interior. The majority of them are ruined and those that have benefited from continuous occupation have naturally been subject to considerable alteration. Much of the interior of Lumley was transformed

[155] Apart from Guy's Tower (completed 1394), this frontage is made up of the gatehouse, barbican and Caesar's Tower, all usually attributed to Thomas, XI earl of Warwick (1329–69). Despite superficial differences of shape, the similarity in the basic planning and purpose of the dominant angle towers, and the use of common window forms, suggest that Caesar's Tower was built not long before Guy's Tower. The chemin-de-ronde and superstructure of Caesar's Tower is also a late rather than a mid 14th century feature. The lack of machicolations protecting the gatehouse or barbican suggest that this was the first work to be raised after the great hall and residential apartments had been built in the mid 14th century. A suggested dating for this frontage, therefore, is gatehouse and barbican c. 1360–9, Caesar's Tower between 1370 at the earliest and 1385, and Guy's Tower c. 1390–4. This important structure still awaits a detailed architectural survey and analysis. In the meantime P. B. Chatwin, *Trans. Birmingham Arch. Soc.* vol. 67 (1947–8) and *V.C.H. Warwickshire*, vol 8 (1969) 455–64 help to fill the gap.

[156] The gatehouses at Hever, Wingfield, and Donnington have also been restored in the 20th century but primarily for reasons of preservation rather than for occupation.

[157] E. W. Tristram, *English Wall Painting of the Fourteenth Century* (1955), 36–8, 194–8.

[158] London Museum, *Medieval Catalogue* (1940), 236.

[159] 56 licences to crenellate were granted between June 1377 and September 1399: 54 by Richard II and 2 by the bishop of Durham. 8 of these licences do not apply to secular residences —3 refer to monastic gatehouses, 2 to the city walls at Salisbury and Canterbury, 2 to town houses in *Fleet Street*, London, and 1 to a bridge tower in Ireland. One of Richard's licences refers to work additional to that already authorized at Penrith, while another duplicates a licence previously granted by the bishop of Durham. To this total of 46 secular buildings licensed during the late 14th century, the pardon and request for a licence for Farleigh Hungerford Castle should be added, and that for Shirburn Castle granted in March 1377 may be included as it covers work undertaken during the years immediately following Richard's accession. The existence of a licence, of course, is not necessarily indicative that the building was constructed: see page 109, note 28. Licences were not required for the work known to have been undertaken at 11 royal castles and 15 royal or semi-royal residences, nor for that believed to have been carried out at Cilgerran Castle. Major building work is also known or firmly believed to have been carried out at 27 private residences during Richard's reign for which no licences are known. Of the 58 residences surviving from the period, 21 were licensed, 13 were for royal or semi-royal buildings and 24 were apparently unlicensed.

by Vanbrugh. Shirburn, Raby, and Brancepeth were scarred by curious interpretations of medievalism in the eighteenth and nineteenth centuries. The gatehouses at Caldicot and Saltwood were rehabilitated in the late nineteenth century with a more sympathetic appreciation of their original form and this approach has been maintained in the present century at Dartington and Norrington.[156] The removal of the house built within the hall at Howden would probably reveal some of its former splendour, and it would not be impossible to restore the interior of Shute Barton to its original condition. Probably Westminster Hall and the roofed parts of Bolton Castle show the least altered interiors today but these, like all other survivals whether ruined or not, should be enlivened by decoration, furniture, and bright colours and peopled with rich dresses, etiquette, and an elaborate ceremonial.

The late fourteenth century wall and ceiling paintings and the contemporary floor tiles found in 1953 in the Byward Tower at the Tower of London are rare survivals.[157] A considerable quantity of heraldic floor tiles were also discovered during the excavation of Baginton Castle, made by an itinerant craftsman from London where tiles from the same moulds have been found.[158] No painted wall cloths are known, and the only glass of this period are fragments that have been found during excavations. Surviving wills show that there was a considerable amount of furniture and furnishing in larger households and that it achieved considerable richness in court circles. Without them, the residences of Richard II's reign can seem gaunt and colourless, but it should always be remembered that they originally displayed qualities that were quite the opposite.

Summary

This survey can only briefly indicate some of the political, financial, and social factors contributing to the building explosion of the late fourteenth century. Nor is it possible to do more than lightly sketch the character and hint at the inventiveness of the architectural style adopted for residential work during this period. What will have emerged is how many powerful and wealthy families were engaged in building activities at this time and how much of their work survives today. Out of the twenty-five or so leading families whose lives span the majority of the period, the work of at least thirteen of them is still extant, and something is known of the work of at least two further magnates which no longer survives. If this analysis is extended a little further, out of the one hundred and two residential buildings known or believed to have been raised by the Crown, baronage, knights, and other landowners during Richard's reign, the remains of at least fifty-eight of them still survive, varying in interest and extent from a fragmentary wall to a complete palace-fortress.[159] Further research, examination, and excavation will doubtless add to these figures, but they are perhaps indicative of the percentage of work that has survived the vagaries of nearly six hundred years. Some of the destroyed buildings such as those at *Highclere*, *Arundel*, and *Fotheringhay* would add considerably to our knowledge of planning and design in Richard's reign. Nevertheless, the extent and range of the surviving structures enable what is probably a reasonably accurate picture to be drawn of the considerations determining the planning and design of many major and a considerable number of minor residences built during the reign of Richard II.

Chapter 7

The Entrance Block and North Courtyard

There is no impressive forecourt or entrance to Dartington Hall. The road curves in front of the Hall and a short approach leads directly to the entrance block. This many-windowed structure is flanked by a short wing on the right and a hexagonal threshing-room on the left projecting from the long low line of the barn. Although these buildings eschew any architectural pretensions, their adoption to different ground levels and their varying roof lines give them a homely character which contrasts sharply with the splendour of the main courtyard.

The Entrance Block

The two-storeyed entrance block is not an integral part of the planning of the Hall, for it is independent of the ranges flanking it. The block consists of a simple entrance passage and two unequal-sized rooms on each floor. Since 1927, the rooms have been used as studios, but for over a century and a half beforehand, the larger one on the ground floor had served as a stable and the room above had been adapted as a hayloft. It is likely that they had been used for such purposes since at least the seventeenth century, and consequently it is difficult to establish their original form and use.

Semicircular arches of undressed local stone[1] frame either end of the passageway admitting both foot and vehicular traffic.[2] The wooden doors, designed by William Weir, hang on an arched frame that appears to be coeval with the wooden trusses of the roof above. The original doors were secured by a wooden bar, but traces of the holes which held it, found by Weir, are no longer visible. The original form of the smaller ground-floor room leading

[1] The underneath of the arches are covered with the remains of the original plaster, partially and inadvertently chipped away in 1928. It is extremely unlikely that these arches ever held inner stone orders.

[2] This was common practice in the west of England as, for example, at Tiverton Castle (mid 14th century), Bradley Manor (*c.* 1420, now destroyed), Shute Barton (probably 15th century), and Weare Gifford Hall (late 15th century) in Devon, Whatley Manor (late 15th century?) and Cothay Manor (*c.* 1485) in Somerset, and Great Chalfield (*c.* 1480) in Wiltshire.

Entrance block from the forecourt

Entrance passage way from the north court

directly off the entrance passage has been entirely obliterated by later changes, although Buck's drawing is evidence that the present entrance was in existence in 1734 and the splay of a narrow window was discovered in the north wall in 1928. It is possible that this room was intended to be occupied by a porter guarding the approach to the Hall.

The principal room on each floor is 40 feet long and 24 feet wide. The present entrance to the ground-floor room was inserted in 1928 but it may have been the site of the original entrance, for a solid flight of stairs to the upper floor precluded a doorway in the usual position at the lower end of the room. There may have been a second entrance in the west wall marked by the pronounced splays on either side of the light wooden door in that wall, the relieving arch above the concrete lintel, and the passageway with its semi-circular roof. However, later buildings and changes in ground level have obliterated all traces of such an approach from the west.[3]

[3] A roof light marks the position of this passage externally.

The ground-floor room is one of considerable height by medieval standards. The open joisted ceiling, restored by Weir, is carried on two bull-like axial timbers supported by a large octagonal wooden pillar[4] with curved braces. The pillar is probably coeval with the roof trusses above, but the pointed stops which terminate the intermediate chamfered planes of the pillar are not closely datable for they persisted throughout the medieval and sub-medieval period. The fact that the axial timbers are two different and ill-matched beams and that the pillar rests on a later base suggest that the whole floor was renewed long ago and that the pillar was probably reset. Urine and dirt from the stables were probably responsible for rotting the bottom of the pillar and making it necessary to replace it with a stone base. There was no evidence of a fireplace in this room before Weir inserted the present one in 1928.

[4] A similar original feature supports the roof of the almost contemporary 'Seventh Chamber' at Winchester College. The beam carrying the first-floor timber complex at the south end of the guest hall at Polsloe Priory near Exeter, is also supported by an octagonal wooden pillar standing on a square stone base. It has been attributed to the late 13th century.

The modern external staircase leading to the first floor roughly follows the line of the old covered one removed in the eighteenth century (see p. 84).[5] There was no half landing

[5] Similar external stairs serving rooms above an entrance gateway in the west of England occur at Whatley Manor, Shute Barton, and Place Farm, Tisbury (all 15th century).

Entrance block from the north court

Entrance block. Principal ground-floor room

Entrance block. Roof of larger first-floor room

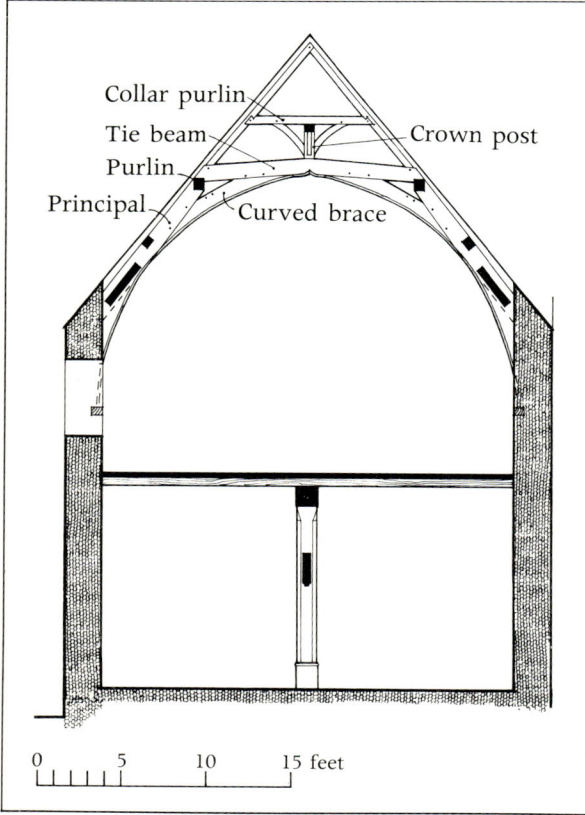

Fig. 23 Entrance block. Central truss including supporting pier to ground-floor room

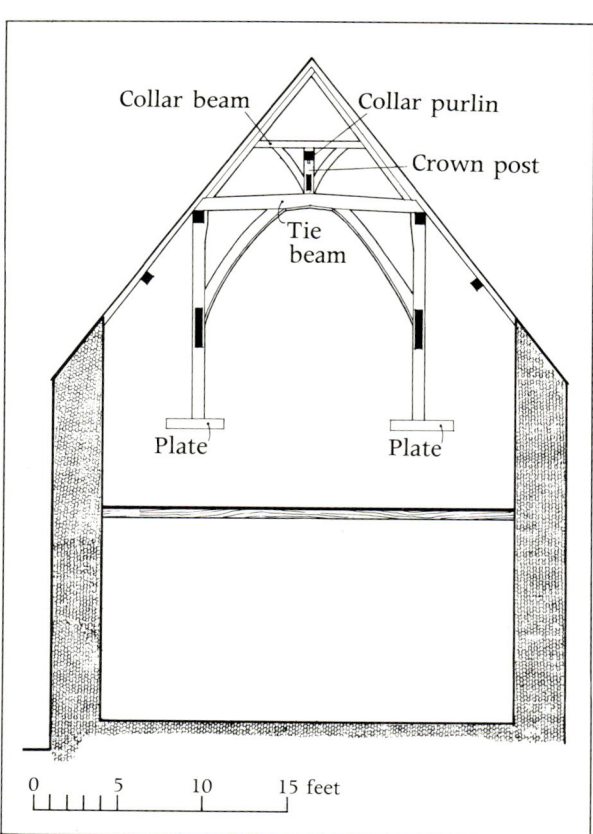

Fig. 24 Entrance block. End truss to west wall

[6] Weir made two attempts at reconstructing the present staircase. The first made no allowance for a half landing and was too steep.

[7] In 1925, this room was the estate carpenter's shop and could only be approached by a ladder on the right-hand side of the outer entrance arch. The wooden gallery, fireplace, and chimney were all inserted by Weir in 1928. The three-way post and corbel on the chimney-flue were brought forward at the same time.

[8] The patterning of the external stonework above this door suggests that it might have been converted from an earlier window.

[9] It is unlikely that certain oddities of construction were the result of 20th-century reconstruction. Weir made it clear to Mr. Elmhirst that despite the substantial replacements necessary to the roofs of the entrance block and the end block of the adjacent west range, he managed to save *in situ* enough pieces of the original work to give anyone in the future an exact picture of the original construction. At least one of every vital piece of roof structure was left where he found it.

[10] J. T. Smith has pointed out to me that these appear to be normal where posts are set in stone walls in the west of England, but not elsewhere. They are also used for the feet of cruck trusses.

originally and the stairs terminated in a landing sufficiently large to provide room for two adjacent doorways.[6] One of these openings, now adapted as a window, led into the larger room of four bays and the other, in use today, led into the smaller room of two bays. Apart from the roof, few early features remain in the smaller of the upper rooms,[7] but the hearth and fireplace in the larger apartment are apparently original. The opening in the first bay from the west, now leading to the upper room of a small projecting wing of later date (right on p. 139), may have formerly given access to a garderobe. The door in the east wall was added in the eighteenth century after the original approach from the courtyard had fallen into disuse.[8]

The two rooms were divided by a stone partition wall that appears to have been modified at a later date. The original partition probably consisted of a low wall at first-floor level on which was set a thinner partition that extended the height of the apartment. This tentative conclusion is based entirely on the way in which the various roof timbers and the relevant truss principals terminate on either side of the present wall.

Beetle-infested timbers made it necessary for Weir to replace many of the members of the roof, but sufficient evidence remained for its early form to be clearly revealed and accurately restored in 1930–1.[9] The three trusses in the larger room support two square-set purlins above which cambered tie-beams carry crown-post and collar-purlin superstructures. Direct support to the purlins is given by short principals which are embedded in the side walls and joined by curved braces to the tie-beams, thus forming a rigid triangle (Fig. 23). Curved wind-braces steady the purlins between each truss and conform to the pitch of the roof. The truss at the west end of the room has the normal complement of tie-beam, crown-post, and collar-purlin, and two principal posts partly embedded in the wall and tenoned at the foot into short horizontal timbers or plates (Fig. 24).[10] The posts terminate a few feet above the present floor level and axial braces rising from them support the

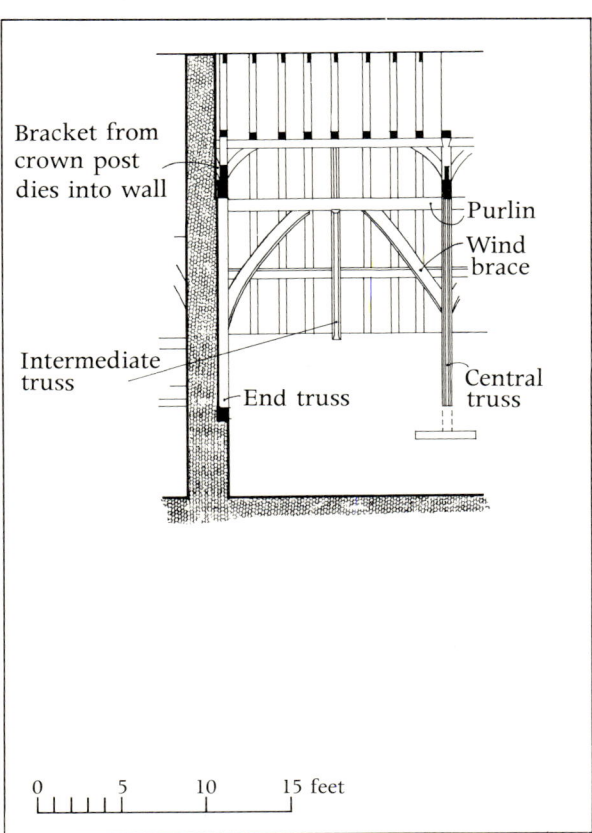
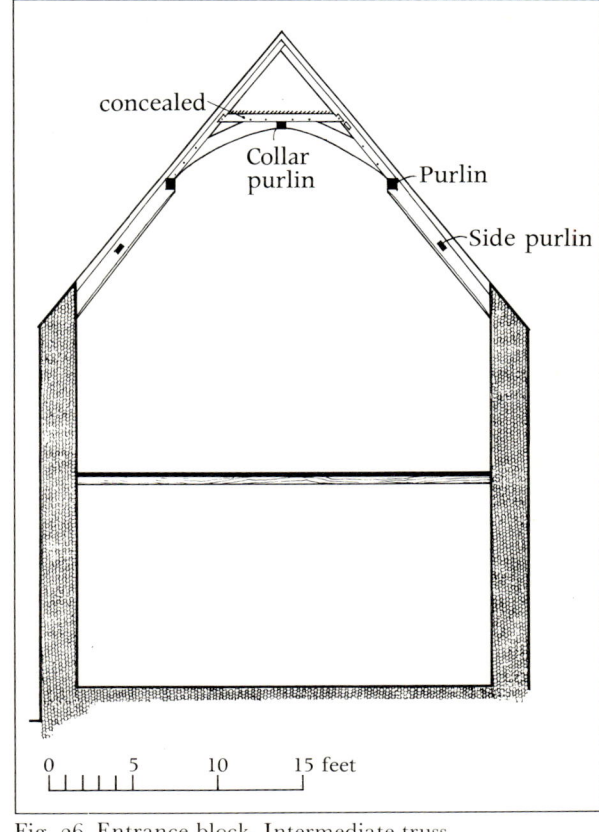

Fig. 25 Entrance block. West bay of room above entrance passage showing end, intermediate, and central trusses

Fig. 26 Entrance block. Intermediate truss

square-set purlins. Except for the short plates, the whole truss resembles that of an aisled timber structure with the principal posts separating the aisles from the nave. Saunders's drawings show that square-set purlins supported by heavy axial braces from the end trusses were formerly present in the roofs of both the great hall and the lower residential block (p. 163), and indeed the similarity between the terminal truss preserved in plaster above the residential block and those in the entrance block is very marked. The west bay of the smaller room above the entrance passage is illustrated as a less restored example than any of those in the large room. The long section illustrates the illogical way in which the axial braces from the neighbouring roof die into the partition wall together with the collar-purlin continuing towards the larger from the smaller room, supported by a brace from the crown-post on that side (Fig. 25).

Apart from the fact that the roof is an extremely heavy one for the building that it covers, it contains two unusual structural features of interest. One is the practice of dividing the collar-purlin into lengths of one bay each and tenoning each end into the crown-post of the central trusses.[11] This very unusual departure from the accepted practice might well have been a local variation and one that could only be reasonably employed where the gable end walls were of stone and able to resist any axial thrust. However, as the crown-posts were supported by braces to the collar-purlins, the axial thrust is almost negligible. The technique therefore suggests some lack of understanding of a crown-post roof. Secondly, the roof over the smaller room has longer bays than that over the larger room and the length necessitated the use of intermediate trusses of a type that was similar to those in the roof of the great hall (Fig. 26).[12] The use of side purlins here is probably due to the combining of certain traditional structural concepts. The use of purlins carried on the backs of principal rafters is almost certainly derived from the cruck truss. In its more refined use the purlin is butt-jointed into each principal, that is to say, it is tenoned through the rafter and not resting in an open rectangular notch on its upper side. The former method post-dates the latter typologically and the same presumably holds good for the collar-purlin and its use in the entrance block in 'bay lengths' described above.

All the windows in this block were renewed in 1928 except for the single lights in the east wall. The opening above the outer entrance arch was enlarged but all the other windows on the north side and the roof lights were new insertions. It is likely that there were hardly any openings on this side in medieval times. Most of the rooms in this block were lit from the south, but a drawing made by Saunders in 1805 shows that the earliest form had been altered in the post-medieval period by the insertion of square-headed windows (p. 84). A drawing made by Arthur Champernowne in 1856 shows that they still retained their roughly shaped semicircular heads internally at that time.

The Date and Purpose of the Entrance Block

Several writers have suggested that the present entrance block is the sole survival of a courtyard residence of the Martin family dating from the late thirteenth or early fourteenth centuries.[13] Few features remain which help to identify the period of its construction, and the absence of any moulded stonework means that the dating of the structure rests essentially on the typological evidence of the roof trusses. The roof is of a

[11] The crown-posts at Dartington are tenoned directly into the collar-beam, whereas that timber is normally dowelled on to the collar-purlin at its central point in common with the remaining collar-beams.

[12] The earliest use of intermediate trusses recorded so far are those at Great Coxwell Barn, attributed to the early 13th century. W. Horn and E. Born, *The Barns of the Abbey of Beaulieu and its Granges of Great Coxwell and Beaulieu St. Leonards* (1965), 6, 7.

[13] J. H. Parker, *Some Account of Domestic Architecture in England*, vol. 3, pt. 2 (1859), 353, refers to it as early 14th century. A. Hamilton Thompson also suggested that it might date from this period, *Arch. Jour.* vol. 70 (1913), 554. Weir favoured a late 13th-century or early 14th-century date, *Country Life* (27 August 1938), 206.

[14] N. Drinkwater, 'The Old Deanery, Salisbury', *Antiquaries Journal*, vol. 44 (1964), 41–59.

[15] The roof at Polsloe Priory, now partly destroyed, covered a first-floor hall of three bays with single-bay rooms at either end. The two central trusses in the hall had principals that lodged directly into the side walls in a similar manner to those at Dartington. Although the trusses no longer exist and the evidence has to be read from their chases, the partition truss at the south end of the hall preserved the original entrance doorways and two large principal posts set 4½ feet in from the side walls. These had been truncated but presumably the post heads supported square-set purlins,

otherwise the position of these posts is hard to explain and the combination of short principal central trusses with such an end framework requires another solution. The missing superstructure of the truss may well have been similar to the crown-post and collar-purlin arrangement at Dartington. Furthermore, the corresponding end of the hall was divided from the north chamber by a cob wall that stood on a substantial stone wall and carried the framework of the terminal truss. Such a wall may have been superseded by the present stone partition between the two rooms of the entrance block at Dartington. The framework at Polsloe Priory is probably no later than the early years of the 14th century and it may be of the preceding century. It is described here solely to illustrate the range typologically speaking that this particular truss covers in the 14th century. Its earlier forms in domestic examples in the west of England have either not survived or await discovery and publication. See A. W. Everett, 'The Priory of St. Catherine, Polsloe', *Proc. Devon. Arch. Exploration Soc.* vol. 2 (1934), 110–19; E. Lega-Weeks, 'The Pre-Reformation History of St. Katherine's Priory, Polsloe', *Trans. Devon Assoc.* vol. 66 (1934), 188–99. Also *Journal of the Royal Institute of British Architects*, vol. 41, no. 17 (July 1924), 9–17; *Devon and Cornwall Notes and Queries* (October 1934), 170–1.

[16] N. W. Alcock has pointed out to me that the roof of the barn at Bishop's Court, Sowton, near Exeter, has several features in common with the entrance roof at Dartington. These include the use of tie-beams, supported by curved braces, and similar but not identical end trusses. But there is no structure above the tie-beam at Sowton comparable with that at Dartington, and both the end truss-braces and the wind-braces are essentially straight whereas those at Dartington are curved. A precise dating of the Sowton barn is not possible, but Alcock considers that it may have been built in the early 14th century. His account of the medieval buildings at Bishop's Court is given in *Trans. Devon Assoc.* vol. 98 (1966), 133–8.

[17] Stables were built not far from the entrance approach at Winchester College (1400–1) and at Howden Manor (between 1388 and 1405) where there were six rooms above them.

[18] J. H. Parker, *Some Account of Domestic Architecture in England*, vol. 3, pt. 2 (1859), 353, refers to it as 'the old hall' and the *Arch. Jour.* vol. 30 (1873), 441, as 'a sort of servants' hall for the retainers'. A. Hamilton Thompson was less certain, *Arch. Jour.* vol. 70 (1913), 554.

form which could have been constructed as early as the second half of the thirteenth century, for it is not unlike the principals of the hall roof of the Old Deanery, Salisbury (1258–74).[14] It is closer in design to that above the hall of Polsloe Priory, Exeter, which is probably not later than the early years of the fourteenth century.[15] A late thirteenth- or early fourteenth-century date cannot therefore be entirely ruled out. On the other hand, there are several marked similarities between the entrance block roof and that built above the great hall and lower residential block at the opposite end of the courtyard during the closing years of the fourteenth century. Both roofs include a superstructure employing collar-beams, collar-purlins, and crown-posts above a cambered tie-beam. The intermediate and terminal trusses of both the entrance and the lower residential block roofs are very similar in design, while the presence of purlins carried on the backs of principal rafters, presumably an original feature, is independent evidence for assigning both structures to the end rather than to the first half of the fourteenth century. The present state of our knowledge does not yet allow the entrance roof to be dated with certainty, but there is no reason to assume that it must necessarily be coeval with early examples simply because it shows similar features of construction. Comparison with other roofs at Dartington suggests that it may well have been raised during the later years of the fourteenth century, but more precise dating must wait until other local examples have been studied in detail.[16]

It is quite likely that the large ground-floor room was originally built as a stable, close to the entrance approach,[17] and it has been suggested that the upper rooms were originally a first-floor hall and solar.[18] The position of the solar at the lower end of a hall is not unusual in thirteenth-century planning and the construction of a fireplace in the second rather than the end bay may well have been dictated by the position of the adjacent door. But the lack of a fireplace and chimney in the smaller room, the probable absence of any windows on the north side of the larger room, the small size of those on the south side, and the very large distance between this block and the only other known building, over 300 feet away, likely to have been built by the late thirteenth century (see Appendix 4) are difficulties in the way of this interpretation. If the roof structure suggests that the block was built in the second half of the fourteenth century, then documentary evidence confines this to a date later than April 1388 when the buildings on the site of the Hall were described as ruined and decayed. Furthermore, the lack of Beer stone, used by the earl of Huntingdon for all his dressed facing, indicates that the entrance block was not built at the same time as the majority of his work during the closing years of the century. Its whole character is indicative of vernacular work carried out by local masons, possibly added after Huntingdon had completed the majority of his work, or more probably built immediately after he had taken possession of the site in 1388.

The planning and use made of rooms in domestic gatehouses have not received the attention given to those guarding military and monastic sites. Barred doors and perhaps a moat were usually sufficient to protect the entrance approach of the smaller house from marauders and vagabonds, and therefore there was no need to make provision for any portcullis or other defensive machinery in the room above the entrance passage. The existence in so many cases of a fireplace in this room and sometimes a garderobe as at

Steeton Hall, Yorkshire (*c.* 1360) indicate that it was intended for residential purposes, and the position of this chamber, as in so many castle gatehouses, must have meant that it was generally used as the lodging of the official responsible for the overall custody of the residence. This would have been a constable in a large household and was the warden at Wykeham's collegiate foundations at Oxford and Winchester. The upper room might also be used as a court room as in the case of the great gatehouse at Ely (1396–1400), but the use of this room as a chapel like that added above the gatehouse at Prudhoe Castle (early fourteenth century?) was rare in domestic residences. The room commanding the approach of the Hall at Dartington may have been used by the constable or permanent custodian of the household, occupying the traditional position above the entrance of a residence. But the adjacent room is so large that it was quite likely that it was used by the grooms of the household, housed directly above the stables.

A curious lack of defence marks the approach to the north court. The entrance block cannot be called a gatehouse for it has no control over the passageway and fails to boast any battlements, portcullis, or other defensive features. There is no conclusive evidence in favour of an outer court, although it is just possible that the short wing projecting north of the entrance block, now devoid of any features of interest, represents the remains of a range or enclosing wall that originally extended further northwards.[19] Yet even this was likely to be no more than a forecourt for stabling and outhouses.[20] The entrance was merely a passage protected by two stout doors and a bar. It was possibly this lack of defensive features which made Hamilton Thompson suggest that the principal approach was situated on the east side of the main courtyard.[21] Apart from the fact that the east face of this range was well endowed with garderobe projections which would make it unlikely that the entrance was adjacent to them, the known form of this range shows that the entrance lay elsewhere. There is no reason to believe that it was anywhere other than in its present position. In any case the symmetrical placing of the entrance almost opposite the hall porch cannot have been coincidence. Of the dozen or so residences built from their foundations during the last quarter of the fourteenth century where the position of the entrance approach and hall can still be identified, nine were planned with these two features opposite or almost opposite each other.[22] It is certainly surprising that Huntingdon should have been satisfied with such a simple approach to his mansion, but Lord Scrope was equally satisfied with a remarkably inconspicuous entrance at Bolton Castle. Perhaps Huntingdon's death prevented him from replacing it with a more elaborate work and his successors were satisfied with the existing building. The whole structure is an unpretentious example of a building which may be compared with the similar but larger fourteenth-century example at Charing Palace (*c.* 1338–48) and the more modest examples at Shute Barton and Whatley Manor, Somerset (both probably fifteenth century).

The entrance block presents one further odd feature of planning. The north wall of the west range only touches the gable-wall of the entrance block, leaving a re-entrant angle at the junction. It is likely that this was simply the result of planning two structures at different times, but it is just possible that closer integration was prevented by the existence of a further structure at this junction. The foundations of a circular structure discovered at the east end of the barn in 1936 may have been those of a dovecote or a tower, and

[19] This small two-storeyed wing had been used for agricultural purposes since at least the early 19th century and nothing was lost in its adoption to different uses in the 20th century. Those roof trusses which were not replaced by Weir appear to be cut down and reused timbers of 17th-century date or even later. Saunders's plan of the Hall shows that there was a small farm building against the west wall of this wing in the early 19th century.

[20] The barn on the east side of the forecourt and two lean-to buildings built up against the north face of the entrance block, removed in 1928, were 19th-century structures. The pits dug for the two trees planted on the west side of the forecourt in 1962 showed that the outcrop of rock there immediately below the present surface had not been disturbed before.

[21] A. Hamilton Thompson, *Arch. Jour.* vol. 70 (1913), 554, followed by N. Pevsner, *South Devon* (1952), 99, also suggested that the existing entrance passage was probably broken through the block at a later period, but neither the plan nor the patterning of the stonework in any way support this view.

[22] Howden Manor, Winchester College, the castles at Bodiam and Lumley, the fortified houses at Farleigh Hungerford, Halnaker, Penrith, Scotney, and almost certainly at Wressell. The exceptions are New College, Oxford, Bolton Castle, and probably Sheriff Hutton Castle.

the possibility that there was a tower in the re-entrant angle at the west end of the entrance block cannot be ruled out until the site has been excavated. There would certainly have been a closer integration between the entrance block and the west range if the Hall had been designed to withstand assault, but although there is no evidence of any contemporary access to a building here from the adjacent blocks, the curious plan at this junction does suggest that some sort of structure may have existed which has no longer survived.

The North Courtyard

The entrance passage opens into the north court, an irregular-shaped quadrangle with sides 243½ feet and 265 feet long and 156 feet and 164 feet wide respectively. At the far end of the court is the late fourteenth-century ensemble of porch tower, great hall, upper and lower residential blocks, and kitchen. The sides of the court are flanked by ranges of lodgings and the fourth side is closed by a barn adjacent to the entrance block. Although the south end of the east range was destroyed in the nineteenth century, it is possible to determine the length of the east and south ranges by reference to a block plan of the Hall made in 1805.[23] Unfortunately, the relevant portion of this plan is now missing, but a small-scale copy of it was published in the *Archaeological Journal* in 1913 and has been incorporated in the plan on page 101.

It is unlikely that the courtyard was ever the tidy sward we see today. Eighteenth-century drawings show that it was slightly higher at the southern than at the western end, and it was not until 1933 that the bank of earth piled up against the lower courses of the great hall and porch tower was removed. The slightly different levels between the east and west ranges still remain although they are now almost concealed by landscaping. The clutter of farm buildings, dividing walls, and agricultural equipment which filled much of the courtyard in 1925 was removed in the following years, and the present lawn and

[23] Exeter City Library: f. 009.4/113547.

North court from the entrance block showing part of west range, hall range with porch tower, and kitchen block

encircling paths, designed by Beatrix Farrand, were laid out in 1935.

A resistivity survey of the area covered by this courtyard was carried out in 1964 to determine whether there was any evidence of earlier buildings beneath the present lawn. Readings made at regular 4-feet intervals showed a general but irregular fall in resistance values from west to east. None of them aligned with any of the present or the earlier medieval buildings, and it is probable that the resistivity meter was detecting the natural layers of Middle Devonian slate near the surface on the western uphill side and an accumulation of more conductive terrace build-up on the eastern side. Any building foundations present should have interrupted this regular pattern, especially if they extended to the eastern half of the courtyard. The only indication of any foundations at all were those of a dividing wall across the middle of the courtyard, and this had been built in the nineteenth century and removed in 1925.

The courtyard is one of the largest areas enclosed within a residential building during the medieval period. Some castle baileys covered a greater area, but their planning was almost entirely dictated by military rather than residential needs.[24] The north courtyard of Dartington Hall was exceeded in area by only a very small number of institutional quadrangles—the contemporary cloister garths at London Charterhouse (1371) and Mount Grace Priory (1398),[25] and the mid fifteenth-century quadrangles planned but not built by Henry VI at Eton College and King's College, Cambridge. At the time of its development during the late fourteenth century, the north courtyard at Dartington enclosed a larger area than the court of any other private residence. It was exceeded in area by only two domestic quadrangles during the later medieval period, the outer court at Thornbury Castle, possibly built by the duke of Buckingham in the early sixteenth century, and the outer court at Eltham Palace, which we first hear about in Richard II's reign although it did not take its final shape until the early Tudor period.[26]

[24] The court at Llangibby Castle in Monmouthshire, for instance, attributed to c. 1310–14, was 540 feet by 270 feet. *Arch. Cambriensis*, vol. 105 (1956), 96–132.

[25] Founded by Huntingdon's nephew, the duke of Surrey and earl of Kent. Although it follows the usual planning of a Carthusian foundation, it shares with Dartington the common planning of an extremely large court from which individual lodgings opened.

[26] A late 16th-century plan shows that the outer court at Eltham Palace was between 264 feet and 319 feet long and 187 feet and 263 feet wide. Part of the existing early Tudor remains show traces of a remodelling from an earlier, possibly mid 15th-century building. The irregularity of this court is almost certainly due to the existence of earlier buildings on the same site and these may date as far back as Richard II's reign when the existence of the outer court is mentioned in the account roll of the controller (June 1387 to June 1389). P.R.O. E 101, 473, 3(i). See also R. A. Brown, H. M. Colvin, and A. J. Taylor, *The History of the King's Works*, vol. 2 (1963), 935; Anthony Emery, 'Eltham Palace', *Arch. Cantiana*, vol. 74 (1960), 101, 103, 107; D. E. Strong, *Eltham Palace: Official Guide* (1958).

North court from the roof of the great hall

Porch tower from the north court

Chapter 8

The Porch Tower and Great Hall

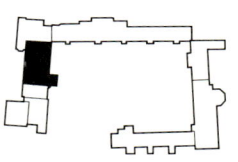

The range on the south side of the north court is composed of five closely associated units. A tall porch tower opens into a passage giving access to the great hall, immediately identifiable from the courtyard by a series of four large windows. The tower and hall separate a group of apartments at either end: the lord's apartments or upper residential block at the west end and the lower residential block with offices beneath it at the east end. The indispensable adjunct of these apartments and offices was the kitchen and this fifth unit, distinguishable from the courtyard by its prominent gable-end, is virtually a detached building, linked internally by a passageway and externally by a low buttressed wall. Since their construction, only the upper residential block has been subject to such drastic changes that it no longer resembles its original form. Apart from this, what exists today, both externally and to a large extent internally, is essentially the range of buildings raised by the earl of Huntingdon in the late fourteenth century. This range is particularly notable for its completeness, the quality of its workmanship, and the existence of a series of closely related apartments of considerable dignity and size, constructed within a very short period of time.

Kitchen, lower residential block, porch tower, and great hall from the north court

The Porch Tower

All the apartments on the south side of the courtyard are approached through an impressive and boldly projecting entrance tower. Like the majority of Devon church towers, it is supported by two slender buttresses set back from the angles. These buttresses, like those supporting the great hall, are not bonded into the walls but are an original feature.[1] The tower consists of a porch opening directly into the screens passage and a single room of similar proportions on the two floors above, reached by a newel staircase which looks as though it has been wedged between the tower and the lower residential block.

Minor alterations have not affected the proportions or character of this late fourteenth-century tower, although the windows lighting the first- and second-floor rooms were replaced by square-headed frames in the sixteenth century.[2] Buck's drawing shows that the tower was formerly crowned with two stone chimneys and a small octagonal-shaped roof above the stair turret (p. 82), but one of the chimneys and the turret roof were probably removed in 1741 when the pretty cupola and weather-vane with that date and the initials A.C. were added by Arthur Champernowne. Battlements were an original feature of the tower, hall, and lower residential block. One or two of the original tower battlements of Beer stone still remain *in situ*, but the remainder were restored in the nineteenth century and replaced again with Bath stone in 1932.

The porch is a fine example of late fourteenth-century domestic work. A single vaulted bay protects the approach to the screens passage and the great hall. The outer archway, heavily weathered both internally and externally, lacks the deep moulding of the inner arch but it is protected and saved from insignificance by a pronounced drip moulding. The wave moulding of this arch is characteristic of west of England workmanship in the late fourteenth century. The inner archway is finer than the outer archway for the continuous roll of deep-cut moulding gives it depth and majesty. This type of moulding is often associated with work of the first half of the fifteenth century, and the fact that the archway is not quite centred in the wall of the porch suggests that it may have been inserted during that period. Yet the close similarity between the moulding of this arch and that at the entrance to the hall of the Vicars Choral at Chichester (1397), the occurrence of two forms of moulding in this arch similar to those used in the screens-passage arches, and the presence of the same mason's mark at the apex of the arch as on the inner arch to the stairs turret and the hall fireplace (see Appendix 8) confirm that the workmanship dates from the late fourteenth century.

The stone vault is divided by eight ribs which meet at a central boss displaying a chained hart on a heraldic rose (p. 97). The junction of the ribs with this boss are filled with wheat-ears, and the pattern of a rose flanked by wheat-ears is repeated at the base of the ribs on each side of the porch. The occurrence of the badges of Richard II and Huntingdon respectively is important evidence for dating this part of the Hall to the years between Huntingdon's receipt of the property in 1388 and the death of Richard II and his half-brother in 1400. There was no indication that the bosses had been coloured before they were painted in 1932, but traces of a pink wash which may have been applied to the plaster walls and stonework several centuries ago, still survive, particularly on the ribs and

---

[1] The batter at the base of all these buttresses and the associated walling was added by Weir in 1933 to strengthen their foundations.

[2] The original relieving arch over the first-floor window is still clearly visible.

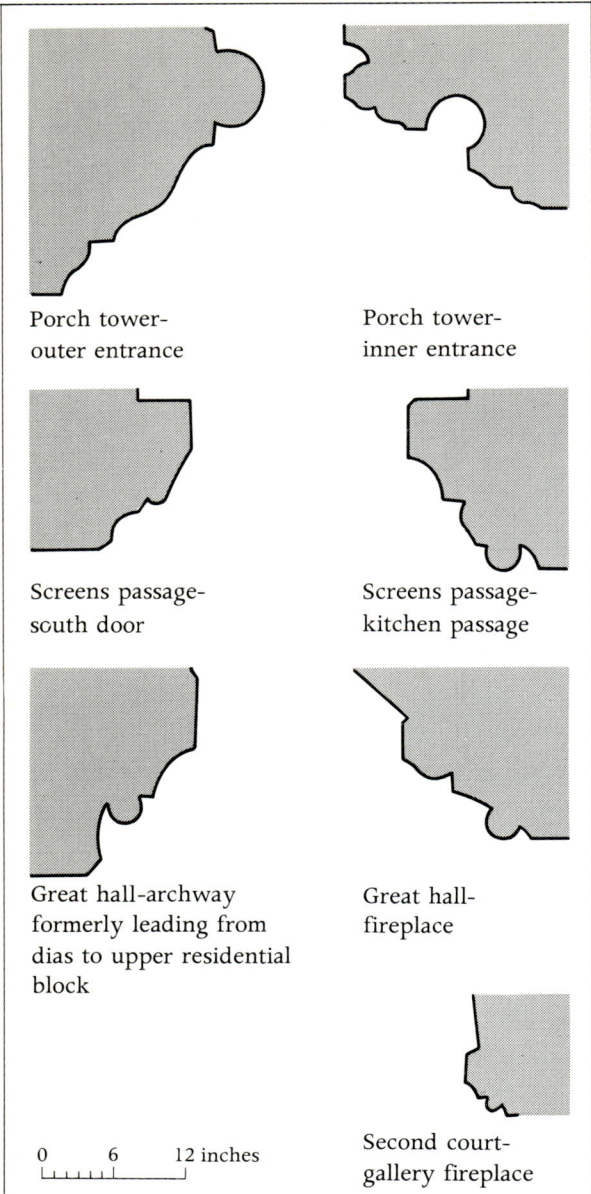

Fig. 27 Profile of mouldings from porch tower, screens passage, great hall, and south court

Porch tower. Vaulted porch opening into screens passage

the rear of the outer arch. Two stone benches line either side of the porch,[3] and it is possible that the oak seats covering them are original. They used to retain traces of former paintwork and part of a chain still exists which may have held one of them to the wall to prevent its theft or more likely, to make it secure to the wall.

Both the rooms above the entrance porch are simple rectangular chambers, approached from the spiral staircase which also gives access to the upper rooms of the lower residential block and the roof. The tower rooms contain fireplaces and were therefore used for residential purposes, but they are otherwise devoid of any original features.[4]

The Great Hall

The entrance porch opens directly into the screens passage, a characteristic feature of medieval domestic planning from at least the early fourteenth century onwards. Such a passage not only screened some of the noise and traffic of the kitchens from the great hall but facilitated access between the north and south courtyards. There are high rear arches with four-centred heads at either end of the passage, similar to the contemporary examples at the entrance to the halls at Halnaker House (c. 1380) and the Vicars Choral, Exeter (1388),

[3] Similar stone benches exist on either side of the contemporary hall porch at Howden Manor.

[4] The moulded Elizabethan ceiling, stated to be in one of the rooms in this tower, *Country Life* (3 September 1938), was an error.

152

Great hall. Screens passage towards the south court

the great hall at Kenilworth Castle (1389–93) and at either end of the entrance passage in the gatehouse of Caldicot Castle (c. 1388).

The screens passage is formed out of the end bay of the great hall. It was easier to appreciate this when the apartment was ruined, since the insertion of the wooden screen and ceiling have given the passage a unity of its own. It is not possible to state whether a screen was an original feature of the hall or not. Comparable examples would suggest that some sort of division of this nature would have formed part of the planning of the hall, but the only evidence in favour of such a partition were two holes in the side walls which might have held the framing for a partition and even these could have been made for a later insertion. In the absence of any drawings or other evidence,[5] the present screen was built by Weir modelled on that in the Church House Inn at Torbryan, three miles north of Totnes. The lack of any chases in the end wall which might have supported a heavy gallery and the absence of a door in the north wall at first-floor level prior to 1932 suggest that a gallery was not an original feature of the hall.

The great hall is a finely proportioned and majestic apartment, $68\frac{3}{4}$ feet long, $37\frac{1}{2}$ feet wide, and 48 feet high. It is divided architecturally into five bays but from the practical

[5] A screen is not included in any of Saunders's drawings of 1805 and therefore could not have been removed by Froude in about 1810 as assumed in *Country Life* (3 September 1938).

Great hall towards the dais: 1925 Great hall. Corbel on north side supporting roof brace

and social points of view, the room may be considered in three parts: the screens passage, the dais, and the body of the hall used for communal eating and entertainment.

Seven tall windows, four on the north and three on the south side, flood the hall with light. They have been subject to considerable alteration since their construction in the late fourteenth century. Only the moulded rear arches remain untouched but fortunately the smaller window on the south side, blocked in the sixteenth century when a new wing was built against it, shows that the splays of all the other windows were formerly much wider. Except for those of the smaller window, they were cut back, probably in the sixteenth century, to allow a different-shaped window to be inserted. The blank walling between the window-sills and the bases of the inner arches, which an examination of the outer north wall shows is made of packing stone, indicates that the windows were originally $2\frac{1}{2}$ feet lower than at present. The additional lengthening would improve their proportions. There is no evidence to show whether window-seats were constructed or not. Nor is there sufficient evidence to indicate the form of the original tracery, for although a fragment of window tracery was found in 1931 which might have come from one of these windows,[6] too little remained for a hypothesis to be based on it with any certainty. The shape and size of the windows at Dartington suggest that they may have been similar in form to those in the dining hall at New College, Oxford (1380–6), Winchester College (1387–94), and the Vicars Choral at Exeter (1388) which are divided by a mullion and transom into four lights with cinquefoiled heads. The fragment of tracery found at Dartington could be part of such a design. The heads of the windows may have been filled with small twin lights as at Winchester or quatrefoils like those at Exeter and Oxford. The Exeter windows have cusped rear arches while the Oxford windows have moulded rear arches similar to those at Dartington (p. 236).

Buck's drawing shows that the hall windows were completely altered in the second half of the sixteenth century when square-headed frames were inserted with two mullions and

[6] It was discovered beneath the floor of the room immediately above the tower porch.

Great hall. Windows from the north court

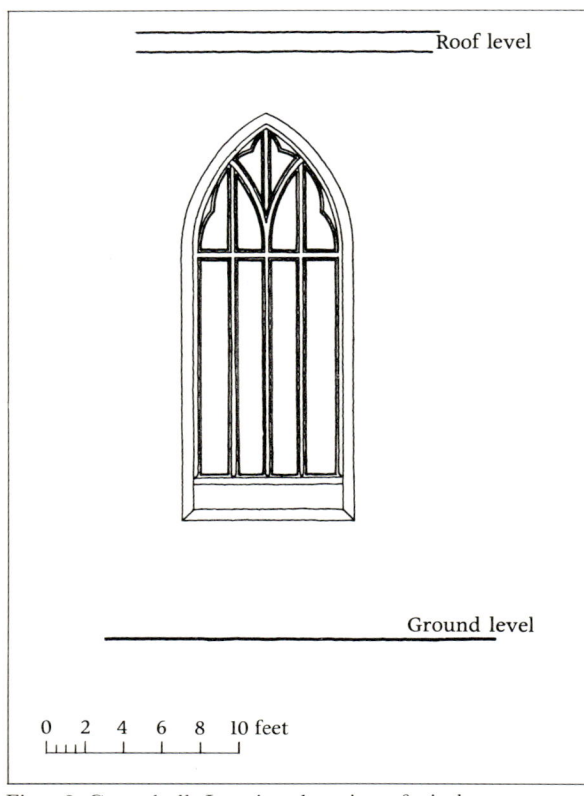

Fig. 28 Great hall. Interior elevation of window

Great hall. South side

[7] This practice was repeated in Devon in the halls at Powderham Castle, Knightstone near Ottery St. Mary, and Blagdon Manor near Paignton.

[8] Several guesses have been made at the date of this tracery. Hamilton Thompson felt that it might be medieval 'in the manner which recalls the work of a century earlier than the actual date of the hall', *Arch. Jour.* vol. 70 (1913), 556. The *Arch. Jour.* vol. 30 (1873), 440, thought that it was inserted in the time of Henry VIII or later, while Christopher Hussey considered that it was introduced by the Champernownes in about 1554, *Country Life* (3 September 1938). Nikolaus Pevsner judged that the tracery was 'a recent innovation', *South Devon* (1952), 100. The existing hand-thrown glass was inserted in the windows in 1932.

[9] The bracket in the side of the fireplace was found in a tip north of the entrance block in the early 1930s and was inserted during the restoration. Buck shows that the chimney serving this fireplace was similar in the early 18th century to that above the lower residential block. The present one was added in the 19th century.

[10] *Arch. Jour.* vol. 70 (1913), 557; *Country Life* (3 September 1938).

[11] The joggling of the stones above the fireplace give the impression of alteration, but they would originally have been covered with plaster and therefore not seen. They were still partly covered with plaster in 1926. The blind spandrels at either end are similar to those in the fireplaces of the hall at Kenilworth Castle.

[12] Dr. Gee has suggested to me that the mason's marks associating the hall fireplace, the inner arch not quite centred in the tower porch, and the arch of the newel stairs which look as though they were wedged in, might indicate slightly later work although the chronological difference could be merely that between two relative parts of the range.

[13] *Arch. Jour.* vol. 70 (1913), 557. Also *Cowdray and Easebourne Priory* (1919), 93 n. 13.

transoms dividing each window into nine lights (p. 82).[7] These were removed nearly two centuries later when the present lights and simple cusped tracery were inserted. This probably took place between 1737 and 1741 when the bell was cast and the weather-vane was raised above the porch tower.[8] Although timid in design, this tracery is far superior to anything we might have expected at a time when the principles of Gothic design were barely appreciated. Champernowne's work is a very fair attempt to reconstruct the windows in keeping with the character of the hall instead of inserting frames of Georgian design, similar to those in the west range of the main courtyard. It should be remembered, however, that the windows now fill the great hall with far more light than was originally the case before the splays were hacked back to their present form.

The level of the fireplace hearth and the stops at the foot of the archway in the south-west corner of the hall suggest that the dais built by Weir restored an original feature. The fireplace in the end wall, 17 feet long, has never been altered and survives in perfect condition. Only the kerb had to be restored and this copies a portion of the original work which still remains on the extreme left-hand side.[9] The shape and moulding of the arch above the fireplace opening has usually been taken as indicative of a date later than the remainder of the hall,[10] but evidence suggests that it was an original feature. Although four-centred arches are characteristic of fifteenth- and early sixteenth-century design, they were coming into fashion during the close of the fourteenth century. It is unnecessary to look any further for examples than the rear arches at either end of the screens passage of the hall. Moreover, the shape and quality of the fireplace moulding strongly resembles that surrounding the door in the south wall and the arches in the screens passage, and substantiates the view that it is coeval with the remainder of Huntingdon's work.[11] The existence of the mason's marks on the right-hand inner wall of the fireplace, identical with that on the inner staircase arch in the screens passage, confirms a late fourteenth-century date for this work (see Appendix 8).[12] William St. John Hope suggested that the fireplace was a later insertion,[13] but this

Great hall. Fireplace

Great hall towards the screens passage

would mean that there was either a central hearth and louvre, or fireplaces in the side walls. The position of the windows immediately precludes the second possibility and Saunders's careful longitudinal drawing of the hall gives no indication that the roof members of the central or the adjacent western bay were patterned differently from the other bays to allow for a louvre (p. 163).[14] Nor is there any indication that the end wall has been rebuilt so that the fireplace and its chimney could be inserted—a formidable task for an internal wall of this size and structural importance. The only alternative is that the present fireplace replaces an earlier and possibly smaller opening in the same position, but the evidence of the mason's marks precludes this possibility.

[14] It is quite likely that traces of the different patterning would still be visible in the drawing even if the louvre had been boarded up. The ashes and cinders found in the centre of the hall before its restoration were not evidence of a central hearth, *Jour. Brit. Arch. Assoc.* vol. 33 (1927), 131, but the remains of bonfires lit in the ruins during the 19th and early 20th centuries.

158

Great hall. Dais door

Penshurst Place, Kent. Stairs to upper residential block

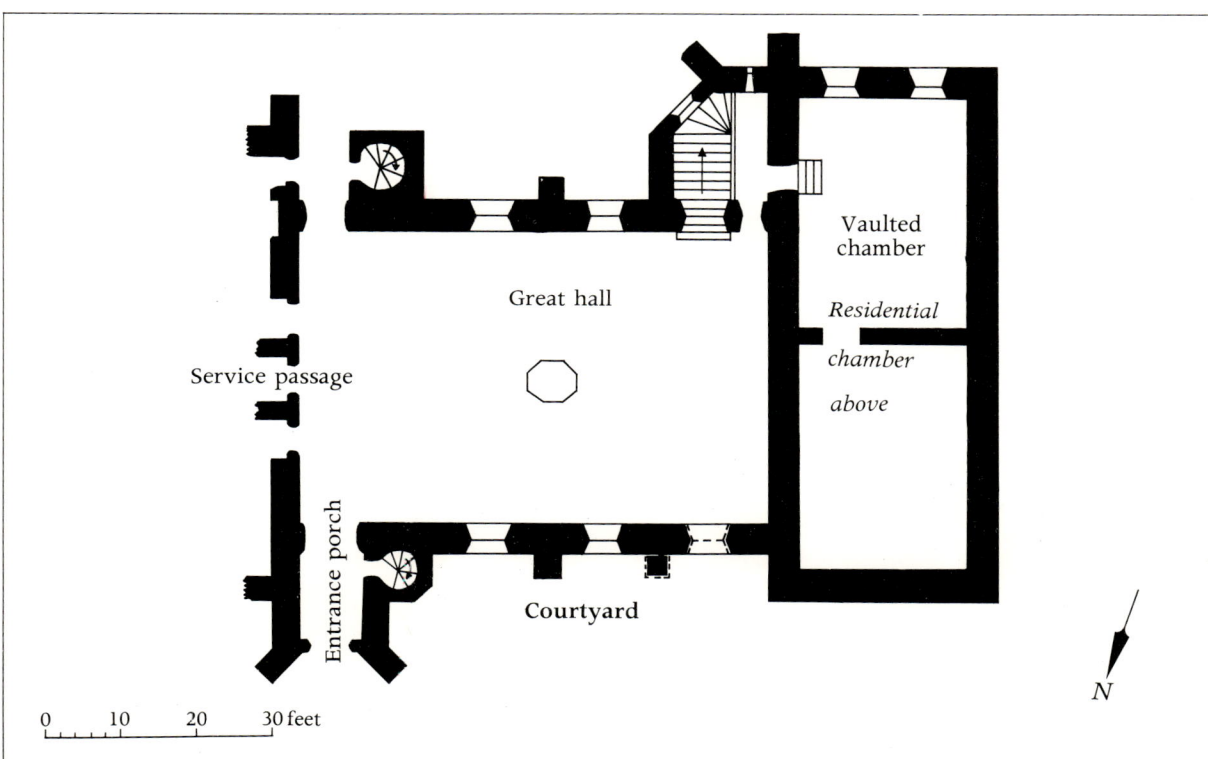
Fig. 29 Penshurst Place, Kent: 1341–9. Ground-floor plan of great hall showing approach to upper residential block

[15] *Proc. Birmingham and Midland Archaeol. Soc.* vol. 77 (1942).

[16] 'Acton Burnell Castle', *Studies in Building History*, ed. E. M. Jope (1961), 101.

[17] The site was excavated in 1953. T. L. Jones informs me that it was found that the hall possessed both a central hearth and an end-wall fireplace projecting into a narrow passageway between the hall and the upper residential block. The presence of both these hearths immediately suggests that the end-wall fireplace was a later insertion, but this was not supported by the site evidence. Furthermore, this fortified house had a short and fairly intense period of occupation going little beyond the 13th century when evidence of habitation suddenly ceased.

In any case, there has been a tradition of wall fireplaces since at least Anglo-Norman times. They were usually inserted in the side walls as in the great hall at Kenilworth Castle, but there is a growing body of evidence to prove the existence of fireplaces in the end walls of halls as early as 1300. S. E. Rigold has drawn my attention to the heavy end-wall fireplace in a ground-floor hall of *c.* 1300 at Shareshill in Warwickshire,[15] while C. A. Ralegh Radford has postulated that two end fireplaces heated the aisled first-floor hall at Acton Burnell Castle (*c.* 1284).[16] Excavations at Whichford Castle in Warwickshire have shown that the end-wall fireplace found in the hall there cannot be later than the early fourteenth century when the whole building seems to have been abandoned.[17] The great hall of the

159

Black Prince's manor at Kennington (1358) was planned with one supporting three chimneys,[18] and surviving examples of end fireplaces of this period can still be seen in the halls of the abbot's house at Croxden Abbey (1360),[19] Harewood Castle (1366), and Norrington Manor (c. 1380).[20]

It is usually assumed that the lord's table was on a dais parallel with the middle of the end wall of the hall, but the proximity of a particularly large fire to the dais suggests that a table directly in front of it must have proved very uncomfortable for some of the diners in winter. If the owner and his family ever ate in the great hall, it is likely that their table was arranged differently from the usual pattern so that their backs could avoid being roasted and some of the heat could percolate into the body of the hall.[21]

The archway on the south side of the dais shows a deep-cut moulding of the same quality as the screens-passage arches, but it is pitted and worn through being open to the elements in the nineteenth century. The opening now serves a small room of no pretensions added in the sixteenth century, but it was almost certainly intended to open on to an internal staircase leading through a right-angled turn to Huntingdon's private apartments in the upper residential block immediately behind the dais. The doorway is offset from the centre line of the window above to allow for the turn of the staircase. Earlier examples of the form and position such a staircase might have taken may still be seen leading from the hall to the upper block at Penshurst Place (1341–9), Berkeley Castle (1340–50 with staircase replaced in 1637), and Compton Castle (attributed c. 1340 and restored in 1955 on original evidence).[22] Unfortunately, any similar feature at Dartington was destroyed and the window immediately above it was filled in when the upper block was extended in Elizabethan times.[23]

[18] R. A. Brown, H. M. Colvin, and A. J. Taylor, *The History of the King's Works*, vol. 2 (1963), 967. Excavations have shown that the hall was a first-floor apartment above an undercroft. *Med. Archaeol.* vol. 11 (1967), 296–7. An impressive fireplace in this position with three chimneys still exists in the great hall of the Palace of Justice, formerly the Ducal Palace, Poitiers, France (probably between 1384 and 1390). The great hall of Hertford Castle also apparently possessed an end-wall fireplace and this might date from the extensive rebuilding programme undertaken by the duke of Lancaster in about 1380. See the plan in *The History of the King's Works* vol. 2 (1963), 679.

[19] *Arch. Jour.* vol. 120 (1963), 278.

[20] The present fireplace at Norrington was inserted in the 16th century and the arch was remade in the 20th century, but there are indications on the right-hand side that the opening is original.

[21] This is always assuming that a fire could burn in the hearth, for Mr. Elmhirst has never been able to achieve this feat.

[22] A contemporary staircase, possibly similar in form to that at Dartington but linking an entrance hall with a great hall also exists in the tower-house at Warkworth Castle.

[23] The moulding of the doorway does not support Hamilton Thompson's suggestion that it was a later insertion, *Arch. Jour.* vol. 70 (1913), 556. Nor is it likely that the window above has been truncated. It was shorter than other windows in the hall in order that it could clear the roof of the staircase beneath it. The window was completely covered over in the 16th century but a note on Saunders's longitudinal section of the hall range indicates that it was uncovered in the 18th century. The moulded stone placed below this window was found during the relaying of the main courtyard in 1935. It bears a strong resemblance to the crowned head shown in Saunders's drawing of a chimney still in existence in the early 19th century.

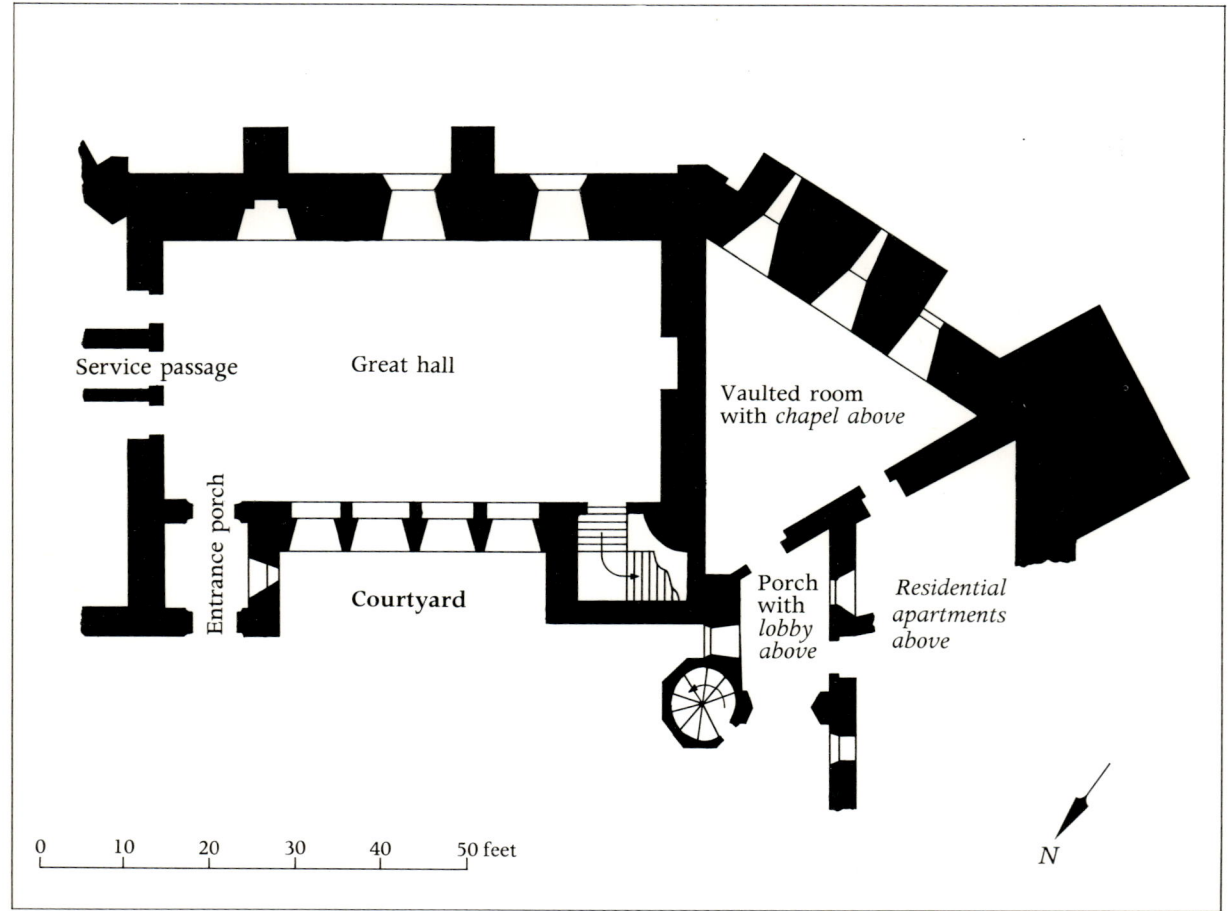

Fig. 30 Berkeley Castle, Gloucestershire: 1340–50. Ground-floor plan of great hall showing approach to upper residential block

The date and purpose of the opening at the north end of the dais is more problematical. This is the usual position for a door opening into the ground-floor room of the upper residential block and occurs, for example, at Amberley Castle (1377–c. 83). If the opening dates from the late fourteenth century, it would certainly have been framed by a finely moulded archway and its absence, particularly as all the other arches in the great hall have survived, is curious. The opening is possibly an original but altered feature of the hall or it may have been broken through in the sixteenth century as part of the reorganization of the upper residential block. The matter will be considered again on page 179.

The original roof of the hall was removed shortly after May 1813 as it was no longer considered safe.[24] The present structure was designed by William Weir in 1931 on lines similar to those chosen by the original master carpenter in the late fourteenth century. The evidence for its original form is twofold. There was the fortunate preservation of the outline of the roof timbers in the plaster at the west end of the hall (p. 155), and of a related but not identical structure in the plaster at the east end wall of the lower residential block.[25] Secondly, among the drawings made by Saunders in 1805 were two cross-sections showing the east and west ends of the hall respectively and a longitudinal section of the south side. Unfortunately, Saunders's drawings were not available for examination at the time of the restoration and it was necessary for Weir to rely entirely on the outline of the timbers in the plastered walls. Using these outlines as a guide and the existing corbels to give him the bay formation, Weir created the present magnificent structure. A study of Saunders's drawings confirms the accuracy of much of Weir's work. It differs from the original structure in four ways. Weir considered that it would be unwise to follow the exact dimensions of the medieval carpenters if he was to guarantee the stability of the whole structure. Therefore,

[24] See p. 87–8.

[25] The design of the late 14th-century roof of the great hall at Lumley Castle may be similarly determined by examining the outlines of the timbers in the plaster on the end walls above the present flat ceiling.

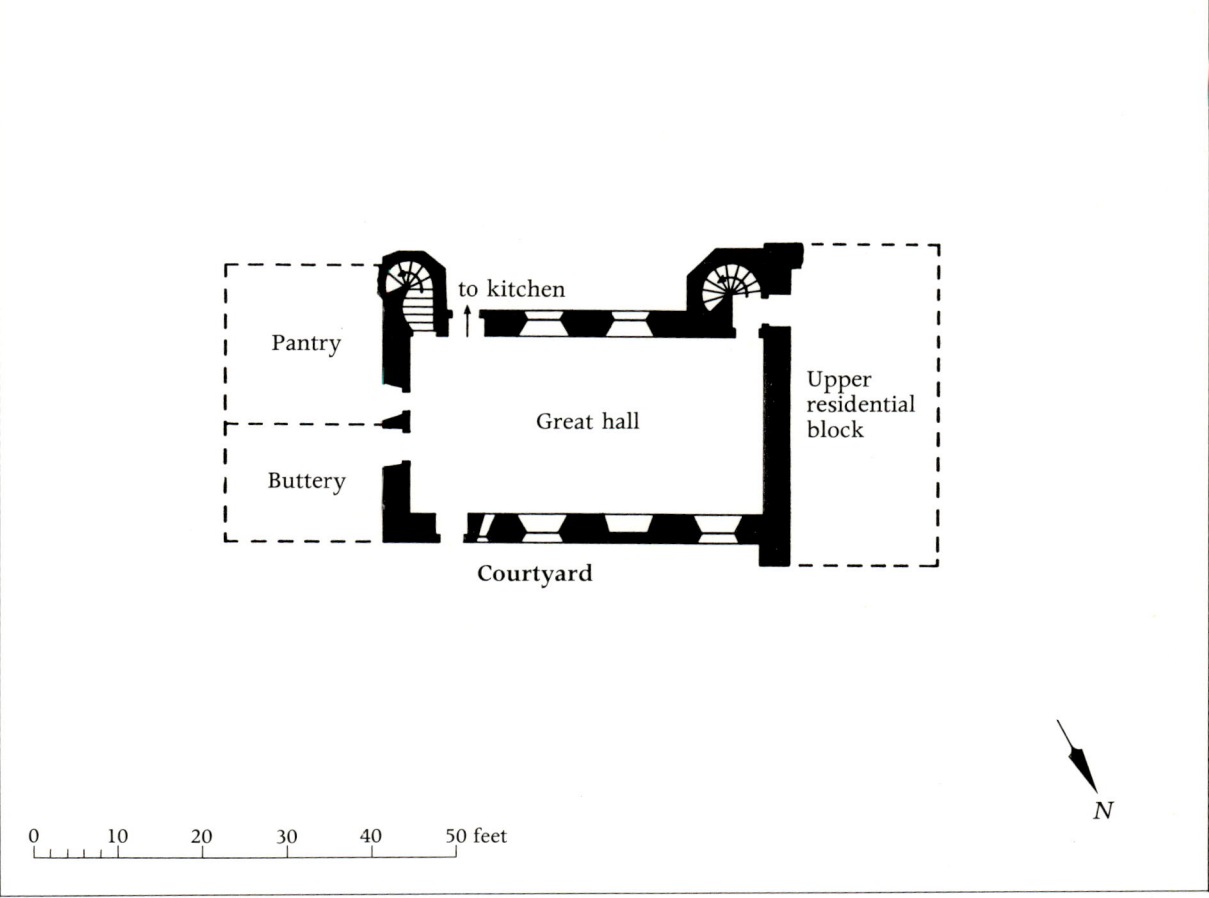

Fig. 31 Compton Castle, Devon: c. 1340. Ground-floor plan of hall, reconstructed on original evidence in 1955, showing approach to upper residential block

Great hall towards the dais: 1805. By G. Saunders   Great hall towards the screens passage: 1805. By G. Saunders

he deliberately created a slightly wider span between the hammer-posts by reducing the hammer-beams by 1¼ feet on either side. Secondly, he omitted the crown-posts braced four ways above the tie-beams for their existence was problematical on the evidence of the end-wall outlines. Thirdly, Weir did not insert the large curved braces rising axially from the hammer-beams to support the square-set purlins, and finally, he added three rows of wind-braces which Saunders's drawings show the original structure did not possess. Nevertheless, the present roof is a masterpiece of architectural reconstruction and a worthy successor to one of the finest medieval roofs built in the west of England.

The original roof was comparatively simple in design but massive in structure. It was divided into five bays separated by hammer-beam trusses supported externally by four narrow-stepped buttresses on either side. Short curved braces below the hammer-beams were supported on corbels carved with angels bearing heraldic shields, and large curved braces rose from the hammer-posts both transversely and axially to support the tie-beam and square-set purlins respectively. Above the cambered tie-beam was a crown-post braced fourways to the collar-purlins and collar-beam and tenoned into the tie-beam. Saunders's drawing appears to incorporate the principal rafters with the roof covering and this exaggerates their size.

Saunders's longitudinal drawing of the hall shows that there were intermediate principal rafters reaching from the top of the wall to the apex of the roof between the main hammer-beam trusses. The foot of each principal is shown notched over the timber wall-plate but that is all that can be seen. Saunders did not draw a cross-section of an intermediate truss, but his longitudinal drawing shows that the latter were broader than the adjacent common rafters. This greater dimension was obviously necessary to give additional support to the

Great hall and lower residential block: 1805. Longitudinal section by G. Saunders

heavy purlin above the hammer-post as well as to the side purlins above and below it on each roof slope. These side purlins are an unusual feature in a roof of this type for the three square-set purlins (one above each hammer-post and the central collar-purlin) were sufficient, structurally, to carry the roof load. Similar side purlins existed in the roof over the adjacent lower residential block and their lodging-holes may still be traced.

Saunders's longitudinal drawing fails to include the common collar-beam that joined each pair of common rafters at a point approximately three-quarters up the roof slope. This might have been because they were not present at the time of the drawing and hence their removal antedates the first years of the nineteenth century, or more likely, the draughtsman omitted them for the sake of clarity.

The pitch of the roof suggests that it was ideally suited to support the considerable weight of the heavy stone slates that were imposed on it, and this may well be the reason for including side purlins as additional bearers. The steeper pitch of the roof over the entrance block suggests that it was more suited to smaller slates or thatch, although the extra purlins are also present in this structure. Crown-post and collar-purlin roofs in the Horsham district of Sussex of comparable pitch to that above the great hall at Dartington appear to have carried heavy stone slates of local origin since their original open-hall phase in the later Middle Ages, whereas other buildings of comparable age in the same county with steeper pitched roofs that employ similar roof trusses are either tiled or thatched.

The lack of carved decoration does not detract from the appeal of the roof but helps to emphasize its massive construction. Weir's decision not to add any pseudo-medieval decoration was not only aesthetically sound but also historically correct. This lack of decorative detail, immediately apparent in Saunders's drawings, was common in later fourteenth-century work and is in contrast with the finely moulded stone archways leading from the entrance porch and the screens passage. Saunders's cross-sections show that there were small pendant projections at the end of the hammer-beams—a feature more usually associated with roofs constructed between the late fifteenth and the early seventeenth centuries. The corbels were the only other decorative feature of the roof, although it is said that it also carried the arms of Richard II and Huntingdon.[26]

It has been suggested by two writers that the hall built by Huntingdon was originally covered with a tie-beam and king-post roof, and that this was replaced by a hammer-beam structure in the second half of the sixteenth century.[27] This view is based entirely on a misinterpretation of the timber outlines in the end wall of the hall and the lower residential block respectively and is totally inaccurate. There is no doubt that a hammer-beam structure was part of the building programme undertaken by the earl of Huntingdon between 1388 and 1400, but what may be suggested is that the need to complete the hall as quickly as possible may have been responsible for a noticeable lack of care in executing its design. The windows are not quite opposite each other, the buttresses are not always central between the windows, and the corbels are not midway between any of the internal window openings. These differences, more appreciable on the south than the north side of the hall, vary between 3 inches and 2 feet. They are not very readily apparent and do not affect the stability of the structure, although the most easterly buttress on the south side is completely off centre from the brace it is intended to support. Comparable irregularities, not uncommon in church plans and repeated in the design of the hall at No. 8 The Close, Exeter (possibly early fifteenth century), usually arose from a less demanding precision in planning than is required today. Nevertheless, the master carpenter insisted that the corbels supporting the main trusses should be inserted irrespective of aesthetic balance to ensure that the roof was divided into five bays of equal length and that the thrust of the timbers was distributed as evenly as possible.

[26] See p. 96, where some doubt is thrown on the accuracy of this statement. The third corbel from the dais on the north side has been cut back and the figure altered, although it still retains its wings. The designs and colouring on the shields were added in 1938 by G. Kruger Gray.

[27] *A Short History of Dartington Hall* (1937), 19. Christopher Hussey, *Country Life* (3 September 1938).

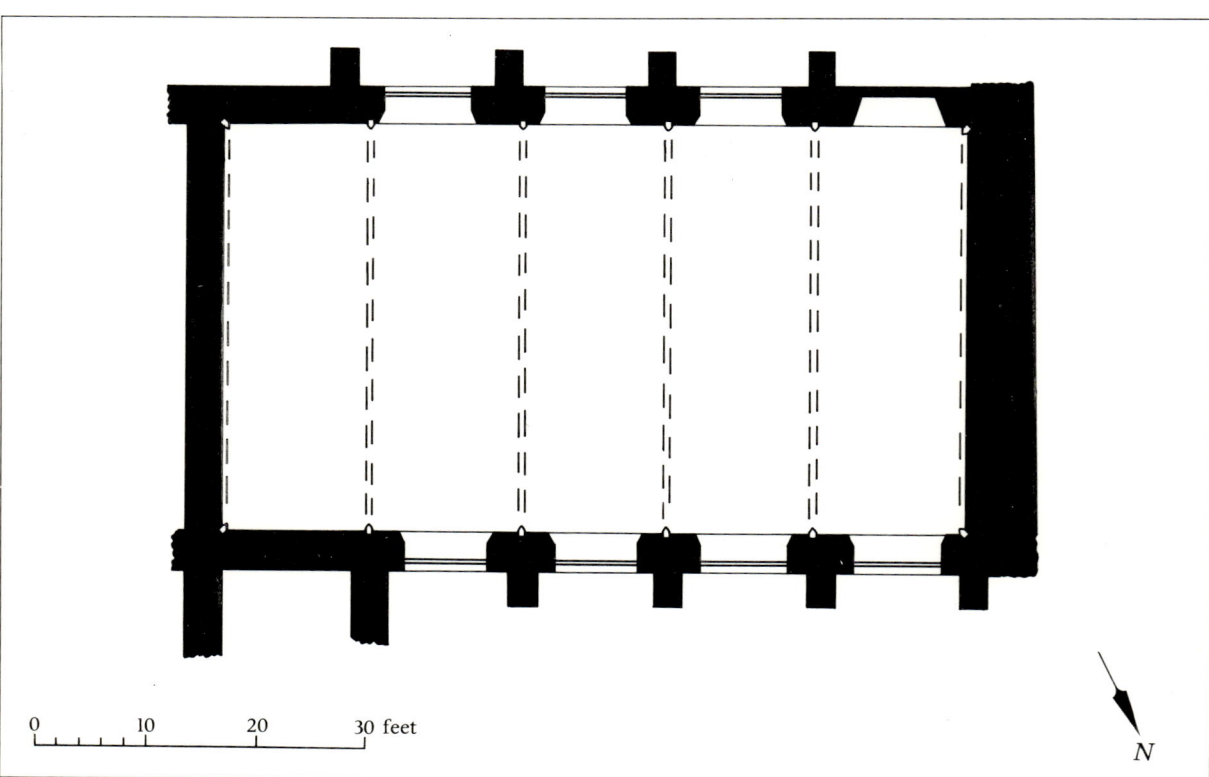

Fig. 32 Great hall. Plan of upper part showing relation between windows, buttresses, corbels, and roof trusses.

Chapter 9

The Lower Residential Block

The term 'lower residential block' is not an entirely adequate description for the group of rooms at the lower end of the hall range, but it defines this feature of late medieval domestic planning reasonably accurately in the absence of a more commonly accepted phrase. The rooms in this position usually consisted of a buttery and pantry at ground-floor level, frequently separated by a central passageway leading to the kitchen, and a single residential apartment above them. At Dartington, there were two such apartments above the service rooms, one on each floor, which makes the description of the block particularly appropriate here.

The entrance to the service rooms and central passageway is marked by the usual late medieval grouping of triple archways in the end wall of the great hall. In this case, the central arch is slightly higher than its neighbours. A fourth arch, close to the entrance porch, opens on to the stairs serving the residential rooms above. The excellent condition of the arches and the survival of the doors opening into the two service rooms form an interesting ensemble of late medieval workmanship (p. 167). The upper part of the north door is bespattered with holes for ventilation, and retains one of a pair of ornamental plates pierced with cusped decoration. The other door is of similar proportions and pattern to its neighbour but lacks the air-holes and metal plate. The hinges for a half door and serving-shelf in this opening were discovered during the course of the restoration in 1926. Vertical lapped doors like these at Dartington were common in the late fourteenth century and other contemporary examples still survive at Winchester College, New College, Oxford, and King's Hostel, Trinity College, Cambridge.[1]

[1] W. D. Caroe, 'King's Hostel, Trinity College, Cambridge', *Cambridge Antiq. Soc.* no. 2 (1909), 15–6. The door at the top of the stair turret opening on to the hall roof at Dartington is also of a considerable age.

The planning of the service rooms and the passageway follows the regular medieval pattern. Although it is not possible to determine which room was used as the buttery and which was the pantry, it is likely that the northern room, screened from the afternoon sun, was used for storing the beer and wine of the buttery. This room has now been divided into a store-room and lavatory, but the room on the south side retains its original proportions. Semicircular relieving arches in both rooms mark the position of the original windows but their frames were replaced by square-headed ones in the sixteenth century. Two further windows were added in the south-facing room in 1926.

The archway near the entrance porch gives access to the spiral staircase leading to the upper rooms, the porch tower rooms, and the hall roof. Originally the arches opening from the stairs into the rooms of this block would have been similar to those opening into the porch tower, but they were replaced by square-headed wooden frames in the sixteenth century. New window-frames were inserted in the stair turret at the same time.

Sixteenth-century changes have so radically altered the appearance of the first-floor room that little of its original character survives. Sir Arthur Champernowne divided the apartment into two rooms, inserted square-headed windows,[2] and added decorative plaster motifs beneath the ceiling in the northern room. These motifs, similar to other sixteenth-century designs in Devon, consisted of alternate fleur-de-lis and leaf and scroll patterns.

[2] The window north of the fireplace in the first-floor chamber did not exist in 1926, but the embrasures for it were found during the restoration. It had been subject to alteration for it extended the full height of the two floors.

Only two motifs survived in 1926, but Weir inserted copies round all the walls of the room after he had restored its original proportions. The insertion by Leonard Elmhirst of oak panelling from the Hall at Shepley near Huddersfield heightens the impression of a late sixteenth-century room (p. 169).

The uncompromising square head of the fireplace suggests that it is also sixteenth-century work but its similarity to the square-headed fireplaces in the third-floor chamber of Nunney Castle (1373), the great chamber in Caldicot Castle gatehouse (c. 1388), and the principal gatehouse chambers at Donnington Castle (1386) suggest that it may be original. It is believed that there was formerly an elaborate plaster overmantle above this fireplace which fell down in the late nineteenth century through damp caused by a blocked roof gutter.[3] There is no reason to doubt that the slender octagonal chimney is an original feature. It is shown in its present form in Buck's drawing of 1734 (p. 82) and although it was built in a more yellow stone than that used elsewhere in the Hall, the decorated pattern and crenellation on each outer face and the cusped design in the gable-head immediately beneath it is consistent with late fourteenth-century work. Traces of an original opening in the south-west corner seem to have led to a range on the east side of the south court (see p. 190) and Weir suggested, probably rightly so, that the door in the south-east corner of the room led to a garderobe. A door in the south-east corner of the room above, slightly to one side of that below, probably served the same purpose (see p. 174).

The second-floor apartment was formerly lit by windows at either end, altered by Sir Arthur Champernowne in the sixteenth century when two more were added in the east wall. The room is now devoid of character and ceiled with a nineteenth-century structure built with typical Victorian thoroughness.[4] Yet an examination of the gable-wall above the present ceiling reveals that the room was formerly covered with an imposing roof of quality and consideration. The impression of the gable-end roof truss in the plaster on the east wall reveals two wall posts with small angle braces supporting a cambered tie-beam.[5] Above this beam rose a crown-post supported by curved brackets. Saunders's longitudinal section of the hall range shows that a similar truss was built against the west wall and that the two trusses were separated by heavy square-set purlins tenoned into the heads of the principal posts and bracketed rigidly to them by deep curved braces. Central support to the purlins was provided by an intermediate truss consisting of a tie-beam with crown-post bracketed to the collar-purlin and beam.[6]

Neither the intermediate nor the terminal trusses were of hammer-beam construction. They were far closer in design to the trusses above the entrance block than to those above the great hall. A major disadvantage of the hammer-beam truss is that the necessary bracketing of the hammer-beam from the side wall posts is extremely wasteful of space and can only be used profitably high above the living area. Fig. 33 shows how this intrusion would have affected the height available in this apartment. The broken line of the central truss has been added to show the type of truss that was probably used at this point.

The employment of trusses that dispensed with the projecting structures of the hammer-beam truss had been adopted in the roof over the great hall where they alternated with the principal hammer-beam trusses. Prior to this, the truss type had been used above the entrance block where the narrower dimensions had considerably reduced the problems of

[3] In 1957, Miss C. E. Champernowne wrote about this room, 'when Mr. Luscombe who was steward for ages and ages, died or was ill before he died, the usual inspection and care was overlooked. The overflow pipe from the battlements got choked and the rain seeped in and brought down the large plaster coat of arms over the chimneypiece.' Historical Papers, Dartington Hall Records Office.

[4] This is the only work remaining at the Hall that can be attributed to Pugin. Arch. Jour. vol. 30 (1873), 441.

[5] There are faint signs of alterations in the wall which suggest that a taller pair of posts may have been intended than those adopted but the evidence is admittedly slight.

[6] This corrects the description given by me in Arch. Jour. vol. 115 (1958), 194, 197.

Great hall. Screens-passage arches to buttery, kitchen passage, and pantry

Tower porch. Inner face of outer arch

Great hall. Screens-passage arch to upper rooms of lower residential block

spanning. That this truss evolved independently from another carpentry tradition rather than as an alternative to the hammer-beam truss or as its successor, can be shown by reference to its use elsewhere in England.[7]

Several writers have referred to an opening in the west wall and it has been conjectured that this was a 'spy hole' for overlooking the activities of people in the great hall. A large relieving arch still exists which may have been part of such an opening. A plan by Saunders showed that there was a cupboard here in 1805 but unfortunately the conversion of this feature into a window with Gothic tracery by Pugin makes it impossible to determine what existed here originally. The tracery has since been blocked up and the opening is now used once more as a cupboard, but whether this was its original purpose or whether there was an opening here giving a view into the great hall can no longer be determined.

[7] An example of its earlier use is that at Great Coxwell Barn, Berkshire, an aisled structure with timber arcade posts, where tall curved principals springing from the side walls serve in an intermediate capacity dispensing with the arcade posts. A date in the first part of the 13th century has been proposed for this structure. W. Horn and E. Born, *The Barns of the Abbey of Beaulieu and its Granges of Great Coxwell and Beaulieu St. Leonards* (1965).

The Purpose of the Residential Rooms

The planning of the lower residential block at Dartington Hall is of considerable interest. The existence of one chamber above the service rooms is common enough in medieval domestic planning, but the existence of two large apartments is unusual and confined to the largest residences. It was almost certainly due to the need for more accommodation, but an examination of the planning at Dartington shows that the two rooms were not

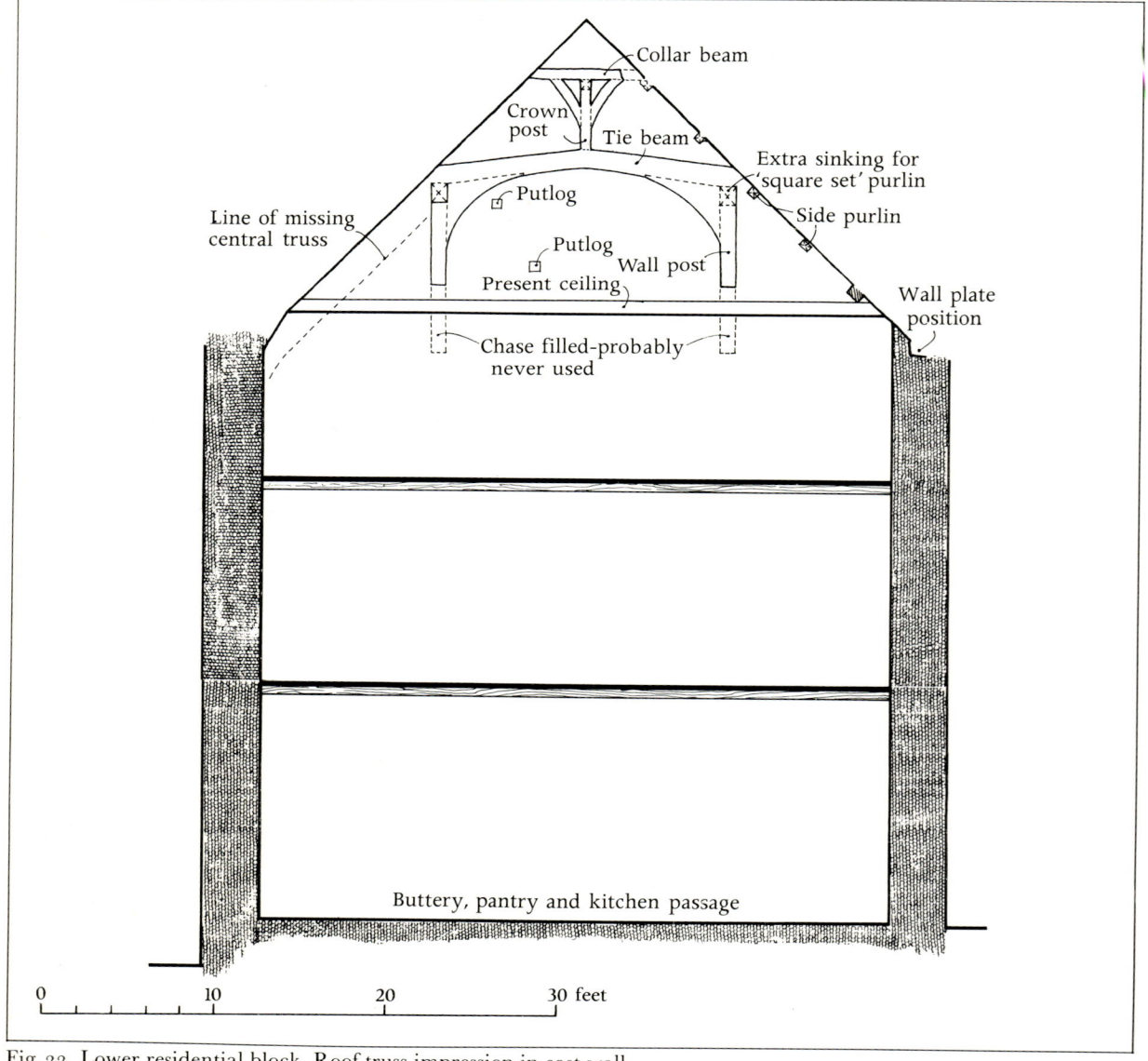

Fig. 33 Lower residential block. Roof truss impression in east wall

[8] Although there was a door in the south wall of the first-floor room which may have given access to the apartments facing the south courtyard, it is quite likely that entry could also be barred here if necessary. In any case, the precaution taken at the foot of the stair turret indicates that it was intended that this group of rooms should be isolated if necessary.

[9] That in the second-floor chamber was still in existence in 1805.

[10] P. A. Faulkner, 'Domestic Planning from the Twelfth to the Fourteenth Centuries', Arch. Jour. vol. 115 (1958), 162–82; Margaret Wood, The English Mediaeval House (1965), 68–73.

[11] P. A. Faulkner, 'Castle Planning in the Fourteenth Century', Arch. Jour. vol. 120 (1963), 221–5.

[12] Faulkner suggests, however, that they may have been intended for the use of Lord Scrope's own household. Ibid., 229.

designed in isolation but in association with the two smaller rooms above the tower porch. They were all served by the same staircase and they could be separated from the remainder of the Hall by inserting a bar into the holes behind the door at the foot of the stairs. The lower residential block was therefore planned as a suite of associated units, two large chambers and two small rooms which could be made independent of the remainder of the Hall.[8] Each unit contained a fireplace[9] and it is extremely likely that there was a garderobe serving each of the larger rooms.

Who originally occupied these chambers? Little attention has so far been paid to this aspect of medieval domestic planning, and therefore it may be helpful to summarize the major reasons for building a residential room or rooms at the lower end of the hall before considering the purpose of those at Dartington. The first-floor chamber was usually used in the thirteenth and early fourteenth centuries as the private room of the owner and his family and it fulfilled this need until the introduction of a second residential block in a more convenient position for them at the upper end of the hall.[10] This development during the late thirteenth century, although earlier examples are not unknown, made it easier to give important guests individual accommodation in a well-planned room. This was probably the case at Goodrich Castle[11] (c. 1290–1310) and the rooms at one end of the inner hall at Bolton Castle (c. 1378–99) (p. 196).[12] With the later development of accommodation for

Lower residential block. First-floor room towards the north court

guests closer to the owner's private rooms and the growth of household officials and staff, the proximity of the lower residential block to the hall, service rooms, and kitchen made it extremely suitable for the steward, particularly in a large household where his management of the economy made him an important official. The accommodation in the three-storeyed block at the lower end of the great hall at Bolton Castle was probably under his control. Other uses to which the chamber above the service rooms could be put included its use by the eldest son of the owner and his family, and the entertainment rather than the accommodation of guests as may have been the case at Bodiam Castle (1385–c. 90) (Fig. 36).[13] This last use emphasizes that the rooms at the lower end of the hall were not necessarily inferior to those at the upper end. After the death of Sir Nigel Loring of Chalgrove, Bedfordshire, in 1386, his house was divided between his two daughters, one taking the hall, screens, chapel, and chambers to the east of the hall, whilst the other took the buttery, pantry, and various chambers to the west of the hall.[14] The use of a large room for entertaining at the lower end of the hall became popular in the following century and is well exemplified in the richly decorated room in this position at South Wingfield Manor House (c. 1440–55). A chapel was raised above the service rooms at Caerphilly Castle (c. 1317–26),[15] while an apartment in that position probably served as a sleeping chamber for scholars in several undergraduate halls at Oxford and Cambridge as at Tackley's Inn, Oxford (c. 1320).[16] At Winchester College (1397–1400) the first-floor room was divided into two (as at Bolton Castle) and used as a bursary and audit room while the second-floor room was used for storing cheeses from at least the early fifteenth century.

Turning now to Dartington Hall, is it possible to suggest who used the rooms above the lower residential block during the closing years of the fourteenth century? Nothing remains of their furnishings or decoration which affords any evidence, apart from the existence of an imposing roof structure, while the lack of certain knowledge of the overall plan of the Hall at the time makes it difficult to come to any firm conclusion. It is clear that the rooms were residential and it is extremely unlikely that one person would have been given such a large amount of accommodation solely for himself and his family. The presence of an upper residential block and probably a group of ranges round a second courtyard rules out their use for Huntingdon and his immediate household. They may have been intended for important guests or for Huntingdon's children. The bar at the foot of the stairs would give these rooms privacy and protection from rowdiness, but if the ranges round the second courtyard formed part of Huntingdon's original design as seems likely (see Chapter 12), such people are more likely to have been given quarters away from the hurly-burly of the service rooms and the main courtyard. In that case, the lower residential block would have been extremely suitable for those members of Huntingdon's staff closely associated with the organization of the household. The two small chambers in the porch tower would have been used by the pages, ready for attendance in the great hall,[17] while the first-floor chamber would have accommodated the squires and men concerned with the domestic life of the Hall.[18] The second-floor chamber would have been occupied by the steward, intimately connected with the economy and organization of the household, and with immediate access to the great hall and service rooms. The possibility that there was an opening in his room overlooking the great hall, as at Bolton Castle, slightly strengthens this suggestion.[19]

[13] *Arch. Jour.* vol. 120 (1963), 233.

[14] Ed. A. L. Poole, *Medieval England*, vol. 1 (1958), 46.

[15] *Bull. of Board of Celtic Studies*, vol. 14 (1952), 299.

[16] *Oxoniensia*, vol. 7 (1942), 80–92.

[17] P. A. Faulkner has suggested that the three chambers in the north turret of Bolton Castle and the two rooms in the postern tower of Bodiam Castle, both located at the lower end of the great hall, may have been used for a similar purpose. 'Castle Planning in the Fourteenth Century', *Arch. Jour.* vol. 120 (1963), 229, 234.

[18] It will be suggested on p. 190 that the door opening from this chamber towards the south court led to a range of residential apartments – a factor compatible with this chamber's use by squires and serving-men.

[19] Margaret Wood has suggested that the bishop of Winchester's staff were accommodated above the service rooms in a double-chamber block at East Meon Court House (first half of the 15th century), *The English Mediaeval House* (1965), 137.

Chapter 10

The Kitchen and Offices

The Kitchen

When Leonard and Dorothy Elmhirst began restoring the Hall in 1926, they intended to leave the kitchen in the same ruined condition that it had been for at least two hundred years. The east and the adjacent half of the north- and south-facing walls survived almost to their full height but only the lower courses remained of the west wall. When it was found that the great hall was useful for purposes other than dining, it was decided to restore the old kitchen and to use it as a student dining-room with a new kitchen on the site of the old offices at the side of it. William Weir rebuilt the walls to their original level and crowned the structure with a roof of his own design. But the original appearance of the kitchen from the courtyard was not necessarily the same as that today. The roof is entirely conjectural, only one chimney has been restored and there was insufficient evidence to indicate that battlements were an original feature of the design, although it is probable that this was so.[1]

[1] Saunders's drawing (p. 174) shows that part of a short arched way leading from the battlements above the lower residential block to the roof of the kitchen still survived in 1805. It no longer existed by the late 19th century. This archway would have facilitated the repair of the kitchen roof and the cleaning of its gutters.

The kitchen, although coeval with the great hall and residential blocks, was not built in line with them but set back from the body of the south range. It was a detached rectangular structure, reached by a passageway continuing the line of the existing one between the buttery and pantry and approached through a door in the middle of the north wall. The opening in this wall is now shorn of its original faced stonework. Nearly all the stonework round the door in the opposite wall was replaced in the nineteenth century, but the opening is an original one and was probably used for conveying food to the apartments round the south court. The significance of this is indicated on page 230.

The kitchen is an impressive and noble apartment, $33\frac{1}{2}$ feet square internally, but the impression of space and quietness which it now gives is the antithesis of the activity that

Kitchen and hall range from the east

Kitchen from the south

Kitchen. Interior showing the adjacent fireplaces

it witnessed during the later Middle Ages. The east and south sides are filled with two gigantic fireplaces, 20 feet wide, spanned by arches 16 feet high at the apex.[2] The hearths were almost certainly covered with large hoods supported by a massive corbel at either end of which two of the present four corbels are original. The reconstruction of one of the hoods by Weir gives an idea of the former appearance of these hearths. The shallow recesses on either side of the fireplaces give the youths who had been ordered to turn the meat-laden spits some comfort and protection from the heat of the fires. Weir found traces of an air-vent within one of them. Dean Milles of Exeter noted in about 1755 that the kitchen had four chimneys but his statement can no longer be confirmed.[3] The *Archaeological Journal* for 1873 also mentions that the kitchen possessed an oven at that time, but the lack of any trace of it in 1926 and its absence from Saunders's drawings of 1805 make the age of such a feature very suspect.[4] Drainage was facilitated by a passage in the north-east corner of the building beginning in the low recess in the north-east corner, but more fully revealed in 1934 when a wine-cellar and an approaching flight of steps were constructed. High

[2] These arches were rebuilt by Weir. The kitchen fireplaces in the tower-house at Warkworth were built in the same position as those at Dartington. Those in the contemporary kitchen at Cockermouth Castle still retain part of their original stone hoods.

[3] Bodleian Library, Oxford, MS. Top. Devon, c. 9, f. 73.

[4] It is quite possible that the writer was referring to the head of the arch in the north-east corner leading to the drain. Saunders's drawings show that the two hearths had been partially filled by 1805 and divided into three smaller fireplaces with nesting-boxes above them. These additions were removed some time in the 19th century, possibly as part of a scheme for restoring the kitchen which was envisaged in 1839. The division of the windows into four lights by a transom and mullion, mentioned in the *Arch. Jour.* in 1873, certainly did not exist in 1805 when their appearance was identical with the present condition. The present entrance, the kitchen hatches, and the staircase leading to the lower residential block were additions made in the early 1930s as part of Weir's sympathetic and imaginative restoration.

172

Kitchen. Interior walling

enough to admit a person on his hands and knees, this passage runs underneath the outer wall and takes a right-angled turn towards the tournament ground. At the turn, it picked up a stone drain, 2 feet square. Blockage does not allow the passage to be explored for any length but there is little doubt that it facilitated drainage much as similar passages did at Baddesley Clinton Hall, Warwickshire (later fifteenth century) and Eltham Palace where the passages were built at the order of Henry VIII.

The kitchen was lit by six tall, single windows with shouldered heads. Weir had to replace much of the stonework in the windows flanking the chimneys in the east and south walls but their original form was quite clear. The lights in the middle of the opposite walls were entirely rebuilt by him although the east side of the window in the north wall still survived intact. Several contemporary kitchens suggest that the heat would escape through a louvre in the roof, although the windows would provide additional ventilation as well as light. Unfortunately, no trace of the original roof has survived and no drawing or other record of its form is known. The two more southerly corbels in the east wall are the only remains

Kitchen. East fireplace: 1805. By G. Saunders

Lower residential block and west wall of kitchen: 1805. By G. Saunders

Kitchen and offices with wall screening them from the north court

of the support necessary for the original covering and guided by these, Weir built the sort of structure which might have been erected in the late fourteenth century. The present beams came from Lord Churston's estate near Brixham, although it was quite a long time before oak trees of sufficient magnitude could be found. Weir was fully aware that his roof was an entirely conjectural reconstruction, but the suggestion that the original structure might have been of hammer-beam design similar to that above the kitchen of the Bishop's Palace, Chichester, is not convincing.[5] The absence of any buttresses, usually necessary to support a roof of hammer-beam construction, is surprising in such a large building and suggests that the structure was originally crowned with a roof of less dramatic design.

There is no reason to doubt that the kitchen was built at the same time as the remainder of the south range. Such an apartment was an essential adjunct to the establishment of a large household and quite commensurate with the size of Huntingdon's great hall. The shouldered heads of the windows are in keeping with a late fourteenth-century date although they are of a form common throughout that century. The kitchen was admirably designed as a spacious workplace where food for a large household could be adequately prepared. Water would be brought from the springs that feed a small stream just over 100 yards south-west of the Hall and which has never been known to dry up. Danger from fire was reduced to a minimum by building the kitchen as a detached structure and inserting the fireplaces in those walls facing away from other immediate buildings. The six windows provide surprisingly ample light and they no doubt helped to take away some of the excessive heat which probably escaped through a central louvre. Whitewashed walls would help to add to the lightness of the apartment as they do today.

The Offices

The constant activities associated with the kitchen and offices in front of it were screened from the main courtyard by a contemporary wall which also served as a linking façade between the lower residential block and the east range. A similar device had been adopted at Haddon Hall in the second quarter of the fourteenth century (p. 233), but that at Dartington was 60 feet long and supported by shallow stepped buttresses at bay intervals. The upper courses have been restored but Buck's drawing shows that it was still topped with battlements in the early eighteenth century. Apart from the evidence of the wall, the line of the roof against the end wall of the lower residential block indicates that the lesser offices were no more than one storey high. They were probably altered in the sixteenth century when the present windows were inserted in the screening wall. No trace remains of their internal plan. Comparison with Haddon Hall and the notes made by Lord Neville for the reconstruction of the hall and kitchen range of Bamborough Castle in 1384[6] suggest that the principal office here was a bakery with possibly a brewhouse nearby.[7]

No traces remain of the corridor or pentice linking the kitchen entrance with the passage between the buttery and pantry. Buck's drawing and that made by Saunders show the line of the sharply pitched corridor roof against the end wall of the hall range and the more shallow-pitched roof above the lesser offices. The construction of the present kitchens, club-room, and other offices in this area in 1934 now make it impossible to determine the form of any earlier buildings on the same site.

[5] Geoffrey Webb, *Architecture in Britain: The Middle Ages* (1956), 189.

[6] L. F. Salzman, *Building in England down to 1540* (1952), 465–6.

[7] Saunders's plan shows two hearths against the inner face of the screening wall, but although he notes that they were apparently flues for boilers, they might have been used for baking purposes.

Chapter 11

The Upper Residential Block

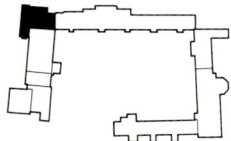

The rooms at the upper end of the hall range have always been reserved for the personal use of the owner and his family. They have been continuously occupied since the mid sixteenth century and probably for much of the time between then and the late fourteenth century. The many changes to which they have been subject are therefore a reflection of the needs and comforts of succeeding generations.

Little remains of the original plan of this block but the evidence suggests that the rooms behind the dais followed the usual pattern of domestic planning in a late medieval house. Behind the hall was a single ground-floor chamber with an important room or rooms above. Such blocks were usually but not invariably two storeys high in the thirteenth and fourteenth centuries, but it is likely that the Dartington block was three storeys high at the upper as well as at the lower end of the great hall.

It has usually been considered that the present south front was built in the sixteenth century and the twin gables, square-shaped windows, ground-floor beams, and panelling are cited as evidence in support of this view (p. 178). A closer examination reveals, however that this frontage includes the work of several periods. The two-storeyed extension built on the west side of the block is nineteenth-century work, but the gable division marks two building periods differentiated by a change in the thickness of the wall from 6 feet to 3 feet. Furthermore, only the lower half of the wall to the west of the division is 6 feet thick whereas the upper half is again 3 feet thick. The deeper part of this frontage is of the same width as the west wall of the upper residential block and the west wall of the great hall and these, together with the hearth-carrying walls of the kitchen and the wall separating the porch tower from the great hall, are not only the thickest walls in the Hall but can in the last three cases be firmly dated to the late fourteenth century. There is little reason to doubt, therefore, that the western part of the south frontage of what is now known as the private house includes the south wall of the original upper residential block, and that the eastern half was added at a later date. The construction of the latter against the end bay of the great hall, blocking one of its windows and incorporating one of the buttresses, confirms that this addition must be later than the fourteenth century.

With the location of the south wall, it is possible to determine the original proportions and design of the block, for there is no reason to doubt that the fourth wall separating the block from the west range, if not original, is built on the site of the original wall.[1] The ground-floor area was approximately 53 feet long and 20 feet wide internally and there were almost certainly two floors above it. That this is likely is suggested in the first instance by a comparison with the contemporary residential block at the lower end of the hall range. An examination of the upper block also reveals that the east and west walls maintain an even thickness to the height of the hall roof, that is to attic level, and although the south front is now only 3 feet thick above first-floor level, it abuts against a $4\frac{1}{2}$-feet-thick wall separating the principal rooms at second-floor level. This suggests that the south front originally rose

[1] See p. 212.

Upper residential block (private house) and great hall from the tournament ground

Private house. Marble hall from dais door of great hall

Private house. Ground-floor library

one floor higher to the level of the hall roof, and that the upper part of the frontage was rebuilt in the sixteenth century when the attic rooms were added. No old roof timbers remain in the short section between the hall gable and the slope of the present roof above this block, but the unweathered appearance of the hall chimney-stack and the gable-end wall indicates that they have never been exposed to the elements. It is likely, in fact, that the block was not only three storeys high but covered by a roof in continuation of the hall roof as at present.[2]

Later alterations have left few original features internally. The ground floor may have been divided internally to form two rooms, one behind the great hall and a lobby giving access to the west range of the south court (see p. 200). However, there is no reason to doubt that the main ground-floor room, now divided into a staircase hall and library, was originally approached by an opening from the great hall. It may have been the present one in the north-west corner of the dais, now bereft of any moulded archway, but the chamber might equally have been approached from a short passageway immediately to the right of the stairs reached through the archway in the south wall of the great hall. A plan somewhat similar to this was adopted at Penshurst Place (1341–9), Compton Castle (c. 1340, restored on original evidence in 1955), and possibly at Norrington Manor House (c. 1380), (pp. 159, 161, 130) but the destruction of the stairs and the adjacent work at Dartington in the sixteenth century makes it impossible to recover the late fourteenth-century plan.[3] Other original features of the ground-floor chamber are minimal. The fireplace in the west wall of the library probably makes use of an original opening, but the present surround is twentieth-century work and the existence of a fireplace here before 1805 cannot be confirmed. The abutment of ranges on two sides and the great hall on the third meant that there could be no windows in these walls. The splay of a window on the fourth side is incorporated in an opening to the twentieth-century extension, but whether this is part of an original feature is conjectural. There is no evidence that the room was vaulted: no doubt the present timber ceiling replaces an earlier similar structure.[4]

Little evidence remains of the original plan and design of the upper rooms. The first-floor room would have been approached by a staircase leading from the opening on the south wall of the great hall, and the windows in this and the second-floor room would have been in the west wall overlooking the churchyard.[5] The contemporary heads of a man and woman flanking one of the present windows in this wall may have formerly been the stops of one of these windows.[6]

An exploration of the roof trusses at the north end of this block reveals two beams, very closely bedded together into the party wall dividing the block from the west range. They are older than the late sixteenth-century trusses above the attic rooms and show crudely chopped-off mortices at their ends. They are built over an opening of some sort, possibly a window or a smoke outlet, but its precise form is concealed by later work. This additional evidence in favour of a second-floor chamber also suggests that it was open to the roof as was the case at the lower end of the hall range. An examination of the hall chimney-stack reveals several further interesting features. The flue is not a single shaft but is bisected, and one half has been truncated immediately below the roof tiles. This half clearly served a fireplace in the upper block, presumably on the first floor although a common flue to a

---

[2] It was usual for residential blocks to be roofed at right angles to the hall, but this was not necessary at Dartington where the roofs of the end blocks were level with the hall roof. The continuation of a hall roof over an adjacent block had been adopted, for example, at Harlech Castle (c. 1290), Compton Castle (c. 1340), and at the lower end of Winchester College hall (1394–1401).

[3] If such a design was adopted, the opening in the north-west corner of the dais would probably have been inserted in the late 16th century. Weir favoured its insertion at that period. It was formerly filled with an elaborately moulded Elizabethan door which was sold in the early 1920s and is now believed to be in the United States.

[4] The medieval-looking arch in the south-west corner of the west range opening into the passage behind the marble hall is a 19th-century insertion.

[5] Buck's drawing of the east frontage of Farleigh Hungerford Castle (c. 1370–83) shows a two-light window in a similar position lighting the first-floor chamber of the upper residential block.

[6] On examining the hairstyle and costume of these two heads, Madeleine Ginsburg of the Department of Textiles, Victoria and Albert Museum, suggests that they are probably late 14th-century work. The lady's head and chin are covered with a *barbe* which seems to have been worn only by widows. See also Arthur Gardner, 'Hair and Head-Dress: 1050–1600', *Jour. Brit. Arch. Assoc.* vol. 13 (1950), 12 and Plate 27.

fireplace on the first and second floor cannot be ruled out.[7] Evidently it was always intended that the stack should serve both the hall and the adjacent block, while the lack of facing stone confirms that the stack was never meant to be exposed and that the hall and residential block are coeval structures.

No trace remains today of the garderobe which must have formerly served this block. Yet a drawing of the south front made in about 1800 clearly show a small projection extending from the west wall of the block in line with the present south wall (p. 84). No other record of this interesting structure survives for it was destroyed before Saunders made his detailed plans of the Hall in 1805. It is possible that it was a staircase turret linking the first and second floors, but its position in a corner of these important rooms and the fact that the projection was only about 5 feet from the line of the west front suggests that it was more likely to be a garderobe serving the private apartments of the owner and his family. Such an amenity, apparently corresponding to a similarly placed feature in the lower residential block, was a necessity in any group of rooms of this nature and was usually part of the planning of such a chamber or group of chambers from the twelfth century onwards. The fact that the projection did not extend to the height of the attic rooms added in the sixteenth century is further evidence that it was built before that time.

Although the evidence is fragmentary, the sum of it indicates that the upper block built for Huntingdon in the late fourteenth century consisted of a spacious apartment on three floors, approximately 53 feet by 20 feet, and a garderobe turret in the south-west angle. The ground-floor chamber probably had a timber ceiling as at present, but it cannot be determined whether the room was residential or not. It is likely that the first floor was approached by a staircase from the south-west angle of the great hall and served by a fireplace in the east wall. The second-floor room may also have possessed a similar fireplace and was probably crowned with an open roof. Both chambers are likely to have been lit on the west side, although a window on the north side of the uppermost chamber cannot be ruled out.

No alterations were made to the block for nearly two centuries, but the accommodation built for Huntingdon's personal use proved unsuited to the needs of the Champernowne family in the second half of the sixteenth century. Substantial changes were made at that time so that the block could form the nucleus of a more up-to-date home, but unfortunately, lack of documentary evidence and further changes by succeeding generations make it difficult to be precise about the extent and nature of these alterations. There is no doubt, however, that Champernowne aimed at providing additional rooms and that he achieved this through internal partitioning, extending the south front and adding a number of attic rooms. Sir Arthur destroyed the staircase leading from the great hall to the first-floor chamber and filled up the south-facing window overlooking the hall dais. The block was then extended in front of the end bay of the great hall to create three further rooms, one on each floor, and a further storey was added to increase the total accommodation from three to four floors.

The new attic rooms were originally open to the roof ridge, but the roof trusses which now exist above ceilings inserted at a later date were clearly never intended to grace rooms of any pretensions. These sixteenth-century trusses have two collar-beams, a

[7] No fireplaces in this east wall are shown in Saunders's plans, but there was one in the marble and inner hall respectively in late Victorian times which may have made use of this flue. The flue was probably truncated in the late 16th century when the attics were added and the lateral chimney-stack added against the west wall of the block.

horizontal lower one tenoned into the principals and a slightly curved upper collar halved and pegged into the same timbers. The precise method of joining the principal rafters to the side walls is unfortunately concealed by the present fourth-storey floor, but there is a short horizontal timber spur at wall-plate level that projects internally and the principal of each truss is apparently tenoned into it. An upright curving timber tenoned into this spur and principal carries its line down to the floor level. In its turn, the spur might be part of, or jointed to a heavy transverse ceiling beam.[8] The additional space obtained through the construction of the fourth storey must be offset by its unfortunate effect on the appearance of the south front of the Hall as an architectural entity. The block is now too tall for the remainder of the frontage. The double-gable division and the additional floor not only emphasize the narrowness of the block but throw it out of balance with the proportions of the great hall and the lower residential block (p. 178).

[8] Sir Cyril Fox and Lord Raglan, *Monmouthshire Houses*, pt. 2 (1953), 34–5. The upper floor of Chapel, Llanelen, which is similar in date, illustrates how the roof principal curves at its foot and is tenoned into the main transverse ceiling beam.

The internal arrangement of the upper block in the sixteenth century cannot be determined. The roof trusses divide it into two areas of seven and two, slightly larger, bays which correspond with the position of the original chambers and the additional south-facing rooms respectively. It is unlikely, however, that this two-room division was common to the lower floors. Apart from the panelling in the small ground-floor room, the only internal feature dating from the sixteenth century is the adjacent library ceiling with its moulded beams, and this does not correspond with the larger bay division although it appears to have been truncated at its northern end. Furthermore, the destruction of the original staircase must have meant the construction of a new one in the body of the house. It is possible that the staircase which existed in the western half of the inner hall until the mid nineteenth century was constructed at this period. The stairs between the first and second floor were built in short flights round a rectangular open well and those between the second and third floor were in two close parallel flights. Both these forms were characteristic of the Elizabethan period.

The date of these alterations cannot be precisely determined. The gables and rectangular windows are characteristic of the sixteenth and early seventeenth centuries but the moulded timbers in the library and the door hinges and simple rectangular panelling in the small ground-floor addition suggest a sixteenth-century date. The trusses may even be more closely dated to the later part of the century. There is no reason why the reconstruction of this block should not be associated with the building work undertaken by Sir Arthur Champernowne at the Hall in 1560–1.[9]

[9] J. H. Butcher, *The Parish of Ashburton in the Fifteenth and Sixteenth Centuries* (1870), 38.

No further changes were made to the block until the mid eighteenth century when Arthur Champernowne carried out a major reconstruction by creating a new entrance hall and staircase and a suite of rooms at the southern end of the west range. As his alterations were part of a plan to confine his residence to this one part of the Hall, it is now more convenient to describe it as the private house rather than as the upper residential block, for the rooms in this block and the adjacent west range were planned as a self-contained residence and are used for this purpose today.

Arthur Champernowne's entrance hall still forms the principal approach to the private house and offers a sharp contrast to the medieval hall from which it opens (p. 176). The new hall was created in the space formerly filled by two floors in the northern part of the block.

A broad flight of stairs rises to a landing giving access to Champernowne's newly formed suite of rooms in the west range on the right-hand side and the body of the house on the left. Built of oak, the staircase is a typical example of mid eighteenth-century workmanship. The treads are not housed into the side of the string but are carried over and rest on it. A carved bracket has been added underneath each of the treads which carry three slender turned balusters. A fluted and two twisted balusters to each tread support the ramped handrail of the staircase but those supporting the handrail on the landing are twisted and fluted alternately. Wainscoting encloses the space underneath the stairs and landing, with that under the stairs carried on a lath and plaster framework.

The ceiling is decorated with a narrow line of moulding with two crossed and bound branches of mistletoe (?) and fronds at the angles and a swirl of acanthus (?) leaves in the centre. A boldly moulded cornice has been added round the edge of the hall. This is restrained plasterwork of good local quality. The white and grey patterned marble floor which gives the hall its name was inserted at the same time as the staircase and ceiling.

It has not been possible to date this work precisely, although its eighteenth-century character is unmistakable. Dean Milles noted in about 1755 that it had not long been

Private house. Morning-room: *c.* 1870

Private house. Morning-room

Private house. Morning-room: *c.* 1870

Private house. Morning-room

completed, and it may therefore be tentatively dated to the years around 1737 and 1741 when Arthur Champernowne raised the bell and weather-vane above the porch tower. The name of his architect has not yet been identified. The staircase is of a style popular during the second quarter of the century and had been adopted, for example, by Francis Smith at Davenport House, Shropshire in 1726. It is probably local workmanship but although the quality of the newels and balusters is high, that of the wainscoting is noticeably poor. The staircase is not unlike that at Old Traine, Modbury, while the ceiling is similar in design and execution to one at Pynes, Upton Pynes, near Exeter, which may also been dated to the mid eighteenth century.

There were two principal rooms at this time on the ground, first, and second floors, similar in proportion to those in the house facing southwards today. The smaller rooms on the first and second floors were reached directly from the larger room (as is still the case on the first floor) but Saunders's plans show that the smaller room on the ground floor could only be approached at that time from the great hall. The drawing of about 1800 shows that the first-floor windows were of Venetian design (p. 84), similar to, but considerably larger than that inserted above one of the projecting porches in the west

Private house. First-floor study: *c.* 1870

Private house. Inner hall: *c.* 1870

Private house. First-floor study

Private house. Inner Hall

range of the main courtyard. No doubt these windows were inserted in about 1740 at the same time as the carved decoration in the present first-floor study.[10]

At least three proposals for improving the family accommodation were put forward during the first half of the nineteenth century. Those submitted by Saunders in 1805 were not accepted, although Joseph Farington noted in his diary after a visit to the Hall that Arthur Champernowne talks 'of doing much to Dartington but has not done anything'. More modest proposals were put forward in February 1839, apparently by Archdeacon Froude[11] for an elevation of the south front of the Hall includes several features which exist later, such as the two-storeyed projection on the west side of the house, Tudor-style windows with heavy drip mouldings lighting the first- and second-floor rooms, a bay-window serving the first-floor study, and a conservatory (p. 89). On the other hand, the elevation also illustrates an open corridor or cloister at ground level spanning the length of the house with a porch midway between the two gables and a projection, possibly for a staircase, serving the first and second floors immediately behind this porch. The fact that there is no evidence supporting the construction of the cloister or the associated projection in any of the drawings submitted by Pugin six years later indicate that the elevation of 1839 is merely a proposal and not a record of the south front at that time.

The grandiose proposals submitted by Pugin in 1845 included re-roofing the great hall and the provision of extensive and impressive domestic accommodation for the Champernowne family in a large court to be constructed on the site of the kitchen and the area immediately southwards.[12] Although these proposals fared no better than those put forward by Saunders, Henry Champernowne decided shortly afterwards to improve the accommodation in the private house in keeping with his needs and comfort. Some of the proposals put forward in 1839 were now carried out. A two-storeyed projection was built on the west side to provide a new approach from the garden and the upper drive. Much of this work was built in a brown-coloured oolitic limestone, not at all in harmony with the remainder of the Hall, and Champernowne inserted an equally jarring Gothic window opposite the church tower to light the inner hall. Tudor-style sash-windows with plaster drip mouldings were inserted in the south-facing wall, and a bay-window was added lighting the first-floor study (p. 92). The inner staircase was replaced at the same time with a new one in red deal with walnut treads. While this work was being carried out between about 1846 and 1851, one of Henry Champernowne's brothers commented that he did not expect to recognize the house after the alterations had been completed.[13]

Changes made to the private house immediately after the Elmhirsts took up residence included removing the Victorian fireplaces in the marble and inner halls and reusing the Victorian treads in a reconstruction of the inner staircase. A more thorough restoration was undertaken by Weir between 1928 and 1930 when all the windows in the south and west fronts were replaced by windows which blended more harmoniously with the earlier work. The morning-room was panelled in elm and a Victorian conservatory adjacent to the garden porch was replaced by a loggia. The block still retains the external imprint of an Elizabethan three-storeyed house with attic rooms, but apart from the early Georgian and early Victorian halls, the present character of the internal rooms arises from their furnishing rather than from decorative walls and ceilings.

[10] Sir Cyril Fox thought that both the mouldings and the fireplace in the study were late 17th century work. This is similar to some of the patterning in the cornice of the marble hall.

[11] Exeter City Library: Champernowne Drawings, no. 18. The drawing is marked R.H.F.(?) for Richard Hurrell Froude.

[12] Ibid., nos. 19–22.

[13] C. E. Champernowne, *The Champernowne Family* (1954), 289.

Chapter 12

The Site of the South Court

Apart from an isolated wall approximately 115 feet from the great hall, there are no buildings today south of the kitchen, hall, or private house. This wall is visible evidence, however, that the Hall formerly covered a larger area than at present. It is pierced by seven openings and part of an eighth one may be traced at its eastern end. The wall is now a forlorn ruin, particularly as the windows are bereft of their wooden frames, badly damaged, and level with the ground on the Hall side owing to the construction of the lawn. Yet its presence immediately raises several questions. Was there a second court? If so, when was it built? What was its plan and purpose? What part did the surviving wall play in its planning, and why was it built at an angle of 11 degrees to the great hall instead of parallel to it?

This wall has been ascribed to dates varying from the late fourteenth to the eighteenth century, principally on the evidence of the four-centred heads of the openings. Several writers have considered that it formed part of a range linked by return wings to the residential blocks at either end of the great hall. Traces of a doorway at first-floor level in the south face of the lower residential block and marks in the lawn during dry weather supported this view.[1] Some writers have suggested that the courtyard was used by the Holand family either for their principal apartments[2] or else as accommodation for their guests.[3] Other writers have suggested that the court was built for servants and that the range of windows was part of a servants' cloister,[4] or that it was intended to provide accommodation for those watching tournaments held in the area below.[5]

It was to prove whether any of these theories was correct or not and whether the plan of the court could be recovered that much of the site was excavated during a three-week

[1] Christopher Hussey, *Country Life* (27 August 1938); Anthony Emery, *Arch. Jour.* vol. 115 (1958), 198.

[2] D. and S. Lysons, *Magna Britannia*, vol. 6, Devon (1822), cccxlviii.

[3] Anthony Emery, *Arch. Jour.* vol. 115 (1958), 192 n. 1.

[4] *Arch. Jour.* vol. 30 (1873), 442.

[5] Christopher Hussey, *Country Life* (27 August 1938). *A Short History of Dartington Hall* (4th ed., 1937), 20.

South court. Inner face of south wall of gallery

period in April 1962.[6] Poor weather conditions and the extent of the remains made it impossible to excavate the whole area in the time available. The excavations therefore by no means resolved all the problems of the site and as they, in turn, raised further problems, a resistivity survey of the area was made by Anthony Clark in October 1963.[7] The plan revealed by these undertakings proved far more complicated than had been anticipated. Evidence was found of at least two different building periods, the thirteenth century and the late Middle Ages. The remains of a rectangular building attributed to the former period are described in Appendix 4, and the complex group of buildings dating from the later period are discussed below.

[6] C. Platt, 'Excavations at Dartington Hall, 1962', *Arch. Jour.* vol. 119 (1962), 208–24.

[7] See Appendix 5.

South court. Detail of gallery window opening

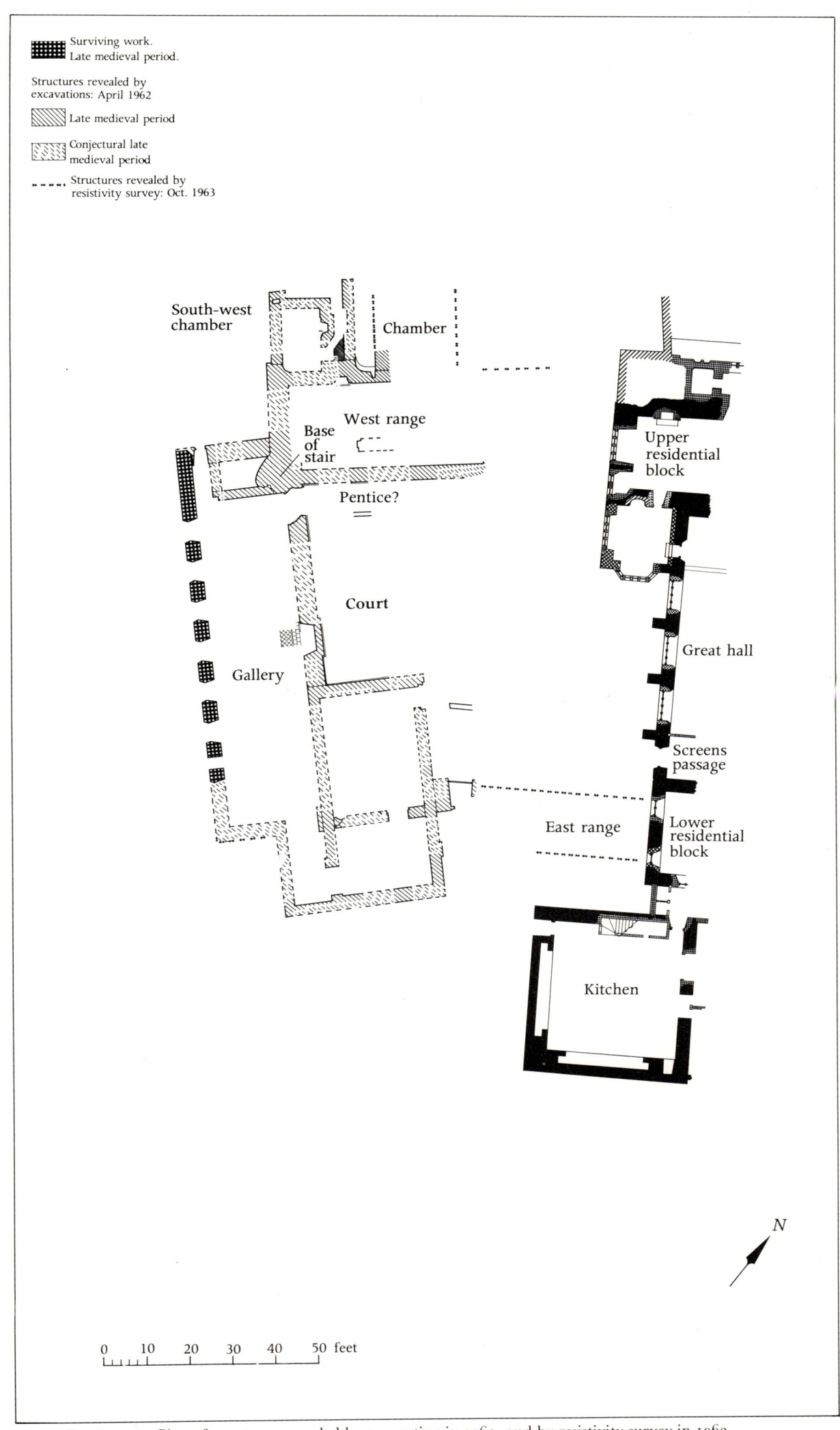

Fig. 34 South court. Plan of structures revealed by excavation in 1962, and by resistivity survey in 1963

The Plan of the Court

The excavations revealed a series of buildings grouped round a courtyard immediately south of the great hall. The principal components of this court were a gallery on the south side, a range on the west side with a projecting block at the south-west angle, and a two-roomed block opening from a small chamber at the east end of the gallery (p. 187).

The full length of the gallery could not be excavated owing to the presence of a Scots pine at the eastern end, but the resistivity survey confirmed the opinion that the rebate in the low outer wall, now the retaining wall of the upper lawn, marked the end wall of this apartment. The gallery was 24 feet wide and 84 feet long internally if its outer wall included all eight surviving windows. The last complete window, however, at the east end is lower and smaller than its neighbours and has straight instead of splayed sides. If it is original, then it suggests that there was some different feature in the planning of the gallery at this point. If it is a later insertion, then the regular spacing between the line of windows was formerly interrupted by several feet of blank walling which still suggests that there was some special feature here. The gallery is 67 feet long internally to this opening and the windows lighting it were originally 3 feet above floor level. The gallery was approached from a lobby at the west end and a small room opening from the north-east corner at the other end.[8] Apart from these entrances, the gallery could also be reached by a large door in the south-west corner of the inner courtyard, approached from a pentice built against the inner wall of the west range. There was a fireplace in the north wall and the excavations revealed part of the surrounding floor, decorated with patterned slates still in good condition. Much of the plaster which covered the walls was recovered but there were no indications that it had ever been painted. The thickness of the walls suggests that the gallery almost certainly supported an upper floor and it is possible that the upper apartment was the gallery and that the area excavated was in fact an undercroft. The proportions of the chamber, the impressive line of windows, the quality of the flooring, and the existence of a large fireplace clearly indicate, however, that the ground-floor room was one of considerable richness and dignity.

[8] There may have also been a small lobby at the east end of the gallery but this would hardly account for the change in the patterning of the windows.

South court. Corner of gallery fireplace

South court. Slate flooring in front of gallery fireplace

The foundations of a large staircase were found at the junction of the gallery and the west range and it is probable that this formed the principal means of access to the upper floor of the gallery. It was not possible to trace the west range for any extent owing to the existence of water-pipes underneath the lawn and a modern garden terrace. It is logical to assume that the range was linked with the upper residential block, but positive indication of the outer walls at the northern end was not revealed by the resistivity survey. The latter suggested the line taken by the west-facing wall, but the destruction of the range in this area seems to have been particularly thorough, possibly because it was very close to the upper block during and after its reconstruction in the later sixteenth century. The excavations indicated that the range was not at right angles to the gallery and that the rooms were approximately $21\frac{1}{2}$ feet wide internally. The east wall of this range, like all those round the courtyard, was marked by a pronounced batter and traces were found of a pentice, 8 feet wide, against its outer face.

The discovery of a chamber projecting from the south-west corner of the range was unexpected. Approximately 23 feet square externally, it consisted of a single room, $10\frac{1}{2}$ feet by $16\frac{3}{4}$ feet internally, warmed by a fireplace. A small drain was found in the thickness of the south-west angle, and a carefully rounded-off chute drain was discovered against the north-east corner of the structure discharging into a ditch which was excavated to a depth of 9 feet below the top of the surviving walls. A doorway in the corner of the room gave access to a narrow passage on the north side. This may have formed the entrance corridor to the tower,[9] but an approach from the west side of the Hall would be a curious one in relation to the remainder of the buildings and difficult of access for the inhabitants of the Hall. It is more likely that the entrance was from the room at the south end of the west range, but the wall common to both this range and the tower was not uncovered and only re-excavation could confirm this suggestion. It is likely that the passageway, only 3 feet wide, was not designed to lead from the chamber towards an outer entrance but towards a projecting garderobe discharging into the ditch continuing round the west face of the tower.[10]

The square plan, the two drains, and the ditch at the north-east corner suggested at first that the structure was a tower, surrounded on each side by a ditch for defensive purposes. However, as the walls were no more than 3 feet thick, the view was also put forward that the structure may have been a garderobe tower.[11] The thinness of the walls show that the structure was not designed primarily with a defensive purpose in mind, while the presence of the fireplace indicates that the ground-floor room was used for residential rather than garderobe purposes. Furthermore, the resistivity survey revealed that the structure was flanked on its north side by a chamber of approximately the same proportions of which the outer wall at the south-east corner was revealed during the excavations. The two projecting structures are therefore likely to have been designed for residential purposes, and the ditch separating them, less than 6 feet wide, was intended to serve garderobe chutes from the chambers flanking its sides.

A small ante-chamber led from the east end of the gallery to a block of two rooms, one of them built against the north face of the gallery range. The larger room was approached from the courtyard by an entrance in the north corner, but few other distinctive features

---

[9] C. Platt, *Arch. Jour.* vol. 119 (1962), 210.

[10] The presence of the ditch on the south side of the chamber was implied by the flattening out of the drain in the south-west angle about 4 feet below the top of the wall. Approximately 40 per cent of all the finds from the site were recovered from within or around this chamber.

[11] C. Platt, *Arch. Jour.* vol. 119 (1962), 209–10.

were revealed. It is likely that the block was two storeys high.

The presence of a large tree made it impossible to excavate the area towards the lower residential block and the kitchen, but the resistivity survey revealed traces of two parallel walls, with centres approximately 14 and 30 feet west of the kitchen. The western wall apparently linked up with the stub end of a wall, $4\frac{1}{2}$ feet thick, found at a low level during the course of the excavations, $46\frac{1}{2}$ feet from the south wall of the lower residential block.[12] It may be tentatively suggested that there was a narrow range, parallel with the kitchen block and stopping a few feet short of the double-room block north of the gallery. The first-floor doorway in the south face of the lower residential block lies astride the west line of this range. The thickness of the wall indicates that it was probably a two-storeyed building. The door may therefore have opened on to a staircase or possibly on to a balcony giving access to the first-floor rooms, as in the fifteenth-century examples at Tretower Court, the New Inn at Gloucester, and Abingdon Abbey.[13]

The plan of the south court, in so far as it has been recovered, shows that it was neither large in area nor regular in plan. The existence of a gallery and a two-roomed block at the east end were firmly established by excavation. It is possible that the west range, partially revealed by excavation, linked the gallery with the upper residential block. Excavation and resistivity work revealed the existence of two chamber blocks projecting from the outer wall of the west range, while the resistivity survey also indicated that the east side of the court was all but closed by a short range linked with the lower residential block.

The Date of the South Court

(i) The architectural and archaeological evidence

No conclusive evidence was found during the excavations which proved when any part of the court had been built. The gallery was a key feature of the site but hardly any architectural stonework was recovered which would identify the period of its construction. It has been suggested, however, that this structure should be ascribed to the early Tudor period, for analogies with other buildings suggest that it is unlikely that a long gallery of this type—particularly a ground-floor gallery—could have existed prior to the sixteenth century, while the style of the flattened rear arches in the surviving wall and a fragment of stone moulding found at the base of the gallery fireplace support a late fifteenth- or early sixteenth-century date.[14]

Galleries were a distinctive feature of Tudor buildings and the earliest known example attributable to that period is the gallery built by Henry VII at Richmond Palace between 1497 and 1501. It was probably a two-storeyed structure built round a garden.[15] A further two-storeyed gallery was built shortly afterwards at Thornbury Castle (1511–21) and galleries were a feature of Henry VIII's additions at Hampton Court (c. 1530–6) and Whitehall (1530–6).[16] But although long galleries were characteristic of sixteenth-century residences, the narrow corridor or gallery was not unknown before that period. A splendid two-storeyed example exists at Much Wenlock Abbey (probably between 1486–c. 1500), and this may be compared with the earlier first-floor galleries raised above the cloisters at Eton College (1441–c. 60) and the complex system of galleries at Hurstmonceaux Castle (c. 1440).[17] All these fifteenth-century examples supported a first-floor gallery such as

[12] The wall was identified by Dr. Platt as 19th-century garden work because the structure was not very substantial and was associated with very late pottery. It was not a certain identification and there was no time to explore it further. However, the thickness of the wall makes it unlikely that it was part of any Victorian garden works.

[13] C. A. Ralegh Radford, *Tretower Court and Castle: Official Guide* (1969), 8, 11, where it is suggested that the balcony may date from the first half of the 15th century. The New Inn was built in about 1450, W. A. Pantin, 'Medieval Inns', *Studies in Building History*, ed. E. M. Jope (1961), 169–73 and 183–6. A. E. Preston, A. C. Baker, and W. H. Godfrey, *Abingdon Abbey* (1963), 14–15, which ascribes the gallery there to the late 15th or early 16th century. See also Margaret Wood, *The English Medieval House* (1965), 337.

[14] C. Platt, *Arch. Jour.* vol. 119 (1962), 216.

[15] G. Webb, *Architecture in Britain: the Middle Ages* (1956), 203–4.

[16] Sir John Summerson considers that the Queen's Gallery at Hampton Court was possibly the first fully developed 'long gallery', but Cardinal Wolsey had built a wooden one at Esher shortly before his fall in 1529. It was taken down by Henry VIII and re-erected at Whitehall not long afterwards. See J. Summerson, *Architecture in Britain: 1530–1830* (4th ed., 1963), 2 n. 1. G. Webb, *Architecture in Britain: the Middle Ages* (1956), 206. G. S. Dugdale, *Whitehall Through the Centuries* (1950), 13–14.

[17] R. A. Brown, H. M. Colvin, and A. J. Taylor, *The History of the King's Works*, vol. 1 (1963) 283, 289; Christopher Hussey, *Country Life* (December 1960); H. Avray Tipping, *English Homes. Period 1 and 2: vol. 2, 1066–1558* (1937), 294.

might have existed at Dartington. Furthermore, it is possible that the 'new alura' built at the Palace of Westminster in 1325–6 to link the royal apartments with St. Stephen's Chapel was a two-storeyed cloister or gallery,[18] while the duke of Lancaster may have also built a cloister court with an upper gallery at Hertford Castle between 1380 and 1383.[19] It is not unlikely, therefore, that the gallery at Dartington is in the tradition of these two-storeyed buildings rather than the Tudor long gallery which may have developed from the rather different medieval conception of a large space capable of subdivision and which certainly tended to be less wide and far longer than the Devon structure.

The rear arches in the surviving wall are difficult to date in their present damaged state, although their form suggests that they were raised some time between the late fourteenth and early sixteenth centuries. It is possible to see, however, that two types of rear arches were used alternately: one was designed with four voussoirs and a keystone and the other was designed with four voussoirs only (p. 186). It will be shown in Chapter 13 that the four-centred arch was in use throughout the last quarter of the fourteenth century, and a comparison between the arches with the keystone and the rear arch of the entrance to the screens passage from the main courtyard, built during the closing years of that century, clearly demonstrates a marked similarity in style. The angles of the splays are similar in both examples and their ground-plans also share the same proportions. None of these characteristics applies to the four-centred arches in the west range of the main courtyard built at a slightly later date. Furthermore, the moulding recovered from the gallery fireplace is almost identical with that of the archway in the great hall which formerly gave access to the staircase leading to the residential rooms behind the dais (p. 152). An examination of the stonework surrounding this archway gives no indication that it was inserted at a date later than the body of the hall and both its form and the character of the moulding give every appearance of being late fourteenth-century work. No firm conclusions on the date of the gallery can be based on the architectural evidence available, but in so far as the present material allows, the remains are closer in style with work known or attributable at Dartington to the late fourteenth century than with that of any other period.

It has been suggested that the precise alignment of some of the ranges round the south courtyard and their apparent similarity of constructional technique indicate a measure of contemporaneity for this complex group of buildings, while the odd relationship between these ranges and the main block of the Hall indicate that they post-date the buildings round the north court.[20] Professor Scott Simpson points out in Appendix 7 that it is not possible to distinguish different periods of construction at Dartington by the stone used or by the method of building. The straight joints which were a feature of the south court suggest a succession of building periods, but apart from the fact that this feature is repeated in buildings facing the main courtyard which were undoubtedly of a single constructional period, no logical sequence of development could be established from these joints during the excavations. In view of the parallel alignment of the gallery and the east block, it is possible that these two structures were built at the same time, and as the outer walls of the west range were thicker than those of the gallery but identical with those of the great hall and upper residential block, this range may have been the first one to be raised.[21] But different alignments between the ranges round the two courtyards at

[18] M. Hastings, *St. Stephen's Chapel* (1955), 66–7. A two-storeyed cloister was also built at St. Paul's Cathedral between 1332 and c. 1335. Both floors were used for ambulatory purposes.

[19] In 1380, William Wintringham agreed to build a chapel and other new buildings of timber at Hertford Castle according to a design made in duplicate. L. F. Salzman, *Building in England down to 1540* (1952), 16, 459–60; J. H. Harvey, *English Mediaeval Architects* (1953), 297. It is likely that the half-timbered domestic buildings round the upper court, shown in an Elizabethan survey, date from this time. It evidently had galleries on the first floor with projecting bays. A. W. Clapham and W. H. Godfrey, *Some Famous Buildings and Their Story* (1913), 145.

[20] C. Platt, *Arch. Jour.* vol. 119 (1962), 217.

[21] The external walls of the court differed in width from 2½ feet to 6 feet. Hardly any two walls were of the same thickness, even within the same range, but insufficient evidence was found to enable any firm conclusions to be drawn from these differences.

Dartington is not necessarily indicative of different periods of construction, or at any rate of no more than different phases of a single operation. The east range of the main courtyard is almost certainly contemporary with the hall range but it was not built at right angles to it. The great hall and the northern ranges of the upper and lower courtyards at Amberley Castle (1377–c. 83) (p. 228) are all contemporary structures but they differ markedly in their alignment to each other. The planning of Sudeley Castle by Ralph, Lord Boteler, in the earlier fifteenth century (p. 229) is an even clearer example of differently aligned ranges of two contemporary courtyards.[22]

Although a large number of fourteenth-century roof tiles were found during the excavation of the second court, no pottery or other finds were discovered attributable to the fourteenth century. Those which could be dated to the fifteenth century were adjudged late in that century and may have been made at the beginning of the next.[23] It has therefore been suggested that the lack of any pottery prior to the early Tudor period is evidence that none of the buildings of the second court were built before the sixteenth or the late fifteenth century at the earliest.[24] It was impossible to establish any dating of the pottery by stratigraphy owing to the very considerable disturbances to which the ground has been subject, and it had to be dated by typological analysis.[25] The lack of fourteenth-century pottery probably arose through the unoccupation of this particular area at that time. The earlier house was in ruins during the third quarter of that century and the site was not inhabited again until 1388. The absence of any sherds dating from the first half of the fifteenth century is not surprising when it is remembered that pottery was not generally left lying around on the floor of a well-ordered residence.[26] Pottery is usually associated with periods of destruction rather than those of construction, and such evidence of inhabitation is therefore less likely to be present during the years immediately after the development of the south court than with a period towards the end of its occupation. Moreover, John Hurst has pointed out to me that discoveries made since the excavations at Dartington suggest that the pottery attributed to the close of the fifteenth century should probably not have been so limited, and that the sherds might now be regarded as earlier.[27] Yet the absence of any large quantities of fifteenth-century material suggests that the site was occupied rather than unoccupied during much of that century, and that the sherds mark the end of its life during the late medieval period.[28]

Two types of glazed ridge tiles were found in great numbers over the site. One was a heavy green glazed tile decorated with deep incisions under a squared-off ridge and the other was a lightly glazed tile with sharply pointed peaks in a rounded ridge decorated immediately below with light incisions. It is not easy to date these tiles as no good sequence of local tiling is known. On examining them, John Hurst has suggested that the decoration indicates that the former were made in the late fourteenth or early fifteenth century. The glaze favours an early fifteenth-century date but there is no reason why they should not be earlier. They were found in two large accumulations, clearly subject to later disturbances. It is almost certain that they were deposited here from elsewhere but owing to the disturbed condition of the site, it is not possible to say when this occurred or whether they formerly covered buildings round the south or the north courtyard.[29] The second type of ridge tile are clearly later in date and the hard, sandy fabric as well as the light incisions

[22] The plan (c. 1930) by W. H. Godfrey in the guide-book by M. Dent-Brocklehurst (c. 1960) should be considered in the light of the comments by P. J. Faulkner, Arch. Jour. vol. 122 (1965), 189–90.

[23] C. Platt, Arch. Jour. vol. 119 (1962), 217–8, 220.

[24] Ibid., 218.

[25] Ibid., 219–20.

[26] The scarcity of 14th- and early 15th-century pottery is characteristic of many sites, and its absence at Dartington can be paralleled elsewhere in Devon. But this gap is so widespread that it reflects the uncertainty of dating pottery rather than the lack of habitation in the county.

[27] See also the note of caution in J. G. Hurst, 'White Castle and the Dating of Medieval Pottery', Med. Archaeol. vols. 6–7 (1962–3), 135–55. On the other hand, the Hispano-Moresque plate originally attributed to the 15th century may be later. Arch. Jour. vol. 119 (1962), 220. Such pieces have been found at many sites of c. 1500–25 at sealed levels and caution must be exercised about their early date.

[28] This association of later pottery with earlier buildings at Dartington is supported by the discovery in 1963 of some later 15th-century sherds in the east range which was probably built in the late 14th century and certainly not after the turn of that century. See p. 217, n. 5.

[29] The only known document referring to the construction of the Hall leaves no

doubt that at least part of the building was roofed in the late 14th century with slates from a quarry at Staverton. It is therefore conceivable that the ranges round the north courtyard were originally roofed with slates and that the earlier tiles were used for roofing the great hall and the ranges round the south courtyard. The great hall was certainly covered with slates in 1813 but this need not always have been so.

and decorative white paint confirm that they were made in the second half of the fifteenth century. They were found in great numbers over the site and could be associated with the destruction of the court.

Fragments of glazed floor tiles of a typical late medieval type were found in several parts of the site, but especially close to the gallery fireplace and in the courtyard immediately north of the gallery. It is possible that many of them had been laid on the floor of the upper gallery. They are larger and thicker than the usual medieval tile and generally seem to have been introduced during the early fifteenth century. They continued in use until the Dissolution but they are not found in Elizabethan times. In the present state of our knowledge, it is not possible to be more precise in dating these tiles than to say that they were made between the close of the fourteenth and the mid sixteenth centuries.

(ii) The historical evidence

The extent and richness of the ranges round the second courtyard indicate that they were constructed by a person of importance, and their position and setting imply a desire for privacy. A survey of the owners of Dartington between 1388 and 1539 may help to limit the field of responsibility, beginning with the Tudor period. An examination of the accounts of Henry Courtenay, marquis of Exeter, who held the manor from 1525 until his execution in 1539, have failed to show that he incurred any sums, large or small, which would have arisen through a heavy building programme such as this. Nor do the minister's accounts for the Devonshire possessions of Margaret, countess of Richmond, who held the property between 1487 and 1509, give any indication of an expenditure commensurate with a large building programme. Although these accounts are often only summary statements, it is likely that they would mention the substantial sums involved in building the second court in some way or other. Nor is there any evidence that Henry or Margaret even visited Dartington.

As far as is known at present, Sir Thomas St. Leger, who held the property from 1476 to 1483, was the last owner to occupy the Hall before it was chosen as the home of the

South court. View of excavations towards gallery wall

South court. Base of staircase

[30] See pp. 69–71.

Champernowne family in 1559.[30] It is difficult to attribute responsibility for the court to St. Ledger unless it is closely supported by the architectural and other evidence, and this is not the case. It is worth noting, moreover, that the alterations to the porch of the fifth block of the west range of the north court which may date from his time, were carried out in timber rather than stone.

Turning now to the dukes of Exeter who held the property for almost a hundred years, it should be emphasized that Dartington Hall reflects a curiously incomplete plan for a major residence of the later Middle Ages if the second court is not considered as an integral part of the building. The private accommodation would be quite inadequate for a family of the standing of any of the dukes of Exeter if it was confined to the two or three rooms in the residential blocks at either end of the great hall, and even more so if the rooms in the lower block were used by the steward and other members of the household. Apart from the chambers necessary for the personal use of the family, they would also need a private chapel and rooms for their guests and their families. Any of the three dukes are likely to have needed accommodation of this nature between the late fourteenth and the late fifteenth centuries, but until his flight to France in 1461, the fourth duke of Exeter had been deeply and continuously embroiled for eleven years in the political troubles of the Wars of the Roses. As a close adherent of the court, his activities were essentially bound up with those of the Crown rather than with his distant estates in Devon. Nor were conditions very propitious for a major building programme during the middle years of the fifteenth century, and there is no evidence to suggest that Exeter's wife needed additional accommodation during her tenure of the estate between the hardly less troubled years from 1461 to 1476.

Youth, imprisonment, and long service abroad confined any building activities of the third duke of Exeter to the few years between 1425 and 1429 and the three years before his death in 1447. Of the two periods, the former is more probable, partly because of Exeter's younger age and partly because of the substantial improvement to his finances in 1426. If there was no other evidence in favour of a building date for the south court before the second quarter of the fifteenth century, then it is most likely that it was constructed shortly after, and perhaps as a result of the third duke of Exeter's marriage to the widow of the earl of March. But the evidence most sharply favours the first duke of Exeter and earl of Huntingdon. He is the only member of the family known to have been responsible for a substantial part of Dartington Hall and some of the major apartments can clearly be attributed to the years between 1388 and 1400. It was essential for Huntingdon to provide adequate family and private rooms, not only for his wife and himself, but also for their five children—three sons and two daughters. It would also have been necessary for him to provide adequate accommodation for guests such as the earl of Devon and Sir Philip Courtenay who are known to have stayed at Dartington in April 1396.[31] As the ranges on either side of the main courtyard were designed for officials, retainers, and servants, it is unlikely that Huntingdon and his wife would be satisfied, or even able to fulfil their needs and those of their family with the few rooms available if the south court had not been an integral part of their home. An inquisition made early in 1400 leaves no doubt that there were a number of richly furnished apartments at

[31] See p. 98.

South court. Approach to court from screens passage

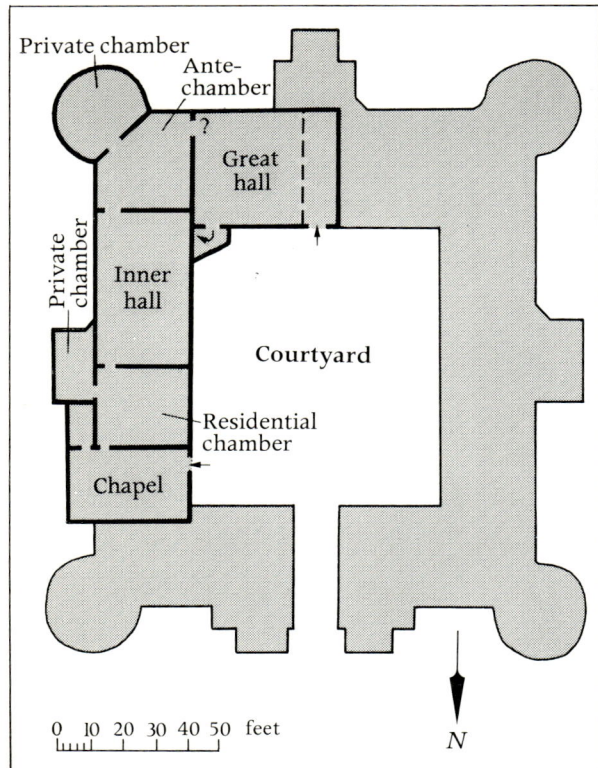

Fig. 35 Bodiam Castle. Ground-floor plan

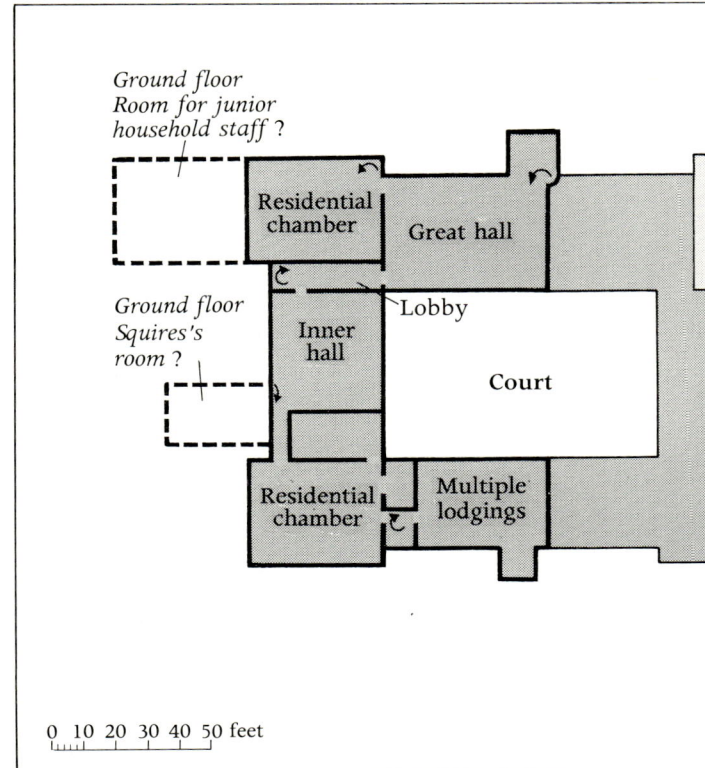

Fig. 37 Bolton Castle. First-floor plan

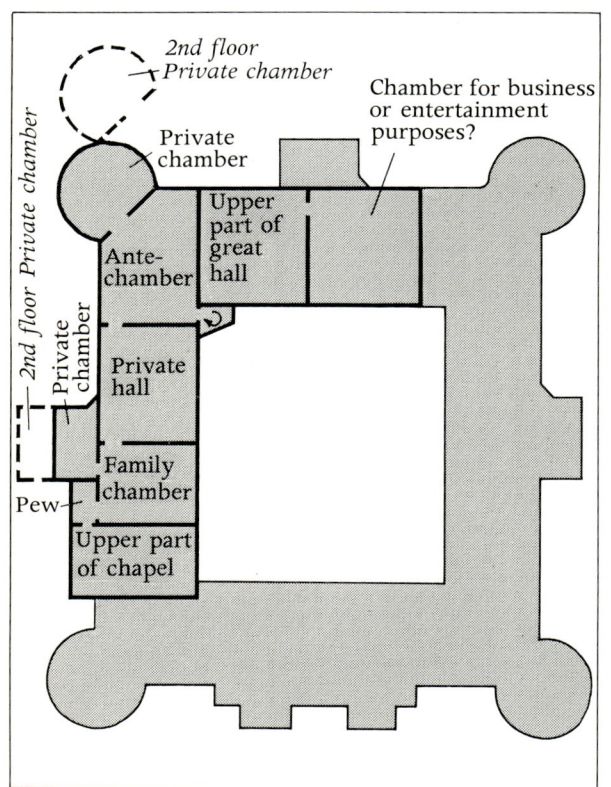

Fig. 36 Bodiam Castle. First-floor plan

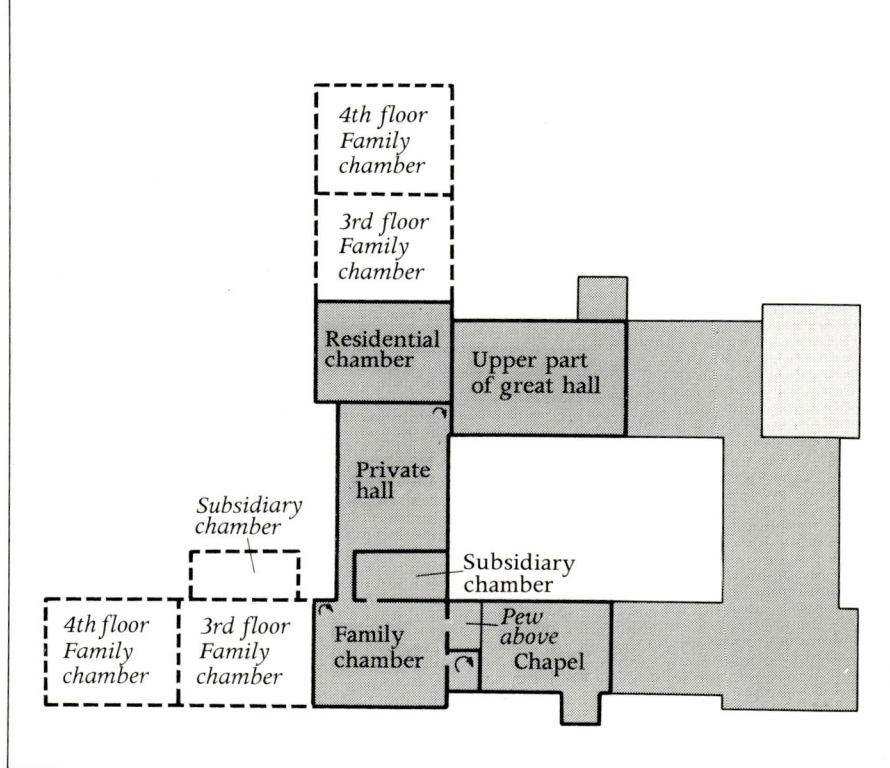

Fig. 38 Bolton Castle. Second-floor plan

Dartington at the time under consideration (see Appendix 6). The enumeration of at least nine beds with curtains and seventy-nine rugs and hangings among Huntingdon's own personal property supports the possibility that there was a greater number of private rooms than exist today.[32] And would not the half-brother of the king, married to the daughter of the premier duke of England, have built a residence with facilities which would to some extent have been comparable with those planned by their contemporaries and equals?

(iii) The comparative evidence

Several late fourteenth-century residences still show considerable evidence of the accommodation needed by a lord for his personal use, and three of them—Bodiam Castle (1385–c. 90), Bolton Castle (c. 1378–c. 99), and Kenilworth Castle (1389–93)—have been chosen to illustrate the design and scale of such accommodation.

Apart from the great hall, Sir Edward Dalyngrigge's accommodation on the ground-floor at Bodiam Castle included an ante-chamber leading to an inner hall, a residential chamber with a private chamber opening from it, and terminated in a chapel. The ante-chamber also gave access to a private room in the south-east tower with two further chambers above it. There was a similar pattern of ante-chamber, private hall, and family chamber on the first floor with the last room giving access to a private pew and two small private chambers in the east turret. The ground-floor rooms were possibly used by important guests staying with Dalyngrigge, while the upper rooms would be occupied by himself and his family. The isolated first-floor room at the lower end of the great hall may have been used by Dalyngrigge for business or possibly for entertainment purposes. Apart from the great hall, Dalyngrigge and his family and their guests therefore occupied two ante-chambers, two further halls, three large chambers, six private chambers, and a chapel with a private pew.

At Bolton Castle, Lord Scrope's accommodation was similar in plan but considerably larger in scale than at Bodiam Castle. The great hall on the first floor of the north range gave access to a series of residential apartments which filled most of the west range and terminated in a chapel in the south range. These apartments, occupying just over a quarter of the total floor area of the castle, may be divided into three suites, each of them with their own hall. The first suite consisted of the great hall and two large residential chambers occupying the usual position of an upper residential block. The second suite, approached from a first-floor lobby, consisted of an inner hall with a large residential and subsidiary chamber at the upper end, and gave access to lodgings for the superior staff attendant on the suite and a ground-floor room for squires. This unit, and possibly the rooms associated with the great hall, may have been used by guests staying with Lord Scrope, with those of the highest rank warranting the inner hall. The first-floor lobby also gave access to the third suite, centred on a private hall on the second floor. This unit, with five large family chambers, two subsidiary chambers, and a private pew was the largest and most remote of the three units and was probably used by Lord Scrope and his wife and their four sons. All these suites were well served with windows, fireplaces, and garderobes and some of them were marked by a very high standard of comfort. Apart from the great hall, the planning of the accommodation for Lord Scrope and his family, their immediate household, and their guests included a lobby, two further halls, eight large chambers with three

---

[32] This ignores those beds, curtains, rugs and hangings etc. owned by Huntingdon and which were simply recorded as being forfeited from his property 'in Devon'. *Cal. Pat. Rolls 1399–1401*, 435, 387, 394. Dartington was Huntingdon's only major residence in the county and a complete inventory of his goods there may have been more extensive than the items listed in P.R.O. Chancery Inq. c. 145/278 no. 26 and *Cal. Pat. Rolls 1399–1401*, 439.

subsidiary chambers, a chapel with a private pew, and three associated staff rooms. All this was planned within a confined site for a person of no greater rank than Huntingdon and amply demonstrates the need for extensive personal accommodation in a baronial household in the late fourteenth century.[33]

Although the residential range at Kenilworth Castle is far less complete now than at Bolton Castle, it possesses the additional interest that it was built by Huntingdon's uncle at precisely the same time that work was in progress at Dartington. As in the previous examples, the accommodation was planned in a two-storeyed range built at right angles or almost at right angles to the great hall and terminated in a chapel built in the preceding century. A porch in the middle of the residential range opened into a large chamber which gave access in one direction to a lobby, an inner hall and chamber for squires, and in the other direction to a second residential chamber close to the chapel. Sixteenth-century alterations and later destruction make it difficult to establish how the range originally terminated. The first-floor apartments were approached from Lancaster's magnificent great hall. This apartment possessed a small chamber at the lower end and a deep oriel-window at its upper end which was almost equivalent to a semi-private dining-room. A narrow projecting tower opposite it was planned with two lobbies on the first floor and a single chamber on the second floor. An ante-chamber behind the great hall gave access to Lancaster's private apartments which followed an identical pattern to those on the floor below. A tower projecting towards the outer court carried garderobes serving the ground- and first-floor suites and a residential chamber on the two floors above. Apart from the great hall, the accommodation for Lancaster and his household and their guests included a semi-private dining-room leading off the great hall, two further halls, four major residential chambers and three associated private chambers, three lesser chambers, four lobbies, and a turret containing an entrance lobby and an upper oriel.

From this summary of the personal accommodation built for a knight, a baron, and a duke respectively during the late fourteenth century, it is possible to establish three broad principles. Firstly, the great hall had tended to become a formal apartment. Secondly, the private accommodation in each case included several family rooms, a number of private rooms, and a chapel if there was not one already in existence. Thirdly, this accommodation extended from behind the great hall through a range at right angles to it and generally followed a common sequence of planning on two floors—an ante-chamber or lobby, an inner hall, one or more residential chambers, and a chapel. Private chambers were generally placed in angle towers or projecting turrets. A similar pattern is reflected in the planning of the royal apartments at Portchester Castle (1396–9) although the design was restricted by the need to build within existing defensive walls.

How do these principles apply to the remains revealed at Dartington? In the first place, it is unlikely that Huntingdon would be satisfied with accommodation built on a less generous scale than that for a knight, and it might be expected that it would be comparable with the accommodation built for members of the baronage such as Scrope and Lancaster. Furthermore, the upper residential block and west range at Dartington was approximately 155 feet long compared with ranges at Bodiam and Bolton castles of approximately 120 feet and at Kenilworth of 170 feet. It is virtually impossible to indicate the internal

[33] There was insufficient residential accommodation in the original specification for building Bolton Castle. As military needs precluded a second court, it was therefore necessary to raise the angle turrets from 50 feet to nearly 100 feet. L. F. Salzman, *Building in England down to 1540* (1952), 454–6.

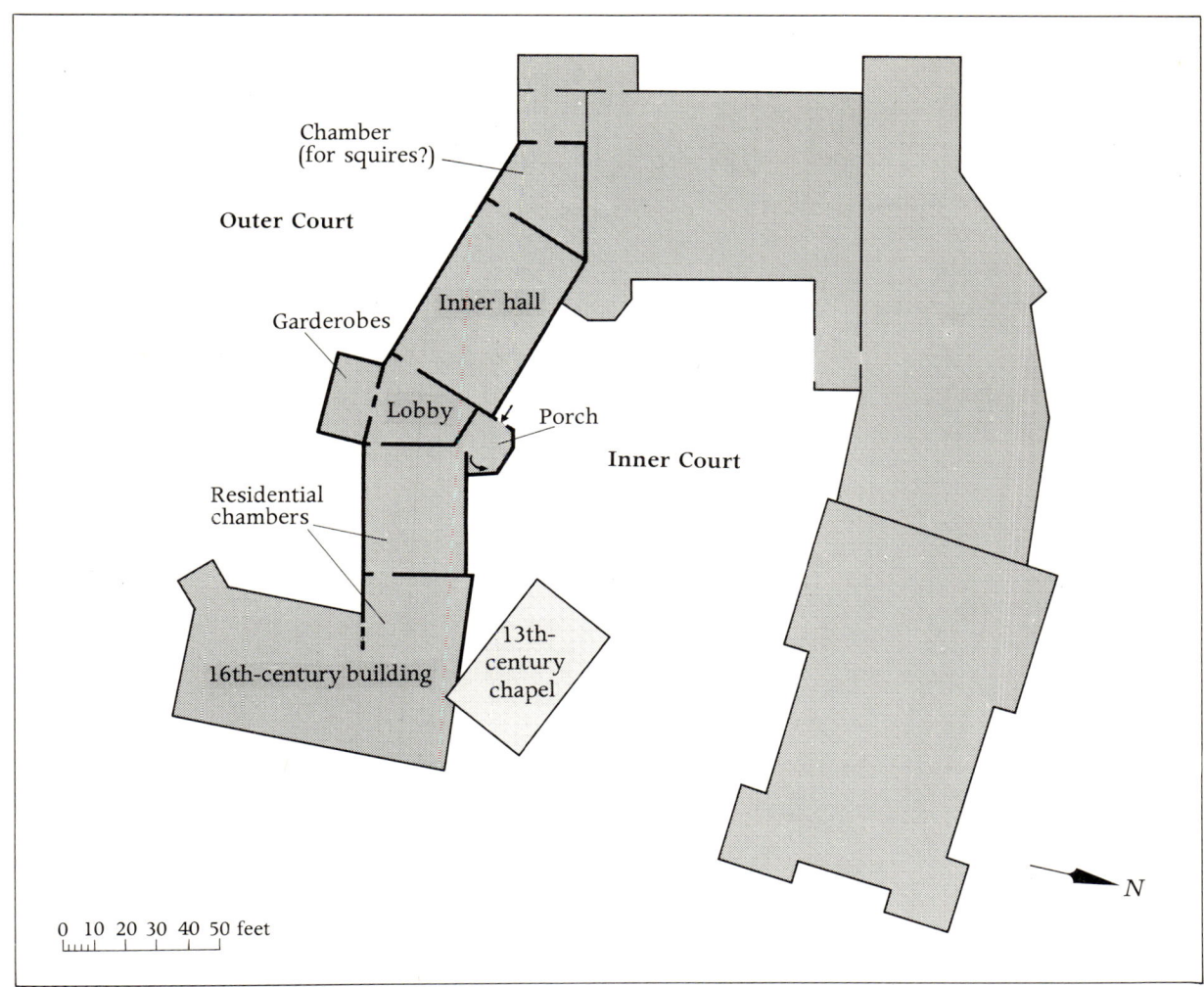

Fig. 39 Kenilworth Castle. Ground-floor plan

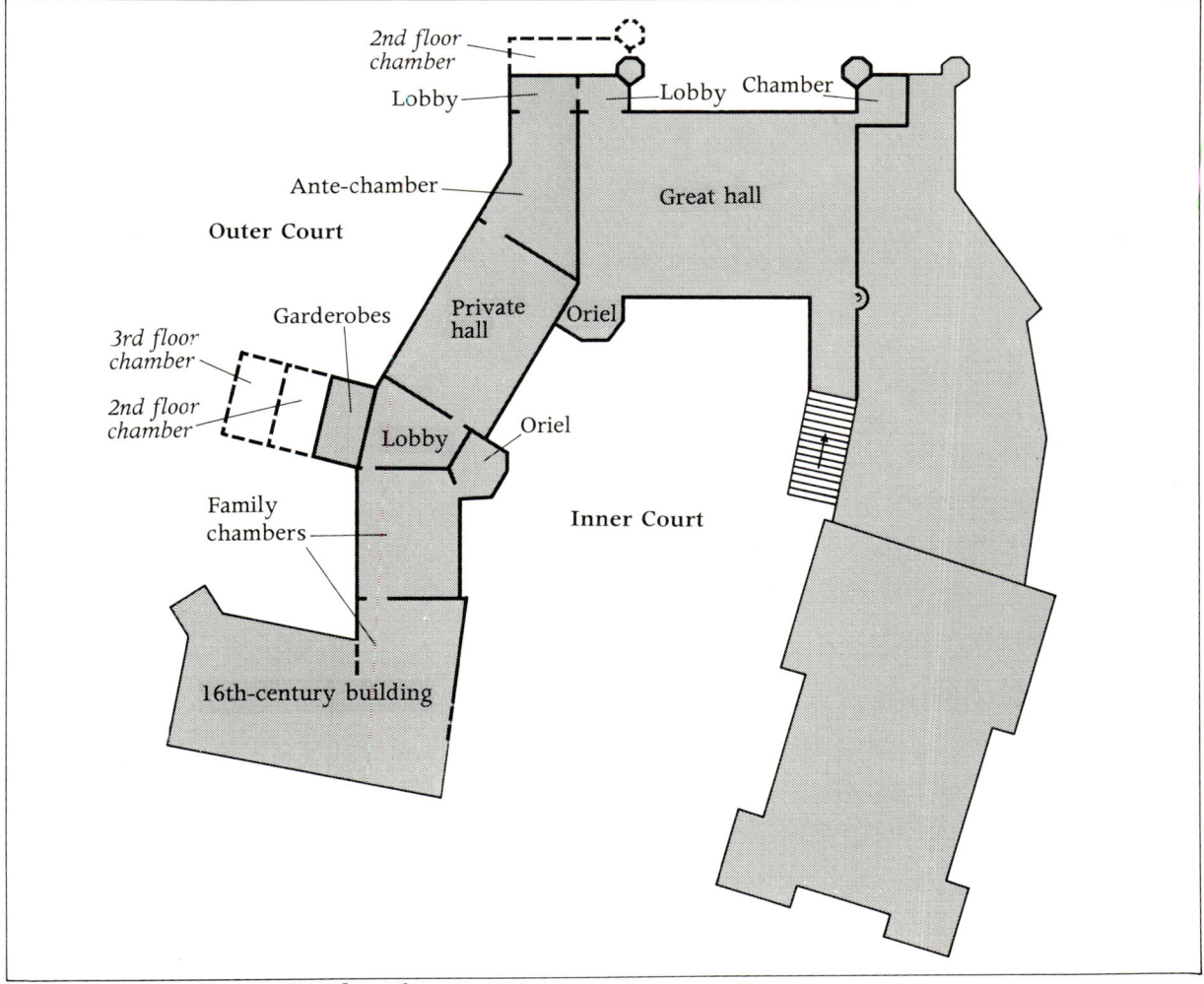

Fig. 40 Kenilworth Castle. First-floor plan

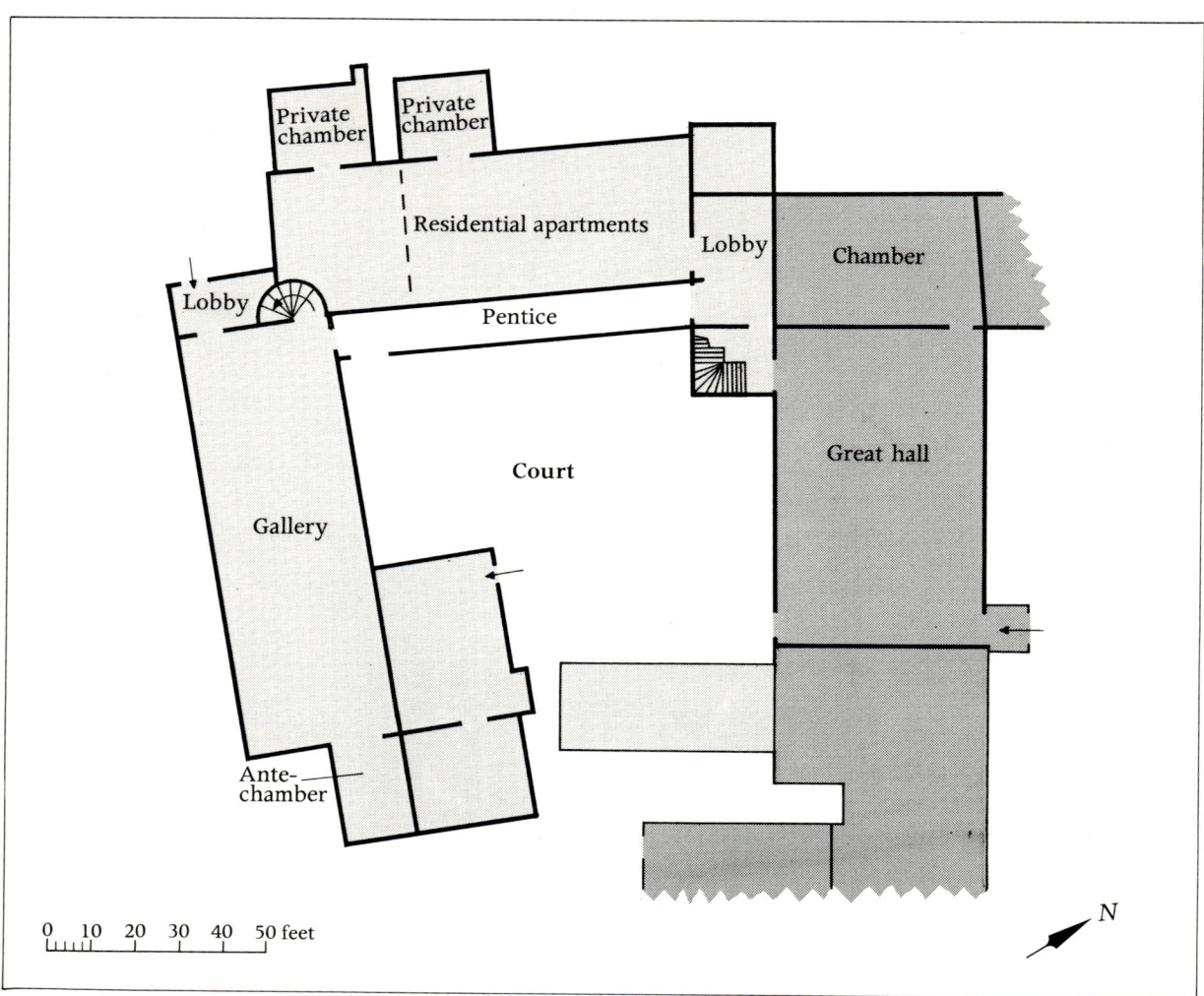

Fig. 41 Dartington Hall. South Court. Conjectural plan of ground-floor

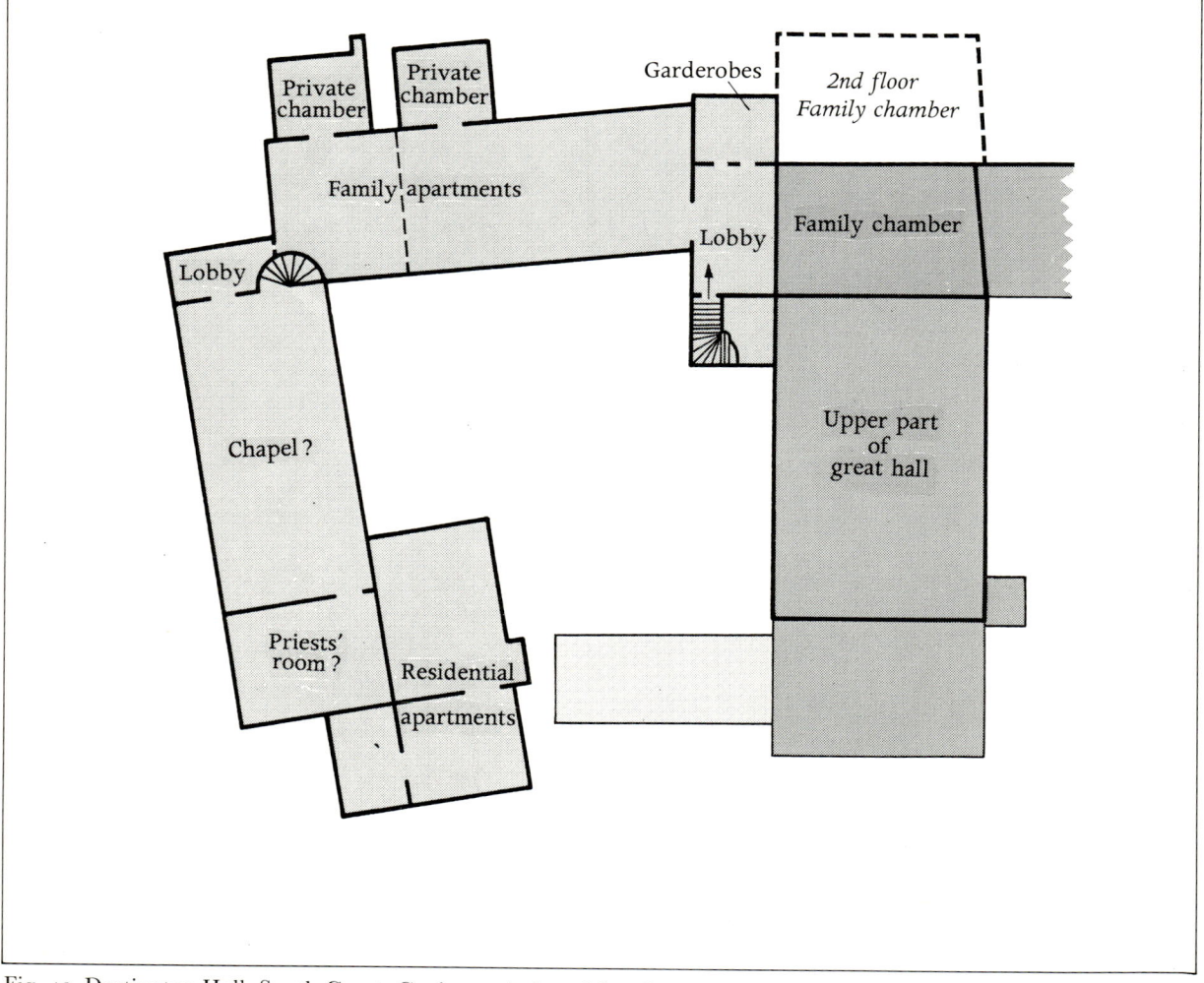

Fig. 42 Dartington Hall. South Court. Conjectural plan of first-floor.

arrangements of the ranges round the south court on the evidence available, but it may be very tentatively suggested that the west range of this court, at right angles to the great hall, was built for residential purposes and that the two structures projecting from it were private chambers. The ground floor of this range may have been approached by a short passageway, at right angles to the stairs opening from the hall dais, to give access to a lobby. Two openings on the site of the present ground-floor windows in the south wall of the upper residential block would lead to a series of residential apartments and a pentice to the gallery respectively. The flight of stairs opening from the great hall would lead to a lobby at first-floor level giving access to a series of private apartments and chambers reserved for Huntingdon and his family. There may have been a further group of private chambers on the east side of the court.

Each of the residential suites at Bodiam, Bolton, Kenilworth, and Portchester castles terminated in a chapel, although Lancaster and Richard II made use of existing structures, extended in the case of that at Portchester at the same time that the royal apartments were built. If a similar pattern of residential planning was adopted at Dartington as in these examples, then it is likely that a private chapel was an integral part of the planning of the second court.[34] No trace of one was discovered during the excavations, although it may have been an upper room and therefore unlikely to be identified. Yet the inquisition post mortem makes it clear that a chapel existed at Dartington Hall in 1400.[35] Could it have been planned in approximately the same position as those in the examples already discussed and built at the end of Huntingdon's private range of apartments above part of the gallery on the south side of the courtyard? It would have been facing eastwards, and the change in the pattern of the windows in the surviving wall hint that the ground-floor gallery may have been partitioned at approximately 65 feet from the west lobby. Lord Scrope's chapel on a restricted site was 50 feet long and one of at least comparable size at Dartington was no more than might befit a pilgrim to Jerusalem and gonfalonier of the Holy Roman Church.[36]

(iv) Summary

It is unfortunate that the dating of the south court cannot be precisely determined but the present evidence is not conclusive enough for any firm strictures to be made. Until further excavations are carried out or new records are discovered, both the date and the responsibility for the ranges round the court must remain an open question. It is possible to suggest, however, that the architectural evidence favours a date in the late fourteenth century in preference to any other period, and it will be shown on page 230 that this is supported by the design of the north court. The tile and other evidence of occupation found on the site does not preclude such a building period while the later fifteenth-century pottery is probably indicative of the time when the area was falling into disuse. A comparison between the arrangement of the rooms round the court and the planning of several late fourteenth-century residential suites reveals a number of similarities. Although the accommodation at Dartington was extensive, it was no greater than in several comparable examples and unlike them, it was not restricted by the need to build within a defensive or confined site. Finally, the existence of a series of rooms such as those round the second court was in keeping with the earl of Huntingdon's position and standing,

---

[34] To the examples given may be added the chapel and other domestic buildings raised by Lancaster at Hertford Castle between 1380 and 1383. See p. 191, n. 19.

[35] There is no record of Bishop Brantingham of Exeter (1370–94) or Bishop Stafford (1395–1419) granting Huntingdon or his son a licence for this chapel, but Huntingdon, especially as gonfalonier, may have obtained a papal licence.

[36] Dr. Pantin points out that a chapel was usually a ground-floor apartment with a raised pew or gallery at the west end for the lord. He has suggested to me that the building discovered midway between the great hall and the gallery (see Appendix 4) might have been a 13th-century structure reused as a chapel. It runs from east to west and the west end was conveniently near the private apartments.

and is supported by the extent of an inventory of his personal goods known to have been kept at the Hall at the time of his death in 1400.

The Later History of the Court

The recovery of a considerable amount of late seventeenth-century pottery and other finds in association with a rubble and mortar floor laid over the majority of the site indicate that it was levelled at that date. This does not mean that the buildings had been in continuous use since their construction and, in fact, it is likely that they had been in ruins for some considerable time. The alterations to the upper residential block by Sir Arthur Champernowne, particularly the insertion of several large windows in the south front, suggest that at least part of the west range of the south court had been pulled down by the mid sixteenth century. Very little dressed stonework of any period was recovered from the site and none that was attributable to the late sixteenth century. Nor were sufficient sherds of pottery and other finds of the late sixteenth or early seventeenth centuries discovered which would indicate or justify continuous occupation of the site during this period.[37] Whatever remained of the south court in the late seventeenth century was almost completely pulled down and the rubble and mortar floor laid over much of the site including some of the walls of the east and west ranges. The floor was not laid over the gallery, however, possibly because it was intended that the remains of this range should become part of a formal garden of which the surviving wall was to be a feature. It is likely that the garden wall enclosing the whole of the site from the outer walls of the upper residential block to the great kitchen was built at this time.[38] A description of Dartington barton in 1663 mentions a wood-house on the south side of the old kitchens,[39] while Prince refers to only one quadrangle in his *Worthies of Devon* (published in 1701), and gives no indication that there was a second court at that time.[40]

Dean Milles's description of the Hall in the third quarter of the eighteenth century makes it clear that there were no buildings on the site by that date, for the south side of the Hall was the only one which did not have a view obstructed by any outhouses or other ancillary buildings.[41] The recovery of a considerable amount of late eighteenth-century pottery over the site mixed with the lawnfill and the debris layer immediately below it shows that the area was remodelled at about that time.[42] Dean Milles had complained that 'as little as can be is done towards improving or even showing the beauty of the situation'.[43] The late eighteenth-century work was an attempt to remedy this condition. The area was evidently dug up, covered with soil which levelled it off and formed a foundation for the lawn which still covers the court today. A description of the Hall in 1803 mentioned that 'the foundations of various walls were also discovered some years ago in digging up the area',[44] and it is likely that this refers to the same operation. The tentative plan of the area made by Saunders in 1805 may also be associated with this work. The foundations shown by him coincide approximately, but not very closely, with those actually recovered during the excavations, possibly because his plan was based on the recovery of isolated fragments of walling. This is all the more likely as the position of the gallery fireplace was accurately marked by Saunders and this is the one part of the site which may not have been completely covered up until the early nineteenth century.[45]

---

[37] C. Platt, *Arch. Jour.* vol. 119 (1962), 213-4.

[38] These walls and a summer-house on the outer face of the west wall were removed during the mid 19th century.

[39] Exeter City Library, 58/3/1/1.

[40] Second ed. (1810), 500.

[41] Bodleian Library, Oxford, MS. Top. Devon, c. 9, f. 73.

[42] C. Platt, *Arch. Jour.* vol. 119 (1962), 214-5.

[43] Bodleian Library, Oxford, MS. Top. Devon, c. 9, f. 73.

[44] J. Britton and E. W. Brayley, *The Beauties of England and Wales*, vol. 4 (1803), 119.

[45] 'Of the inner quadrangle . . . little remains except a wall with a pointed-arch window that formed part of a gallery, 100 feet long.' *Devonshire Illustrated* (early 1800s), 72. Among Saunders's proposals in 1805 was one for rebuilding the gallery on the site of the original structure.

Chapter 13

The West Range of Lodgings

The two-storeyed ranges on either side of the north courtyard were designed as a parallel series of household lodgings. These ranges are a most remarkable survival of late medieval domestic architecture, and although they have been subject to many changes, their original plan can be determined with a fair degree of accuracy. They were built to a similar but not identical plan and each contains features not paralleled in the opposite range. As the lodgings on the west side have been subject to far less alteration than those on the east side, it is preferable to consider them first.

The west range, nearly 250 feet long, was originally divided into five groups of chambers. Each group consisted of four rooms, two at ground- and two at first-floor level, occupying the full depth of the range. The upper rooms were reached by an external staircase over a projecting porch, and the four porches which remain—formerly matched by a fifth one in the middle of the range—mark the entrance to each group of lodgings. Only the rooms adjacent to the upper residential block were built to a different plan from the others, so that there were twenty chambers—of which at least sixteen were of uniform design— enclosing the west side of the court. Many of these chambers have been altered to meet

West range, entrance block and barn from the kitchen offices

West range from the great hall

West range from the east

Fig. 43 West range. Suggested design of original elevation to north court

the needs of later generations and much of the original work has been so drastically altered that their former character is difficult to discern. Fortunately, this does not apply to the group of rooms at the north end of the range and an examination of their form will enable the remainder of the range to be more readily appreciated.

First Group of Lodgings

The planning of the four chambers in the north-west angle of the courtyard is indicated by the arrangement of the doors in pairs. There is no reason to believe that the arched porch or the external stone staircase are not original.[1] The small gabled roof above the landing shown in Buck's engraving of 1734 was probably the original structure (p. 83), but the present lean-to roof was inserted later in the eighteenth century. Each chamber, approximately 22 feet by 20 feet internally, was a self-contained unit with its own entrance, window, fireplace, and garderobe. The doorways have four-centred heads, and there is a narrow rebate for the doors in the adjacent dividing wall. The transomed two-light windows overlooking the courtyard are set in deep internal splays and characterized by shouldered heads. The wooden strengthening above the openings is possibly an original feature, but none of the shutters, indicated by internal rebates, has survived. Each window was subject to some restoration by Weir in 1934 but sufficient evidence remained for this to be completed with confidence. The fireplaces were built in the rear wall with a single massive stone lintel above them.[2] The chimneys projecting above the line of the roof form a distinctive feature of the range as seen from the churchyard. The garderobes were accommodated in a narrow projection built between the fireplaces. They were approached from a single four-centred arch divided by a partition to create a pair of privies on each floor opposite the entrance doors. Unfortunately, the form of this projection is unknown for only its foundations and the arches opening into it survive. The footings, 9 inches thick and standing 3 feet outside the line of the rear wall, are hardly substantial enough to support a stone wall. If the present remains are reliable, it is possible that the projection was built of wood on stone foundations.

[1] The impression given by Buck in his engraving that the steps formerly cut across the line of the ground-floor windows is probably due to faulty draughtsmanship. There is no reason why the steps should originally have been wooden ones as suggested in *Arch. Jour.* vol. 30 (1873), 441.

[2] The purpose of the external projection at the rear of the northernmost ground-floor fireplace is unknown.

West range: first group of lodgings

The first-floor chambers were formerly separated by a timber-framed partition, but both the timbers and the lath within the framework were so badly infested that the division had to be removed in 1934. These chambers are open to the roof and this was the original arrangement throughout the range. Each chamber was divided by two central trusses into three equal bays and a further truss, now restored to match the remaining trusses, marks the position of the central partition. Each truss is formed by a cambered collar-beam into which curved braces are tenoned creating a flattened arch. The lower part of the braces are tenoned into rafters set well into the wall. The arch form of the braces is continued into the face of the wall by means of a lower shaped timber piece tenoned to

West range: first group of lodgings. External window

West range: first group of lodgings. Internal window

West range: first group of lodgings. Upper floor

[3] There are similar collar-beam trusses above the first-floor hall and chamber block at Leigh, Churchstow, a late medieval stone house and probably a former grange of Buckfast Abbey.

[4] Although it was necessary for Weir to replace most of the timbers in 1934, the restoration was an accurate copy of the earlier work.

[5] A similar arrangement exists in one of the ground-floor rooms of the fourth block.

the base of each principal rafter. This form of truss of a well-established type was common throughout the fourteenth and fifteenth centuries and was fairly widely distributed throughout the country.[3] The absence of wind-braces between the principal rafters and the purlins is probably due to the fact that the trusses are sited with very close 'centres', roughly 7 feet apart, and possibly because the need for such braces, intended primarily for stiffening the roof, was considered superfluous above the lodgings.[4] It is interesting to compare the lightness of these trusses with those above the entrance block.

The floor of the northernmost upper chamber is carried on two substantial beams and it is probable that this was the original arrangement.[5] One of these has been replaced by a beam similar to that in the ground-floor room of the entrance block and was probably inserted at the same time. Weir replaced the beams in the adjacent room with a single member. One other feature of interest remains. The internal walls were originally covered with plaster which has survived in parts, particularly on the south wall of the upper chamber which is decorated with scratch drawings of late medieval ships.[6]

Second, Third, and Fourth Group of Lodgings

Apart from those rooms adjacent to the upper residential block, the remainder of the range was made up of three groups of lodgings similar to that already described. Buck's engraving gives an excellent impression of the original external character of the range for it still retained many of its original doorways and windows in the early eighteenth century (pp. 82–3). The present character of this part of the range is essentially due to changes made a few years later when many of the rooms in the centre and at the southern end of the range were modified. The central porch was taken down and the staircases of two of the remaining porches were removed and the landings enclosed to create small rooms lit by Venetian-type windows. The outer faces of the enclosing walls were hung with tiles which add substantially to the present character of the courtyard. Most of the windows in the body of the range were replaced by large square-headed openings,[7] and a number of staff rooms were

[6] Later alterations have not seriously interfered with the original plan of these chambers. The opening in the north wall of the upper chamber was inserted in the 19th century when part of this room was used for storing apples preparatory to crushing them in the cider-press in the room below. This press is now preserved as an ornamental feature in the garden, but the cutting back of the window splay in the ground-floor room to allow a donkey to turn the press still remains. The removal of the partition between the upper rooms, the insertion of the ground-floor partition, the wooden staircase, and the roof lights date from 1934. One of the ground-floor fireplaces was replaced by a window at the same time, but the chimney-shaft was left to indicate its former position.

[7] A plain pediment, removed in 1934, had been inserted in the roof above the central porch. The upper windows on either side of the present entrance in the middle of the range are replacements by Weir of a single square-headed window directly above the present doorway.

West range: first group of lodgings.
Scratch drawing on south wall

West range: second group of lodgings.
Scratch drawings on north wall

West range: second group of lodgings.
Inserted chimney-stack

[8] The staff rooms at the south end of the range were inserted in 1925–6. At the suggestion of a local resident, the end of a bottle was inserted in the peak of the gable to ward off the 'evil eye'.

[9] One of the upper openings has been blocked and the other has been adapted as a window. The rear arches of the ground-floor openings have survived.

created in the roof lit by gabled dormer-windows.[8] Despite these and later minor changes, each block still retains some evidence of its former plan.

Many of the rooms retain their original proportions and several of the window openings have their original splays. All the doorways opening into the second block survive, although the upper ones are now concealed externally by the tile-hung porch room. Internally, two of the rooms have kept so little of their medieval character that they were almost entirely reconstructed in 1934. Fortunately, the other two rooms of this block have not been inhabited for several centuries and apart from the group of chambers already described, they retain far more of their earlier character than any other part of the range. The windows lighting them have been subject to less restoration than others in the range and the lower one still retains the hooks which supported the shutters. The insertion, probably in the sixteenth century, of a massive fireplace with three differently shaped ovens and a stepped flue rising through both rooms, made it necessary to remove the floor between the two chambers and concealed the original fireplaces. Instead of a single arch opening into the garderobes, there were two arches on each floor and the position of all four openings can be clearly seen on the external face of the rear wall.[9] There are substantial remains of the plaster covering the walls of these lodgings, and in the case of the upper room, the lower part is incised with a drawing of a ship and a series of numerals which may date

West range and private house from the churchyard

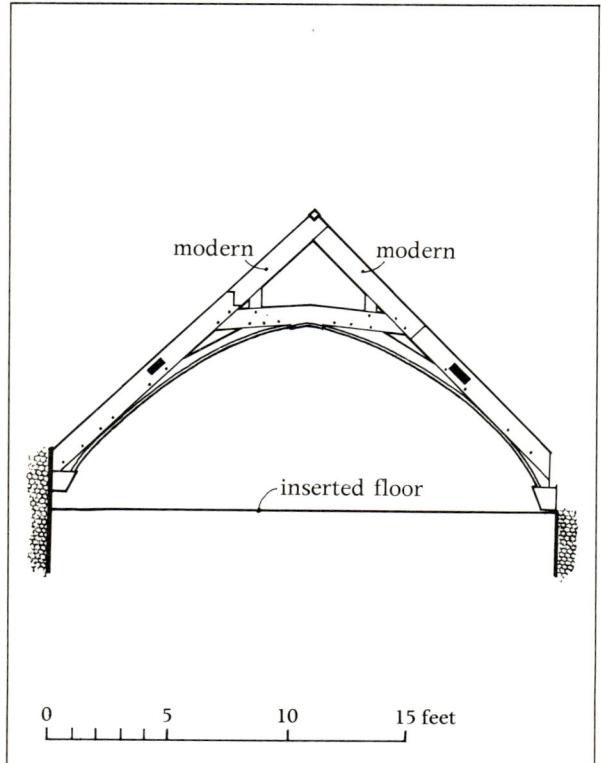
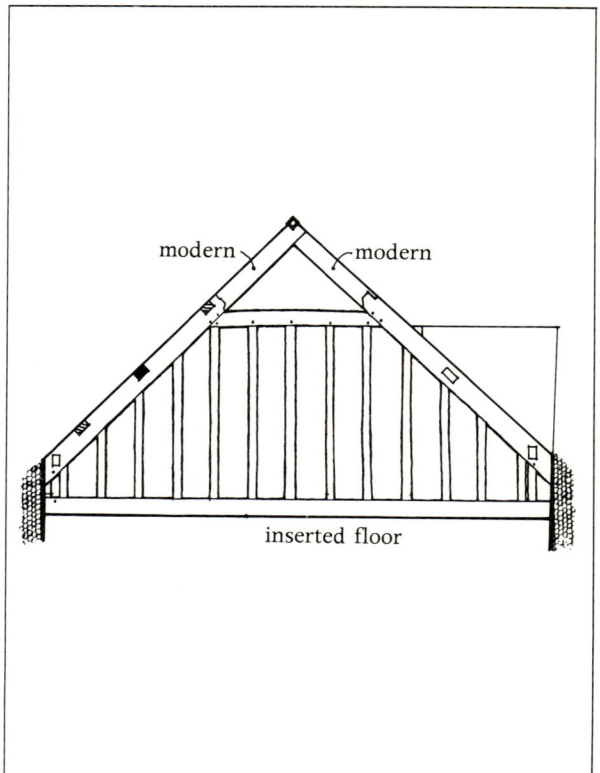

Fig. 44 West range: third group of lodgings. Central truss Fig. 45 West range: third group of lodgings. End truss

from the first quarter of the sixteenth century.[10]

The third block served as part of the barton farm throughout the nineteenth century and it was almost entirely reconstructed internally in 1933–4. The remains of the internal partition wall were removed at that time so that apart from traces of the relieving arches of the lower courtyard openings and the re-used arch inserted between them, little evidence of the original character of that block now remains.

All the courtyard and garderobe openings of the fourth block survive. The lower garderobe openings are particularly well preserved in this block but otherwise the ground-floor rooms are devoid of any distinctive features.[11] One of the upper rooms was panelled in the eighteenth century and the other one was divided into two rooms in the nineteenth century.

The proportions and planning of these three blocks are identical with the first one apart from three features. Firstly, the garderobes serving the first block were designed with single arched openings between each pair of rooms, probably with wooden doors inset within them, whereas those in the other blocks were planned with separate stone doorways opening from each chamber.

Secondly, the roof trusses over the central block differ slightly from those over the first one. All these trusses are now concealed from view except for one which has a cambered collar-beam with dowel-holes and mortices for short vertical timbers between the beam and the principal rafters. The upper part of the truss has been restored and it is not at all certain what the original appearance of the roof to the ridge piece was like.[12] The employment of short horizontal timber 'spurs' in this particular truss close to the attic-floor level and projecting from the side walls is an intriguing feature. The lower part of the principal rafters tenon into these 'spurs' in such a way that the work could either be a repair to the rafters and braces, which might have previously continued downwards to a lower point in the wall similar to the trusses in the first block, or this 'spur' arrangement could be coeval

[10] Photographs of the graffito on this wall were submitted to the Director of the National Maritime Museum who prepared the following report:

Lieut.-Commander G. P. B. Naish in charge of the Department of Models, Draughts, and Relics, suggests that the drawing was made in the early 16th century This view is supported by Lieut.-Commander D. W. Waters. Mr. M. S. Robinson, Curator of Pictures, suggests that if the rectangular lines above the stern represent an after castle, then he would think the ship is of the late 15th century. He also thinks that the size of the main mast and the fact that the fore and mizzen masts are near the ends of the vessel, are also a sign of her being an early ship. Mr. A. W. H. Pearsall, Custodian of Manuscripts, suggests that the shape of the hull has affinities with that of a galley, but that the rigging does not support this view. The Museum's Education Officer, Mr. D. Proctor, also thinks that the hull has something of the lines of a galley or galleass, but the graffito shows no oars, and the rigging does not fit. Mr. John Munday, Librarian, has carefully examined the characters inscribed between the fore and main masts, and he suggests that these appear to be a set of numerals, perhaps from 7 to 20. The characters would support an early 16th-century date. Although it is not possible to be too positive, the most likely dating which can be suggested for this graffito is sometime during the first quarter of the 16th century.

[11] The plans of 1805 show that the fireplaces in the rear wall were still in existence at that date.

[12] Early 19th-century drawings made by J. Buckler (B.M. Add. MSS. 36436, fols. 394 and 627) illustrate roof trusses at Butleigh Court, Somerset, and a building near the bridge at Butleigh which includes the use of separate upper members. Such an arrangement may have existed above the collar-beam trusses at Dartington. Neither of the buildings at Butleigh survive.

West range: fifth group of lodgings. Entrance porch   West range: second group of lodgings. Entrance porch

with the truss as in similar examples where arch-braced collar-beam trusses are tied into the side wall by such a method.[13]

Thirdly, a corridor was added against the rear wall at the south end of the range in the mid eighteenth century, but the section abutting against the garderobe arches of the fourth block and part of the fifth block opens into a curious projection with walls between 2 and 5 feet thick. The proximity of the churchyard, almost level with the upper rooms, was probably taken into consideration when planning this part of the range and the thickness of some of the walls may be due to this factor. The existence of the paired garderobe arches serving the fourth block makes it unlikely that a projection built against them is medieval, but it might be sixteenth- rather than eighteenth-century work. Later alterations now make it difficult to clarify the age or former plan of this particular part of the range.[14]

Fifth Group of Lodgings

The four blocks examined so far conform to a similar pattern, but the fifth block was built to quite a different plan distinguished by the arrangement of the porch and the rooms on either side of it. There is only one archway under the porch opening from the courtyard and although it now leads into a short corridor giving access to offices, it formerly led directly into a single room, 30 feet by 20 feet, which extended to the end of the range. The proportions of this room and that directly above it were similar, and in the latter case have remained unaltered. Access to the second room on each floor in this block is made directly from the larger ones. This gives a pattern for the fifth block of four rooms, two of them similar in proportion to those in the other four blocks but approached from two larger chambers instead of directly from the courtyard. The question arises whether this is the original plan and whether the porch, so different from those already considered, is original or not.

The size of the present room over the porch and the slope of the wall above part of the outer arch suggests that there was only one doorway at first-floor level and that it was

[13] More usually encountered in timber-framed houses where the arch brace, usually a timber of some size, is carried down into the side walls to a point a few feet below the wall-plate, e.g. Dun Cow Inn, Coventry and Solihull Hall, Warwickshire, destroyed in 1966.

[14] The widely splayed opening in the outer wall of the ground-floor corridor looks medieval but is 19th-century work. The large corbel in an exterior wall immediately outside this window is a curious feature.

West range: fifth group of lodgings. First-floor music-room

West range: fourth group of lodgings. First-floor reception room

approached by a staircase on the right- instead of the left-hand side of the porch. No trace of a second door at either ground- or first-floor level can be identified in the walling on either side of the porch. It seems likely, therefore, that the plan of the fifth block has always followed a different pattern from the other four blocks (see also p. 253). The removal of the external stairs and the alterations to the upper landing must have been among the earliest modifications made to the original plan of the Hall. The use of timber framing here, a form of construction not found externally elsewhere in the Hall, suggests a fifteenth- or sixteenth-century date, while more particularly, the framing for a three-light window immediately below the gable and the cusped head between the two wooden mullions points to a date not later than the close of the fifteenth century.[15]

Hardly any medieval features can be traced internally, apart from the position of the upper fireplaces and the head of one of the garderobe arches. The roof is entirely modern and there are no clues as to the original character of the trusses at this end of the range. This is particularly regrettable as the south wall of the range is also common with that of the upper

[15] It is similar to the framing of the windows at 13 Higher Street, Dartmouth, attributed to the mid 15th century. *Trans. Devon Assoc.* vol. 91 (1959), 110–11. The present windows and glass were probably inserted in the 16th century. Buck's engraving shows that the lower porch has been subject to alteration but it probably follows the overall pattern of the original design.

residential block, but as the wall is set square with the range and not with the residential block, it presumably post-dates the latter. The wall separating the fifth from the fourth block was replaced, possibly in the sixteenth century, by a massive fireplace and flue. This substantially altered the character of the two more northerly rooms, but more radical changes were made after 1805 by piercing the flue with a narrow passage at both ground- and first-floor level and inserting a medieval-style window overlooking the courtyard at the end of the first-floor passage. The ground-floor rooms are now used as offices and are featureless, while the upper rooms were altered by Arthur Champernowne in the mid eighteenth century when he created a new suite of rooms here. The windows and woodwork which he inserted make them essentially Georgian in character. The wainscoting is divided into simple rectangular panels, topped by a modillion cornice. Fluted pilasters and capitals were added on either side of the fireplaces. The ceiling in the present dining-room was inserted in the nineteenth century and replaced a more ornate one.

The Date of the West Range

The original plan of the range is reasonably clear. It consisted of four groups of four identical rooms, two on each floor, approached directly from the courtyard. Two more rooms of similar proportions and two larger rooms adjacent to the upper residential block formed a fifth group at the south end of the range. This series of chambers is to be associated with a further series on the opposite side of the court, built to a slightly different plan, and their purpose will be discussed in the following chapter. What needs to be considered here is the date of the west range.

Its construction has been attributed to several occasions within a period spanning nearly 150 years. J. H. Parker favours the mid fourteenth century,[16] Hamilton Thomson,[17] Christopher Hussey,[18] and W. A. Pantin[19] prefer the late fourteenth century, while a date not earlier than the close of the fifteenth century has been proposed by two architectural historians in discussion with the author. It is noticeable that the range is not set square to the upper residential block and great hall which suggests that the same date cannot be claimed for both these buildings. The awkward junction between the two ranges, clearly visible from the courtyard, would certainly be unlikely if they were of one build. If the great hall is to be dated to about 1390, the west range must therefore be later. On the other hand, the abutment of the slaughter-house (finished 1397–8) and the stables (1400–1) on two sides of the Outer Court of Winchester College in a manner similar to that at Dartington shows that the junction does not necessarily indicate widely separated periods of construction (p. 133).

The type of roof truss used throughout the range cannot be closely dated for it was a form extensively used in England with minor variations from the fourteenth to the sixteenth centuries.[20] However, the use of four-centred heads for all doorways and shouldered heads for all windows throughout the range helps to determine the period of its construction. Four-centred heads are usually associated with fifteenth-century work, but they had already been used in several buildings, particularly in southern England, during the last quarter of the fourteenth century. They occur, for example, at Scotney Castle (*c.* 1378–80), Amberley Castle (1377–*c.* 83), Donnington Castle (1386), Winchester College (*c.* 1390),

[16] *Domestic Architecture of the Middle Ages*, vol. 3, pt. 2 (1859), 353.

[17] *Arch. Jour.* vol. 70 (1913), 556.

[18] *Country Life* (27 August 1938).

[19] 'Chantry Priests' Houses and Other Medieval Lodgings', *Med. Archaeol.* vol. 3 (1959), 251–3.

[20] Numerous examples have been recorded in the systematic county surveys carried out by the Royal Commission on Historical Monuments. In the volume dealing with Herefordshire, the majority appear to belong to a date before about 1500. J. T. Smith, 'Medieval Roofs: A Classification', *Arch. Jour.* vol. 115 (1958), 111–48, suggests that the distribution of arch-braced collar-beam roofs generally follows that of cruck roofs and their hybrid forms.

213

and Portchester Castle (1396–9). As this form was also adopted at Dartington Hall in the early 1390s for the rear arches at either end of the screens passage and for the doorways leading to the tower rooms and hall roof, their occurrence in the west range does not make a late fourteenth-century date at all unlikely although it precludes an earlier period.[21] The shouldered arch was a popular and widely distributed design for window and door openings throughout the late thirteenth and fourteenth centuries. It occurs in the north during the last quarter of the fourteenth century at Bolton and Cockermouth castles and Preston Patrick Hall, and in the south at Caldicot Castle, Winchester College, and part of the cloisters of Gloucester Cathedral. The design seems to have gone completely out of fashion shortly afterwards and no examples attributable to the fifteenth century have been traced.[22] A date later than this for the windows in the west range is therefore unlikely, while the presence of shouldered heads in the kitchen at Dartington which may be reasonably assigned to the late fourteenth century, and in the windows of the contemporary east range, suggests that those in the west range may well have been raised at about the same time or not very long afterwards. The construction of this range can therefore be confined to a period between about 1390 at the earliest and the first years of the following century at the latest. Can historical evidence limit this period still further?

As the great hall and entrance porch were built in the years following Huntingdon's acquisition of the property in 1388, it is very probable that the upper residential block and the kitchen were constructed at the same time. The east range probably followed immediately afterwards and on its completion, it is likely that work would begin on the comparable range on the other side of the courtyard. Huntingdon's death in 1400 and the forfeiture of all his estates would have meant an immediate cessation of all building activities. His wife sought to recover as much of his property as possible during the following years, and it is unlikely that she would have spent any income from the estates on starting or continuing to build an extended range of apartments for a household that was now greatly reduced in size. Her first priority was to conserve all her financial resources for the benefit of her family rather than expend them on a series of apartments which neither she nor her young son needed. The childhood of John Holand II during the first fifteen years of the new century and his almost continuous absence abroad between 1415 and 1425 make any building programme at Dartington during the first quarter of the fifteenth century extremely improbable. Further absences abroad between 1429 and about 1445 confine any building activities to the four years following Holand's return from imprisonment in 1425. Historical evidence therefore indicates that the west range is likely to have been constructed between about 1393 and 1400, with the period from 1425 to 1429 as no more than a rank outsider. The use of architectural forms in the range which occur in other late fourteenth-century buildings at Dartington, and the adoption of a window-head which was rapidly becoming old fashioned by the close of the century strongly support the earlier dating. Finally, it may be noted that the mason's marks on the upper right-hand archway of the first group of lodgings are identical with those on two arches in the screens passage which can be dated with confidence to the last years of the century. The mark is merely a cross, however (Appendix 8), and its simplicity precludes it from being offered as more than tentative supporting evidence.

[21] The historical evidence given on p. 95 also tends to rule out a mid 14th-century date. The conjunction of two- and four-centred heads in buildings which cannot be more than a few years apart occurs at Winchester College.

[22] Margaret Wood attributes the shouldered lights at Woodsford Castle, Dorset, to the early 15th century, *The English Mediaeval House* (1965) 360, but they are coeval with the majority of the structure crenellated in 1337.

Chapter 14

The East Range of Lodgings

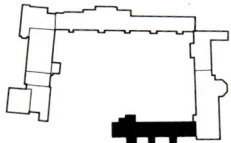

The two conjoined blocks which make up the east range bear little resemblance today to the buildings originally enclosing this side of the courtyard. They were already decayed by the beginning of the eighteenth century and after part of the range had been pulled down in the early nineteenth century, the remainder was drastically reconstructed as a coach-house, harness-room, stabling, cow-house and hayloft. The different roof and window levels are indicative of two building phases during this period, while the abundance of mortar and the dishevelled pattern of stonework testify to workmanship of an inferior quality.[1] The range was still used for stabling and shippens when the Elmhirsts purchased the estate in 1925 and its condition and lack of any interesting internal features made it possible for them to carry out extensive alterations and to convert it into a students' hostel.[2] The interior was reconstructed again in 1963 when it was redesigned as a Devon County Residential Centre for Further Education.

The early form of the range can be recovered from three sources—an eighteenth-century description of the Hall, three drawings of the same period, and a block plan of the Hall made in 1805. Were it not for these records, it is extremely unlikely that the original character of the range could be accurately determined from the existing remains. The earliest reliable pictorial evidence is again Buck's engraving of 1734 which shows part of the dilapidated roof of the range in the foreground (pp. 82–3). It gives little idea of the design of the range, although the continuous roof ridge and the regular positioning of several chimneys are suggestive of repetitive planning in a two-storeyed building. However, the engraving is important because it shows that the range filled most of the east side of the courtyard, and although it does not show the re-entrant angles with the barn and kitchen offices, their existence can be established by examining one of the other drawings and the plan of 1805 (incorporated in that on p. 101).

The description of Dartington by the dean of Exeter in about 1755 confirms the evidence deduced from Buck's engraving and indicates that the range was planned on similar lines to that on the opposite side of the courtyard.

> On each side of the arched entrance are stables, and outhouses from whence the two sides adjoining extended in a plain manner, built two storeys high and consisting of   small houses, each house consisting only of one room below and one above, the communication between the rooms being a stone staircase of 8 or 10 steps built out into the court. . . . Some of these little houses continue in their original condition; many of them on the south side are fallen down.[3]

Two drawings made during the second half of the eighteenth century illustrate the dean's description. A general view of the main courtyard from the entrance arch shows that the south end of the range adjacent to the kitchen offices terminated in two projecting and covered staircases, similar to those which existed on the other side of the courtyard. The second drawing marked 'offices opposite the present dining room at Dartington taken

---

[1] After the remains at the south end had been cleared in the early 19th century, new roof trusses were raised over the central portion and the opportunity was taken to insert a 16th-century window in the wall at the south end. The floor of the upper room was carried on new walls built against the inner faces of the original outer walls, whereas the earlier floor had been supported on beams fitted into sockets 6 inches above the present floor level. Until 1963, it was possible to see that a small upper window in the north wall of the central part of the range had been blocked by the construction of the adjacent roof at a lower level. This evidence and the fact that the poor stonework of the central part of the range was formerly hidden beneath a veneer of plaster, suggest that this work preceded the rebuilding at the north end. This incorporated the remains of a medieval projection at the rear and a fragment of a medieval window.

[2] The courtyard entrance and nearly all the window-frames were inserted at this time. An old timber beam, removed from the north-facing office in the lower residential block, was placed above the ground-floor opening in a projection at the rear which had been used for the previous 100 years as a coach-house. The reconstruction of a complete window in the rear wall on the pattern of those in the west range was due to the enthusiasm of a foreman who made and inserted it during a week-end in 1927 when both Mr. Weir and Mr. Elmhirst were absent.

[3] Bodleian Library, Oxford, MS. Top. Devon, c. 9, f. 72. If Dean Milles had added his estimate of the number of houses in the courtyard, we would have a better idea of the number of rooms originally planned in these two ranges

down in 1792' and attributed to Mrs. Champernowne, apparently shows two groups of lodgings in the centre of the range.[4] It confirms that each group consisted of four rooms, two at ground- and two at first-floor level, approached by an external staircase under a gabled roof. Each roof was lit by a small two-light window with shouldered heads and possessed a fireplace in the rear wall.

None of the evidence considered so far indicates the form of the garderobe accommodation which must have served these rooms. However, three projections at the rear of the range have survived the drastic alterations of the early nineteenth century which destroyed most

North court from entrance block showing destroyed part of east range: late 18th century. By T. Bonner

East range. Middle group of lodgings: 1792. By Mrs. Champernowne

[4] As the drawing shows that the chambers were unattached on the left-hand side, it has always been assumed that Mrs. Champernowne made her drawing from one of the windows of the present dining-room and that it illustrated the south end of the range which no longer exists. Doubt is cast upon this interpretation by Bonner's drawing which shows that the doorways at the south end of the range were still protected by porches and gables during the later 18th century whereas the doors in Mrs. Champernowne's sketch lack any such protection. Further doubt is thrown on this interpretation by Saunders's ground-plan of the Hall made in 1805 (reprinted before its mutilation in *Arch. Jour.* vol. 70 (1913), 554, and incorporated in the plan on page 101), which shows that there was no gap at that time at the south end of the range and that the drawing cannot therefore have illustrated this part of the building. However, Saunders's plan does show a gap not far from the north end and it is likely that Mrs. Champernowne's drawing represents the central part of the range immediately to the right of this gap. A comparison between the 1805 plan and the present structure shows that the change in the roof level almost exactly coincided with the beginning of this gap. The omission of the ruins of the northernmost projection which must still have existed at that time might have been made on aesthetic grounds or because they were not clearly visible from the artist's position. If this interpretation is correct, the pencil note on the drawing is extremely suspect. Architectural evidence makes it impossible for this view to represent any part of the Hall other than the east range. Saunders's plan shows that the only part of the range that had been taken down by 1805 was the section close to the north end and the drawing shows far too much of the range to have filled that gap. The offices illustrated, therefore, were not 'taken down' in 1792 but rather 'drastically reconstructed after 1805'. The position of the dining-room at the time of the drawing is not known, even assuming that the artist sat in a dining-room window as the drawing states. There is no evidence that the room used as a dining-room today served the same purpose before the mid 19th century. One of the other rooms on the first floor of the west range, altered by Arthur Champernowne in the mid 18th century could easily have served as the same venue from which Mrs. Champernowne made her sketch.

of the other original work. Both their position and their plan suggest that they were built as garderobe accommodation, with the upper privies built directly against the rear wall and those below built against a dividing wall separating them from the upper drainage shafts. The discovery in 1927 of a complete two-seat lavatory on the upper floor of the northernmost projection was practical confirmation of their former purpose. Unfortunately, both the lavatory and the broad steep steps leading to it had to be removed to allow for more modern sanitation, but the foundations of the dividing wall were discovered during further alterations in 1963.[5] The arch visible externally at the foot of the rear wall of the middle projection

[5] Parts of a large jar or jars decorated with white paint were found at the time beneath the floor of this projection. John Hurst considers them 15th-century work, possibly dating from the second half of the century.

East range from the north court: 1925

East range from the north court

was a drainage outlet, facilitated here by the fall in the ground. It is unlikely that there were any windows in the rear walls and the present blank walling of the middle projection is probably its original appearance.[6] Although oddly unequal in size,[7] there is no reason to doubt that each garderobe projection served four rooms, two at ground- and two at first-floor level. If Mrs. Champernowne's drawing represents the lodgings in the centre of the range, the likelihood that the end wall shown in her elevation is common with the dividing wall in the present range means that the garderobe and entrance doors were opposite each other.

The range is 20 feet deep internally, and the position of the garderobe projections helps to postulate the possible width of some of the rooms. The grouping of the four external doors in each block of chambers presupposes one wall between each pair of doors and another one midway between the projections separating each block from its neighbour. Such walls, equidistant between the three existing projections create four rooms, approximately 17 feet wide respectively. The existence until 1963 of three ground-floor fireplaces in the walls between the projections support this measurement. Such a regular pattern suggests that this may originally have been the width of some and possibly all the rooms in this range but the point cannot be proved.

One further feature revealed by Mrs. Champernowne's drawing is that the doorways opening from the courtyard possessed two-centred heads.[8] The survival of such an arch *in situ*, opening into the ground floor of the middle garderobe projection, indicates that this pattern was adopted internally as well as externally.[9] It is similar in form to the more elaborate arches in the screens passage and, more particularly, similar in design and proportions to that at the foot of the porch tower stair. None of these arches can be earlier than 1388 and there is no reason why this arch in the east range and its companions should not have been constructed at about that same time. Architectural evidence suggests therefore that the east range may have been built shortly before or immediately after work had been completed on the great hall and the adjacent residential block.

[6] It is similar, for example, to the rear wall of the garderobe projection of the late 15th-century chantry at Combe Raleigh, Devon. The rear wall of the northernmost projection was also blank until the insertion of two windows in 1927 and the arch of the drainage outlet was visible here until 1963.

[7] Their internal measurements from north to south are 8½ feet by 11 feet, 6 feet by 11 feet, and 12 feet by 11 feet respectively. Part of the southernmost projection may have been rebuilt but there is no visible evidence that this applies to the other projections. The garderobes in the west range were apparently 5½ feet by 8 feet internally.

[8] Two of the present ground-floor doors at the north end of the west range were obviously made for doorways with two-centred arches, and shoulders were added to make them fit their present openings. They may have been brought from the east range at the time of its reconstruction in the early 19th century. The red paint still discernible on one of them may have been a preservative, similar to that used on some of the doors at Lord Leycester's Hospital, Warwick. *Trans. Birmingham Arch. Soc.* vol. 70 (1952), 40.

[9] The removal of the plaster surround in 1963 confirmed that the doorway was bonded into the adjacent walling and that it had not been brought from elsewhere.

East range. Garderobe projections from the north-east

East range. Garderobe projections from the south

The Comparative Plan of the East and West Ranges and Their Purpose

Both the east and west ranges originally consisted of a series of lodgings arranged in pairs on two floors, approached directly from the courtyard. Each room possessed a two-light window and there was a fireplace and garderobe opening in the rear wall with the latter almost certainly opposite the entrance door. Four differences, however, may be distinguished between these two series of lodgings. Those on the east side were approached by two-centred instead of four-centred arches and opened into rooms which were possibly 4 feet narrower than those on the other side of the court. Both ranges were lit by windows with shouldered heads, but those on the east side were smaller and lacked transoms. Finally, the garderobes in the east range were built in large stone projections whereas those opposite were possibly built of wood on stone foundations and were less than half the size internally.

It is these differences which suggest that the west range was built after the east range had been completed. The four-centred arch was a development of the long-fashionable two-centred arch,[10] and although there was an overlapping of the two styles in the last quarter of the fourteenth century, the exclusive use of the more flattened arch throughout the west range strongly suggests a constructional date later than that for the east range. The larger sized rooms and windows support this proposition, and in so far as it is possible to distinguish a pattern, paired garderobe projections serving corporate accommodation tended to become smaller as the Middle Ages drew to a close.[11] To the architectural and historical evidence already deduced in the previous chapter, the wider rooms, the larger windows, and the more sophisticated garderobe accommodation in the west range are further evidence that the lodgings were built slightly later than those on the east side of the courtyard.

On the evidence available, any estimation of the total number of chambers surrounding the main courtyard at Dartington Hall must be conjectural. It is certain that there were ten pairs of lodgings in the west range of which two were larger than the remainder, but the

[10] Examples are given in Margaret Wood, *The English Mediaeval House* (1965), 340.

[11] The following list of garderobes is confined to those serving different types of lodgings. Areas refer to the upper floor except where stated.
- *c.* 1310 Vicars' Court, Lincoln, 72 square feet (ground floor).
- *c.* 1377–83, Amberley Castle, 32 square feet.
- *c.* 1387–94, Winchester College, 55 square feet (110 square feet for 2 rooms).
- *c.* 1388–93, East Range, Dartington Hall, 66, 47, and 32 square feet.
- *c.* 1393–1400, West Range, Dartington Hall, 22 square feet.
- *c.* 1445, Hospital of St. Cross, Winchester, 18 square feet.
- Late 15th century, Lower Court, Haddon Hall, 27 square feet.
- 1511–21, Thornbury Castle, 27 square feet (ground floor).

East range from the kitchen offices

drastic changes made to the lodgings in the east range make any estimation of their number hypothetical. If the chambers were approximately 17 feet wide and built on a regular pattern throughout the length of the range, then there was space for fourteen pairs of lodgings. This would make a total of forty-eight lodgings, and even if this number can only be tentatively suggested, it is clear that the main courtyard of the Hall was flanked by an extremely large number of rooms of a well-developed and regular pattern. For what purpose were they built?

The household of a late fourteenth-century magnate was a complicated hierarchy in which officials and retainers expected better accommodation than that allocated to yeomen, grooms, pages, and servants. Several contemporary castles such as Bolton, Lumley, and Amberley have a large number of independent chambers scattered throughout them which reflect these and other household positions, but a series of between forty and fifty lodgings at Dartington poses a different problem. It is obvious that they were too large, too comfortable, and too numerous to have been intended for Huntingdon's servants. Their number also makes it extremely unlikely that they were planned solely for household officials or guests of the family.[12] Nor are any comparable series of lodgings known to have been built before the second half of the fourteenth century, and those which do survive on any scale are confined to large residences built between the later fourteenth and earlier sixteenth centuries. Lodgings of this design and extent therefore must be closely identified with circumstances in the organization of a magnate's household which were peculiar to the last 150 years of the Middle Ages.

During the fourteenth century, the principle of payment for service between a lord and a vassal was established in place of the old feudal principle of tenurial loyalty. Among the changes this brought about in the structure of society was the development of a lord's retinue into three distinct groups—the officials of his household, the men bound by written indenture to serve him in times of peace and war, and those who accepted his fees and wore his livery. The last-named were not usually resident with their lord and they need not concern us here. But permanent residence was obviously essential for household officials and was sometimes, but by no means always the case with indentured retainers. Regular attendance on his lord in private as well as in public life was a characteristic of a retainer's service, and household service at Huntingdon's command is expressly stated, for instance, in the contract between Thomas Proudfoot and the earl in 1399.[13] It was necessary therefore for Huntingdon to provide accommodation for those indentured retainers attendant upon him as well as for his household officials, and both the number and amenities of the lodgings at Dartington Hall support the view that they were designed for their accommodation. Huntingdon's semi-royal position, the size of his household, and the chance survival of several indentures suggest that his retinue was appreciable in size and that he would have needed lodgings for them commensurate with the number built at Dartington. Any estimation of the size of his household based on the number of lodgings, however, is quite speculative for neither their total nor the number of occupants to a room is known. It is likely that at least one family would occupy a chamber and several bachelor officials or soldiers would share a room together as members of a college did at Oxford or Cambridge and the priests at Bolton Castle,[14] but more than that cannot yet be determined.

[12] As suggested by C. A. Ralegh Radford, *Arch. Jour.* vol. 114 (1957), 133. Although some of the rooms may have been used by officials, it is far more likely that guests would have been accommodated in ranges round the south court away from the hurly-burly of the main court.

[13] *Cal. Pat. Rolls 1399–1401*, 244, and Patent Roll, 1 Henry IV, pt. 6, mem. 18, for full details.

[14] The majority of chambers at New College, Oxford were 20 feet by 30 feet. Those on the ground floor were intended to hold four fellows and those on the upper floor accommodated three fellows. A. H. Smith, *New College Oxford and Its Buildings* (1952), 48–9. Among the regulations for King's College, Cambridge, laid down by Henry VI in 1443 was the rule that there should be at least two fellows or scholars in each of the upper chambers and three in the lower chambers. R. Willis and J. W. Clark, *History of Cambridge University*, vol. 1 (1886), 368. The six priests who served the chantry founded by Lord Scrope in 1399 doubtless shared the three small lodgings, 7 feet by 9 feet, opening out of or directly above the chapel.

Chapter 15

The Barn

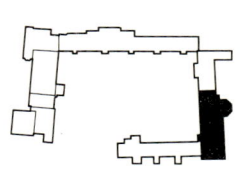

The entrance block and the east range are linked by a long, low barn which forms an integral part of the courtyard complex. It was possibly the last part of the Hall to be built, other than the attractive six-sided projection added on the north side of the barn as a threshing-house in the nineteenth century.

Like so much of the Hall, the barn is an unbuttressed building, 111 feet long and $23\frac{1}{2}$ feet wide internally. The sloping nature of the ground made a batter at the foot of the east wall necessary. A large square-headed opening in either side, oppositely sited but not centrally positioned, formerly gave access to the interior. That in the south wall has been blocked but the opposite entrance is still partially open. This is the traditional position for barn openings in England, but necessary as they are to the function of the structure, it is by no means certain that they are an original feature. Apart from the fact that such openings would have minimized the security of the courtyard, it is noticeable that their

The barn from the entrance approach

jambs are not splayed. This suggests a post-medieval date.[1] On the other hand, the angles of the large opening at the west end of the building are splayed and may therefore be original. This entrance would have been of little use if the side openings had been in existence at the same time, and the fact that it could only be reached after passing through the outer entrance doors of the Hall would have maintained the basic security of the precincts which the side openings rendered vulnerable.

The interior is divided into fourteen bays. Each truss consists of two large principal rafters between 4 and 5 inches wide, which taper from 14 inches at the base to 4 inches at their junction at the apex of the roof.[2] Two cambered collar-beams, notched across the principals, tie the rafters together. The lower collar-beam of every alternate truss is braced to the principal with an angle bracket.[3] Each slope has three purlins, all in bay lengths and resting on the back of the principals so that their ends are either above or below those of the adjoining bay purlins. There are no wind-braces. Vertical timbers, tenoned into the underside of the rafters ensure that the lower extremities of both the truss and the common rafters are rigidly secured in the top of the wall. The tapering principals show the carpenters' concern with the need to reduce the weight of timber towards the crown of the roof,

[1] They may be as late as the similar opening inserted in the kitchen screen wall not long before 1800.

[2] The trusses restored in 1937 do not repeat this feature.

[3] Whereas the collar-beams are both notched, the angle brackets are mortised and tenoned into the principals and collar-beams so that the use of the notched joint is not necessarily restricted to timber with scantling which did not permit deep mortises.

The barn. Interior towards the east

but this is a general feature of western roofs and is not found elsewhere in association with stone or slate roofs. It is this factor which is responsible for the use of smaller and therefore lighter slates at the apex of the roof and larger, heavier ones towards the eaves. Evidence of the narrow slits which allowed air to circulate within the barn are traceable in the north wall and the east gable-head.

There is a total absence of any dating criteria in the masonry of the walls. The present trusses with their tapered principals are probably the work of the Champernowne family in the second half of the sixteenth century. The small size of the angle brackets and their carefully rounded ends are usually an indication of a late medieval date. The notching of the collar-beams across the principals is a practice that became universal in west Devon in the seventeenth century, but it was doubtless widely employed in preceding centuries.[4]

[4] It appears, for example, in Midland cruck-trussed houses of medieval date and beams of similar age and construction.

Even if the roof may be attributed to the Elizabethan period, it does not follow that the same applies to the walls. The barn is of the same width as the adjoining block, it shares a common wall, and the pitch of the roof corresponds closely with that over the entrance block. These facts suggest that both structures could be coeval. It is usual for the trusses of a barn with low walls to spring from a point below the level of the wall top and it is likely that cruck trusses or their related forms, such as the short principals of the gate-house roof, would have been used in the fourteenth century. However, extensive patching of the walls makes it difficult to determine whether they originally supported this form or not. The present evidence is not conclusive enough to determine the date of the structure, but a late medieval date cannot be ruled out, and even if it was not built in the late fourteenth century, the existence of a precinct wall on the same site at that time may be postulated.

A barn was often built next to the entrance block of a large residence. There was a long house, used as a cowshed, next to the outer gatehouse at the royal manor of Burstwick in the fourteenth century,[5] and a granary with stables underneath was built during the same period adjacent to the entrance approach of the Bishop's Palace at Norwich. The south end of the precincts of Ely Cathedral was closed in about 1375 by a two-storeyed barn not far from the great gatehouse, while a barn-like building was erected close to the gatehouse at South Wingfield Manor in the mid fifteenth century. The relationship between the entrance block and the barn is also interesting in considering the development of the 'long house' where the cattle were housed at one end and the farmer and his family at the other, although it is not suggested that the gatehouse and barn at Dartington ever functioned in this way.

[5] R. A. Brown, H. M. Colvin, and A. J. Taylor, *The History of the King's Works*, vol. 2 (1963), 905.

The external reconstruction of the barn was carried out in 1930–1 and its conversion into a theatre was undertaken by Walter Gropius and Robert Hening between 1933 and 1938. Five bays were used for the stage, seven bays for the auditorium, and an end bay for the foyer.[6] The eastern half of the passageway on the north side was converted from a nineteenth-century bull-pen, and the remainder was built to complete the link between the annexe and the dressing-rooms. The change in the pitch of the roof marks the line of the original outer wall of the barn on the north side which still remains 10 feet behind the present outer wall. A nineteenth-century threshing-house was converted at the same time into an annexe to the auditorium. The massive beam spanning this room formerly supported a horse-powered rotary structure operating a threshing-machine in the west end of the barn.

[6] The four-centred doorway, now forming the courtyard approach to the stage and dressing-rooms, was removed from the adjacent first-floor wall of the east range where it had been inserted in the 19th century.

Chapter 16

Dartington Hall and Aspects of Residential Design in the Late Fourteenth Century

The Development of the Double Courtyard Plan

Very few residences of an entirely domestic character built during the late fourteenth century survive today, and none comparable in extent or magnificence with that raised by Huntingdon. Of its type, it is almost the sole survival of its age, and therein lies its importance in the study of English domestic architecture. Unfortunately, it is not yet possible to determine the exact plan of his mansion in the absence of a firm dating criteria for the south court. It may be suggested, however, that as the evidence strongly favours Huntingdon's responsibility for that work, his residence probably consisted of a larger and smaller court, separated by the present hall range. If this interpretation is correct, Dartington Hall was an early example of the double courtyard plan.

The origins and development of this form have not yet been traced in detail, but it was clearly a major development in residential planning in the second half of the fourteenth century and became a popular form for larger houses for nearly two hundred years. The planning of Sudeley Castle, South Wingfield Manor, and Cotehele House in the fifteenth century, the palaces of Cardinal Wolsey and Henry VIII in the early sixteenth century, and the mansions at Theobalds and Holdenby in the later sixteenth century were all based on a pattern established by the last quarter of the fourteenth century.

The decline of military considerations in fourteenth-century England meant that compactness was no longer essential in residential planning. Buildings could be designed more spaciously and with better lighting than hitherto. This trend is observable even in defensive structures where their principal function still demanded restricted planning. The increasing luxury, display, and lavish hospitality of the age encouraged the need to provide extensive and splendid accommodation. Ostentation was encouraged for its own sake as well as an outward display of power and wealth.[1] Not surprisingly, the pattern of life during this period became more elaborate and fostered the development of a plan which differentiated more keenly than hitherto the different scale of accommodation befitting the hierarchy of a household. Accommodation reflected rank and responsibility. It varied from individual rooms for important officials such as the steward, treasurer, and butler, to communal rooms for lesser staff such as esquires, retainers, priests, grooms, and pages. The extension of a residence round two courtyards, separated by the hall and offices, not only gave scope for planning according to the ranks of a household, but it furthered the separation of the owner and his family and their guests from the staff who served them.

Designing a residence round two courtyards had been axiomatic of much castle-planning since the late eleventh and twelfth centuries with the residential buildings grouped round an inner courtyard and protected by an outer courtyard. But this did not become a common pattern in domestic architecture until considerably later. The additions made to Clarendon

[1] M. McKisack, *The Fourteenth Century* (1959), 262–4. See also G. Mathew, *The Court of Richard II* (1968), which surveys the richness of English culture, art and literature during the late 14th century.

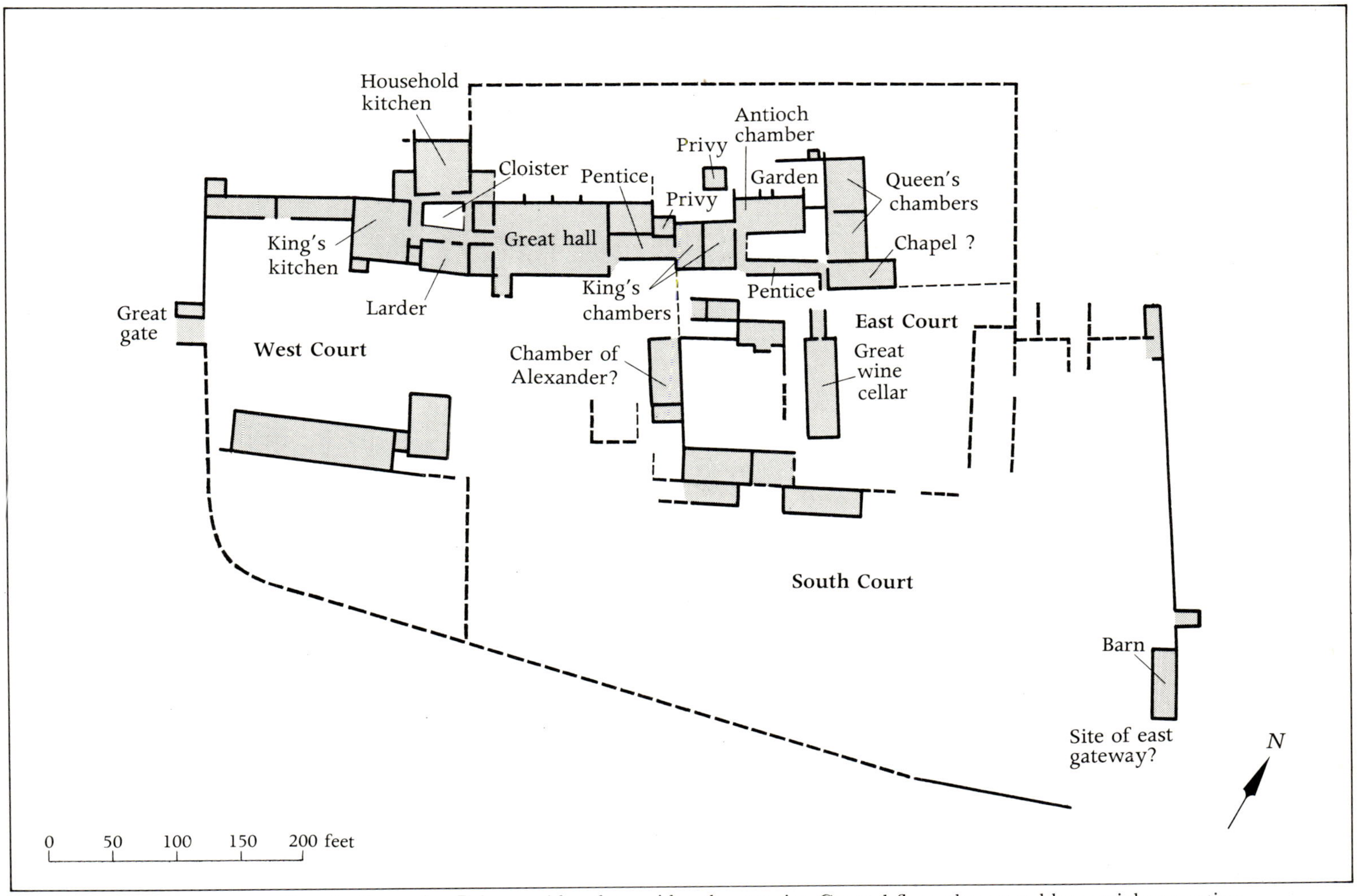

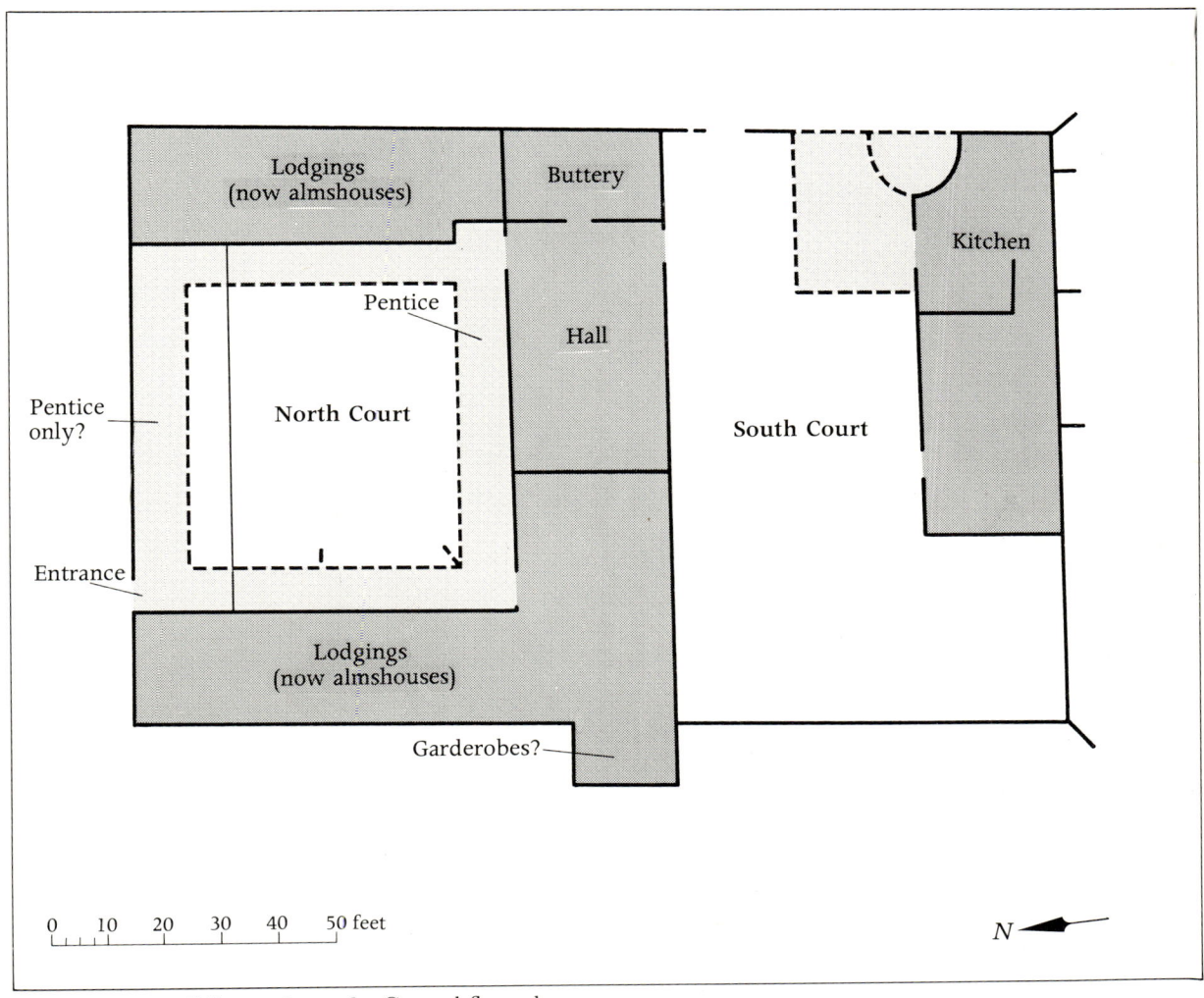

Fig. 46 Clarendon Palace: mid 12th to mid 13th centuries. Ground-floor plan traced by partial excavation

Fig. 47 Cobham College: after 1362. Ground-floor plan

Palace by Henry III in the mid thirteenth century created two courtyards but this was due to haphazard and not conscious planning. By the close of the thirteenth century, the royal manor of Kings Langley had an outer, middle, and inner court, of which one, much larger and known as the great court, contained the royal apartments.[2] The planning of domestic residences round two rather than a single courtyard was not uncommon in the fourteenth century and occurred, for example, at the royal palaces of Sheen and East Tytherley,[3] but the residential ranges were usually confined to the inner court and were separated by a gatehouse or gateway from the barns, sheds, and out-buildings grouped round the outer area. A closer integration between the two courts was adopted at the chantry college at Cobham founded in 1362, where the lodgings were ranged round the first court, and the hall and offices separated them from the second court containing the kitchen and other offices.[4] The new pattern established in the last quarter of the fourteenth century, however, was the planning of the residential apartments round both courtyards, separated by the great hall but with the screens passage providing a line of communication between the two courts. Among the earliest examples of this fully developed form is a group of southern castles built in the 1370s and early 1380s at Farleigh Hungerford (p. 124), Amberley, and Scotney.

One further factor encouraged the development of the double courtyard plan during the fourteenth and fifteenth centuries—the growth of the indentured retinue, for large retinues created accommodation problems. A magnate had to build chambers which ensured privacy and sometimes security for himself and his family. His followers needed stables

[2] R. A. Brown, H. M. Colvin, and A. J. Taylor, *The History of the King's Works*, vol. 2 (1963), 970–3. The courts were so named in 1305–6, but the plan had been established during the last quarter of the 13th century.

[3] Ibid., 994, 928. The addition of a range dividing the courtyard area of a more modest manor-house into two parts in the mid 14th century was discovered during excavations at Northolt Manor in 1962–3. This work was carried out to an existing building by Simon Fraunceys, a prominent London merchant, but it did not result in an orderly plan and the range was levelled in the late 14th century. *Med. Archaeol.* vol. 5 (1961), 211–99, and vol. 8 (1964), 272.

[4] P. J. Tester, 'Notes on the Medieval Chantry College at Cobham', *Arch. Cantiana*, vol. 129 (1964), 109–20.

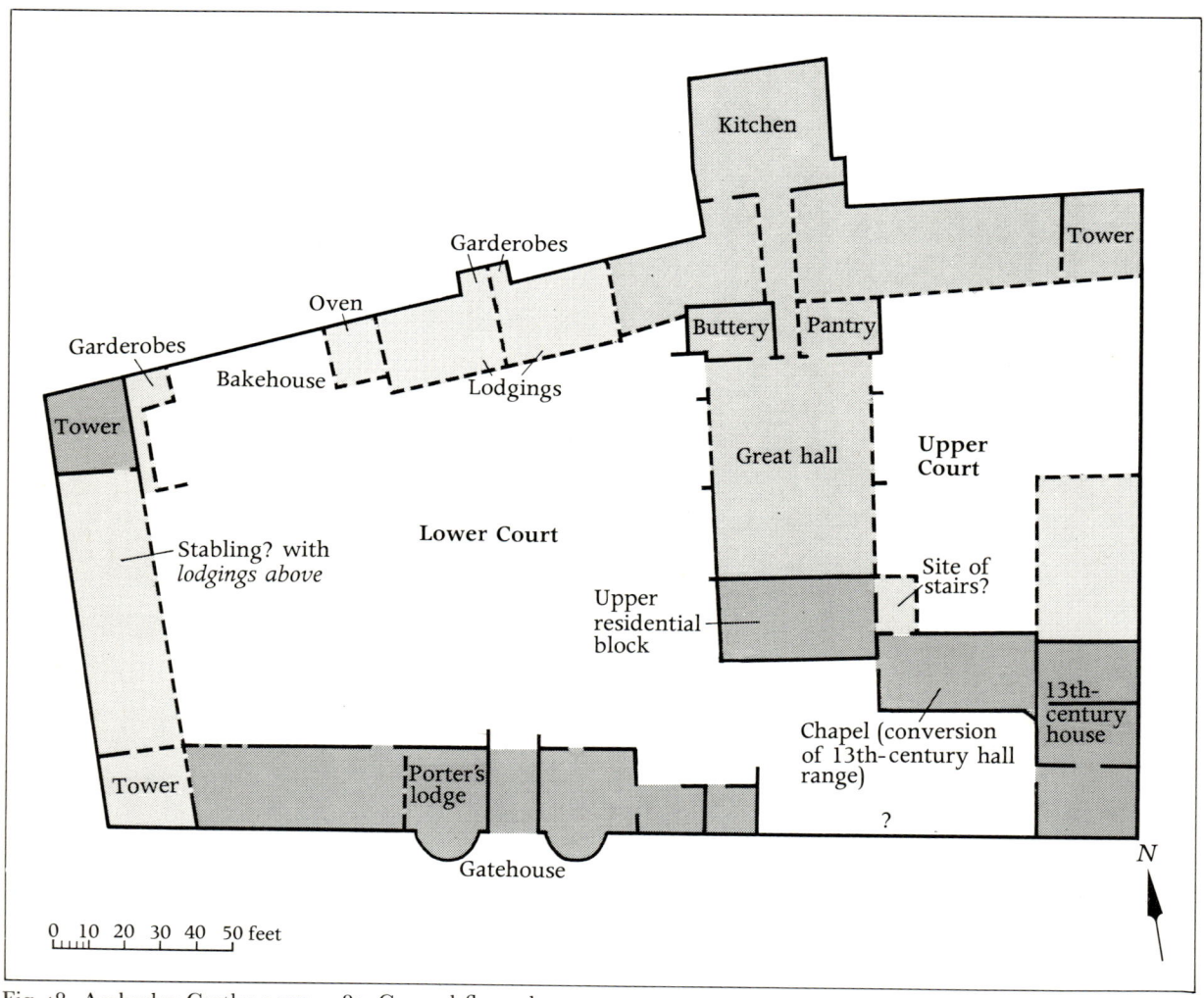

Fig. 48 Amberley Castle: 1377–c. 83. Ground-floor plan

and other offices as well as adequate lodgings, and separate dining accommodation usually had to be built for a magnate so that the great hall could be used by his retinue. On the whole, the lawlessness frequently associated with the practices of retaining and wearing livery, two of the principal characteristics of bastard feudalism, did not become widespread until the fifteenth century, but the statutes passed against the practice in 1377 and 1390 were indicative that the system could get out of hand. There was always the possibility —not unknown in the fifteenth century—that supporters would change their allegiance, and several magnates took precautions which ensured that they could isolate themselves from their retinues if the need arose.

The immediate influence of bastard feudalism on residential planning was twofold. It was necessary for a magnate to provide adequate quarters for his retinue, and it became equally necessary for him to build those quarters as far from his own apartments as possible.[5] These requirements were most difficult to achieve on a restricted military site. A second hall, intended for the personal use of a magnate and his household, might be built above an earlier one which could then be set aside for his retainers. This occurred in the 1370s at both Raby and Tantallon castles. In the case of a newly defensive site, as at Bolton and Bodiam castles, the second hall, kitchen, and associated residential quarters were built on the opposite side of the courtyard from the lord's apartments (pp. 118 and 127). Most satisfactory of all was the construction of two courtyards with the lord's apartments ranged round the upper one and the retainers and subsidiary offices confined to the lower one. This plan was adopted at Amberley Castle in the late fourteenth century,

[5] A third and slightly later influence of the indentured retinue on residential planning may already be distinguished by the close of the 14th century. This was the need for a lord's accommodation to be designed so that he could completely isolate himself from his retinue should the need arise. This pattern may be distinguished in the planning of the tower-house at Warkworth Castle and in the later examples at Ashby de la Zouch and Raglan castles. Some of the effects of bastard feudalism on military architecture are discussed by W. Douglas Simpson in '"Bastard Feudalism" and the Later Castles', *The Antiq. Jour.* vol. 26 (1946), 145–71.

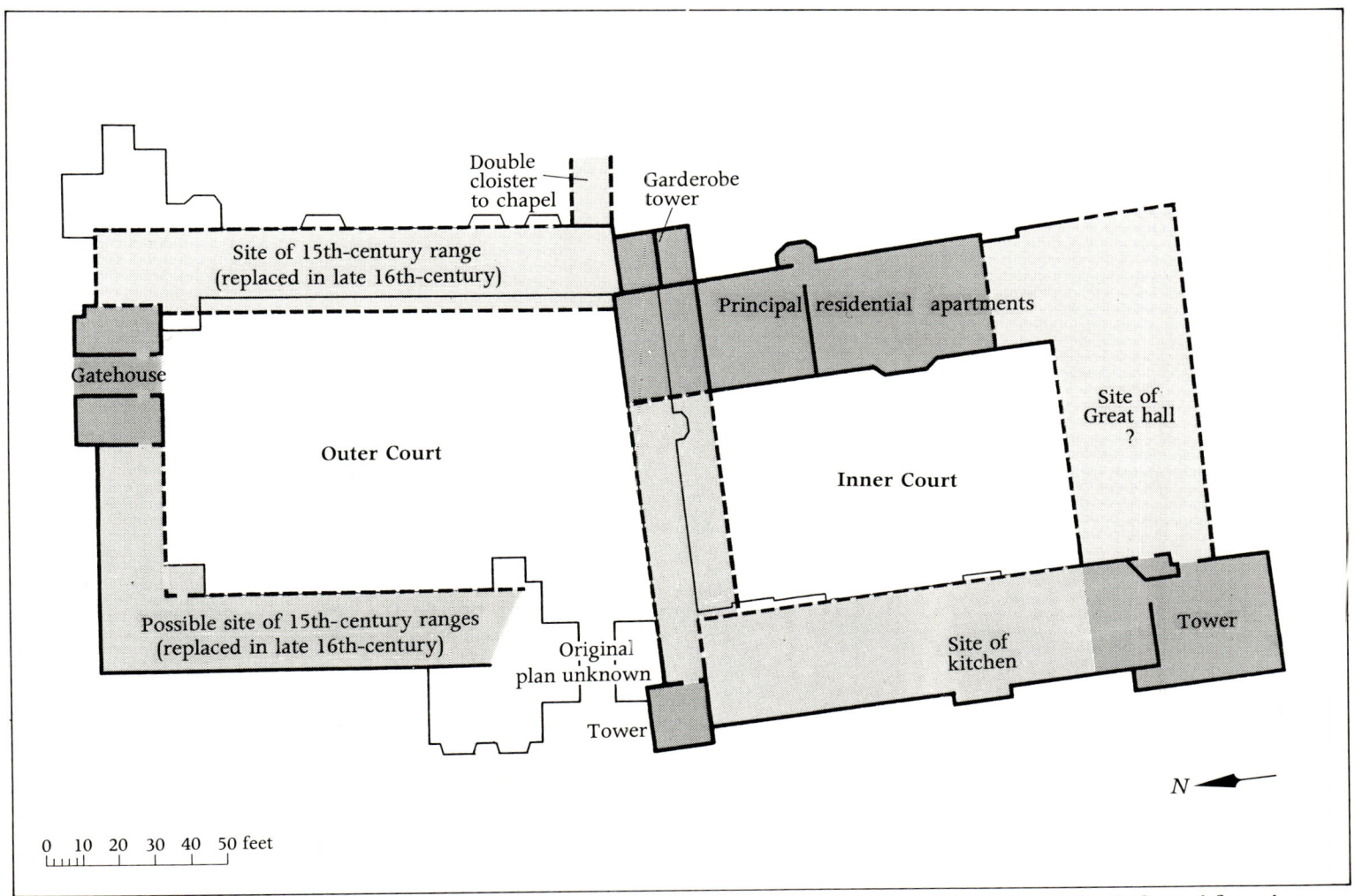

Fig. 49 Sudeley Castle: outer court and mid towers: early 15th century, inner court: 1469–78. Ground-floor plan

Sudeley and Raglan castles, South Wingfield Manor, Haddon Hall and Eltham Palace in the fifteenth century, and at Thornbury Castle and Hampton Court in the early sixteenth century.

The existence of a double courtyard plan during the later Middle Ages does not necessarily imply that the accommodation in the outer court was intended for retainers and servants, although this is frequently true of major residences. On the other hand, the existence of a series of lodgings for retainers built round a court does imply that a second court was an integral part of the overall design of the residence. To the evidence already considered therefore in Chapter 12 as to whether the second court at Dartington was part of Huntingdon's original plan, it may now be added that the construction of an extended series of two-storeyed lodgings for retainers on the east and probably the west side of the main courtyard by the earl, implies the existence of a second court to provide adequate accommodation for Huntingdon and his family that would separate him from his retinue. Furthermore, the absence of any special hall for his retainers means that they would have probably used the existing great hall and *inter alia*, a second smaller hall or chamber for Huntingdon's own use would have formed part of the second courtyard complex. The door in the south-west corner of the kitchen would facilitate the movement of food to the apartments round this court.

The position and planning of the great hall at Dartington indicates that it was never intended that Huntingdon should be completely isolated from his retinue. This residence was not therefore designed so that the lord could withdraw from the great hall and dine in a separate chamber for reasons of security, but it was designed to ensure that Huntingdon could enjoy the privacy and comfort for himself and his family that a magnate of his standing now demanded. This movement, the subject of a contemporary complaint in *Piers the Plowman*,[6] quickened in the fifteenth century, but Huntingdon's mansion is an early example of its application to the planning of a large and entirely non-fortified residence.

The Non-defensive Character of the Mansion

The lack of any defensive features at Dartington is immediately apparent, although the site would not be an easy one to defend. The Hall is built on the side of a low hill above a wide loop of the river Dart and is overlooked by rising ground towards the west and south-west. Furthermore, the whole of the west range of the main courtyard and the upper residential block are overtopped by the church tower, less than 20 yards away, although a similar factor had not deterred Bishop Rede from fortifying his residence at Amberley.

No evidence has been found that a defensive ditch or moat surrounded the site. A channel ran between the west range and the churchyard on the site of the present passageway, but this was merely to allow for clearance of the garderobes. The drainage of the garderobes at the back of the east range was helped by the natural slope of the ground and no trace of a ditch has been found there. Evidence of a ditch or moat was found against the outer face of the west range during the excavation of the south court, but the resistivity survey and other evidence indicates that it was intended for drainage purposes.

The lack of a gatehouse or fortified gateway is unusual in an age that continued to build

[6] 'And the rich have a habit nowadays of eating by themselves in private parlours ... or in a special chamber with a fireplace of its own. So they abandon the main hall which was made for men to eat their meals in.' Langland, *Piers the Plowman*, ed. J. F. Goodridge (1959), 153.

them in residences which otherwise paid only lip-service to defence. It is all the more surprising in a county where they were a particularly common feature throughout the fifteenth and sixteenth centuries. They were not usually defended with a portcullis or other defensive apparatus but just a pair of stout doors, even in such an important residence as Tiverton Castle (mid 14th century). Some foundations were discovered in 1936 at the east end of the barn which may have been the lower courses of a circular tower.[7] No detailed record was kept of their form or position and it is now impossible to say much about their date or purpose. Such a tower may have been built to defend the entrance approach, but the absence of a fortified gateway and the weak re-entrant angles between the entrance block and the west range and between the east and south ranges, do not support this view. The foundations could have been those of a dovecot, for instance, and their position in relation to the barn supports this possibility. It is known that there was a dovecot at Dartington in 1326, valued at 40*d.* a year.[8] Yet a drawing of the Hall made two centuries later indicates that the roof line was broken by three rather than by a single tower. They are shown in a representation of the Hall included in a panoramic view of the coast from Exeter to Land's End, prepared in about 1540 (p. 225).[9] The interpretation, however, of this part of this drawing is uncertain. It is noticeable that none of the three towers is embattled like those of Dartmouth Castle and some of the neighbouring church towers. Assuming therefore that the drawing is an accurate one,[10] it might be thought that the three Dartington towers represent the church and porch tower and possibly the dovecot or whatever structure existed on that site. Both the church and the porch tower, however, were embattled at the time[11] and the dozen or so dovecotes still in existence in Devon are certainly nowhere near so tall as the tower shown in the drawing. Whatever the interpretation of this representation of the Hall proves to be, it seems clear that any tower next to the barn was completely subservient to the domestic character of the building.

The reasons why Huntingdon decided to build a non-defensive residence can only be conjectured now, but factors which may have influenced him were the lack of any disturbances in Devon during the recent Peasants' Revolt, the more peaceful conditions following Richard II's assumption of control in 1389, the unlikelihood of any inland attacks from French shipping, and the absence of any turbulent neighbours. Both the Courtenays, the pre-eminent family at the time in the west of England, and the de la Pomerais were friends of the earl and his wife. The only apparent sign of a defensive feature were the battlements of the great hall and lower residential block and these were entirely decorative, added for aesthetic effect and reasons of prestige.

In one respect the design of Dartington clung to an outdated characteristic which must have tended to give the Hall a more severe appearance than it now possesses. The outer faces of the north, east, and west ranges surrounding the main courtyard originally lacked any windows, or else they were merely broken by the smallest openings. Only one of those in the entrance block existed before 1928 and even that might not be very old. The only openings in the barn were slits for ventilation, and there are no traces of any medieval windows in the rear wall of the west range, although the garderobes presumably possessed some sort of openings for purposes of ventilation and light. As far as the present evidence allows, the same applies to the east range. The only substantial outward-facing windows in

[7] Anthony Emery, *Arch. Jour.* vol. 115 (1958), 188. One-quarter of a complete circle was found. Mr. Elmhirst remembers its discovery and position.

[8] P.R.O. C 134/99, no. 14.

[9] B.M. MS. Cott. Augustus I. 1, art. 39.

[10] B. H. St. J. O'Neil noted in a study of the defences at Dartmouth that there were difficulties in reconciling this map with existing remains. *Archaeologia*, vol. 85 (1936), 133.

[11] The church was despoiled during Richard III's brief reign and a considerable amount of repair work, both internal and external, was necessary. The principal work was the restoration of the church tower between 1485 and 1493 and replacing the bell with a new one. Dartington Church Wardens Accounts, fols 9, 10, and 14.

the north courtyard were those on the east and west side of the south range lighting the kitchen and upper residential block respectively. In so far as the ranges round the north courtyard were concerned, Dartington, like several contemporary palace-fortresses and colleges, was an inward- rather than an outward-looking building.

The Design of the Great Hall and the Residential Blocks

During the early Middle Ages, two forms of residential planning had been favoured. One was a unified block with rooms on two floors, generally a greater and a lesser chamber in each case, of which the greater one on the first floor was the hall. This was already a popular design in the late eleventh century and was widely adopted until the mid fourteenth century. The alternative plan was dominated by a ground-floor hall rising through the height of the building with a domestic block at one and later at both ends. The earliest surviving examples of this plan date from the late twelfth century,[12] but it was subject to a series of major developments during the thirteenth and early fourteenth centuries and gradually became the standard plan during the later medieval period. At first, halls of any appreciable size were generally divided by two rows of columns into a central nave flanked by aisles so that the width of the block could be adequately spanned, but the development of building techniques in the thirteenth century made the inclusion of arcades unnecessary. Commensurate with the development of the hall was that of the residential block. At first it was built at one end of the hall only as at Crowhurst Manor (c. 1250) and usually consisted of one or two chambers at ground-floor level and a single residential room above. Gradually

[12] The arrangement, however, is much earlier. A hall and upper residential block have been excavated at Sulgrave, Northamptonshire, attributable to the late pre-Conquest period. *Arch. Jour.* vol. 125 (1968), 305-6.

Haddon Hall, Derbyshire. Great hall from upper court: second quarter of 14th century. Staircase tower: early 17th century

Fig. 50 Haddon Hall: between 1325 and 1350. Ground-floor plan

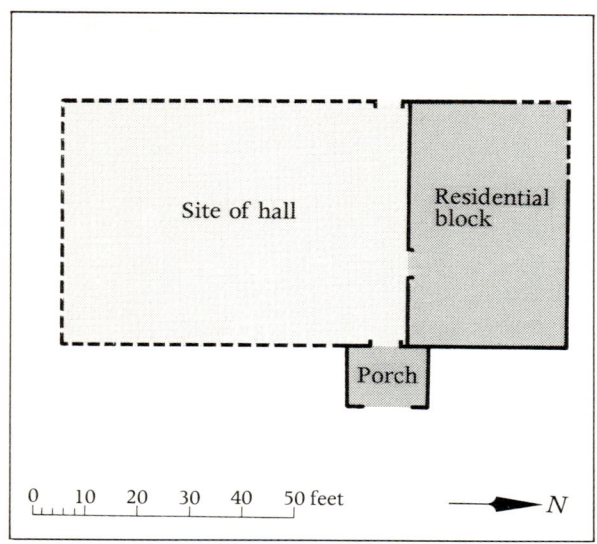

Fig. 51 Crowhurst Manor: *c.* 1250. Ground-floor plan

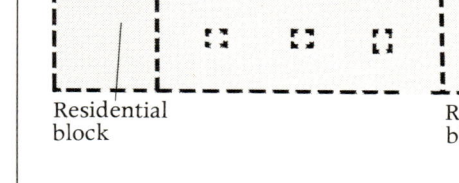

Fig. 52 Kirkstall Abbey Guest House: early 13th century. Ground-floor plan

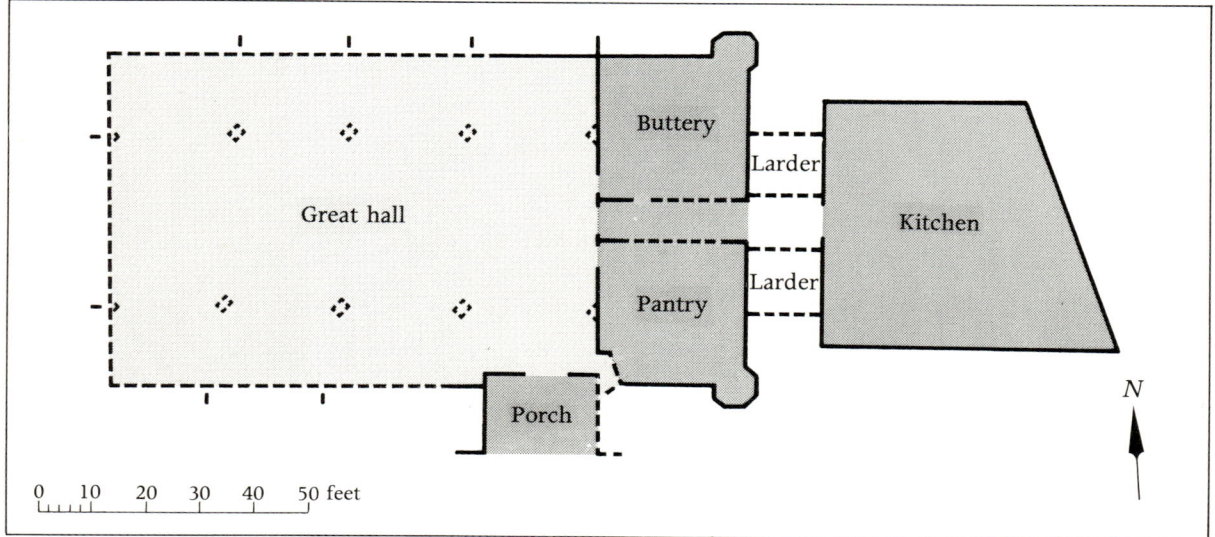

Fig. 53 Bishop's Palace, Lincoln: *c.* 1224. Ground-floor plan

Penshurst Place, Kent. Great hall, porch, and lower residential block: 1341–9

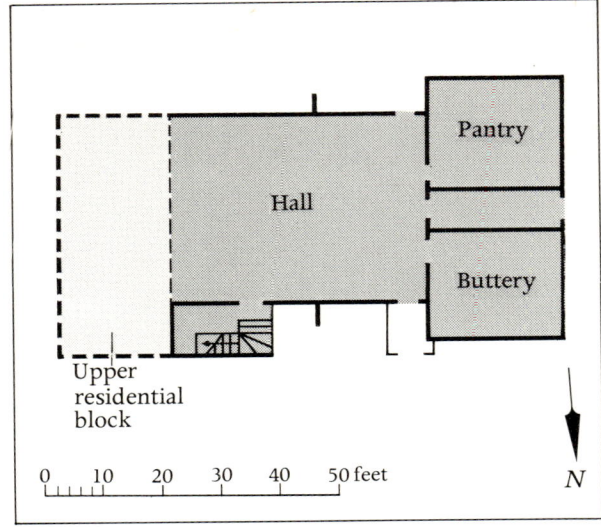

Fig. 54 Northborough Manor House: c. 1340. Ground-floor plan

Raby Castle, Co. Durham. Lower hall: c. 1325–30. Upper hall: c. 1378–c. 90

it became more convenient to build chambers at both ends of the hall, as at Kirkstall Abbey Guest House constructed in the early thirteenth century, and to use the ground-floor rooms at the lower end for service rooms and those at the upper end for the lord. The practice of inserting a passageway between the service rooms at the lower end to facilitate access between a detached kitchen and the hall may have been adopted as early as the late twelfth century and had certainly become a common practice by the mid thirteenth century as the planning of the Bishop's Palace at Lincoln indicates (c. 1224). A screen was added still later at the lower end of the hall to form a passage separating the service rooms from the body of the hall. All these elements were usually present in the planning of large domestic houses from the beginning of the fourteenth century onwards and the plan may be seen in full flower at Clevedon Court, Haddon Hall, and Penshurst Place built in the years immediately after 1320, 1325, and 1341 respectively.

These principles of planning are also to be found in the design of Dartington Hall, for they had been subject to little development since the second quarter of the fourteenth century. The planning of the great hall, offices, and associated residential blocks at Haddon, in particular, is similar to that in Huntingdon's residence. Not only is there a close parallel between the overall concept of a central hall with a residential block at either end and a detached rectangular kitchen, but the analogy is still closer through the planning of the approach to the rooms of the upper block, the layout of the screens passage with four contemporary doors, the location of the bakery adjacent to the kitchen, and the construction of a buttressed wall to screen the offices and kitchen from the adjacent court.

Where Dartington principally differs from these and other fourteenth-century examples is in the generosity of its accommodation. Firstly, the entrance tower was not two but three storeys high. A vaulted porch with a room over it was popular in larger houses such as the Bishops' Palaces at Wells (c. 1274–92) and Norwich (1318–25) and at Penshurst Place (1341) and Howden Manor (1388–1405), but a three-storeyed porch is almost unknown before the fifteenth century. It is possible that it was so designed to provide accommodation for those members of the household attendant upon the great hall and offices and therefore intended for use by the pages of Huntingdon's household.

Secondly, although Dartington lacks the elaborate decoration found in many houses such as the porch at Penshurst Place (1341), the screens passage at Northborough Manor

New College, Oxford. Great hall: 1380–6

(*c.* 1340), or the great hall at Kenilworth Castle (1389–93), there are indications that the great hall was used for events of a ceremonial nature as well as for purposes of dining and entertainment. Few halls built in the fourteenth century were larger than Huntingdon's great apartment. The exceptions during the first half of the century include those built for the archbishop of Canterbury at Charing (*c.* 1300) and Mayfield (*c.* 1320–30), for the bishops at Durham (*c.* 1300, enlarged in *c.* 1350), Norwich (1318–25), and St. David's (*c.* 1327–45), and for Hugh Despenser at Caerphilly Castle (*c.* 1317–26). Only two larger structures were built before that at Dartington during the second half of the century, the hall for Edward III at Windsor Castle (1357–65) and that for Lord Neville at Raby Castle (*c.* 1378–90), but immediately after the completion of Huntingdon's apartment, it was surpassed by the royal halls at Kenilworth Castle (1389–93) and Westminster (1394–1401).[13] No larger structures were then raised for nearly fifty years until Lord Cromwell built his hall at South Wingfield Manor between about 1440 and 1456. The standing of this small group of owners is indicative that their halls were intended to serve a ceremonial as well as a domestic purpose. Huntingdon's apartment was probably built with a dais, not a very common feature at this time.[14] The position of the fireplace in the end wall, comparable in position and accent with that in the Black Prince's manor at Kennington and with the magnificent example in the great hall of the Ducal Palace at Poitiers in France (probably

[13] Charing, 69½′ × 35′, Mayfield, 69½′ × 39¼′; Durham, 101′ × 35′, enlarged to 132′ × 35′; Norwich (aisled), 121½′ × 58½′, St. David's, 119′ × 31′; Caerphilly Castle, 70′ × 35′; Windsor Castle, 85′ × 32′; Raby Castle, 90′ × 35′; Kenilworth Castle, 90′ × 45′ (the predecessor of 1347 was 89′ × 46′); Westminster Hall, 239½′ × 67¼′. The hall at Dartington, 68¾′ × 37½′, may also have been exceeded by the hall at Arundel Castle (*c.* 1380) but lack of records make verification impossible. It was also slightly smaller than the dining hall at New College, Oxford (1380–6), 79′ × 32½′, but this served a somewhat different purpose.

[14] P. A. Faulkner, 'Domestic Planning From the Twelfth to the Fourteenth Centuries', *Arch. Jour.* vol. 115 (1958), 180.

between 1384 and 90), suggests an aesthetic as much as a practical purpose. Furthermore, the likelihood that there was a rich staircase leading from the dais to the private quarters, a feature which had been designed in earlier times to avoid pomp and ceremony, emphasizes the ceremonial purpose of this apartment. The absence of a second hall for retainers and junior members of the household such as existed at Bolton and Bodiam castles, indicates that the existing one at Dartington must have been used every day by the majority of Huntingdon's household. Nevertheless, it was more than adequately designed to serve as a status symbol of its owner and a background to the pomp and ceremony beloved of the age.

Thirdly, the two residential blocks were larger than most of those built in the fourteenth century such as the blocks at Northborough Manor (*c*. 1340) and Amberley Castle (1377–*c*. 83), and was exceeded only by that at Goodrich Castle (*c*. 1300).[15] Moreover, most blocks were only two storeys high whereas those at Dartington were built with an additional storey. A similar plan had been adopted many years before at Ludlow Castle (p. 248). The lower block there had probably been built at the same time as the great hall in the late thirteenth century[16] but about thirty years later, Roger Mortimer, earl of March and the most powerful baron of the time, added two further blocks, back to back, at the upper end of the hall. The kitchen and offices built at Harewood Castle for Sir William Aldeburgh in 1366 supported two residential floors at the lower end of his hall. Further north, a three-storeyed block was built at the lower end of the great hall at Bolton Castle and a double two-storeyed block at the upper end with the lower one approached directly from the hall giving access to a third room for staff at ground-floor level (p. 196). The need for a large amount of accommodation also made a three-storeyed block necessary at Winchester College, but the feature was not usually adopted unless the household was a particularly large one.

The Development of the Hammer-Beam Roof

The dating of the great hall at Dartington to the years between 1388 and 1400, and possibly more precisely to the early 1390s is particularly important in considering the development of the hammer-beam roof. Only a handful of such structures are known to have been raised before the remarkable technical and aesthetic achievement at Westminster Hall, and that at Dartington preceded it by no more than a few years.

The origin of this roof form still awaits detailed investigation, but the outline of its development is becoming fairly clear. A number of thirteenth- and early fourteenth-century carpenters made use of hammer-beam trusses in a very tentative way. An incipient form, for instance, is used to support the upper part of the intermediate truss of the roof of Great Coxwell Barn (possibly earlier part of the thirteenth century).[17] A rudimentary form also occurs as part of the complicated roof structure of the chapter house at York Minster (closing years of the thirteenth century),[18] and it is used more dramatically at Ely Cathedral where elaborate brackets support the remarkable octagonal lantern (1323–42).[19] None of these examples, however, incorporates the basic combination of hammer-post, hammer-beam, and square-set purlin.

It is possible that the beginning of the hammer-beam roof is to be found in the development of the great hall from its nave and aisle form. In its essentials, a hammer-beam roof is

---

[15] Northborough Manor, 36′ × 16′; Amberley Castle, 38′ × 17′; Dartington Hall, 53′ × 20′; Goodrich Castle, 57′ × 22′.

[16] W. H. St. John Hope, 'The Castle of Ludlow', *Archaeologia*, vol. 61 (1908), 281, 325 considered that it may have been begun in the late 13th century, but that it was completed shortly after Roger Mortimer acquired the property in 1314. C. A. R. Radford concurred: *Arch. Jour.* vol. 113 (1956), 198. Margaret Wood and A. J. Taylor favour its construction by Peter de Genevill between 1283 and 1292: *The English Mediaeval House* (1965), 69–70.

[17] W. Horn and E. Born, *The Barns of the Abbey of Beaulieu and its Granges of Great Coxwell and Beaulieu St. Leonards* (1965), 7, 17–35. The structure is more usually attributed after less careful study, to varying dates in the 14th century.

[18] J. Quentin Hughes, 'The Timber Roofs of York Minster', *Yorks. Arch. Jour.* vol. 38 (1958), 474–95.

[19] J. T. Smith has pointed out to me that the Ely lantern does not incorporate the hammer-beam principle. The crude model in the cathedral, in so far as it is possible to discern anything from it, suggests that the lantern is related to the earlier passing brace system.

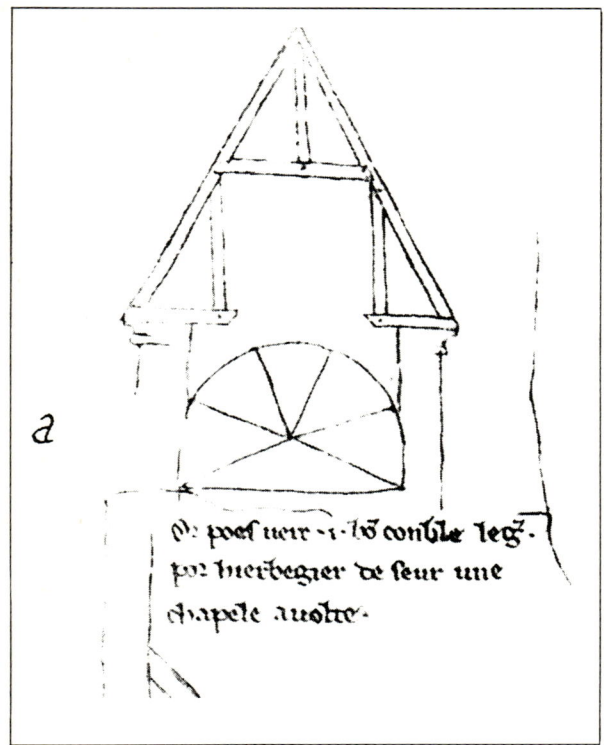
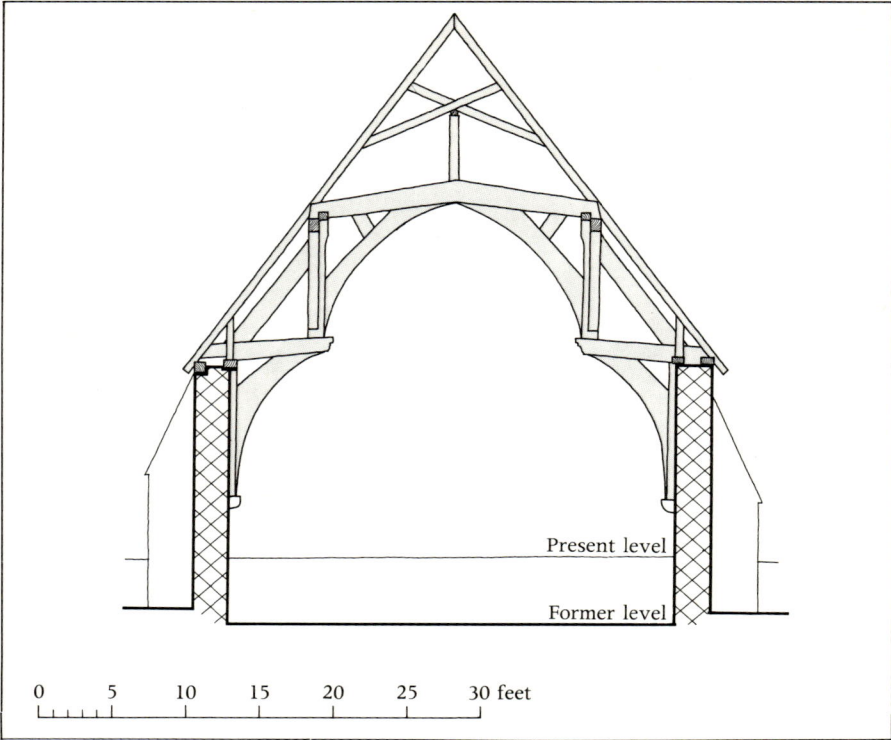

Fig. 55 Sketchbook of Villard de Honnecourt: c. 1235–45

Fig. 56 'Pilgrims' Hall', Winchester: 1325–6. Transverse section of hall

simply an aisled structure raised on tie-beams and lacking the support of any aisle pillars. It is significant that early examples of this roof tend to preserve the nave and aisle proportions of aisled halls. It has usually been considered that the first example of a roof clearly illustrating the hammer-beam principle is that drawn by the French mason, Villard de Honnecourt, in his sketchbook (c. 1235–45). But Villard's small sketch is described by him as 'a good light roof to raise over a vaulted chapel' which is hardly applicable to a hammer-beam roof. His drawing, in fact, shows a simple trussed rafter roof, and it is notable that no roof designed on the hammer-beam principle has yet been discovered in France. Yet the great timber brackets supporting the roof above the kitchen of the Bishop's Palace at Chichester, possibly built in the second half of the thirteenth century,[20] show that the principle of this form of construction had already been assimilated in England and that its technical development was being explored.

The 'Pilgrims' Hall' in the close of Winchester Cathedral (probably 1325–6)[21] is the earliest known example of the fully developed hammer-beam roof in England, but it is extremely unlikely that earlier structures of this form have not survived—it is probable that they have not yet been discovered and recorded. The Winchester roof is of orthodox hammer-beam design with scissor-braces above a tie-beam and crown-post. A more elaborate example survives in Essex at Tiptofts Manor House (possibly 1348–67) where the hammer-posts support axial as well as transverse braces and the tie-beams support crown-posts braced four ways as at Dartington.[22] A slightly later structure, dating from between 1370 and 1385, was discovered in 1962 during the destruction of Balle's Place, Salisbury. It is similar to the Winchester roof but with the crown-post braced four ways and lacking the carved heads at the end of the hammer-beams.[23] This is the sum of existing structures known to have preceded the design of that raised by Huntingdon, although a further example, no longer existing but to be numbered among them, is discussed below. Furthermore, at least two and possibly three other roofs raised in the

[20] The dating of this structure has varied considerably. W. H. Godfrey and J. W. Bloe suggested that the walls may have been built in the 13th century, and inclined towards a 15th-century date for the roof. *V.C.H. Sussex*, vol. 3 (1935), 148. W. H. Godfrey pointed out the similarity between this roof and that at St. Mary's Hospital, Chichester, which he dated to the early 14th century, *Arch. Jour.* vol. 92 (1935), 390. He subsequently amended this to the late 13th century, *The English Almshouse* (1955), 21–2, and finally to the years between 1232 and 1248, *Sussex Arch. Coll.* vol. 97 (1959), 134. J. T. Smith, *Arch. Jour.* vol. 115 (1958), 115–6, and I. Nairn and N. Pevsner, *Sussex* (1965), 174, prefer a date in about 1290. The construction of the kitchen roof during the second half of the 13th century seems likely, possibly during the last quarter of the century if the cinquefoil segmental arch in the west wall is a contemporary feature.

[21] This is the date when the roofing slates were ordered. *Med. Archaeol.* vol. 1 (1957), 152.

[22] *Arch. Jour.* vol. 112 (1955), 90; Margaret Wood, *The English Mediaeval House* (1965), 315–6. The truss of what has been described as a 14th-century hammer-beam roof survives at Tendring Church. N. Pevsner confines it to a date before 1350, *Essex* (1954), 28. Stanley Jones informs me, however, that it is probably an altered tie-beam truss type. The mid 14th-century roof at Market Deeping Rectory, Lincolnshire, has incipient hammer-beam trusses, but it is

essentially an arch-braced collar-beam roof.

[23] H. Bonney, 'Balle's Place, Salisbury', *Wilts Arch. and Nat. Hist. Mag.* vol. 59 (1964), 155–67. The roof has been preserved for re-erection.

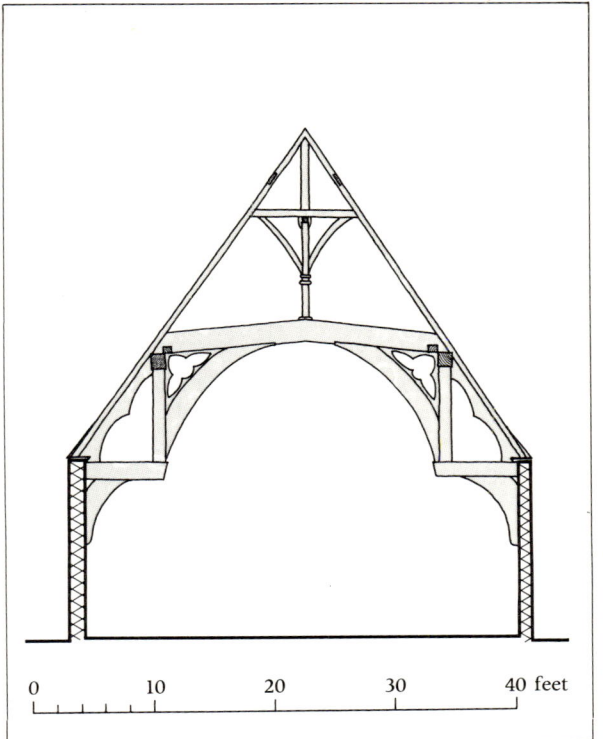

Fig. 57 Tiptofts Manor House: 1348–67. Transverse section of hall

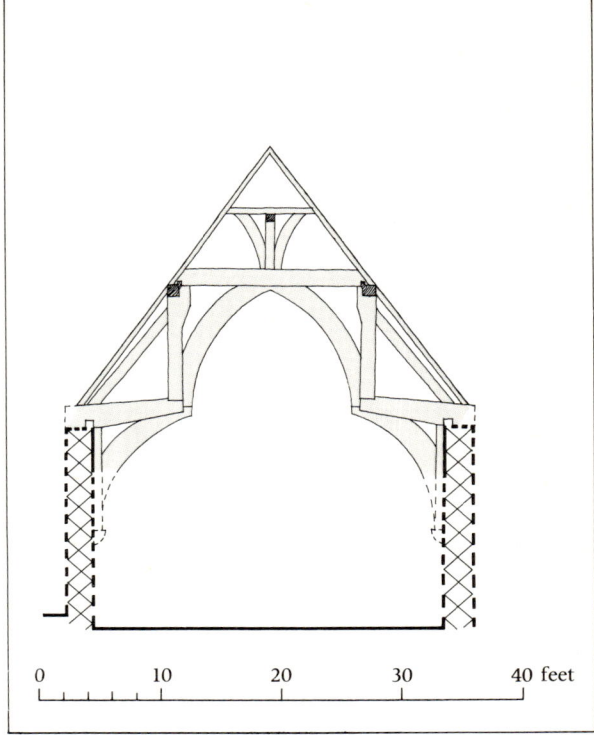

Fig. 58 Balle's Place, Salisbury: 1370–85. Transverse section of hall

[24] Only the corbels survive.

[25] T. W. Horsfield, *History, Antiquities and Topography of the County of Sussex* (1835), 126, quoting J. Cartwright, *History of the Western Division of Sussex* (1830).

[26] It is possible that the kitchen at Cockermouth Castle (*c.* 1388) was also covered with a roof based on the hammer-beam principle.

late fourteenth century may have been of hammer-beam design. That designed by Hugh Herland for the chapel at New College, Oxford (1380–6), destroyed in 1790 and not recorded in detail, may have been of comparable design,[24] while it is difficult to see how the 45 feet of Lancaster's great hall at Kenilworth Castle (1389–93) could have been spanned except by a roof of hammer-beam form. Thirdly, as the roof of the hall at Arundel Castle, destroyed in 1643–4 was described as resembling those at Westminster and Eltham Palace,[25] it is possible that a hammer-beam structure like those raised at the royal palaces was an integral part of the great hall built by the earl of Arundel in about 1380.[26]

By the close of the century, this form of roof had been adopted by a prior and chapter, a manorial lord, a wool merchant, two or three magnates, and possibly an academic foundation. Other experimental and early forms that made Richard II's achievement possible will undoubtedly be discovered, precursors of the great design at Westminster Hall. But the design of the roofs being constructed for Huntingdon and Lancaster at the beginning of the last decade of the fourteenth century would certainly not have gone unnoticed by the king, and it is possible that the principle which had proved so successful in the hall of Richard's half-brother and possibly in that of his uncle, encouraged its application to the unprecedented width of nearly 70 feet at the Palace of Westminster (1394–1401).

The measure of Hugh Herland's achievement for Richard II may be gauged by comparing the confidence of his design with some of the features of the Devon structure. One or two elements in the construction of the roof at Dartington suggest that the master carpenter there was still grappling with the problems of an experimental form. Saunders's drawings leave no doubt that the builders were particularly anxious to ensure that the roof was thoroughly sound. It was securely braced with timbers of considerable dimensions and strengthened on each slope with two side purlins that were not structurally necessary.

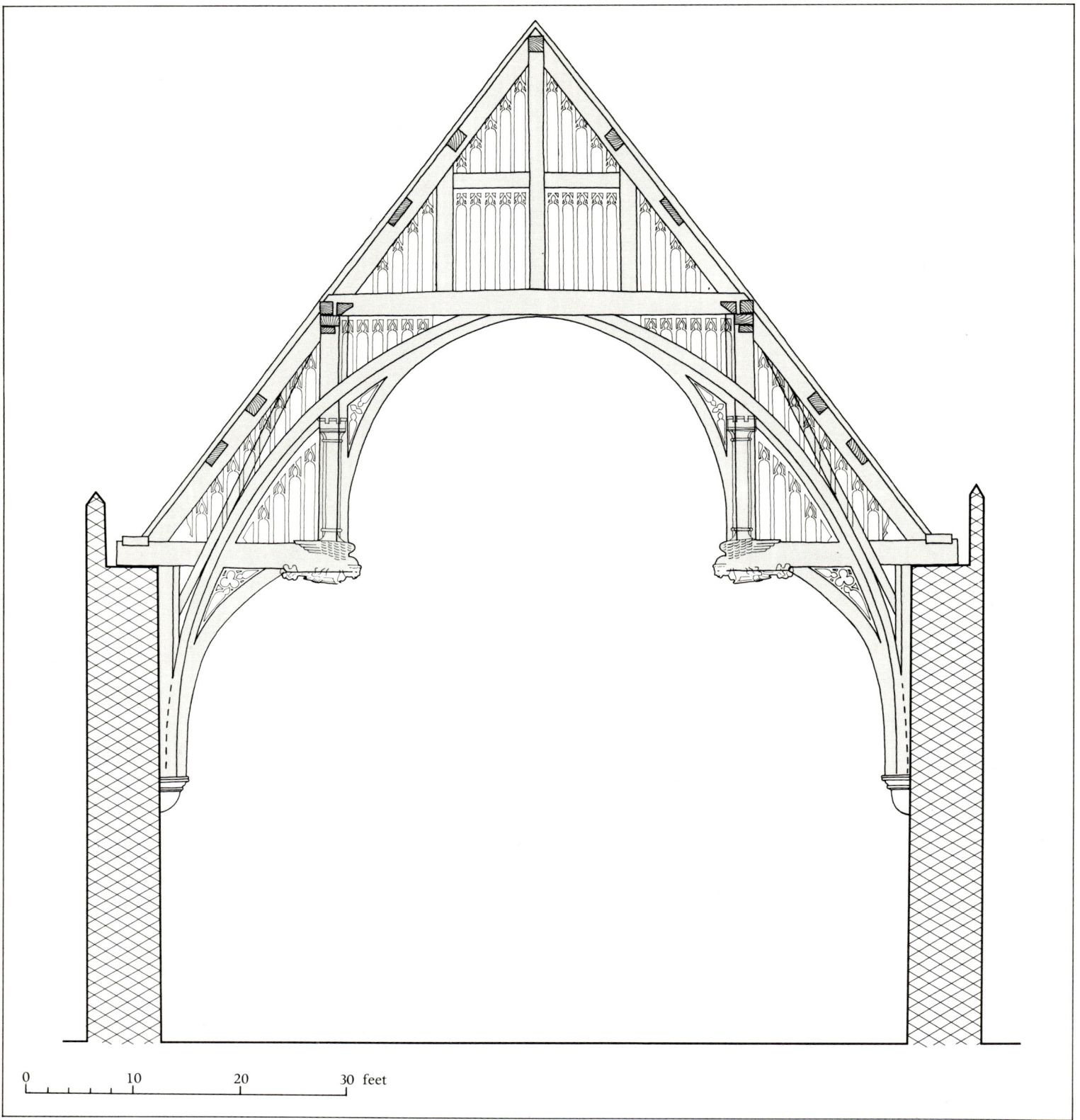

Fig. 59 Westminster Palace: 1394–1401. Transverse section of great hall

The pair of braces which rose from the hammer-posts tend to meet at the centre point of the member that they support. Both these features may be local forms but they indicate an emphasis on structural rigidity rather than finesse of detail. Yet Saunders's drawings show that an attempt was made to minimize the apparent weight of the structure by cutting back the underside of the hammer-beam on each side to create the illusion of a lighter structural member.[27]

In all probability erected immediately before that at Westminster, the Dartington roof was conceived quite independently of the royal design. It lacks the elaborately moulded timbers and the profusion of traceried lights which are a feature of the royal work and

[27] J. T. Smith has suggested to me that it is possible that the hammer-beam trusses were designed to make an impressive effect and that the roof chiefly relied on the intermediate trusses for its strength.

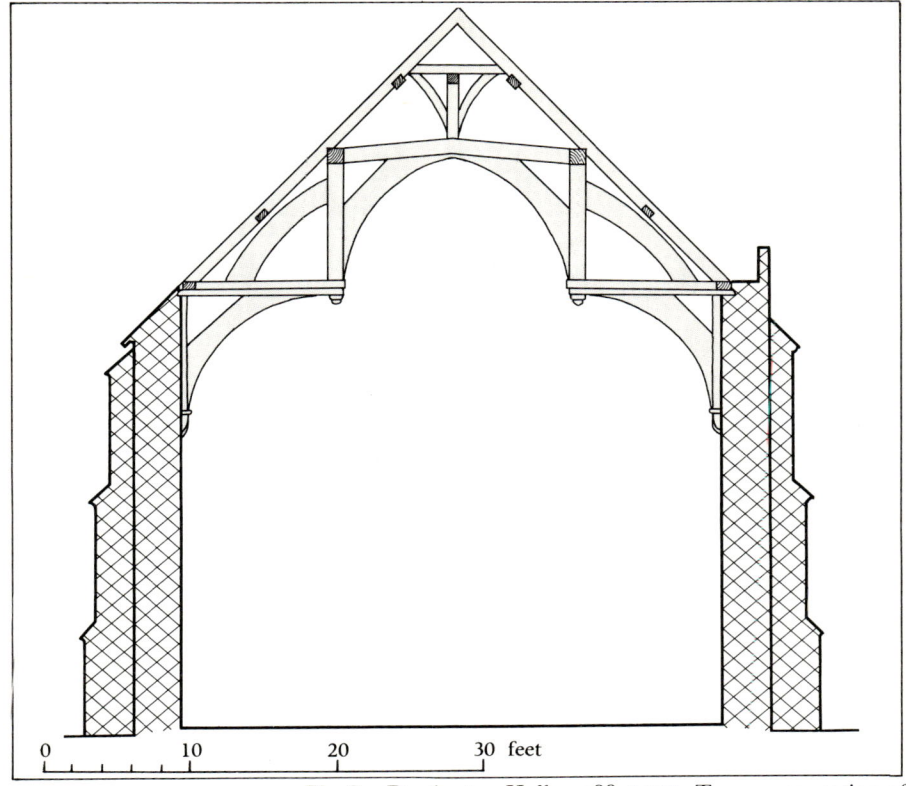

Fig. 60 Dartington Hall: 1388–1400. Transverse section of great hall. Taken from G. Saunders, 1805

Westminster Abbey. Roof of dorter: 14th century

more fundamentally, it lacks the arch-braces that are a structural characteristic of Herland's work. It was a country cousin compared with the sophisticated royal design and were it not for other evidence, its robustness would suggest that the roof was built in the mid rather than the late fourteenth century. Its heaviness indicates that it was certainly not the work of the king's master carpenter,[28] and it is most likely that it was the creation of a highly competent local craftsman. This is supported by the narrow width of the central span which appears as a local deviation from the normal proportions established for hammer-beam roofs in south-east England.

It is possible, however, that Westminster is not devoid of all association with Huntingdon's residence, for the roof of the dorter at Westminster Abbey was formerly covered with a structure of comparable design. The dorter, originally 173 feet long by 34½ feet wide, was badly damaged in a fire in 1298 which destroyed many of the monastic buildings. It was possibly at the time of its reconstruction in the fourteenth century that the dorter was divided into two apartments, a smaller one now used as the chapter library and a larger one, 124 feet long, now used as the hall of Westminster School. The roof above the larger room was divided into eleven bays by identical hammer-beam trusses, but unfortunately they were destroyed in 1941 and no detailed drawings of them exist. Large curved braces rose transversely from the hammer-posts to support a tie-beam. The hammer-beams were supported by braces rising from simple corbels and above the tie-beam was an unbraced crown-post. The abbey roof lacked the transverse braces rising from the hammer-posts and the bracing of the crown-posts that were a feature of the Dartington structure. The Westminster design also apparently possessed a row of wind-braces between the side purlins. However, the massiveness of the design and the lack of almost any form of decoration were common to both the Westminster and Dartington structures. No detailed attempt was made to date the abbey roof while it existed, although a fifteenth- or

[28] It is unlikely that Hugh Herland was even consulted, vide J. H. Harvey, *English Mediaeval Architects* (1954), 129, for he would have favoured a far more sophisticated design than that adopted.

sixteenth-century date was sometimes hazarded.[29] Even though there is no documentary evidence to clarify the period of its construction, its form and robustness suggest that it was built in the fourteenth century. It was obviously necessary to reconstruct the dorter after the fire of 1298 as soon as funds permitted, and the alterations to the windows in the east and west walls point to a date early in that century. Furthermore, the similarity between the form of the hammer-beam roof at the abbey and that within the close at Winchester makes its construction during the first quarter of the century not impossible. The work would certainly have been completed during the great reconstruction of the monastic buildings between about 1345 and 1393, and it may have been carried out at the same time that the eastern walk of the cloister was built in the years immediately after 1345.[30] The similarity between the form of the Dartington and the Westminster roofs suggest that they were members of a common line of development and it is possible that Huntingdon may have expressed a preference for a design that he had seen in the abbey during one of his frequent visits to the adjacent royal court.

Fully developed by 1400, the hammer-beam form of construction was adopted with enthusiasm, mainly in the eastern and south-eastern counties. Suffolk had certainly welcomed it by 1421 when the roof of Bardwell Church was raised, and the form had been chosen by a wealthy yeoman family at Crowhurst Place in Surrey only about thirty years after Huntingdon had completed that at Dartington.[31] Yet the Devonshire example did not really lead to its adoption elsewhere in the west of England. There are no hammer-beam roofs in Cornwall or Somerset, and only one or two comparable structures in Devon and Dorset. Apart from the roof at Dartington, the only other structure of an almost similar design in the west of England is the little-known roof at Winterborne Clenston in Dorset. This may have been moved after the Dissolution from Milton Abbey some two and a half miles away, for it was certainly never intended to crown the barn that supports it now. The hammer-posts are plain, but the braces and tie-beam are finely

[29] F. Bond, *Westminster Abbey* (1909), 298, suggested that it was probably built in the late 16th century. *R.C.H.M. London*, vol. 1 (1924), 83 was more cautious. It dated the moulded wall-plates to the 15th century and suggested that the rest of the roof was later. F. H. Crossley attributed the whole roof to the 15th century, *Timber Building in England* (1951), 61. The low-pitched hammer-beam roof above the chapter library is of a later design than that formerly above the dorter. It is possibly mid 15th-century work built after a fire in 1449.

[30] W. R. Lethaby, *Westminster Abbey and the King's Craftsmen*, (1906), 201.

[31] H. Munro Cautley, *Suffolk Churches and Their Treasures* (3rd ed., 1954), 221; H. Avray Tipping, *English Homes, Periods I and II, Vol. 2, 1066–1558* (1936), 155–62

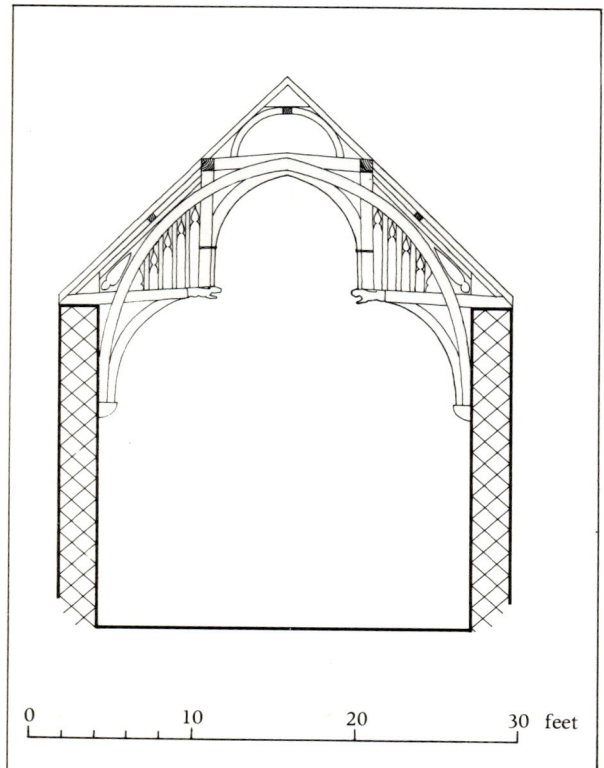 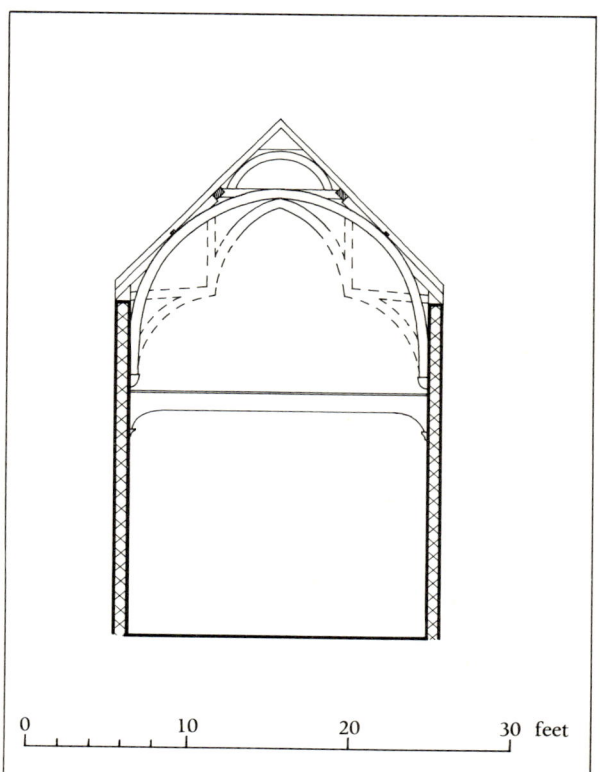

Fig. 61 No. 8, The Close, Exeter: first half of 15th century. Transverse section of hall

Fig. 62 Cadhay: late 15th century. Transverse section of hall

Winterborne Clenston Manor, Dorset. Roof of barn: possibly early 15th century

Milton Abbey, Dorset. Roof of abbot's hall: 1498

Weare Gifford Hall, Devon. Roof of great hall: third quarter of 15th century

moulded. Its sturdiness suggests a date in the second half of the fourteenth century, but the moulding of the beams favours the close of the century or the early fifteenth century when compared with the plainness of those at Balle's Place and Dartington.

There is a group of roofs related to that at Dartington but they are essentially arch-braced structures, despite the presence of hammer-beam trusses. They include No. 8, The Close in Exeter, Cadhay and Weare Gifford Hall in Devon, and the abbot's hall at Milton Abbey in Dorset. All these structures were raised during the fifteenth century. That in The Close at Exeter was constructed in the first half of the fifteenth century[32] and the roof at Cadhay, almost a copy of it, may date from the end of the century.[33] In both cases, the hammer-beam units are closely associated with large curved braces rising from corbels to form two-centred arches meeting at heavy collar-beams. This immediately indicates that the main trusses are different from those at Dartington, and the removal of the hammer-beams and posts at Cadhay in the eighteenth century demonstrates that they were not an essential part of the structure but added primarily for effect. At Exeter, the effect was heightened by including features used by Hugh Herland at Westminster Hall, particularly the angels at the end of the hammer-beams and the vertical tracery between the beams and the curved braces.[34] The roof at Weare Gifford Hall, probably dating from the third quarter of the fifteenth century,[35] is an even clearer example of an arch-braced roof with false hammer-beam trusses. Its encrustation with tracery, cusping, pendants, figures, and other ornamentation creates an overwhelmingly rich effect. The roof above the abbot's hall at Milton Abbey, built in 1498, is a more restrained version of the same design.[36]

The Kitchen

Few medieval kitchens have survived for many of them were timber-framed structures which have either been burnt down or replaced by later buildings. A dozen or so stone kitchens of the twelfth and thirteenth centuries remain, and not many more for the following century. Where the site was a defensive one, the kitchen was usually tightly integrated with the overall planning of the building as, for example, at Berkeley, Bodiam, Cockermouth, and Wardour castles. Where space was not restricted, however, it was generally separated from the offices and associated residential block and built as a detached structure so as to reduce the smell, noise, and danger from fire to a minimum. Examples of this form occur at Haddon Hall, Dartington Hall, Ashby de la Zouch Castle, and Trinity Hall, Cambridge which all follow the common fourteenth-century pattern of siting the kitchen beyond the line of the hall and offices and connecting it with them by a covered way.[37] At New College, Oxford, the kitchen was free standing on three sides but conjoined with the hall by a two-storeyed buttery and pantry block. Wherever possible, kitchens were tall single-storey structures, and if they had to be built at first-floor level as at Raby, Cockermouth, and Wardour castles, they were raised above a vaulted chamber. Only the kitchens at Ashby de la Zouch, Lumley, and probably Bolton Castle supported living accommodation above them.

Dartington is among the small group of independent or nearly independent structures that have survived from the fourteenth century. They are all built on a comparable scale,[38]

---

[32] Sir Cyril Fox, *Arch. Jour.* vol. 114 (1957), 138–9. The house is usually known as the Law Library. Sir Cyril suggests that the roof may have been built during the first quarter of the century, but Margaret Wood favours the later 15th century, *The Mediaeval House* (1965), 317.

[33] M. Baldwin and S. D. T. Spittle, *Arch. Jour.* vol. 114 (1957), 162–3.

[34] It is interesting to note that the roofs at Exeter and Cadhay follow the great hall at Dartington in having a narrow central span. Their intermediate trusses are similar to those of the larger roof above the entrance block at Dartington

[35] H. Avray Tipping, *English Homes, Period 2, 1485–1558*, vol 1 (1924). The roof was built after the Fortescues acquired the estate in 1454

[36] A. Oswald, *Country Houses of Dorset* (1959), 111–2 and *Country Life* (July 1962 and June 1966)

[37] The principal exception in secular architecture in the second half of the century was at Winchester College (see p. 133).

[38] Glastonbury Abbey, $33\frac{1}{2}'$ square; Durham Cathedral Priory, $36\frac{1}{2}'$ diameter; Raby Castle, 30' square; Ashby de la Zouch Castle, $50\frac{1}{2}' \times 28'$; Haddon Hall, $28' \times 24'$; New College, Oxford, $40' \times 25'$; Dartington Hall, $33\frac{1}{2}'$ square. The kitchen at Trinity Hall, Cambridge (1374) was $25' \times 22'$ but it no longer retains any ancient features. It is unfortunate that the contemporary kitchen at Penshurst Place was destroyed in the mid 19th century.

Glastonbury Abbey, Somerset. Great kitchen: c. 1340

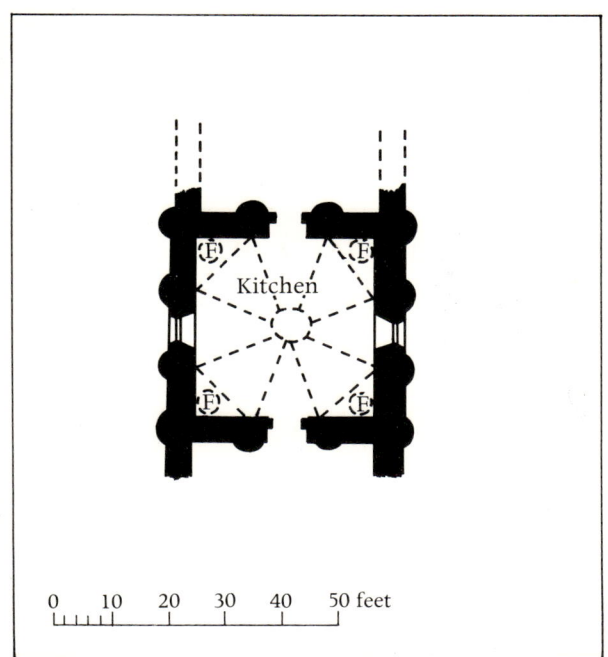
Fig. 63 Glastonbury Abbey. Kitchen. Ground-floor plan

Raby Castle, Co. Durham. Great kitchen: c. 1378–c. 90

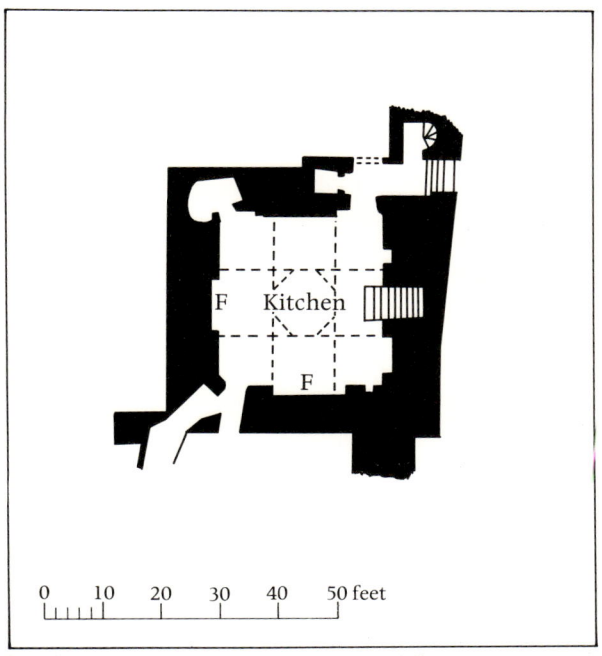
Fig. 64 Raby Castle. Kitchen. Ground-floor plan

Haddon Hall, Derbyshire. Kitchen: between 1325 and 1350

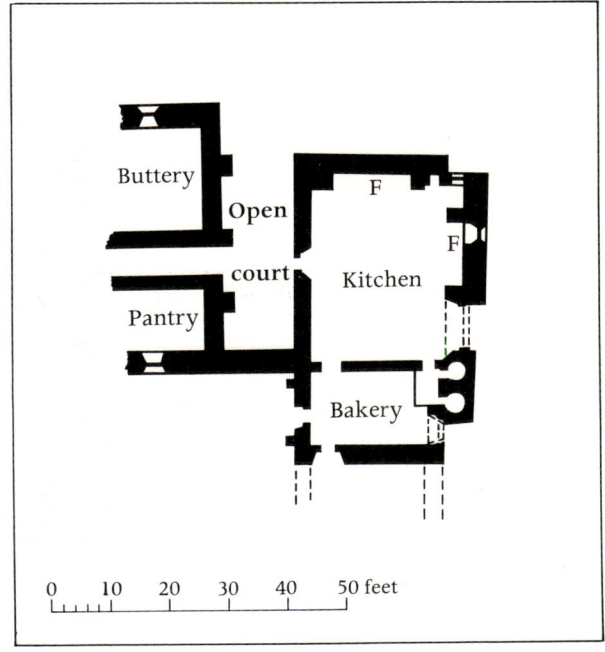
Fig. 65 Haddon Hall. Kitchen. Ground-floor plan

Durham Cathedral Priory. Great kitchen: mainly 1366–71

generally square in plan, and retain many of their original fittings. Those at Glastonbury Abbey (c. 1340),[39] Durham Cathedral Priory (mainly 1366–71),[40] Raby Castle (c. 1378–c. 90), and Ashby de la Zouch (later fourteenth century),[41] possess stone-ribbed roofs, and in all but the last example, support a central louvre. The kitchen at Haddon Hall (between 1325 and 1350), New College, Oxford (c. 1386), and Dartington Hall were built with wooden roofs, but the insertion of a low ceiling at Haddon in the sixteenth century now makes it difficult to recover the original form of the upper windows or roof.

The kitchen, offices, and hall at Ashby de la Zouch are ruined. The splendid monastic structures at Glastonbury and Durham have been subject to remarkably few alterations since their construction, but the halls and offices they served have disappeared. The windows at Raby have been enlarged and the offices, passage, and flight of steps to the upper hall no longer exist. The fireplaces and windows at New College, Oxford, are later insertions but the apartment still retains much of its original character. The entirely free-standing kitchens at Haddon and Dartington are the only other major fourteenth-century examples which still exist in association with their contemporary halls and offices,

[39] The date of its construction is still problematical. As the window tracery is similar to that at the near-by Manor House at Meare, probably built by Abbot Sudbury (1322–35), the kitchen may have been built by his successor, Abbot Beynton (1335–41) who completed the adjacent great hall.

[40] Mainly built between 1366 and 1371, but not finished until the episcopate of Bishop Langley (1406–37) who contributed to the work. See *Durham Account Rolls* (Surtees Society), vol. 2 (1833), 57, and *Historiae Dunelmensis Scriptores Tres.* (Surtees Society, vol. 3 (1838), 146; ibid., vol. 9 (1839), 132 n. Canon Greenwell, *Durham Cathedral* (1897), 104, and *V.C.H. Durham*, vol. 3 (1928), 129.

[41] Attributed to the later 14th century by T. L. Jones, *Ashby de la Zouch Castle: Official Guide* (1953), 5, 12. This dating should be treated with some reservation for although the size of the building is strong evidence for the attribution, the architectural evidence is scanty.

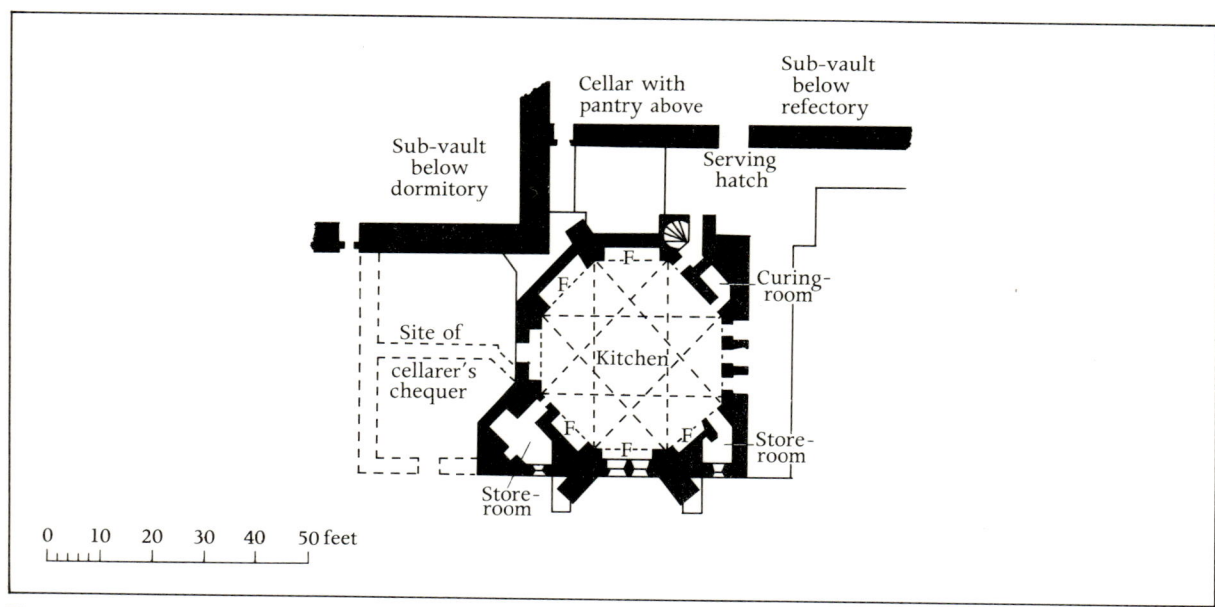
Fig. 66 Durham Cathedral Priory. Kitchen. Ground-floor plan

Ashby de la Zouch Castle, Leicestershire. Kitchen: later 14th century

Pickering Castle, Yorkshire. Rosamund Tower: 1323–4

although later additions have enveloped that at Haddon and the roof at Dartington is a conjectural restoration. Only Berkeley Castle (1340–50) can show a comparable grouping of hall, kitchen, and offices, even though the offices have been altered several times.

The Development of Retainers' Lodgings

The retainers' lodgings at Dartington are a very early example of a specialized type of accommodation, but similar lodgings on a much smaller scale had been built a few years beforehand in the lower court at Amberley Castle. The particular value of those at Dartington lies in the fact that the lodgings on the east side of the north courtyard are one of the first examples of this type of accommodation to be built in an extended form, while those on the opposite side of the courtyard, constructed at a slightly later date, are among the finest examples to have survived.

Retainers' lodgings are associated with a system of indenture that was well established by the reign of Edward II. Although no examples have yet been traced in a domestic residence earlier than the closing years of Edward III's reign, the source of their development may be sought in the lodgings built earlier in the century for the guests and officials of important households, and in the accommodation provided for corporate clergy, chantry priests, and college members respectively.[42]

The planning of single private rooms for members of a family, their guests, and important household officials occurs in the planning of several castles by Edward I in Wales and it had become an established practice by the beginning of the fourteenth century. Roger Mortimer, for instance, had built six single rooms at Ludlow Castle in about 1320 for members of his family and their guests in the tower projecting from the two residential blocks at the upper end of the great hall.[43] There were four small identical lodgings on the ground and first floor furnished with window-seats and garderobes, and a single chamber on the second and third floors with a garderobe and fireplace. The upper floors of the Rosamund and Diate Hill Tower at Pickering Castle, built by Edward II between 1323 and 1324, similarly consisted of a single chamber furnished with a garderobe and

[42] The origins and development of lodgings are also discussed by W. A. Pantin, 'Chantry Priests' Houses and Other Medieval Lodgings', *Med. Archaeol.* vol. 3 (1959), 216–58.

[43] W. H. St. John Hope, 'The Castle of Ludlow', *Archaeologia*, vol. 61 (1908), 281–94; P. A. Faulkner, 'Domestic Planning from the Twelfth to the Fourteenth Centuries', *Arch. Jour.* vol. 115 (1958), 177–8.

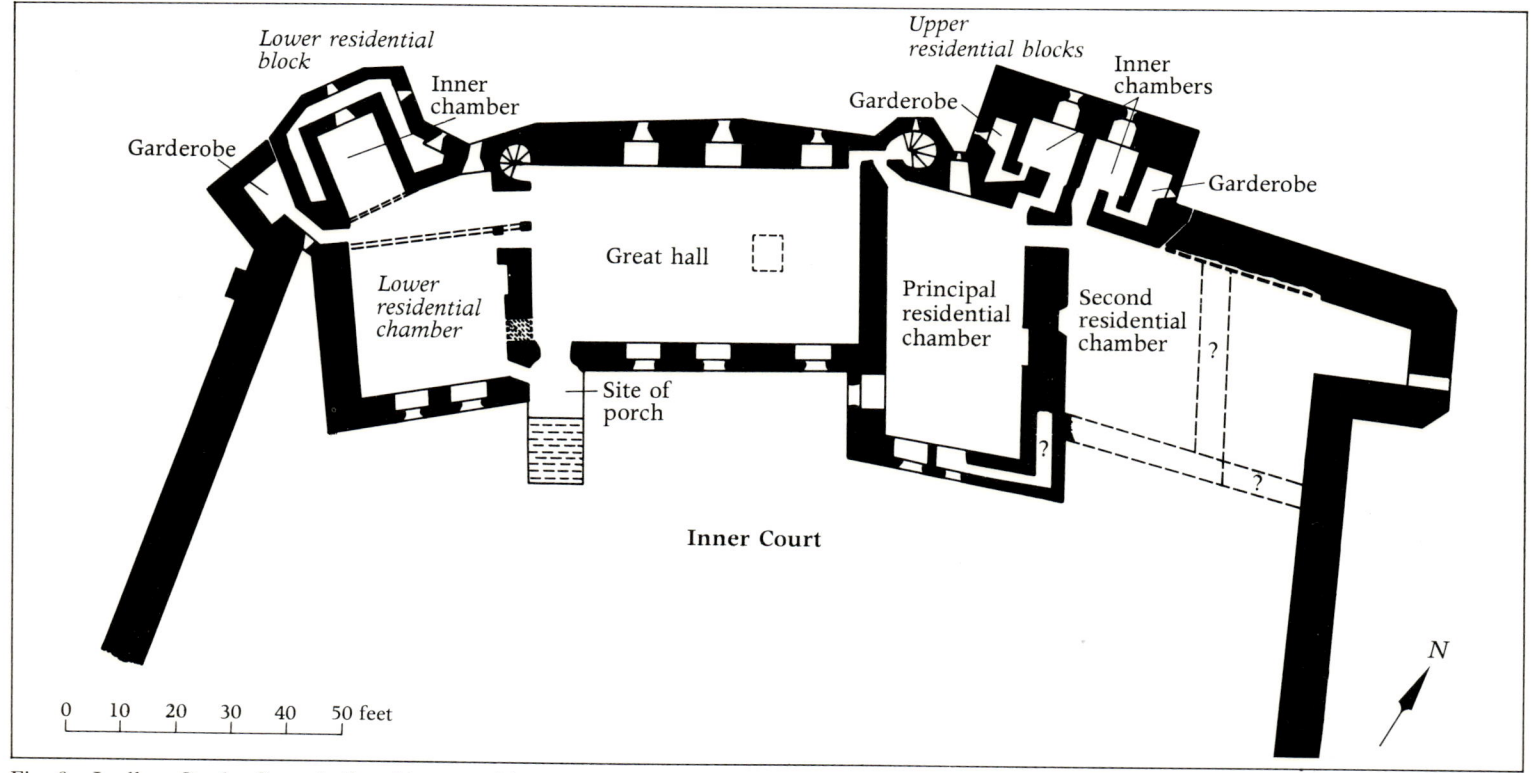

Ludlow Castle, Shropshire. Great hall and lower residential block: late 13th century. Upper residential blocks: *c.* 1320

Fig. 67 Ludlow Castle. Great hall and lower residential chamber: late 13th century. Upper residential blocks and tower: *c.* 1320. Flanking curtain wall and towers: 12th century. First-floor plan

Warwick Castle. Caesar's Tower: between 1370 and 1385

Fig. 68 Warwick Castle. Caesar's Tower. Elevation

[44] M. W. Thompson, *Pickering Castle, Yorkshire: Official Guide* (1958), 9, 20–1.

in one room with a fireplace.[44] It is probable that they were intended for officials rather than for guests as the towers were built on the enceinte of the outer ward. Later in the century, two massive towers were built at Warwick Castle to guard the river and town approach and to provide seven suites of apartments tiered above each other for household officials and possibly for retainers. The earlier of these, Caesar's Tower, contains a basement, three suites of rooms, a store, and a guard-room at the highest level. Each suite was vaulted and contained a large and well-lit central room with a fireplace, flanked by a mural bedroom and a garderobe. Guy's Tower, completed in 1394, was constructed with four suites of rooms and a guard-room.

The practice of building lodgings in two-storeyed ranges for a particular class of person had been firmly established by the early fourteenth century. The Vicars' Court at Lincoln, built in about 1310 for members of the clergy serving the near-by Minster, was apparently intended to consist of two-storeyed ranges grouped round three sides of a courtyard.[45] The plan is most clearly preserved on the south side where the range consists of three chambers on each floor, each vicar apparently occupying a single chamber. The two eastern chambers formed a pair of lodgings, served by a common door and an internal

[45] Margaret Wood, '3, Vicars' Court, Lincoln', *Lincolnshire Historian* (1951), 281–6.

Vicars' Close, Lincoln. South side: c. 1310

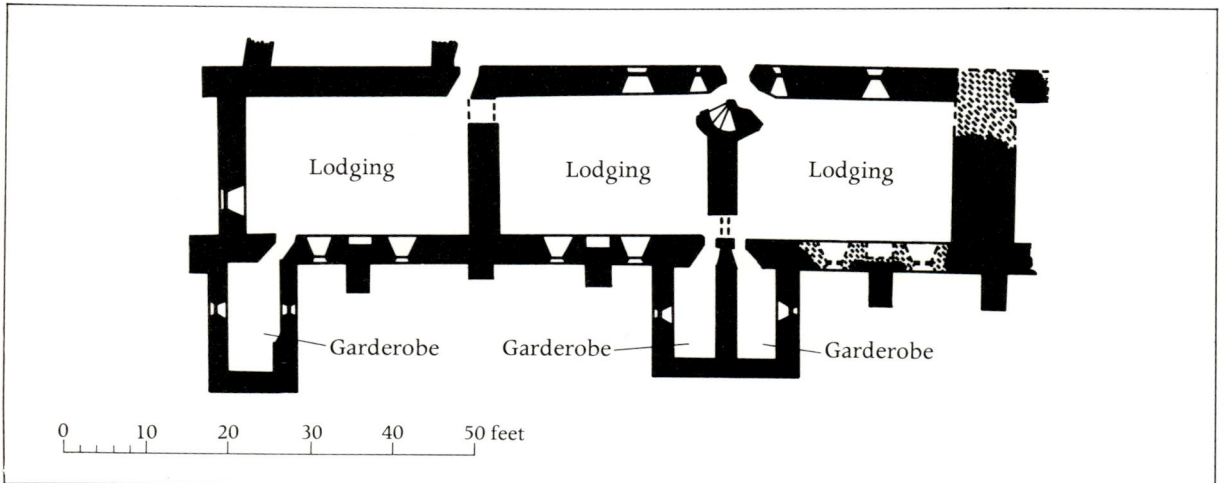

Fig. 69 Vicars' Court, Lincoln. South range: c. 1310. Ground-floor plan

newel staircase. Every room was well lit and possessed a fireplace and garderobe. The latter was built in a common projection with an arched opening at ground level for cleaning purposes. Although larger than the east lodgings built by Huntingdon, most of the features adopted at Dartington Hall exist in embryo form in the Lincoln residence. The accommodation provided about forty years later for the vicars choral at Wells is not strictly comparable, for each vicar occupied a self-contained two-storeyed house.[46] Nevertheless, it is interesting to observe that there were forty-two identical residences at Wells, twenty on the west side and twenty-two on the east side. Despite the addition of the front gardens and the chapel in the early fifteenth century, the close at Wells was essentially an elongated quadrangle with self-contained residences on either side and a communal hall at one end—a plan which was adopted on a smaller scale at the Vicars Choral at Exeter in 1388[47] and was not unlike that adopted immediately afterwards at Dartington Hall.

The planning of a series of lodgings for three or four occupants was a basic tenet of collegiate planning at Oxford and Cambridge throughout the medieval period. Built in two-storeyed ranges of one-room thickness round two and occasionally three sides of a

[46] These houses have been subject to many alterations but No. 22 was restored as far as possible to its original design in 1863. W. A. Pantin suggests that the houses were probably rebuilt in the third quarter of the 15th century by Bishop Beckington or his executors, Med. Archaeol. vol. 3 (1959), 248. W. H. Godfrey agrees, The English Almshouse (1955), 45–7, although he had previously confined Beckington's work to remodelling, Arch. Jour. vol. 107 (1950), 112. N. Pevsner prefers a mid 14th-century date and limits the bishop's additions to the chapel and hall at either end of the Close, North Somerset and Bristol (1958), 319–20. This is also the view of Joan Evans, English Art: 1307–1461 (1949), 187–8, and R. D. Reid, Wells Cathedral (1963), 120–1, 187–8. The moulding of the windows, quite unlike Beckington's work elsewhere at Wells, supports a mid 14th-century date. Beckington's work was probably confined to the insertion or replacement of the fireplaces and chimneys, but the Close must have been enlarged after its foundation as it was originally intended for no more than 13 priests.

[47] Similarly, the houses built for the accommodation of chantry priests at Cobham after 1362 and at Arundel in 1380 were a series of two-storeyed lodgings grouped round a small quadrangle.

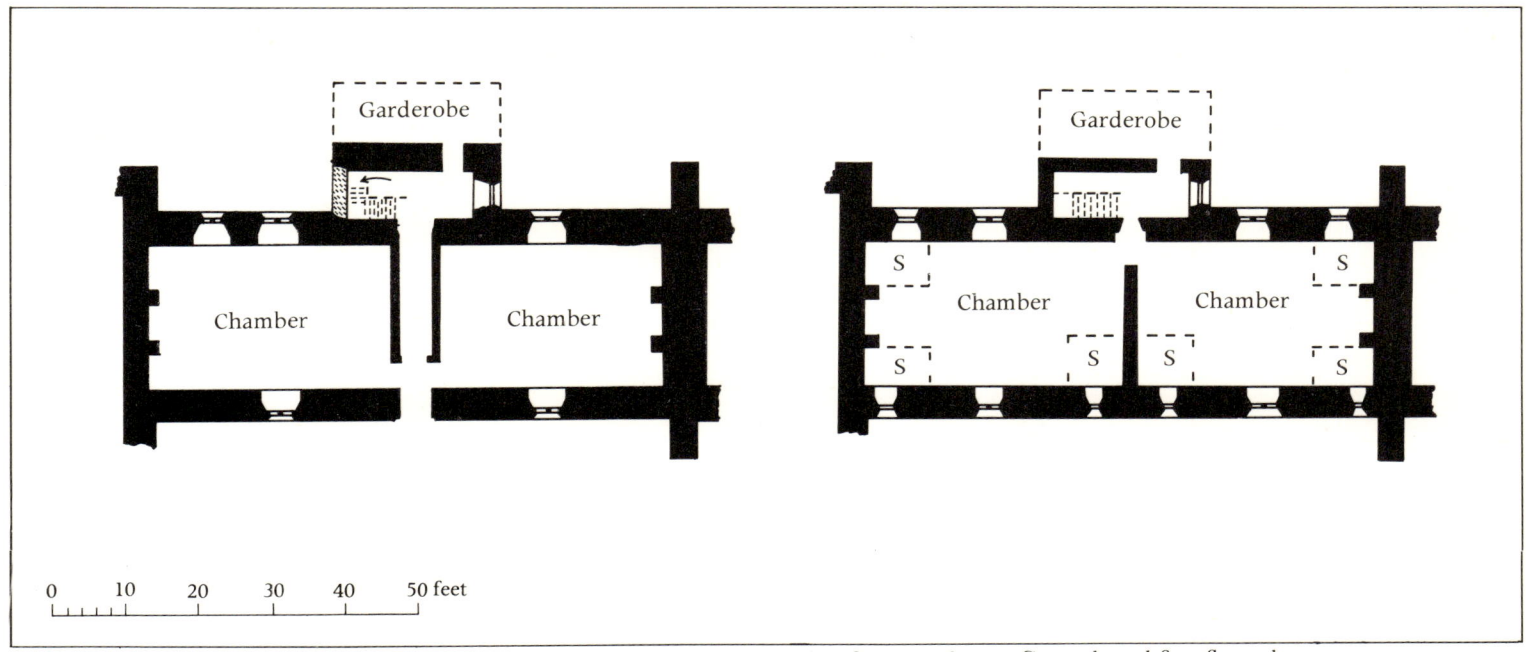

Fig. 70 Winchester College. East range of Chamber Court: 1387–94. Ground- and first-floor plans

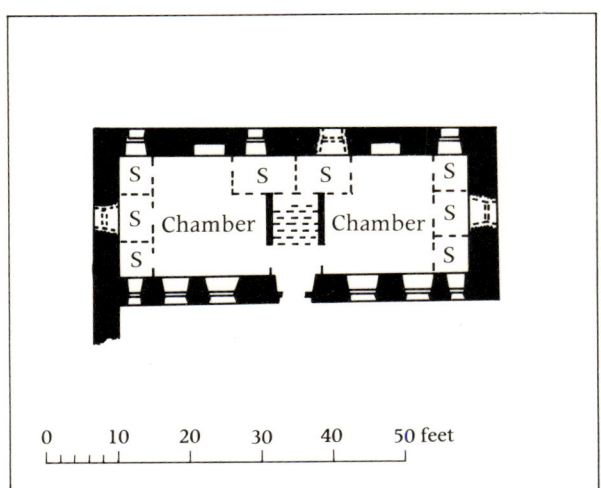

Fig. 71 Merton College, Oxford. North range of Mob Quad: 1304–7. Ground-floor plan

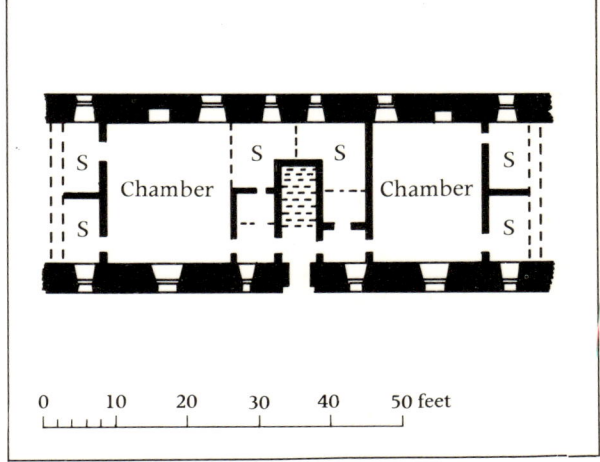

Fig. 72 New College, Oxford. South range of Great Quad: 1380–6. Ground-floor plan

quadrangle, these lodgings were arranged in pairs, served by a common door from the courtyard and divided by a straight internal staircase. Each chamber, lit by a two-light window, was used by several fellows or undergraduate scholars as a bed-sitting room, but the corners were partitioned off to form a number of small study cubicles with their own windows where members could work undisturbed. The origin of these lodgings needs further investigation, for the earliest surviving example on two sides of Mob Quad at Merton College, Oxford, shows the fully developed plan. Built about 1304–7 and now drastically altered, each range formerly consisted of two chambers on each floor, 22 feet by 17 feet, separated by a steep flight of stairs.[48] Each chamber was probably partitioned to create four study cubicles. The chambers built in the third quarter of the century at Corpus Christi College, Cambridge, are better preserved,[49] but the finest examples attributable to this century are those at Wykeham's foundations at Oxford and Winchester where the original pattern of paired chambers, staircase, fireplaces, studies, and garderobe accommodation can be distinguished.[50]

It is probable that household retainers were originally accommodated in large corporate rooms as at Bodiam and possibly Warwick castles, but the practice quickly grew up of

[48] *V.C.H. Oxfordshire*, vol. 3 (1954), 100; *R.C.H.M. City of Oxford* (1939), 81–2.

[49] *R.C.H.M. City of Cambridge* (1959), 54–7. R. Willis and J. W. Clarke, *The University of Cambridge*, vol. 3 (1886), 297–327, traces the evolution of student accommodation.

[50] A. H. Smith, *New College Oxford and its Buildings* (1952), 48–51. The rooms at New College were probably whitewashed or decorated with fresco of which a fragment survives in a room on staircase 2. The garderobes were contained in a separate building, but they were built at the rear of the east chambers at Winchester College.

Vicars' Close, Wells. Towards the chapel: mid 14th century

providing them with individual lodgings based on antecedents from which they differed little in purpose, scale, or amenities. Some of the two-storeyed lodgings built for Edward III between 1365 and 1368 round two sides of the upper ward at Windsor Castle may well have been intended for retainers as well as for members of the court and household,[51] and there is no doubt about the examples built between 1377 and about 1383 on the north side of the outer court of Amberley Castle. Each of these four lodgings, built in pairs in a two-storeyed block, was approximately 13 feet by 31 feet. Each chamber contained its own fireplace, a single loophole or window in the outer wall, and a garderobe which was grouped with its neighbour in a projecting tower. The destruction of the south-facing wall makes any reconstruction of their approach from the courtyard entirely conjectural.[52]

The destruction or total alteration of so much lesser household accommodation, even when the hall and residential block have survived, severely limits the number of early lodgings extant, but the remains of the east range at Dartington Hall make it clear that household retainers were now provided with the same standard of accommodation that

[51] R. A. Brown, H. M. Colvin, and A. J. Taylor, *The History of the King's Works*, vol. 2 (1963), 880.

[52] The presence of fireplaces, loopholes, and a garderobe chute in the upper part of the outer wall of the west range is evidence of further lodgings but they were clearly not so elaborate as those on the north side of the courtyard and may have been general service accommodation above ground-floor stables. A further residential range was also built against the south wall, west of the gatehouse, but the site is overgrown and awaits excavation.

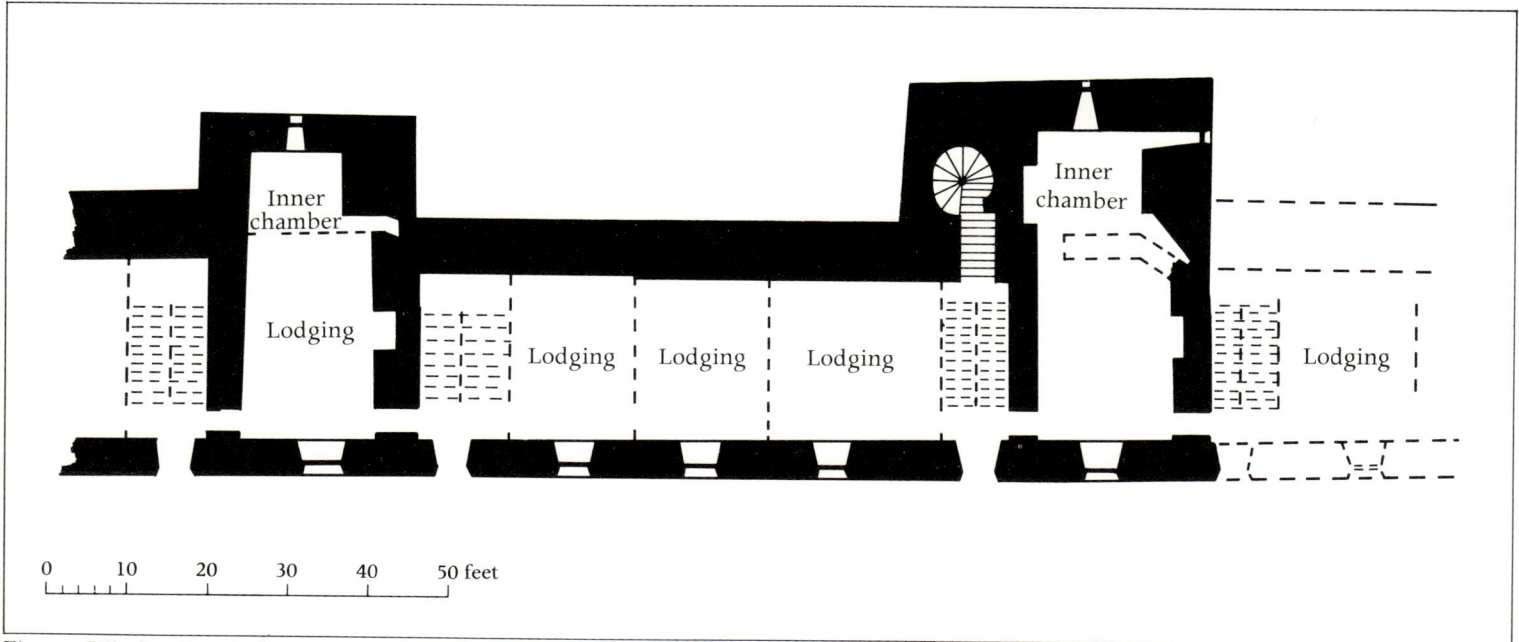
Fig. 73 Windsor Castle. South range of upper court: 1365–8. Ground-floor plan before post medieval alterations

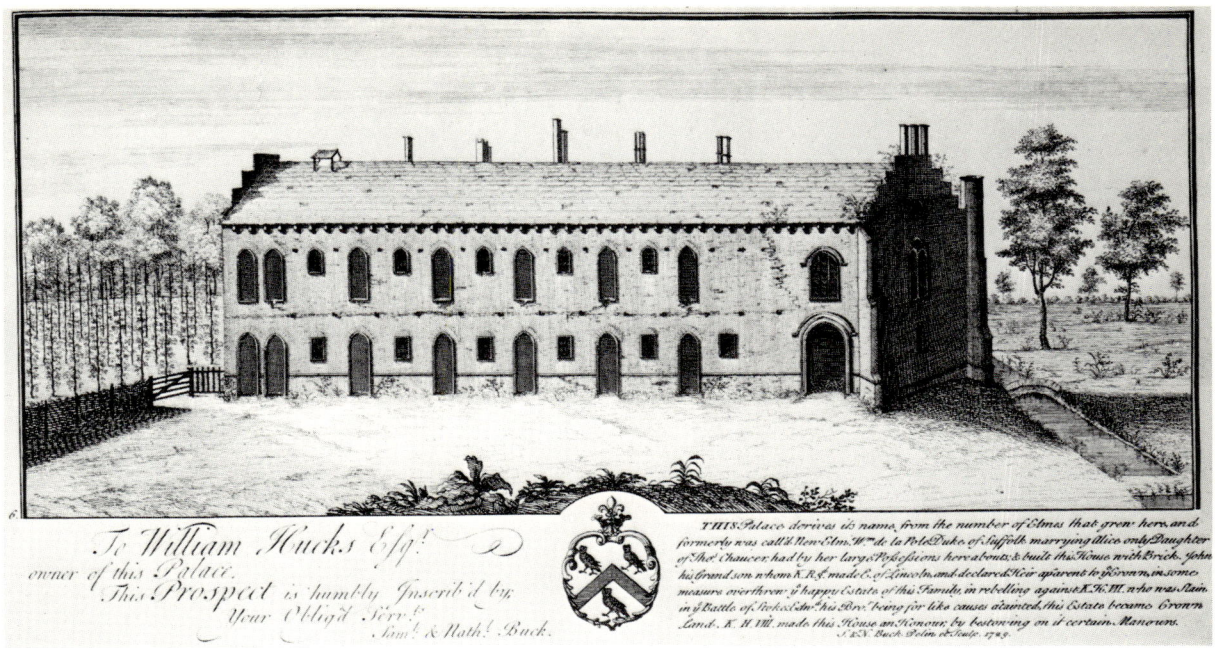

Ewelme Palace, Oxfordshire. Range of lodgings: second quarter of 15th century. By S. and N. Buck, 1729

53 Buck's engraving shows a two-storeyed brick range divided into a series of six lodgings on each floor. Those on the upper floor were served by a covered gallery which had disappeared by the early 18th century. Each room had a fireplace and was lit by a small window overlooking the courtyard. The pattern was broken at one end by two paired doors at both levels, one of them on each floor possibly leading to a communal garderobe. At the other end were two larger rooms, marked by a more elaborate entrance at ground level and a window above in place of the usual door. The range no longer exists. It was probably built by the 4th earl (later 1st duke) of Suffolk who obtained Ewelme through his marriage to the daughter of Thomas Chaucer in 1430, founded the near-by brick almshouses in 1437, and was murdered in 1450.

had been accorded to guests or important officials earlier in the century. The two larger chambers at the south end of the west range at Dartington were possibly intended as spacious accommodation for important officials or, more likely, as communal rooms for lesser members of the household. They are comparable in size with those chambers at Winchester College intended for between ten and thirteen scholars at ground level and three fellows at first-floor level. The Dartington rooms were clearly unconnected with the lord's apartments in the upper residential block, for this would have destroyed the basis on which the whole range was planned.

Retainers' lodgings were an integral part of several major residences in the fifteenth century. The range of twelve lodgings at Ewelme Palace, Oxfordshire, built in the second quarter of the century was similar in several ways to those at Dartington Hall,[53] but the foundations of the slightly later and larger communal lodgings built by Lord Cromwell on either side of the outer courtyard at South Wingfield Manor (c. 1440–56) is a reminder that not all retainers were accommodated in individual rooms. Some of the ground-floor

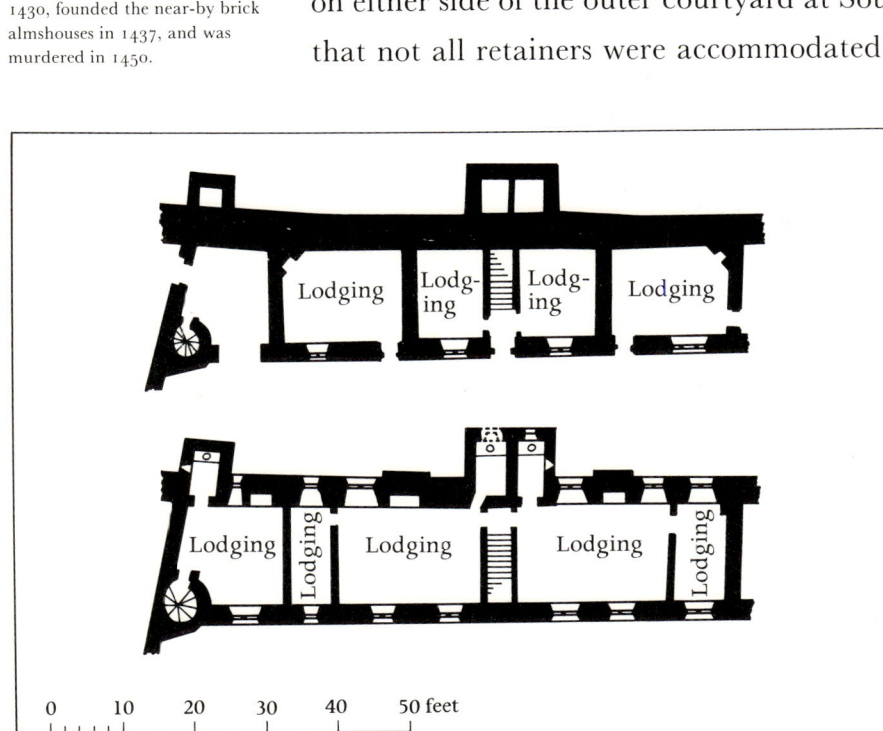

Fig. 74 Haddon Hall. West range of lower court: late 15th century. Ground- and first-floor plans

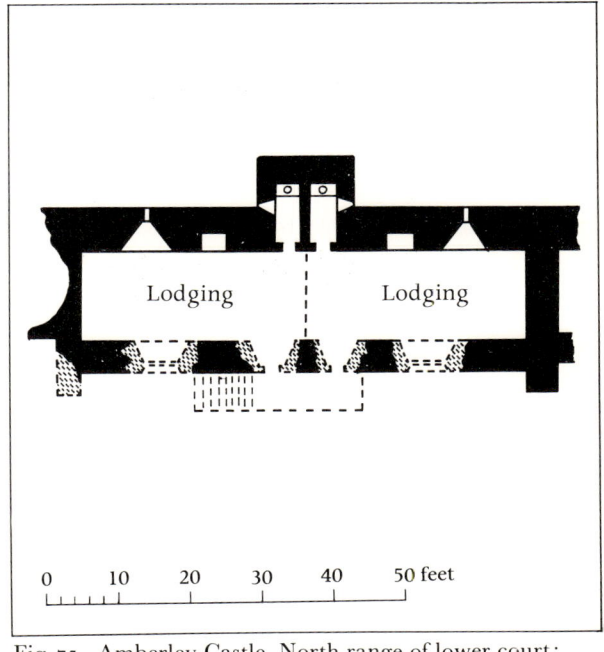

Fig. 75 Amberley Castle. North range of lower court: 1377–c. 83. Ground-floor plan

Haddon Hall, Derbyshire. West lodgings, lower court: late 15th century

rooms in the west range of the lower court at Haddon Hall, built by Sir Henry Vernon towards the close of the fifteenth century, were probably single lodgings for retainers, but the paired chambers above them may have been intended for guests or important household officials.[54] The planning of accommodation in this form, also distinguishable at Eltham Palace,[55] Raglan Castle,[56] and Bishop's Waltham Palace[57] marks a further stage in the development of a residence to keep pace with the increasing number of social grades in a large household. Yet the lodgings built round the outer court at Thornbury Castle between 1511 and 1521 by the third duke of Buckingham in that last magnificent

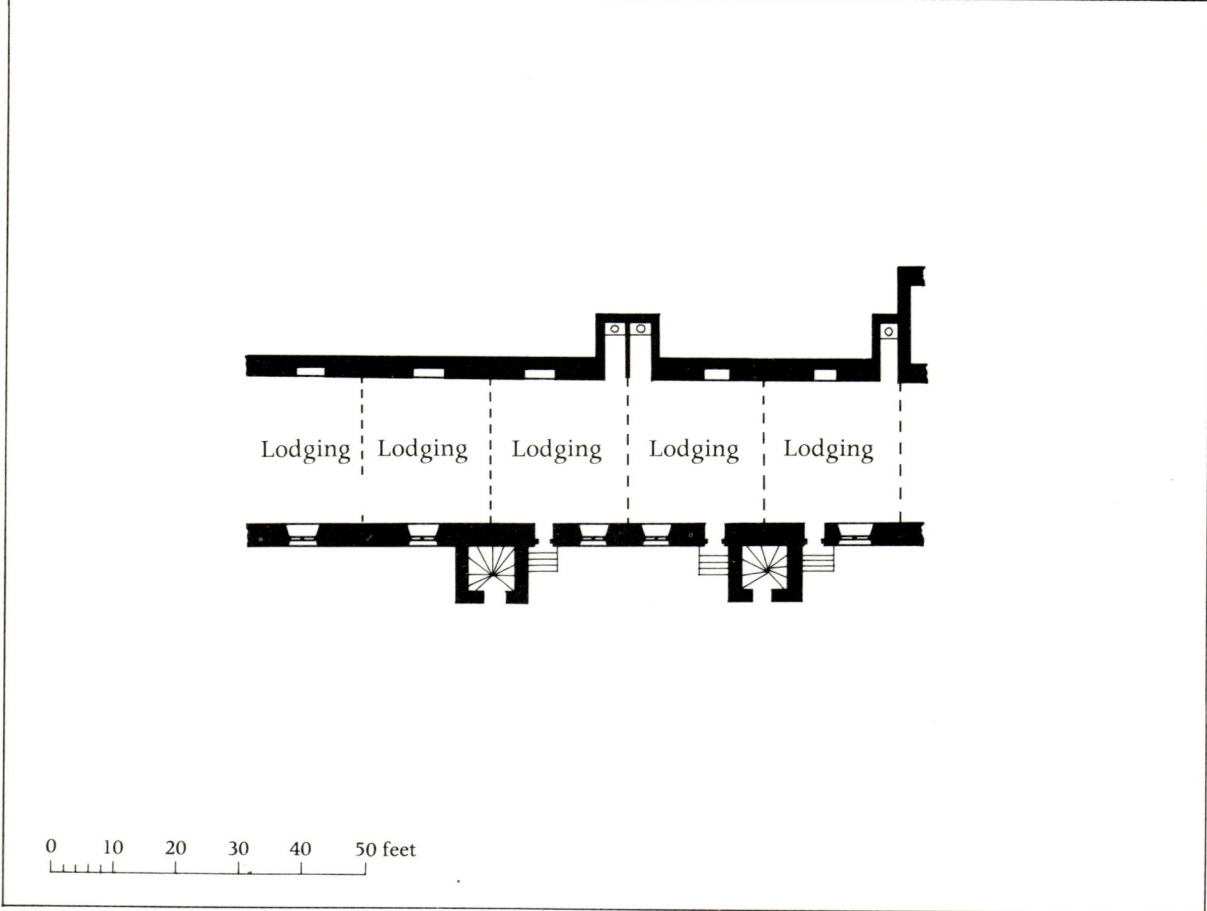

Fig. 76 Thornbury Castle. North range of outer court: 1511–21. Ground-floor plan

[54] P. A. Faulkner, 'Haddon Hall and Bolsover Castle', *Arch. Jour.* vol. 118 (1961), 194–7. Further contemporary lodgings, similar in design but sometimes lacking the second chamber, were built in the north-west tower and the adjacent north wing. Ibid., 96.

[55] The date of the timber-framed lodgings which surrounded the outer court is not clear. None of the buildings mentioned round the outer court in Richard II's reign were lodgings, but it is almost certain that their final form had been established by the close of the 15th century. See p. 148, n. 26. The lodgings on the eastern side had been completed by 1501 when an account book refers to their repair, B.M. Eg. 2358, f. 50. The plan drawn by John Thorpe in 1590, reproduced in A. W. Clapham and W. H. Godfrey, *Some Famous Buildings and Their Story* (1913), 54–5, shows that the lodgings on the south and east sides of the court differed from each other. Some may have been single lodgings but others were large enough to house a number of people. The upper chambers were reached by straight internal staircases, although an outside staircase in the corner of the courtyard is similar to that at Dartington. There was probably a series of lodgings on the upper floor of the north range, but much more pretentious accommodation forming a self-contained residence and still in existence, was built at the west end of this range.

[56] The eight lodgings built by the earl of Pembroke on the east side of the Fountain Court (c. 1461–5?) were probably intended for guests, with four upper chambers reserved for special visitors. It is likely that the earl's retainers were lodged in the contemporary north range of the Pitched Stone Court, replaced in the later 16th century by the existing office range.

[57] The range, adjacent to the gatehouse and enclosing the north side of the palace, was built by Bishop Langton in the 1490s. Only the foundations of the outer wall remain.

[58] W. Douglas Simpson, *The Antiq. Jour.* vol. 26 (1946), 165-70.

fling of an over-mighty subject,[58] are comparable in their siting, scale, and purpose with those built more than a century earlier at Dartington Hall.

The strong government of the early Tudor rulers was responsible for the elimination of armed retainers and Thornbury Castle was the last major residence to provide accommodation for them. A lord's household was now made up of his officials and servants, and the latter could be housed in dormitories under the roof. Lodgings were only provided for guests, courtiers, and household officials, and whereas the forty or more chambers at Dartington had been ranged round the courtyard, Lord Marney solved the problem at Layer Marney in about 1520-3 by building a comparable number vertically in an eight-storeyed gatehouse.

The Designer of Dartington Hall

No documentary evidence has yet come to light which gives any indication of the master mason responsible for the design of the Hall. There were three leading master masons in England during the last quarter of the fourteenth century: Henry Yevele, who dominated the architecture of the court and south-east England, William Wynford, who was pre-eminent in southern and south-west England, and John Lewyn, who was responsible for many of the principal buildings in the north of England. Neither Yevele's nor Lewyn's work is at all like that at Dartington and they can be dismissed from consideration. Wynford was responsible for several major works in the west of England and probably for New College, Oxford. There are several parallels between the Devonshire house and the contemporary Oxford foundation. The halls were almost identical in size, the design of the hall windows may have been similar, corporate lodgings and hammer-beam roofs were common to both buildings and there was a common association of barn and entrance approach. But Dartington can show none of Wynford's decorative characteristics nor that compact planning and massing of components which mark his domestic work. Nor is there any known association between Wynford's patron, the bishop of Winchester, and the earl of Huntingdon. It is quite likely that the master mason responsible for Dartington Hall is a figure little known to us, such as Master Fawley who was responsible for the accomplished design of St. Mary's College as St. David's (c. 1384) but of whom little else is known.[59]

[59] J. H. Harvey, *English Mediaeval Architects* (1954), 105.

What does Dartington Hall tell us about its designer? The general plan shows that he was a local rather than a leading mason used to working close to metropolitan developments. The plan of the Hall, in so far as it can be established, was not a particularly compact one like those designed by Wynford at Winchester and Oxford or by the author of Wardour Castle. Furthermore, the design of the hall range shows little advance on that adopted at Penshurst Place and Haddon Hall nearly half a century earlier. The heavy design and lack of assurance in handling the hall roof indicate that the master carpenter was also a local rather than a metropolitan figure.

Four features of the Hall design are particularly characteristic of the west of England. Firstly, the position of the barn in line with a residential block on a sloping site is not unlike the design of the Devon long-house where the cattle occupied one end and the family the other. This pattern extended throughout the medieval period and beyond, and although it is not claimed that this plan was consciously followed at Dartington, its occurrence is of regional significance. Secondly, the usual hall porch of two storeys was replaced at Dartington by a three-storeyed tower. The penchant for towers in the west of England during the Perpendicular period was reflected in a number of private residences as well as in numerous churches. Both Devon and Somerset possess several examples of halls approached through three- or even four-storeyed towers but that at Dartington is the earliest known example of this regional characteristic in a private mansion.[60] Thirdly, the prominent polygonal stair turret set against the main show side was a popular local feature, repeated in a group of church towers not far from the Hall in the fifteenth century and already present in the outer entrance gate at Tiverton Castle in the mid fourteenth century. Fourthly, the outer arch of the hall porch is distinguished by wave moulding, one of the more important forms of moulding in south-west England during the Perpendicular period, although it is not unknown in other parts of the country. This form was used on the piers at Dartmouth and Brixham churches which have been attributed to 1372[61] and 1377 respectively.[62] It also characterizes the choir piers of Crediton Church, apparently built during the late fourteenth century,[63] and is a feature of many of the contemporary arches at Wardour Castle. This suggests that a number of local masons in the west of England had adopted the Perpendicular style and created local forms of it during the last thirty years of the fourteenth century. It is possible that one of them was responsible for undertaking the important commission at Dartington. He may have also been responsible for the contemporary work at Crediton, but the compactness and individuality of the design of Wardour Castle compared with that of Dartington seems to preclude a common responsibility for both of these buildings. The names of only two masons working in the west of England at that time are known so far and none of their work accords with that carried out for Huntingdon.[64] It is to be hoped, however, that the name of the person responsible for the Hall will yet be discovered so that he may be credited with this important work.

The Influence of Dartington Hall on Regional Design

The period of modest economic prosperity that Devon enjoyed between about 1150 and 1350 suffered a severe setback during the following thirty years from which it did not fully recover until just before 1400.[65] The effects of this economic ebb and flow are still visible today. Many churches show evidence of reconstruction between about 1300 and 1350, but very little work was undertaken during the third quarter of the fourteenth century and it was not until about 1380 that a further wave of rebuilding began which continued for nearly 150 years. A similar but not such a distinctive fluctuation of prosperity is reflected in the pattern of residential building. The county is not rich in major medieval mansions but it shows considerable evidence of minor work. The great hall and apartments at Okehampton Castle may date from about 1300 and the small tower at Gidleigh was probably built at about the same time. Application was made to crenellate six residences between 1334 and 1340, although the only evidence today are the fragments at Modbury (1340) and Bere Ferers (1340). Considerable work of the early and mid fourteenth century survives at Tiverton Castle and the foundations of the hall at Compton Castle may be attributed to about 1340. Building activity fell sharply in Devon,

[60] A three-storeyed entrance tower leading directly to the screens passage had been built 20 years earlier at Harewood Castle, with a portcullis chamber and chapel on the two upper floors. However, the design had been determined by special considerations of tight planning and defence. Probably the earliest three-storeyed porch in Devon after Dartington was that at Shilton Barton. Four-storeyed porches survive at Holcombe Court (c. 1530) and Powderham Castle. The last-named was rebuilt in brick in 1766 but it is obviously a late medieval feature and is shown as such in Buck's engraving of 1734. It is unlikely that it was as early as the main body of the castle, c. 1400. In Somerset, there are late medieval three-storeyed porch towers at Clapton Court and Hutton Court, and a four-storeyed example at Birdcombe Court which formerly belonged to the Courtenay family of Powderham Castle. There is also a three-storeyed tower of late 15th-century date at the Bishop's Palace, Salisbury.

[61] Work was begun on an enlargement of Dartmouth Church in 1370 which was dedicated in October 1372. A. Hamilton Thompson does not ascribe any of the present building to that time, *Arch. Jour.* vol. 70 (1913), 461, 541, N. Pevsner does *South Devon* (1952), 113.

[62] This is Pevsner's B-type pier—a form not used in granite areas, *South Devon* (1952), 23–4; *North Somerset and Bristol* (1958), 45.

[63] In 1399, Bishop Stafford of Exeter directed that the canons of Crediton should contribute to the cost of completing the choir of the church. F. C. Hingeston-Randolph, *Episcopal Registers of the Diocese of Exeter: Bishop Stafford* (1906), 75. Also *Arch. Jour.* vol. 114 (1957), 141. The nave, built between 1413 and 1418, had piers of similar design.

[64] The more important was Robert Lesyngham who was responsible for the cloisters (now destroyed), the upper part of the screen of the west front, and the great east window of Exeter Cathedral between 1376 and 1394. The second mason was Nicholas Waleys who had a private practice in the west of England and was responsible for the spire of Bridgwater Church in 1366. J. H. Harvey, *English Mediaeval Architects* (1954), 166, 275.

[65] W. G. Hoskins, *Devon* (1954), 58–62.

as in most other parts of the country, during the third quarter of the century, but work was in progress on several residences in the 1380s, particularly on a minor group close to the Dorset border and on three major dwellings in south Devon.

Despite the local interest aroused by the construction of such a large residence as Dartington and the wider impact in the county of a large number of craftsmen and workmen engaged on a major project, the building of Dartington Hall had little effect on regional architecture. The one residence not far away known to have been under construction at about the same time was the bishop of Exeter's palace at Chudleigh. It might be expected that the residence for such a wealthy and powerful landowner would be fairly reasonable in size, but nothing is known of its plan and the two or three scraps of walling that remain are of indeterminate age and without meaning until the site has been excavated. As the licence to crenellate the palace was granted nine years before work had begun at Huntingdon's mansion, any influence that the latter might have had on it would have been minimal. The only other residence firmly attributable to the closing years of the century is at Holditch (1397) and the surviving angle tower bears little relation to any work that had recently been completed near Totnes.[66]

The one local family that might have emulated Huntingdon's work was the Courtenay

[66] It is said that Huntingdon built a stately home for himself within the precincts of Exeter Castle after he was created duke of Exeter in 1397. *Arch. Jour.* vol. 70 (1913), 510. Joan Sinar informs me that research into the history of the castle has not revealed any evidence to support this statement.

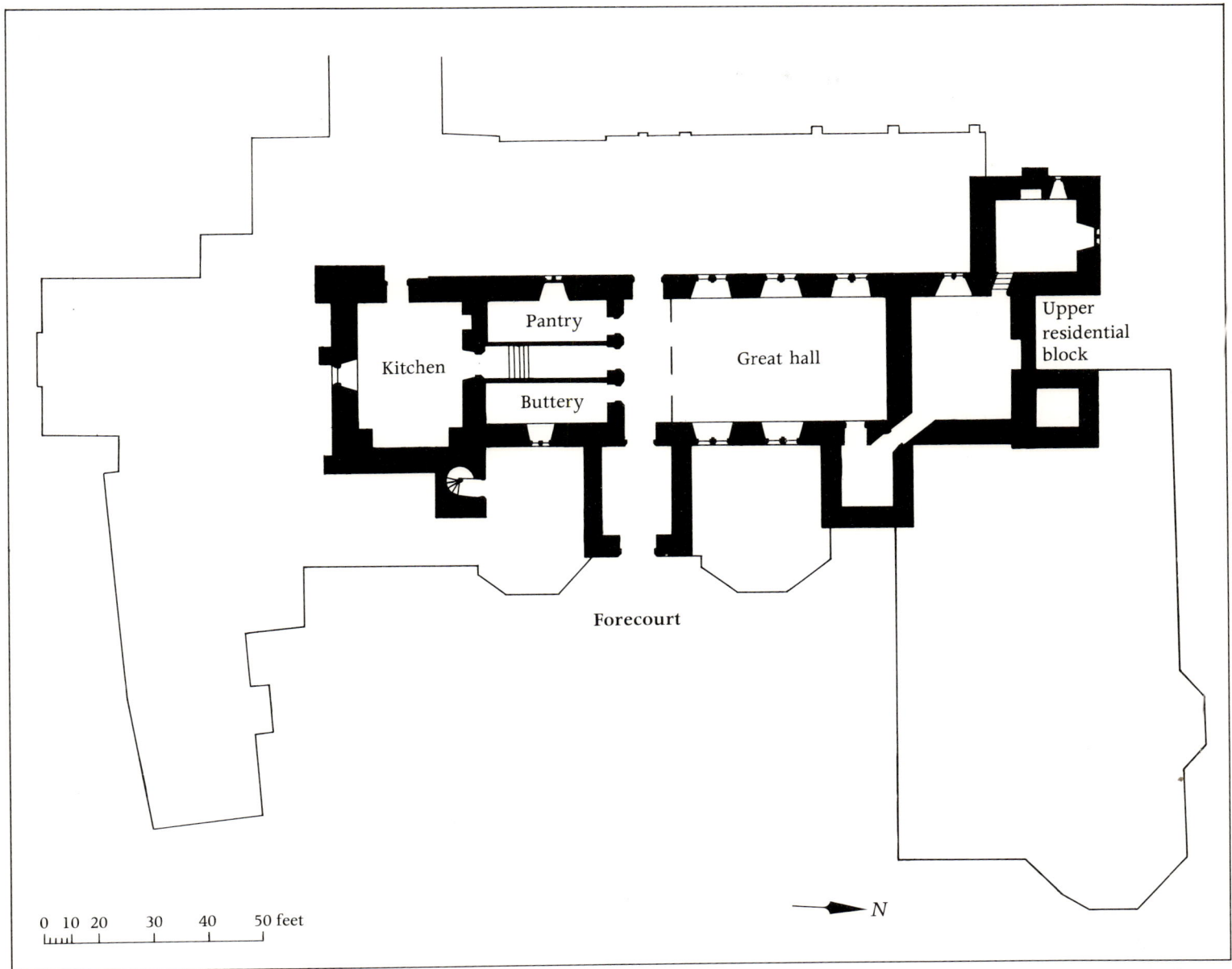

Fig. 77 Powderham Castle: possibly between 1391 and 1406. Ground-floor plan

family who acquired the Powderham estate in 1391. Powderham Castle, bordering the estuary of the river Exe, is about twenty miles north-east of Dartington. Its construction is usually attributed to Sir Philip Courtenay, the sixth son of the earl of Devon, who held the property between 1391 and 1406. There is no supporting documentary evidence for this attribution,[67] but if any residence was likely to be influenced by work at Dartington, it is the house built by one of the leading families in the west of England, a friend of Huntingdon and his wife, and possibly begun only a few years after their mansion. Yet Powderham follows the popular hall and end-block plan with an entrance porch, through screens passage with three office archways, and great hall. This was certainly the plan of the range separating the two courts at Dartington, and the pattern of three-storeyed residential blocks at either end of the hall was repeated. But the hall was much smaller, 49 feet by 23 feet internally, and the kitchen was built directly at the end of the kitchen passage (as at the Vicars Choral, Exeter). The parlour at the upper end of the hall was approached from a lobby outside the line of the hall wall, and had the unusual feature of a small residential tower projecting from it as well as the more usual garderobe tower. There is no evidence of any ranges enclosing a courtyard area, and the whole plan is closer to that at Compton Castle (*c.* 1340[68] (p. 161)) and Knighstone near Ottery St. Mary (possibly late fourteenth century)[69] than Huntingdon's residence.

The considerable number of fifteenth- and sixteenth-century residences remaining in Devon is partly a reflection of the growing prosperity of the county, and partly attributable to their remoteness and the chance of time. They tended to be modest in scale and adopt the single courtyard plan, modified by local characteristics such as the position of the kitchen on the far side of the courtyard. A gatehouse, so noticeably absent at Dartington, was often an important feature of the design. The Old Manor at Little Hempston on the opposite side of the river from Dartington looks at first like a small-scale version of its powerful neighbour.[70] It has two small courts separated by a hall range, but the wall creating the outer court is of no antiquity and was probably added in the nineteenth century. Without it, the orthodox west of England quadrangular plan is created with the kitchen on the far side of the courtyard as at Compton Castle (in the fifteenth century), Bladgon Manor near Paignton, and Widworthy Barton near Honiton. Even the end-wall fireplace in the hall is not an ancient feature. It was inserted in the 1920s and in the absence of any other evidence, presumably replaced a central hearth.

One other later residence which seems as though it may have been influenced by the plan at Dartington was Cotehele House, not far from the Cornish border. This was also designed round two courtyards and boasted an additional retainers' court. Yet it had originally been a modest quadrangular house for well over a hundred years before the major additions of 1485 to 1539 converted it to the present extensive structure.[71] There was, in fact, no reason why local residences in the fifteenth century should follow the design adopted by Huntingdon, for it had been dictated by considerations of wealth, size, and display that applied to very few people. The Hall has certain vernacular characteristics, but it was essentially a spectacular importation developing a plan found in other parts of southern England and marked by an individuality that had hardly any effect on local practice or design.

---

[67] As an example of medieval domestic architecture, Powderham Castle is not now of much account owing to a series of drastic alterations made between the mid 18th and mid 19th centuries. A small portion of one of the original hall windows and its relieving arch survive above the present hall roof. It is a square-headed window of two lights with cinquefoil openings and no hood mouldings. It possibly dates from about 1400. I am most grateful to A. W. Everett for giving me details of his researches at Powderham and for the provision of photographs and a plan of the structure on which my modified drawing is based after examining the site. For descriptions of the castle, see M. Girouard, *Country Life* (July 1963), and *Trans. Exeter Diocesan Soc.* (1867), 170–83.

[68] *Compton Castle: Official Guide* (1962); A. W. Everett, 'The Rebuilding of the Hall at Compton Castle', *Trans. Devon Assoc.* vol. 88 (1956), 75–85.

[69] Christopher Hussey, *Country Life* (September 1950).

[70] Christopher Hussey has suggested that it was built as a manor-house by Sir John Stretch in about 1360, *Country Life* (August 1933). A. W. Everett considers that it was intended to serve as a priest's house, although it is larger than most priests' houses built in south-west England, particularly in such a remote country parish. See W. A. Pantin, *Med. Archaeol.* vol. 1 (1957), 118–46. The parish is a large and scattered one but the house is extremely isolated and nearly a mile from the church and village it is supposed to have served. It was certainly used as a parsonage in the second half of the 15th century when the wall painting was added in the hall but was it built for this purpose? See also *Arch. Jour.* vol. 70 (1913).

[71] T. Garner and A. Stratton, *The Domestic Architecture of England during the Tudor Period*, vol. 1 (2nd ed., 1928), 40.

Appendixes

Appendix 1

The Charter of 833

There is no reason to doubt the authenticity of this charter, even though it is only known through its inclusion in a late medieval cartulary of Shaftesbury Abbey.[1] There would be no motive for its forgery and its formulae cause no difficulty. A spurious charter to Winchester of 825,[2] which is certainly based on a genuine text of Egbert, agrees with the Dartington charter in its dating clause. Such an agreement could be obtained only by collusion between the two monastic houses and that is extremely unlikely. The charter of 833 is written in a mixture of corrupt Latin and Anglo-Saxon, but although the Shaftesbury cartulary is notoriously corrupt in its copying, early ninth-century charters—even in their original form—were frequently written in corrupt Latin.[3]

The existence of this document in a cartulary of a house not founded until between 871 and 877 is probably because Wennland was among the estates later held by the abbey of Shaftesbury. Cartularies often include deeds prior to the foundation of the house and these are usually the previous title-deeds of estates which came into their possession.

I, Egbert, by the grace of God king of the West Saxons with the consent and common counsel of my bishops and ealdormen and the elders of all my people have ordered to be drawn up this deed of witness, namely of ten hides of that land which is called *Wennland*, so that it may remain firmly assigned according to the ancient document to those possessors whose own inheritance [it is], namely three sisters Beornwynn, Aelfflaed and Wealhburh [?], [and] should continue with the boundaries of the same and all things belonging to it with firm stability and without any contradiction.

And we have done this for the reason that it happened—we know not for what cause—that the earlier deeds have been lost. And if it ever happen that they are found again by any man, unless they come into the possession [?] and support of these same heirs, they are to be judged invalid and rejected by all catholics practising the true faith; In either case, the aforesaid sisters dividing that land between them, each of them received three hides and the third part of a fourth in her own right.

It happened however after the passage of years that when the same afore-mentioned sisters received more of their paternal inheritance, Beornwynn withdrew into Devon and took her share there in the place which is called Dartington-*homm* and allowed the other two to divide these ten hides as they pleased. But when they indeed shared it between them, Aelfflaed took for herself into her own ownership two hides in the western part.

The boundaries truly of this estate are these: First from the alder-stream up on to a thorn-tree,[4] thence on to a wall ditch; then through the hedgerow [?] on to the middle of *delesburg*; thence to *cylberg*; then on to the *wyrtruma*; then on to the *burg*; then on to a ditch; [then] on to the old enclosure; thence along this enclosure as far as a thorn-tree in *hacggenhamm*; thence on to a hedge; thence straight on to an oak; then east[5] over melenbroc on to an . . . .; thence to a post back to an alder stream.

This charter of privilege was written in the year of our Lord's incarnation 833, the twelfth indiction on the day on which the festival of St. Stephen the first martyr is celebrated, in the royal town of Dorchester, in the presence of suitable witnesses whose names are disclosed noted below.

But if anyone puffed up by tyrannical power or deceived by the fraud of the devil should dare to infringe or diminish this, let him know that he is excommunicated and separated from the communion of saints and must give an account before the judgment seat of Christ.

I, King Egbert, thus confirm this our common confirmation with my own hand with the sign of the holy cross.
I, Bishop Ealhstan, have consented and subscribed.

[1] B.M. Harl. 61, f. 17b. This early 15th-century register includes charters, rentals, etc. from Anglo-Saxon times to the reign of Richard II. The charter is printed in *Cartularium Saxonicum*, ed. by W. de Gray Birch, vol. 1 (1885), 572–3, and in a more corrupt form in *Codex Diplomaticus Aevi Saxonici*, ed. by J. M. Kemble, vol. 1 (1839), 300–1, and vol. 3 (1845), 390.

[2] *Cartularium Saxonicum*, ed. by W. de Gray Birch, vol. 1 (1885), 541–4.

[3] F. M. Stenton, *Latin Charters of the Anglo-Saxon Period* (1955), 39–42.

[4] *Poure* must be corrupt: it is probably *porne*. The boundaries refer to those of *Wennland* and not to those of Dartington.

[5] Or possibly 'back' if *est* is the common error for *eft*.

Appendix 2

The Estates and Income of John Holand, Earl of Huntingdon, in the late Fourteenth Century

Estates

c. 1360–1388. John Holand was a very modest landowner during his youth. A scattered manor or two in Berkshire, Bedfordshire, and Hertfordshire, and a small group of holdings in Cheshire and Flintshire, valued in July 1388 at no more than £200 a year,[1] was the sum of his holdings.

Holand received three manors when he was still a child. His tenure was brief of the two that his parents granted him in November 1360, North Weald in Essex and Whissendine in Rutland,[2] but he retained the manor of Great Gaddesden which Joan settled on him in 1361 for the remainder of his life.[3]

On approaching manhood, he was awarded two manors, Ardington and Philiberts Court in Berkshire which Alice Perrers, Edward III's mistress, had forfeited shortly before December 1378.[4] Twenty months later, he obtained a small group of manors in Cheshire and Flintshire for the maintenance of his estate during his life. They were the town of Northwich, Cheshire,[5] the lordship of Hope and Hopedale, Flintshire, and the revenue of £7. 6s. 8d. per annum from the profits of land at Overmarsh, Cheshire.[6] These lands had formerly belonged to Richard Stafford who had spent his life in the Black Prince's service, and although

[1] *Cal. Pat. Rolls 1385–89*, 494–5.

[2] *Cal. Pat. Rolls 1358–61*, 480. The grant had been for life but both of these manors had reverted to Joan by the time of her death in 1385 when they passed to her elder son. *V.C.H. Essex*, vol. 4 (1956), 287, and *V.C.H. Rutland*, vol. 2 (1935), 158.

[3] Before her death in 1385, Joan had also granted him the manor of Stevington in Bedfordshire. *Cal. Inq. Misc. 1377–88*, 179. In 1388 the grant for life was changed to one in fee. *Cal. Pat. Rolls 1385–89*, 494. Huntingdon held it until his death when his wife successfully claimed it as part of her dower. It remained in the Holand family until 1461. *V.C.H. Bedfordshire*, vol. 3 (1912), 101.

[4] *Cal. Pat. Rolls 1377–81*, 141, 324. Richard II gave up all his rights in the manor of Ardington to his half-brother in June 1385. *Cal. Pat. Rolls 1381–85*, 577. Philiberts Court is part of the manor of East Hanney. The reversion was granted to William Windsor, Alice Perrers's husband. *Cal. Pat. Rolls 1377–81*, 504. The grant in fee tail of this manor in 1388 to Holand and his wife was therefore invalid. *V.C.H. Berkshire*, vol. 4 (1927), 270, 288. Huntingdon still held the property at the time of his death. *Cal. Pat. Rolls 1399–1401*, 233.

[5] Wood from the forest of Delamare was granted to Holand by Richard in August 1389 for the repair of the mill, and 12 months later for repairing the mill weir at Northwich, P.R.O. Chester Rolls 2/61 and 2/62.

[6] *Cal. Pat. Rolls 1377–81*, 539. P.R.O. Chester Rolls 2/52. It proved difficult to obtain the annual rent from the revenues of the lands of Overmarsh for, in 1394, the chamberlain of Chester was ordered to pay Huntingdon the arrears from this land since 2 June 1388. *Cal. Close Rolls 1392–96*, 194.

[7] *Cal. Pat. Rolls 1385–89*, 130. *Cal. Fine Rolls 1383–91*, 120–1. P.R.O. Chester Rolls 2/57.

[8] *Cal. Pat. Rolls 1385–89*, 494–5. Also *Cal. Pat. Rolls 1391–96*, 102.

[9] *Cal. Close Rolls 1396–99*, 342.

[10] *Cal. Pat. Rolls 1385–89*, 494–5.

[11] December 1390. *Cal. Pat. Rolls 1388–92*, 364

[12] *Cal. Pat. Rolls 1391–96*, 102. This was the only manor granted to Huntingdon in December 1384 which he did not receive in the award of July 1388.

[13] *Cal. Pat. Rolls 1399–1401*, 244. In April 1399, Huntingdon was also granted £20 per annum from the fee farm of Exeter. *Cal. Pat. Rolls 1396–99*, 537.

[14] P.R.O. Misc. Inq. C 145/274, no. 16 and C 145/275, no. 18.

[15] *Cal. Pat. Rolls 1391–96*, 102.

[16] Ibid., 600.

[17] *Cal. Pat. Rolls 1396–99*, 526.

[18] *Cal. Pat. Rolls 1391–96*, 102.

[19] *Cal. Close Rolls 1396–99*, 342.

[20] *Cal. Pat. Rolls 1388–92*, 91.

[21] Ibid., 423.

[22] *Cal. Close Rolls 1396–99*, 372.

Richard II seized them together with the remainder of Holand's property after the murder of Sir Ralph Stafford in 1385, they were restored to him on 6 April 1386.[7]

1388–1397. Huntingdon became a landowner of some importance in July 1388, when his elevation to the peerage at the beginning of the previous month made it essential for him to be awarded estates sufficient to maintain his new dignity and position. Richard II made him a grant of sixteen manors in the west of England, mainly in Devon but including four in Somerset and one in Cornwall. They were valued at £1,333. 6s. 8d. per annum, but as it was known that they were worth only £646. 13s. 4d., it was intended that the deficit should be made up by a claim on the petty customs of London, Southampton, and Bristol until lands to that value could be conveyed to him.[8] This grant formed the basis of Huntingdon's tenurial holdings for the remainder of his life. The intention to make up the deficit was honoured during the following twelve years by the award of a number of smaller grants with the result that at the time of his death, the basis of Huntingdon's tenure, although still predominantly in Devon, had been extended by a group of holdings in Suffolk and a number of manors in the southern counties and Westmorland.

All the property granted to him in July 1388 had formerly belonged to James, Lord Audley except for two manors in Devon forfeited to the king by Sir John Cary, and the manor of Haslebury Plucknet in Somerset which had formerly belonged to the late earl of Suffolk.[9] Audley's lands were valued at £400, Cary's two manors at £200, and Haslebury Plucknet at £46. 13s. 4d.[10]

Huntingdon's *Devonshire* property included the manors of Bovey Tracey, Holsworthy, Northlew, Langgacre (in Broad Clyst), Barnstaple, Combe Martin, Fremington, South Molton, Dartington, Blackborough, Torrington, Cockington, and the hundreds of Fremington and South Molton. All these manors had formerly been held by the late Lord Audley, except the manors of Torrington and Cockington which had formerly been in Sir John Cary's possession. Before he had died, Edward III had purchased the reversion of Audley's four manors in Somerset and Cornwall and the manors of Bovey Tracey, Holsworthy, Northlew, and Langgacre in Devon as part of his endowment of the abbey of St. Mary Graces by the Tower founded by him in 1350. In order that Richard could give his half-brother a more homogeneous holding, he revoked his grandfather's bequest and added these manors to the Audley estates he already intended giving to Huntingdon and which, in fact, he had held for a short time between December 1384 and April 1385. The monks received the farm of the church of Scardeburgh in exchange, although it was worth only just over half the value of Edward III's grant.[11] Three additions were made to Huntingdon's holdings in Devon before 1400. He obtained the manor of Winkleigh in June 1392[12] and granted it to Thomas Proudfoot in September 1399.[13] He and his wife were bequeathed the manor of Staverton by the earl of Kent in 1397, and Huntingdon also held the manor of Harberton at the time of his death.[14]

In *Cornwall*, the castle and manor of Trematon and the manors of Calstock and Assheburgh (Saltash?) were added to the single manor of Tackbear in June 1392,[15] and the manors of Tewington, Moresk near Truro, Tintagel, the reversion of the manor and borough of Helston, and the borough of Bossiney and Trevailly were transferred to him in July 1395.[16] The final grant of land in Cornwall and the last one made to Huntingdon during his lifetime was the manor of Helston in Trigare, with the parks of Lanteglos and Helsbury, previously held by Sir Richard Abberbury (April 1399).[17]

In *Somerset*, the original grant included the manors of Blagdon, Lydford, Staundon by Dunster, and Haslebury Plucknet, but the hundreds of Stone and Catash were added four years later.[18] Owing to the annulment of the judgment against Suffolk in 1398, Huntingdon was ordered to restore Haslebury Plucknet to Michael de la Pole, Suffolk's heir,[19] and by the first days of 1400, he had also given up the manor of Staundon by Dunster.

The only other county where Huntingdon held an appreciable amount of property was in *Suffolk*. Almost exactly a year after the major grant in 1388, it was discovered that the annual value of the manors of Torrington and Cockington in Devon, originally estimated at £200 was worth only £129. 6s. 8d. Richard therefore granted Huntingdon the manors of Benhall and Stratford, formerly held by the earl of Suffolk, and the manor of Icklingham, alias Bernershall, forfeited by Sir James Berners, so that the value of these properties at £70 compensated Huntingdon for the loss which he would otherwise have sustained over Cary's lands in Devon.[20] A further grant was made in June 1391, when Huntingdon and his wife were granted the reversion of the manor of Lowestoft and the hundred of Lothingland after the death of Queen Anne.[21] They were valued at £70 but the earl and his wife did not enter into the property until 1394. The final change in his Suffolk holding occurred during the last year of Huntingdon's life when he had to relinquish the manor of Icklingham on the reversal of the earl of Suffolk's attainder.[22]

The remainder of Huntingdon's property was scattered. He held a share in the manor of Milton-next-

Gravesend, *Kent* which had formerly been held by Sir Simon Burley,[23] the manor of Stevington, *Bedfordshire*,[24] the manor of Bereford St. Martin, *Wiltshire*,[25] the manor of Langton, *Yorkshire*,[26] and the manor of Marton, *Westmorland*.[27] It is also known that Huntingdon received £16. 13s. 4d. from the rent of a moiety of Coventry, *Warwickshire* called Earl's Park,[28] and that he held property in the county from which he took his title,[29] but no details have yet come to light. It is also possible that he held some property in *Ireland* for his goods and chattels there were seized in 1400 by Lord Grey of Ruthin on behalf of the king.[30] Finally, Huntingdon held the castles of Berkhamsted, Tintagel, Horston, and Trematon, and a house in London called Cold Harbour.[31]

1397–1399. During the two years between the late summer of 1397 and 1399, it seemed as though Huntingdon was destined to become one of the leading landowners in England, for his estates were considerably enlarged by the receipt of much of the property formerly held by the appellant earl of Arundel, and for a short time by the earl of Warwick. They were swollen still further by the grant of all the estates in South Wales formerly held by the duke of Lancaster. But Huntingdon had hardly begun to enjoy the benefits from these acquisitions before he was ordered to forfeit them by the new régime in November 1399, and he died only two months later as a landowner of far more modest proportions.

Huntingdon had been granted the keeping of Arundel Castle in August 1397 and received the honour of Arundel immediately after the earl's execution in the following month.[32] Some of the contents of the castle that he had seized in August were granted to him in October.[33] At the beginning of December, he received the rents and services due from the manor, honour, and barony of Petworth and from all the manors, lands, and holdings in Sussex and Surrey belonging to Arundel which the earl of Northumberland had been holding until then on behalf of the king.[34] Ten months later, the castle, town, and lordship of Lewes were added to this large group of estates, as well as a number of properties in Kent, Sussex, and Surrey, originally granted to the duke of Norfolk, but after his banishment, transferred to Huntingdon.[35] The last Arundel addition was in January 1399 when the castle, honour, and lordship of Reigate, Surrey was granted to him in exchange for the lands in Cheshire and Flintshire which he had held for nearly twenty years and which Richard wished to annex to the county palatine of Chester.[36]

Less than seven weeks after Lancaster's death early in 1399, Richard had granted Huntingdon all the estates held by the duke in South Wales, including Monmouth, White Castle, Skenfrith, Grosmont, Kidwelly, Ogmore, and Carreg Cennen with their castles.[37] These, together with the properties he held during the wardship of the earl of March, made Huntingdon a formidable landowner in South Wales, but his tenure of them proved too short for him to derive much benefit from them. By the judgment given in November 1399, all estates which Huntingdon had acquired since his creation as duke of Exeter were to be forfeited. Once more he became primarily a west of England landowner, but this time without his properties in Cheshire and Flintshire which never seem to have been returned to him.

Income

Any estimation of the income Huntingdon might expect in a year is fraught with difficulty owing to the incompleteness of the records and the amount of conjecture necessary. None of his financial accounts have survived, and even if they had, we should not find them the carefully balanced and accurate records demanded today. During the earlier days of his career, Huntingdon's small territorial revenue was supplemented by direct financial grants from the Crown. A grant of £100 per annum made in March 1378[38] had been replaced in the following December by the award of two Berkshire manors,[39] but a further grant of £166. 13s. 4d. per annum was made two years later.[40] All grants ceased with the confiscation of his goods and estates in September 1385, but when the latter were restored in March 1386 he was allowed to claim the residue from the Exchequer if the total value of his lands came to less than £333. 6s. 8d.[41]

Any estimation of his total income subsequent to his elevation to the peerage naturally depends on economic fluctuations and the size of his holdings. To lessen the many unknown factors involved, the estimation is confined to a point at the beginning of 1397 shortly before he received a number of temporary additions to his estates. Generally speaking, Huntingdon could expect a regular annual income from five sources: his estates, the sale of the produce from them, his courts and franchises, castle fees, and feudal incidents.

Every year, Huntingdon's accounting officers—his reeves, bailiffs, and receivers—would visit all those estates within their purview to collect the rents due to their overlord. Their value, estimated at £846. 13s. 4d. in 1388, had been increased by several grants in the following eight and a half years worth at least £228,[42] with the result that they brought in an accountable income of at least £1,074 by the beginning of 1397.

---

[23] *Cal. Pat. Rolls 1388–92*, 418.

[24] See p. 260, n. 3 above.

[25] *Cal. Pat. Rolls 1396–99*, 152.

[26] *Cal. Pat. Rolls 1401–05*, 111. *Cal. Fine Rolls 1399–1405*, 58.

[27] Ibid., 59.

[28] 12 March 1399. *Cal. Close Rolls 1396–99*, 382.

[29] Ibid., 343. Also *Cal. Close Rolls 1422–29*, 436.

[30] *Cal. Close Rolls 1399–1402*, 145.

[31] He had held it since 1389. W. Dugdale, *The Baronage of England*, vol. 2 (1676), 79a. It was described by the author of the *Traison et Mort* as 'a very beautiful residence'. It had formerly been owned by Sir John Poulteney and the Black Prince, and was destroyed in the late 16th century. See also *Survey of the Cities of London and Westminster*, ed. C. L. Kingsford (1908), vol. 1, 236; vol. 2, 321; *Archaeologia*, vol. 57 (1901), 257–84, and 'A Sketch Map of London under Richard II', *London Topographical Society* (1960), no. 93.

[32] *Cal. Pat. Rolls 1396–99*, 176. The castle, town, and lordship of Arundel included all the lands appertaining thereto in Surrey, Sussex, Essex, and Herts. They were valued at £600 a year. V. Gibbs and H. A. Doubleday, *The Complete Peerage*, vol. 1 (1910), 245.

[33] *Cal. Fine Rolls 1391–99*, 227. *Cal. Pat. Rolls 1396–99*, 216.

[34] *Cal. Pat. Rolls 1396–99*, 266. B.M. MS. Cott. Vespasian, F. XIII, no. 30.

[35] *Cal. Pat. Rolls 1396–99*, 458.

[36] Ibid., 467.

[37] *Cal. Fine Rolls 1391–99*, 293–4.

[38] *Cal. Pat. Rolls 1377–81*, 141.

[39] Ibid., 324.

[40] Ibid., 492, 497.

[41] *Cal. Pat. Rolls 1385–89*, 130.

[42] The three manors in Suffolk granted in June 1391 were valued at £70, and the lands in Cornwall and Somerset granted in June 1392 were valued at £157. 6s. 8d. He received a further grant of land in Cornwall of unknown value in July 1395.

[43] *Cal. Pat. Rolls 1391–96*, 102.

[44] Particularly valuable in Devon. At the time of his forfeiture in 1400, Huntingdon had 200 pieces of oak, 26 oak planks, 8,000 laths, and 6 oak trunks at Bovey Tracey. P.R.O. Misc. Inq.

The claim on the petty customs, which had been making up the balance to £1,333. 6s. 8d. was therefore gradually reduced.[43] The income associated with these estates also included the sale of produce from them and included grain, cattle, timber,[44] and wool, as well as the farm from dovecotes, ferries, mills, fishing rights, mines[45] and quarries, and the dues from the commutation of labour services. Furthermore, there was the revenue from his courts, including fines for non-attendance and offences against the courts, and franchises or liberties such as the proceeds from the chattels of fugitives or permission to hold a fair or market. Only two or three scattered figures exist for these sources,[46] but research on the Clare estates has suggested that out of a total income of £2,500 per annum in the mid fourteenth century, about half this amount came from rents and the remainder from the profits of manorial courts, produce, mills, wood, and other minor sources.[47] Huntingdon's manors in the west of England were likely to have been rather less profitable than those in the more wealthy region of East Anglia,[48] but on this basis we may hazard a guess that at the beginning of 1397, he could anticipate a total revenue from his estates of between £2,000 and £2,500 per annum.

The fees attached to castles of which Huntingdon held the custody were substantial. That for Conway Castle was £40 a year.[49] The total fees for holding the castles of Tintagel for eleven years, Rockingham for nine years, Conway, Horston, and Brest for over eight years must have been a welcome addition to his finances, and he was also able to claim an annual grant of £20 on the Exchequer from June 1392 onwards in compensation for the non-receipt of any fees attached to the custody of Haverford Castle which he had held since the previous January.[50]

Finally, there were the valuable profits from feudal incidents—aids, reliefs, wardships, and the marriage of heirs—attached to any lands held by knight's service. Generally, the right of exacting a substantial fee for the marriage of an heir or heiress and the wardship of an heir or heiress during their minority was highly profitable. The latter proved particularly so in the case of Huntingdon. The estates of any fatherless heir were automatically held in trust by the king during his minority and were usually farmed to royal servants or members of the nobility. Except in the case of forfeiture where no reservation was usually made, only two-thirds of an estate was usually entrusted to a keeper[51] and the remaining one-third of the inheritance was devoted to the maintenance of the widow. Keepers were expected to maintain the estates, particularly buildings and fences, and the rights of their wards, but in return they could claim all the rents from those estates. Quite obviously, such grants frequently proved extremely profitable and large sums were sometimes paid for the grant of a valuable ward. In June 1391, Huntingdon was willing to pay £300 for the manor of Buckland, Surrey and the marriage rights of the heir of Sir John Arundel;[52] evidently the lands he already held in trust for this heir since November 1390 had proved financially profitable. He paid £133. 6s. 8d. in February 1392 for the lands of Sir Robert Luton during the minority of his son,[53] and was fortunate enough to obtain three Devon properties in trust for the two daughters of Guy of Brienne rent free.[54] The income from wardships varied from the reversion of a single manor such as Old Shoreham valued at £20 per annum[55] to the lucrative grant of the lands in South Wales held by Richard Mortimer, the heir of the earl of March.[56]

Incomplete evidence makes it impossible to suggest the sum of Huntingdon's financial resources but whatever his income, there is little doubt that his expenditure was particularly heavy. In addition to the cost of administering his estates and maintaining the property on them, he had to pay his servants, members of his 'company', and the additional forces, for example, which accompanied him on his military expeditions. There was also his own position to maintain, his clothes and furnishings and those of his family and household, his armour, horses, and the building of his splendid new mansion at Dartington. There were also numerous annuities and gifts including some very substantial ones of jewels, clothes, silver and gold plate.[57] It was probably more than a mark of favour which made it necessary for Richard II to pardon Huntingdon of all his debts due to the Crown in May 1393 and again in April 1399.[58]

Appendix 3

The Authorship of the *Chronique de la Traison et Mort de Richard II*

The author of this valuable chronicle covering the last three years of Richard II's life gives no indication of his name, position, or rank. The chronicle, written in French, occasionally makes use of a French poem attributed to a person known as 'Creton', but it also includes a great deal of information which is obviously the record of an eye-witness who was in close touch with several of the participants.

C 145/275, no. 16. He also held timber worth £7. 7s. 8d. at Trematon and Saltash. Ibid., C 145/278, nos. 6, 17, 18, 20.

[45] He obtained a licence in March 1393 to exploit a tin-mine in Cornwall for 7 years without payment of any fee. *Cal. Pat. Rolls 1391–96*, 226. Such a venture could be extremely profitable because of its necessity in plumbing and the manufacture of pewter.

[46] At the beginning of 1400, jurors assessed the revenue from the assize of Bovey Tracey, with perquisites of the court, at £45 per annum. P.R.O. Misc. Inq. C 145/275, no. 19.

[47] G. A. Holmes, *The Estates of the Higher Nobility in Fourteenth-Century England* (1957), Ch. IV, particularly 109.

[48] According to the reports made after the inquisitions held in the west of England in 1400, local jurors evaluated Huntingdon's property in Devon at £436. 13s. 4d. (North Lew, Blackborough, and Torrington were not included). His property in Cornwall was valued at £163. 18s. 3d. (Helston and Helston in Trigare were omitted), and that in Somerset was valued at £126. 14s. 0d. Their total value was £727 5s. 7d. P.R.O. Misc. Inq. C 145/274–277. The manor of Dartington was valued at £66. 13s. 4d. and at £40 without the advowson of the church. P.R.O. Misc. Inq. C 145/275, nos. 16 and 18.

[49] *Cal. Pat. Rolls 1391–96*, 208.

[50] Ibid., 70.

[51] This is specifically stated in the grant vesting control of Sir John Arundel's lands to Huntingdon during the minority of his son. *Cal. Close Rolls 1389–92*, 213.

[52] *Cal. Pat. Rolls 1388–92*, 430

[53] *Cal. Pat. Rolls 1391–96*, 20.

[54] Ibid., 218.

[55] Huntingdon held the property from September 1397. *Cal. Pat. Rolls 1396–99*, 198.

[56] Ibid., 408.

[57] On 4 February 1400, the mayor of London delivered goods to the king from the London property of Huntingdon and Sir Andrew Hake worth £409 5s. 3d. P.R.O. E 364/34. Some of the gifts distributed by Huntingdon before the January rising are mentioned on page 51.

[58] *Cal. Pat. Rolls 1391–96*, 263. *Cal. Pat. Rolls 1396–99*, 540.

This work has been sadly underestimated by most late nineteenth- and early twentieth-century historians.[1] On the evidence of its French authorship and the eye-witness description of Richard's parting from his consort in 1399 prior to his second Irish expedition, it has been suggested by A. Steel, *Richard II* (1941), 299, that the *Traison et Mort* was written by a member of Queen Isabelle's household. The fact that the work includes a detailed account of the dismissal of the queen's governess and that the time covered by the chronicle approximately coincides with Isabelle's life in England, tends to support this view. On the other hand, it is surprising that a member of the queen's entourage should omit any reference to Isabelle's return to France in 1400, particularly as it is described in detail in 'Creton's' poem. Nor does it explain how the author came to be so well informed about Bolingbroke's movements if he was with the queen in the south of England throughout the summer of 1399.

In addition to the vivid description of Richard's parting from his consort, there is another equally vivid description of a similar parting between the earl of Huntingdon and his wife immediately before the Holand rising in 1400. If the author was a member of the queen's household as suggested by Steel, it is odd that he should have been able to witness this incident when he was presumably with the queen at Sonning during what must necessarily have been an extremely difficult time for her. On the other hand, if the author was a member of Huntingdon's household, he could have witnessed his master's leave-taking as well as the royal parting, for Huntingdon was amongst those who accompanied the king on his expedition to Ireland in 1399.

Although the chronicle is essentially an account of the events leading up to the deposition and death of Richard II, the earl of Huntingdon appears in a subsidiary yet important role throughout the story in the same way that Bishop Odo does in the Bayeaux Tapestry record of the Norman Conquest. The author is the only chronicler who gives any reason for the appellants' arrest in 1397 and who indicates that Huntingdon was Richard's leading supporter in their downfall. The earl's participation in Richard's own downfall in the summer of 1399 is carefully minuted, while the rising at the beginning of 1400 is described in greater detail than in any other record. A particularly lengthy and precise description is given of Huntingdon's death, while passing references to such matters as Huntingdon's London residence, the name of his butler, and his wife's ability at dancing, suggest an intimate knowledge of the earl and his household far beyond that of a disinterested chronicler. Furthermore, the author obviously had an extensive knowledge of Bolingbroke's movements after his landing in Yorkshire and was able to include copies of letters he had issued. One of the few people who must have been at least as interested in the success of Bolingbroke's enterprise as in that of Huntingdon's rebellion, was the countess of Huntingdon. She was Bolingbroke's sister as well as the wife of one of Richard's principal supporters. The author's attachment to Elizabeth's household would not only account for this dual interest—one which is reflected throughout the chronicle—but it would also explain his concern with Huntingdon's fortunes. No personal details are given of the earl's visit to Ireland in 1399, but this is not surprising if the author was attached to Elizabeth's household rather than to that of her husband, and it would also account for his copying this section from 'Creton' who was with Richard and Huntingdon at that particular time.

[1] There are two surviving copies of the chronicle: MS Ancien 5327 and 5028 in the Bibliotheque Nationale, Paris. Each of them is preceded by a chronicle covering the early history of Normandy from the time of Rollo to the reign of Henry III of England, and followed by a chronicle of the duchy from 1414 to 1422. The differences between the two texts, both written on 15th-century paper, do not appear to be substantial. B. Williams based his text of 1846 on MS 5327.

Appendix 4

An Early Medieval Building on the Site of Dartington Hall

During the excavations on the site of the second court in 1962, the foundations were discovered of an apparently rectangular building bearing little relation to the remainder of the courtyard complex.[1] Three sides of the building were clearly traced by excavation and the position of the west wall was established by the discovery of the north-west angle. This independent building, standing approximately 35 feet south of the great hall, was 20 feet wide and over 40 feet long internally. The discovery at foundation level of part of a French jug attributed to the late thirteenth century, sherds of a thirteenth-century cooking-pot, and a spoon handle of the same century suggest the occupational date for this area. A silver penny of Edward I was also found close to the south wall but it was only discovered at the point of infilling. It has been suggested that these finds need not necessarily have any connection with the building near which they were found which has been attributed to the general development of the site in the late fifteenth or early sixteenth century.[2] It has been pointed out that there was no difference between the masonry or construction technique of the rectangular building and the adjacent ranges, and that the wall width was the same. The batter, characteristic of the external walls on other parts of the site was repeated

[1] Colin Platt, 'The Excavations at Dartington Hall, 1962', *Arch. Jour.* vol. 119 (1962), 212.

[2] Ibid.

[3] Ibid.

here, and there seems to have been some sort of flagstone floor linking the south-east corner of the rectangular building with the near-by range and implying a contemporary existence, if not origin.[3]

The use of local limestone for all external walls of the Hall at whatever period they were built and the likelihood that the majority of the work was undertaken by local labour which preferred to use well-established techniques, are major factors contributing to the similarity between buildings which were undoubtedly constructed at quite different periods. Professor Scott Simpson points out in Appendix 7 that it is not possible to distinguish different periods of wall-building at Dartington, either by the type of local stone used or by the method of building, and it is likely that this applies as much to the ranges round the south court as to those round the north court.

The thickness of two walls of the rectangular building were established by excavation, but only the outer face of the north wall was revealed. The east wall was 3 feet wide and the adjacent south wall increased in width after 14 feet from a thickness of $3\frac{1}{2}$ to 4 feet. The inner walls of the adjacent south, east, and west ranges were 5 feet, $3\frac{1}{2}$ feet, and $3\frac{3}{4}$ feet wide respectively.

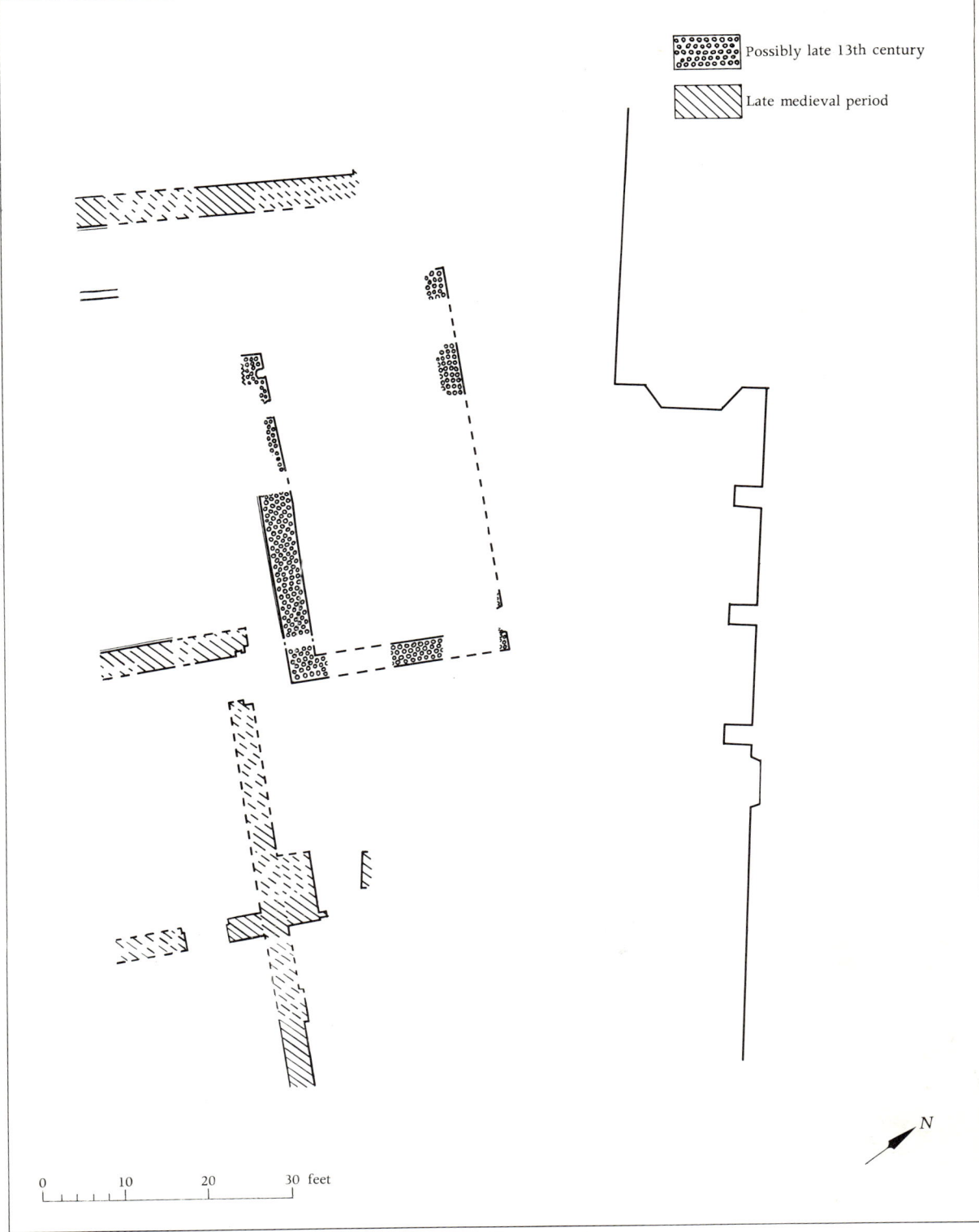

Fig. 78 Site of south court. Plan of early structure revealed by excavation

265

The flagstone floor which appears to have been laid between the rectangular building and the adjacent range of the south court may have been part of the approach to the entrance in that range. The existence of an entrance at this point is not in doubt and therefore it is rather unlikely that these two adjacent buildings would have been built at the same time, when the rectangular structure was less than 5 feet away from the entrance of the larger range and completely blocked it.

Although it is possible that the rectangular building may have been raised two or more centuries later than the earliest known occupation of this particular part of the site, the lack of co-ordination between this building and the ranges round the south court, the recovery on this site of part of a jug, sherds of pottery, and a spoon handle dating from the thirteenth century, and a coin of Edward I, suggests that this building may have been constructed as early as the last quarter of the thirteenth century and that it may have been pulled down when the majority of the south court was planned and built.

Appendix 5

Report of a Resistivity Survey at Dartington Hall

The South Court Area

This survey was undertaken in October 1963 with the object of trying to elucidate some of the problems which could not be solved during the earlier excavation of the south court because of physical obstacles or lack of time. A Martin-Clark Type 1C resistivity meter was used throughout this and the later survey undertaken on the north courtyard area.

A stable geological 'background' resistivity is necessary to obtain a clear indication of any ancient remains. At first, it seemed that this would not be the case at Dartington. The subsoil consists of tilted strata of rock of irregular profile, and the site is complicated by the fact that it has been levelled to form a terrace, partially made up by the dumping of assorted loads of material. Attention will be drawn to these factors in the report where their effect demands special caution in interpretation. Nevertheless, parts of the buildings already excavated were clearly indicated as the work proceeded, so that the reliability of the survey as a whole is probably high. This is almost certainly due in part to the wet conditions that prevailed at the time, for such conditions tend to emphasize masonry and suppress resistivity changes due to soil variation.

The Wenner probe configuration was used and, after careful trials, a probe spacing of 4 feet was chosen as the standard distance, while important points were checked at 3-feet and 2-feet intervals. Both the latter spacings were affected by unimportant variations. The main concern was to confirm or define the limits of the remains. A number of linear traverses were made at the east and west ends of the excavated site respectively. The surveys were plotted on tracing paper to the same scale as the excavation plan to facilitate direct comparison (see p. 187).

The Gallery

It was possible to confirm the western limit of the gallery, as revealed by the excavations, and the eastern limit as surmised from the offset in the terrace wall. Additional confirmation of the eastern limit was obtained by probing.

The 'Tower'

The survey of the eastern area strongly indicates that the room referred to in Dr. Platt's report as a 'tower',[1] is flanked on its north side by a room of about the same size. It possibly projects a little further west than the west wall line of the 'tower', although this suggestion is confused by possibly anomalous readings under the large tree near by. The possibility that this limited area is an outcrop of rock cannot be ruled out but, if so, it is a very singular and isolated one. However, the plan of the excavations indicates that the south-east corner of the feature was where it seems to be shown as a wall.

The indications that have led the draughtsman to interpolate the exceedingly thin length of the north wall of the 'tower' would perhaps be more creditably interpreted as a garderobe entrance associated with the 'ditch'. Perhaps the character of this 'ditch' should also be reconsidered. It is only clearly indicated on the resistivity plan at its eastern end, and it is so narrow that one could almost lean across to touch the 'tower'. This is narrower than any defensive ditch I have ever seen. Furthermore, note the thinness of the wall of the main building where the 'defensive ditch' joins it. I would very tentatively suggest that the 'ditch' is a garderobe

[1] Colin Platt, 'The Excavations at Dartington Hall, 1962', *Arch. Jour.* vol. 119 (1962), 209-10.

channel, and that we have two rooms here, built on to the main block for domestic purposes and requiring ample drainage.

West Range

Positive indication of the outer wall passing under the modern terrace was absent. Its projected line was marked by a slight fall in readings from west to east suggesting that, although the wall has probably been removed, excavation of the ground during the building construction had left a tenuous outline to be detected by the resistivity meter. The lack of remains suggested by the resistivity results is supported by the limited excavation in the north-west area of the site. The removal of the remains seems to have been particularly thorough in this area.

East Block of Gallery Building and Adjacent Area

Four linear traverses at the east end of the lawn, and an area 20 feet beyond the excavated end of the building, revealed no sign of its continuing. The outer wall of the east block was not clearly marked and must have been dismantled down to a low level; but readings rose rapidly within the building and the burnt floor area was very apparent. A sharp rise in readings away from the building along a line running north-east to south-west through the area immediately east of the gallery, and aligned quite differently from the building, is probably due to material used to build up the terrace towards its highest point above the natural ground, an effect noticed elsewhere near the outer edge of the terrace.[2] It is possible that material from the dismantled building was used in this area.

[2] It is naturally not impossible that this could mask further separate structures.

East Range

Five linear traverses were made, parallel to the path along the north side of the lawn. One was south of the path and the others were between the path and the great hall. These confirmed the outline of the rectangular building that partly underlies the path, and they also suggest the presence of a pair of parallel walls running out from the hall with centres approximately 14 and 30 feet west of the west wall of the kitchen (see p. 187). The easternmost of these was traced to the path parallel with the hall but no further, but the western one seems to continue and would link up with the wall end excavated on Dr. Platt's plan at 029.[3] It is possible that both these walls were linked with the body of the hall range.

[3] *Arch. Jour.* vol. 119 (1962), 211.

The North Courtyard Area

The whole of the lawn of the main courtyard was surveyed in April 1964 except for a few feet at the northern end which were rather encumbered by the roots of the large tree. When the readings, made at 4-feet intervals, were plotted as a contour plan, they showed a general but irregular fall from west to east. Nothing aligned at all convincingly with the present buildings. I think, therefore, that I was detecting the natural layers of Middle Devonian slate, near the surface on the western uphill side, and with an accumulation of more conductive material forming the build-up of the lawn on the eastern side. If building foundations were present, they should have interrupted this regular pattern, especially if they extended to the eastern half of the courtyard. It is possible that foundations could have been masked by the generally high readings on the east, but my impression is that there is nothing of any substance there. Some indication was obtained, however, of the east-west dividing wall, erected in the nineteenth century and removed in 1925.

ANTHONY CLARK

Appendix 6

Furnishings at Dartington Hall: 1400–1401

As the Hall was Huntingdon's principal residence, it was furnished in a manner appropriate to his position. Two inventories, made in 1400 and 1401 respectively, offer further proof, if proof was still needed, of the love of fourteenth-century magnates for rich furnishings. According to the 1400 inventory, Huntingdon's own goods at Dartington included 9 beds, each with its own set of curtains, 79 rugs and hangings, 40 cushions, and 8 carpets, as well as a tapestry in the great hall, books, armour, and kitchen equipment. Further inquisitions relating to the earl's goods have also survived but only these two inventories specifically refer to his property at the Hall. A third inquisition refers to a locked chest found by the escheator in the church at Dartington containing goods belonging to Huntingdon, but no further details are given.[1]

[1] P.R.O. Chancery Inq. C 145/278, no. 26.

The principal inventory is by no means a complete one, for there are items in the second list which do not tally with those in the first one. Nor is any mention made of tables, chairs, benches, or ornaments, other than those maintained in the chapel. It is hardly surprising that Huntingdon's furnishings have not survived the vicissitudes of nearly six centuries but timber insertions which would carry the hooks for a tapestry were found in 1933 above the fireplace in the great hall. It is possible that some fragments of contemporary stained glass, either from the Hall or the church, have survived at Weare Gifford Hall near Bideford where four badges have been inserted in a window in the great hall showing Huntingdon's wheat-ears enlaced with the gold letters I and E—the initials of John Holand and his wife Elizabeth.[2]

Inquisition taken at Dertyngton on Monday next before the feast of St. Mathias the Apostle I Henry IV [24 February 1400] ... that there are on the day of the present Inquisition within the manor of Dertyngton divers goods and chattels which were of the same late Earl of Huntingdon ... namely one bed of silk embroidered with bulls and divers other arms with iii curtains of tarteryn covered with gold foil with bulls, with two rugs[3] [tapeta] of tapestry [tapiserie] with bulls and viii cushions of silk embroidered with bulls. Also one bed of baudekyn[4] embroidered with the arms of England and Hainault with iii curtains of red sendell. Also one bed of red tarteryn embroidered with letters with a curtain of red tarteryn belonging to the same bed. Also xix white rugs of Arace of parrots [papeiays]. Also xiiii rugs of red tapestry with the arms of the same late Earl of Huntingdon and of the lady his wife and with the livery of the same late Earl, namely wheat ears [wheteneris] with ii 'festienys'.[5] Also xii rugs of blue tapestry and of the arms of the same late Earl of Huntingdon. Also ii long cushions of red cloth of gold. Also ii long cushions of red velvet and viii short cushions of the same cloth. Also viii short cushions of red cloth of gold and xii cushions of white cloth of gold. Also iiii long white cushions of white Damask cloth embroidered with M's with golden crowns and ii short cushions of the same suit. Also ii long cushions of green Damask cloth. Also i cushion of black Damask cloth. Also iii golden rugs of Arace. Also i long cushion of old damask. Also i hanging [coster] of tapestry for the Hall. Also i velvet covering for the lady's chariot [quadriga] i 'pal'[6] of white and red. . . . Also iiii green rugs of tapestry. Also vii rugs of white Worsted embroidered with black Ragged Staves. Also iii curtains with i valance [travers] of white tarteryn of the same work of Ragged staves. Also i bed of baudekyn with iii curtains of red tarteryn. Also xi old rugs of linsey-woolsey [stamyn] of white and blue i 'woun . . .'. Also viii old . . . of red worsted. Also i bed of green baudekyn with a canopy [celer] and iii curtains of green tarteryn. Also viii 'carpes'.[7] Also i old bed torn [dilacerat] of baudekyn with iii curtains of blue tarteryn. Also i other old bed of Norfolk with iii old curtains of 'card'[8] Also an old bed of red worsted embroidered with iii curtains of the same suit. Also iii white Irish mantles. Also i horse-trapper of red and black buckram. Also an old bed of red worsted embroidered with oak leaves with iii curtains of tarteryn of the same suit and vii old rugs of Worsted of the same suit. Also i old back-cloth [doser] and ii side-hangings [coster] of the same suit abovesaid of oak leaves. Also i old covering of blue cloth for the lord's chariot. Also i covering for a bed of silk 'pal' of red and white. Also i missal, i antiphonal with a psalter contained within it and i gradual. Also i set of vestments of red baudekyn and ii altar coverings of the same suit and i frontal of baudekyn and ii towels for the altar and ii curtains of red tarteryn and iiii surplices. Also viii table cloths [nappa] and six hand towels and v cloths [savenappes]. Also ii silver bowls with i silver washbasin [lavator]. Also i pot and i covered salt of silver. Also one cup with a cover of silver gilt. Also ii other silver cups, vi silver spoons. Also vi plates [disci] and iiii saucers of silver. Also iiii chests bound with iron and another chest bound with iron. Also i travelling cheste [trussigcoffre]. Also ii jousting saddles with ii head pieces [testeres] for horse. Also ii helms, vi gauntlets [maynfers] and iii pairs of plate gloves, vii vambraces[9] and ii pairs of rerebraces[10] and one pair of poleyns[11] and xvii vamplates.[12] Also in the kitchen iiii great standard pots of bronze and v smaller standard pots of bronze and vi small bronze pots and v very small pots [olliole] of bronze. Also ii great cooking vessels [cacobi] and ii small cooking vessels and iiii great ladles of copper and iiii small ladles of bronze and iiii frying pans [frixor] and iii great griddles of iron and i old griddle of iron, vi iron rakes, xix iron jacks [verna] and v leaden pipes for gutters for the Hall. Also v great mortars, xiii dozen of tin plates. Also i 'pollax' of copper.[13] Also ii mattresses and i canvas [canevaces] . . . .[14]

The second inquisition was made in 1401 when some of Huntingdon's furnishings from Dartington were granted to Henry IV's son, Humphrey. The grant included

three cloths of gold worked with oaks, six red rugs worked with tapestry of the arms of the earl and his wife, a bed with a canopy and tester of red tarteryn[15] embroidered with letters with three curtains of red tarteryn, a bed of silk with a canopy and three curtains of blue tarteryn, a trapping of red velvet embroidered with stags, a coverlet for a car palled with white, black and red velvet, a bed of silk with a white and red canopy with curtains of the same suit, a canopy with a tester of red embroidered worsted and three old rugs of red worsted embroidered with oak leaves, in the hands of William Hody, late escheator in the county of Devon, and all other parcels of money and moveable goods late of the said John within his manor of Dertyngton on the day of his forfeiture and not granted by the king to anyone else. . . .[16]

Appendix 7

The Building Stones of Dartington Hall

This report contains an account of all the various sorts of stone that have been used either in the construction of the main fabric of the buildings or in their ornamentation. Where possible the source quarries of the different types of stone have been identified, and attention has been drawn to the preference of the builders for different sorts of stone at different periods in construction and reconstruction. Some conclusions are drawn about the history of the use of different sorts of stone, and some points of particular interest are mentioned. However, the object of this report is not to discuss historical or architectural matters, though it is to be hoped that the data contained in it may be of some interest to those who are versed in them.

In all periods of the construction of the buildings which are preserved today, natural stone has been used for the load-bearing walls, for paving, for roofing, and for ornamental features such as fireplaces. Except

---

[2] A. W. B. Messenger, 'A Survey of the Heraldry at the Hall, Weare Gifford, Devon', *Trans. Devon Assoc.* vol. 75 (1943), 179, 205.

[3] Mats on tables and floors or hangings on walls.

[4] A bed with a coverlet and perhaps a back cloth and canopy of baudekyn, a richly patterned silk material.

[5] Possibly 'fusillys', a heraldic bearing in the form of an elongated lozenge or 'lusuenys', a lozenge.

[6] Possibly 'pallum', a piece of rich material, or 'paly', i.e. striped.

[7] Presumably carpets, i.e. thick materials for use on tables or floors.

[8] A coarse unpatterned woven material thought to have been of linen, used in England between about 1250 and 1450.

[9] A defence for the lower arm.

[10] A defence for the upper arm and shoulder.

[11] Plate defence for the knees.

[12] A hand defence attached to a lance.

[13] It is difficult to understand the use of a pole-axe of copper unless it was intended for ceremonial purposes only.

[14] P.R.O. Chancery Inq. C 145/278, no. 37.

[15] An unpatterned material, apparently of silk, current in England between about 1350 and 1550.

[16] *Cal. Pat. Rolls 1399–1401*, 439.

for concrete lintels to some modern doors and windows opened in the ancient walls, fire-bricks in some modern hearths, and a few brick partitioning walls, man-made building materials are virtually absent.

A particularly noteworthy feature is that all external walls at whatever period they have been built are of the same materials, used in the same way as in the earliest fourteenth-century construction. These walls are built of the local limestone in irregular untrimmed blocks as they came from the quarry, all sizes of stone being used, the small pieces placed between the larger to fill gaps. Selected large stones are used at corners and these may be slightly dressed to give two faces at right angles, but otherwise very little trimming of the blocks has been undertaken.

There are six sorts of building stone to be considered. These are:

1. The local limestone, which has been quarried on the estate from earliest times.
2. Beer stone, the medieval freestone.
3. Oolitic freestone, used for sixteenth-century and later door and window jambs, sills, lintels, etc., and for restoration of Beer stone structures.
4. Slate, used for paving and roofing.
5. Dartmoor granite, used only for a few corbels by the medieval builders.
6. Marble used for paving and fireplaces.

The Local Limestone

This is a very hard, dense limestone of dark bluish colour when freshly broken but developing a characteristic grey colour on weathered surfaces. There is considerable variation in the stone from different quarries and in the different beds within a single quarry. Some of the stone is quite uniform and fine grained, some is highly fossiliferous containing corals and stromatoporoids. It is always thoroughly re-crystallized, and this is the explanation of its density and impermeability. For the same reason, it will take a good polish and can be used as an ornamental stone. The Ashburton marble, referred to below under the heading 'Marbles' is identical with some of the local stone which has been used in the walls of the Dartington buildings.

The limestone is of Middle and Upper Devonian age, and constitutes a formation several hundred feet thick which extends over a large area in this part of Devonshire, forming Berry Head and much of Torquay as well as occurring as far east as Chudleigh and as far west as Plymouth. In the lower part of the limestone, of Middle Devonian age, the limestone tends to occur in thin beds alternating with slate. These thin beds yield tabular blocks or flags which have often been used for paving.

All the main structural walls throughout the buildings of the north court, and presumably originally of the south court also, are built of undressed blocks of local limestone. Dressed blocks are seen in the quoins of some rebuilt walls, as in the medieval kitchen, and in the modern additions connected with the outside staircase of the entrance block and the entrance to the barn on its south side, but otherwise not at all. It is not possible to distinguish different periods of wall-building by the stone used or by the method of building. Thin tabular limestone blocks have been used to terminate the weatherings of the buttresses of the great hall so as to produce a slight overhang.

Limestone flags were probably extensively used for paving. Examples can still be seen in the porch below the clock-tower, at the entrance to the marble hall in the upper residential block, and in the treads of the external staircase at the end of the west range.

The quarries from which the local limestone was won are all within the estate. The biggest of these, and perhaps the oldest, is at Shinner's Bridge. Other important quarries are two in Symon's Tree Wood—one at its north end and another by the stream below Shinner's Bridge—and the one, now used as a dump, known as Pit Park Quarry. Some of the rock from the last-named quarry was highly dolomitic and coarse grained. There is also an old overgrown quarry containing very massive limestone due east of the Hall in Hill Park. Thinner bedded, more flaggy limestones can be seen in the small quarry which is still occasionally worked, at the bend of the road south of the Hall.

A geological account of these quarries is given in a paper by A. J. Jukes-Browne entitled 'The Devonian Limestones of Dartington, and their equivalents at Torquay' published in the *Proceedings of the Geologists' Association*, volume 24 (1913), 14–32.

The Beer Stone

This is a white limestone belonging to the lower part of the Middle Chalk formation which occurs in a limited area near Beer in east Devon. It is a particularly hard variety of chalk consisting largely of small shell fragments.

All the Beer stone that has been used in the buildings dates back to the sixteenth century or to the original structure built by the earl of Huntingdon. While in interior work it has remained very well preserved, where it has been exposed to the weather it has crumbled badly and has had to be extensively restored. A characteristic cavernous weathering makes it possible to recognize this stone from a distance in certain places where it is not readily accessible.

The following is a list of the more important structures of Beer stone:

West range
All the doorway arches from the court.
(There is some restoration in oolite.)
Six medieval windows in the six apartments at the north end of the range.
(All heavily restored in oolite.)
Coping-stones of stair turret roof.

Porch tower
Porch archways, ribs and carvings of vaulting.
All windows. (Much restored in oolite.)
Fireplace in room over porch.
Steps of spiral staircase in turret—the only original steps remaining.
Doorway arch from staircase on to tower roof.
Parapet to tower roof, except battlements.
Coping-stones of stair turret roof.

Great hall
All doorway arches.
Fireplace.
Internal window arches.
(Some restoration in oolite.)

Lower residential block
Windows facing north court on ground floor and first floor (not second-floor window).
East ground-floor window facing south court.
First-floor window facing south court (with oolite restoration).

Kitchen
Arches of niches on either side of both fireplaces.

South court
Arches of windows overlooking supposed tournament ground.
Pedestals to arches seen in 1962 excavations.

The Oolitic Freestone

This type of limestone, consisting largely of small spherical bodies and thus having the appearance of fish roe when examined closely, is called oolite. Oolitic limestone of Middle Jurassic age has provided many famous freestones from quarries which have been worked from medieval times in Somerset, Gloucestershire, Oxfordshire, Rutland, and Lincolnshire. There are distinct differences of colour and grain in the stone from different areas, but the differences between some of the stones from widely separated quarries are often extremely subtle. I have not been able to determine the undoubted provenance of any of the oolites of Dartington Hall though they are all certainly from the Middle Jurassic of some of the counties mentioned. I have, however, noticed three apparently different types of stone which I describe below. Further research might show that the differences are due to different sources which might perhaps ultimately be identified.

Type 1: Fine-grained, very uniform, densely oolitic limestone, rather pale in colour, showing very little evidence of bedding, containing few shell fragments. Often with calcite veins. Possibly Bath stone.

Type 2: Slightly shelly, medium-grained oolite generally showing traces of bedding by streaky concentrations of shelly fragments. Colour similar to Type 1. No calcite veins.

Type 3: Fine- to medium-grained oolite of uniform texture. Warm brownish colour. With calcite veins. Very similar to Type 1 except in colour—but richer colour may be due to lack of weathering.

Type 1 oolite has been used in the great hall for the exterior window arches and their mullions, tracery, etc., and also for the restorations to the internal window arches. Repairs have clearly been made in the tracery, etc. of the external windows, and the new stone is somewhat yellower in colour than the old, but as I have been able to detect no other difference this may be due to lack of weathering.

The same stone has been used for the string-course above the windows and the associated gargoyles and carved bosses of the lower residential block. It has also been used for the battlements on the parapets of the great hall and the porch tower, and for the jambs of the doors into the spiral staircase of the tower from the parapet walk. The windows of the kitchen and its external door on the south side are again of Type 1.

Outside the south range, this stone is only seen in the restorations to the Beer stone work in the west range and in an imitation medieval window, a copy of those of the west range, which has been provided for a ground-floor room on the outside of the east range. This imitation is entirely of oolite.

Type 2 oolite has been used for two windows on the ground floor of the east range, one facing into the court and one facing outwards. It has also been used for all the windows in the lower residential block which are not of Beer stone. That is: on the ground floor, the western one of the two windows facing south; on the second floor, all four windows. The first-floor windows facing north and south are of Beer stone restored with Type 2 oolite. I have not been able to examine the window facing east.

Type 3 oolite is confined to the upper residential block and has been used for its Venetian windows on the first floor as for all the other windows facing south and east and for six windows facing west. It is also used for the garden porch and steps, and for the pillars of the adjacent shelter.

Slate

Two kinds of slate have been used in the buildings. These are:

1. Local slate of Middle Devonian age. 2. Cornish slate of Upper Devonian age.

The local slate occurs on the estate in the immediate vicinity of the Hall and elsewhere. However, good-quality hard stone yielding large slabs is only obtainable in a few places, and the quality improves with depth. No quarries appear to have been opened on the estate, probably because better stone could always be obtained from deep pre-existing quarries. Thus it is known that Huntingdon got slate from an existing quarry at Staverton, and it is probable that any later needs for slate will have been supplied from the same quarry.

The local slate is of a dark blue-black colour. It is rather soft for roofing and is weak when cleaved thin. Though it was probably used for this purpose in medieval times, none of the existing roofs are covered with it. However, it was probably much used for paving, and floors of small square slates were uncovered in the excavation of the south court site in 1962.

The Cornish slate is a splendid roofing material with a pleasant greenish-grey colour, owing its hardness to metamorphism by the Bodmin Moor granite. It is now the only type of slate to be seen on the roofs of Dartington Hall. A number of quarries have been worked in the past, all in the country between Camelford and Tintagel. The best known, and by far the largest, is Delabole, and it is from this only remaining working quarry that the slates for the roof of the great hall and the barn have come. Judging by the small size of the slates, and the way the roofs have been secured by concreting them over, the oldest roofs surviving today are those of the entrance block and the south part of the upper residential block.

Granite

The characteristic 'giant granite' of Dartmoor with its enormous feldspar phenocrysts was used by the medieval builders for the row of corbels which support the parapet walk where it overhangs the eastern end of the lower residential block, and also for the huge corbels which supported the hoods over the fires in the kitchen. From their battered appearance, the left-hand corbel of the east wall fireplace and the right-hand corbel of the south wall fireplace are original. The other two are in such perfect condition that they are replacements. Granite has been used for the flight of steps (1960) leading up to the porch tower entrance. This does not appear to be a Dartmoor granite. Another example of granite used in recent improvements is to be found in the hearth of the great hall fireplace.

Marble

The ground-floor hall in the upper residential block as it is today has a marble floor which was probably laid in the eighteenth century. Two sorts of stone, one white and the other grey veined with white, have been used. At the door there is some paving of local limestone. While I have made no attempt to see all the rooms which may contain marble fireplaces, I note here one or two examples which may be of interest. In the first-floor rooms at the south end of the west range, there are very similar fireplaces in local Devonshire marble. While there are very many places where rock can be obtained which cannot be distinguished from that which the fireplaces are made of (including some of the quarries on the estate), it is almost certain that this particular stone came from the quarry which is still worked at Ashburton. It is possible to say this because, as with slate quarries, large slabs of good quality can only be obtained from a few places, and in the case of the marble there are colour differences by which the stone from particular quarries can be recognized.

Also worthy of note is the marble fireplace in the present first-floor dining-room. This is a serpentine breccia with black fragments set in a green matrix—it is possibly a variety of the Verde antico from Greece. The same stone is seen in the fireplace of the morning-room.

Though not of marble, it is convenient to record here that the fireplace in the library, which is modelled on that of the great hall, is made of a fine oolitic freestone.

Some Miscellaneous Points

The central wooden post in the ground-floor room of the entrance block stands on a rough stone pedestal. This is a large piece of local Devonian limestone. Since dressed freestone has not been used, this was probably inserted as a makeshift expedient on cutting away the bottom of the post either because it had been damaged or perhaps in connection with changing the level of the floor.

There are three windows which at first sight appear to be made of oolitic freestone, but which on closer examination can be seen to be imitations in concrete. These are:

1. The window facing south to the ground-floor room at the south end of the east range on the court side.
2. The window facing east at the north-east corner of the south range on the ground floor.
3. The window immediately above the last on the first floor.

Conclusions

The medieval builders of Dartington Hall used only one kind of stone, the Beer stone, when carved or shaped stone was required. Beer stone was again used in the sixteenth century when the lower residential block was improved. The use of oolitic freestone came later. It may be presumed that it was employed in a separate phase of building in the eighteenth century, when the great hall received its outer window arches, with their mullions and tracery, and when the present string-course and the battlements above were built. It is of some interest, however, that while the battlements of the porch tower parapet are similar to those round the hall, the parapet itself is of Beer stone ashlar work on the tower, but of rough local limestone round the hall. It is probable that repairs in oolite to the medieval windows of the west range were carried out at this time. All this work was in Type 1 oolite.

At some later date, oolite from another source (Type 2) was acquired for windows in the east range, and some was also used for new windows, and repairs to old ones, in the lower residential block.

Finally, in the twentieth century, the upper residential block was renovated and received its present windows, garden porch, and shelter. In this work, Type 3 stone was used.

The absence of any sign of restorations in oolite to the arches of the south court suggests strongly that at least this part of the court was already a ruin at the end of the sixteenth century. (Incidentally, no sign of oolite was noticed in the 1962 excavation of the south court.) The possibility suggests itself that the Beer stone employed in the new windows of the lower residential block in the sixteenth-century reconstruction may have been taken from the ruined south court.

SCOTT SIMPSON

Appendix 8

Masons Marks at Dartington Hall

Group 1	Cross	Group 3	Reverse z
✗	Screens passage 3 arch 5 course (L)	⊂	Screens passage - 2 arch 5 course (L)
✗	Screens passage between 3 and 4 arches 3 course	⊂	Screens passage - 3 arch 5 course (R)
✗ ✗ ✗	West range. 1st group of lodgings - upper r.h. arch 1,2,4 courses (L)	⊂	Screens passage - 4 arch 6 course (R)
Group 2	Cross with hook	Group 4	Other marks
⊣ ⊣	Porch tower-inner arch 6 and 7 courses (L)	⋀	Screens passage - 1 arch 5 course (R)
✗ ✗ ✗	Great hall-fireplace 2, 3 and 4 courses (R)	⅀	Screens passage - 4 arch 3 course (L)
⊢	Screens passage-1 arch 3 course (L)		
⋈	Screens passage-1 arch 2 course (L)	↑	Screens passage - between 3 and 4 arches 4 course
⋁	Screens passage-3 arch 3 course (L)		
✗	Great hall-fireplace 1 course (R)	✓	Porch tower - stairs to roof underside of 15 step from roof

List of Plates

Frontispiece Dartington Hall. Hall range from the north court. *Humphrey Sutton*

Page 2 Dartington Hall. North court from the entrance passage: 1925

5 Dartington Hall. Porch tower: 1925

6 Dartington Hall. Interior of great hall: 1925

7 Dartington Hall. West range from the north court: 1925

8 Dartington Hall. East range from the rear: 1925
Dartington Hall. Reconstruction of the roof of the great hall: 1932
Dartington Hall. Restoration of the private house and great hall: 1933
Dartington Hall. Private house, great hall and kitchen from the stone terrace. *Chaplin Jones*

9 Dartington Hall. The Hall and tournament ground from the upper terrace

10 Dartington Hall. The gardens from the roof of the great hall. *Chaplin Jones*

11 Dorothy and Leonard Elmhirst. *Bryan Heseltine*

12 Dartington. The deer-park wall looking towards Staverton. *Humphrey Sutton*

25 Edward, the Black Prince: 1377–80. Canterbury Cathedral. *National Portrait Gallery*
Joan, the 'Fair Maid of Kent': *c.* 1380. Catalogue of Benefactors of St. Albans Abbey. B.M. MS. Cott. Nero D. VII, f. 7v
John, duke of Lancaster. Early 15th century. Ante-chapel, All Souls College, Oxford

26 Berkhamsted Castle. Remains of motte, encircling bailey wall, earthworks and moats. *Aerofilms Ltd.*

27 The Peasants' Revolt. John Ball and Wat Tyler leading the insurgents, 1381. *c.* 1460–80. Jehan Froissart, *Chroniques de France et d'Angleterre*; B.M. MS. Royal 18, E. I, f. 165v

29 Richard II: *c.* 1390–95. Artist unknown. Westminster Abbey. *The National Gallery*

32 English ships arriving at Lisbon in 1385 to support the Portuguese against Castile. Late 15th century. Jean de Wavrin, *Chronique d'Angleterre*; B.M. MS. Royal 14, E. IV, f. 195

33 João I entertaining the duke of Lancaster, 1386. Late 15th century. Jean de Wavrin, *Chronique d'Angleterre*; B.M. MS. Royal 14, E. IV, f. 244v

34 Joust between John Holand and Regnault de Roye, 1387. Late 15th century. Jean de Wavrin, *Chronique d'Angleterre*; B.M. MS. Royal 14, E. IV, f. 293v

35 The siege of Ribadavia, 1386. Late 15th century. Jean de Wavrin, *Chronique d'Angleterre*; B.M. MS. Royal 14, E. IV, f. 281v

41 The arrest of the duke of Gloucester, 1397. *c.* 1460–80. Jean Froissart, *Chroniques de France et d'Angleterre*; B.M. MS. Royal 18, E. II, f. 328v

42 Royal retinues watching Edward III paying homage to Philip VI of France, 1331. Late 14th century. *Chronique de France*; B.M. MS. Royal 20, C. VII, f. 72v

45 Richard II prepares to leave for Ireland, 1399. *c.* 1460–80. Jehan Froissart, *Chroniques de France et d'Angleterre*; B.M. MS. Royal 18, E. II, f. 382r

47 The Seal of John Holand, 1st duke of Exeter: 1399. Engraving from Sandford, *Genealogical History of the Kings and Queens of Great Britain* (1707) 214

48 Richard II at Conway Castle, 1399. Early 15th century. Creton, *The Deposition of Richard II*; B.M. MS. Harley 1319, f. 19b
The dukes of Exeter and Surrey leave for Chester, 1399. Early 15th century. *Ibid.*, f. 25

49 Henry Bolingbroke receives the dukes of Exeter and Surrey at Chester Castle, 1399. Early 15th century. *Ibid.*, f. 30b
Henry Bolingbroke delivers Richard II to the citizens of London, 1399. Early 15th century. *Ibid.*, f. 53b

50 The Holand rebellion, 1400. *c.* 1460–80. Jehan Froissart, *Chroniques de France et d'Angleterre*; B.M. MS. Royal 18, E. II, f. 411v

52 Pleshey Castle: *c.* 1803. Richard Gough, *The History and Antiquities of Pleshey* (1803) 158. *Essex Record Office*

54 The jousts of St. Inglevert, 1390. *c.* 1460–80. Jehan Froissart, *Chroniques de France et d'Angleterre*; B.M. MS. Royal 18, E. II, f. 50v

56 Elizabeth Holand, 1st duchess of Exeter: *c.* 1425. Burford Church, Shropshire. *National Monuments Record*

57 Elizabeth Holand and Sir John Cornwaille: mid 15th century. Window formerly in Ampthill Church. Engraving from Sandford, *Genealogical History of the Kings and Queens of Great Britain* (1707) 259

All illustrations are taken from the collection of the Dartington Hall Trustees unless otherwise stated

59 The siege of St. James de Beuvron, Normandy, 1418. 1487. *Chronique de France*; B.M. MS. Royal 20, E. VI, f. 20

60 The Tower of London: *c.* 1500. *Poems of Charles d'Orléans*, B.M. MS. Royal 16, F. ii, f. 73

62 The seal of John Holand, earl of Huntingdon: 1436–44. B.M. D.C.G. 265
The signature of John Holand, earl of Huntingdon: *c.* 1432. B.M. Cott. Vespasian F. VII, f. 49v

63 John Holand, 3rd duke of Exeter: *c.* 1447. St. Peter ad Vincula, Tower of London. *Ministry of Public Building and Works*

64 Henry VI and Queen Margaret of Anjou receiving a book from the earl of Shrewsbury: 1445. B.M. MS. Royal 15, E. VI, f. 2b

67 The seal of Henry Holand, 4th duke of Exeter: 1447–57 or 1460–1. Ashmolean Museum, Oxford. *Ashmolean Museum*
The battle of Barnet, 1471. Late 15th century. Ghent MS. 236, Bibliothek Universiteit, Ghent

68 The duchess of Exeter and Sir Thomas St. Leger: *c.* 1483. St. George's Chapel, Windsor Castle

70 Panoramic view of lower Dart valley showing Dartington Hall in upper left-hand corner: *c.* 1540. B.M. MS. Cott. Augustus I. vol. 1, art. 39

76 Sir Arthur Champernowne, d. 1578. Artist unknown. David Champernowne, Esq.

77 Gawen Champernowne, d. 1592. Artist unknown. David Champernowne, Esq.

82 Dartington Hall. The north court from the east: 1734. By S. & N. Buck, *Antiquities*, vol. 2, no. 19.

84 Arthur Champernowne, d. 1766. By Thomas Hudson. University of Exeter
His wife, Jane Champernowne. By Thomas Hudson. University of Exeter
Dartington Hall and church from the south: *c.* 1800. By R. H. Froude.
Dartington Hall. The entrance block and north end of west range: 1805. By G. Saunders. Exeter City Libraries

86 Arthur Champernowne, d. 1819. By William Brockedon. David Champernowne, Esq.
Louisa Champernowne, d. 1870. By William Brockedon. David Champernowne, Esq.

87 Dartington Hall. The north court from the entrance block: 1797. By T. Bonner for R. Polwhele, *History of Devonshire*. Exeter City Libraries

89 Dartington Hall. The south front of the Hall: 1839. Artist unknown. Exeter City Libraries

91 Dartington Hall. The great hall and porch tower from the north court: *c.* 1870
Dartington Hall. West range from the north court: *c.* 1870

92 Dartington Hall. Private house and great hall from the south: *c.* 1870
Dartington Hall. Private house. Interior of the morning room: *c.* 1870. *Miss C. E. Champernowne*
Dartington Hall. West range, great hall and kitchen from the east: *c.* 1900

94 Dartington Hall. North court from the entrance passage

97 Dartington Hall. Porch tower vault. The badge of Richard II. *Humphrey Sutton*

100 Aerial view of Dartington Hall. *Aerofilms Ltd.*

105 Sheriff Hutton Castle, Yorkshire: 1382–after 1402. *A. H. Emery*
Carlisle Castle, Cumberland. Outer gatehouse: 1378–83. *Ministry of Public Building and Works*
Cockermouth Castle, Cumberland. Inner entrance range: 1383–5. Kitchen tower: *c.* 1388. Outer court: before 1408. *Aerofilms Ltd.*
Dunstanburgh Castle, Northumberland. Gatehouse of 1313–6 converted into keep: 1380–3. *Ministry of Public Building and Works*

106 Workington Hall, Cumberland. Lower ground floor of pele-tower: 1380. *National Monuments Record*
Carisbrooke Castle, Isle of Wight. Gatehouse of 1335–7 heightened in 1380–4. *Ministry of Public Building and Works*

107 Cooling Castle, Kent: 1381–*c.* 85. *Aerofilms Ltd.*
Amberley Castle, Sussex: 1377–*c.* 83. *Aerofilms Ltd.*

108 Halnaker House, Sussex. Entrance front: *c.* 1380. *A. H. Emery*
Scotney Castle, Kent. *c.* 1378–80. *British Travel Association*
Hever Castle, Kent. Gatehouse: 1383. *The Times*

109 Shute Barton, Devon. Residential ranges: *c.* 1385–90. *Country Life*

110 Lumley Castle, Co. Durham: 1389–*c.* 92. *Aerofilms Ltd.*

111 Tabley Old Hall, Cheshire. Main truss of great hall: *c.* 1380. Taken in 1923. *Country Life*
Tabley Old Hall, Cheshire. Taken in 1968. *A. H. Emery*

275

Shirburn Castle, Oxfordshire: 1377.
National Monuments Record
North Elmham Saxon Cathedral, Norfolk.
Residential conversion: 1387.
Ministry of Public Building and Works

113 Caldicot Castle, Monmouthshire. Gatehouse: c. 1388. *National Monuments Record*
Warwick Castle. Guy's Tower: 1394. *National Monuments Record*
Palace of Westminster. Great Hall: 1394–1401. *Ministry of Public Building and Works*

114 Kenilworth Castle, Warwickshire. Great hall: 1389–93. *Ministry of Public Building and Works*
Scarborough Castle, Yorkshire. Hall and residential block: 1396–1400. *National Monuments Record*
Penshurst Place, Kent. Mid 14th-century manor with one of the additional defensive towers: 1392. *National Monuments Record by permission of Lord de l'Isle*
Carisbrooke Castle, Isle of Wight. Upper residential block: 1385–97. *Central Office of Information*
New College, Oxford. Great quadrangle: 1380–6. *Ministry of Public Building and Works*

115 Winchester College, Hampshire. Middle gate from Chamber Court: 1387–94. *Central Office of Information*

118 Bolton Castle, Yorkshire: c. 1378–99. *Aerofilms Ltd.*

119 Brancepeth Castle, Co. Durham. South front: c. 1391–8. *National Monuments Record*

120 Raby Castle, Co. Durham. Neville gateway and west front: 1378–c. 90. *National Monuments Record*

121 Bodiam Castle, Sussex. Entrance and east frontages: c. 1385–c. 90. *A. F. Kersting*

122 Penrith Castle, Cumberland: 1397. *Aerofilms Ltd.*
Wressell Castle, Yorkshire. South front: c. 1380–90. *A. H. Emery*

123 Wingfield Castle, Suffolk. Entrance front: 1385. *A. F. Kersting*

124 Farleigh Hungerford Castle, Somerset. Site of gatehouse and inner court: c. 1370–83. *Ministry of Public Building and Works*

125 Warkworth Castle, Northumberland. Tower-house: c. 1377–84. *Ministry of Public Building and Works*

126 Baginton Castle, Warwickshire. Foundations of west front: c. 1390–5. *A. H. Emery*
Wardour Castle, Wiltshire. Tower-house: 1393. *Ministry of Public Building and Works*

127 Donnington Castle, Berkshire. Gatehouse: 1386. *Ministry of Public Building and Works*
Saltwood Castle, Kent. Gatehouse: c. 1382. *Country Life*

128 Dartington Hall, Devonshire. Great hall, entrance porch and lower residential block: 1388–c. 1400. West range: c. 1393–1400.

129 Howden Manor, Yorkshire. Great hall and entrance porch: 1388–1405. *A. H. Emery*

130 Norrington Manor, Wiltshire. Great hall: c. 1380. *National Monuments Record*

131 Kenilworth Castle, Warwickshire. Great hall and residential range: 1389–93. *Ministry of Public Building and Works*
Portchester Castle, Hampshire. Great hall, entrance porch and lower residential block: 1396–9. *Ministry of Public Building and Works*

132 Winchester College, Hampshire: 1387–1401. Engraving by David Loggan, 1675. *Courtauld Institute of Art*

134 Warwick Castle. Caesar's Tower: c. 1370–85. Gatehouse and barbican: c. 1360–9. Guy's Tower: c. 1390–4. *A. F. Kersting*

135 Kenilworth Castle, Warwickshire. Windows of great hall: 1389–93. *A. H. Emery*
Tower of London. Byward Tower; painted wall decoration: c. 1380, with superimposed figures: c. 1400.
Ministry of Public Building and Works

138 Dartington Hall. Entrance passageway from the north court. *Humphrey Sutton*

139 Dartington Hall. Entrance block from the forecourt

140 Dartington Hall. Entrance block from the north court

141 Dartington Hall. Entrance block. Principal ground-floor room. *Humphrey Sutton*

142 Dartington Hall. Entrance block. Roof of larger first-floor room. *Humphrey Sutton*

147 Dartington Hall. North court from the entrance block showing part of west range, hall range with porch tower, and kitchen block. *Humphrey Sutton*

148 Dartington Hall. North court from the roof of the great hall

149 Dartington Hall. Porch tower from the north court. *Humphrey Sutton*

150 Dartington Hall. Kitchen, lower residential block, porch tower and great hall from the north court. *Humphrey Sutton*

152 Dartington Hall. Porch tower. Vaulted porch opening into screens passage

153 Dartington Hall. Great hall. Screens passage towards the south court. *Humphrey Sutton*

154 Dartington Hall. Great hall towards the dais
155 Dartington Hall. Great hall towards the dais: 1925
Dartington Hall. Great hall. Corbel on north side supporting roof brace
156 Dartington Hall. Great hall. Windows from the north court. *Humphrey Sutton*
Dartington Hall. Great hall. South side
157 Dartington Hall. Great hall. Fireplace
158 Dartington Hall. Great hall towards the screens passage
159 Dartington Hall. Great hall. Dais door. *Humphrey Sutton*
Penshurst Place, Kent. Stairs to upper residential block. *A. F. Kersting*
162 Dartington Hall. Great hall towards the dais: 1805. By G. Saunders. Exeter City Libraries
Dartington Hall. Great hall towards the screens passage: 1805. By G. Saunders. Exeter City Libraries
163 Dartington Hall. Great hall and lower residential block: 1805. Longitudinal section by G. Saunders. Exeter City Libraries
167 Dartington Hall. Great hall. Screens-passage arches to buttery, kitchen passage and pantry. *Humphrey Sutton*
Dartington Hall. Tower porch. Inner face of outer arch
Dartington Hall. Great hall. Screens-passage arch to upper rooms of lower residential block. *Humphrey Sutton*
169 Dartington Hall. Lower residential block. First-floor room towards the north court
171 Dartington Hall. Kitchen and hall range from the east
Dartington Hall. Kitchen from the south
172 Dartington Hall. Kitchen. Interior showing the adjacent fireplaces. *Humphrey Sutton*
173 Dartington Hall. Kitchen. Interior walling. *Humphrey Sutton*
174 Dartington Hall. Kitchen. East fireplace: 1805. By G. Saunders. Exeter City Libraries
Dartington Hall. Lower residential block and west wall of kitchen: 1805. By G. Saunders. Exeter City Libraries
Dartington Hall. Kitchen and offices with wall screening them from the north court. *Humphrey Sutton*
176 Dartington Hall. Private house. Marble hall
178 Dartington Hall. Upper residential block (private house) and great hall from the tournament ground
Dartington Hall. Private house. Marble hall from dais door of great hall
Dartington Hall. Private house. Ground-floor library
182 Dartington Hall. Private house. Morning-room: *c.* 1870. *Miss C. E. Champernowne*
Dartington Hall. Private house. Morning-room
Dartington Hall. Private house. Morning-room: *c.* 1870. *Miss C. E. Champernowne*
Dartington Hall. Private house. Morning-room.
183 Dartington Hall. Private house. First-floor study: *c.* 1870. *Miss C. E. Champernowne*
Dartington Hall. Private house. Inner hall: *c.* 1870. *Miss C. E. Champernowne*
Dartington Hall. Private house. First-floor study
Dartington Hall. Private house. Inner hall
185 Dartington Hall. South court. Inner face of south wall of gallery
186 Dartington Hall. South court. Detail of gallery window opening
188 Dartington Hall. South court. Corner of gallery fireplace
Dartington Hall. South court. Slate flooring in front of gallery fireplace
193 Dartington Hall. South court. View of excavations towards gallery wall
Dartington Hall. South court. Base of staircase
194 Dartington Hall. South court. Approach to court from screens passage. *Humphrey Sutton*
203 Dartington Hall. West range, entrance block and barn from the kitchen offices. *Humphrey Sutton*
204 Dartington Hall. West range from the great hall
Dartington Hall. West range from the east
206 Dartington Hall. West range: first group of lodgings. *Humphrey Sutton*
207 Dartington Hall. West range: first group of lodgings. External window. *Humphrey Sutton*
Dartington Hall. West range: first group of lodgings. Internal window. *Humphrey Sutton*
Dartington Hall. West range: first group of lodgings. Upper floor. *Humphrey Sutton*
208 Dartington Hall. West range: first group of lodgings. Scratch drawing on south wall. *Humphrey Sutton*
Dartington Hall. West range: second group of lodgings. Scratch drawings on north wall
Dartington Hall. West range: second group of lodgings. Inserted chimney-stack
209 Dartington Hall. West range and private house from the churchyard
211 Dartington Hall. West range: fifth group of lodgings. Entrance porch. *Humphrey Sutton*

Dartington Hall. West range: second group of lodgings. Entrance porch. *Humphrey Sutton*

212 Dartington Hall. West range: fifth group of lodgings. First-floor music-room
Dartington Hall. West range: fourth group of lodgings. First-floor reception room

216 Dartington Hall. North court from entrance block showing destroyed part of east range: late 18th century. By T. Bonner. *Exeter City Libraries*
Dartington Hall. East range. Middle group of lodgings: 1792. By Mrs. Champernowne. *Exeter City Libraries*

217 Dartington Hall. East range from the north court: 1925
Dartington Hall. East range from the north court. *Humphrey Sutton*

218 Dartington Hall. East range. Garderobe projections from the north-east
Dartington Hall. East range. Garderobe projections from the south. *Humphrey Sutton*

219 Dartington Hall. East range from the kitchen offices. *Humphrey Sutton*

221 Dartington Hall. The barn. Threshing-house. *Humphrey Sutton*

222 Dartington Hall. The barn from the entrance approach

223 Dartington Hall. The barn. Interior towards the east. *Humphrey Sutton*

225 Dartington Hall: c. 1540. B.M. MS. Cott. Augustus I. vol. 1, art 39

232 Haddon Hall, Derbyshire. Great hall from upper court: second quarter of 14th century. Staircase tower: early 17th century. *National Monuments Record*

234 Penshurst Place, Kent. Great hall, porch and lower residential block: 1341–9. *National Monuments Record by permission of Lord de L'Isle*

235 Raby Castle, Co. Durham. Lower hall: c. 1325–30. Upper hall: c. 1378–c. 90. *National Monuments Record*

236 New College, Oxford. Great hall: 1380–6. *Ministry of Public Building and Works*

241 Westminster Abbey. Roof of Dorter: 14th century. *Ministry of Public Building and Works*

243 Winterborne Clenston Manor, Dorset. Roof of barn: possibly early 15th century. *Country Life*
Milton Abbey, Dorset. Roof of abbot's hall: 1498. *Country Life*
Weare Gifford Hall, Devon. Roof of great hall: third quarter of 15th century. *Country Life*

245 Glastonbury Abbey, Somerset. Great kitchen: c. 1340. *National Monuments Record*
Raby Castle, Co. Durham. Great kitchen: c. 1378–c. 90. *National Monuments Record*
Haddon Hall, Derbyshire. Kitchen: between 1325 and 1350. *National Monuments Record*

246 Durham Cathedral Priory. Great kitchen: mainly 1366–71. *A. F. Kersting*

247 Ashby de la Zouch Castle, Leicestershire. Kitchen: later 14th century. *Ministry of Public Building and Works*
Pickering Castle, Yorkshire, Rosamund Tower: 1323–4. *Ministry of Public Building and Works*

248 Ludlow Castle, Shropshire. Great hall and lower residential block: late 13th century. Upper residential blocks: c. 1320. *Country Life*

249 Warwick Castle. Caesar's Tower: between 1370 and 1385. *National Monuments Record*

250 Vicars' Close, Lincoln. South side: c. 1310. *National Monuments Record*

252 Vicars' Close, Wells. Towards the chapel: mid 14th century. *A. F. Kersting*

253 Ewelme Palace, Oxfordshire. Range of lodgings: second quarter of 15th century. By S. & N. Buck, 1729

254 Haddon Hall, Derbyshire. West lodgings, lower court: late 15th century. *National Monuments Record*

List of Figures and Maps

Page 4	South Devon showing the position of Dartington Hall
14	Map showing places mentioned in Chapter I
17	The Martin succession from the 11th to the 14th centuries
19	The deer-park wall at Dartington
21	The Audley succession in the 14th century
24	The Royal and Holand families in the 14th century
34	Map of the Castilian campaign: 1386–7
46	Map showing the routes of Richard II and Bolingbroke in 1399, and the Holand rebellion in 1400
58	The Exeter branch of the Holand family in the late 14th and 15th centuries
72	The Dartington branch of the Champernowne family from the 16th to the 20th centuries
101	Dartington Hall. General plan of existing and other known buildings
102	Major residential building activity: 1377–99
118	Bolton Castle. First-floor plan
120	Raby Castle. Ground-floor plan
121	Bodiam Castle. Ground-floor plan
123	Wingfield Castle. Ground-floor plan
124	Farleigh Hungerford Castle. Ground-floor plan
127	Baginton Castle. Lower ground-floor plan
	Wardour Castle. Ground-floor plan
129	Howden Manor. Ground-floor plan
130	Norrington Manor. Ground-floor plan
133	Winchester College. Ground-floor plan
142	Dartington Hall. Entrance block. Central truss including supporting pier to ground-floor room
	Dartington Hall. Entrance block. End truss to west wall
143	Dartington Hall. Entrance block. West bay of room above entrance passage showing end, intermediate, and central trusses
	Dartington Hall. Entrance block. Intermediate truss
152	Dartington Hall. Profile of mouldings from porch tower, screens passage, great hall and south court
156	Dartington Hall. Great hall. Interior elevation of window
158	Penshurst Place, Kent: 1341–9. Ground-floor plan of great hall showing approach to upper residential block
160	Berkeley Castle, Gloucestershire: 1340–50. Ground-floor plan of great hall showing approach to upper residential block
161	Compton Castle, Devon: c. 1340. Ground-floor plan of hall, reconstructed on original evidence in 1955, showing approach to upper residential block
164	Dartington Hall. Great hall. Plan of upper part showing relation between windows, buttresses, corbels and roof trusses
168	Dartington Hall. Lower residential block. Roof truss impression in east wall
187	Dartington Hall. South court. Plan of structures revealed by excavation in 1962, and by resistivity survey in 1963
196	Bodiam Castle. Ground-floor plan
	Bodiam Castle. First-floor plan
	Bolton Castle. First-floor plan
	Bolton Castle. Second-floor plan
199	Kenilworth Castle. Ground-floor plan
	Kenilworth Castle. First-floor plan
200	Dartington Hall. South court. Conjectural plan of ground floor
	Dartington Hall. South court. Conjectural plan of first floor
204	Dartington Hall. West range. Suggested design of original elevation to north court
210	Dartington Hall. West range: third group of lodgings. Central truss
	Dartington Hall. West range: third group of lodgings. End truss.
227	Clarendon Palace: mid 12th to mid 13th centuries. Ground-floor plan traced by partial excavation
	Cobham College: after 1362. Ground-floor plan
228	Amberley Castle: 1377–c. 83. Ground-floor plan
229	Sudeley Castle: outer court and mid towers, early 15th century; inner court, 1469–78. Ground-floor plan
233	Haddon Hall: between 1325 and 1350. Ground-floor plan
234	Crowhurst Manor: c. 1250. Ground-floor plan
	Kirkstall Abbey Guest House: early 13th century. Ground-floor plan
	Bishop's Palace, Lincoln: c. 1224. Ground-floor plan
235	Northborough Manor House: c. 1340. Ground-floor plan

238	Sketchbook of Villard de Honnecourt: 1235–45	249	Warwick Castle. Caesar's Tower. Elevation
	'Pilgrims' Hall', Winchester: 1325–6. Transverse section of hall	250	Vicars' Court, Lincoln. South range: *c.* 1310. Ground-floor plan
239	Tiptofts Manor House: 1348–67. Transverse section of hall	251	Winchester College. East range of Chamber Court: 1387–94. Ground- and first-floor plans
	Balle's Place, Salisbury: 1370–85. Transverse section of hall		Merton College, Oxford. North range of Mob Quad: 1304–7. Ground-floor plan
240	Westminster Palace: 1394–1401. Transverse section of great hall		New College, Oxford. South range of Great Quad: 1380–6. Ground-floor plan
241	Dartington Hall: 1388–1400. Transverse section of great hall. Taken from G. Saunders, 1805. Exeter City Libraries	252	Windsor Castle. South range of upper court: 1365–8. Ground-floor plan before post-medieval alterations
242	No. 8 The Close, Exeter: first half of 15th century. Transverse section of hall	253	Haddon Hall. West range of lower court: late 15th century. Ground- and first-floor plans
	Cadhay: late 15th century. Transverse section of hall		Amberley Castle. North range of lower court: 1377–*c.* 83. Ground-floor plan
245	Glastonbury Abbey. Kitchen. Ground-floor plan	254	Thornbury Castle. North range of outer court: 1511–21. Ground-floor plan
	Raby Castle. Kitchen. Ground-floor plan	257	Powderham Castle: probably between 1391 and 1406. Ground-floor plan
	Haddon Hall. Kitchen. Ground-floor plan	265	Dartington Hall. Site of south court. Plan of early structure revealed by excavation
246	Durham Cathedral Priory. Kitchen. Ground-floor plan		
248	Ludlow Castle. Great hall and lower residential chamber: late 13th century. Upper residential blocks and tower: *c.* 1320. Flanking curtain wall and towers: 12th century		Dartington Hall. Ground-, first-, and second-floor plans

Bishop's Waltham Palace (Hants.) 254
Blackborough (Devon) 56 f. 21, 261
Blagdon (Somerset) 19 f. 33, 261
Blagdon Manor (Devon) 157 f. 7, 258
Blakesley, Thomas 43
Blount, Sir Thomas (d. 1400) 50
Bodiam Castle (Sussex): *121*; building materials 134; date of construction 109; design 118, 119, 135, 136; financing 117; kitchen 244; lower residential block 170; plan *121, 196*; postern tower 170 f. 17; reflection of bastard feudalism 229; residential accommodation 197; restoration 6; retainers' hall 237
Bohun, Eleanor de, duchess of Gloucester (d. 1399) 112 f. 52
Bolingbroke, Henry, *see* Henry IV
Bolton Castle (Yorks.): *118*; building costs 116; chapel 201; entrance 146; financing 116; general plan 118, 119, 135, 136, 137; household chambers 220; kitchen 244; pages' rooms 170 f. 17, period of construction 104, 106; plans *118, 196*; position 96; priests' lodgings 220; reflection of bastard feudalism 229; residential accommodation analysis 197-8; residential blocks 169-70, 237; retainers' hall 237; shouldered arch 214
Bonham-Carter, Victor 4
Boniface IX, pope (d. 1404) 40
Bonville, Sir William 109
Bony, Thomas 33 f. 43
Bordeaux (France) 36 f. 46, 47
Bossiney (Cornwall) 261
Boteler, Ralph, Lord (d. 1473) 192
Bouer, Alexander 43
Boulogne (France) 73
Bovey Tracey (Devon) 52, 55, 261
Bradley Manor (Devon) 139 f. 2
Braganza (Portugal) 34
Brancepeth Castle (Durham): *119*; financing 117; general plan 118, 119; later additions 137; period of construction 103, 111
Braybrooke, Robert, bishop of London (d. 1404) 32
Breauté, Fawkes de (d. 1226) 19 f. 35
Brest (France) 33, 40
– Castle 263
Bridgwater Church (Somerset) 256 f. 64
Bridlington Priory (Yorks.) 125 f. 130
Brienne, Guy of 263
Bristol (Somerset) 45, 51
Brittany, duke of 33, 40, f. 31
Brixham (Devon) 80
– Church 256
Brochall (Kent) 109 f. 27
Brockedon, William (d. 1859) 86
Brook, Sir Thomas 112
Brooking Church (Devon) 89
Buchanan, W. 85
Buck, Samuel (d. 1779) and Nathaniel (d. 1753); engraving of Dartington Hall: 81, *82-3*, 99; east range 215; entrance block 140; great hall 155; lower residential block 166; offices 175; porch tower 151; west range 205, 208
Buckfast Abbey (Devon) 22
Buckingham, Edward, 3rd duke of (d. 1521) 254-5
– Henry, 2nd duke of (d. 1483) 69
Buckland (Surrey) 263
Buckland Abbey (Devon) 81
Buller family 86, 90
Burci, Serlo de 16, 18
Burford Church (Salop) 56
Burgundy, Charles, duke of (d. 1477) 67
– Philip, duke of (d. 1467) 61
Burley, Sir Simon (d. 1388) 30 f. 24, 262
Burstwick Manor (Yorks.) 224
Butleigh Court (Somerset) 211 f. 12
Butler, James, earl of Wiltshire (d. 1461) 66
Bygrave Manor (Herts.) 102

Cade, Hugh 43
Cadhay (Devon) *242*, 244
Caerphilly Castle (Glamorgan) 170, 236
Calais (France) 41, 61, 66, 68, 85
Caldicot Castle (Mon.): *113*; date of residential additions 104, 112; decoration 136; financing 117; fireplace 166; gatehouse design 125, 153; restoration 137; shouldered arch 214
Calstock (Cornwall) 261
Camaes (Pemb.) cantref of 18, 19
Cambernon (Normandy) 73
Cambridge 85
– Corpus Christi College 251
– King's College 148, 220 f. 14
– Pembroke College 115 f. 72
– Trinity College 115 f. 72, 165
– Trinity Hall 244
Campden, John 133 f. 146
Canaletto, Antonio (d. 1768) 87
Cane, Percy 11
Canterbury, archbishop of, *see* Arundel, Courtenay, Reynolds, Sudbury, Walden, Winchelsey
– Cathedral 136
– St. Augustine's Abbey 125 f. 130
– West Gate 106, 136
Cardigan 18
Carew family 75
– Sir George (d. 1545) 74 f. 16
– Richard (d. 1620) 74, 78
Carisbrooke Castle (Isle of Wight): defensive additions 106, *106*; residential additions 114, *114*, 128
Carlisle (Cumb.) 66
– bishop of (d. 1419) 50, 111
– Castle gatehouse 105, *105*, 116
Carr, W. H. (d. 1830) 85
Carracci, Ludovico (d. 1619) 87
Carreg Cennen Castle (Carmarthen) 262
Cary, Sir John (d. 1395) 43 f. 61, 261
– Robert 43
Castile (Spain) 31-5, *34, 35*
Catash (Somerset) hundred of 261
Catherine Howard, queen of England (d. 1542) 71
Catherine Parr, queen of England (d. 1548) 71
Cawood Castle (Yorks.) 106
Cecil, William, Baron Burghley (d. 1598) 75, 76, 77, 78
Cely, Sir Benedict 43

Index

Abberbury, Sir Richard (d. c. 1400) 110, 116, 261
Abingdon Abbey (Berks.) 190
Acton Burnell Castle (Salop) 159
Adams, Nicholas 71
Admirals: 1st duke of Exeter 39; 3rd duke of Exeter 61, 64; 4th duke of Exeter 64
Admiralty, court of 39, 75
Aelfflaed, sister of Beornwynn 13, 260
Agincourt (France) battle of 58
Aldburgh, Sir William (d. 1388) 237
Alexander, earl of Huntingdon's wardrober 43
Aller Park (Devon) 87
Allington, William 43
Alva, duke of (d. 1582) 75–6
Alwine, thegn of Devon 15
Amberley Castle (Sussex): *107*; date of erection 104, 109; defences 230; double courtyard plan 125, 192, 228, 229; four-centred arches 213; household chambers 220; plan *228*; residential block 161, 237; retainers' lodgings 132, 219 f. 11, 247, 252, *253*
Ampthill (Beds.) 65
Anglo-Saxon charter (833) 260
Anschetil, under-tenant of William of Falaise 15, 16
Antony (Cornwall) 74
Appellants 36–7, 40–2
Aquitaine (France) 24, 61
Ardington (Berks.) 260
Arras, congress of 61
Artois, Jacobus (d. 1684) 87
Arundel Castle (Sussex): great hall rebuilt 110, 116; great hall roof 239; occupied by Huntingdon 41, 262
– College: design 132; foundation 115; lodgings 250 f. 47
– earl of, see Fitzalan
– honour of, 116 f. 89, 262
– Sir John 263
– Thomas (d. 1414) archbishop of Canterbury 41–2, 45
Ashburnham, Roger (d. 1392) 109

Ashburton (Devon), churchwardens' accounts 74, 99
Ashby-de-la-Zouch Castle (Leics.): kitchen 244–7, *247*; tower-house 229 f. 5
Assheburgh (Cornwall) 261
Assheton, Henry 71
Asthorp, Sir William 110
Audley family 21–2
– Isobel, 2nd wife of 2nd Lord Audley 21
– James, 2nd Lord Audley (d. 1386) 20, 21–2, 30, 55, 95, 261
– Joan, 1st wife of 2nd Lord Audley 20
– Nicholas, 3rd Lord Audley (d. 1391) 20
Aumale, duke of, *see* York
Aylworth, John 71, 74
Ayton Castle (Yorks.) 125

Baddesley Clinton Hall (War.) 173
Baginton Castle (War.) 112, 125, *126*, *127*, 137
Bagot, Sir William (d. 1407) 112
Bamburgh Castle (Northumb.): date of additions 110; financing 117; offices 175; present remains 128
Bampton (Oxon.) 51
Bardwell Church (Suffolk) 242
Barnet (Herts.) battle of 67, *68*
Barnstaple (Devon) 52
– barony of 20
– manor of 20, 21, 56 f. 21, 261
– member of parliament (1547) 78
Baronage: income in 1436, 60; organisation in late 14th century 38
Bastard feudalism: development in late 14th century 43–4; effect on residential planning 220, 229–30
Bath, bishop of (d. 1166) 18 f. 27
Baugé (France) 59
Bayonne (France) 36 f. 46
Bays, Robert 43
Beauchamp, Thomas, 11th earl

of Warwick (d. 1369) 136 f. 155
– Thomas, 12th earl of Warwick (d. 1401); appellant 36, 37; arrest and banishment 41–2; forfeited estates 262; work at Warwick Castle 112, 116, 136 f. 155
Beaufort, Edmund, 2nd duke of Somerset (d. 1455) 64
– Henry, bishop of Winchester (d. 1447) 61 f. 53
– John, earl of Somerset (d. 1410) 42 f. 36, 55
– Margaret, countess of Richmond (d. 1509) 69, 193
– Thomas, 2nd duke of Exeter (d. 1427) 61 f. 57
Bedford, John, duke of, *see* John of Lancaster
Bedfordshire, shire elections 62
Beer stone 145, 151, 269–70
Bek, Antony, bishop of Durham (d. 1311) 236
Belle, John 43
Benavente (Spain) 34
Benhall (Suffolk) 261
Beornwynn, sister of Aelfflaed 13, 14, 260
Bere Ferers Castle (Devon) 256
Bereford St. Martin (Wilts.) 262
Berkeley Castle (Glos.): 15th century staffing 118 f. 94; kitchen 244, 247; plan *160*; staircase 160
– William, Lord (d. 1492) 118 f. 94
Berkhamsted Castle (Herts.): *26*; Black Prince at 23, 24; granted to Huntingdon 38, 262; 4th duke of Exeter confined at 65
Berners, Sir James 261
Bernershall (Suffolk) 261
Berry, John duc de (d. 1416) 117
Berwick-on-Tweed 31, 40
– Castle 105
Betchworth Castle (Surrey) 102
Binbury (Kent) 50 f. 81
Birdcombe Court (Somerset) 256 f. 60
Bishops Canning Castle (Wilts.) 102

Page numbers in italic *type refer to plates or figures*

Chalgrove (Beds.) 170
Chamber, under Richard II 39
Chamberlain, king's 38, 39
Champernowne family 73–92
— Sir Arthur (d. 1578): 71, 73–8, 76: alters Dartington Hall 98–9; lower residential block 165, 166; south court block 202; upper residential 180, 181
— Arthur (d. 1650) 79–80
— Arthur (d. 1697) 80
— Arthur (d. 1766): 80–5, 84; alters Dartington Hall 99; great hall 157; porch tower 151; upper residential block 181–3; west range 213
— Arthur (d. 1819) 85–8, 86, 90
— Arthur (d. 1831) 88
— Arthur (d. 1887) 89–90, 144
— Arthur (d. 1946) 90–2
— Bridgett (d. 1667) 80
— Charles (fl. 1578) 73 f. 1
— Elizabeth (d. 1968) 90, 166 f. 3
— Francis (d. 1687) 79–80
— Gawen (d. 1592) 77, 77, 78–9
— George (d. 1589) 73 f. 1
— Henry (d. 1851) 88–90, 184
— Jane, wife of Arthur (d. 1766) 81, 84, 85, 86
— Jane, daughter of Arthur (d. 1766) 82, 85, 215–16, 217, 218
— John (d. 1732) 85
— Louisa (d. 1870) 85, 86, 86
— Rawlin (d. 1774) 85
— Robarda (d. c. 1600) 78, 79
Chardstock Castle (Dorset) 102
Charing Palace (Kent) 146, 236
Charles I, king of England (d. 1649) 80
Charles VI of France (d. 1422) 59
Chaucer, Geoffrey (d. 1400) 33 f. 41, 43
Cheshire, justice of 39
Chester, abbot of 112
— Castle 47–8, 49
Cheyne, Sir Hugh 112
Cheyney Longville Castle (Salop): date of construction 112; financing 117; general plan 119, 122
Chichester (Sussex), bishop of (d. 1385) 109, 230
Chidiock Castle (Dorset) 109, 117
— Sir John 109
Vicars Choral 132, 151
— St. Mary's Hospital 238 f. 20
— city walls 106
— Bishop's Palace kitchen 136, 175, 238
Chillenden, prior of Canterbury (d. 1411) 104 f. 5
Chivalry, court of 39
Chronique de la Traison et Mort de Richard II, 263–4
Chudleigh Palace (Devon) 109, 257
Churchstow (Devon) 207 f. 3
Churston, Lord 10, 175
Cilgerran Castle (Pemb.) 107 f. 18
Cirencester (Glos.) 51
Ciudad Rodrigo (Spain) 34
Clanvowe, Sir John 30 f. 21
Clapton Court (Somerset) 256
Clare estates in mid 14th century 263
Clarendon Palace (Wilts.) 226, 227
Clark, Anthony 186, 266–7
Clevedon Court (Somerset) 99, 235
Clinton, Edward, earl of Lincoln (d. 1585) 74
Cnut, king (d. 1035) 15
Cobham College (Kent) 132, 135, 227, 228, 250 f. 47
— John, Lord (d. 1408) 106
Cockermouth Castle (Cumb.): date of additions 103, 104, 106; gatehouse design 105; date of additions 103, 125: kitchen 172 f. 2, 239 f. 26, 244: shouldered arch 214
Cockington (Devon) 261
Coggeshall, Sir William 43
Combe Martin (Devon) 52
— manor of 19, 20, 21, 56 f. 21, 261
Combe Ralegh (Devon) 218 f. 6
Commynes, Philippe de (d. 1511?) 67
Compiègne (France) 61
Compton Castle (Devon): date 256; kitchen 258; plan 161, 258; roofs 179 f. 2; stairs 160, 179
Concressault Castle (France) 117
Constanza of Castile, duchess of Lancaster (d. 1394) 31
Conway Castle (Caern.) 38, 47–8, 48, 263
Cooling Castle (Kent) 107, 109, 119
Corfe Castle (Dorset) 112 f. 57
Cornwaille, Sir John (d. 1443) 57, 57, 58, 59, 60
Coruña, La (Spain) 33
Cosin, John 51 f. 86
Cotehele House (Cornwall) 226, 258
Cothay Manor (Somerset) 139 f. 2
Council, king's under Richard II 39–40
Courtenay family 98, 117, 231
— Edward, earl of Devon (d. 1419) 23 f. 7, 53 f. 100, 195
— Henry, marquis of Exeter (d. 1539) 71, 193
— Sir Peter (d. 1409) 53
— Sir Philip (d. 1406): custody of Dartington park 22, 69; and death of friar 30 f. 24; guest at Dartington 193; possibly builder of Powderham Castle 258
— Sir William (d. 1762) 81–2
— William, archbishop of Canterbury (d. 1396): builds Saltwood gatehouse 109; and Saltwood chapel and hall 112; founder of Maidstone College 104, 115; possibly builder of Croydon Palace hall 112; witness of Holand's pardon 32
Coveley, Ranlin 43 f. 63, 52
Coventry (War.) 44, 65, 262
— Dun Cow Inn 211 f. 13
Cowick, King's House (Yorks.) 110
Cowley (Devon) 88
Crediton Church (Devon) 256
Crenellate, licences to 103–4
Creshill, William 43
Creton 53, 263–4
Crispin, Miles (d. 1107) 16 f. 20
Cromwell, Ralph Lord (d. 1456) 65, 236, 253
Crowhurst Manor (Sussex) 232, 234
Crowhurst Place (Surrey) 242
Croxden Abbey (Staffs.) 160

Architectural History: prior to 1388: 14, 17, 18, 20, 95; 1388–1400: 37, 42, 95–8; 1400–1559: 56, 104, 263; 1400–1559: 57, 61, 69, 70, 71, 225; 1559–1717: 74, 79, 80, 1559–1717: 74, 79, 80, 1717–1925: 81, 96–8; 1717–1925: 81, 82–4, 85–9, 87, 89, 91–2, 99; 1925–1970: 2, 3, 5, 6–8, 9–10, 99
Architectural Significance 99–101
Building Stones 268–72
Description 100–101, 128, 135, 255
Barn 3, 10, 83, 222–4, 221–3
Buttery 165
East range 3, 9, 10, 82, 215–18, 216–19, 219–20
Entrance Block 9, 83–4, 138, 139–47, 139–43
Garderobes 166, 180, 205, 210, 216–18, 219, 219, 230
Graffiti 208, 208, 209–10
Great Hall 3, 6, 8, 9–10, 82, 87, 89, 91, 128, 136, 150, 152–64, 154–8, 162–4, 236–7, 239–41, 241
Kitchen 3, 10, 89, 92, 171–5, 171–4, 244–7, Lodgings 42, 203–20, 247, 252–5
Lower residential block 3, 9, 82, 87, 89, 91, 128,
Mason's marks 151, 157, 158, 214, 272
Non-defensive character 230–2
Periods of construction 95–9
Pottery: East range 217
Resistivity survey 266–7
Roofing tiles 192–3
— Manor of: prior to 1388: 13–22; 1388–1559: 22, 23–69, 69–71, 261; 1559–1925: 73–92; 1925 onwards: 3, 11, 92
— Deer Park 12, 17, 19, 20
— Hall (1447) 61
— nowne 78; vestment bequest (1400) 267; illustrated (c. 1800) 84; pulled down 89–90; tomb of Sir Arthur Champernowne 78; vestment bequest (1447) 61
— history 19; Holand's goods at Dartington Church (Devon): churchwardens (1588) 79; early Roofs 143–5, 161–4, 166–8, 173–5, 180–1, 206–7, 210–11, 223–4, 239–41
Screens passage 152–3, 153, 167
Service rooms 165
South court 185–202, 185–8, 193–4, 200, 264–6, 266–7
Threshing house 221, 224
Upper residential block 3, 6, 8, 9, 84, 89, 92, 176, 177–84, 178, 182–3, 237
West range 3, 7, 10, 82–3, 84, 87, 91, 92, 203–14, 203–12, 219
Designer 255–6
Double courtyard plan, significance of 226, 230
Dovecot 231
Early medieval building, on site of 264–6
Floor tiles 193
Furnishings at: (1400–1) 195, 267–8; (1774) 87; (1809) 86–7
Gardens 9, 10–11
Mason's marks 151, 157, 158, 214, 272
Non-defensive character 230–2
Periods of construction 95–9
Pottery: East range 217
Resistivity survey 266–7
Roofing tiles 192–3
— Manor of: prior to 1388: 13–22; 1388–1559: 22, 23–69, 69–71, 261; 1559– (Northumb.) 105, 106, 125
Dart, river 13, 15, 18, 70
Dartington Church (Devon): churchwardens (1588) 79; early history 19; Holand's goods at (1400) 267; illustrated (c. 1800) 84; pulled down 89–90; tomb of Sir Arthur Champernowne 78; vestment bequest (1447) 61
— Deer Park 12, 17, 19, 20
— Hall
Dalyngrigge, Sir Edward (d. 1394) 106, 117, 197
Danes, early raids of 14–15
Dart, river 13, 15, 18, 70
Dartington Church (Devon): churchwardens (1588) 79; early history 19; Holand's goods at (1400) 267; illustrated (c. 1800) 84; pulled down 89–90; tomb of Sir Arthur Champernowne 78; vestment bequest (1447) 61
Dartmouth (Devon) 52, 55, 70, 75, 79
— Castle 109, 231
— Church 256
— Higher Street 212 f. 15
Davenport House (Salop) 183
Dean (Devon) 15
Delabole (Cornwall) 271
Derby, earl of, see Henry IV
Derentune-homm (Devon) 13–14
Dereland (Devon) 18
Despenser, Henry, bishop of Norwich (d. 1406) 28, 40, 110–11
— Sir Hugh (d. 1326) 236
— Thomas, Lord (d. 1400) 23 f. 7, 42 f. 36, 45, 50
Devereux, Sir John (d. 1393) 112
Devon, county of: commissioner of peace (16th century) 78; Danish raids 14–15; Domesday Survey 15–16; justice of the peace (1633) 79; prosperity in Middle Ages 256: residential building activity in late Middle Ages 256–8; Saxon settlement 13–14; sheriff of (1561) 78, (1811) 86
— earl of, see Courtenay
— long house 224, 255
Dieppe (France) merchants of 75
Dodgson, J.McN. 13
Domesday Book 15–16
Donnet, Margery 69
Donnington Castle Gatehouse (Berks.) 127; building material 134; date of construction 110; design 125; financing 116; fireplace 166; four centred arches 213
Dorchester (Dorset) 13, 260
Dormston Castle (Worcs.) 102
Douglas, James, earl of (d. 1491) 65 f. 72
Drake, Sir Francis (d. 1596) 75, 79
Dudley, Sir Henry (d. 1565?) 74
Dunstanburgh Castle (Northumb.) 105, 106, 125
Durham, bishop of, see Bek, Hatfield, Skirlaw
Durham Castle 236

Eure, Sir Ralph 124 f. 122
Eu, count of 24
Elton, Thomas de 124 f. 121
Eton College (Bucks.) 148, 190
Essex, escheator of 55
Esher Palace (Surrey) 190 f. 16
English Place Name Society 13
146; octagon 237
Ely Cathedral Priory (Cambs.):
    barn 224; gatehouse 125 f. 130,
    retainers' lodgings 254; Richard
    II's additions 112
Eltham Palace (Kent): drainage
    passage 173; multiple court-
    yard plan 230; outer court 148;
    3–11, 11, 92
Elmhirst, Dorothy and Leonard
    62
— Sir William 30 f. 24
Elmham, Thomas of (d. 1440?)
    (d. 1603) 75–6, 79
Elizabeth I, queen of England
Elford, Sir William (d. 1837) 87
(d. 839) 13, 14, 260
Egbert, king of West Saxons
    24, 25, 26, 43
— prince of Wales (d. 1376) 23,
    24
Edward of Angoulême (d. 1371)
    (d. 1553) 73
Edward VI, king of England
    (d. 1483) 66, 67, 68
Edward IV, king of England
Mary Graces, London 55, 261
earls 42 f. 38; endows St.
building activity 104–5; creates
(d. 1377): 21, 23, 26, 42;
Edward III, king of England
Pickering Castle 247–9
(d. 1327): 20, 37; additions to
Edward II, king of England
at Dartington 264–6
Faringdon, Joseph (d. 1821)
1307): 20, 247; silver penny of,
Edward I, king of England (d.
Kent (d. 1330) 23
Edmund of Woodstock, earl of
East Tytherley (Hants.) 228
170 f. 19
East Meon Court House (Hants.)
(d. 867) 260
Eahlstan, bishop of Sherborne
246
111 f. 48; kitchen 136, 246,
— Cathedral Priory: dormitory

Ewelme Palace (Oxon.) 253, 253
Exeter, bishop of (d. 1394) 109
— Castle 257 f. 66
— Cathedral 52, 256 f. 64
— 8 The Close, 164, 242, 244
— duke of, see Beaufort and
    Holand
— marquis of, see Courtenay
— Vicars Choral: design 132,
    250; hall 152, 155; kitchen
    258
Faringdon (Berks.) 51
Farleigh Hungerford Castle
    (Somerset): design 124;
    119, 125, 228; period of
    construction 103, 110; plan
    124; window in upper
    residential block 179 f. 5
Farrand, Beatrix 11, 148
Fastolf, Sir John (d. 1459) 66
Fawley, Master (fl. 1384) 255
Fenna (Devon) 18
Fenwick Castle (Northumb.)
    106, 117, 125
— John 106
Ferriby, Robert 43 f. 63
Fishguard (Pemb.) 18
Fitzalan, Richard, 4th earl of
    Arundel (d. 1397): appellant
    36, 37, 39, 41–2; besieges St.
    Malo 27; establishes Arundel
    College 115; estates 39, 262;
    his influence 38; rebuilds
    Arundel Castle hall 110, 116,
    239
— Thomas, 5th earl of Arundel
    (d. 1415) 42, 45, 47, 53
Flanders 28
Flint Castle 47
— Justice of 39
Flushing (Netherlands) 75
Flute Daumarie (Devon) 44
Follaton (Devon) 15
Fonthill (Wilts.) 85
Forde Abbey (Dorset) 81
Fotheringhay Castle (Northants.)
    65, 112, 125 f. 123
Four-centred arches 213–14
Fowey (Cornwall) 75
Frankfurt (Germany) 85
Fraunceys, Simon (d. 1358)
    228 f. 3

Gropius, Walter 10, 224
— Sir Thomas 67 f. 96
262
Grey, Lord, of Ruthin (d. 1440)
— Sir Richard 78 f. 28
Greville family 75
Green, Sir Henry 30 f. 24
Great Gaddesden (Herts.) 260
f. 12, 168 f. 7, 237
Great Coxwell Barn (Berks.) 144
139 f. 2
Great Chalfield Manor (Wilts.)
(d. 1369) 96
Grandisson, bishop of Exeter
Gower, John (d. 1408) 41 f. 33
237
Goodrich Castle (Hereford.) 169,
Gonfalonier 40, 201
Golafré, Sir John 98
Godmerock (Devon) 80
— New Inn 190
— earl of, see Despenser
    Thomas
— duke of, see Humphrey and
— Cathedral 98, 214
Gloucester Castle 112 f. 57
— abbot of (d. 1166) 18 f. 27
245, 246
Glastonbury Abbey (Somerset)
f. 110
Gillow Manor (Hereford.) 122
Gilling Castle (Yorks.) 125
Gilbert family 75
Gidleigh Castle (Devon) 256
Falaise 15, 16
Geva, wife of William of
Genoese bankers 75
Gaywood Castle (Norfolk) 102
Gawen, John 111, 118
Gatehouses 145–6
Gascony (France) 24, 67
Galleries 190–1
Gall, Simon 52

— Sir Thomas (fl. 1600) 80
66–7
Fulford, Sir Baldwin (d. 1461)
18 f. 26
Fulchard, abbot of St. Dogmael
84, 88, 89, 184
Froude, Rev. R. H. (d. 1849)
34 f. 45
Froissart, Jean (d. 1400?) 28,
f. 21, 261
Fremington (Devon) 21, 56

Grosmont (Mon.) 262

Haddon Hall (Derby.): 232;
design 235; gardrobes 219
f. 11; kitchen 244-7, 245;
offices 175; reflection
of bastard feudalism 230;
retainers' lodgings 253, 254
Hadleigh Castle (Essex) 52
Halnaker House (Sussex): 108;
decoration at 136; financing
117; gatehouse design 125;
period of construction 109;
screens arches 152
Hamm, origin of place name
13–14
Hammer-beam roofs 161–4,
237–44
Hampton Court (Middlesex)
190, 230
Hams, The (Devon) 13
Harberton (Devon) 261
Harbertonford (Devon) 55
Hare, Captain 86
Harewood Castle (Yorks.):
design 124 f. 122; entrance
tower 256 f. 60; hall fireplace
160; lower residential block
237
Harfleur (France) 58
Harlech Castle (Merioneth.)
179 f. 2
Harrington, Richard 85, 87
Harringworth Castle (Northants.)
102
Haslebury Plucknet (Somerset)
261
Hastinges, Lord (d. 1325) 20
Hastings, John, earl of Pembroke
(d. 1389) 33 f. 41
Hatfield, Thomas, bishop of
Durham (1381) 236
Haughton Castle (Northumb.)
124 f. 122
Haverford Castle (Pemb.) 38, 263
Hawkins, Sir John (d. 1595) 75
Haye, John de la 23
Heidelberg (Germany) 85
Helsbury (Cornwall) 261
Helston (Cornwall) 261
Hemyock Castle (Devon) 110,
117, 122
Hening, Robert 10, 224
Henry III, king of England
(d. 1272) 19
Henry IV, king of England (d.
1413) earl of Derby, duke of
Hereford 36, 38, 44–9, 46, 49,
51–2, 54, 55–6, 58
Henry V, king of England (d.
1422) 58, 59, 61
Henry VI, king of England (d.
1471) 61, 64, 65, 66
Henry VIII, king of England
(d. 1547) 71, 73, 226
Hereford, duke of, see Henry IV
– Joan countess of (d. 1419) 52
– Vicars Choral 133 f. 150
Herland, Hugh (d. c. 1405) 239,
241, 244
Hertford Castle: chapel 201 f. 34;
cloister court 191; date of
residential additions 110;
hall fireplace 160 f. 18
– earl of, see Seymour
Hever Castle (Kent) 108, 109,
122
Highclere Castle (Hants.) 112
Hilton (Cornwall) 44
Hingston Down (Cornwall)
battle of 14
Hobildoe, John 43 f. 63
Holand, Anne, countess of
Huntingdon (d. 1432) 60, 62
f. 65
– Anne (d. c. 1474) daughter of
4th duke of Exeter 67, 96,
69
– Anne, duchess of Exeter (d.
1476) 64, 67, 68, 69
– Anne (d. 1486) daughter of
3rd duke of Exeter 65 f. 72
– Beatrice, countess of Huntingdon (d. 1439) 62 f. 65
– Constance (d. 1437) daughter
of 1st duke of Exeter 57 f. 25
– Edmund (c. 1370) 23 f. 4
– Edmund (fl. 1415) 57 f. 29
– Elizabeth, countess of Huntingdon (d. 1425) : in Castile 35;
chronicle in household 264;
dancer 42; death 60;
first marriage 33; possible
building activity 214;
recovers husband's estates
and chattels 56–7; relationship with husband 55;
second marriage 57, 57;
tomb 56
– John, chaplain 43
– John, earl of Huntingdon and
1st duke of Exeter (d. 1400):
activity and life up to 1377;
23–6, 1377–88: 27–37, 34;
1388–1400: 38–54, 47, 48,
49, 50, 264; appointments
36–7, 38–40; building
activity at Dartington 95–8,
145, 195–6, 198–202, 214;
character 53–4; debts 263;
estates 22, 30, 260–62;
and chattels forfeited 55;
gonfalonier 40, 201; goods
household 42–4; income 38,
262–3; retainers 43–4, 220
– John, earl of Huntingdon and
3rd duke of Exeter (d. 1447):
activity and life 57–62, 62,
63; building work at
Dartington 195, 214
– Henry, 4th duke of Exeter
(d. 1475): activity and life
57, 64–9, 67; building work
at Dartington 195
– Maud (fl. 1400) 53 f. 100
– Richard (d. 1400) 57
– Sir Robert (d. 1328) 23
– Sir Thomas (d. 1360) 23, 24
– Thomas, earl of Kent (d.
1397) 23–4, 96 f. 4, 261
– Thomas, earl of Kent (d.
1400) 42 f. 36, 47, 48, 50–1,
148 f. 25
– Thomas, illeg. son of 3rd duke
of Exeter 62
– William, illeg. son of 3rd duke
of Exeter 62
Holbeton (Devon) 44
Holcombe Court (Devon) 256
f. 60
Holdenby House (Northants.)
226
Holditch Castle (Dorset) 112,
117, 125, 257
Hollings, Dr. John (d. 1739) 81
Holne (Devon) 18
Holsworthy (Devon) 261
Honiton (Devon) 88
Honnecourt, Villard de (d. c.
1250) 238, 238
Hope (Flint) 260
– William St. John 157
Hopedale (Flint) 260
Horsey, Jasper 71
Horston Castle (Derby.) 38, 261-3

Houghton, Adam, bishop of St.
    David's (d. 1389) 115 f. 75
Howden Manor (Yorks.): 129;
    design 128; hall porch 152 f. 3,
    235; period of construction
    104, 112; present condition
    137; plan 129; stables 145
f. 17
Howell, William 44
Hudson, Thomas (d. 1779) 84
Huguenots, massacre of 78
Hull (Yorks.) 110 f. 35
Humphrey, duke of Gloucester
    (d. 1447) 55, 62, 268
Hundred Years War 23, 28,
    58–61
Hungary, Holand's visit to 40
Hungerford, Sir Thomas (d.
    1398) 110, 116
Huntingdon, earl of, see Holand
Huntingfield Castle (Suffolk)
    102
Hurst, John G. 192
Hurstmonceux Castle (Sussex)
    190
Hutton Court (Somerset) 256
f. 60
Icklingham (Suffolk) 261
Ince Grange (Cheshire) 113 f. 70
Ireland, Richard II's expedition
    to 40 f. 25, 45
Irvine, James 85
Isaac, John 44
Isabelle, queen of England
    (d. 1409) 51 f. 85, 264
Isle of Man, Warwick's banish-
    ment to 42
Jerusalem, Holand's pilgrimage
    to 40
Joan of Arc, St. (d. 1431) 61
Joan, princess of Wales (d. 1385)
    23–4, 25, 26, 31, 54, 96 f. 4,
    260
João I, king of Portugal (d. 1433)
    33, 33–4, 53
John II, king of France (d.
    1364) 23
John of Ghent, duke of Lancaster
    (d. 1399): 25; arms at Lincoln
    98; building activity at Cowick
    Manor 110; Dunstanburgh
    Castle 106; Hertford Castle
    110; Kenilworth Castle 112,

Kenilworth Castle (War.):
    great hall and apartments
    114, 131; comparison with
    Dartington Hall 100; date
    104, 112; decoration 135,
    136, 236; design 119, 128,
    135, 136, 198, 236; entrance
    arch 153; financing 117;
    fireplaces 159; plans 199; roof
    239
Kennington Manor (Surrey)
    160, 236
Kent, earl of, see Holand
—escheator of 55
Kidwelly (Carmarthen) 262
Killigrew, John 75
King's Langley, King's House
    (Herts.) 112, 228
Kingston (Devon) 20
Kingston upon Thames (Surrey)
    51
Kingswear (Devon) 80
Kirkstall Abbey Guest House
    (Yorks.) 234, 235
Kitchens 244–7
Knightstone (Devon) 131 f. 141,
    157 f. 7, 258

Lambard, Walter 43
Lancaster, duke of, see Henry IV
    and John of Ghent
—earl of, see Thomas of Wood-
    stock
Langland, William (d. c. 1400)
    230 f. 6
Langley, Edmund 1st duke of
    York (d. 1402) 23 f. 7, 37, 38,
    51, 112
—Edward, 2nd duke of York
    (d. 1415) 38, 42 f. 36, 45, 50
—Richard, 3rd duke of York

Langley Castle (Northumb.)
    124 f. 122
Langton (Yorks.) 262
Lankey, John 43
Lanteglos (Cornwall) 261
Larkfield (Kent) 131 f. 142
Latimer, John 30 f. 21
Lavenden (Bucks.) 71
Layer Marney Towers (Essex)
    255
Leger, Sir Thomas St. (d. 1483)
    68, 69, 193, 195
Leicester, hunting party at 37
—Sir John 110
—Sir Peter 110 f. 42
Leigh (Devon) 207 f. 3
Leland, John (d. 1552): on
    Bolton Castle 116; on Darting-
    ton Hall 66, 69, 71; on
    Wressell Castle 135
Lesparre (France) 61
Lesyngham, Robert (d. c. 1396)
    256 f. 64
Lewes (Sussex) 262
Lewyn, John (d. c. 1398) 111
    f. 48, 116, 255
Licences to crenellate 103–4,
    137 f. 159
Lincoln, Bishop's Palace 234, 235
—earl of, see Clinton
—Vicars Court 133 f. 150, 219
    f. 11, 249–50, 250
Lisle, Warin, Lord (d. 1382) 110
Lillington, Thomas 53
Little Hempston (Devon) 22,
    258
Livery 43–4
Llanteen, Chapel (Mon.) 181 f. 8
Llangibby Castle (Mon.) 148
    f. 24
Llawhaden Castle (Pemb.) 125
    f. 130
Lodgings 203–20, 247–55
London, bishop of, see Bray-
    brooke
—Bridge 53, 60
—Charterhouse 148
—Cold Harbour 41 f. 33, 64, 67,
    262
—customs of the port of 56
—mayor of 55
—Montague Square 88
—St. Mary Graces by the Tower
    53, 261

198; Pontefract Castle and
    Savoy Palace 118 f. 95;
    career 26–8, 30, 31–6, 33,
    34, 37, 38, 45; establishes
    St. David's College 115;
    estates granted to Huntingdon
    262; income 38; retainers 43
John of Lancaster, later duke of
    Bedford (d. 1435) 55
Ken, John 51

287

Market Deeping Rectory 67
March, earl of, see Mortimer
Margaret of Anjou, queen of England (d. 1482) 64, 65, 66,
Mallock, Margaret 85
Maintenance 44
f. 148
gatehouse design 132, 133
date of erection 104, 115;
Maidstone College (Kent):
Maidenhead (Berks.) 51
Magnates, organisation in late 14th century 38
Lydford (Somerset) 19, 261
Luton, Sir Robert 263
Darlington Hall 99
Luscombe, Mr. steward of
Luscombe (Devon) 15, 16
— Ralph, Lord (d. 1400) 111
alterations 136
reconstruction 111; subsequent
220; kitchen 244; period of
161 f. 25; household chambers
general plan 119; hall roof
Lumley Castle (Durham): 110;
248
Ludlow Castle (Salop) 237, 247,
Lowestoft (Suffolk) 261
117
Lovel, John Lord (d. 1408) 112,
Louis XI of France (d. 1483) 66
of 261
Lothingland (Suffolk) hundred
Loring, Sir Nigel (d. 1386) 170
Lopes, Fernão 33 f. 44, 53 f. 104
Lonlay Abbey (France) 16 f. 20
Long-houses 224
Longford Castle (Wilts.) 85
Champernowne at 74, 75
use of 28, 41; Sir Arthur
(c. 1500) 60; Richard II's
112 f. 57; representation
made to in late 14th century
and imprisoned in 68; repairs
61, 64; and constable of 64;
Exeter buried at 62; and
constable of 59, 61, 62, 64;
4th duke of Exeter born at
Tower 135, 137; 3rd duke of
— Tower of: decoration of Byward
— Soho Square 81
— Savoy Palace 118 f. 95
— St. Paul's Cathedral 191 f. 18

Marney, Lord (d. 1523) 255
(Lincs.) 238 f. 22
Marshal of England, deputy 61
Martin family 17-20, 95
— Alice (d. after 1175) wife of Robert 18
— Eleanor (d. 1342) daughter of 1st Lord Martin 20
— Margaret (d. 1359) wife of 2nd Lord Martin 20
— Maud (d. before 1159) wife of Robert 18
— Nicholas (d. 1282) 19-20
— Robert (d. 1159) 16, 18
— Robert (fl. 1170) 18
— William (d. 1208) 18, 19
— William (d. 1216) 19
— William 1st Lord Martin (d. 1324) 20
— William, 2nd Lord Martin (d. 1326) 20
Marton (Westmor.) 262
Mary I, queen of England (d. 1558) 74, 75
Mary, queen of Scots (d. 1587) 77
Mason's marks 151, 157, 158, 214, 272
Mayfield Palace (Sussex) 236
Maynard, Lady 87
Meare Manor House (Somerset) 99, 246 f. 39
Mézières, Phillippe de (d. 1405) 40 f. 26
Milanese ambassador to Burgundy (c. 1470) 66, 68
Milles, Jeremiah (fl. 1755): describes Dartington Hall 99; east range 215; kitchen 172; south court 202; upper residential block 182
Milton Abbey (Dorset) 243, 244
Milton-next-Gravesend (Kent) 261-2
Modbury (Devon) 73, 74
— Castle 256
— Church 74
— Old Traine 183
Monmouth 262
Montague, Sir John 30 f. 24
— John, 3rd earl of Salisbury (d. 1400) 42 f. 36, 50-51, 53 f. 100

Montgomery, count de (d. 1574) 78-9
Moresk (Cornwall) 261
Morieux, Sir Thomas 32
Mortimer, Edmund, 5th earl of March (d. 1425) 60, 262
— Roger, 1st earl of March (d. 1330) 237, 247
— Roger, 4th earl of March (d. 1398) 43
Morval (Cornwall) 86
Mount Grace Priory (Yorks.) 148
Mowbray, John, 3rd duke of Norfolk (d. 1461) 61, 62
— Thomas, 2nd earl of Nottingham, duke of Norfolk (d. 1399) 36, 38, 41, 42 f. 36, 44, 53, 262
— Thomas, 3rd earl of Nottingham (d. 1405) 57 f. 25
Mount Sinai (Egypt) 40
Much Wenlock Abbey (Salop) 190

Nevern (Pemb.) 19
Neville family in later 14th century 117
— Alexander, archbishop of York (trans. 1388) 106
— John, Lord (d. 1388): additions to Bamburgh Castle 110, 175; and Raby Castle 106, 236; builds Sheriff Hutton Castle 106; financial resources 117, 118
— Ralph, 1st earl of Westmorland (d. 1425) 111
— Richard, 16th earl of Warwick (d. 1471) 65, 66, 67
Newbury (Berks.) 66
Newport (Pemb.) 19, 20
— Castle 20 f. 49
— Nonant, Alice de 18
— Roger de 18
Nonsuch Palace (Surrey) 74 f. 19
Norfolk, duke of, see Mowbray
Norrington Manor (Wilts.) 130; design 131; fireplace 160; period of construction 111; plan 130; restoration 137; upper residential block 179
Northborough Manor

289

Northants, 235, 237
North Elmham Castle (Norfolk) 111, 119
North Ford, Totnes (Devon) 19
Northlew (Devon) 261
Northolt Manor (Middx.) 228
Northumberland, earl of, see Percy
Norwich, Bishop's Palace: granary 224; hall 236; porch 235
– bishop of (d. 1406) 28, 40, 110–11
Nottingham, earl of, see Mowbray
Nunney Castle (Somerset) 124 f. 122, 166

Ogmore (Glamorgan) 262
Okehampton Castle (Devon) 256
Old Shoreham (Sussex) 263
Orleans, duke d' (d. 1793) 85
Otham, Wardes (Kent) 131 f. 142
Overmarsh (Cheshire) 260
Oxford, university of 61 f. 50
– Balliol College 115 f. 72
– Canterbury College 115 f. 72
– earls of, see Vere
– Exeter College 115 f. 72
– Merton College 251, 251
– New College 114; chapel 239; comparison with Dartington Hall 100, 255; design 131; doors 165; entrance gate 146; hall 155, 236; kitchen 244–6; lodgings 220 f. 14, 251, 251; period of construction 104, 114; workmanship 136
– The Queen's College 115 f. 72
– Tackley's Inn 170
– University College 115 f. 72

Parliament: (1384) 28–30; (1388) 36, 37; (1388–99) 39; (1397) 41–2; (1398) 44
Pasford, John 43 f. 63
Peasants' Revolt 27–8, 27
Peckham, Sir Edmund (d. 1564) 71
Pedro the Cruel, king of Castile and Leon (d. 1369) 31
Pembrokeshire 18, 47
Pembroke, earl of, see Hastings
Penrith Castle (Cumb.) 111, 122, 125
Penryn (Cornwall) 71
Penshurst Place (Kent): 114, 234; defensive improvements added 112; design 235; financing 116; hall porch 235; plan 159; upper residential block staircase 159, 160, 179
Percy family in later 14th century 117
– Henry, 1st earl of Northumberland (d. 1408): additions to Cockermouth Castle 106; and Warkworth Castle 106, 117; his capabilities 117; chivalric character 54; interviews Richard II 47–8
– Sir Richard (d. 1461) 65
– Sir Thomas, earl of Worcester (d. 1403) 37 f. 53, 110
Perpendicular style, character-istics of 134
Perrers, Alice (d. 1400) 260
Peter, Sir John 74
Petworth (Sussex) 262
Peverel, Maud 18
Philiberts Court (Berks.) 260
Philip II, king of Spain (d. 1598) 75–6, 79
Philip, Thomas 67 f. 95
Philippa of Hainault, queen of England (d. 1369) 96 f. 4
Philippa Lancaster, queen of Portugal (d. 1415) 33
Pickering Castle (Yorks.) 247–9, 247
Pleshey Castle (Essex) 41, 52, 52
– Church 53
– College 115
Plowman, Piers 230
Plymouth (Devon) 32, 34
Plympton (Devon) 18
– member of parliament (1555) 78
– prior of 57
– Priory 80
Poitiers (France), battle of (1356) 23
– Ducal Palace 160 f. 18, 236

Pole, Michael de la, 1st earl of Suffolk (d. 1389) 110, 117, 118, 261
Polsloe (Devon) 74
– Priory: exchanged for Darting-ton 71, 74, 78; hall 140 f. 4, 144 f. 15, 145
Polwhele, Richard (d. 1838) 85
Pomerai family in later 14th century 231
– Henry de la 20
– Sir John de 57
Pontefract Castle (Yorks.) 53, 65, 118 f. 95
Pope, see Boniface
Porchester Castle (Hants.) 131; chapel 201; comparison between residential additions and Dartington Hall 100; cost 116; date 96, 112; four-centred arches 214; general design of additions 119, 128, 198
Portugal 31–6, 32
Poterne Castle (Wilts.) 102
Powderham Castle (Devon): description 258; engraving (1734) 81; hall 157 f. 7; plan 257; porch 256 f. 60
– rector of 85
Poynington Court House (Dorset) 131 f. 141
Prayer Book Rebellion 73–4
Preston Patrick Hall (Westmor.) 131 f. 141, 214
Prince, John (d. 1723) 202
Prittlewell (Essex) 52
Privy Council in 16th century 74, 75
Proudfoot, Thomas 43, 55, 220, 261
Prouse, John 44
Prudhoe Castle (Northumb.) 146
Pudhaven (Devon) 79
Pugin, A. W. N. (d. 1852) 88–9, 168, 184
Pynes (Devon) 183

Queenborough Castle (Kent) 116

Raby Castle (Durham): 120; date of additions 104, 106; design 119; financing 117; great hall 229, 235, 236; kitchen 244–6, 245; plan 120; subsequent alterations 137

Radcot Bridge, battle of 22, 36
Radford, C. A. Raleigh 159
Raglan Castle (Mon.) 229 f. 5,
  230, 254
Ragley Castle (War.) 103
Raleigh family in the 16th
  century 75
Ramsbury Castle (Wilts.) 102
Rattery (Devon) 15
Rede, William, bishop of
  Chichester (d. 1385) 109, 230
Regate Castle (Surrey) 41, 42
  f. 41, 262
Rembrandt, H. van Rhyn (d.
  1669) drawings of 90
Residential blocks: development
  during Middle Ages 232–7;
  purpose 168–70
Resistivity survey at Dartington
  Hall 148, 186–90, 230, 266–7
Rest Manor (Yorks.) 106, 125,
  135
Retainers: 42; development of
  the retinue 43–4; effect on
  residential planning 220,
  228–30; lodgings 251–5
Reynolds, Sir Joshua (d. 1792)
  87
— Walter, archbishop of Canterbury (d. 1327) 236
Rheims (France) 85
Rhys, Lord 18
Ribadavia (Spain) 34, 35
Richard I, King of England
  (d. 1199) 18
Richard II, king of England
  (d. 1400) 22, 24, 29; badge of
  96, 97, 98; building activity
  112; deposition 46, 47–9, 48,
  49, 53; early years 26, 27, 28,
  30–2, 36, 37; grants of land
  38–42, 44–5, 45
by 55, 261–2; personal rule
  38–42, 44–5, 45
Richard III, king of England
  (d. 1485) 69
Richmond, Margaret, countess
  of, see Beaufort
— Palace (Surrey) 190
Rigold, S. E. 159
Rochelle, La (France) 79
Rochester (Kent) city walls 106
— Castle 107 f. 19
Rockingham Castle (Northants.)
  38, 263
Roger of Nonant 18

Roos, Lord 69 f. 108
Rosa, Salvator (d. 1673) 87
Rouen, merchants of (1577) 75
Roxburgh Castle 105
Roye, Sir Reginald de 34, 53
Rubens, Peter Paul (d. 1640) 85
Russell, John, 1st earl of Bedford
  (d. 1555) 71
Rutland, earl of, see Langley

Sackville, Sir Richard 74 f. 16
Saighton Grange (Cheshire) 113
  f. 70
St. Albans chronicler (1428) 62
St. Bartholomew's Day, massacre
  of 78
St. David's, Bishop's Palace
  (Pemb.) 236
— St. Mary's College 115, 132,
  255
St. Dogmael's Abbey (Pemb.) 18
St. Inglevert (France) 53, 54
St. James de Beuvron (France) 59
St. John, Lord (d. 1429) 109
St. Leger, Sir Thomas (d. 1483)
  68, 69, 74, 193, 195
St. Malo (France) 27
Salisbury (Wilts.) 28
— Balle's Place 238, 239
— bishop of (trans. 1388) 109, 118
— Bishop's Palace 256 f. 60
— Castle 30
— earls of, see Montague
— Old Deanery 145
Saltash (Cornwall) 75, 86, 261
Saltwood Castle (Kent): 127;
  date of gatehouse 103, 104,
  109; design 125, 136; restoration 137; date of hall and
  chapel 112; present remains
  128; financing 117
Santiago de Compostela (Spain)
  33
Saunders, George (d. 1839)
  drawings and plans of Dartington Hall 85–6, 147, 184,
  215; entrance block 84, 144;
  great hall 144, 158, 161–3,
  162–3, 164, 239, 240; kitchen
  and offices 172, 174, 175;
  lower residential block 144,
  163, 166, 168; south court
  202; upper residential block
  180, 183
Savage, John 43 f. 63

Savery, Christopher 87
Saxons, settlement of Devon 13
Scarborough (Yorks.) 261
— Castle 112, 114, 128
Scardeburgh, see Scarborough
Schevele, John 43 f. 63
Scotland 28, 31
Scotney Castle (Kent): 108; date
  of erection 103, 109; financing
  117; four-centred arches 213;
  general plan 125, 228
Scrope, Richard Lord (d. 1403)
  96, 106, 116, 146, 197
Scrope, Sir Stephen 50 f. 81
— Sir William 42 f. 36
Serlo de Burci 16
Seymour family in the 16th
  century 75, 78
— Sir Edmund 79
— Edward, earl of Hertford
  (d. 1552) 73
Shaftesbury Abbey (Dorset)
  cartulary of, 260
Shareshill Manor (War.) 159
Sheen, King's House (Surrey)
  112
— Palace 228
Shelley, Richard 43
— Sir Thomas 43, 52, 55 f. 2
Shepley Hall (Yorks.) 166
Sherbourne Castle (Dorset) 102
Sheriff Hutton Castle (Yorks.)
  105, 106, 117, 119, 135
Shilston Barton (Devon) 256
  f. 60
— Sir John 71
Shirburn Castle (Oxon.) 110
Shirburn Castle (Kent) 102
Shoford Castle (Kent) 102
Shouldered arches 213–14
Shrewsbury 44
— earl of, see Talbot
Shute Barton (Devon): 109;
  design 125, 137; entrance
  block 139 f. 2; 140 f. 5, 146;
  period of erection 109
Sigismund, king of Hungary
  (d. 1437) 40
Simpson, Professor Scott 191,
  268–72
Skenfrith (Mon.) 262
Skirlaw, Walter, bishop of
  Durham (d. 1406) 112
Slade (Devon) 78
Smallbridge Manor (Suffolk) 102

Wallingford (Berks.) 112 f. 57
Walsingham, Thomas (d. c. 1422): 30 f. 21; quoted 30, 50 f. 81, 51, 52, 53
Wantage (Berks.) 51
Warde, William 43
Wardes (Kent) 131 f. 142
Wardour Old Castle (Wilts.): *126*; date of construction 112; decoration 136; design 125; designer 255; financing 117; general plan *127*; kitchen 244; wave moulding 256
– New Castle 85
Warkworth Castle (Northumb.): *125*; date of tower-house 104, 106; decoration 136; design 125, 135, 136, 229 f. 5; financing 117; kitchen fireplaces 172 f. 2; staircase 160 f. 22
Warwick Castle: Caesar's Tower *249*; date 136 f. 155; described 249; elevation *249*. Entrance frontage *134*, 136. Guy's Tower *113*; cost 116; date 103, 111–2; described 249
– countess of (d. 1422) 118 f. 94
– earl of, *see* Beauchamp and Neville
– estates in mid 14th century 116 f. 89
– Leycester's Hospital 218 f. 8
Wealden houses 131
Wealhburgh, sister of Beornwynn 13, 260
Weare Gifford Hall (Devon) 139 f. 2, *243*, 244, 268
Weir, William, restores Dartington Hall 6–10; entrance block 139, 140, 143; great hall 153, 157, 161–2; kitchen 171, 172, 173, 175; lower residential block 166; upper residential block 184; west range 205, 208
Wells, Bishop's Palace (Somerset) 99, 235
– Vicars Choral 250, *252*
Wennland (Dorset) 13, 260
Wessex, kings of 13
West Lydford (Somerset) 19, 55
Westminster Abbey: 65, 68; dorter roof 241–2, *241*; Sir John Golafré's tomb 98; Richard II's badge 98;

Richard II's tomb 98
– Chronicle 30 f. 21
– Palace of: 65; Gallery 191, Great Hall *113*; comparison with Dartington Hall 100; cost 116; date 41, 112; design 128, 136, 236; Richard II's badge 98; roof 239–40, *240*, 244; St. Stephen's Chapel 64
Westmorland, earl of, *see* Neville
West Welsh of Cornwall 13, 14
Whatley Manor (Somerset) 139 f. 2, 140 f. 5, 146
Whichford Castle (War.) 159
Whissendine (Rutland) 260
White Castle (Mon.) 262
Whitehall Palace 190
White, William 96
Widworthy Barton (Devon) 258
Wigmore Abbey (Hereford) 114 f. 71, 125 f. 130
Wilkins, William (d. 1839) 87–8
Willes, Charles 81 f. 51
William of Falaise 15, 16
William III, king of England (d. 1702) 76, 80
Wilson, Richard (d. 1782) 87
Wilton Diptych 98
Wiltshire, earl of, *see* Butler
Winchelsey, Robert, archbishop of Canterbury (d. 1313) 236
Winchester, bishop of, *see* Wykeham
– Castle 112
– Cathedral 136
– Charter of 825, 260
– City Walls 111 f. 46
– College: *132*; building materials 134; badge of Richard II 98; comparison with Dartington Hall 100; design 131; dining hall 155; doors 165; four-centred arches 213; lodgings 219 f. 11, 251, *251*, 253; lower hall block 170, 237; middle gate *115*, 146; outer court 213; period of construction 104, 114–15; plan *133*; roofs 179 f. 2; seventh chamber 140 f. 4; shouldered arch 214; stables 145 f. 17; workmanship 136
– Hospital of St. Cross 132, 219 f. 11

– Pilgrims Hall 238, *238*
– West Gate 98, 111 f. 46
– Wolvesey Palace 112
Windsor Castle (Berks.): great hall 236; Henry IV at 51; lodgings 252, *252*; plan compared with Wykeham's colleges 131; St. George's Chapel 69 f. 109
– Park 112
Wingfield Castle (Suffolk): *123* building materials 134; date of erection 110; design 118, 122; financing 117; plan *123*
Winkleigh (Devon) 55, 261
Winterbourne Clenston Manor (Dorset) 242, *243*
Wolsey, Thomas, Cardinal (d. 1530) 226
Woodford Castle (Wilts.) 102
Woodland (Devon) 53 f. 102
Woodsford Castle (Dorset) 99, 214 f. 22
Woodville, Elizabeth, queen of England (d. 1492) 67 f. 96
Woolland (Dorset) 13 f. 2
Workington Hall (Cumb.) 106, *106*, 125
Wressell Castle (Yorks.): *122* building materials 135; design 119, 122; period of construction 103, 110
Wyatt, Sir Thomas (d. 1554) 74
Wykeham, William of, bishop of Winchester (d. 1404): establishes New College, Oxford 114–15, and Winchester College 114–15; financial resources 117; his collegiate design 131, 136; improves Wolvesey Palace 112; patron of Wynford 255; rebuilds Highclere Castle 112
Wynford, William (d. 1404) 255

Yard, Sir John 43 f. 48
Yerde, William 43 f. 63, 55
Yevele, Henry (d. 1400) 136, 255
York 31
– archbishop of, *see* Neville
– duke of, *see* Langley
– Minister 237

Zouche, Lord (d. 1396) 30

Smith, Francis (d. 1738) 183
Solihull Hall (War.) 211 f. 13
Somerset, earl and duke of, see
　Beaufort
Sonning Palace (Berks.) 51 f. 85,
　102
Southampton (Hants.) 75
– Castle 106, 125 f. 123
South Molton (Devon) 19, 56
　f. 21, 261
South Wales, Norman conquest
　of 18, 19
Southwark (Surrey) 66
South Wingfield Manor (Derby):
　hall 236; lower residential
　block 170; plan reflects
　bastard feudalism 226, 230;
　retainers' lodgings 253;
　servants barn-like quarters 224
Sowton, Bishop's Court (Devon)
　145 f. 16
Spain 33–5, 75, 79
Spanish Armada, defeat of 79
Spicer, Richard 44
Stafford, Edmund, bishop of
　Exeter (d. 1419) 41 f. 33
– Humphrey, 6th earl of
　　(d. 1460) 62
– Sir Ralph (d. 1385) 31, 261
– Richard 260
Stanley Pontlarge (Glos.) 103 f. 2
Staundon (Somerset) 261
Staverton (Devon) 22, 95, 261
Steel, A. 264
Steeton Hall (Yorks.) 146
Sternfield Castle (Suffolk) 102
Stevington (Beds.) 262
Stone (Somerset) 261
Stonor, Anne, wife of Sir William
　Stonor 69
Stourhead (Wilts.) 85
Stratford (Suffolk) 261
Stratton (Cornwall) 44
Strensham Castle (Worcs.) 119
Strickland, William, bishop of
　Carlisle (d. 1419) 50, 111
Stubbs, William, bishop of
　Oxford (d. 1901) 53
Sudbury, Simon, archbishop of
　Canterbury (d. 1381) 106
Sudeley Castle (Glos.) 192, 226,
　229, 230
Suffolk, earl of, see Pole
Sulgrave Castle (Northants.)
　232 f. 12

Surrey, duke of, see Thomas
　Holand
Sutton Grange (Cheshire) 113
　f. 70
– King's House (Middx.) 112
– John of 98
Syon Abbey (Devon) 3

Tabley Old Hall (Cheshire) 110,
　111, 131
Tackbear (Cornwall) 261
Talbot, John, 2nd earl of
　Shrewsbury (d. 1460) *64*, 66
Tantallon Castle (E. Lothian)
　229
Tattershall Castle (Lincs.) 6
Tavistock, abbot of 57
Teignton (Devon) 16 f. 20
Tendring Church (Essex) 238
　f. 22
Teniers, David (d. 1649) 87
Tewington (Cornwall) 261
Theobalds (Herts.) 226
Thomas, earl of Lancaster (d.
　1322) 23
Thomas of Woodstock, duke of
　Gloucester (d. 1397): an
　appellant 36, 37, 40–2, *41*;
　character and influence 38,
　54; establishes Pleshy College
　115; gatehouse and tower
　added at Caldicot Castle 112
Thompson, A. Hamilton 146
Thornbury Castle (Glos.):
　gallery 190; garderobes 219
　f. 11; outer court 148; plan
　reflects bastard feudalism 230;
　retainers' lodgings 254–5, *254*
Thornton Abbey (Lincs.) 125
　f. 130
Tintagel (Cornwall) 261
– Castle 38, 42, 112 f. 57, 262
Tiptofts Manor House (Essex)
　238, *239*
Tisbury Place Farm (Wilts.)
　140 f. 5
Titian, Vecelli (d. 1576) 85
Tiverton Castle (Devon) 139
　f. 2, 231, 256
Tong Castle (Salop) 102
Torbay (Devon) 75
Torbryan, Church House
　Inn (Devon) 153
Toriton, Avice de 19 f. 35
Torrington (Devon) 261

Totnes (Devon) 15, 20
– members of parliament 78, 79
– North Ford 19
– Priory 18
Tower of London, see London
Towton, battle of 66
Traison et Mort, authorship:
　50 f. 81, 263–4; quoted 40, 53
　54, 56
Treguz (Glamorgan) 16 f. 20
Trematon Castle (Cornwall) 38,
　261, 262
Tremayn, Nicholas 44
Trenarke, John 43
Tretower Court (Brecon) 190
Trevailly (Cornwall) 261
Trubleville, Henry de (d. 1239)
　19 f. 35
Tuchet, Sir John 22 f. 66
Turkey 40
Tynemouth Priory (Northumb.)
　111 f. 49

Ufford family in late 14th
　century 117
Ulcombe (Kent) 69
Upholland (Lancs.) 23
Upton Pynes (Devon) 183
Upton Scudmore, Manor Farm
　(Wilts.) 131 f. 141
Usk, Adam of (d. after 1402) 50
　f. 81, 51

Valderas (Spain) 35
Vanbrugh, Sir John (d. 1726)
　137
Vendôme, count of 59
Venton (Devon) 18 f. 25
Verdon, John 43 f. 63
Vere, Aubrey de, 10th earl of
　Oxford (d. 1400) 39 f. 19, 52
– Richard de, 11th earl of
　Oxford (d. 1417) 52, 55
– Robert, 9th earl of Oxford
　(d. 1392) 22, 30, 36
Vernon, Sir Henry (d. 1515) 254
Vice-Admiral of the West in
　late 16th century 75, 78

Waldegrave, Warin 43, 55
Walden, Roger, archbishop of
　Canterbury (deprived
　1399) 50
Waleys, Nicholas 256 f. 64